CONTENTS

NOTE TO STUDENTS

As writers, you already know that to express your ideas clearly, you need to understand the basic principles of grammar, mechanics, and style. In addition, however, writers in the digital age also need to know how computers can help them communicate their ideas to others more effectively. Today, new computer software makes it possible for you to manipulate text and visuals as previously only professionals could.

In your personal writing, you may already have experimented with clip art, special formatting elements, and other functions of your word-processing or email applications. When you are writing for an academic audience (or, on the job, for a business audience), visual elements—graphics, icons, highlighted and boxed text, and so on—can play a significant role in helping you to communicate. In fact, in all the writing you do—regardless of your purpose or audience—technology plays an ever-increasing role in helping you to convey your ideas. For this reason, it is very important that you have a clear understanding of the relationship between technology and writing.

We wrote *The Wadsworth Handbook* with this idea in mind. The result is a book that you can depend on to give you sound, sensible advice about grammar and usage as well as about the electronic tools available to you as a writer. We hope you will find *The Wadsworth Handbook* a resource that you can turn to again and again as you write in college and beyond.

Laurie Kirszner
Steve Mandell
April 2004

Features of This Book

• *Frequently Asked Questions (FAQs)* appear at the beginning of each chapter. A marginal FAQ icon appears in the chapter beside each answer.

• *Computer tips* highlight specific ways in which technology can help you throughout the writing, revising, and editing processes. Each computer tip includes the URL for the book's companion Web site <http://kirsznermandell.wadsworth.com>, which contains a wealth of online resources.

• *Numerous checklists* summarize key information that you can quickly access as needed.

• *Close-up boxes* provide an in-depth look at some of the more perplexing writing-related issues you will encounter.

• *Case study icons* in the writing and research process sections direct you to examples in the two chapter-length case studies: one in Chapter 6 that follows a student's writing process as she drafts and revises a short essay, and another in Chapter 17 that traces her progress as she expands her essay into a research paper.

• *Part 3, "Documentation Styles,"* includes the most up-to-date documentation and format guidelines from the Modern Language Association, the American Psychological Association, the University of Chicago Press, and the Council of Science Editors. (A discussion of Columbia Online Style appears in Chapter 18, "MLA Documentation Style.")

• *Newly designed documentation directories*—including a specific icon that designates print sources

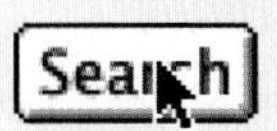

and a different icon that designates electronic sources—make it easy for you to locate models for various kinds of sources, including those found online from library subscription services such as InfoTrac® and Lexis-Nexis™. In addition, annotated diagrams of sample works-cited entries clearly illustrate the elements of proper documentation.

- *A large thumb cut* enables you to move directly to Chapter 18, "MLA Documentation Style."

See 7a

- *Marginal cross-references* throughout the book allow you to flip directly to other sections that treat topics in more detail.

ESL 61c

- *Marginal ESL cross-references* throughout the book direct you to sections of Part 11, "Bilingual and ESL Writers," where concepts are presented as they apply specifically to second-language writers.

- *ESL tips* are woven throughout the text to explain concepts in relation to the unique experiences of bilingual students.

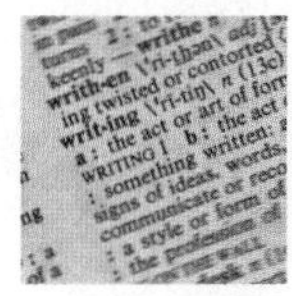

- *Getting Help from the Dictionary boxes* appear throughout Chapter 61, "Grammar and Style for ESL Writers," offering bilingual students practical advice for using a dictionary effectively.

- *Numerous exercises* throughout the text allow you to practice at each stage of the writing, revising, and editing processes.

- A *Student Writer at Work exercise* appears at the end of each of the eleven parts of the book, enabling you to practice what you have learned in the context of actual writing assignments.

- *Numerous annotated sample documents,* created by both student and professional writers, illustrate the principles of effective print and electronic document design.

- *An extensive writing-centered treatment of grammar, punctuation, and mechanics,* including hand-edited examples, explains and illustrates specific strategies for improving your writing.

- *A free four-month access card for InfoTrac® College Edition* comes with your new copy of *The Wadsworth Handbook.* An invaluable research tool, InfoTrac® College Edition offers you twenty-four-hour-a-day access to millions of full-text articles.

PART 1

Writing Essays

Chapter 1

Understanding Purpose, Audience, and Tone

Frequently Asked Questions

Everyone who sets out to write confronts a series of choices. Some choices are based on fairly obvious factors, such as how much you know about your subject and how much time you have. Others are determined by more subtle and far-reaching considerations, such as your purpose for writing and the audience you are addressing. In the writing you do in school, on the job, and in your personal life, your understanding of purpose and audience is essential, influencing the choices you make about content, emphasis, organization, style, and tone.

See 2b, 29d

Like written texts, visual texts—fine art, charts and graphs, photographs, maps, advertisements, and so on—are also created with specific purposes and audiences in mind. The advertisement reproduced in Figure 1.1, sponsored by the National Center for Family Literacy, was designed to appeal to a particular audience and to serve a variety of purposes. The ad addresses educated adults who value reading as a pastime and who understand how illiteracy limits people economically and socially. Its purposes are to identify a problem and suggest a solution, to persuade people to donate money, and perhaps to inspire them to volunteer their time. Notice how the different words and images in this advertisement work together to achieve these purposes and appeal to the target audience.

Like this ad, every written text you create addresses a particular audience and sets out to achieve one or more specific purposes.

1a Determining Your Purpose

In simple terms, your **purpose** for writing is what you want to accomplish. For instance, your purpose may be to *reflect*, to express private feelings, as in the introspective or meditative writing that appears in personal journals, diaries, and memoirs. Or your purpose

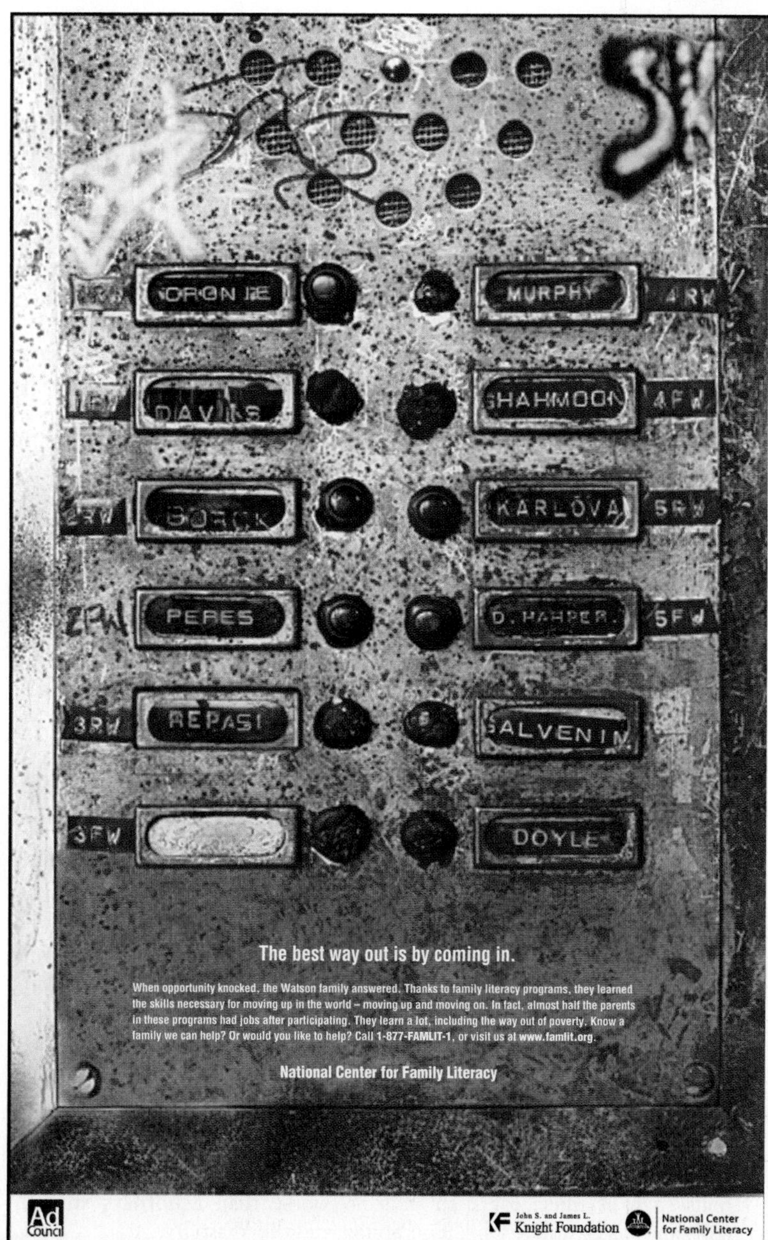

Figure 1.1 Ad for the National Center for Family Literacy.

may be to *inform*, to convey factual information as accurately and as logically as possible, as in the informational or expository writing that appears in reports, news articles, encyclopedias, and textbooks. At other times, your purpose may be to *persuade*, to convince your readers, as in advertising, proposals, editorials, and some business communications. Finally, your purpose may be to *evaluate*, to make a judgment about something, as in a recommendation report or a comparative analysis.

(1) Writing to Reflect

In diaries and journals, writers explore ideas and feelings to make sense of their experiences; in autobiographical memoirs and in personal letters, they communicate their emotions and reactions to others.

> At the age of five, six, well past the time when most other children no longer easily notice the difference between sounds uttered at home and words spoken in public, I had a different experience. I lived in a world magically compounded of sounds. I remained a child longer than most; I lingered too long, poised at the edge of language—often frightened by the sounds of *los gringos*, delighted by the sounds of Spanish at home. I shared with my family a language that was startlingly different from that used in the great city around us. (Richard Rodriguez, *Aria: A Memoir of a Bilingual Childhood*)

(2) Writing to Inform

In newspaper articles, writers report information, communicating factual details to readers; in reference books, instruction manuals, textbooks, and the like, as well as in catalogs, cookbooks, and government-sponsored Web sites, writers provide definitions and explain concepts or processes, trying to help readers see relationships and understand ideas.

> Most tarantulas live in the tropics, but several species occur in the temperate zone and a few are common in the southern U.S. Some varieties are large and have powerful fangs with which they can inflict a deep wound. These formidable-looking spiders do not, however, attack man; you can hold one in your hand, if you are gentle, without being bitten. Their bite is dangerous only to insects and small mammals such as mice; for man it is no worse than a hornet's sting. (Alexander Petrunkevitch, "The Spider and the Wasp")

(3) Writing to Persuade

In proposals and editorials, as well as in advertising, writers try to convince readers to accept their position on an issue.

Testing and contact tracing may lead to a person's being deprived of a job, health insurance, housing and privacy, many civil libertarians fear. These are valid and grave concerns. But we can find ways to protect civil rights without sacrificing public health. A major AIDS-prevention campaign ought to be accompanied by intensive public education about the ways the illness is *not* transmitted, by additional safeguards on data banks and by greater penalties for those who abuse HIV victims. It may be harsh to say, but the fact that an individual may suffer as a result of doing what is right does not make doing so less of an imperative. (Amitai Etzioni, "HIV Sufferers Have a Responsibility")

(4) Writing to Evaluate

In reviews of books, films, or performances and in reports, critiques, and program evaluations, writers assess the validity, accuracy, and quality of information, ideas, techniques, products, procedures, or services, perhaps assessing the relative merits of two or more things.

Kingston, Jamaica-based reggae label Phase One never got the credit it deserved for bridging the gap between dub and vocal reggae, but *We Are Getting Bad: The Sound of Phase One* might remedy the oversight. Phase One vocal groups like the Chantells and the Untouchables are backed by production as eerie as anything done by better-known auteurs. And the Untouchables' version of "Sea of Love" provides one of the most unexpected payoffs since the Human League covered "Reach Out (I'll Be There)." (Ethan Brown, "The War at Home," *New York* magazine)

Close-up: Purpose and Content

Your purpose for writing determines the material you choose and the way you organize and express your ideas.

- A memoir *reflecting* on the negative aspects of summer camp might focus on mosquitoes, poison ivy, homesickness, institutional food, and so on.
- A magazine article about summer camps could *inform*, presenting facts and statistics to show how camping has changed over the years.
- An advertising brochure designed to recruit potential campers could *persuade*, enumerating the benefits of the camping experience.
- A nonprofit camping association's Web site could *evaluate* various camps, assessing facilities, costs, staff-to-camper ratios, and activities in order to assist parents in choosing a camp.

Although writers do write to reflect, to inform, to persuade, and to evaluate, these purposes are certainly not mutually exclusive, and writers may have other purposes as well. For example, writers may also write to *discover*, to gather ideas or record observations, as in a scientist's laboratory notes, a scholar's preliminary research, or a student's class notes. Or writers may *affirm*, expressing strongly held beliefs or values, as in manifestos, declarations, or position papers. And, of course, in any piece of writing a writer may have a primary aim and one or more secondary purposes; in fact, a writer may even have different purposes in different sections—or different drafts—of a single document.

Checklist: Determining Your Purpose

Is your purpose:

- ☐ to express emotions?
- ☐ to inform?
- ☐ to persuade?
- ☐ to explain?
- ☐ to amuse or entertain?
- ☐ to evaluate?
- ☐ to discover?
- ☐ to analyze?
- ☐ to debunk?
- ☐ to draw comparisons?
- ☐ to make an analogy?
- ☐ to define?
- ☐ to criticize?
- ☐ to motivate?
- ☐ to satirize?
- ☐ to speculate?
- ☐ to warn?
- ☐ to reassure?
- ☐ to take a stand?
- ☐ to identify problems?
- ☐ to suggest solutions?
- ☐ to identify causes?
- ☐ to predict effects?
- ☐ to reflect?
- ☐ to interpret?
- ☐ to instruct?
- ☐ to inspire?

http://kirsznermandell.wadsworth.com

Computer Tip: Achieving Your Purpose

Your computer can help you achieve your purpose. For example, if your purpose is to recruit new members to a campus organization, you can use a desktop publishing program to create a brochure or flyer. In this document, you may use visuals as well as text (for example, photographs of social events) to help persuade students to join your organization. You can also use formatting features (such as bold or italic type or tables and borders) to emphasize the most important information.

Exercise 1

Read the following excerpts carefully. Try to put yourself in each writer's position, considering the purpose or purposes he or she had in mind when writing. For what purpose or purposes do you think each passage was written? What makes you think so?

1. Of course, short people have been looked down upon for years. In the matter of language, for example . . . one does not wish to be found short-tempered, short-winded or shortsighted. One does not wish to be left with the short end, caught short-handed or given short shrift. Shortages, short circuits and shortfalls are universally deplored. On the other hand, one takes pride in filling a tall order, gapes at the tall ships, admires a tall tale and—out here in the Wild West—sits tall in the saddle. Although brevity is the soul of wit and one strives to make a long story short, this quality is not equally appreciated when manifested in human form. Just as we habitually use the masculine gender to denote all people, we use tallness to measure height. Thus there are those who say they are "4 feet tall" when they are clearly 4 feet short. (Beth Luey, "Short Shrift," *Newsweek*)
2. Radio began with the transatlantic "wireless" communication of Guglielmo Marconi (1874–1937) in 1901 and the development of the vacuum tube in 1904, which permitted the transmission of speech and music. But it was only in 1920 that the first major broadcasts of special events were made in Great Britain and the United States. Lord Northcliffe, who had pioneered in journalism with the inexpensive, mass-circulation *Daily Mail,* sponsored a broadcast of "only one artist . . . the world's very best, the soprano Nellie Melba." Singing from London in English, Italian and French, Melba was heard simultaneously all over Europe on June 16, 1920. This historic event captured the public's imagination. The meteoric career of radio was launched. (McKay, Hill, Buckler, *A History of Western Society*, Vol. II)
3. ★★★★★ **One of Grisham's Best,** April 29, 2003

   Reviewer: **CHARLES H. PETERSON** from METAIRIE, LOUISIANA, United States

   Grisham is not going to win any prizes for literature, but when he tries, he can sure win a prize for page turners. This one was better thought out than most of his recent efforts. He clearly knew how he was going to end it before he started writing which is not always the case with Grisham. While there may be literary flaws in his character development, the book proceeds at a lively and generally logical pace. It also sheds some light on the problems associated with the "class action" mentality in our legal system these days.

   It is what it is, and it is an excellent read. (Amazon.com customer review of John Grisham's *The King of Torts*)

Exercise 2

The two student paragraphs below treat the same general subject, but their purposes are different. What do you see as the primary purpose of each paragraph? What other purposes might each writer have had?

1. Answer to an essay examination question: "Identify the Boston Massacre."

   The Boston Massacre refers to a 1770 confrontation between British soldiers and a crowd of colonists. Encouraged by Samuel Adams, the citizens had become more and more upset over issues like the British government's stationing troops and customs commissioners in Boston. When angry colonists attacked a customhouse sentry on March 5, 1770, a fight broke out. Soldiers fired into the crowd, and five civilians were killed. Although the soldiers were found guilty only of manslaughter and given only a token punishment, Samuel Adams's propaganda created the idea of a "massacre" in the minds of many Americans.

2. From "The Ohio Massacre: 1770 Revisited" (student essay):

   In two incidents that occurred exactly two hundred years apart, civilian demonstrators were shot and killed by armed troops. Although civilians were certainly inciting the British troops, starting scuffles and even brawls, these actions should not have led the Redcoats to fire blindly into the crowd. Similarly, the Ohio National Guard should not have allowed themselves to be provoked by students who were calling names, shoving, or throwing objects, and Governor Rhodes should not have authorized the troops to fire their weapons. The deaths—five civilians in Boston, Massachusetts, in 1770, and four students in Kent, Ohio, in 1970—were all unnecessary.

Exercise 3

The primary purpose of the following article from the *New York Times* is to present information. Suppose you were using the information in an orientation booklet aimed at students entering your school, and your purpose was to persuade students of the importance of maintaining a good credit rating. How would you change the original article to help you achieve this purpose? Would you reorder any details? Would you add or delete anything?

What Makes a Credit Score Rise or Fall?

By JENNIFER BAYOT

Your financial decisions can affect your credit score in surprising ways. Two credit-scoring simulators can help consumers understand the potential impact.

The Fair Isaac Corporation, which puts out the industry-standard FICO scores, offers the myFICO simulator. A consumer with a score of 707 (considered good) and three credit cards would be likely to add or lose points from his score by making various financial moves. Following are some examples:

- By making timely payments on all his accounts over the next month or by paying off a third of the balance on his cards, he could add as many as 20 points.
- By failing to make this month's payments on his loans, he could lose 75 to 125 points.
- By using all of the credit available on his three credit cards, he could lose 20 to 70 points.
- By getting a fourth card, depending on the status of his other debts, he could add or lose up to 10 points.
- By consolidating his credit card debt into a new card, also depending on other debts, he could add or lose 15 points.

The other simulator, the What-If, comes from CreditXpert, which designs credit management tools and puts out its own, similar credit score. A consumer with a score of 727 points (also considered good) would be likely to have her score change in the following ways:

- Every time she simply applied for a loan, whether a credit card, home mortgage or auto loan, she would lose five points. (An active appetite for credit, credit experts note, is considered a bad sign. For one thing, taking on new loans may make borrowers less likely to repay their current debts.)
- By getting a mortgage, she would lose two points.
- By getting an auto loan or a new credit card (assuming that she already has several cards) she would lose three points.
- If her new credit card had a credit limit of $20,000 or more, she would lose four points, instead of three. (For every $10,000 added to the limit, the score drops a point.)
- By simultaneously getting a new mortgage, auto loan and credit card, she would lose seven or eight points.

Exercise 4

Look closely at the visuals reproduced in Figures 1.2 and 1.3, and consider for what purpose or purposes each might have been created. (You can consult the checklist on page 6 to help you identify the purpose or purposes that best apply.)

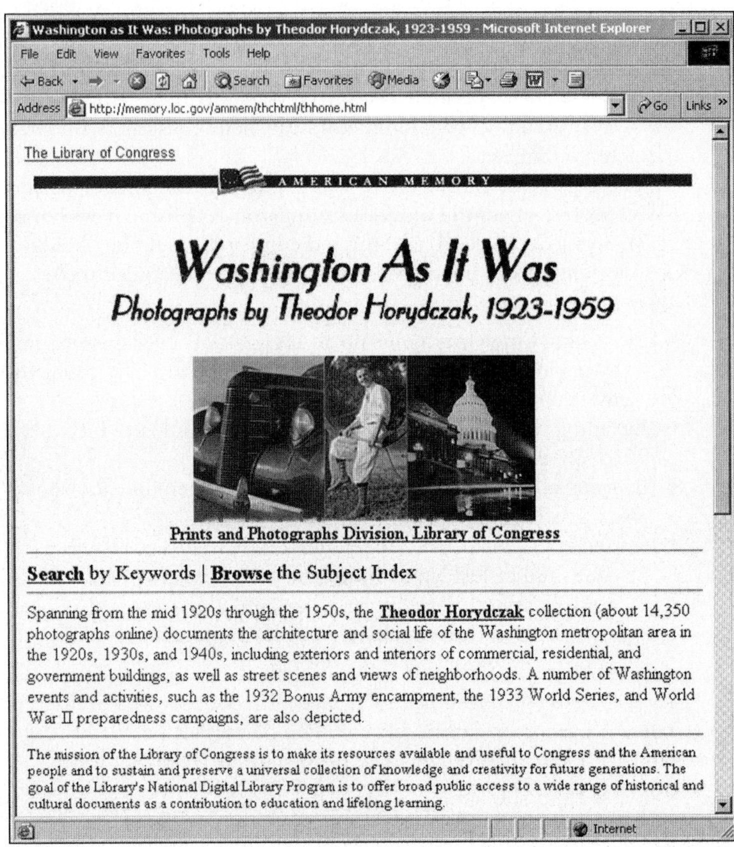

Figure 1.2 Home page for The Library of Congress American Memory project's Theodor Horydczak collection.

OVERALL RATINGS — Excellent · Very good · Good · Fair · Poor

BRAND AND MODEL	PRICE	OVERALL SCORE (0–100: P F G VG E)	EASE OF USE	BATTERY LIFE	DISPLAY	IN SYNC	CONVENIENCE
PALM-OS MODELS							
Sony CLIE PEG-SJ20	$150.00		Very good	Excellent	Good	Very good	Very good
Palm i705	$180.00		Good	Excellent	Very good	Excellent	Very good
Palm Zire	$100.00		Good	Excellent	Good	Excellent	Good
Sony CLIE PEG-NZ90	$800.00		Very good	Good	Good	Excellent	Very good
Palm Zire 71	$300.00		Good	Good	Very good	Excellent	Good
Sony CLIE PEG-SJ33	$300.00		Very good	Good	Good	Very good	Very good
Palm Tungsten T	$400.00		Good	Good	Good	Very good	Very good
Palm m515	$300.00		Good	Good	Good	Very good	Very good
Sony CLIE PEG-NX70V CLIE PEG-NX60	$500.00		Very good	Good	Good	Very good	Good
Sony CLIE PEG-TG50	$400.00		Good	Good	Good	Excellent	Very good
Sony CLIE PEG-SJ22	$200.00		Very good	Good	Good	Excellent	Good
Palm m130	$200.00		Good	Good	Fair	Very good	Good

Figure 1.3 Part of *Consumer Reports* ratings chart for Palm-OS PDA models.

1b Identifying Your Audience

When you are in the early stages of a writing project, staring at an empty computer screen or a blank sheet of paper, it is easy to forget that what you write will have an audience. But except for diaries and private journals, you always write for an **audience**, a particular reader or group of readers. In this sense, writing is a public rather than a private activity.

(1) Writing for an Audience

At different times, in different roles, you address a variety of audiences.

- As a citizen, consumer, or member of a community, civic, political, or religious group, you may respond to pressing social, economic, or political issues by writing letters to a newspaper, a public official, or a representative of a special interest group.
- In your personal life, you may write notes and email messages to friends and family.
- As an employee, you may write letters, memos, and reports to your superiors, to staff members you supervise, or to coworkers; you may also be called on to address customers or critics, board members or stockholders, funding agencies or the general public.
- As a student, you write essays, reports, and other papers addressed to one or more instructors, and you may also participate in peer review, writing evaluations of classmates' essays and writing responses to their comments about your own work.

See 5d2

As you write, you shape your writing in terms of what you believe your audience needs and expects. Your assessment of your readers' interests, educational level, biases, and expectations determines not only the information you include but also what you emphasize and how you arrange your material. For example, in an email to a friend, you take into account the experiences you share, what your friend knows about you, and how much you need to explain. In a letter of complaint, you try to present the evidence that will convince your reader that your complaint is justified. In a job application letter, you decide how to make your reader see you in the best possible light. And this is true of all the other writing you do in your daily life.

See 9c

See 28b

At work, the demands and expectations of your audience affect your writing even more directly. Whether you write for your peers, your immediate supervisor, your subordinates, or the public, you tailor your style and content directly to them. In each case, you ask yourself what information your audience needs and what language and format will communicate this information to them most effectively.

Most of the writing you do as a student also has an audience. Whether you are writing for your instructor, as in the case of a midterm exam, or for the entire university community, as in the case of an article for your school newspaper, the challenge remains the same: trying to communicate ideas and information effectively to readers.

(2) The College Writer's Audience

Writing for Your Instructor As a student, you usually write for an audience of one: the instructor who assigns the paper. Instructors want to know what you know and whether you can express what you know clearly and accurately. They assign written work to encourage you to use critical thinking skills, so the way you organize and express your ideas can be as important as the ideas themselves.

As a group, instructors have certain expectations. Because they are trained as careful readers and critics, your instructors expect accurate information, standard grammar and correct spelling, logically presented ideas, and a reasonable degree of stylistic fluency. They also expect you to define your terms and to support your generalizations with specifics. Finally, every instructor also expects you to draw your own conclusions and to provide full and accurate documentation for ideas that are not your own.

If you are writing in an instructor's academic field, you can omit long overviews and basic definitions. Remember, however, that outside their areas of expertise, most instructors are simply general readers. If you think you may know more about a subject than your instructor does, be sure to provide background, and to supply the definitions, examples, and analogies that will make your ideas clear.

ESL Tip

If you did not attend school in the US, you may have trouble identifying your instructor's expectations. You may also have difficulty determining how much background information your instructor knows about a specific topic, especially if that topic relates to your own cultural background, native language, or home country. In these situations, it is usually a good idea to ask your instructor for advice.

NOTE: Keep in mind that because different academic disciplines have their own document design formats, documentation styles, methods of reporting data, technical vocabularies, and stylistic conventions, instructors' expectations may vary according to their discipline.

Writing for Other Students Before you submit a paper to an instructor, you may have an opportunity to participate in **peer review,** sharing your work with your fellow students and responding in writing to their work. In both these cases, you need to see your classmates as an audience whose needs you must take into account.

- **Writing Drafts** If you know that other students will read a draft of your paper, you need to consider how they might react to your ideas. For example, are they likely to agree with you? To be shocked or offended by your paper's language or content? To be confused, or even mystified, by any of your references? Even if your readers are your own age, you cannot assume that they share your cultural frame of reference. It is therefore very important that you maintain an appropriate tone and use moderate language in your paper and that you explain any historical, geographical, or cultural references that might be unfamiliar to your audience.

See 1c

- **Writing Comments** When you respond in writing to other students' papers, you need to take into account how this audience will react to your comments. Here too, your tone is important: you want to be as encouraging (and as polite) as possible. In addition, keep in mind that your purpose is not to show how clever you are but to offer constructive comments that can help your classmate write a stronger essay.

Checklist: Audience Concerns for Peer Review Participants

- ☐ **Know your audience.** To be sure you understand what the student writer needs and expects from your comments, read the paper several times before you begin writing your response.
- ☐ **Focus on the big picture.** Don't get bogged down on minor problems with punctuation or mechanics or become distracted by a paper's proofreading errors.
- ☐ **Look for a positive feature,** zeroing in on what you think is the paper's greatest strength.

(continued)

Audience concerns for peer review participants (continued)

- ☐ **Be positive throughout.** Try to avoid words like *weak*, *poor*, and *bad*; instead, try using a compliment before delivering the "bad news": "Paragraph 2 is very well developed; can you add this kind of support in paragraph 4?"
- ☐ **Show respect.** It is perfectly acceptable to tell a student that something is confusing or inaccurate, but don't go on the attack.
- ☐ **Be specific.** Avoid generalizations like "needs more examples" or "could be more interesting"; instead, try to offer helpful, focused suggestions: "You could add an example after the second sentence in paragraph 2"; "Explaining how this process operates would make your discussion more interesting."
- ☐ **Don't give orders.** Ask questions, and make suggestions.
- ☐ **Include a few words of encouragement,** emphasizing the paper's strong points.

Checklist: Identifying Your Audience

- ☐ Who will read your paper?
- ☐ What are your audience's needs? Expectations? Biases? Interests?
- ☐ Does your audience need you to supply definitions? Overviews? Examples? Analogies?
- ☐ What does your audience expect in terms of document design? Format? Documentation style? Method of collecting and reporting data? Use of formulas and symbols or specialized vocabulary?

Exercise 5

Look again at the excerpts and visuals in Exercises 1 through 4 on pages 7–10. This time, try to decide what audience or audiences each seems to be aimed at. Then, consider what (if anything) might have to be changed to address the needs of each of the following audiences:

- College students
- Middle-school students
- The elderly
- People with limited English skills
- People who do not live in the US

1c Setting Your Tone

FAQs links

Tone conveys your attitude. The attitude, or mood, that you adopt as you write may be serious or frivolous, respectful or condescending, intimate or detached. Because tone tells your readers how you feel about your material, it must remain consistent with your purpose and your audience as you write and revise.

When your general purpose is to present information, you choose words and construct sentences that make your writing objective and informative. Your choice of a factual, straightforward, reasonable—even impersonal—tone will convey your no-nonsense attitude. In such a situation, a sarcastic or playful tone would be inappropriate. When, however, your primary purpose is to influence your readers—for example, to sway their opinions or appeal to their emotions, to make them angry or sympathetic—you select words and shape sentences that serve this end. Your tone could be ironic or harsh, sentimental or cold, bitter or compassionate: whatever best reflects your attitude and serves your purpose.

Your tone also reveals how you feel toward your readers—sympathetic or superior, concerned or indifferent, friendly or critical. For instance, if you identify with your readers or feel close to them, you use a personal and conversational tone. When you address a general reader indirectly or anonymously, you use a more distant, formal tone.

When your audience is an instructor and your purpose is to inform (as is often the case in college writing situations), you should generally use an objective tone—neither too personal and informal nor too detached and formal—as the following student paragraph does.

> One of the major characteristics of streptococci is that they are gram-positive. This means that after a series of dyes and rinses they take on a violet color. (Gram-negative organisms take on a red color.) Streptococci are also nonspore forming and nonmotile. Most strains produce a protective shield called a capsule. They use organic substances instead of oxygen for their metabolism. This process is called fermentation.

An English composition assignment asking students to write a short, informal essay expressing their feelings about the worst job they ever had calls for an entirely different tone. In the paragraph that follows, the student's tone effectively conveys his attitude toward his job, and his use of the first person encourages his audience to identify with him. Sarcastic comments ("good little laborer," "Now here comes the excitement!") contribute to the informal effect.

> Every day I followed the same boring, monotonous routine. After clocking in like a good little laborer, I proceeded over to a gray file cabinet, forced open the half-caved-in doors, and removed a staple gun, various packs of size cards, and a blue ballpoint pen. Now here comes the excitement! Each farmer had a specific number assigned to his name. As his cucumbers were being sorted according to their particular size, they were loaded into two-hundred-pound bins, which I had to label with a stapled size card with the farmer's number on it. I had to complete a specific size card for every bin containing that size cucumber. Doesn't it sound wonderful? Any second grader could have handled it. And all the time I worked, the machinery moaned and rattled, and the odor of cucumbers filled the air.

In a letter applying for a job, however, the same student would have a different purpose—and, therefore, would use a different tone. In this situation, his distance from his audience and his desire to impress readers with his qualifications would call for a much more objective and straightforward tone.

> My primary duty at Germaine Produce was to label cucumbers as they were sorted into bins. I was responsible for making sure each two-hundred-pound bin bore the name of the farmer who had grown those cucumbers and also for keeping track of the cucumbers' sizes. Accuracy was extremely important in this task.

Checklist: Setting Your Tone

- ☐ What is your attitude toward your readers?
- ☐ Do you feel close to or distant from your audience?
- ☐ Do you know your readers well, or are they just acquaintances (or even strangers)?
- ☐ Does your audience command a high degree of respect or deference?
- ☐ Do your audience and purpose call for an objective tone?
- ☐ Is your purpose to present information, or are you intending to persuade your readers?

☐ Do you have another, more specific purpose that might influence your tone?
☐ Does your audience expect a formal or informal tone?
☐ Will your audience be likely to accept slang or sarcasm?

http://kirsznermandell.wadsworth.com

Computer Tip: Conveying Your Tone

Your computer gives you options—different type sizes and typefaces, for example—that can help you convey a particular tone. For example, if you are applying for a job in business or industry and want to write a **résumé**, you would select a conservative typeface such as Times New Roman rather than a more decorative font. A plain, businesslike typeface tells readers that you are a serious applicant.

See 28c–d

Exercise 6

1. Focus on a book that you liked or disliked very much. How would you write about the book in each of the following writing situations? Consider how each writing situation would affect your choice of content, style, organization, tone, and emphasis.
    - A journal entry reflecting on your impressions of the book
    - An exam question that asks you to summarize the book's ideas
    - A book review for a composition class in which you evaluate the book's strengths and weaknesses
    - A letter in which you try to convince your local school board that the book should (or should not) be purchased for a public high school's library
    - An editorial for your school newspaper in which you try to persuade other students that the book is worth reading
    - An email to a friend recommending (or criticizing) the book
2. Choose two of the writing situations listed above, and write a paragraph in response to each specified assignment.

Chapter 2

Reading to Write

Frequently Asked Questions

What is active reading? (p. 18)
How do I preview a text? (p. 18)
How do I highlight a text? (p. 19)
How do I annotate a text? (p. 22)
How do I interpret a visual image? (p. 27)

Central to becoming a critical reader is learning the techniques of active reading. **Active reading** means reading with pen in hand, physically marking the text in order to identify parallels, question ambiguities, distinguish important points from not-so-important ones, and connect causes with effects and generalizations with specific examples. The understanding you gain from active reading prepares you to think (and write) critically about a text.

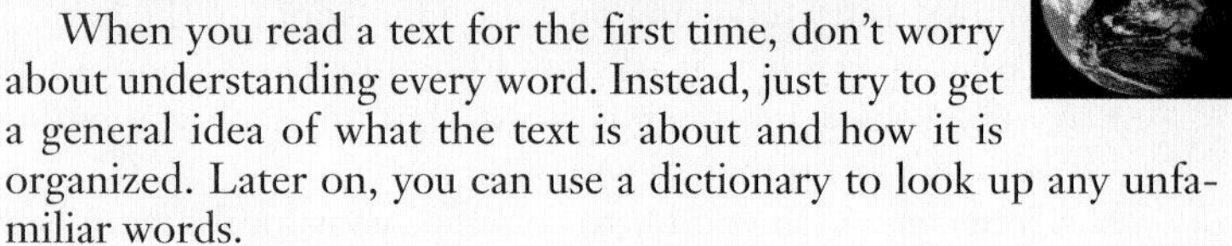

ESL Tip

When you read a text for the first time, don't worry about understanding every word. Instead, just try to get a general idea of what the text is about and how it is organized. Later on, you can use a dictionary to look up any unfamiliar words.

2a Reading Texts

(1) Previewing a Text

The first time you encounter a text, you should **preview** it—that is, skim it to get a sense of the author's subject and emphasis.

When you preview a *book*, begin by looking at its table of contents, especially at the sections that pertain to your topic. Then, turn to its index. A quick glance at the index will reveal the amount of coverage the book gives to subjects that may be important to you. As you leaf through the chapters, look at pictures, graphs, or tables, and read the captions that appear with them.

When you preview a *magazine article*, scan the introductory and concluding paragraphs for summaries of the author's main points. (Journal articles in the sciences and social sciences often begin with summaries called abstracts.) Thesis statements, topic sentences, repeated key terms, transitional words and phrases, and transitional paragraphs can also help you to identify the points a writer is making. In addition, look for the visual cues—such as headings and lists—that writers use to emphasize ideas.

Close-up: Visual Cues

When you preview a text, don't forget to note its use of color as well as its use of various typographical elements—typeface and type size, boldface and italics—to emphasize ideas.

(2) Highlighting a Text

When you have finished previewing a work, you should **highlight** it—that is, use a system of graphic symbols and underlining—to identify the writer's key points and their relationships to one another. (If you are working with library material, photocopy the pages you need before you highlight them.) Be sure to use symbols that you will understand when you reread your material later on.

Checklist: Using Highlighting Symbols

- ☐ Underline to indicate information you should read again.
- ☐ Box or circle key words or important phrases.
- ☐ Put question marks next to confusing passages, unclear points, or words you need to look up.
- ☐ Draw lines or arrows to show connections between ideas.
- ☐ Number points that appear in sequence.
- ☐ Draw a vertical line in the margin to set off an important section of text.
- ☐ Star especially important ideas.

The student who highlighted the following passage used many of the symbols listed in the checklist above to help her isolate the author's key ideas and clarify the progression of ideas in the passage.

Public zoos came into existence at the beginning of the period which was to see the disappearance of animals from daily life. The zoo, to which people go to meet animals, to observe them, to see them, is, in fact, a monument to the impossibility of such encounters. Modern zoos are an epitaph to a relationship which was as old as man. They are not seen as such because the wrong questions have been addressed to zoos.

When they were founded—the London Zoo in 1828, the Jardin des Plantes in 1793, the Berlin Zoo in 1844—they brought considerable prestige to the national capitals. The prestige was not so different from that which had accrued to the private royal menageries. These menageries, along with gold plate, architecture, orchestras, players, furnishings, dwarfs, acrobats, uniforms, horses, art and food, had been demonstrations of an emperor's or king's power and wealth. Likewise in the 19th century, public zoos were an endorsement of modern colonial power. The capturing of the animals was a symbolic representation of the conquest of all distant and exotic lands. "Explorers" proved their patriotism by sending home a tiger or an elephant. The gift of an exotic animal to the metropolitan zoo became a token in subservient diplomatic relations.

Yet, like every other 19th century public institution, the zoo, however supportive of the ideology of imperialism, had to claim an independent and civic function. The claim was that it was another kind of museum, whose purpose was to further knowledge and public enlightenment. And so the first questions asked of zoos belonged to natural history; it was then thought possible to study the natural life of animals even in such unnatural conditions. A century later, more sophisticated zoologists such as Konrad Lorenz asked behavioristic and ethological questions, the claimed purpose of which was to discover more about the springs of human action through the study of animals under experimental conditions. (John Berger, *About Looking*)

Exercise 1

Preview the following passage, and then read it more carefully, highlighting it to help you understand the writer's ideas. Next, compare your highlighting with a classmate's. When you are satisfied that you have identified the most important ideas and that you both understand the passage, work together to answer the following questions.

- What is the writer's subject?
- What is the writer's most important idea?
- How does he support this key idea?
- How does the writer make connections among related points clear?

"Go to Wall Street," my classmates said.

"Go to Wall Street," my professor advised.

"Go to Wall Street," my father threatened.

Whenever I tell people about my career indecisiveness, their answer is always the same: Get a blueprint for life and get one fast. Perhaps I'm simply too immature, but I think 20 is far too young to set my life in stone.

Nobody mentioned any award for being the first to have a white picket fence, 2.4 screaming kids, and a spanking new Ford station wagon.

What's wrong with uncertainty, with exploring multiple options in multiple fields? What's wrong with writing, "Heck, I don't know," under the "objective" section of my résumé?

Parents, professors, recruiters and even other students seem to think there's a lot wrong with it. And they are all pressuring me to launch a career prematurely.

My sociology professor warns that my generation will be the first in American history not to be more successful than our parents' generation. This depressing thought drives college students to think of success as something that must be achieved at all costs as soon as possible.

My father wants me to emulate his success: Every family wants its children to improve the family fortune. I feel that desire myself, but I realize I don't need to do it by age 25.

This pressure to do better, to compete with the achievements of our parents in a rapidly changing world, has forced my generation to pursue definitive, lifelong career paths at far too young an age. Many of my friends who have graduated in recent years are already miserably unhappy.

My professors encourage such pre-professionalism. In upper level finance classes, the discussion is extremely career-oriented. "Learn to do this and you'll be paid more" is the theme of many a lecture. Never is there any talk of actually enjoying the exercise.

Nationwide, universities are finally taking steps in the right direction by re-emphasizing the study of liberal arts and a return to the classics. If only job recruiters for Wall Street firms would do the same.

"Get your M.B.A. as soon as possible and you'll have a jump on the competition," said one overly zealous recruiter from Goldman Sachs. Learning for learning's sake was completely forgotten: Goldman Sachs refused to interview anybody without a high grade-point average, regardless of the courses composing that average.

In other interviews, it is expected that you know exactly what you want to do or you won't be hired. "Finance?" they say, "What kind of finance?"

A recruiter at Dean Witter Reynolds said investment banking demands 80 to 100 hours of work per week. I don't see how anyone will ever find time to enjoy the gobs of money they'll be making.

The worst news came from a partner at Salomon Brothers. He told me no one was happy there, and if they said they were, they're lying. He said you come in, make a lot of money and leave as fast as you can.

Two recent Wharton alumni, scarcely two years older than I, spoke at Donaldson, Lufkin & Jenrette's presentation. Their jokes about not having a life outside the office were only partially in jest.

Yet, students can't wait to play this corporate charade. They don ties and jackets and tote briefcases to class.

It is not just business students who are obsessed with their careers. The five other people who live in my house are not undergraduate business majors, but all five plan to attend graduate school next year. How is it possible that, without one iota of real work experience, these people are willing to commit themselves to years of intensive study in one narrow field?

Mom, dad, grandpa, recruiters, professors, fellow students: I implore you to leave me alone.

Now is my chance to explore, to spend time pursuing interests simply because they make me happy and not because they fill my wallet. I don't want to waste my youth toiling at a miserable job. I want to make the right decisions about my future.

Who knows, I may even end up on Wall Street. (Michael Finkel, "Undecided—and Proud of It")

(3) Annotating a Text

After you have read through a text once, read it again—this time, more critically. At this stage, you should **annotate** the pages, recording your responses to what you read. This process of recording notes in the margins or between the lines will help you understand the writer's ideas and your own reactions to those ideas.

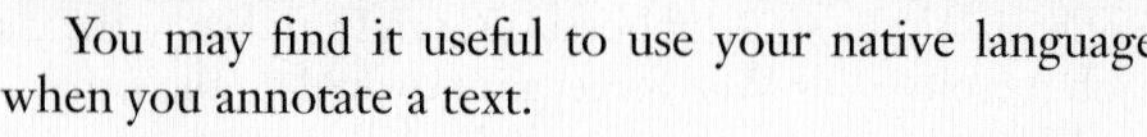

You may find it useful to use your native language when you annotate a text.

Some of your annotations may be relatively straightforward. For example, you may define new words, identify unfamiliar references, or jot down brief summaries. Other annotations may be more personal: you may identify a parallel between your own experience and one described in the reading selection, or you may record your opinion of the writer's position.

Close-up: Reading Critically

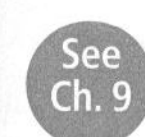

See Ch. 9

When you start to think critically about a text, your annotations may identify points that confirm (or dispute) your own ideas, question the appropriateness or accuracy of the writer's support, uncover the writer's biases, or even question (or challenge) the writer's conclusion.

The following passage illustrates a student's annotations of an article about the decline of American public schools.

> One of the most compelling arguments about the Vietnam War is that it lasted as long as it did because of its "classist" nature. The central thesis is that because neither the decision makers in the government *nor anyone they knew* had children fighting and dying in Vietnam, they had no personal incentive to bring the war to a halt. The government's generous college-deferment system, steeped as it was in class distinctions, allowed the white middle class to avoid the tragic consequences of the war. And the people who did the fighting and dying in place of the college-deferred were those whose voices were least heard in Washington: the poor and the disenfranchised.
>
> Is this comparison valid? (seems forced)
>
> I bring this up because I believe that the decline of the public schools is rooted in the same cause. Just as with the Vietnam War, as soon as the middle class no longer had a stake in the public schools, the surest pressure on school systems to provide a decent education instantly disappeared. Once the middle class was gone, no mayor was going to get booted out of office because the schools were bad. No incompetent teacher had to worry about angry parents calling for his or her head "downtown." No third-rate educationalist at the local teachers college had to fear having his or her methods criticized by anyone that mattered. } bias
>
> The analogy to the Vietnam War can be extended even to the extent of the denial. It amuses me sometimes to hear people like myself decry the state of the public schools. We bemoan the lack of money, the decaying facilities, the absurd credentialism, the high foolishness of the school boards. We applaud the burgeoning reform movement. And everything we say is deeply, undeniably true. We can see every problem with the schools clearly except one: the fact that our decision to abandon the schools has helped create all the other problems. One small example: In the early 1980s, Massachusetts passed one of those

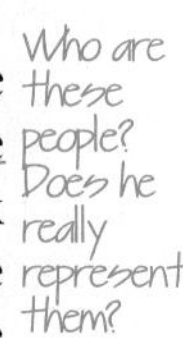

Who are these people? Does he really represent them?

Is this "one small example" * enough to support his claim?

bias

Oversimplification—Do all parents have the same motives?

tax cap measures, called Proposition 2 1/2, which has turned out to be a force for genuine evil in the public schools. Would Proposition 2 1/2 have passed had the middle class still had a stake in the schools? I wonder. I also wonder whether 20 years now, in the next round of breast-beating memoirs, the exodus of the white middle class from the public schools will finally be seen for what it was. Individually, every parent's rationale made impeccable sense—"I can't deprive my children of a decent education"—but collectively, it was a deeply destructive act.

Is this a valid assumption?

Why does he assume intent was "good" + "moral"? Is he right?

The main reason the white middle class fled, of course, is race, or more precisely, the complicated admixture of race and class and good intentions gone awry. The fundamental good intention—which even today strikes one as both moral and right—was to integrate the public classroom, and in so doing, to equalize the resources available to all school children. In Boston, this was done through enforced busing. In Washington, it was done through a series of judicial edicts that attempted to spread the good teachers and resources throughout the system. In other big city districts, judges weren't involved; school committees, seeing the handwriting on the wall, tried to do it themselves.

?

Interesting point—but is it true?

However moral the intent, the result almost always was the same. The white middle class left. The historic parental vigilance I mentioned earlier had had a lot to do with creating the two-tiered system—one in which schools attended by the kids of the white middle class had better teachers, better equipment, better everything than those attended by the kids of the poor. This did not happen because the white middle-class parents were racists, necessarily; it happened because they knew how to manipulate the system and were willing to do so on behalf of their kids. Their neighborhood schools became little havens of decent education, and they didn't much care what happened in the other public schools.

Slanted language (over emotional)

Generalization

Slanted language (over emotional)

In retrospect, this behavior, though perfectly understandable, was tragically short-sighted. When the judicial fiats made those safe havens untenable, the white middle class quickly discovered what the poor had always known: There weren't enough good teachers, decent equipment, and so forth to go around. For that matter, there weren't even enough good students to go around; along with everything else, middle-class parents had to start worrying about whether their kids were going to be mugged in school.

Either/or fallacy? Were there other choices?

Faced with the grim fact that their children's education was quickly deteriorating, middle-class parents essentially had two choices: They could stay and pour the energy that had once gone into improving the neighborhood school into improving the

Oversimplification? No exceptions?

entire school system—a frightening task, to be sure. Or they could leave. Invariably, they chose the latter.

And it wasn't just the white middle class that fled. The black middle class, and even the black poor who were especially ambitious for their children, were getting out as fast as they could too, though not to the suburbs. They headed mainly for the parochial schools, which subsequently became integration's great success story, even as the public schools became integration's great failure. (Joseph Nocera,"How the Middle Class Has Helped Ruin the Public Schools")

Exercise 2

Read the following article. Then, reread it, highlighting it as you read. When you have finished, annotate the article.

My father loved to tell the story of how he got into college. It was 1947 and my father, poor, black and brilliant, was a 15-year-old high school senior in rural Sylvester, Ga. One day he was called into the principal's office to meet a visiting state education official, a white bureaucrat who had learned of my father's academic prowess. The state, the official said, had decided that it wanted to send "a nigra" to college. "You can go to any college in the state," the official told my father. "Except . . . for the University of Georgia, Georgia Tech, Georgia A & M, Emory. . . ."

My father was happy and proud to attend Atlanta's Morehouse, perhaps the finest black college in America. But there was always a trace of bitterness when he told this story since his choice of college had, in effect, been made for him.

Times had changed when I applied to college in 1978. Thanks to my father's success as a financial consultant, I grew up in a solidly middle-class home in the Bronx, and, thanks largely to the social advances wrought by the civil rights movement, I was able to attend private school and get into Harvard.

I arrived in Cambridge just as the national backlash against affirmative action was gaining momentum. Many critics were suggesting that African-Americans were inherently inferior students, below the standards of the great universities. I found this argument fatuous, particularly when I encountered some of the less illustrious white students who had allegedly been accepted on "merit." There was, for example, the charming, wealthy young man I'll call "Ted." Intellectually incurious, struggling in most of his courses, Ted said he had been rejected by every college to which he had applied, except Harvard, the alma mater of his father and grandfather.

Ted was what is known as a "legacy." According to Harvard's dean of admissions, William Fitzsimmons, approximately 40 percent of alumni children who apply are admitted each year as against 14 percent of non-alumni applicants.

So Ted and I were beneficiaries of two different forms of affirmative action. He was accepted largely because his forebears had attended Harvard. I was accepted largely because my father had been denied the chance to apply to any predominantly white universities. Yet the type of affirmative action that benefited me is relentlessly assailed while the more venerable form of preferential treatment that Ted enjoyed goes virtually unchallenged.

Whether one is listening to Clarence Thomas's tortuous rationalizations about how he didn't really benefit from affirmative action, or George Bush's railing against racial quotas, which have never been widely supported by Americans, white or black, the underlying message is the same: were it not for affirmative action, America would function as a perfect meritocracy.

Of course there are people of all backgrounds who have succeeded solely through talent and perseverance. But at least as many have been assisted by personal connections, old-boy networks, family ties and the benefits traditionally accorded certain, primarily white, primarily male segments of the American population. Why, in the interminable debate over affirmative action, have these historic advantages generally been brushed aside?

I am not suggesting that most "legacies" or other beneficiaries of long-established de facto affirmative action programs are unqualified for the placements and positions they get. Most of the "legacies" I met at Harvard did just fine there, but so did the great majority of African-Americans. The difference was that the "legacies" were not stigmatized by their extra edge and the black students were. (Jake Lamar, "Whose Legacy Is It, Anyway?")

Checklist: Reading Texts

- ☐ Does the writer provide any information about his or her background? If so, how does this information affect your reading of the text?
- ☐ Are there parallels between the writer's experiences and your own?
- ☐ What is the writer's purpose? How can you tell?
- ☐ What audience is the text aimed at? How can you tell?
- ☐ What is the text's most important idea? What support does the writer provide for that idea?
- ☐ What information can you learn from the text's introduction and conclusion?
- ☐ What information can you learn from the thesis statement and topic sentences?

See 1a–b

See 4a

- ☐ What key words are repeated? What does this repetition tell you about the writer's purpose and emphasis?
- ☐ How would you characterize the writer's tone?
- ☐ Where do you agree with the writer? Where do you disagree?
- ☐ What, if anything, is not clear to you?

See 1c

2b Reading Visuals

The texts you read in college courses—books, newspapers, and articles, in print or online—are often accompanied by visual images. For example, textbooks often include illustrations to make complex information more accessible, and newspapers use photographs to break up columns of written text as well as to add interest. Currently, more and more information is being presented in visual form—not just on billboards and in magazines and other print media, but also on the Web and even in cell phones that can store and send images. Because the world audience is becoming increasingly visual, it is important for you to acquire the skills needed to read and interpret visuals as well as to use them in your own written work. (For information on incorporating visuals into your own writing, **see 5b3.**)

Close-up: Reading Visuals

Visuals (such as those listed below) have long been used to persuade as well as to entertain and to convey information.

Photographs	Flowcharts	Advertisements
Maps	Fine art	Scientific diagrams
Cartoons	Bar and line graphs	Tables

The powerful newspaper photograph shown in Figure 2.1, which depicts a Marine in front of the Vietnam Veterans Memorial, uses a variety of techniques to convey its message. To interpret this photograph, you need to determine exactly how it achieves its effect. You might notice right away that contrasts are very important in this picture. In the background is the list of soldiers who died in the war; in the foreground, a lone member of a Marine honor guard stands in silent vigil, seemingly as unmoving as the names carved in granite. Still, those who view this photo know that the Marine is motionless only in the picture; when the photographer puts the camera

The whole world is watching

Member of Marine honor guard passes the Vietnam memorial on which names of casualties of the war are inscribed

Figure 2.1 Newspaper photograph taken at the Vietnam memorial.

down, the Marine lives on, in contrast to his comrades whose names are listed behind him. The large close-up of the Marine set against the smaller names in the background also suggests that the photographer's purpose is at least in part to contrast the past and the present, the dead and the living. Thus, the photograph has a persuasive purpose: it suggests, as its title states, that "the whole world is watching" (and, in fact, *should* be watching) this scene in order to remember the past and honor the dead.

To convey their ideas, visuals often rely on contrasting light and shadow and on the size and placement of individual images (as well as on the spatial relationship of these images to one another and to the whole). In addition, visuals often use color as well as captions and other verbal elements, and they may also include animation, audio narration, and even musical soundtracks. When you analyze a visual text, you may need to consider many—or even all—of these elements. Given the complexity of most visuals and the number of individual elements each one uses to convey its message, analyzing (or "reading") visual texts can be challenging. This task will be easier, however, if you follow the same active reading process you use when you read a written text.

(1) Previewing a Visual

Just as with a written text, the first step in analyzing a visual text is to preview it, scanning it to get a sense of its subject and emphasis. At this stage, you may notice little more than the visual's major features: its central image, its dominant colors, its use of empty space, and the largest blocks of written text. Still, even these elements can give you a general idea of what the focus of the visual is and what purpose it might have.

See 2a1

(2) Highlighting and Annotating a Visual

When you highlight a visual text, you mark it up to help you identify key images and their relationship to one another. You might, for example, use arrows to point to important images or written elements, or you might circle smaller details. When you annotate a visual text, you record your reactions to the images and words you see. (If a visual's background is dark, or if you are not permitted to write directly on it, you can do your highlighting and annotating on small self-stick notes.)

See 2a2

See 2a3

A student in a composition class was asked to analyze the magazine advertisement for Phoenix Wealth Management shown in

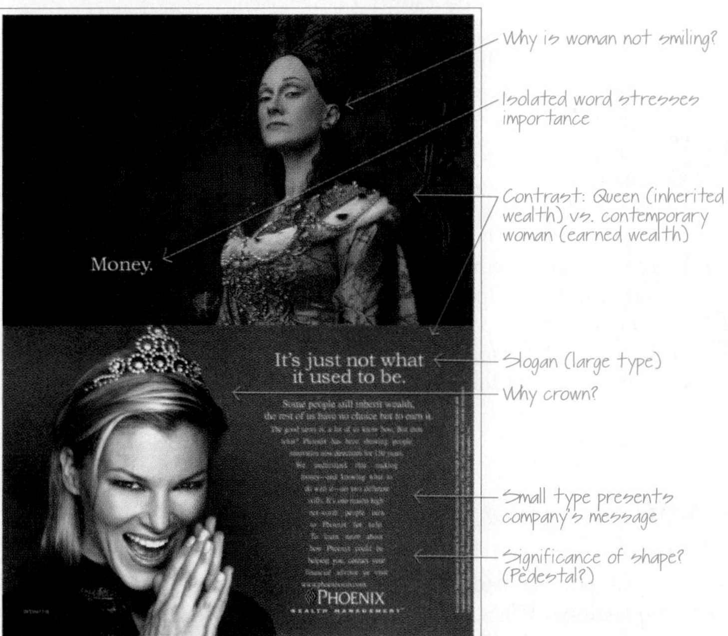

Figure 2.2 Magazine ad for Phoenix Wealth Management.

Figure 2.2. When she went to Phoenix's Web site, she learned that the company's mission is to offer investment advice to affluent people who want to become more financially secure. The student's highlighting and annotating focus on the relationship between the text and visuals and how they work together to present the company's message: that investing with Phoenix will make women financially independent and secure.

Checklist: Reading Visuals

See 1a–b

- ☐ Who owns or has created the visual?
- ☐ For what purpose was the visual created? For example, does it seem to be designed primarily to inform? To persuade? To entertain or amuse?
- ☐ Where did the visual originally appear? What is the target audience for this publication?
- ☐ What scene does the visual depict?
- ☐ What kinds of people appear in the visual? What do they suggest about its target audience? What is their relationship to the scene and to one another? What are they doing?
- ☐ How would you describe the people's facial expressions? Their positions? Their body language?
- ☐ Does the visual include a lot of blank space?
- ☐ How large are the various elements (words and images)?
- ☐ Is the background light or dark? Clear or blurred? What individual elements stand out most clearly against this background?
- ☐ What general mood is suggested by the visual's use of color and shadow?
- ☐ Does the visual include a written message? How large is it? How prominently is it placed? What is its purpose?
- ☐ In general terms, what is the visual's message? How do its individual elements help to communicate this message?
- ☐ What associations do the individual images have for you?
- ☐ How would the visual's message or impact be different if something were added? If something were deleted?

Exercise 3

Write a paragraph in which you analyze the *Runner's World* magazine ad for New Balance sneakers shown in Figure 2.3. Consider the following questions: What audience is being addressed? What is the ad's primary purpose? What message is being conveyed? How do the various visual elements work together to appeal to the ad's target audience?

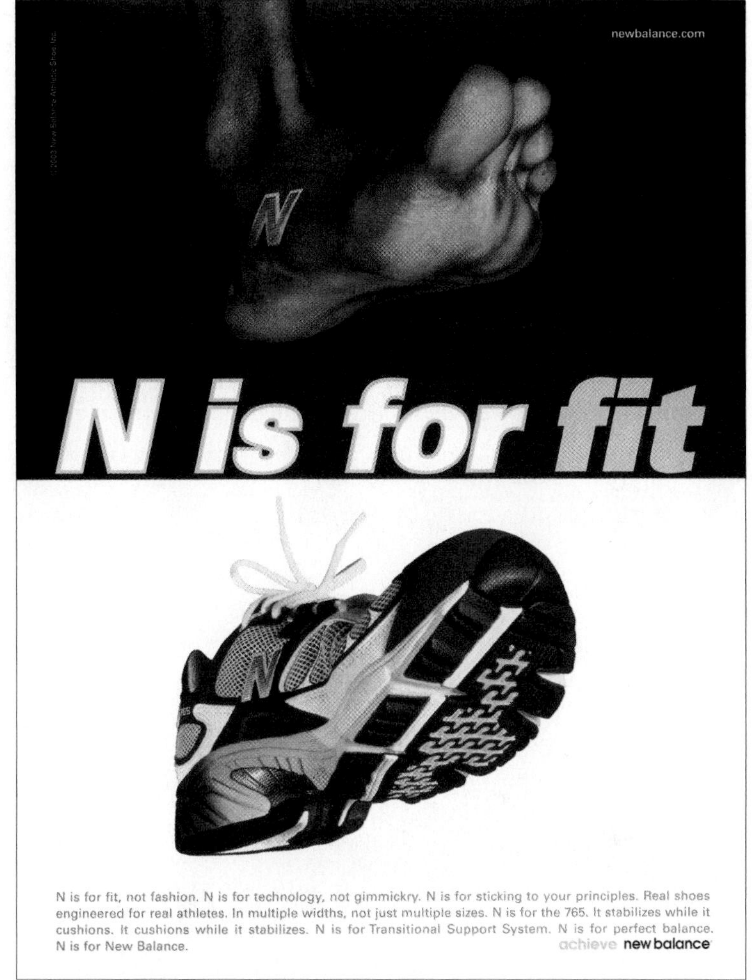

Figure 2.3 Magazine ad for New Balance sneakers.

Exercise 4

Use the checklist on page 30 to help you write a paragraph in response to each of the following.

1. On your way to campus or work, locate a billboard or a prominent sign (for example, on a train platform or bus shelter). What product or service does it promote? To what audience is it directed? How do you know? What does the image seem to assume about its intended audience (age, class, gender, and so on)?

2. Compare and contrast two magazine, television, or Internet advertisements for the same type of product (an automobile or cologne, for instance) that are aimed at two different audiences. How are the two ads different? How does each aim to reach its audience? What elements contribute to the persuasive message of each ad?
3. Select a Web site related to your major or to a paper you are currently working on. What elements of the site—visuals, typeface and type size, color, audio and video components—contribute to the site's usefulness as an information resource? How might the site benefit from additional (or fewer) visual features?
4. Select a chapter from a textbook in your major, and examine the way in which content is arranged on the pages. What visual elements (headings, lists, charts, tables, photographs, and so on) can you identify? How do these elements highlight important information?

Chapter 3

Planning an Essay

Frequently Asked Questions

3a Understanding the Writing Process

Writing enables you to discover ideas, make connections, and see from new perspectives. In this sense, writing is a demanding, creative process of thinking and learning—about yourself, about others, and about your world. In another sense, writing is a tool that empowers you: it enables you to participate in the ongoing dialogue among people who communicate in letters, emails, memos, petitions, reports, articles, editorials, and books.

See Ch. 9

Writing presents many situations in which you must think critically: make judgments, weigh alternatives, analyze, compare, question, evaluate, and engage in other decision-making activities. Virtually all writing demands that you make informed choices about your subject matter and about the way you present your ideas. In fact, writing is a constant process of decision making—of selecting, deleting, and rearranging material.

Close-up: The Writing Process

The writing process includes the following stages:

Planning: Consider your purpose, audience, and tone; choose your topic; discover ideas to write about.

Shaping: Decide how to organize your material.

Drafting: Write your first draft.

Revising: "Re-see" what you have written; write additional drafts.

Editing: Check grammar, spelling, punctuation, and mechanics.

Proofreading: Check for typographical errors.

The neatly defined stages listed on the previous page communicate neither the complexity nor the flexibility of the writing process. These stages actually overlap: as you look for ideas, you begin to shape your material; as you shape your material, you begin to write; as you write a draft, you reorganize your ideas; as you revise, you continue to discover new material. Moreover, these stages may be repeated again and again throughout the writing process.

During your college years and in the years that follow, you will develop your own version of the writing process and use it whenever you write, adapting it to the audience, purpose, and writing situation at hand.

NOTE: The writing process that is explained in Chapters 3 through 5 will be illustrated in Chapter 6, "Writing an Essay: A Case Study," which follows a student as she plans, writes, and revises an essay.

ESL Tip

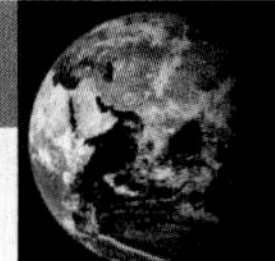

In many high school and college writing classes in the US, classroom and homework activities are organized around the stages of the writing process outlined in this text. For more information, **see Chapter 61.**

Exercise 1

1. Write a paragraph in which you describe your own writing process. (If you prefer, you may draw a diagram that represents your process.) What do you do first? What steps do you return to again and again? Which stages do you find most satisfying? Which do you find most frustrating?
2. Write a paragraph in which you focus on the visual aspects of your writing process. For example, do you find yourself making charts or diagrams as you write? Do you use arrows to connect ideas? How do these strategies help you to generate ideas and identify connections between them?

3b Computers and the Writing Process

Computers have changed the way we write and communicate in both academic and workplace settings. In addition to using word-processing applications for typical writing tasks, writers may rely on programs such as *PowerPoint*® for presentations, *Publisher*® for creating customized résumés or brochures, and Web-page authoring software such as *FrontPage*® for creating Internet-accessible documents that include images, movies, and a wide range of visual effects.

With the expanding role of the Internet in professional, academic, and personal communication, it is becoming increasingly likely that some of the feedback you receive on your writing will be electronic. For example, you may receive personal email from your instructor about a paper draft that you have submitted to a digital drop box, a tool often associated with course management software such as *WebCT*™ or *Blackboard*™. Or, you may use discussion boards for attaching or sharing your documents in a whole-class or small-group forum or for later review and discussion with others. Chat room and Net meeting software also allow you to discuss topic ideas collaboratively and to offer and receive feedback on drafts. Although the specific tools you use may be course- or workplace-specific, the writing process will be similar.

Not all electronic collaboration is Internet based, however. For example, it is also possible to use *Microsoft Word*®'s Comment feature to give and receive feedback on drafts. You may save the marked-up document to disk or email it as an attachment to a peer or instructor. Whatever tools you have at your disposal, there are clear advantages to online dialogue with others, including the immediacy of feedback and a potentially larger number (and broader range) of responses from readers.

Exercise 2

To what extent does your writing process rely on the computer? Look back at the two paragraphs you wrote for Exercise 1, and add details about how you use the computer in your writing process.

3c Analyzing Your Assignment

Planning your essay—thinking about what you want to say and how you want to say it—begins well before you actually start recording your thoughts in any organized way. This planning is as important a part of the writing process as the writing itself. During this planning stage, you determine your purpose for writing, identify your audience, and decide on an appropriate tone. Then, you go on to focus on your assignment, choose and narrow your topic, and gather ideas.

Before you begin writing, be sure you understand the exact requirements of your assignment, and keep those guidelines in mind as you write and revise. Don't assume anything; ask questions, and be sure you understand the answers.

Checklist: Analyzing Your Assignment

- ☐ Has your instructor assigned a specific topic, or can you choose your own?
- ☐ What is the word or page limit?
- ☐ How much time do you have to complete your assignment?
- ☐ Will you get feedback from your instructor? Will you have an opportunity to participate in peer review? See 5d2
- ☐ Does your assignment require research?
- ☐ What format (for example, MLA) are you supposed to follow? Do you know what its conventions are? See Ch. 18
- ☐ If your assignment has been given to you in writing, have you read it carefully and highlighted key words?

3d Choosing and Narrowing a Topic

If your instructor allows you to choose a topic, choose one you know something about—or, at least, one you want to learn about. Perhaps a class discussion or reading assignment will suggest a topic; maybe you have seen a movie or television program or had a conversation (or an argument) about a topic you could explore.

Most of the time your instructor will steer you toward a topic by giving you an assignment that specifies a length, format, and general subject; gives a list of general subjects from which to choose; or poses a question for you to answer.

> Write a two-page critical analysis of a film. (Specifies length, format, and general subject)
>
> Write an essay explaining the significance of one of these court decisions: *Marbury* v. *Madison*, *Baker* v. *Carr*, *Brown* v. *Board of Education*, *Roe* v. *Wade*. (Gives list of general subjects from which to choose)
>
> How did the boundaries of Europe change after World War I? (Poses a question)

Even if your instructor gives you a very specific assignment, however, you may not be able to start writing immediately. First, you must determine whether the topic this assignment suggests is narrow enough for your purpose, your audience, and your page limit. If it is not, you will need to narrow it further.

Narrowing a Topic

Course	Assignment	Topic
American History	Analyze the effects of a social program on one segment of American society.	How did the GI Bill of Rights affect American service-women?
Sociology	Identify and evaluate the success of one resource available to the homeless population of one major American city.	The role of the Salvation Army in meeting the needs of Chicago's homeless
Psychology	Write a three- to five-page paper assessing one method of treating depression.	Animal-assisted therapy for severely depressed patients
Composition	Write an essay about your childhood.	My parents' divorce

(To see how a student writer moved from a broad assignment to a narrow topic, **see 6a1.**)

Exercise 3

Read the following excerpt, and study the photograph in Figure 3.1. Then, list ten possible essay topics about your own childhood suggested by the photo or by the writer's memories. (Your assignment is to write a three-page essay about your childhood; your purpose is to give your audience—your composition instructor and possibly members of your peer-review group—a vivid sense of what some aspect of your childhood was like.) Finally, choose the one topic that you feel best qualified to write about, and write a few sentences explaining why you selected it.

When we weren't down at the field or watching the Yankees on TV, we were playing whiffle ball and climbing trees checking out birds' nests, going down to Fly Beach in Mrs. Zimmer's old car that honked the horn every time it turned the corner, diving underwater with our masks, kicking with our rubber frog's feet, then running in and out of our sprinklers when we got home, waiting for our turn in the shower. And during the summer nights we were all over the neighborhood, from Bobby's house to Kenny's, throwing gliders, doing handstands and backflips off fences, riding to the woods at the end of the block on our bikes, making rafts, building tree forts, jumping across the streams with tree branches, walking and balancing along the back fence like Houdini, hopping along the slate path all around the back yard seeing how far we could go on one foot.

And I ran wherever I went. Down to school, the candy store, to the deli, buying baseball cards and Bazooka bubblegum that had the little fortunes at the bottom of the cartoons.

When the Fourth of July came, there were fireworks going off all over the neighborhood. It was the most exciting time of year for me next to Christmas. Being born on the exact same day as my country I thought was really great. I was so proud. And every Fourth of July, I had a birthday party and all my friends would come over with birthday presents and we'd put on silly hats and blow these horns my dad brought home from the A&P. We'd eat lots of ice cream and watermelon and I'd open up all the presents and blow out the candles on the big red, white, and blue birthday cake and then we'd all sing "Happy Birthday" and "I'm a Yankee Doodle Dandy." At night everyone would pile into Bobby's mother's old car and we'd go down to the drive-in, where we'd watch the fireworks display. Before the movie started, we'd all get out and sit up on the roof of the car with our blankets wrapped around us watching the rockets and Roman candles going up and exploding into fountains of rainbow colors, and later after Mrs. Zimmer dropped me off, I'd lie on my bed feeling a little sad that it all had to end so soon. As I closed my eyes I could still hear strings of firecrackers and cherry bombs going off all over the neighborhood. . . . (Ron Kovic, *Born on the Fourth of July*)

Figure 3.1 Children on the beach, posing for the camera.

3e Finding Something to Say

Once you have a topic, you can begin to collect ideas for your paper, using one (or several) of the strategies discussed in the pages that follow.

ESL Tip

Some ESL students spend little time generating ideas for their writing because they are primarily concerned about writing grammatically correct sentences. But remember, the purpose of writing is to convey ideas. If you want to find material to write about, you will need to devote plenty of time to the activities described in this section.

(1) Reading and Observing

The best way to find material to write about is to open your mind to new ideas. As you read textbooks, magazines, and newspapers and visit the library or browse the Internet, be on the lookout for ideas that relate to your topic, and make a point of talking informally with friends or family about it.

Films, television programs, interviews, telephone calls, letters, emails, and questionnaires can also provide material. But be sure your instructor permits such research—and remember to document ideas that are not your own. If you do not, you will be committing plagiarism.

See Ch. 16

(2) Keeping a Journal

Many professional writers keep **journals** (print or electronic), writing in them regularly whether or not they have a specific project in mind. Such a collection of thoughts and ideas can be a valuable resource when you run short of material. Journals, unlike diaries, do more than simply record personal experiences and reactions. In a journal, you explore ideas, ask questions, and draw conclusions. You might, for example, analyze your position on a political issue, try to solve an ethical problem, or trace the evolution of your ideas about an academic assignment. You can also record quotations that have special meaning to you or make notes about your reactions to important news events, films, or conversations. (In addition to writing, you can illustrate your journal by drawing pictures or diagrams or pasting in photos or cartoons.) A good journal is a scrapbook of ideas that you can leaf through in search of new material and new ways of looking at old material. The important thing is to write regularly—every day if possible—so that when a provocative idea comes along, you won't miss the opportunity to record it. (For an example of a student's journal entry, **see 6a2.**)

(3) Freewriting

Another strategy that can help you discover ideas is **freewriting.** When you freewrite, you let yourself go and write nonstop about anything that comes to mind, moving as quickly as you can. Give yourself a set period of time—say, five minutes—and don't stop to worry about punctuation, spelling, or grammar, or about where your mind is wandering. This strategy encourages your mind to make free associations; thus, it helps you to discover ideas you probably aren't even aware you have. When your time is up, look over what you have written, and underline, bracket, or star the most promising ideas. You can then use each of these ideas as the center of a focused freewriting exercise.

When you do **focused freewriting,** you zero in on your topic. Here too you write without stopping to reconsider or reread, so you have no time for counterproductive reactions—no time to be self-conscious about style or form, to worry about the relevance of your ideas, or to count how many words you have and panic about how many more you think you need. At its best, focused freewriting can suggest new details, a new approach to your topic, or even a more interesting topic. (For examples of a student's freewriting exercises, **see 6a2.**)

(4) Brainstorming

One of the most useful ways to accumulate ideas is by brainstorming (either on your own or in a group). This strategy enables you to recall pieces of information and to see connections among them.

When you **brainstorm,** you list all the points you can think of that seem pertinent to your topic, recording ideas—comments, questions, single words, symbols, or diagrams—as quickly as you can, without pausing to consider their relevance or trying to understand their significance. (For an example of a student's brainstorming notes, **see 6a2.**)

(5) Clustering

Clustering—sometimes called *webbing* or *mapping*—is similar to brainstorming. As with brainstorming, you don't need to worry about writing complete sentences, and you jot ideas down quickly, without pausing to evaluate their usefulness or to analyze their logical relationships to other ideas. However, clustering encourages you to explore your topic in a somewhat more systematic (and more visual) manner.

Begin making a cluster diagram by writing your topic in the center of a sheet of paper. Then, surround your topic with related ideas as they occur to you, moving outward from the general topic in the center and writing down increasingly specific ideas and details as you move toward the edges of the page. Eventually, following the path of one idea at a time, you create a diagram (often lopsided rather than symmetrical) that arranges ideas on spokes or branches radiating out from the center (your topic). (For an example of a student's cluster diagram, **see 6a2.**)

http://kirsznermandell.wadsworth.com

Computer Tip: Generating Ideas

You can use your computer to help you find material to write about. For example, you can set up a computer journal, and you can also use your computer for freewriting and brainstorming.

When you freewrite or compose a journal entry, try turning down the brightness of the monitor, leaving the screen blank to eliminate distractions and encourage spontaneity. When you reread what you have written, you can boldface or underline important ideas. You can also experiment with other word-processing formatting features (such as colored text) to emphasize key ideas—or even create columns or tables to highlight parallels between related points.

When you brainstorm, type your notes randomly. Later, after you print them out, you can add more notes and graphic elements (arrows, circles, and so on) by hand to indicate parallels and connections. If you prefer to do all your brainstorming electronically, you can use the drawing tools available with most word-processing programs. These drawing tools typically enable you to create shapes, arrows, and lines as well as to fill lines and shapes with colors. Such visual elements can help you distinguish the relationships among ideas and their relationship to your essay's main idea.

(6) Asking Journalistic Questions

Journalistic questions offer an orderly, systematic way of finding material to write about. Journalists are trained to ask the questions *Who? What? Why? Where? When?* and *How?* to ensure that they have explored all angles of a story, and you can use these questions to make sure you have considered all aspects of your topic. (For an example of a student's use of journalistic questions, **see 6a2.**)

Journalistic Questions

Who?	Why?	When?
What?	Where?	How?

(7) Asking In-Depth Questions

If you have time, you can ask a series of more focused questions about your topic. These in-depth questions not only can give you a great deal of information but also can suggest ways for you to eventually shape your ideas into paragraphs and essays. (For an example of a student's use of in-depth questions, **see 6a2.**)

In-Depth Questions

Questions	Suggestions
What happened? When did it happen? Where did it happen?	Suggest narration (an account of your first day of school; a summary of Emily Dickinson's life)
What does it look like? What does it sound like, smell like, taste like, or feel like?	Suggest description (of the Louvre; of the electron microscope; of a Web site)
What are some typical cases or examples of it?	Suggests exemplification (three infant day-care settings; four popular fad diets)
How did it happen? What makes it work? How is it made?	Suggest process (how to apply for financial aid; how a bill becomes a law)
Why did it happen? What caused it? What does it cause? What are its effects?	Suggest cause and effect (the events leading to the Korean War; the results of global warming; the impact of a new math curriculum on slow learners)

How is it like other things? How is it different from other things?	Suggest comparison and contrast (of the popular music of the 1970s and 1980s; of two paintings)
What are its parts or types? Can they be separated or grouped? Do they fall into a logical order? Can they be categorized?	Suggest division and classification (components of the catalytic converter; kinds of occupational therapy; kinds of dietary supplements)
What is it? How does it resemble other members of its class? How does it differ from other members of its class?	Suggest definition (What is Marxism? What is photosynthesis? What is a MOO?)

ESL Tip

If your instructor allows it, you may sometimes use your native language for planning activities. This strategy has both advantages and disadvantages. On the one hand, if you do not have to contend with the strain of trying to think in English, you may be able to come up with better ideas. Additionally, using your native language may help you record your ideas more quickly and keep you from losing your train of thought. On the other hand, using your native language extensively while planning may make it more difficult for you to move from the planning stages of your writing to drafting. After all, you will eventually have to write your paper in English.

Exercise 4

List all the sources you encounter in one day (specific people, books, magazines, Web sites, and so on) that could provide you with useful information for the essay you are writing. Exchange lists with a classmate, and add two sources to his or her list.

Exercise 5

Make a cluster diagram and brainstorming notes for the topic you selected in Exercise 3. If you have trouble thinking of material to write about, try freewriting. Then, write a journal entry assessing your progress and evaluating the different strategies for finding something to say. Which strategy worked best for you? Why?

Exercise 6

Using the question strategies described on pages 42–43 to supplement the work you did in Exercises 4 and 5, continue generating material for a short essay on your topic from Exercise 3.

Exercise 7

See 5b3

Consider what kinds of visual images might enhance your essay-in-progress. For example, would a photograph of a particular person or place be helpful? List several possibilities, and write a few sentences explaining what each visual might add to your essay.

Exercise 8

Choose one visual to use in your essay. Using the visual as a focus, brainstorm to find additional ideas for your essay.

Chapter 4

Shaping Your Material

Frequently Asked Questions

What is a thesis? (p. 45)
How do I know if I have an effective thesis? (p. 46)
Do I need an outline? (p. 52)

After you have gathered material for your essay and begun to see the direction your ideas are taking, you start to sift through these ideas and choose those you can use in your essay. As you do this, you begin to shape your material into a thesis-and-support essay.

4a Understanding Thesis and Support

Your **thesis** is the main idea of your essay, the central point your essay supports. The concept of **thesis and support**—stating the thesis and then supplying information that explains and develops it—is central to much of the writing you will do in college.

As the following diagram illustrates, the essays you will write will consist of an introductory paragraph, which opens your essay and states your thesis; a concluding paragraph, which closes your essay and gives it a sense of completion, perhaps restating your thesis; and a number of **body paragraphs,** which provide the support for your thesis statement.

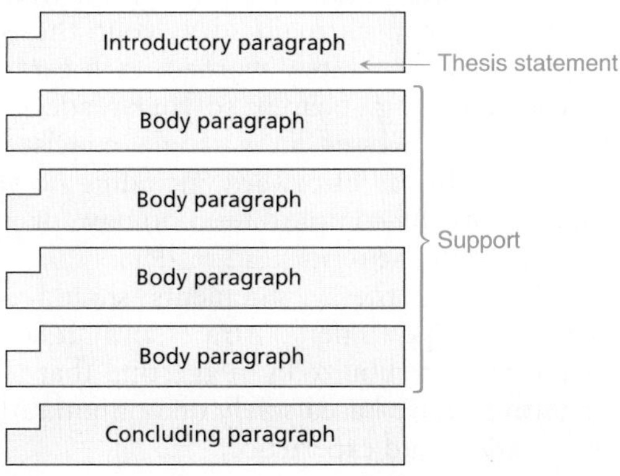

4b Developing a Thesis

(1) Stating Your Thesis

An effective thesis statement has four characteristics.

1. **An effective thesis statement clearly communicates your essay's main idea.** It tells readers what your essay's topic is and suggests what you will say about it. Thus, your thesis statement reflects your essay's purpose.
See 1a
2. **An effective thesis statement is more than a general subject, a statement of fact, or an announcement of your intent.**

Stating Your Thesis

Subject	Statement of Fact	Announcement
The Military Draft	The United States currently has no military draft.	In this essay, I will reconsider our country's need for a draft.

Thesis statement Once the military draft may have been necessary to keep the armed forces strong; however, today's all-volunteer force has eliminated the need for a draft.

3. **An effective thesis statement is carefully worded.** Because it communicates your paper's main idea, your thesis statement should be clearly and accurately worded, with careful phrasing that makes your meaning apparent to your readers. Your thesis statement—usually expressed in a single concise sentence—should be direct and straightforward, including no vague or abstract language, overly complex terminology, or unnecessary details that might confuse or mislead readers.

   Moreover, effective thesis statements should not include phrases such as "I hope to demonstrate" and "It seems to me," which weaken your credibility by suggesting that your conclusions are tentative or are based solely on opinion rather than on reading, observation, and experience.

Close-up: Avoiding Vague Wording

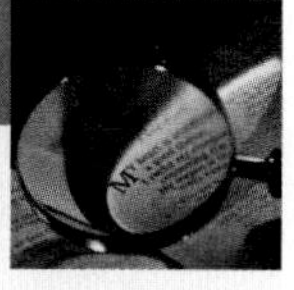

Try to avoid vague, wordy phrases—*centers on*, *deals with*, *involves*, *revolves around*, *has a lot to do with*, *is primarily concerned with*, and so on. Be direct and forceful.

> The real problem in our schools ~~does~~ *is* not ~~revolve around~~ the absence of nationwide goals and standards; the problem is ~~primarily concerned with~~ the absence of resources with which to implement them.

4. **Finally, an effective thesis statement suggests your essay's direction, emphasis, and scope.** Your thesis statement should not make promises that your essay will not fulfill. It should suggest how your ideas are related, in what order your major points will be discussed, and where you will place your emphasis, as the following thesis statement does.

   Effective Thesis Statement

   > Widely ridiculed as escape reading, romance novels are becoming increasingly important as a proving ground for many never-before-published writers and, more significantly, as a showcase for strong heroines.

   This effective thesis statement tells readers that the essay to follow will focus on two major new roles of the romance novel: providing markets for new writers and (more important) presenting strong female characters; it also suggests that the role of the romance novel as escapist fiction will be treated briefly. This effective thesis statement, as the diagram on page 48 shows, also indicates the order in which the various ideas will be discussed.

Checklist: Stating Your Thesis

- ☐ Does your thesis statement clearly communicate your essay's main idea? Does it suggest the approach you will take toward your material? Does it reflect your essay's purpose?
- ☐ Is your thesis statement more than a subject, a statement of fact, or an announcement of your intent?
- ☐ Is your thesis statement carefully worded?
- ☐ Does your thesis statement suggest your essay's direction, emphasis, and scope?

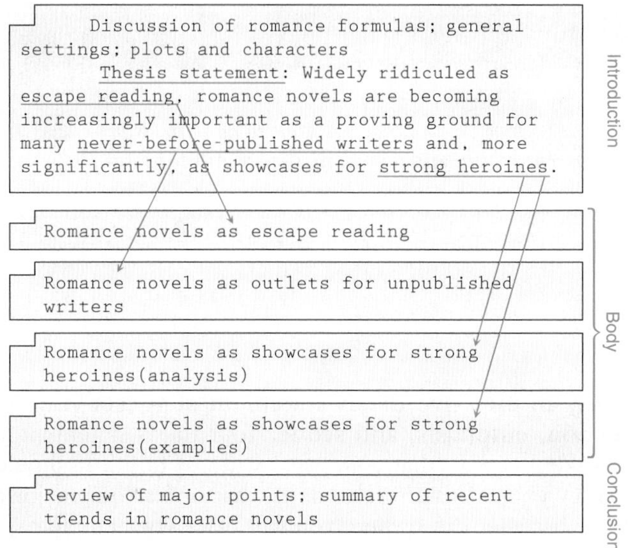

(2) Revising Your Thesis Statement

Occasionally—especially if you know a lot about your topic—you may begin writing with a thesis in mind. Most often, however, your thesis evolves out of the reading, questioning, and grouping of ideas that you do during the planning stage of the writing process.

The thesis statement that you develop as you plan your essay is only tentative. As you write and rewrite, you often think of new ideas and see new connections. As a result, you may modify your essay's direction, emphasis, and scope several times, and if you do so, you must reword your thesis statement as well. (For an example of a student's tentative thesis statement, **see 6b1;** for an example of a student's revised thesis statement, **see 6c4.**)

Notice how the following thesis statements changed as the writers moved through successive drafts of their essays.

Revising Your Thesis Statement

Tentative Thesis Statement (rough draft)	**Revised Thesis Statement (final draft)**
Professional sports can easily be corrupted by organized crime.	Although supporters of legalized sports betting argue that

Tentative Thesis Statement (rough draft)	Revised Thesis Statement (final draft)
	organized crime cannot make inroads into professional sports, the way in which underworld figures compromised the 1919 World Series suggests the opposite.
Laboratory courses provide valuable educational experiences.	By providing students with the actual experience of doing scientific work, laboratory courses encourage precise thinking, careful observation, and creativity.
It is difficult to understand Henry James's short novel <u>The Turn of the Screw</u> without examining the personality of the governess.	A careful reading of Henry James's <u>The Turn of the Screw</u> suggests that the governess is an unreliable narrator, incapable of distinguishing appearance from reality.

Close-up: Using Original Phrasing

Moving from a tentative to a final thesis statement often means moving from a "three points" thesis to something more original.

The familiar three points (or "four reasons" or "five examples") thesis lists each of the specific points to be discussed ("Hot air ballooning is an exciting sport for three reasons: x, y, and z"), and the paper that follows goes on to cover each of these points, using the same tired language: "The first reason hot air ballooning is so exciting is x"; "Another reason is y"; "The most important reason is z." Although this kind of formulaic thesis statement can be a very useful strategy for a rough draft, as you revise, you should substitute fresher, more interesting, and more original language.

4c Using a Thesis Statement to Shape Your Essay

The wording of your thesis statement often suggests not only a possible order and emphasis for your essay's ideas, but also a specific pattern of development—*narration*, *description*, *exemplification*, *process*, *cause and effect*, *comparison and contrast*, *division and classification*, or *definition*. These familiar patterns of development may also shape individual paragraphs of your essay.

Using a Thesis Statement to Shape Your Essay

Thesis Statement	Pattern of Development
As the months went by and I grew more and more involved with the developmentally delayed children at the Learning Center, I came to see how important it is to treat every child as an individual.	Narration
Looking around the room where I spent my childhood, I realized that every object I saw told me I was now an adult.	Description
The risk-taking behavior that has characterized the past decade can be illustrated by the increasing interest and involvement in such high-risk sports as mountain biking, ice climbing, sky diving, and bungee jumping.	Exemplification
Armed forces basic training programs take recruits through a series of tasks designed to build camaraderie as well as skills and confidence.	Process
The gap in computer literacy between rich and poor has had many significant social and economic consequences.	Cause and Effect

Thesis Statement	Pattern of Development
`Although people who live in cities and people who live in small towns have some similarities, their views on issues like crime, waste disposal, farm subsidies, and educational vouchers tend to be very different.`	Comparison and Contrast
`The section of the proposal that recommends establishing satellite health centers is quite promising; unfortunately, however, the sections that call for the creation of alternative educational programs, job training, and low-income housing are seriously flawed.`	Division and Classification
`Until quite recently, most people assumed that rape was an act perpetrated by a stranger, but today's wider definition encompasses acquaintance rape as well.`	Definition

Exercise 1

Analyze each of the following items, and explain why none of them qualifies as an effective thesis statement. How could each be improved?

1. In this essay, I will examine the environmental effects of residential and commercial development on the coastal regions of the United States.
2. Residential and commercial development in the coastal regions of the United States
3. How to avoid coastal overdevelopment
4. Coastal Development: Pro and Con
5. Residential and commercial development of America's coastal regions benefits some people, but it has a number of disadvantages.
6. The environmentalists' position on coastal development
7. More and more coastal regions in the United States are being overdeveloped.
8. Residential and commercial development guidelines need to be developed for coastal regions of the United States.

9. Coastal development is causing beach erosion.
10. At one time I enjoyed walking on the beach, but commercial and residential development ruined the experience for me.

Exercise 2

For three of the following topics, formulate a clearly and carefully worded thesis statement.

1. A local or national event that changed your life
2. Cheating in college
3. The validity of SAT scores as the basis for college admissions
4. Should women in the military serve in combat?
5. Private versus public education
6. Should college health clinics provide birth control services?
7. Is governmental censorship of the Internet justified?
8. The role of the individual in saving the earth
9. The portrayal of an ethnic group in film or television
10. Should smoking be banned in bars?

4d Constructing an Informal Outline

Once you have decided on a thesis statement, you may want to construct an informal outline. An **outline** is a blueprint for an essay, a plan that gives you more detailed, specific information about structuring your essay than a thesis statement does. You don't always need to prepare an outline; a short essay on a topic with which you are very familiar may require nothing more than a thesis statement and a list of your three or four main supporting points. Often, however, you will need the additional help of an **informal outline,** one that arranges your essay's main points and major supporting ideas in an orderly way to guide you as you write. (For an example of a student writer's informal outline, **see 6b2.**)

Checklist: Constructing an Informal Outline

- ☐ Copy down the most important ideas from your notes.
- ☐ Arrange the notes into categories and subcategories in the order in which you plan to discuss them.
- ☐ Expand the outline with additional material from your notes, adding any new ideas that come to mind.

NOTE: Sometimes—particularly when you are writing a long or complex essay—you will need to construct a formal outline, which indicates both the exact order of all the ideas you will explore and the relationship of those ideas to one another. You can construct such an outline either before you draft your paper (to guide your rough draft) or later on (to guide your revision).

See 5d4

Exercise 3

Look carefully at the visual you chose in Chapter 3, Exercise 8. In one sentence, state the main idea that this visual communicates to its audience. Then, list the individual images and details in the visual that support this main idea.

Exercise 4

Review all the notes you have accumulated so far, and use them to help you develop a thesis for an essay on the topic you chose in Chapter 3, Exercise 3.

http://kirsznermandell.wadsworth.com

Computer Tip: Outlining

Although you may be used to constructing outlines for your written work by hand, a number of software applications and formatting features can help in this process, including the outlining feature in some desktop publishing and word-processing programs (such as *Microsoft Word*). Another useful tool for outlining (particularly for oral presentations), is *Microsoft PowerPoint*, presentation software that enables you to format information on individual slides with major headings, subheadings, and bulleted lists.

See Ch. 31

Exercise 5

Find an editorial in the newspaper or on the Internet. Then, prepare an informal outline that includes all the writer's main points and major supporting ideas. (Use the model outline in 6b2 as a guide.)

Exercise 6

Prepare an informal outline for the paper you have been developing in Chapters 3 and 4.

4e Constructing a Storyboard

If you are visually oriented, you might try using storyboarding to help you shape your material. **Storyboarding** is a way of graphically organizing material into a series of boxes or panels. This technique has long been used in outlining scenes and plot developments for films and commercials, and it can be adapted, with some modifications, into a useful outlining tool for an essay or a Web site.

Unlike a strictly text-based outline, which uses words, phrases, or sentences to plot the organization of material in a linear way, a storyboard uses pictures and diagrams, either electronically generated or drawn by hand, to map out an arrangement of material. As a tool for shaping an essay, a storyboard can use lines and shapes or blocks of text as well as pictures. Storyboarding can help you plan the placement of your ideas; in addition, it can help you visualize the placement of potential source information and illustrations. Thus, storyboarding enables you to see how the various elements of your paper—your own ideas, source material, and visuals—work together. (For an example of a student writer's storyboard, **see 6b3.**)

Checklist: Constructing a Storyboard

- ☐ Use a large sheet of paper to represent your essay.
- ☐ On the paper, draw a box to represent each major section of the paper; better yet, use self-stick notes or index cards as boxes.
- ☐ Fill in each box with a combination of words, shapes, and symbols to represent key ideas, sources, and visuals.
- ☐ If you like, use the visuals themselves—such as printouts of clip art or images cut from magazines—in your boxes.
- ☐ Leave blank space (or even a blank box) for undeveloped sections; label blank spaces "to come."
- ☐ Rearrange boxes on the page if necessary.
- ☐ Number the boxes if necessary.
- ☐ Use arrows to indicate possible relocation of elements within boxes.

Exercise 7

Construct a storyboard for the paper you have been developing in Chapters 3 and 4. Use the model storyboard in 6b3 as a guide.

http://kirsznermandell.wadsworth.com

Computer Tip: Storyboarding

In a multimedia or Web-based project, storyboards map the relationship between text, visuals, audio, and video in formats as diverse as *PowerPoint* presentations, Web sites, and *QuickTime* movies.

Exercise 8

Which did you find most useful in helping you shape your ideas—your informal outline or your storyboard? Write a paragraph explaining the strengths and weaknesses of each strategy.

Chapter 5

Drafting and Revising

Frequently Asked Questions

5a Writing a Rough Draft

(1) Understanding Drafting

As its name implies, a rough draft is far from perfect; in fact, it usually includes false starts, irrelevant information, and unrelated details. At this stage, though, the absence of focus and order is not a problem. You write your rough draft simply to get your ideas down on paper so that you can react to them. You should expect to add or delete words, to reword sentences, to rethink ideas, and to reorder paragraphs. You should also expect to discover some new ideas—or even to take an unexpected detour.

When you write your rough draft, concentrate on the body of your essay, and don't waste time mapping out your introduction and conclusion. The effort to write the perfect opening and closing paragraphs will slow you down; besides, these paragraphs are likely to change substantially in subsequent drafts. For now, focus on drafting the support paragraphs of your essay. (For an example of a student writer's rough draft, **see 6c1.**)

(2) Developing Drafting Strategies

Taking a systematic approach to writing your first draft will greatly simplify the revision process.

Checklist: Drafting Strategies

The following suggestions should help you revise effectively:

- ☐ **Prepare your work area.** Once you begin to write, you should not have to stop because you need better lighting, important notes, or anything else.
- ☐ **Fight writer's block.** An inability to start (or continue) writing, writer's block is usually caused by fear that you will not write well or that you have nothing to say. If you really don't feel ready to write, take a short break. If you decide that you really don't have enough ideas to get you started, use one of the strategies for finding something to say.

- ☐ **Get your ideas down on paper as quickly as you can.** Don't worry about sentence structure, about spelling and punctuation, or about finding exactly the right word—just write. Writing quickly helps you uncover new ideas and new connections between ideas. You may find that following an informal outline enables you to move smoothly from one point to the next, but if you find this structure too confining, go ahead and write without consulting your outline.

- ☐ **Write notes to yourself.** As you type your drafts, get into the habit of including bracketed, boldfaced notes to yourself. These comments, suggestions, and questions can help you later, when you revise.
- ☐ **Take regular breaks as you write.** Try writing one section of your essay at a time. When you have completed a section—for example, one paragraph—take a break. Your mind will continue to focus on your assignment while you do other things. When you return to your essay, writing will be easier.
- ☐ **Leave yourself enough time to revise.** All writing benefits from revision, so be sure you have time to reconsider your work and to write as many drafts as you need.
- ☐ **Save your drafts.** Using the Save option in your word processor's file menu saves only your most recent draft. If you prefer to save every draft you write (so you can return to an earlier draft to locate a different version of a sentence or to reconsider a section you have deleted), use the Save As option instead.
- ☐ **Label your files.** To help you keep track of which version of your paper is which, label every file in your folder by content and date (for example, `first draft, 10/20`).

Exercise 1

Write a rough draft of the essay you began planning in Chapter 3.

ESL Tip

Using your native language occasionally as you draft your paper may keep you from losing your train of thought. However, writing most or all of your draft in your native language and then translating it into English is generally not a good idea. This process will take a long time, and the translation into English may sound awkward.

5b Revising Your Drafts

(1) Understanding Revision

Revision is a process you engage in from the moment you begin to discover ideas for your essay. As you work, you are constantly rethinking your ideas and reconsidering their relevance, their relative importance, the logical and sequential relationships between them, and the patterns in which you arrange them. Revision is a creative part of the writing process, and everyone does it somewhat differently. You will have to experiment to find the techniques that work best for you.

Inexperienced writers often do little more than change a word here and there, correct grammatical or mechanical errors, and reprint their papers to make them neater. Experienced writers, however, expect revision to involve a major reworking of their papers, so they are willing to rethink a thesis statement or even to completely rewrite and rearrange an essay.

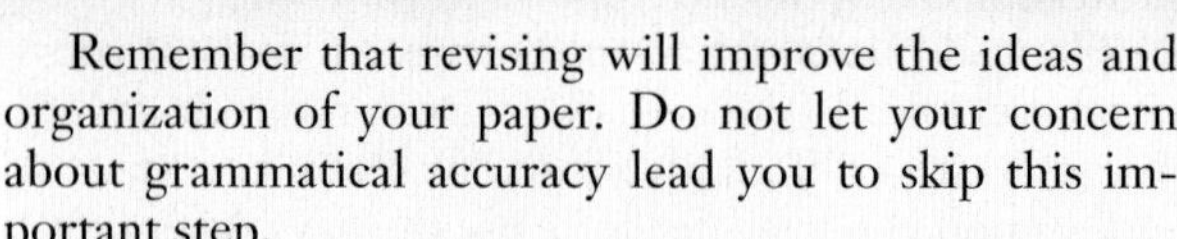

Remember that revising will improve the ideas and organization of your paper. Do not let your concern about grammatical accuracy lead you to skip this important step.

(2) Accommodating Your Audience

Often, you write your rough draft without thinking much about your audience. When you revise, however, you should begin to make the kinds of changes that your readers need in order to understand and appreciate your ideas. Thus, revision should reflect not only your own evaluation of your first draft but also your anticipation of your readers' needs and reactions.

Checklist: Revising to Accommodate Your Readers

- ☐ **Be sure you have presented one idea at a time and summarized when necessary.** When you overload your paper with more information than readers can take in, you lose their attention. Readers should not have to backtrack constantly to understand your message.
- ☐ **Be sure you have organized your ideas clearly.** Readers expect your essay to do what your thesis statement says it will do, with major points introduced in a logical order and supported in your body paragraphs.
- ☐ **Add clear signals to establish coherence.** Repeating key points, constructing clear topic sentences, using transitional words and phrases to link ideas logically, and providing verbal cues that indicate the precise relationships among ideas all help establish continuity and coherence.
- ☐ **Consider using visuals to illustrate or clarify ideas.**

(3) Adding Visuals

FAQs

As you write and revise, you should consider whether one or more **visuals** might enhance your paper. Sometimes you may want to use a visual that appears in one of your sources; at other times, you may be able to create a visual (for example, a photograph or a chart) yourself; at still other times, you may need to search a clip-art database to find an appropriate visual.

http://kirsznermandell.wadsworth.com

Computer Tip: Using Clip Art

Many software suites, such as *Microsoft Office*® and *WordPerfect*®, have clip-art databases that you can search to find appropriate visuals for use in your essays. Although inserting clip art is a simple process of browsing for files in the same way you would browse for other documents on your computer, some clip art may appear too cartoonish and may therefore be inappropriate in academic papers. Before selecting a visual to use, consider the role it will play in helping your readers understand the comparison you are making, the story you are relating, or the setting you are describing. Above all, do not use a visual just because you can; use a visual only when it strengthens your paper.

Once you have decided to add a visual to your paper, the first step is to determine at what point in the text you want to insert the visual and to make sure your cursor is at that point. Within *Microsoft Word*, for example, you can double-click on an image to call up a picture-editing menu that allows you to alter the size, color, and position of your visual within your essay—and even permits you to wrap text around the image. After you insert a visual into a document, you need to format it. The visual should be closely aligned in size and placement with the part of the essay where it will have the greatest impact in terms of conveying information to or persuading your audience. Next, you should make sure that the visual stands out in your paper: surround it with white space, add ruled lines, or enclose it in a box.

http://kirsznermandell.wadsworth.com

Computer Tip: Inserting Visuals

Most software applications have an Insert menu that allows you to insert pictures or other visual data, either from an accompanying clip-art database or from your own collection of visuals that you yourself have created or selected to accompany text. Usually, this option involves clicking on the Insert menu and selecting options for Picture or Image. Just as you are able to open print documents by browsing to either a disk or desktop file, you can browse for clip art, for pictures that you have taken with a digital camera, or for photographs and line art that you have scanned into your computer. Once you have inserted a visual in your document, it is easy to position it at a point where it is best integrated with your text in terms of both content and format.

Once the visual has been inserted where you want it, you need to integrate it into your paper. You can include a sentence that introduces the visual (`The following table illustrates the similarities between the two health plans`), or you can refer to it in your text (`Figure 1 shows Kennedy as a young man`) to give it some context and explain why you are using it. You should also identify the visual by labeling it (`Fig. 1. Photo of John F. Kennedy, 1937`). In addition, if the visual is not one you have created yourself, you must document it. In most academic disciplines, this means including full source information directly below the image and sometimes in the list of references as well. (For an example of a visual in a student paper, **see 6c5.**)

Checklist: Inserting Visuals

- ☐ Select an appropriate visual.
- ☐ Place the image in a suitable location.
- ☐ Make sure the image is easily distinguished from the written text.
- ☐ Introduce the visual with a sentence (or refer to it in the text).
- ☐ Label the visual.
- ☐ Document the visual (if necessary).

5c Moving from Rough Draft to Final Draft

As you revise successive drafts of your essay, you should shift your focus from larger elements, such as overall structure and content, to increasingly smaller elements, such as sentence structure and word choice. (For examples of successive drafts of a student paper, **see 6c.**)

(1) Revising Your Rough Draft

After you finish your rough draft, set it aside for a day or two if you can. When you return to it, focus on only a few areas at a time. As you review this first draft, evaluate the thesis-and-support structure of your essay and your paper's general organization. Once you feel satisfied that your thesis statement says what you want it to say and that your essay's content supports this thesis and is logically arranged, you can turn your attention to other matters.

As you reread this draft, you may want to consult the questions in the "Revising the Whole Essay" checklist on page 70. If you have the benefit of a peer-review session or a conference with your instructor, consider your readers' comments carefully, focusing for now on their suggestions about content, organization, and thesis and support.

http://kirsznermandell.wadsworth.com

Computer Tip: Moving Text

Use the Copy, Cut, and Paste features found under your word processor's Edit menu to help you move text within a single document or between documents.

(2) Writing and Revising Additional Drafts

After you have read over your rough draft several times, making notes about plans for revision, you are ready to write a second draft.

Close-up: Making Handwritten Revisions

Because it can be more difficult to see errors on the computer screen than on hard copy, some writers prefer to print out every draft, making revisions by hand on printed drafts and then returning to the computer to type these changes into the document.

If you plan to use this strategy, be sure to triple-space your draft. This will make any errors or inconsistencies more obvious and at the same time give you plenty of room to write questions, add new material, or try out new versions of sentences.

You will also find it helpful to develop a system of symbols, each designating a different type of revision. For instance, you can circle individual words or box longer groups of words (or even entire paragraphs) that you want to relocate. You can use an arrow to indicate the new location, or you can use matching numbers or letters to indicate how you want to rearrange ideas. When you want to add words, use a caret like ^this. (For an example of an excerpt from a student's draft that includes handwritten revisions, **see 6c4.**)

As you assess your rough draft, as well as any drafts that follow, you will narrow your focus to your essay's individual paragraphs, sentences, and words; if you like, you can use the "Revising Paragraphs," "Revising Sentences," and "Revising Words" checklists on pages 70–71 to guide your revision.

http://kirsznermandell.wadsworth.com

Computer Tip: Revising

If you revise directly on the computer, be very careful not to delete any material that you may need later; instead, move this material to the end of your document so that you can assess its usefulness later on and retrieve it if necessary. Or, use the Save As feature to save each new version of your essay under a different file name each time you revise.

5d Using Specific Revision Strategies

Everyone revises differently, and every writing task demands a slightly different process of revision. Five strategies in particular can help you revise at any stage of the writing process.

(1) Using Word-Processing Tools

Your word-processing program includes a variety of tools designed to make the revision process easier. For example, *Microsoft Word*'s **Track Changes** feature allows you to make changes to a draft and to see the original version of the draft and the changes simultaneously. Changes appear in color as underlined text, and writers have the option of viewing the changes on the screen or in print. Other options include the ability to accept or reject all changes or just specific changes. (For an example of how the Track Changes feature is used in a student paper, **see 6c2.**)

Another useful revision tool is the **Compare Drafts** feature. Whereas Track Changes allows you to apply the tracking feature in a single document as you make changes, Compare Drafts allows you to analyze the changes in two completely separate versions of a document, usually an original and its most recent update. Changes appear in color as highlighted text.

http://kirsznermandell.wadsworth.com

Computer Tip: Tracking Changes versus Comparing Documents

Where you are in the writing process can help you decide whether to track your changes or to compare one complete version of your document with another. Tracking changes is especially useful in helping you follow sentence-level changes as you draft and revise; it can also be helpful later on, when you edit words and phrases. Comparing documents is most helpful when you are comparing global changes, such as paragraph unity and thesis-and-support structure, between one draft and another.

(2) Participating in Peer Review

Peer review—a collaborative revision strategy that enables you to get feedback from your classmates—is another useful activity. With peer review, instead of trying to imagine an audience for your paper, you address a real audience, exchanging drafts with classmates and commenting on their drafts. Such collaborative work can be formal or informal, conducted in person or electronically. For example, you and a classmate may email drafts back and forth, perhaps using *Word*'s Comment feature, or your instructor may conduct the class as a workshop, assigning students to work in groups to critique other students' essays. (For an example of a student draft that illustrates peer review, **see 6c4.**)

http://kirsznermandell.wadsworth.com

Computer Tip: Peer Review

Certain features in word-processing programs are particularly useful for peer review. For example, the Comment tool allows several readers to insert comments at any point, or to highlight a particular portion of the text they would like to comment on and then insert annotations. To write comments, a reviewer clicks the Insert menu and selects Comment.

A particular advantage of this function for peer-review groups is that a single paper can receive comments from multiple readers. Comments are identified by the initials of the reviewer and by a color assigned to the reviewer, so the paper's author can go to the View menu, select Comments, and then select the reviewer's comments he or she wants to view (or select All Reviewers to see all comments at once).

Other online programs have been developed specifically for the purpose of electronic peer review. Some programs, such as *InSite* (see Figure 5.1), mirror the traditional peer-review process by allowing readers to insert comments anywhere within an essay or to mark up a document with standard correction symbols.

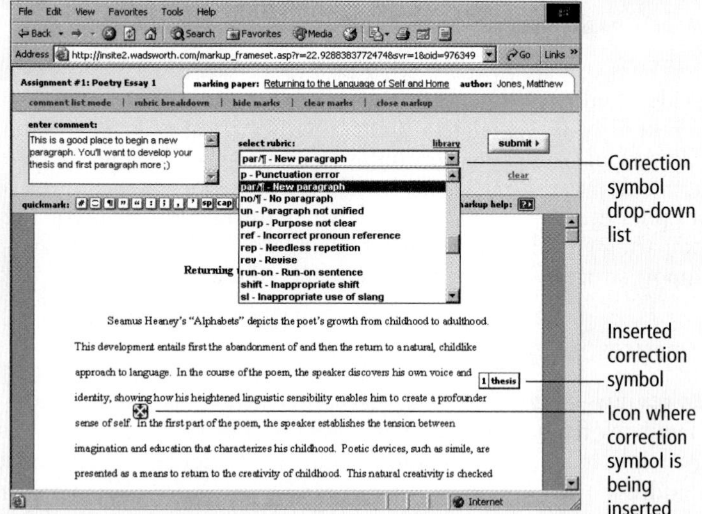

Figure 5.1 *InSite* Paper Markup tool.

Checklist: Questions for Peer Review

The following questions can help guide you through the peer-review process.

- ☐ What is the essay about? Does the topic fulfill the requirements of the assignment?
- ☐ What is the essay's main idea? Is the thesis clearly worded? If not, how can the wording be improved?
- ☐ Is the essay arranged logically? Do the body paragraphs appear in an appropriate order?
- ☐ What ideas support the thesis? Does each body paragraph develop one of these ideas?
- ☐ Is any necessary information missing? Identify any areas that seem to need further development. Is any information irrelevant? If so, suggest possible deletions.
- ☐ Can you think of any ideas or examples from your own reading, experience, or observations that would strengthen the writer's essay?
- ☐ Can you follow the writer's ideas? If not, would clearer connections between sentences or paragraphs be helpful? Where are such connections needed?
- ☐ Is the introductory paragraph interesting to you? Would another opening strategy be more effective?
- ☐ Does the conclusion leave you with a sense of closure? Would another concluding strategy be more effective?
- ☐ Is anything unclear or confusing?
- ☐ What is the essay's greatest strength?
- ☐ What is the essay's greatest weakness?

(3) Using Instructors' Comments

Instructors' comments—in correction symbols, in marginal comments, or in conferences—can also help you revise. (Note that some instructors may prefer to record their comments electronically, perhaps using the Comment feature described in **5d2.** For an example of a student paper that includes such instructor commentary, **see 6c3.**)

Correction Symbols Your instructor may indicate concerns about style, grammar, mechanics, or punctuation by using the correction symbols listed on the inside back cover of this book. Instead of correcting a problem, the instructor will simply identify it and supply the number of the section in this handbook that deals with the error. After reading the appropriate pages, you should be able to make the necessary corrections on your own. For example, the symbol and number beside the following sentence referred a student to **42e2,** the section in the handbook that discusses sexist usage.

Draft with Instructor's Comment: `Equal access to jobs is a desirable goal for all mankind.` *Sxt—see 42e2*

After reading section 42e2, the student made the following change.

Revised: `Equal access to jobs is a desirable goal for all people.`

Marginal Comments Instructors frequently make handwritten marginal comments on your essays to suggest changes in content or structure. Such comments may ask you to add supporting information or to arrange paragraphs differently within the essay, or they may recommend stylistic changes, such as more varied sentences. Marginal comments may also question your logic, suggest a more explicit thesis statement, ask for clearer transitions, or propose a new direction for a discussion. In some cases, you can consider these comments to be suggestions rather than corrections. You may decide to incorporate these ideas into a revised draft of your essay, and then again, you may not. In all instances, however, you should take your instructor's comments seriously. (For an example of a student draft with marginal comments, **see 6c3.**)

Conferences Many instructors require or encourage one-on-one conferences, and you should certainly schedule a conference if you can. During a conference, you can respond to your instructor's questions and ask for clarification of marginal comments. If a certain section of your paper presents a problem, use your conference time to focus on it, perhaps asking for help in sharpening your thesis or choosing more accurate words.

Checklist: Getting the Most Out of a Conference

- ☐ **Make an appointment.** If you are unable to keep your appointment, be sure to call or email your instructor to reschedule.
- ☐ **Review your work carefully.** Before the conference, reread your notes and drafts and go over all your instructor's comments and suggestions. Make all the changes you can on your draft.

- ☐ **Bring a list of questions.** Preparing a list in advance will enable you to get the most out of the conference in the allotted time.
- ☐ **Bring your paper-in-progress.** If you have several drafts, you may want to bring them all, but be sure you bring any draft that has your instructor's comments on it.
- ☐ **Take notes.** As you discuss your paper, write down any suggestions that you think will be helpful so you won't forget them when you revise.
- ☐ **Participate actively.** A successful conference is not a monologue; it should be an open exchange of ideas.

http://kirsznermandell.wadsworth.com

Computer Tip: Online Conferences

Conferences can also take place online, in virtual chat rooms or in synchronous online communication sessions in which you and your instructor are online at the same time and engage in real-time dialogue about your paper. You can also discuss your writing online by posting your questions about your work-in-progress to a discussion board for both instructor and peer review. (In this case, hours or even days may pass before a question is answered.)

Perhaps the most common way to discuss a paper online is through email. If you send emails to your instructor or to members of your peer-review group, don't forget to include a specific subject line that clearly identifies the message as coming from a student writer (for example, "question about assignment" or "comments on your paper"). This is especially important if your email address does not include your name. And when you attach a document to an email and send it to your instructor for comments, mention the attachment in your subject line (for example, "first draft—see attachment")—and be sure your name appears on the attachment itself, not just on the email.

(4) Constructing a Formal Outline

A formal outline can help you to plan and shape a draft before you write it, but an outline can also guide you as you revise. Outlining can be helpful early in the revision process, when you are reworking the larger structural elements of your essay, or later on, when you are checking the logic of a completed draft. For example, a formal outline reveals at once whether points are irrelevant or poorly placed—or, worse, missing. It also reveals the hierarchy of your ideas—which points are dominant and which are subordinate.

A **formal outline** uses a system of letters and numbers to indicate the order of your ideas and the relationship of main ideas to supporting details. A formal outline is more polished and much more detailed than an informal outline. It is more strictly parallel and more precise, pays more attention to form, and presents points in the exact order in which you plan to present them in your draft.

See 4d

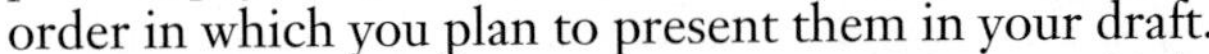

A formal outline may be a **topic outline,** in which each entry is a single word or a short phrase, or a **sentence outline,** in which each entry is a complete sentence. (For an example of a student's sentence outline, **see 6c4.**) A sentence outline is a more fully developed guide for your paper; you have a head start on your paper when you are able to use the sentences of your outline in your draft. Because it is so polished and complete, however, a sentence outline is more difficult and time consuming to construct, especially at an early stage of the writing process.

Close-up: The Conventions of Outlining

Formal outlines conform to specific conventions of structure, content, and style. If you follow the conventions of outlining carefully, your formal outline can help you make sure that your paper presents all relevant ideas in an effective order, with appropriate emphasis.

Structure

- Outline format should be followed strictly.

  I. First major point of your paper
  - A. First subpoint
  - B. Next subpoint
    - 1. First supporting example
    - 2. Next supporting example
      - a. First specific detail
      - b. Next specific detail

  II. Second major point

- Headings should not overlap.
- No heading should have a single subheading. (A category cannot be subdivided into one part.)
- Each entry should be preceded by an appropriate letter or number, followed by a period.
- The first word of each entry should be capitalized.

Content

- The outline should include the paper's thesis statement.
- The outline should cover only the body of the essay, not the introductory or concluding paragraphs.
- Headings should be concise and specific.
- Headings should be descriptive, clearly related to the topic to which they refer.

Style

- Headings of the same rank should be grammatically parallel.
- A **sentence outline** should use complete sentences, with all sentences in the same tense.
- In a sentence outline, each entry should end with a period.
- A **topic outline** should use words or short phrases, with all headings of the same rank using the same parts of speech.
- In a topic outline, entries should not end with periods.

http://kirsznermandell.wadsworth.com

Computer Tip: Formatting an Outline

If you use your computer's word-processing program to construct a formal outline, the Bullets and Numbering feature and the Auto Format feature will help you to format it properly. Usually found in the Format menu, Bullets and Numbering allows you to select the format type of your outline, including styles that use roman numerals, letters, and/or numbers. Once you have selected your outline style, Auto Format will arrange what you type in the selected format and allow you to customize the formatting further.

(5) Using Checklists

A revision checklist—one that your instructor prepares or one that you develop yourself—enables you to examine your writing systematically by helping you to focus on revising one element at a time. Depending on the problems you have and the amount of time you have to deal with them, you can use all the questions on a checklist or only some of them.

The four revision checklists that follow are keyed to sections of this text. They parallel the normal revision process, moving from global to specific concerns. As your understanding of the writing process increases and you become better able to assess the strengths and weaknesses of your writing, you may want to add items to (or delete items from) one or more of the checklists. You can also use your instructors' comments to tailor these checklists to your own needs.

Checklist: Revising the Whole Essay

- ☐ Have you maintained an appropriate distance from your readers? **(See 1b.)**
- ☐ Is your tone consistent with your purpose? **(See 1c.)**
- ☐ Are thesis and support logically related, with each body paragraph supporting your thesis statement? **(See 4a.)**
- ☐ Is your thesis statement clearly and specifically worded? **(See 4b1.)**
- ☐ Have you discussed everything promised in your thesis statement? **(See 4b1.)**
- ☐ Have you presented your ideas in a logical sequence? Can you think of a different arrangement that might be more appropriate for your purpose? **(See 4c.)**
- ☐ Do clear transitions between paragraphs allow your readers to follow your essay's structure? **(See 7b6.)**
- ☐ Are the patterns of paragraph development you use in your essay consistent with your assignment and purpose? **(See 7d.)**

Checklist: Revising Paragraphs

- ☐ Does each body paragraph have one main idea? **(See 7a.)**
- ☐ Are topic sentences clearly worded and logically related to your thesis? **(See 7a1.)**
- ☐ Are your body paragraphs developed enough to support your points? **(See 7c.)**
- ☐ Does your introductory paragraph arouse reader interest and prepare readers for what is to come? **(See 7e2.)**
- ☐ Does each body paragraph have a clear organizing principle? **(See 7b1.)**
- ☐ Are the relationships between sentences within paragraphs clear? **(See 7b2–5.)**
- ☐ Are your paragraphs arranged according to familiar patterns of development? **(See 7d.)**
- ☐ Does your concluding paragraph sum up your main points? **(See 7e3.)**
- ☐ Have you provided transitional paragraphs where necessary? **(See 7e1.)**

Checklist: Revising Sentences

- ☐ Have you strengthened your sentences with repetition, balance, and parallelism? (**See 35c–d, 40a.**)
- ☐ Have you avoided overloading your sentences with too many clauses? (**See 36c.**)
- ☐ Have you used correct sentence structure? (**See Chs. 37 and 38.**)
- ☐ Have you placed modifiers clearly and logically? (**See Ch. 39.**)
- ☐ Have you avoided potentially confusing shifts in tense, voice, mood, person, or number? (**See 41a1–4.**)
- ☐ Are your sentences constructed logically? (**See 41b–d.**)
- ☐ Have you used emphatic word order? (**See 35a.**)
- ☐ Have you used sentence structure to signal the relative importance of clauses in a sentence and their logical relationship to one another? (**See 35b.**)
- ☐ Have you avoided wordiness and eliminated unnecessary repetition? (**See 36a–b.**)
- ☐ Have you varied your sentence structure? (**See Ch. 34.**)
- ☐ Have you combined sentences where ideas are closely related? (**See 34b.**)

Checklist: Revising Words

- ☐ Is your level of diction appropriate for your audience and your purpose? (**See 42a–b.**)
- ☐ Have you selected words that accurately reflect your intentions? (**See 42b1.**)
- ☐ Have you chosen words that are specific, concrete, and unambiguous? (**See 42b3–4.**)
- ☐ Have you enriched your writing with figurative language? (**See 42c.**)
- ☐ Have you eliminated jargon, neologisms, pretentious diction, clichés, mixed metaphors, ineffective figures of speech, and offensive language from your writing? (**See 42c–e.**)

Exercise 2

Revise your rough draft, using one or more of the strategies for revision discussed in 5d. At this point, focus on your paper's thesis and support and on content and arrangement of ideas. Try not to worry now about stylistic issues, such as sentence variety and word choice.

Exercise 3

Review the second draft of your paper, this time focusing on paragraphing, topic sentences, and transitions and on the way you structure your sentences and select your words. If possible, ask a friend to read your draft and to respond to the peer-review questions in 5d2. Then, revise your draft, incorporating any suggestions you find helpful.

Exercise 4

Using the revision checklists in 5d5 as a guide, create a customized checklist—one that reflects the specific concerns that you need to consider when you revise an essay. Then, use this checklist to help you in your revision.

5e Editing and Proofreading

Once you have revised your drafts to your satisfaction, two final tasks remain: editing and proofreading.

Editing When you edit, you concentrate on grammar and spelling, punctuation and mechanics. You will have done some of this work as you revised previous drafts of your paper, but now your focus is on editing. Approach your work critically, reading each sentence carefully. As you proceed, consult the items on the checklist on pages 73–74. Keep your preliminary notes and drafts and your reference books (such as this handbook and a current dictionary) nearby as you edit.

ESL Tip

Editing can be difficult if you did not grow up speaking English as your primary language. For strategies to help you with this step of the writing process, **see 61a.**

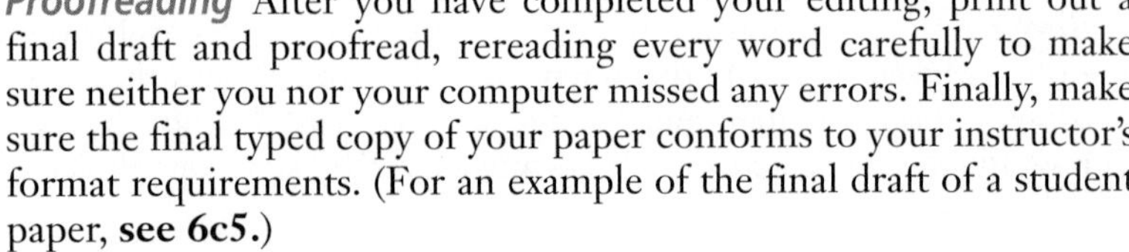

Proofreading After you have completed your editing, print out a final draft and proofread, rereading every word carefully to make sure neither you nor your computer missed any errors. Finally, make sure the final typed copy of your paper conforms to your instructor's format requirements. (For an example of the final draft of a student paper, **see 6c5.**)

http://kirsznermandell.wadsworth.com

Computer Tip: Editing and Proofreading

- As you edit and proofread, try looking at only a small portion of text at a time. If your software allows you to split the screen and create another window, create one so small that you can see only one or two lines of text at a time. If you use this technique, you can dramatically reduce the number of surface-level errors in your paper.
- Use the Search or Find command to look for usage errors you commonly make—for instance, confusing *it's* with *its*, *lay* with *lie*, *effect* with *affect*, *their* with *there*, or *too* with *to*. You can also uncover sexist language by searching for words like *he*, *his*, *him*, or *man*.

- Finally, keep in mind that neatness does not equal correctness. The computer's ability to produce clean-looking text can mask flaws that might otherwise be readily apparent; for this reason, it is up to you to make sure spelling errors and typos do not slip by.

Checklist: Editing and Proofreading

Grammar

- ☐ Have you used the appropriate case for each pronoun? (**See 46a–b.**)
- ☐ Are pronoun references clear and unambiguous? (**See 46c.**)
- ☐ Are verb forms correct? (**See 47a.**)
- ☐ Are tense, mood, and voice of verbs logical and appropriate? (**See 47b–d.**)
- ☐ Do subjects and verbs agree? (**See 48a.**)
- ☐ Do pronouns and antecedents agree? (**See 48b.**)
- ☐ Are adjectives and adverbs used correctly? (**See Ch. 49.**)

Punctuation

- ☐ Is end punctuation used correctly? (**See Ch. 50.**)
- ☐ Are commas used correctly? (**See Ch. 51.**)
- ☐ Are semicolons used correctly? (**See Ch. 52.**)
- ☐ Are apostrophes used correctly? (**See Ch. 53.**)
- ☐ Are quotation marks used where they are required? (**See Ch. 54.**)
- ☐ Are quotation marks used correctly with other punctuation marks? (**See 54e.**)
- ☐ Are other punctuation marks—colons, dashes, parentheses, brackets, slashes, and ellipses—used correctly? (**See Ch. 55.**)

(continued)

Editing and proofreading (continued)

Mechanics

- ☐ Is capitalization consistent with standard English usage? (**See Ch. 56.**)
- ☐ Are italics used correctly? (**See Ch. 57.**)
- ☐ Are hyphens used where required and placed correctly within and between words? (**See Ch. 58.**)
- ☐ Are abbreviations used where convention calls for their use? (**See Ch. 59.**)
- ☐ Are numerals and spelled-out numbers used appropriately? (**See Ch. 60.**)

Spelling

- ☐ Are all words spelled correctly? (**See Ch. 44.**)

http://kirsznermandell.wadsworth.com

Computer Tip: Using Spell Checkers and Grammar Checkers

FAQs

Spell checkers and grammar checkers can make the process of editing and proofreading your papers a lot easier. Remember, though, that both have limitations. Neither a spell checker nor a grammar checker is a substitute for careful editing and proofreading.

- **Spell Checkers** A spell checker simply identifies strings of letters it does not recognize; it does *not* distinguish between homophones or spot every typographical error. For example, it does not recognize *there* in "They forgot there books" as incorrect, nor does it spot a typo that produces a correctly spelled word, such as *word* for *work* or *thing* for *think*. Moreover, a spell checker may not recognize every technical term, proper noun, or foreign word you may use.
- **Grammar Checkers** Grammar checkers scan documents for certain features (the number of words in a sentence, for example); however, they are not able to read a document to see if it makes sense. For this reason, grammar checkers are not always accurate. For example, they may identify a long sentence as a run-on when it is in fact grammatically correct, and they generally advise against using passive voice—even in contexts where it is appropriate. Moreover, grammar checkers do not always supply answers; often, they ask questions—for example, whether *which* should be *that* or whether *which* should be preceded by a comma—that you must answer. In short, grammar checkers can guide your editing, but you should be the one who decides when a sentence is (or is not) correct. (For more information on the advantages and limitations of your grammar checker, consult the charts on pages 728 and 868–69.)

Close-up: Choosing a Title

When you are ready to decide on a title for your essay, keep these criteria in mind.

- A title should be descriptive, giving an accurate sense of your essay's focus. Whenever possible, use one or more of the key words and phrases that are central to your paper.
- A title's wording can echo the wording of your assignment, reminding you (and your instructor) that you have not lost sight of it.
- Ideally, a title should arouse interest, perhaps by using a provocative question or a quotation or by taking a controversial position.

Assignment: Write about a problem faced on college campuses today.

Topic: Free speech on campus

Possible titles:

`Free Speech: A Problem for Today's Colleges` (echoes wording of assignment and includes key words of essay)

`How Free Should Free Speech on Campus Be?` (provocative question)

`The Right to "Shout 'Fire' in a Crowded Theater"` (quotation)

`Hate Speech: A Dangerous Abuse of Free Speech on Campus` (controversial position)

Exercise 5

Using the checklist on pages 73–74 as a guide, edit your essay. Then proofread it carefully, give it an appropriate title, and print out your final draft.

Exercise 6

Review your responses to Exercises 1 and 2 in Chapter 3. Write a paragraph explaining how your personal writing process has changed since you wrote that response.

Chapter 6

Writing an Essay: A Case Study

Frequently Asked Questions

This chapter follows the writing process of Kimberly Romney, a first-year composition student. Kimberly's instructor gave the class the following assignment:

> College broadens your horizons and exposes you to new people, places, and experiences. At the same time, it can also create problems. Write a short essay (3–5 pages) about a problem you (and perhaps others) have encountered since coming to college. Be sure that your essay has a clearly stated thesis and that it helps readers to understand your problem.

The class was given two weeks to complete the assignment. Students were expected to do some research and to have the instructor read and comment on at least one draft.

Because this paper was the class's first full-length assignment, the instructor asked students to approach the writing process systematically, experimenting with different kinds of activities designed to help them plan, shape, write, and revise their essays. Of course, not all these strategies would work equally well for each student, but the instructor wanted students to discover which activities worked best for them. For this reason, she asked them to record their thoughts about each activity as they completed it. In addition to illustrating each writing activity Kimberly tried, the pages that follow also reproduce computer screens that show her reactions to these activities.

6a Planning an Essay

(1) Choosing and Narrowing a Topic

I had no trouble thinking of a problem I've encountered in college. I come from a small town, and our college is located in a much larger city, so I've had to make a lot of adjustments. One adjustment that has been particularly difficult is that I've had to use computers on a daily basis. In my high school, computers were not very important. There were a few computers at school, and I'd been exposed to *Microsoft Word*, email, and the Internet, but my parents didn't own a computer, so I never became really familiar with a wide range of software programs or the Internet. In college, students are expected to have a high degree of computer literacy. Many professors and administrators incorrectly assume that students have a basic knowledge of computers, but this isn't true for me. So, I decided my topic would be my problems with computers.

(2) Finding Something to Say

Reading and Observing

In our composition reader, I came across an article by Henry Louis Gates Jr. titled "One Internet, Two Nations." Gates observes that there is a division between those who are Internet savvy and those who are not, and he's particularly concerned with the fact that most Internet content is not aimed at African Americans. He thinks that this is why many African Americans aren't accessing the Internet. I think that I could use this article in my paper to help me move outside my personal experience with computers and the Internet.

Keeping a Journal

Professor Wilson told us to use *Microsoft Word* instead of a paper notebook for our journals, and this presented a problem for me. My typing skills are poor, so I was worried that it would be really time consuming to constantly have to correct myself. After a while, though, I found that keeping a computer journal actually helped me to improve my typing skills. The more I forced myself to work with the computer, the more familiar the process became. I also realized that the spell check and grammar check features made it possible for me to review my work in a really efficient way. At the same time, keeping a journal gave me some ideas for my paper.

Writing Activity: Journal Entry

I'm not really comfortable writing about my own poor computer skills, but I have to admit it's a good topic for a paper about a problem I have. What I really want to focus on, though, is the ways in which computer illiteracy is a big problem not just for me but for many college students. I don't want to write about the hours it took me to register for classes online or the fact that it took me an hour to figure out how to email my professor and then save that email to a disk. I don't want this paper to be about me and my problems. What I want to do is write about the difficulties students with low computer skills have and mention a few things about my own life to illustrate these general ideas.

Freewriting

I like freewriting because it allows me to write without worrying—a real benefit given the anxiety I often feel when I write on a computer. In freewriting, you don't have to worry about grammar or spelling. This exercise helped me to see that there are two groups of students on campus: those who are computer literate and those who are not.

Writing Activity: Freewriting (Excerpt)

This isn't so bad because I finally don't have to worry about typing perfectly. I can make mistakes, and I won't have to stop writing and then correct myself. That's how I feel using computers: anxious. We had a few computers at my high school, but we didn't have to take a computer class, or even a typing class. Maybe we should have! When I got to college, I felt like such an idiot. Everyone else seemed to have no trouble using the Internet for research, creating PowerPoint presentations, and creating their own Web sites for class projects. All of a sudden I was expected to use computers to register, for research, and to communicate with my professors. It was horrible! Most other students didn't ever have to ask a question about computers. It's like there are two groups when you get to college: the people who are computer literate and those who aren't.

Writing Activity: Focused Freewriting (Excerpt)

The first day of orientation we were told to use the computers to register. It's not like I'd never used a computer before or seen the Internet. Our high school had a few computers, and I'd accessed the Internet a few times. Still, I had to raise my hand and get the proctor in the computer room to come help me click on the right icon. And then I had to ask a lot of questions to figure out how to access two Web sites at the same time so that I could look at both the online course catalog and the registration program. Meanwhile, most of the other students were already finished and on their way to dinner. When I asked if I could get a copy of the course schedule on paper, the proctor told me that the university had recently gone "paperless." I realized then and there that I was going to have to do a lot of extra work to make myself computer literate. I started by asking the proctor about classes I could take at the college that might help.

Brainstorming

I like brainstorming because it allows me to think freely and write quickly, starting and stopping when I feel like it instead of writing in sentences and paragraphs.

Writing Activity: Brainstorming Notes

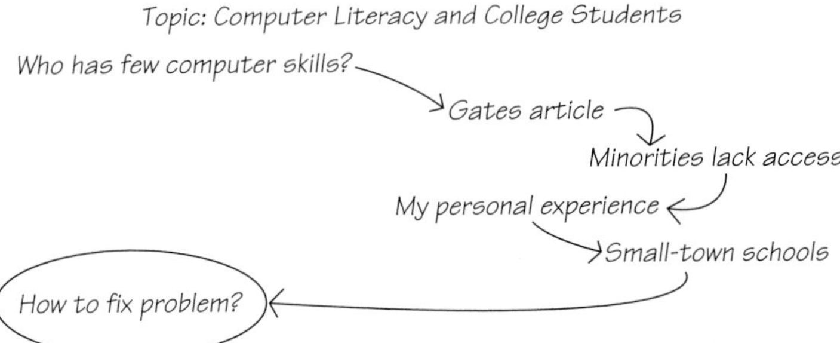

Clustering

Making a cluster diagram didn't take much time, and it showed me that I have basically three parts to my topic—the belief that most students are computer literate, the reality that many students aren't, and the ways in which this problem is being addressed.

Writing Activity: Cluster Diagram

Topic: Computer Literacy and College Students

Understanding basic word processing
Internet savvy
Assumptions that all are computer literate

Minorities
Small-town students
Me: problems

College Students and Computers

Ways of fixing the problem
Programs at school
High school?

Asking Questions

These questions took a lot of time, but they did help me to see a possible shape for my essay. I thought the *Why?* and *How?* questions were the most interesting of the journalistic questions. When I went through the in-depth questions, those that suggested causes and effects seemed most useful.

Writing Activity: Journalistic Questions

- Who stereotypes college students? Who is familiar with computers and the Internet and who is not?
- What are some of the assumptions people make about college students? What is computer illiteracy? What kinds of programs exist to help those who are computer illiterate at the college level?
- When did computers become essential for college students?
- Where are students most likely to learn computer skills?
- Why is familiarity with the Internet so important in college? Why is there a gap between those who are computer savvy and those who are not?
- How can we bridge this gap?

Writing Activity: In-Depth Questions (Excerpt)

What causes the gap between those who are computer savvy and those who are not? Differences in family income, parents' education level, quality of public education, regional differences.

What are the effects of the gap? Differences in achievement in college, performance on the job; differences in access to information; differences in earning power.

6b Shaping Material

(1) Developing a Thesis

I tried different ways to word my tentative thesis, but I wanted to make sure it included the most important ideas I was going to talk about—that I've faced problems in college because I don't know a lot about computers.

Writing Activity: Tentative Thesis Statement

I was at a real disadvantage when I entered college because I lacked important computer skills.

(2) Constructing an Informal Outline

My outline seemed kind of short, but I thought I could follow it pretty easily as I wrote my rough draft, maybe getting a paragraph out of each section.

Writing Activity: Informal Outline

College Students and Computer Literacy

Thesis statement: I was at a real disadvantage when I entered college because I lacked important computer skills.

Students are expected to be familiar with computers

- Basic word-processing programs
- Internet
- Email

Many students have very little or no experience with computers

- No access at home
- No access at school

Consequences of computer illiteracy

- Difficulty with everyday tasks
- Embarrassment
- Missed opportunities

Possible solutions to problem

- Classes
- ??????

Personal experience

- Few computer skills
- Classes in computer lab

(3) Constructing a Storyboard

I'd never even heard of a storyboard, but I had to make one for my essay. Following Professor Wilson's advice, I used sticky notes to represent the individual parts of my paper, and I liked being able to move them around.

FAQs

Writing Activity: Storyboard

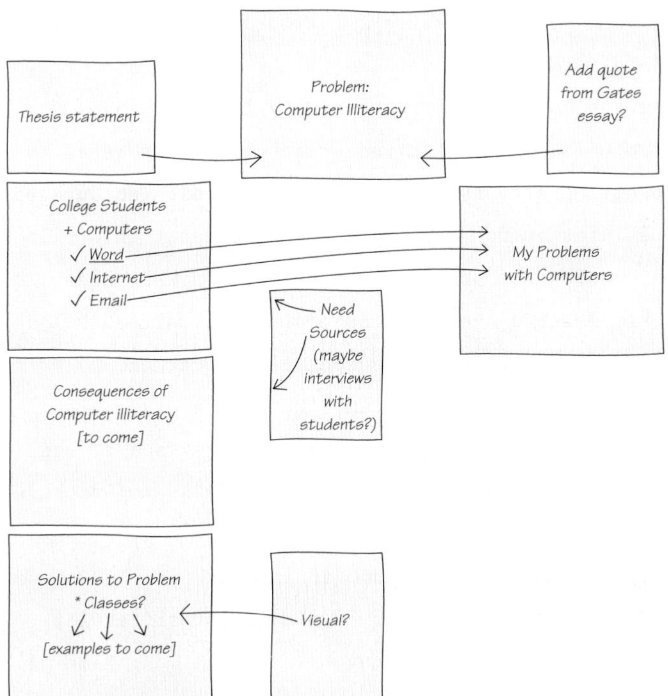

6c Drafting and Revising

(1) Writing a Rough Draft

As I wrote my first draft, I tried to write quickly. Still, I checked my outline as I wrote so that I wouldn't wander off my topic. I also made boldfaced and bracketed notes to myself so I wouldn't forget to add or double check information later.

Rough Draft

College Students and Computer Literacy

Today, most colleges expect their entering students to be familiar with computers. From registering for courses to contacting professors, students are required to use computers on a daily basis. I was at a real disadvantage when I entered college because I lacked important computer skills. [Add more here]

Computers have become increasingly important on college campuses. When I arrived at school, I was asked to use Microsoft Word to type my papers. I was also encouraged to use the Internet for research. [Do I document this?] In fact, many professors posted their syllabi on Web pages. I also quickly learned the importance of email. Although I'd been exposed to email in high school, I'd never had to learn how to use an email program like Eudora or download it to my computer. I had to call the help desk and it was really embarrassing. All of my other friends seemed to have few problems doing this.

If you don't have high computer literacy skills, there are many consequences. Students have a lot of difficulty completing everyday tasks. It may take them a long time to email a professor or register for a course simply because they are unfamiliar with the software being used. Students who feel uncomfortable using computers also feel embarrassed. They may not want to admit that they don't understand how to use particular software programs. If they don't seek help, they miss out on a lot of opportunities. Computers are so important in school that students who don't understand them may avoid taking exciting classes that require a working knowledge of specific computer programs.

The reality is that a lot of students don't have a lot of experience with computers. Students who do understand computers are usually math and science people. If you're interested in English, you probably aren't familiar with computers. Even if they are familiar with computers, she may have never used the Internet. In small towns, students probably don't have access to a computer at home. Many high schools also have trouble providing their students with computer access, which is a big problem for many students. **[Need more/better support here]**

Our school does provide students with several opportunities to improve their computer skills, but most students don't know about them. The library offers several classes that teach students how to access useful information online. The computer lab also holds classes on how to use software programs like Microsoft Word and Microsoft Publisher. Students can even learn how to design their own Web pages. Unfortunately, these classes are not well advertised. Course listings appear on the Information Technology Web site, but for those students who avoid using the Internet, finding out when and where to take classes is difficult. Ironically, students who need these classes will probably not be using the Internet a lot to get information about the university. **[Check on all of this to make sure]**

When I arrived at college, I had very few computer skills. Our high school had a couple of computers, but we didn't have Internet access. My first required class was a writing course and was held in a computer lab. I was forced to learn how to use computers and the Internet to write my papers. After a few weeks of pretending to know what I was doing, I decided to try to find some help. I was too embarrassed to ask my professor where to go for help, so it took me a few days to find out when and where the classes were. I ended up going to the library and asking the librarian. She was really helpful and I enrolled in a couple of them. After a course on Microsoft Word and the Internet, I felt much more comfortable using computers.

It is important to remember that some students arrive at college with few computer skills and that they are at a significant disadvantage. [Add more!]

This first draft really only got me started writing. I wrote a short introduction to get into the subject and identify the problem, but I really didn't have a clear idea of where my paper was headed or how I was going to incorporate my outside sources.

(2) Revising the Rough Draft

Professor Wilson asked us to turn in a copy of the changes we decided to make on our paper and suggested that we use the Track Changes feature in *Word.* Since my handwriting is fairly messy, I was excited about the opportunity to make changes that I could actually read. The color contrast between the text and the changes also made it easy for me to distinguish my original work from my changes.

Using the Track Changes feature was easy. All I had to do was open my rough draft, click the Tools menu, and then select Track Changes and Highlight Changes.

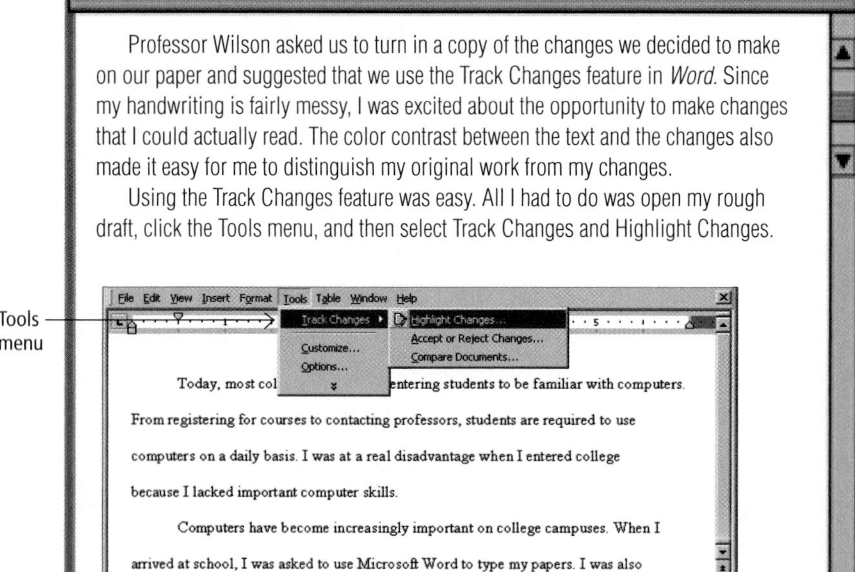
Tools menu
File Edit View Insert Format Tools Table Window Help
Track Changes
Highlight Changes...
Accept or Reject Changes...
Compare Documents...
Customize...
Options...
Today, most col
entering students to be familiar with computers.
From registering for courses to contacting professors, students are required to use
computers on a daily basis. I was at a real disadvantage when I entered college
because I lacked important computer skills.
Computers have become increasingly important on college campuses. When I
arrived at school, I was asked to use Microsoft Word to type my papers. I was also

When I revised my rough draft, I added a reference to the article by Henry Louis Gates Jr. to the beginning. Also, there were many places where I thought my paper didn't flow, so I added more transitions and revised some topic sentences to give more focus to my paragraphs. I made these few changes and then handed in my revised draft to Professor Wilson.

Rough Draft with Student's Revisions

College Students and Computer Literacy

Today, most colleges expect their entering students to be familiar with computers. From registering for courses to contacting professors, students are required to use computers on a daily basis. I was at a real disadvantage when I entered college because I lacked important computer skills.

Computers have become increasingly important ~~on college campuses~~ in today's society. Consequently, many scholars and public officials are concerned that those without access to computers will be at a disadvantage. Henry Louis Gates Jr., for example, argues in "One Internet, Two Nations" that the content on the Internet, which is primarily aimed at whites, threatens to leave African Americans behind. Similarly, college students who arrive with low computer literacy skills are at a disadvantage.

When I arrived at school, I was asked to use computers in several ways. First, I was required to use Microsoft Word when typing~~to type~~ my papers. I was also encouraged to use the Internet for research. In fact, many professors posted their syllabi on Web pages. I also quickly learned the importance of email. Although I'd been exposed to email in high school, I'd never had to learn how to use an email program like Eudora or download it to my computer. I had to call the help desk and it was really embarrassing. All of my other friends seemed to have few problems doing this.

If you don't have high computer literacy skills, there are many consequences. Students who aren't familiar with the Internet or email may have a lot of difficulty completing everyday tasks. For example, i~~I~~t may take them a long time to email a professor or register for a course simply because they are unfamiliar with the software being used. Students who feel uncomfortable using computers also feel embarrassed. They may not want to admit that they don't understand how to use particular software programs. If they don't seek help, they miss out on a lot of opportunities. Computers are so important in school that students who don't understand them may avoid taking exciting classes that require a working knowledge of specific computer programs.

There are many reasons why a student entering college might have low computer literacy skills. ~~The reality is that a lot of students don't have a lot of experience with computers.~~ Students who do understand computers are usually math and science people. If you're interested in English, you probably aren't familiar with computers. Even if they are familiar with computers, she may have never used the Internet. In small towns, students probably don't have access to a computer at home. Many high schools also have trouble providing their students with computer access, which is a big problem for many students.

There are many steps a student can take to improve his or her computer skills. ~~Our school does provide students with several opportunities to improve their computer skills, but most students don't know about them.~~ The library offers several classes that teach students how to access useful information online. The computer lab also holds classes on how to use software programs like

Microsoft Word and Microsoft Publisher. Students can even learn how to design their own Web pages. Unfortunately, these classes are not well advertised. Course listings appear on the Information Technology Web site, but for those students who avoid using the Internet, finding out when and where to take classes is difficult. Ironically, students who need these classes will probably not be using the Internet a lot to get information about the university.

When I arrived at college, I had very few computer skills. Our high school had a couple of computers, but we didn't have Internet access. My first required class was a writing course and was held in a computer lab. I was forced to learn how to use computers and the Internet to write my papers. After a few weeks of pretending to know what I was doing, I decided to try to find some help. I was too embarrassed to ask my professor where to go for help, so it took me a few days to find out when and where the classes were. I ended up going to the library and asking the librarian. She was really helpful and I enrolled in a course~~couple of them~~ about~~After a course on~~ Microsoft Word and a course that taught students the basics of email and the Internet. After taking these two classes, I felt much more comfortable using computers.

It is important to remember that some students arrive at college with few computer skills and that they are at a significant disadvantage.

(3) Writing a Second Draft

Professor Wilson used the Comment feature in *Microsoft Word* when she reviewed my draft. This was really helpful because the boxed comments linked to specific words and sentences made it easy for me to see and keep track of her suggestions.

Second Draft with Instructor's Comments

College Students and Computer Literacy

Today, most colleges expect their entering students to be familiar with computers. From registering for courses to contacting professors, students are required to use computers on a daily basis. I was at a real disadvantage when I entered college because I lacked important computer skills.

Comment: This thesis is very personal and limits you in terms of what you can talk about in this paper. Try broadening your thesis so that it moves beyond your personal experience and thus broadens your paper's focus.

Computers have become increasingly important in today's society. Consequently, many scholars and public officials are concerned that those without access to computers will be at a disadvantage. Henry Louis Gates Jr., for example, argues in "One Internet, Two Nations" that the content on the Internet, which is primarily aimed at whites, threatens to leave African Americans behind. Similarly, college students who arrive with low computer literacy skills are at a disadvantage.

When I arrived at school, I was asked to use computers in several ways. First, I was required to use <u>Microsoft Word</u> when typing my papers. I was also encouraged to use the Internet for research. In fact, many professors posted their syllabi on Web pages. I also quickly learned the importance of email. Although I'd been exposed to email in high school, I'd never had to learn how to use an email program like <u>Eudora</u> or download it to my computer. I had to call the help desk and it was really embarrassing. All of my other friends seemed to have few problems doing this.

Comment: In your final draft, edit out all contractions. (Contractions are too informal for most college writing.) See 53b1.

Comment: Consider making this point less personal. Use this paragraph to talk about all of the reasons a student might use a computer in college. Remember, you are moving from general to specific. See 7b1.

If you don't have high computer literacy skills, there are many consequences. Students who aren't familiar with the Internet or email may

Comment: Consider switching this paragraph with the one above it. Remember, you are moving from general to specific. See 7b1.

have a lot of difficulty completing everyday tasks. For example, it may take them a long time to email a professor or register for a course simply because they are unfamiliar with the software being used. Students who feel uncomfortable using computers also feel embarrassed. They may not want to admit that they don't understand how to use particular software programs. If they don't seek help, they miss out on a lot of opportunities. Computers are so important in school that students who don't understand them may avoid taking exciting classes that require a working knowledge of specific computer programs.

There are many reasons why a student entering college might have low computer literacy skills. Students who do understand computers are usually math and science people. If you're interested in English, you probably aren't familiar with computers. Even if they are familiar with computers, she may have never used the Internet. In small towns, students probably don't have access to a computer at home. Many high schools also have trouble providing their students with computer access, which is a big problem for many students.

Comment: These two sentences are generalizations. Is this really true? What are some other reasons students might have low computer literacy skills? Think about your own situation.

Comment: Incorrect pronoun reference. See 46c.

Comment: You need one more outside source, Kimberly, and this is a good place to add information to back yourself up. I suggest going to the library and asking the librarian to help you search one of our online indexes.

Comment: This sentence is too wordy. Condense it and make it more specific. See 36a.

There are many steps a student can take to improve his or her computer skills. The library offers several classes that teach students how to access useful information online. The computer lab also holds classes on how to use software programs like Microsoft Word and Microsoft Publisher. Students can even learn how to design their own Web pages. Unfortunately, these classes are not well advertised. Course listings appear on the Information Technology Web site, but for those students who avoid using the Internet, finding out when and where to take classes is difficult. Ironically, students who need these classes will probably not be using the Internet a lot to get information about the university.

Comment: You need a transition at the end of this paragraph. See 7b6.

When I arrived at college, I had very few computer skills. Our high school had a couple of computers, but we didn't have Internet access. My first required class was a writing course and was held in a computer lab. I was forced to learn how to use computers and the Internet to write my papers. After a few weeks of pretending to know what I was doing, I decided to try to find some help. I was too embarrassed to ask my professor where to go for help, so it took me a few days to find out when and where the classes were. I ended up going to the library and asking the librarian. She was really helpful and I enrolled in a course about <u>Microsoft Word</u> and a course that taught students the basics of email and the Internet. After taking these two classes, I felt much more comfortable using computers.

Comment: When we spoke last, you mentioned that your high school was instituting a new computer literacy class. Consider contacting one of your high school teachers and asking if the class was instituted and how it is working.

It is important to remember that some students arrive at college with few computer skills and that they are at a significant disadvantage.

Comment: This conclusion is very brief. Use this paragraph to summarize all of the points that you made in the paper.

Comment: Don't forget to add a works-cited list. See 18a2.

After reading Professor Wilson's comments, I decided that the three most important things I needed to do were revise my thesis, ask a librarian to help me find another source, and check with one of my high school teachers to find out about the new computer literacy class.

(4) Revising the Second Draft

One way to revise is to print out a hard copy of the paper and then hand-edit it. I used this method to make some of the changes Professor Wilson recommended.

Old Version:

```
     There are many reasons why a student entering college
might have low computer literacy skills. Students who do
understand computers are usually math and science people.
If you're interested in English, you probably aren't
familiar with computers. Even if they are familiar with
computers, she may have never used the Internet.
```

Revised Version:

Despite the necessity of a strong working knowledge of computers and the Internet, many students arrive at college with very little to no experience of either.

^There are many reasons why a student entering college might have low computer literacy skills. Students *might not, for example, have had access to a computer in their home.* ^~~who do understand computers are usually math and science people. If you're interested in English, you probably aren't familiar with computers.~~ Even if they are familiar with computers, ^~~she~~ *they* may have never used the Internet.

When I went to the library to try to find another source, one of the librarians, Jocelyn Miller, was very helpful. She showed me how to use my university ID to log onto a computer. Next, she showed me how to access the online indexes and databases. She told me about *Expanded Academic ASAP*, a very helpful database that she thought would suit my purposes. This database contains articles from the arts, the humanities, the social sciences, and science and technology. Its articles are often full text and may contain visuals as well.

When I told her about my paper, Ms. Miller told me that the gap between computer-savvy people and others is commonly referred to as the *digital divide*. Gates uses this term in his essay, but I didn't know that it was the standard term used to define the problem. Ms. Miller said this term would be really helpful when we did our search, and it was. When we did a search using the term *digital divide*, it yielded thousands of results, and on the first page of results, I found an article that sounded promising. It turned out to be inappropriate for my paper, but at the end of the article, *Expanded Academic ASAP* lists the topics that the article covered. One of them was "digital divide and social aspects." The database had an icon that said there were thirty-seven other articles about the digital divide and social aspects.

When I clicked that icon, another list appeared, and I found an article titled "Educators and Technology Standards: Influencing the Digital Divide." After reading the article, I realized it was exactly what I was looking for because it talked about computer illiteracy in K–12 schools.

This weekend, I emailed my old high school English teacher, Vicky Wellborn, to find out how the local high school is tackling the problem of computer illiteracy. She told me that all freshmen in high school now have to take a class that teaches them basic computer skills and gives them hands-on experience and that all teachers are now required to take a computer course during the summer. She also emailed me a photo of students in the lab, which I think might come in handy later to show the changes that are taking place.

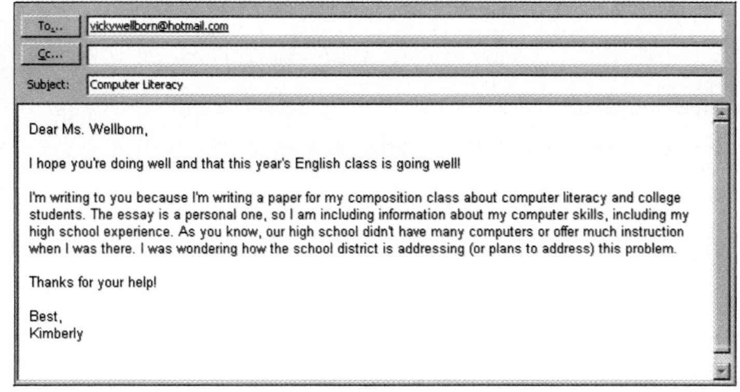

To... vickywellborn@hotmail.com
Cc...
Subject: Computer Literacy

Dear Ms. Wellborn,

I hope you're doing well and that this year's English class is going well!

I'm writing to you because I'm writing a paper for my composition class about computer literacy and college students. The essay is a personal one, so I am including information about my computer skills, including my high school experience. As you know, our high school didn't have many computers or offer much instruction when I was there. I was wondering how the school district is addressing (or plans to address) this problem.

Thanks for your help!

Best,
Kimberly

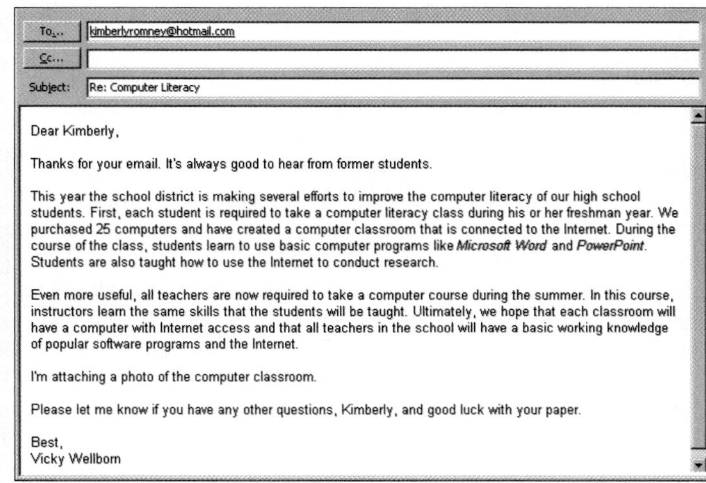

To... kimberlyromney@hotmail.com
Cc...
Subject: Re: Computer Literacy

Dear Kimberly,

Thanks for your email. It's always good to hear from former students.

This year the school district is making several efforts to improve the computer literacy of our high school students. First, each student is required to take a computer literacy class during his or her freshman year. We purchased 25 computers and have created a computer classroom that is connected to the Internet. During the course of the class, students learn to use basic computer programs like *Microsoft Word* and *PowerPoint*. Students are also taught how to use the Internet to conduct research.

Even more useful, all teachers are now required to take a computer course during the summer. In this course, instructors learn the same skills that the students will be taught. Ultimately, we hope that each classroom will have a computer with Internet access and that all teachers in the school will have a basic working knowledge of popular software programs and the Internet.

I'm attaching a photo of the computer classroom.

Please let me know if you have any other questions, Kimberly, and good luck with your paper.

Best,
Vicky Wellborn

After getting this new information, I added it and my two new sources. I also revised my tentative thesis. My new thesis statement is more consistent with my essay, which I wanted to focus not just on my personal experience with computers but also on the idea that the problem is faced by many other students as well. My main goal now is to make my paper flow smoothly, moving from broad, general ideas to my own personal experience with computers.

Writing Activity: Revised Thesis Statement

Students who enter college with weak computer skills are at a significant disadvantage.

After revising my second draft and incorporating Professor Wilson's comments, I asked three of my classmates to look over my paper. Each student used a different color to indicate what he or she thought of my paper. I found this process very helpful. If one student didn't say a lot about a particular problem in the paper, someone else did. The comments about how students use email were really helpful. When Professor Wilson asked me to make this paragraph less personal, I just took the information out, but then the paragraph looked too short. The student comments helped me think about ways to expand my discussion.

Second Draft with Peers' Comments (Excerpt)

When I arrived at school, I was asked to use computers in several ways. That's for sure ☺! First, I was required to use Microsoft Word when typing my papers. I was also encouraged to use the Internet for research. In fact, many professors posted their syllabi on Web pages. I also quickly learned the importance of email. Although I'd been exposed to email in high school, I'd never had to learn how to use an email program like Eudora or download it to my computer. I had to call the help desk and it was really embarrassing. All of my other friends seemed to have few problems doing this.

There's a lot more to talk about here. What about listservs? PowerPoint?

Talking w/profs. is another imp. use of email.

Yes! I emailed Prof. Wilson when I had to go out of town and couldn't make office hrs.

After my peer-review session, I felt ready to write my final draft. First, though, I was required to write a sentence outline. I thought the effort of a sentence outline would really pay off because it would help me check the organization of my ideas one more time. Besides, I might be able to use sentences from my outline in my paper.

Writing Activity: Sentence Outline

College Students and Computer Literacy

Thesis statement: Students who enter college with weak computer skills are at a significant disadvantage.

I. Computers are increasingly important in today's society.
   A. According to Gates, many are concerned about the division between those who have access to the Internet and those who do not.
   B. This "digital divide" exists among college students.

II. College students are expected to be familiar with computers.
   A. Students are expected to be familiar with basic computer programs.
      1. Students are expected to use Microsoft Word to type their papers.
      2. Instructors ask their students to use PowerPoint for their presentations.
   B. Students are expected to be familiar with the Internet.
      1. Students register for classes on the Internet.

```
      2. Announcements for campuswide events are
         posted on the Internet.
      3. Professors post their syllabi on Web pages.
      4. Students are expected to use the Internet to
         conduct research.
   C. Students are expected to be familiar with
      email.
      1. Discussion questions are posted on
         listservs.
      2. Students need to communicate with one
         another via email.
      3. Students need to communicate with their
         professors via email.
III. The reality is that many students arrive at
   college with very little experience with
   computers or the Internet.
   A. They might not have access at home.
      1. Many families are not able to afford a
         computer.
      2. Computers might not be seen as a necessity.
   B. College students may have had limited access to
      computers in elementary or high school.
      1. K-12 schools are getting more computers.
      2. However, these computers are often obsolete
         or not connected to the Internet.
 IV. There are many consequences for students with low
   computer skills.
   A. Students may have difficulty with everyday
      tasks.
      1. Registering for classes is difficult.
      2. Contacting professors and other students is
         difficult.
```

B. Students feel embarrassed.
   1. Students do not want to ask for help.
   2. Students do not improve their skills.
C. Students miss out on opportunities.
   1. They miss out on the benefits of using the Internet to do research.
   2. They miss out on the benefits of sophisticated software programs.

V. Our school has an outreach program.
   A. Many classes are available.
      1. Students can learn how to use basic computer programs.
      2. Students can learn how to use email.
      3. Students can learn to use the Internet for library research.
   B. Publicity for the outreach program is poor.
      1. The administration needs to advertise these programs during freshman orientation.
      2. The administration needs to understand the embarrassment that some students might feel.

VI. I have personal experience with this problem.
   A. I came to school with few computer skills.
   B. I took a writing class in a computer lab.
   C. I took classes on <u>Word</u>, email, and the Internet.
   D. I now realize that more efforts should be made at the high school level.
      1. My high school is now making such efforts.
      2. My high school now requires computer literacy classes for both students and teachers.

```
VII. The future is hopeful.
     A. High schools are making changes.
     B. College students will be better prepared.
```

(5) Preparing a Final Draft

As I wrote the final draft, I really tried to keep my personal reactions about this topic in check. Because it is such a personal topic, I found that I often began to rant and get off topic. When this happened, I stopped writing. I took a break. I tried to imagine myself as an observer rather than someone actually experiencing the problem. This was difficult, but I think it allowed me to write a good paper as opposed to an angry complaint against my high school and my college.

Magazine articles were also helpful in forcing me to maintain my distance from the paper. The articles helped me see that this problem goes beyond me and affects the lives of many Americans. Using some of them in my paper also helped me show that this problem is well documented and how it is being addressed. This tells my readers that this paper isn't just my opinion, but a balanced discussion of a problem that many people are aware of and trying to fix.

Professor Wilson reminded me that I needed to document my sources. She told me that not only the Gates piece and the article by Swain and Peterson but also Ms. Wellborn's email need to be documented both in the essay and on a separate works-cited page. She referred me to Chapter 18 of the handbook for guidance.

As I revised, I decided to use the photo Ms. Wellborn sent. I thought it would be a good way to give readers a visual example of the changes that have occurred at my high school. Before I could insert the photo into my paper, I had to figure out how to download it from Ms. Wellborn's email. I went to the computer lab, and they helped me save the photo to disk. I was then able to insert it into my paper. It was really much easier than I thought it would be.

After I finished printing out my final draft, I read it through one more time and noticed a few typos. So I corrected them and printed it out again—and then I really had a final draft.

FAQs links

Romney 1

Kimberly Romney

Professor Wilson

English 101

10 October 2003

College Students and Computer Literacy

Introduction

Today, most colleges expect their entering students to be familiar with computers. From registering for courses to contacting professors, students are required to use computers on a daily basis. For this reason, those students who enter college with weak computer literacy skills are at a significant disadvantage.

Thesis statement

Importance of computers in society

Computers are increasingly important in today's society. As Henry Louis Gates Jr. writes in his article "One Internet, Two Nations," many people are concerned that there is a division between those who have access to the Internet and those who do not. He writes, "Today we stand at the brink of becoming two societies, one largely white and plugged in and the other black and unplugged" (500). This gap is often referred to as the "digital divide." The gap between those who are technologically literate and those who are not extends beyond race and ethnicity to include the elderly, the disabled, and those who live in rural areas. This division is particularly apparent among college students.

Importance of computers in college

As students enter higher education, they are expected to be familiar with a variety of software programs as well as with the Internet. Most

Romney 2

professors, for example, require their students to use Microsoft Word to write their papers. Further, instructors often ask their students to use PowerPoint to present their papers or research projects.

Importance of the Internet

Students are also expected to be familiar with the Internet. For example, registration for classes is often conducted online. Professors and administrators use the Internet to post information about campuswide events, and many professors create their own Web pages where they post their syllabi and class assignments. Finally, most professors ask their students to use the Internet when conducting research.

Importance of email

A good understanding of how email works is also necessary for a student to be successful in college. Discussion questions for class are often posted on listservs. If a student wants to communicate with someone in the class, email is one of the most efficient ways to do so. Communicating with the professor is also easier if one uses email. For example, if a student cannot attend office hours, he or she can still ask the professor a question.

Reason for students' poor skills: lack of access at home

Despite the importance of a strong working knowledge of computers and the Internet, many students arrive at college with very little experience with either. There are several reasons why students might have poor computer skills. They might not, for example, have had access to a computer at

Romney 3

home. Many families cannot afford computers, and others simply do not see a computer as a necessity.

In many cases, students may not have been taught computer skills in elementary or high school. A recent study of efforts to bridge the "digital divide" in elementary and high schools reported that although many schools are improving their access to computers, the computers they have may be obsolete models or not connected to the Internet (Swain 328). According to the report, "even though 98% of all schools have computers, as of fall 2000, only 77% of instructional rooms have Internet access" (Swain 328).

Reason for students' poor skills: lack of access at school

For those students who arrive at college with weak computer skills, there are many consequences. They may have difficulty completing everyday tasks in a timely manner. Registering for classes on the Internet and contacting professors or other students via email become time-consuming (rather than timesaving) tasks. Students may also be embarrassed by their weak computer skills. As a result, they often do not ask for help. Without help, they have difficulty improving their skills. As a result, they do not benefit from the opportunities offered by the Internet (such as faster and more thorough research) or by sophisticated software programs (such as professional-looking papers and presentations).

Problems caused by weak computer skills

Our college does have an outreach program aimed at students with sub-par computer skills. Once a week, the computer lab offers classes on software

Possible solution to problems: classes

Romney 4

programs such as Microsoft Word, PowerPoint, and Dreamweaver. There is also a class about email that not only gives students basic information (such as how to send and open attachments), but also tells them how to use programs (such as Outlook Express) to track their daily schedules and appointments. The library also offers several classes, both broad research classes and more discipline-specific ones, about how to use the Internet for research.

Limitations of classes

While the college's outreach program provides students with many opportunities to improve their skills, the publicity for this program is very poor. Students are not given information about these classes at orientation, and they are not well advertised in the student newspaper, or even at the computer lab and library. The administration is also not very sensitive to the embarrassment that many students might feel about having poor computer skills. Many students might avoid asking a librarian or computer lab proctor for information about these programs, and this is a problem that a good advertising campaign would remedy.

Personal experience: problems in college

As a student from a small town where computer classes were not a part of the high school curriculum, I have personal experience with this problem. I came to college with few computer skills. Although I had a basic working knowledge of Microsoft Word and had used the Internet and email a few times, I was not very comfortable using computers. One of my first classes here was a writing class that was held

Romney 5

in a computer lab. I was confronted with my problem every Monday, Wednesday, and Friday, and because I was embarrassed about my poor computer skills, I did not want to ask the professor for help. Trying to find help on my own was difficult. It took me two weeks to figure out when and where classes on Microsoft Word and the Internet were held. However, after taking these classes, my skills were greatly improved.

Personal experience: changes in high school

Through my experience at school, I have come to realize that more efforts need to be made to educate students about technology at the high school level. In my hometown, the school district instituted a computer literacy class for all high school freshmen the year after I graduated.

Fig. 1. Student in the Woodrow Wilson High School computer lab, personal photograph by Vicky Wellborn, 5 Sept. 2003.

Romney 6

According to my high school English teacher, Vicky Wellborn, students really enjoy this class: they go to the new computer lab during breaks or after school, and the lab is frequently full (see fig. 1). Even better, the district now requires teachers to take a computer literacy class so that they are better prepared to answer students' questions (Wellborn).

Conclusion

Despite my own frustrating experiences, I believe the future is hopeful. As high schools continue to make efforts to incorporate technology into the classroom, students entering college will be better prepared for the technological challenges they will face. And as they become more competent computer users, they will narrow the "digital divide."

Romney 7

Works Cited

Gates, Henry Louis Jr. "One Internet, Two Nations." The Blair Reader. 4th ed. Ed. Laurie G. Kirszner and Stephen R. Mandell. Upper Saddle River, NJ: Prentice, 2002. 499-501.

Swain, Colleen, and Tamara Pearson. "Educators and Technology Standards: Influencing the Digital Divide." Journal of Research on Technology in Education 34.3 (2002): 326-35. Expanded Academic ASAP. Gale Group Databases. U of Texas Lib. System, TX. 15 Sept. 2003 <http://www.galegroup.com>.

Wellborn, Vicky. "Re: Computer Literacy." Email to the author. 23 Sept. 2003.

Chapter 7

Writing Paragraphs

Frequently Asked Questions

When do I begin a new paragraph? (p. 106)
What transitional words and phrases can I use to make my paragraphs flow? (p. 115)
How do I know if I have enough information to support my paragraph's main idea? (p. 120)
How do I write a good introduction for my paper? (p. 135)
How do I write an effective conclusion? (p. 138)

A **paragraph** is a group of related sentences. It may be complete in itself or part of a longer piece of writing.

Checklist: When to Paragraph

- ☐ Begin a new paragraph whenever you move from one major point to another.
- ☐ Begin a new paragraph whenever you move your readers from one time period or location to another.
- ☐ Begin a new paragraph whenever you introduce a new step in a process or sequence.
- ☐ Begin a new paragraph when you want to emphasize an important idea.
- ☐ Begin a new paragraph every time a new person speaks.
- ☐ Begin a new paragraph to signal the end of your introduction and the beginning of your conclusion.

ESL Tip

Indent the first line of each paragraph one-half inch (or five spaces). When you type, set the margin at one-half inch, and press the return key on your computer every time you start a new paragraph. Do not add extra lines of space between paragraphs.

http://kirsznermandell.wadsworth.com

Computer Tip: Auto Formatting

Microsoft Word's Formatting Palette (see Figure 7.1) allows you to customize paragraph spacing and indentation as well as other document design options. Once you set your preferences, *Word* will automatically format the rest of your document accordingly.

See Ch. 29

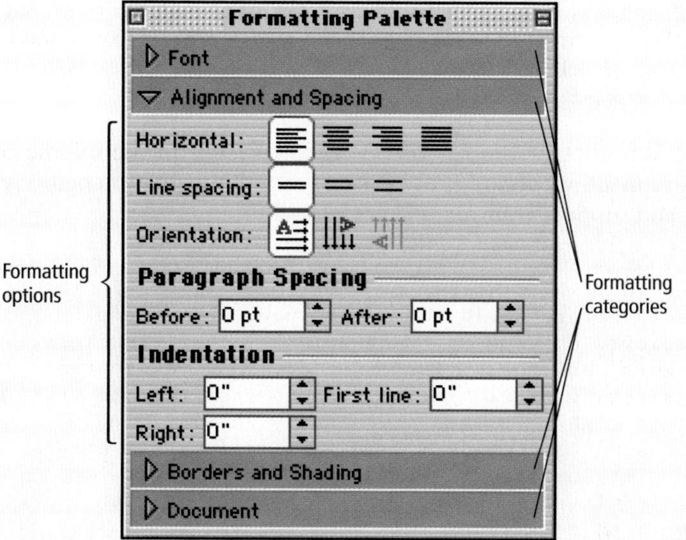

Figure 7.1 ***Microsoft Word*'s Formatting Palette.**

7a Writing Unified Paragraphs

A paragraph is **unified** when it develops a single main idea. The **topic sentence** states the main idea of the paragraph, and the other sentences in the paragraph support that idea.

(1) Using Topic Sentences

Topic sentences can be placed at the beginning, in the middle, or at the end of a paragraph. In some cases, the paragraph's main idea may even be implied; if so, there is no explicitly stated topic sentence.

Topic Sentence at the Beginning A topic sentence at the beginning of a paragraph tells readers what to expect and helps them to understand your paragraph's main idea immediately.

> I was a listening child, careful to hear the very different sounds of Spanish and English. Wide-eyed with hearing, I'd listen to sounds more than words. First, there were English (*gringo*) sounds. So many words were still unknown that when the butcher or the lady at the drugstore said something to me, exotic polysyllabic sounds would bloom in the midst of their sentences. Often the speech of people in public seemed to me very loud, booming with confidence. The man behind the counter would literally ask, "What can I do for you?" But by being so firm and so clear, the sound of his voice said that he was a *gringo;* he belonged in public society. (Richard Rodriguez, *Aria: A Memoir of a Bilingual Childhood*)

Topic Sentence in the Middle A topic sentence in the middle of a paragraph allows you to provide background information before you state and support your main idea.

> African-American servicemen have played a role in the US military since revolutionary times. In the years before World War II, however, they were employed chiefly as truck drivers, quartermasters, bakers, and cooks. Then, in July 1941, a program was set up at Alabama's Tuskegee Institute to train black fighter pilots. Eventually, nearly one thousand flyers—about half of whom fought overseas—were trained there; sixty-six of these men were killed in action. Ironically, even as African-American servicemen were fighting valiantly against fascism in Europe, they continued to experience discrimination in the US military. Black officers encountered hostility and even violence at officers' clubs. Enlisted men and women were frequently the target of bigoted remarks. Throughout the war, in fact, African-American servicemen were placed in separate, all-black units. This segregation was official army policy until 1948, when President Harry S. Truman signed an executive order to desegregate the military. (student writer)

Topic Sentence at the End If you are presenting an unusual or hard-to-accept idea, you may decide to place the topic sentence at the end of a paragraph. If you present a logical chain of reasoning and then state your conclusion in the topic sentence, you are more likely to convince readers that your conclusion is reasonable.

> These sprays, dusts and aerosols are now applied almost universally to farms, gardens, forests, and homes—nonselective chemicals

that have the power to kill every insect, the "good" and the "bad," to still the song of birds and the leaping of fish in the streams, to coat the leaves with a deadly film, and to linger on in soil—all this though the intended target may be only a few weeds or insects. Can anyone believe it is possible to lay down such a barrage of poisons on the surface without making it unfit for life? They should not be called "insecticides," but "biocides." (Rachel Carson, "The Obligation to Endure," *Silent Spring*)

Main Idea Implied In some cases, you may not need a topic sentence. For example, in some narrative or descriptive paragraphs, an explicit topic sentence might seem forced or unnatural. In these situations, a writer will omit the topic sentence entirely if readers can easily infer it from the details in the paragraph. For example, in the following paragraph, the writer wants readers to conclude for themselves (as she did) that because she was female, she was considered inferior.

I am eight years old and a tomboy. I have a cowboy hat, cowboy boots, checkered shirt and pants, all red. My playmates are my brothers, two and four years older than I. Their colors are black and green, the only difference in the way we are dressed. On Saturday nights we all go to the picture show, even my mother; Westerns are her favorite kind of movie. Back home, "on the ranch," we pretend we are Tom Mix, Hopalong Cassidy, Lash LaRue (we've even named one of our dogs Lash LaRue); we chase each other for hours rustling cattle, being outlaws, delivering damsels from distress. Then my parents decide to buy my brothers guns. These are not "real" guns. They shoot "BBs," copper pellets my brothers say will kill birds. Because I am a girl, I do not get a gun. Instantly I am relegated to the position of Indian. Now there appears a great distance between us. They shoot and shoot at everything with their new guns. I try to keep up with my bow and arrows. (Alice Walker, "Beauty: When the Other Dancer Is the Self," *In Search of Our Mothers' Gardens*)

(2) Testing for Unity

Each sentence in a paragraph should support the main idea, whether that idea is stated in a topic sentence or implied. The following paragraph is not unified because it includes sentences that do not support the main idea.

Paragraph Lacking Unity

One of the first problems I had as a college student was learning to use a computer. All students were required to buy a computer before school started. Throughout the first semester, we took a special course to teach us to use a computer. My laptop has a large memory and can do word processing and spreadsheets. It has a large screen and a DVD drive. My parents were happy that I had a computer, but they were concerned about the price. Tuition was high, and when they added in the price of the computer, it was almost out of reach. To offset expenses, I got a part-time job in the school library. I am determined to overcome "computer anxiety" and to master my computer by the end of the semester. (student writer)

The lack of unity in the preceding paragraph becomes obvious when you **chart** its structure. Begin charting paragraph structure by assigning the sentence that expresses the main idea of the paragraph to level 1. (If no sentence in the paragraph expresses the main idea, compose a sentence that does.) Indent and assign to level 2 any sentences that qualify or limit the main idea. Indent again, and assign to level 3 any sentences that support level-2 sentences. Do this for every sentence in the paragraph, assigning increasingly higher numbers to more specific sentences.

1 One of the first problems I had as a college student was learning to use a computer.
  2 All students were required to buy a computer before school started.
    3 Throughout the first semester, we took a special course to teach us to use a computer.
1 My laptop has a large screen and a DVD drive.
  2 It has a hard drive and a modem.
1 My parents were happy that I had a computer, but they were concerned about the price.
  2 Tuition was high, and when they added in the price of the computer, it was almost out of reach.
    3 To offset expenses, I got a part-time job in the school library.
1 I am determined to overcome "computer anxiety" and to master my computer by the end of the semester.

Each level-1 sentence represents a main idea that could be developed in its own paragraph; in other words, the paragraph has not one but four topic sentences. Instead of writing one unified paragraph, the writer has made a series of false starts.

After the writer decided what his main idea actually was, he deleted the sentences about his parents' financial situation and the computer's characteristics, including only those details related to the main idea (expressed in his topic sentence).

Revised Paragraph

One of the first problems I had as a college student was learning to use a computer. All first-

```
year students were required to buy a computer before
school started. Throughout the first semester,
we took a special course to teach us to use the
computer. In theory this system sounded fine, but
in my case it was a disaster. In the first place, I
had never owned a computer before. The closest I
had ever come to a computer was the computer lab in
high school. In the second place, I could not type
well. And to make matters worse, many of the people
in my computer orientation course already knew
everything there was to know about operating a
computer. By the end of the first week, I was
convinced that I would never be able to keep up
with them.
```

NOTE: A logically constructed paragraph has only one level-1 sentence. If your charting reveals more than one level-1 sentence, you need to revise your paragraph, perhaps dividing it into two paragraphs.

http://kirsznermandell.wadsworth.com

Computer Tip: Charting Paragraph Structure

You can chart the structure of a paragraph by setting the tabs in your word-processing document to correspond to the different levels of sentences you need to chart. By hitting the return key and then adjusting the tab key, you can place the sentences in proper relationship to one another.

Exercise 1

Each of the following paragraphs is unified by one main idea, but that idea is not explicitly stated. Identify the main idea of each paragraph, write a topic sentence that expresses it, and decide where in the paragraph to place it.

A. The narrator in Ellison's novel leaves an all-black college in the South to seek his fortune—and his identity—in the North. Throughout the story, he experiences bigotry in all forms. Blacks as well as whites, friends as well as enemies, treat him according to their preconceived notions of what he should be, or how he can help to advance their causes. Clearly this is a book about racial prejudice. However, on another level, *Invisible Man* is more than the account of a young African American's initiation into the harsh realities of life in the United States before the civil rights movement. The narrator calls himself invisible because others refuse to see him. He becomes so alienated from society—black and white—that he chooses to live in isolation. But, when he has learned to see himself clearly, he will emerge demanding that others see him too.

B. "Lite" can mean that a product has fewer calories, or less fat, or less sodium, or it can simply mean that the product has a "light" color, texture, or taste. It may also mean none of these. Food can be advertised as 86 percent fat free when it is actually 50 percent fat because the term "fat free" is based on weight, and fat is extremely light. Another misleading term is "no cholesterol," which is found on some products that never had any cholesterol in the first place. Peanut butter, for example, contains no cholesterol—a fact that manufacturers have recently made an issue—but it is very high in fat and so would not be a very good food for most dieters. Sodium labeling presents still another problem. The terms "sodium free," "very low sodium," "low sodium," "reduced sodium," and "no salt added" have very specific meanings, frequently not explained on the packages on which they appear.

7b Writing Coherent Paragraphs

A paragraph is **coherent** when all its sentences are logically related to one another. You can achieve coherence by arranging details according to an organizing principle, by using transitional words and phrases, by using pronouns, by using parallel structure, and by repeating key words and phrases.

(1) Arranging Details

Even if its sentences are all about the same subject, a paragraph lacks coherence if the sentences are not arranged according to a general organizing principle—*spatial*, *chronological*, or *logical*.

Spatial order establishes the perspective from which readers will view details. For example, an object or scene can be viewed from top to bottom or from near to far. Spatial order is central to descriptive paragraphs. Notice how the following descriptive paragraph begins on top of a hill, moves down to a valley, follows a river through the valley into the distance, and then moves to a point behind the speaker.

See 7d2

East of us rose another hill like ours. Between the hills, far below, was the highway which threaded south into the valley. This was the

> Yakima valley; I had never seen it before. It is justly famous for its beauty, like every planted valley. It extended south into the horizon, a distant dream of a valley, a Shangri-la. All its hundreds of low, golden slopes bore orchards. Among the orchards were towns, and roads, and plowed and fallow fields. Through the valley wandered a thin, shining river; from the river extended fine, frozen irrigation ditches. Distance blurred and blued the sight, so that the whole valley looked like a thickness or sediment at the bottom of the sky. Directly behind us was more sky, and empty lowlands blued by distance, and Mount Adams. Mount Adams was an enormous, snow-covered volcanic cone rising flat, like so much scenery. (Annie Dillard, "Total Eclipse")

Chronological order presents events in sequence, using transitional words and phrases that establish the time order of events—*at first*, *yesterday*, *later*, *in 1930*, and so on. Chronological order is central to narrative paragraphs and process paragraphs. The following narrative paragraph gains coherence from the orderly sequence of events.

See 7d1, 4

> They married in February, 1921, and began farming. Their first baby, a daughter, was born in January, 1922, when my mother was 26 years old. The second baby, a son, was born in March, 1923. They were renting farms; my father, besides working his own fields, also was a hired man for two other farmers. They had no capital initially, and had to gain it slowly, working from dawn until midnight every day. My town-bred mother learned to set hens and raise chickens, feed pigs, milk cows, plant and harvest a garden, and can every fruit and vegetable she could scrounge. She carried water nearly a quarter of a mile from the well to fill her wash boilers in order to do her laundry on a scrub board. She learned to shuck grain, feed threshers, shuck and husk corn, feed corn pickers. In September, 1925, the third baby came, and in June, 1927, the fourth child—both daughters. In 1930, my parents had enough money to buy their own farm, and that March they moved all their livestock and belongings themselves, 55 miles over rutted, muddy roads. (Donna Smith-Yackel, "My Mother Never Worked")

Logical order presents details or ideas in terms of their logical relationship to one another. For example, the ideas in a paragraph may move from *general to specific*, as in the conventional topic-sentence-at-the-beginning paragraph, or the ideas may progress from *specific to general*, as they do when the topic sentence appears at the end of the paragraph. A writer may also choose to begin with the *least important* idea and move to the *most important*. Logical order is central to exemplification paragraphs and comparison-and-contrast paragraphs. The following paragraph moves from a general statement about the need to address the problem of the injury rate in boxing to specific solutions.

See 7d3, 6

    Several things could be done to reduce the high injury rate in boxing. First, all boxers should wear protective equipment—head gear and kidney protectors, for example. This equipment is required in amateur boxing and should be required in professional boxing. Second, the object of boxing should be to score points, not to knock out opponents. An increased glove weight would make knockouts almost impossible. And finally, all fights should be limited to ten rounds. Studies show that most serious injuries occur in boxing between the eleventh and twelfth rounds—when the boxers are tired and vulnerable. By limiting the number of rounds a boxer could fight, officials could substantially reduce the number of serious injuries. (student writer)

(2) Using Transitional Words and Phrases

Transitional words and phrases clarify the relationships between sentences by identifying spatial, chronological, and logical connections. The following paragraph, which has no transitional words and phrases, illustrates just how important these elements are.

Paragraph without Transitional Words and Phrases

Napoleon certainly made a change for the worse by leaving his small kingdom of Elba. He went back to Paris, and he abdicated for a second time. He fled to Rochefort in hope of escaping to America. He gave himself up to the English captain of the ship *Bellerophon.* He suggested that the Prince Regent grant him asylum, and he was refused. All he saw of England was the Devon coast and Plymouth Sound as he passed on to the remote island of St. Helena. He died on May 5, 1821, at the age of fifty-two.

In the preceding narrative paragraph, the topic sentence clearly states the main idea of the paragraph, and the rest of the sentences support this idea. However, not only is the paragraph choppy, but it also is difficult to understand. Because of the absence of transitional words and phrases, readers cannot tell exactly how one event relates to another in time. Notice how much easier it is to read this passage once transitional words and phrases (such as *after*, *finally*, *once again*, and *in the end*) have been added to indicate the order in which events occurred.

Paragraph with Transitional Words and Phrases

Napoleon certainly made a change for the worse by leaving his small kingdom of Elba. After Waterloo, he went back to Paris, and he abdicated for a second time. A hundred days after his return from Elba, he fled to Rochefort in hope of escaping to America. Finally, he gave himself up to the English captain of the ship *Bellerophon.* Once again, he suggested that the Prince Regent grant him asylum, and once again, he was refused. In the end, all he saw of England was the Devon coast and Plymouth Sound as he passed on to the remote island of St. Helena. After six years of exile, he died on May 5, 1821, at the age of fifty-two. (Norman Mackenzie, *The Escape from Elba*)

Frequently Used Transitional Words and Phrases

FAQs links

To Signal Sequence or Addition

again
also
besides
first . . . second . . . third
furthermore
in addition
moreover
one . . . another
too

To Signal Time

afterward
as soon as
at first
at the same time
before
earlier
finally
in the meantime
later
meanwhile
next
now
soon
subsequently
then
until

To Signal Comparison

also
by the same token
in comparison
likewise
similarly

To Signal Contrast

although
but
despite
even though
however
in contrast
instead
meanwhile
nevertheless
nonetheless
on the contrary
on the one hand . . . on the other hand
still
whereas
yet

To Introduce Examples

for example
for instance
namely
specifically
thus

(continued)

Frequently used transitional words and phrases (continued)

To Signal Narrowing of Focus

after all
indeed
in fact
in other words
in particular
specifically
that is

To Introduce Conclusions or Summaries

as a result
consequently
in conclusion
in other words
in summary
therefore
thus
to conclude

To Signal Concession

admittedly
certainly
granted
naturally
of course

To Introduce Causes or Effects

accordingly
as a result
because
consequently
hence
since
so
then
therefore

(3) Using Pronouns

By referring to nouns or other pronouns, pronouns establish connections between sentences. Clear, well-placed pronoun references, such as those in the following paragraph, can eliminate unnecessary repetition and make a paragraph's ideas easier to follow.

> Like Martin Luther, John Calvin wanted to return to the principles of early Christianity described in the New Testament. Martin Luther founded the evangelical churches in Germany and Scandinavia, and John Calvin founded a number of reformed churches in other countries. A third Protestant branch, episcopacy, developed in England. Its members rejected the word *Protestant* because they agreed with Roman Catholicism on most points. All these sects rejected the primacy of the pope. They accepted the Bible as the only source of revealed truth, and they held that faith, not good works, defined a person's relationship to God. (student writer)

(4) Using Parallel Structure

Parallelism—the use of matching words, phrases, clauses, or sentence structures to express similar ideas—can help to increase coherence in a paragraph. Note in the following paragraph how parallel constructions beginning with "He was . . ." link Thomas Jefferson's accomplishments.

> Thomas Jefferson was born in 1743 and died at Monticello, Virginia, on July 4, 1826. During his eighty-four years, he accomplished a number of things. Although best known for his draft of the Declaration of Independence, Jefferson was a man of many talents who had a wide intellectual range. He was a patriot who was one of the revolutionary founders of the United States. He was a reformer who, when he was governor of Virginia, drafted the Statute for Religious Freedom. He was an innovator who drafted an ordinance for governing the West and devised the first decimal monetary system. He was a president who abolished internal taxes, reduced the national debt, and made the Louisiana Purchase. And, finally, he was an architect who designed Monticello and the University of Virginia. (student writer)

(5) Repeating Key Words and Phrases

Repeating **key words and phrases**—those essential to meaning—throughout a paragraph connects the sentences to one another and to the paragraph's main idea. The following paragraph repeats the key word *mercury* to help readers focus on the subject. (Notice that to avoid monotony the writer sometimes refers indirectly to the subject of the paragraph with such phrases as *similarly affected* and *this problem*.)

> Mercury poisoning is a problem that has long been recognized. "Mad as a hatter" refers to the condition prevalent among nineteenth-century workers who were exposed to mercury during the manufacturing of felt hats. Workers in many other industries, such as mining, chemicals, and dentistry, were similarly affected. In the 1950s and 1960s, there were cases of mercury poisoning in Minamata, Japan. Research showed that there were high levels of mercury pollution in streams and lakes surrounding the village. In the United States, this problem came to light in 1969, when a New Mexico family got sick from eating food tainted with mercury. Since then, pesticides containing

mercury have been withdrawn from the market, and chemical wastes can no longer be dumped into the ocean. (student writer)

(6) Achieving Coherence between Paragraphs

The same methods you use to establish coherence within paragraphs may also be used to link paragraphs in an essay. (You can also use a transitional paragraph as a bridge between two paragraphs.)

See 7e1

The following group of related paragraphs shows how some of the strategies discussed in 7b1–5 work together to create a coherent unit.

> A language may borrow a word directly or indirectly. A direct borrowing means that the borrowed item is a native word in the language it is borrowed from. *Festa* was borrowed directly from French and can be traced back to Latin *festa*. On the other hand, the word *algebra* was borrowed from Spanish, which in turn borrowed it from Arabic. Thus *algebra* was indirectly borrowed from Arabic, with Spanish as an intermediary.
>
> Some languages are heavy borrowers. Albanian has borrowed so heavily that few native words are retained. On the other hand, most Native American languages have borrowed little from their neighbors.
>
> English has borrowed extensively. Of the 20,000 or so words in common use, about three-fifths are borrowed. Of the 500 most frequently used words, however, only two-sevenths are borrowed, and because these "common" words are used over and over again in sentences, the actual frequency of appearance of native words is about 80 percent. Morphemes such as *and, be, have, it, of, the, to, will, you, on, that,* and *is* are all native to English. (Victoria Fromkin and Robert Rodman, *An Introduction to Language*)

These paragraphs are arranged according to a logical organizing principle, moving from the general concept of borrowing words to a specific discussion of English. In addition, each topic sentence repeats a variation of the word group *A language may borrow.* Throughout the three paragraphs, some form of this word group (as well as *word* and the names of various languages) appears in almost every sentence.

Exercise 2

A. Read the following paragraph, and determine how the author achieves coherence. Identify parallel elements, pronouns, repeated words, and transitional words and phrases that link sentences.

> Some years ago the old elevated railway in Philadelphia was torn down and replaced by the subway system. This ancient El with its barnlike stations containing nut-vending machines and scattered food scraps had, for generations, been the favorite feeding ground of flocks

of pigeons, generally one flock to a station along the route of the El. Hundreds of pigeons were dependent upon the system. They flapped in and out of its stanchions and steel work or gathered in watchful little audiences about the feet of anyone who rattled the peanut-vending machines. They even watched people who jingled change in their hands, and prospected for food under the feet of the crowds who gathered between trains. Probably very few among the waiting people who tossed a crumb to an eager pigeon realized that this El was like a food-bearing river, and that the life which haunted its banks was dependent upon the running of the trains with their human freight. (Loren Eiseley, *The Night Country*)

B. Revise the following paragraph to make it more coherent.

The theory of continental drift was first put forward by Alfred Wegener in 1912. The continents fit together like a gigantic jigsaw puzzle. The opposing Atlantic coasts, especially South America and Africa, seem to have been attached. He believed that at one time, probably 225 million years ago, there was one supercontinent. This continent broke into parts that drifted into their present positions. The theory stirred controversy during the 1920s and eventually was ridiculed by the scientific community. In 1954, the theory was revived. The theory of continental drift is accepted as a reasonable geological explanation of the continental system. (student writer)

Exercise 3

Read the following group of related paragraphs. Then, revise as necessary to increase coherence among paragraphs.

Leave It to Beaver and *Father Knows Best* were typical of the late 1950s and early 1960s. Both were popular during a time when middle-class mothers stayed home to raise their children while fathers went to "the office." The Beaver's mother, June Cleaver, always wore a dress and high heels, even when she vacuumed. So did Margaret Anderson, the mother on *Father Knows Best*. Wally and the Beaver lived a picture-perfect small-town life, and Betty, Bud, and Kathy never had a problem that father Jim Anderson couldn't solve.

The Brady Bunch featured six children and the typical Mom-at-home and Dad-at-work combination. Of course, Carol Brady did wear pants, and the Bradys were what today would be called a "blended family." Nevertheless, *The Brady Bunch* presented a hopelessly idealized picture of upper-middle-class suburban life. The Brady kids lived in a large split-level house, went on vacations, had two loving parents, and even had a live-in maid, the ever-faithful, wisecracking Alice. Everyone in town was heterosexual, employed, able-bodied, and white.

The Cosby Show was extremely popular. It featured two professional parents, a doctor and a lawyer. They lived in a townhouse with original art on the walls, and money never seemed to be a problem. In addition to warm relationships with their siblings, the Huxtable children also had close ties to their grandparents. *The Cosby Show* did introduce problems, such as son Theo's dyslexia, but in many ways it replicated the 1950s formula. Even in the post-1980s family, it seemed, father still knew best. (student writer)

Exercise 4

Consider the possible use of a visual in each of the three paragraphs in Exercise 3. What visuals would you use? How might these visuals increase the coherence of the entire passage?

7c Writing Well-Developed Paragraphs

A paragraph is **well developed** when it includes all the supporting information—examples, statistics, expert opinion, and so on—that readers need to understand and accept its main idea.

Close-up: Well-Developed Paragraphs

Keep in mind that length does not determine whether a paragraph is well developed. To determine the amount and kind of support you need, consider your audience, your purpose, and your paragraph's main idea.

- **Consider your audience.** Will readers be familiar with your subject, or will it be new to them? Should the paragraph give readers detailed information, or should it just present a general overview of the topic? Given the needs of your audience, is your paragraph well developed?
- **Consider your purpose.** Is your purpose to inform or to persuade, or is it something else? Given your purpose, is your paragraph well developed?
- **Consider your paragraph's main idea.** Do you need to explain this idea more fully? Do you need another example, a statistic, an anecdote, or expert opinion? Given the complexity and scope of your main idea, is your paragraph well developed?

(1) Testing for Adequate Development

Just as charting paragraph structure can help you see whether a paragraph is unified, it can also help you determine whether or not a paragraph is well developed. At first glance, the following paragraph may seem adequately developed.

See 7a2

Underdeveloped Paragraph

From Thanksgiving until Christmas, children and their parents are bombarded by ads for violent toys and games. Toy manufacturers persist in thinking that only toys that appeal to children's aggressiveness will sell. Despite claims that they (unlike action toys) have educational value, video games have escalated the level of violence. The real question is why parents continue to buy these violent toys and games for their children. (student writer)

Charting the underlying structure of the paragraph, however, reveals a problem.

1 From Thanksgiving until Christmas, children and their parents are bombarded by ads for violent toys and games.
   2 Toy manufacturers persist in thinking that only toys that appeal to children's aggressiveness will sell.
   2 Despite claims that they (unlike action toys) have educational value, video games have escalated the level of violence.
   2 The real question is why parents continue to buy these violent toys and games for their children.

As charting reveals, the paragraph does not contain enough support to convince readers that children and parents are "bombarded by ads for violent toys." The first sentence of this paragraph, the topic sentence, is a level-1 sentence. The level-2 sentences do qualify this topic sentence, but the paragraph offers no level-3 sentences (specific examples). What kinds of toys appeal to a child's aggressive tendencies? What particular video games does the writer object to?

(2) Revising Underdeveloped Paragraphs

You can strengthen underdeveloped paragraphs like the preceding one by adding specific examples that illustrate the statements made in the level-2 sentences.

Revised Paragraph (Examples Added)

From Thanksgiving until Christmas, children and their parents are bombarded by ads for violent toys and games. Toy manufacturers persist in thinking that only toys that appeal to children's aggressiveness will sell. One television commercial praises the merits of a commando team that attacks and captures a miniature enemy base. Examples Toy soldiers wear realistic uniforms and carry automatic rifles, pistols, knives, grenades, and ammunition. Another commercial shows laughing children shooting one another with plastic rocket launchers and tanklike vehicles. Despite claims that they (unlike action toys) have educational value, video games have escalated the level Examples of violence. The most popular video games involve children in strikingly realistic combat simulations. One game lets children search out and destroy enemy fighters on the ground and in the air. Other best-selling games graphically simulate hand-to-hand combat on city streets and feature dismembered bodies and the sound of breaking bones. The real question is why parents continue to buy these violent toys and games for their children.

You can also use expert opinion and statistics to develop the paragraph further.

Revised Paragraph (Expert Opinion and Statistics Added)

From Thanksgiving to Christmas, children are bombarded by ads for violent toys and games. Toy manufacturers persist in thinking that only toys that appeal to children's aggressiveness will Expert opinion sell. The president of one large toy company recently observed that in spite of what people may say, they buy action toys. This is why toy companies spend so much money on commercials that promote them (Wilson 54). One such television commercial features a commando team that attacks and captures a miniature enemy base. Toy soldiers wear realistic uniforms and carry automatic rifles, pistols, knives, grenades, and ammunition. Another commercial shows laughing children shooting one another with plastic rocket launchers and tanklike vehicles. Despite claims that they (unlike action toys) have educational value, video games have escalated the level of violence. Statistic A parents' watchdog group has estimated that during the past three years, violent video games have increased sales by almost 20 percent ("Action Toys Sell" 17). The most popular video games involve children in strikingly realistic combat situations. One game lets children search out and destroy enemy fighters on the ground and in the air. Other best-selling games graphically simulate hand-to-hand combat on city streets and feature dismembered bodies and chilling sound effects. The real question is why parents continue to buy these violent toys and games for their children.

Along with several specific examples, this revised paragraph now includes an expert opinion—a statement by a toy manufacturer—and a statistic that shows the extent to which sales of violent video games have increased.

NOTE: The writer documents both the expert opinion and the statistic because she got them from outside sources.

See 18a

Exercise 5

Write a paragraph for two of the following topic sentences. Make sure you include all the examples and other support necessary to develop the paragraph adequately. Assume that you are writing your paragraph for the students in your composition class.

1. First-year students can take specific steps to make sure that they are successful in college.
2. Setting up a first apartment can be quite a challenge.
3. Whenever I get depressed, I think of __________, and I feel better.
4. The person I admire most is __________.
5. If I won the lottery, I would do three things.

Exercise 6

Chart the two paragraphs you wrote for Exercise 5. If your charting indicates that either paragraph is not adequately developed, revise it, adding the necessary detail.

7d Patterns of Paragraph Development

Patterns of paragraph development—*narration*, *exemplification*, and so on—reflect the way a writer arranges material to express ideas most effectively. These patterns can also reflect the way material is arranged in visuals.

(1) Narration

A **narrative** paragraph tells a story by presenting events in chronological (time) order. Sometimes a narrative begins in the middle of a story, or even at the end, and then moves back to the beginning. Most narratives, however, move in a logical, orderly sequence from beginning to end, from first event to last. Clear transitional words and phrases (*later, after that*) and time markers (*in 1990, two years earlier, the next day*) establish the chronological sequence and the relationship of each event to the others.

Topic sentence establishes subject of narrative

Sequence of events

My academic career almost ended as soon as it began when, three weeks after I arrived at college, I decided to pledge a fraternity. By midterms, I was wearing a pledge cap and saying "Yes, sir" to every fraternity brother I met. When classes were over, I ran errands for the fraternity members, and after dinner I socialized and worked on projects with the other people in my pledge class. In between these activities, I tried to study. Somehow I managed to write papers, take tests, and attend lectures. By the end of the semester, though, my grades had slipped, and I was exhausted. It was then that I began to ask myself some important questions. I realized that I wanted to be popular, but not at the expense of my grades and my future career. At the beginning of my second semester, I dropped out of the fraternity and got a job in the biology lab. Looking back, I realize that it was then that I actually began to grow up. (student writer)

Figure 7.2 Student in pledge cap; one event in narrative sequence.

(2) Description

A **descriptive** paragraph communicates how something looks, sounds, smells, tastes, or feels. The most natural arrangement of details in a description reflects the way you actually look at a person, scene, or object: near to far, top to bottom, side to side, or front to back. This arrangement of details is made clear by transitions that identify precise spatial relationships: *next to, near, beside, under, above,* and so on.

NOTE: Sometimes a descriptive paragraph does not have an explicitly stated topic sentence. In such cases, it is unified by a **dominant impression**—the effect created by all the details in the description.

When you are inside the jungle, away from the river, the trees vault out of sight. It is hard to remember to look up the long trunks and see the fans, strips, fronds, and sprays of glossy leaves. Inside the jungle you are more likely to notice the snarl of climbers and creepers round the trees' boles, the flowering bromeliads and epiphytes in every bough's crook, and the fantastic silk-cotton tree trunks thirty or forty feet across, trunks buttressed in flanges of wood whose curves can make three high walls of a room—a shady, loamy-aired room where you would gladly live, or die. Butterflies, iridescent blue, striped, or clear-winged, thread the jungle paths at eye level. And at your feet is a swath of ants bearing triangular bits of green leaf. The ants with their leaves look like a wide fleet of sailing dinghies—but they don't quit. In either direction they wobble over the jungle floor as far as the eye can see. I followed them off the path as far as I dared, and never saw an end to ants or to those luffing chips of green they bore. (Annie Dillard, "In the Jungle")

Topic sentence implied

Details that convey dominant impression

Figure 7.3 Vividly detailed close-up of Blue Morpho butterfly in Costa Rican rainforest.

(3) Exemplification

An **exemplification** paragraph supports a topic sentence with a series of specific examples (or, sometimes, with a single extended example). These examples can be drawn from personal observation or experience or from research.

Illiterates cannot travel freely. When they attempt to do so, they encounter risks that few of us can dream of. They cannot read traffic signs and, while they often learn to recognize and to decipher symbols, they cannot manage street names which they haven't seen before. The same is true for bus and subway stops. While ingenuity can sometimes help a man or woman to discern directions from familiar landmarks, buildings, cemeteries, churches, and the like, most illiterates are virtually immobilized. They seldom wander past the streets and neighborhoods they know. Geographical paralysis becomes a bitter metaphor for their entire existence. They are immobilized in almost every sense we can imagine. They can't move up. They can't move out. They cannot see beyond. Illiterates may take an oral test for drivers' permits in most sections of

Topic sentence

Series of examples

Figure 7.4 Street signs illustrate one area of confusion for illiterates.

America. It is a questionable concession. Where will they go? How will they get there? How will they get home? Could it be that some of us might like it better if they stayed where they belong? (Jonathan Kozol, *Illiterate America*)

(4) Process

Process paragraphs describe how something works, presenting a series of steps in strict chronological order. The topic sentence identifies the process, and the rest of the paragraph presents the steps involved. Transitional words such as *first*, *then*, *next*, *after this*, and *finally* link steps in the process.

Some process paragraphs give **instructions,** providing all the specific information that enables readers to perform a procedure themselves. Instructions use commands and the present tense. Other process paragraphs simply explain the process to readers, with no expectation that they will actually perform it. These process paragraphs may use first or third person and past tense (for a process that has been completed) or present tense (for a process that occurs regularly).

Topic sentence identifies process

Steps in process

Members of the court have disclosed, however, the general way the conference is conducted. It begins at ten A.M. and usually runs on until late afternoon. At the start each justice, when he enters the room, shakes hands with all others there (thirty-six handshakes altogether). The custom, dating back generations, is evidently designed to begin the meeting at a friendly level, no matter how heated the intellectual differences may be. The conference takes up, first, the applications for review—a few appeals, many more petitions for certiorari. Those on the Appellate Docket, the regular paid cases, are considered first, then the pauper's applications on the Miscellaneous Docket. (If any of these are granted, they are then transferred to the Appellate Docket.) After this the justices consider, and vote on, all the cases argued during the preceding Monday through Thursday. These are tentative votes, which may be and quite often are changed as the opinion is written and the problem thought through more deeply. There may be further discussion at later conferences before the opinion is handed down. (Anthony Lewis, *Gideon's Trumpet*)

Figure 7.5 US Supreme Court justices after handing down opinion in Gideon v. Wainwright, November 1962.

Close-up: Instructions

When a process paragraph presents instructions to enable readers to actually perform the process, it is written in the present tense and in the imperative mood—"*Remove* the cover . . . and *check* the valve."

(5) Cause and Effect

A **cause-and-effect** paragraph explores causes or predicts or describes results; sometimes a single cause-and-effect paragraph does both. When cause-and-effect relationships are complex, clear, specific transitional words and phrases such as *one cause*, *another cause*, *a more important result*, *because*, and *as a result* are essential.

Some paragraphs examine causes.

> The main reason that a young baby sucks his thumb seems to be that he hasn't had enough sucking at the breast or bottle to satisfy his sucking needs. Dr. David Levy pointed out that babies who are fed every 3 hours don't suck their thumbs as much as babies fed every 4 hours, and that babies who have cut down on nursing time from 20 minutes to 10 minutes . . . are more likely to suck their thumbs than babies who still have to work for 20 minutes. Dr. Levy fed a litter of puppies with a medicine dropper so that they had no chance to suck during their feedings. They acted just the same as babies who don't get enough chance to suck at feeding time. They sucked their own and each other's paws and skin so hard that the fur came off. (Benjamin Spock, *Baby and Child Care*)

Topic sentence establishes major cause

Cause explored in detail

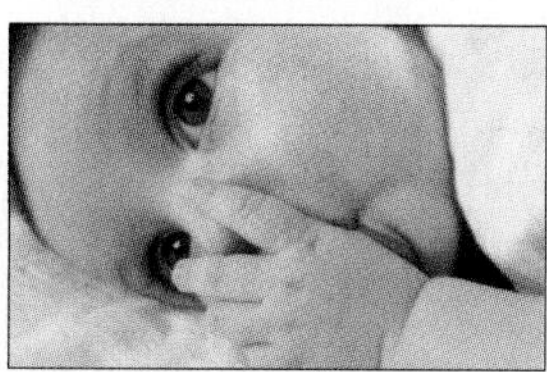

Figure 7.6 Baby sucking thumb (effect).

Other paragraphs focus on effects.

> On December 8, 1941, the day after the Japanese attack on Pearl Harbor in Hawaii, my grandfather barricaded himself with his family—my grandmother, my teenage mother, her two sisters and two brothers—inside of his home in La'ie, a sugar plantation village on Oahu's North Shore. This was my maternal grandfather, a man most villagers called by his last name, Kubota. It could mean either "Wayside Field" or else "Broken Dreams," depending on which ideograms he used. Kubota ran La'ie's general store, and the previous night, after a long day of bad news on the radio, some locals had come by, pounded on the front door, and made threats.

Topic sentence establishes major effect

Discussion of other effects

One was said to have brandished a machete. They were angry and shocked, as the whole nation was in the aftermath of the surprise attack. Kubota was one of the few Japanese Americans in the village and president of the local Japanese language school. He had become a target for their rage and suspicion. A wise man, he locked all his doors and windows and did not open his store the next day, but stayed closed and waited for news from some official. (Garrett Hongo, "Kubota")

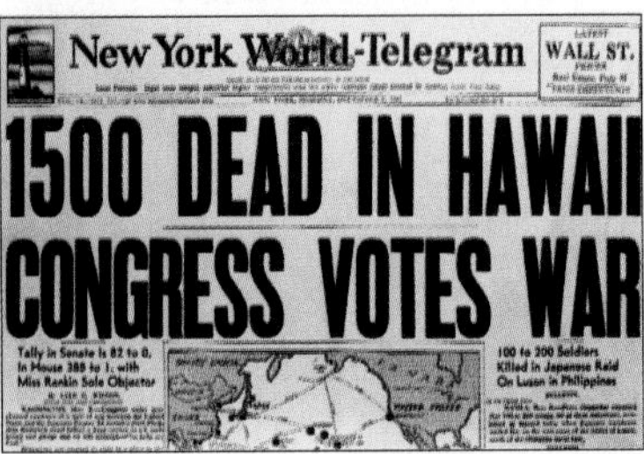
New York World-Telegram

WALL ST.

1500 DEAD IN HAWAII

CONGRESS VOTES WAR

Tally in Senate Is 82 to 0, In House 388 to 1, with Miss Rankin Sole Objector

100 to 200 Soldiers Killed in Japanese Raid On Luzon in Philippines

Figure 7.7 Headline announcing US entry into World War II after Pearl Harbor (cause).

(6) Comparison and Contrast

Comparison-and-contrast paragraphs examine the similarities and differences between two subjects. **Comparison** focuses on similarities; **contrast** emphasizes differences.

Comparison-and-contrast paragraphs can be organized in one of two ways. Some paragraphs, **point-by-point** comparisons, discuss two subjects together, alternating points about one subject with comparable points about the other.

Topic sentence establishes comparison

Alternating points about the two subjects

There are two Americas. One is the America of Lincoln and Adlai Stevenson; the other is the America of Teddy Roosevelt and the modern superpatriots. One is generous and humane, the other narrowly egotistical; one is self-critical, the other self-righteous; one is sensible, the other romantic; one is good-humored, the other solemn; one is inquiring, the other pontificating; one is moderate, the other filled with passionate intensity; one is judicious and the other arrogant in the use of great power. (J. William Fulbright, *The Arrogance of Power*)

Figure 7.8 Abraham Lincoln (left) and Theodore Roosevelt (right) symbolize the contrast between the two Americas.

Other paragraphs, **subject-by-subject** comparisons, treat one subject completely and then move on to the other subject. In the following paragraph, notice how the writer shifts from one subject to the other with the transitional word *however*.

First, it is important to note that men and women regard conversation quite differently. For women it is a passion, a sport, an activity even more important to life than eating because it doesn't involve weight gain. The first sign of closeness among women is when they find themselves engaging in endless, secretless rounds of conversation with one another. And as soon as a woman begins to relax and feel comfortable in a relationship with a man, she tries to have that type of conversation with him as well. However, the first sign that a man is feeling close to a woman is when he admits that he'd rather she please quiet down so he can hear the TV. A man who feels truly intimate with a woman often reserves for her and her alone the precious gift of one-word answers. Everyone knows that the surest way to spot a successful long-term relationship is to look around a restaurant for the table where no one is talking. Ah . . . now that's real love. (Merrill Markoe, "Men, Women, and Conversation")

Topic sentence establishes comparison

First subject discussed

Second subject introduced

Figure 7.9 Man using mute button to halt conversation (illustrates contrast between conversation styles of men and women).

An **analogy** is a special kind of comparison that explains an unfamiliar concept or object by likening it to a familiar one. In the following paragraph, the writer uses the behavior of people to explain the behavior of ants.

Ants are so much like human beings as to be an embarrassment. They farm fungi, raise aphids as livestock, launch armies into wars, use chemical sprays to alarm and confuse enemies, capture slaves. The families of weaver ants engage in child labor, holding their larvae like shuttles to spin out the thread that sews the leaves together for their fungus gardens. They exchange information ceaselessly. They do everything but watch television. (Lewis Thomas, "On Societies as Organisms")

Topic sentence establishes analogy

Analogy explained in detail

Figure 7.10 Tailor ants sewing leaves together illustrates analogy between ants and people.

(7) Division and Classification

A **division-and-classification** paragraph **divides** (breaks a subject into its component parts) and **classifies** (groups individual terms into categories). Division and classification are closely related processes. For example, when you *divide* the English language into three historical categories (Old English, Middle English, and Modern English), you can then *classify* examples of specific linguistic characteristics by assigning them to the appropriate historical period. Transitional words and phrases help to distinguish categories from one another: *one kind, another group, a related category, the most important component.*

Division paragraphs take a single item and break it into its components.

Topic sentence establishes categories

Categories discussed

The blood can be divided into four distinct components: plasma, red cells, white cells, and platelets. Plasma is 90 percent water and holds a great number of substances in suspension. It contains proteins, sugars, fat, and inorganic salts. Plasma also contains urea and other by-products from the breaking down of proteins, hormones, enzymes, and dissolved gases. In addition, plasma contains the red blood cells that give it color, the white cells, and the platelets. The red cells are most numerous; they get oxygen from the lungs and release it in the tissues. The less numerous white cells are part of the body's defense against invading organisms. The platelets, which occur in almost the same number as white cells, are responsible for clotting. (student writer)

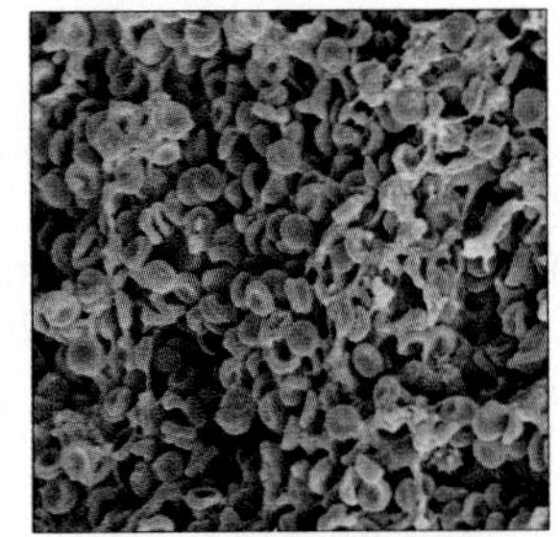

Figure 7.11 Components of blood—blood cells and platelets—in vein.

Classification paragraphs take many separate items and group them into categories according to qualities or characteristics they share.

Topic sentence establishes categories

Charles Babbage, an English mathematician, reflecting in 1830 on what he saw as the decline of science at the time, distinguished among three major kinds of scientific fraud. He called the first "forging," by which he meant complete fabrication—the recording of observations that were never made. The second category he called "trimming"; this consists of manipulating the data to make them look better, or, as Babbage wrote, "in clipping off little bits here and there from those observations which differ most in excess from the mean and in sticking them on to those which are too small." His third category was data selection, which he called "cooking"—the choosing of those data that fitted the researcher's hypothesis and the discarding of those that did not. To this day, the serious discussion of scientific fraud has not improved on Babbage's typology. (Morton Hunt, *New York Times Magazine*)

Categories discussed

Figure 7.12 The FeJee mermaid illustrates "forging," one of three categories of scientific fraud.

(8) Definition

A **formal definition** includes the term defined, the class to which it belongs, and the details that distinguish it from other members of its class.

(term) (class to which it belongs) (distinguishing details)
Carbon is a nonmetallic element sometimes occurring as diamond.

Definition paragraphs develop the formal definition with other patterns—for instance, defining *happiness* by telling a story (narration) or defining a diesel engine by telling how it works (process).

The following definition paragraph is developed by means of exemplification: it begins with a straightforward definition of *gadget* and then cites an example.

Figure 7.13 Rural mailbox with semaphore (term defined by means of exemplification).

A gadget is nearly always novel in design or concept and it often has no proper name. For example, the semaphore which signals the arrival of the mail in our rural mailbox certainly has no proper name. It is a contrivance consisting of a piece of shingle. Call it what you like, it saves us frequent frustrating trips to the mailbox in winter when you have to dress up and wade through snow to get there. That's a gadget! (*Smithsonian*)

Topic sentence gives general definition

Definition expanded with examples

Checklist: Developing Paragraphs

- ☐ **Narration** Do you present enough explanation to enable readers to understand the events you discuss?
- ☐ **Description** Do you supply enough detail about what things look like, sound like, smell like, taste like, and feel like? Will your readers be able to visualize the person, object, or setting that your paragraph describes?
- ☐ **Exemplification** Do you present enough individual examples to support your paragraph's main idea? If you use a single extended example, is it developed in enough detail to enable readers to understand how it supports the paragraph's main idea?
- ☐ **Process** Do you present enough steps to enable readers to understand how the process is performed? Is the sequence of steps clear? If you are writing instructions, do you include enough explanation—as well as reminders and warnings—to enable readers to perform the process?
- ☐ **Cause and Effect** Do you identify enough causes (subtle as well as obvious, minor as well as major) to enable readers to understand why something occurred? Do you identify enough effects to show the significance of the causes and the impact they had?
- ☐ **Comparison and Contrast** Do you supply a sufficient number of details to illustrate and characterize each of the subjects in the comparison? Do you present a similar number of details for each subject? Do you discuss the same or similar details for each subject?
- ☐ **Division and Classification** Do you present enough information to enable readers to identify each category and distinguish one from another?
- ☐ **Definition** Do you present enough support (examples, analogies, descriptive details, and so on) to enable readers to understand the term you are defining and to distinguish it from others in its class?

Exercise 7

Determine one possible pattern of development for a paragraph on each of these topics. Then, write a paragraph on one of the topics.

1. What success is (or is not)
2. How to prepare for a job interview
3. The kinds of people who appear on TV reality shows

4. My worst experience
5. American versus British spelling
6. The connection between coffee consumption and heart disease
7. Budgeting money wisely
8. Junk food
9. Dressing for success
10. The dangers of using a cell phone while driving

Exercise 8

A. Read each of the following paragraphs, and then answer these questions: In general terms, how could each paragraph be developed further? What pattern of development might be used in each case?

B. Choose one paragraph, and rewrite it to develop it further.

1. Many new words and expressions have entered the English language in the last ten years or so. Some of them come from the world of computers. Others come from popular music. Still others have politics as their source. There are even some expressions that have their origins in films or television shows.
2. Making a good spaghetti sauce is not a particularly challenging task. First, assemble the basic ingredients: garlic, onion, mushrooms, green pepper, and ground beef. Sauté these ingredients in a large saucepan. Then, add canned tomatoes, tomato paste, and water, and stir. At this point, you are ready to add the spices: oregano, parsley, basil, and salt and pepper. Don't forget a bay leaf! Simmer for about two hours, and serve over spaghetti.
3. High school and college are not at all alike. Courses are a lot easier in high school, and the course load is lighter. In college, teachers expect more from students; they expect higher quality work, and they assign more of it. Assignments tend to be more difficult and more comprehensive, and deadlines are usually shorter. Finally, college students tend to be more focused on a particular course of study—even a particular career—than high school students are.

Exercise 9

Choose one of the four visuals shown in Figures 7.14–7.17, and write a paragraph developed according to a pattern the visual suggests. (Note that each visual may suggest more than one pattern.)

Figure 7.14 New college graduate pondering his future.

Figure 7.15 Goldilocks eating porridge.

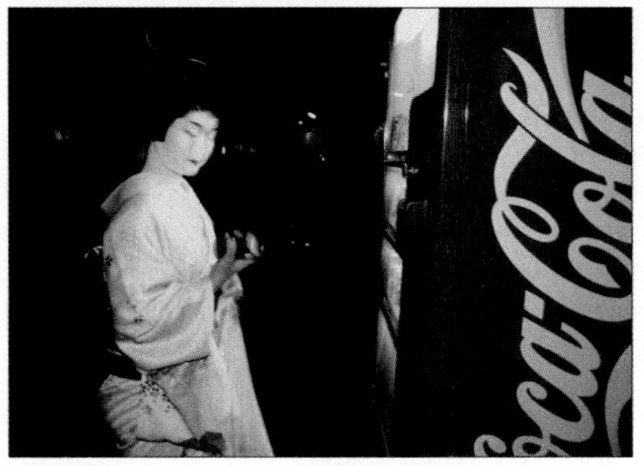

Figure 7.16 Japanese geisha in front of soda machine.

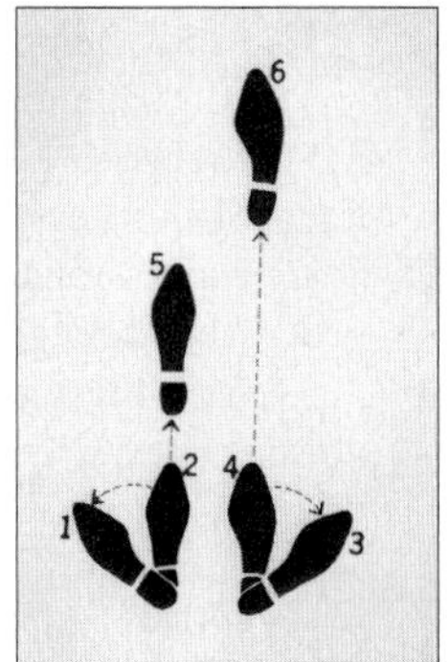

Figure 7.17 Basic steps of the hustle.

7e Writing Special Kinds of Paragraphs

So far, this chapter has focused on **body paragraphs,** the paragraphs that carry the weight of your essay's discussion. Other kinds of paragraphs—*transitional paragraphs*, *introductory paragraphs*, and *concluding paragraphs*—have special functions in an essay.

http://kirsznermandell.wadsworth.com

Computer Tip: Alternative Formats

When you draft a traditional academic paper, you double-space text and indent paragraphs. As upcoming chapters on writing in the disciplines, preparing for the workplace, and designing effective documents will show, other kinds of documents may require the use of additional formatting options (such as headings and subheadings, bold and italics, and numbers and lists) to highlight and emphasize meaningful units of information.

(1) Transitional Paragraphs

A **transitional paragraph** connects one section of the essay to another. At their simplest, transitional paragraphs can be single sentences that move readers from one point to the next.

What is true for ants is also true for people.
This idea works better in theory than in practice.
Here are several examples.

More often, writers use transitional paragraphs to present concise summaries of what they have already said before they move on to a new point. The following transitional paragraph uses a series of questions to sum up some of the ideas the writer has been discussing. In the next part of his essay, he goes on to answer these questions.

> Can we bleed off the mass of humanity to other worlds? Right now the number of human beings on Earth is increasing by 80 million per year, and each year that number goes up by 1 and a fraction percent. Can we really suppose that we can send 80 million people per year to the Moon, Mars, and elsewhere, and engineer those worlds to support those people? And even so, nearly remain in the same place ourselves? (Isaac Asimov, "The Case against Man")

(2) Introductory Paragraphs

An **introductory paragraph** prepares readers for the essay to follow. It typically introduces the subject, narrows it, and then states the essay's thesis.

> Christine was just a girl in one of my classes. I never knew much about her except that she was strange. She didn't talk much. Her hair was dyed black and purple, and she wore heavy black boots and a black turtleneck sweater, even in the summer. She was attractive—in spite of the ring she wore through her left eyebrow—but she never seemed to care what the rest of us thought about her. Like the rest of my classmates, I didn't really want to get close to her. It was only when we were assigned

to do our chemistry project together that I began to understand why Christine dressed the way she did. (student writer)

ESL Tip

A **thesis statement** is a carefully worded sentence (or two) that clearly communicates your essay's main idea and forecasts the direction of your essay. Thesis statements, which usually appear in introductory paragraphs, are an important part of US academic writing that most students are familiar with if they were educated in the United States.

To arouse their audience's interest, writers may vary this direct approach by using one of the following introductory strategies.

Strategies for Effective Introductions

Quotation or Series of Quotations

When Mary Cassatt's father was told of her decision to become a painter, he said: "I would rather see you dead." When Edgar Degas saw a show of Cassatt's etchings, his response was: "I am not willing to admit that a woman can draw that well." When she returned to Philadelphia after twenty-eight years abroad, having achieved renown as an Impressionist painter and the esteem of Degas, Huysmans, Pissarro, and Berthe Morisot, the *Philadelphia Ledger* reported: "Mary Cassatt, sister of Mr. Cassatt, president of the Pennsylvania Railroad, returned from Europe yesterday. She has been studying painting in France and owns the smallest Pekingese dog in the world." (Mary Gordon, "Mary Cassatt")

Question or Series of Questions

Of all the disputes agitating the American campus, the one that seems to me especially significant is that over "the canon." What should be taught in the humanities and social sciences, especially in introductory courses? What is the place of the classics? How shall we respond to those professors who attack "Eurocentrism" and advocate "multiculturalism"? This is not the sort of tedious quarrel that now and then flutters through the academy; it involves matters of public urgency. I propose to see this dispute, at first, through a narrow, even sectarian lens, with the hope that you will come to accept my reasons for doing so. (Irving Howe, "The Value of the Canon")

Definition

Moles are collections of cells that can appear on any part of the body. With occasional exceptions, moles are absent at birth. They first appear in the early years of life, between ages two and six. Frequently, moles appear at puberty. New moles, however, can continue to appear throughout life. During pregnancy, new moles may appear and old ones darken. There are three major designations of moles, each with its own unique distinguishing characteristics. (student writer)

Unusual Comparison

Once a long time ago, people had special little boxes called refrigerators in which milk, meat, and eggs could be kept cool. The grandchildren of these simple devices are large enough to store whole cows, and they reach temperatures comparable to those at the South Pole. Their operating costs increase each year, and they are so complicated that few home handymen attempt to repair them on their own. Why has this change in size and complexity occurred in America? It has not taken place in many areas of the technologically advanced world (the average West German refrigerator is about a yard high and less than a yard wide, yet refrigeration technology in Germany is quite advanced). Do we really need (or even want) all that space and cold? (Appletree Rodden, "Why Smaller Refrigerators Can Preserve the Human Race")

Controversial Statement

Something had to replace the threat of communism, and at last a workable substitute is at hand. "Multiculturalism," as the new menace is known, has been denounced in the media recently as the new McCarthyism, the new fundamentalism, even the new totalitarianism—take your choice. According to its critics, who include a flock of tenured conservative scholars, multiculturalism aims to toss out what it sees as the Eurocentric bias in education and replace Plato with Ntozake Shange and traditional math with the Yoruba number system. And that's just the beginning. The Jacobins of the multiculturalist movement, who are described derisively as P.C., or politically correct, are said to have launched a campus reign of terror against those who slip and innocently say "freshman" instead of "freshperson," "Indian" instead of "Native American" or, may the Goddess forgive them, "disabled" instead of "differently abled." (Barbara Ehrenreich, "Teach Diversity—with a Smile")

Close-up: Introductory Paragraphs

An introductory paragraph should make your readers want to read further. For this reason, you should try to avoid opening statements that simply announce your subject ("In my paper, I will talk about Lady Macbeth") or that undercut your credibility ("I don't know much about alternative energy sources, but I would like to present my opinion about the subject").

Checklist: Revising Introductions

- ☐ Does your introduction include your essay's thesis statement?
- ☐ Does it lead naturally into the body of your essay?
- ☐ Does it arouse your readers' interest?
- ☐ Does it avoid statements that simply announce your subject or that undercut your credibility?

(3) Concluding Paragraphs

A **concluding paragraph** typically begins with specifics—reviewing the essay's main points, for example—and then moves to more general statements. Whenever possible, it should end with a sentence that readers will remember, one that encourages them to think about the implications of what you have written.

> As an Arab-American, I feel I have the best of two worlds. I'm proud to be part of the melting pot, proud to contribute to the tremendous diversity of cultures, customs and traditions that makes this country unique. But Arab-bashing—public acceptance of hatred and bigotry—is something no American can be proud of. (Ellen Mansoor Collier, "I Am Not a Terrorist")

Writers may also use one of the following concluding strategies.

Strategies for Effective Conclusions

Prediction

Looking ahead, [we see that] prospects may not be quite as dismal as they seem. As a matter of fact, we are not doing so badly. It is something of a miracle that creatures who evolved as nomads in an intimate, small-band, wide-open-spaces context manage to get along at all as villagers or surrounded by strangers in cubicle apartments. Considering that our genius as a species is adaptability, we may yet learn to live closer and closer to one another, if not in utter peace, then far more peacefully than we do today. (John Pheiffer, "Seeking Peace, Making War")

Warning

The Internet is the twenty-first century's talking drum, the very kind of grassroots communication tool that has been such a powerful source of education and culture for our people since slavery. But this talking drum we have not yet learned to play. Unless we master the new information technology to build and deepen the forms of social connection that a tragic history has eroded, African-Americans will face a form of cybersegregation in the next century as devastating to our aspirations as Jim Crow segregation was to those of our ancestors. But this time, the fault will be our own. (Henry Lewis Gates Jr., "One Internet, Two Nations")

Contradiction or Paradox

A piece of writing is never finished. It is delivered to a deadline, torn out of the typewriter on demand, sent off with a sense of accomplishment and shame and pride and frustration. If only there were a couple more days, time for just another run at it, perhaps then. . . . (Donald Murray, "The Maker's Eye: Revising Your Own Manuscripts")

Recommendation for Action

Computers have revolutionized learning in ways that we have barely begun to appreciate. We have experienced enough, however, to recognize the need to change our thinking about our purposes, methods, and outcome of higher education. Rather than resisting or postponing change, we need to anticipate and learn from it. We must harness the technology and use it to educate our students more effectively than we have been doing. Otherwise, we will surrender our authority to those who can. (Peshe Kuriloff, "If John Dewey Were Alive Today, He'd Be a Webhead")

Quotation

When we let freedom ring, when we let it ring from every village and every hamlet, from every state and every city, we will be able to speed up that day when all of God's children, black men and white men, Jews and Gentiles, Protestants and Catholics, will be able to join hands and sing in the words of the old Negro spiritual, "Free at last! Free at last! Thank God almighty, we are free at last!" (Martin Luther King Jr., "I Have a Dream")

Close-up: Concluding Paragraphs

Because a good conclusion provides closure to an essay, it makes no sense for you to introduce new points or to go off in new directions. A dull conclusion can weaken an otherwise strong essay, so try to make your conclusion as interesting as you can. Your conclusion is your essay's last word; don't waste time simply repeating your introduction in different words or apologizing or in any other way undercutting your credibility ("I may not be an expert" or "At least, this is my opinion").

Checklist: Revising Conclusions

- ☐ Does your conclusion remind readers of the primary focus of your essay?
- ☐ Does it review your essay's main points?
- ☐ Does it end memorably?
- ☐ Does it do more than repeat the introduction?
- ☐ Does it avoid apologies?

Chapter 8

Combining Paragraphs: The Writer's Purpose

As you learned in Chapter 7, writers use various patterns—narration, description, exemplification, process, cause and effect, comparison and contrast, division and classification, and definition—to help them organize and develop paragraphs. Although any one of these patterns might determine the structure of an entire essay, most of the time in your college assignments you will need to use a combination of patterns to help you achieve your purpose.

Close-up: Identifying Your Purpose

When you receive an essay assignment, look for key words that will help you identify your purpose.

- To reflect: *interpret, analyze, explore, examine, recount*
- To inform: *tell, explain, record, demonstrate, explicate, describe*
- To persuade: *persuade, argue, debate, dispute, challenge, convince, take a stand*
- To evaluate: *evaluate, assess, criticize, appraise, compare*

The four essays that follow illustrate four purposes that are often used in writing assignments across the disciplines. Each writer uses a number of different patterns of paragraph development to accomplish his or her essay's purpose.

8a Writing to Reflect

When you write to reflect, you explore ideas and feelings in order to communicate your emotions (and perhaps convey their significance).

In a first-year composition class, Vanessa Sam read and discussed an essay about a Latino family's struggle to reclaim property that had once belonged to them. The class was then given the following assignment.

> Write an essay in which you recount a crisis or struggle that your own family has encountered. This could be something that happened to your immediate family, or it could be something involving more distant relatives, even those you have never met. In your essay, write about what the conflict signified or represented to your family, how they overcame (or did not overcome) the struggle, and what personal significance their experience has for you today. If possible, interview one or more family members, and include their comments in your essay, following MLA (Modern Language Association) guidelines for formatting and documenting your quotations.

Genocide: A Narrative

Introduction: background (narration)

It was 1975, and a group called the Khmer Rouge, also known as the Democratic Republic of Kampuchea, had taken over the country of Cambodia. Their motive was to overthrow the government that they disagreed with. The outcome was not pretty. More than two million people died between 1975 and 1979. The Khmer Rouge would kidnap innocent Cambodians and take them to the "killing fields" and rape them, kill them, or beat them until they could no longer walk. My family, as well as millions of other Cambodian families, experienced this terrible treatment. This was genocide, and it should never happen again.

Thesis statement

Background (cause and effect)

Every Cambodian family has its own recollection of what happened during this time and of how many family members were killed. Because of the Khmer Rouge's brutality, my family suffered throughout this period; they had to escape from the terror by moving to Thailand. As a result, they lost everything they had: their homes, clothing, food, and money. Grandma's version of the story was an emotional one; in fact, she had to fight back tears when she spoke to me:

> Those bastards took over our country and lied to us while doing so. They said they were going to help us, but instead, they killed us and stole our belongings. Our family was torn apart by members of the Khmer Rouge, and no one helped because journalists were killed on the spot if they did any reports. They told us to leave our homes within two days or else they would kill us and anyone who refused to leave. The walk to the country was very tiring; we were sweating and did not have much to eat, but we kept on going because we were afraid that if we stopped, the Khmer Rouge would notice us and then kill us. I picked up any piece of fruit from the ground because I knew if I picked it from the tree, they would see me. There were thousands that were dying left and right of me; I couldn't bear to see it anymore, so I just kept on looking forward, praying that I would not be one of those people. (Sam, S.)

First example: grandmother's story

I almost cried with her when my grandmother told me this story, but I held back my tears so that she could finish. I knew the story would never come up again. I would never dare to ask my grandmother for more information because I knew how hard it was for her to tell her story.

Reactions to story (cause and effect)

When my mother was a teenager, she was forced to marry my father. If she refused, the members of the Khmer Rouge would have raped her, so she had no choice but to do what they told her. Her marriage was not the fairy-tale wedding with white orchids and ornate traditional outfits that many girls hope

Narrative (introduces mother's story)

theirs will be. Instead, she was taken at the age of eighteen, and with a gun to her head told to marry a man she had known for only a week. I asked my mother for details, and this is what she told me:

Second example: mother's story

> I think it's about time you should know this; you're old enough to understand what I'm going to tell you. If I didn't tell you now, you would eventually find out from someone. I was eighteen when the Khmer Rouge took over. Our economy was already going down the drain, and the people were becoming poorer in a country that was already one of the poorest countries in the world. I had to help support my brothers and sisters because your grandma and grandpa were working. When they invaded, I was forced to marry your father without a choice. We soon had a daughter, and she was so beautiful. A year after she was born, she died of malnutrition and starvation. We did not have any food to give her, except for rice, but since she was so young, it was not enough. We buried her and held a small ceremony when the Khmer Rouge weren't looking. It was the hardest thing I ever had to do. I wanted to destroy the Khmer Rouge; I wanted to kill them because they killed my baby. (Sam, T.)

Reactions to story (cause and effect)

I had two emotions after my mother told me her story. One feeling was sadness for my mother who had experienced this terrible time during her childhood. The other feeling was hatred for the Khmer Rouge even though I had not experienced the pain firsthand as she had.

During the four years of the war, my mother and grandmother were separated for approximately three years. My mother had to survive with her new husband, and my grandmother had to find a way to feed her other three children without money. She did not have a husband to support her, either; he had been murdered because he had held a high rank in the government. They would have lived a happy, quiet life if the war had not begun.

Family's wartime experiences (narration, comparison and contrast)

Recently, there were stories about remaining members of the Khmer Rouge killing six people in the city. These people tried to restart the Khmer Rouge reign because they believed everyone would still listen to them as they had almost thirty years ago. These people who think they will regain power are wrong. Genocide programs have now been set up to prevent such events from happening again. The new Khmer Rouge supporters may try, but they will not get too far. This horrific period was something that no one should have to experience, and with the help of genocide programs, we can hope it will not happen again.

Concluding paragraphs (cause and effect)

I did not experience the unexplainable events of 1970s Cambodia myself, but my hatred of the Khmer Rouge has grown with each story told to me. Those stories have helped me understand the troubles my people have gone through and how it has affected their lives—and, in a sense, my own life—today.

Works Cited

Sam, Sitha. Personal interview. 22 Oct. 2003.

Sam, Thuy. Personal interview. 24 Oct. 2003.

Exercise 1

1. Interview a friend, coworker, or relative. Then, write an essay that explores that person's reasons for making a serious life choice that goes against the social norm (such as a choice not to have children, to home school children, or to live a life without technology).
2. Write an essay in which you reflect upon a cultural or historical event that is significant to your family. If possible, include properly documented visuals of your family members to support your discussion.

8b Writing to Inform

When you write to inform, your goal is to convey factual information as accurately as possible.

In a cultural anthropology class, Erin Lansmon was given the following assignment.

> Choose a specific location in your community (such as a block, an apartment complex, or a park), and describe it in terms of how it reflects the cultures of those who use or inhabit it. Include a visual, such as a photograph or map, to illustrate your essay. Use APA (American Psychological Association) style to document the visual.

Mapping a Block: Field Exercise 1

Introduction

Thesis statement

My city block consists of four corners. I chose to observe activity at the intersection of Fort Worth Drive and Collins, here in Denton, Texas. Each corner has its own distinct details, and each corner (like its people) has its own culture.

Description

A house sits on one particular corner on this block. It is high on a hill, and there are trees all around it. The house, made of wood, looks old, and it is in need of many repairs. There are trees all around the property, which make it seem as if it is under a canopy. There are always several cars and trucks parked in the side yards, and many of them are also old and rusty. The house is occupied, and the people who live there are very physically active. I imagine that there is little or no air-conditioning, as there are always people sitting outside, even on the hottest days. Many of the windows are boarded up as well, so it is likely that there is poor ventilation throughout the house. Outside, there is a barbecue grill as well as several lawn chairs. The occupants seem to enjoy the outdoors: there is even a large red boxing bag hanging outside. Many times there are children outside talking or climbing trees, or adults working on the engine of a car. The large number of people moving about the property helps to create a sense of community.

On another corner, directly across the street from the house, is undeveloped land. Much of it is thickly treed, somewhat like a small forest. As the hill slopes downward toward the street, the trees disappear and are replaced by grass. The land is for sale, and it is likely that it will soon become either a residential or a commercial property. On this corner, I heard sounds of chirping birds and, at night, the sounds of crickets.

Description

Across the larger road, Fort Worth Drive, is a totally different picture. This corner is commercial, not residential. On one side of the intersection is a gas station. During my observations (both in the evening and in the morning), the station was never busy. Sometimes there was no one there at all, but usually there was at least one person filling up her or his car or entering the convenience store. Based on its physical appearance, the store is between three and five years old.

Description; comparison and contrast (between residential and commercial corners)

Figure 1. City of Denton's shelter for day workers.

Description

Process

On the fourth corner is my favorite city block "culture." At first sight, someone might guess that the area, as shown in Figure 1, is a picnic site because it includes a large covered area with picnic tables. In fact, however, the area is a shelter for day workers that was constructed by the City of Denton to protect workers from the elements. I do not know much about day workers, but I do know that large numbers of men, young and old, head to this corner every morning, Monday through Sunday. They arrive in the early morning, around 7:30 a.m., and they wait there until work finds them. They never seem to tire of waiting. When promise of work, usually in the form of a pickup truck, pulls up to the curb, the men surround it. Usually, there are men there even late into the afternoon, and if they finish their first job in the afternoon, they return to the shelter and visit with others. Many times I saw a truck parked on the concrete grounds, selling food and beverages to waiting workers. This corner of the block is my favorite because I learned the most from it. Also, although each of the other locations remains pretty much the same throughout the course of the day, the day worker's shelter site is always changing. Comparison and contrast

During my field observations, I learned a lot about each of the four locations but particularly about the fourth corner. I learned that each place, no matter how small, has its own individual culture, and I also learned that residential, commercial, and recreational land can exist side by side. Finally, I learned the importance of patience, which enabled me to really see the individual details that characterize each corner of the block I observed. Conclusion

Exercise 2

1. Write a similar essay in which you inform readers of the cultural significance of a particular location in your community: a building, an apartment complex, a park, or any other specific location.
2. Examine a group of advertisements (on television or in print or electronic media) that either target the same consumer (children, for example) or focus on a similar product (teeth whiteners, for example). Write an essay in which you assess the ads in terms of how effectively they present information.

8c Writing to Persuade

When you write to persuade, you try to convince readers to accept a debatable, or even controversial, position. See 1a3

In an introduction to psychology class, Heather Renee Thornton was given the following assignment.

> Choose an area of controversy in psychology that you have encountered in your reading so far this semester. Review and summarize the literature on this topic in an essay that takes a stand on this issue. Use APA (American Psychological Association) documentation for any references you cite.

See 19a

Spirituality in Therapy:
Should Secular Psychologists Accommodate Religious Patients?

Introduction

The field of psychology is based on constant exploration of the different aspects that make a human being unique. One of these unique characteristics is the belief in a higher power (and the accompanying desire to please a deity). Those who are religiously inclined have motivations for their actions that are different from those of their secular counterparts, and psychologists may gain new knowledge from the understanding of these motivations. Therefore, it is possible that the incorporation of spirituality in a therapy setting (assuming the patient agrees) would be beneficial not only to religious patients, but also to the psychologists who treat them.

Thesis statement

Incorporation of spirituality into psychotherapy sessions will enable religious individuals to gain access to a more professional level of treatment. A great many Americans believe in a higher power (Kanz, 2001) and are looking for psychologists who are sympathetic to religious problems. Due to the scarcity of professionals of this nature, 40 percent of religious people would prefer to consult a member of the clergy (Genia, 1994; Kanz, 2001). However, as Domino (as cited in Genia) discovered, clergy generally do not receive psychopathological training. Therefore, patients who are counseled by a member of the clergy do not usually get adequate help for their psychological problems (Kanz, 2001). This situation presents religious people who have such problems with a dilemma: they must choose which problem—spiritual

Cause and effect (beneficial results of spirituality in therapy; cause of dilemma)

or psychological—they want adequately addressed (Kanz).

Another advantage for patients who incorporate spirituality in therapy is their ability to use their belief in a higher power as an effective method for coping with stress (Fallot, 2001). The idea that God helps those in need gives patients hope that the outcome of therapy will be successful. For example, Christians believe humans feel more "whole" as they draw closer to God (Fallot). Social support from the local spiritual community also helps patients to achieve their goal of mental health.

Cause and effect (benefits of spirituality in therapy)

Of course, the incorporation of spirituality in counseling is not without problems. For one thing, most psychologists are not trained in theology (Genia, 1994; Shafransky & Maloney as cited in Kanz, 2001). Holden, Watts, and Brookshire (as cited in Genia, 1994) proposed that although methods are available to train psychology students and those currently in the field, there is no assurance that psychologists will be able to confront spiritual matters in counseling. In fact, Genia argued that a healthy personal religious connection is more beneficial to a psychologist's level of competence than is any training he or she might receive. Currently, there is resistance both within and outside the field to training psychologists to include spirituality along with current secular treatment methods.

Exemplification (examples of problems)

Moreover, the belief in a higher power can sometimes cause great emotional distress in clients. Failing to reach the ideal of perfection established by most religions can create feelings of guilt (Kanz, 2001). This guilt can escalate into serious problems

Cause and effect (origins and results of distress)

when some patients begin to feel they are sinful beyond redemption (Fallot, 2001). These are problems that psychologists may not be able to treat.

Exemplification (psychologists' views)

Overall, psychologists do not support the incorporation of spirituality in counseling. Only 25 percent of the psychotherapists who participated in Bergin and Jenson's study (as cited in Genia, 1994) believed that addressing spiritual concerns would be useful in therapy. Psychologists' reluctance to combine spirituality with therapy may be explained by the low percentage of psychologists who believe in a supreme being (Weaver as cited in Kanz, 2001). McMinn (as cited in Kanz, 2001) suggested that even psychologists who want to embrace religion have no idea how to use it in therapy or do not feel equipped to approach topics they know little about (Kanz, 2001).

Cause and effect (origins of psychologists' views)

Exemplification (religious community's objections)

Negative opinions about the current format of psychotherapy have formed within the religious community. Secular psychologists are seen by some as instruments of the devil designed to lead moral people astray (Kanz, 2001). The suspicion exists that psychologists will encourage their patients to engage in sinful behaviors (Kanz). Although psychologists may not encourage sinful behaviors, studies have shown that clients do tend to adopt the beliefs of the counselor (Kanz, 2001), so it is important for religious patients to find a counselor who shares similar moral standards.

Conclusion

Despite these objections, the incorporation of spirituality in a psychotherapeutical setting can have significant benefits for both patient and

Recommendations

psychologist. Religious individuals with emotional and psychological problems will freely seek treatment without worrying about their religious beliefs being challenged. Psychologists will receive more trust from the religious community and will therefore have more patients. In this way, the field of psychology can only stand to benefit from the incorporation of spirituality: cooperation with the religious community will help to expand the field, and ultimately, psychologists will have the opportunity to explore mind, body, and spirit.

References

Fallot, R. D. (2001). Spirituality and religion in psychiatric rehabilitation and recovery from mental illness. *International Review of Psychiatry, 13*, 110-116. Retrieved March 3, 2003, from Academic Search Premier database.

Genia, V. (1994). Secular psychotherapists and religious clients: Professional considerations and recommendations. *Journal of Counseling & Development, 72*, 395-398. Retrieved March 18, 2003, from Academic Search Premier database.

Kanz, J. E. (2001). The applicability of individual psychology for work with conservative Christian clients. *The Journal of Individual Psychology, 57*(4), 342-353. Retrieved March 18, 2003, from Academic Search Premier database.

Exercise 3

1. Imagine your favorite television show has just been cancelled. Write a letter to the network executives persuading them to reconsider their decision.

2. Write an essay in which you present your position on a controversial issue now affecting your campus (curriculum changes, tuition hikes, limited parking spaces, and so on) and try to convince your readers to support this position.

8d Writing to Evaluate

When you write to evaluate, you make judgments, assessing the quality and accuracy of information, ideas, and so on.

In a women in sports class, Shabrielle Morris was given the following assignment.

> Select a Web site that focuses on some aspect of women's sports. Evaluate that site in terms of how well it meets the objectives of the sponsoring institution and the visitors it serves as well as in terms of how easy the site is to access and navigate, and suggest changes that might improve the site. Finally, evaluate the site in terms of its contribution to the field of women's athletics. If you like, you may use descriptive headings to separate the sections of your paper. If you use outside sources, be sure to use MLA (Modern Language Association) documentation style.

Web Site Evaluation:

The Women's Basketball Hall of Fame

Introduction (description)

The Women's Basketball Hall of Fame is a 32,000-square-foot building in Knoxville, Tennessee, capped by a thirty-foot-tall, ten-ton basketball sitting on top of a glass staircase designed to look like a basketball net. For those who cannot visit the actual museum, or for those who want to know what to expect when they do make it there, the museum's Web site is a useful tool for exploring this celebration of women's basketball.

Thesis statement

Design

Narration (site loads)

After entering the address <http://www.wbhof.com/>, viewers are first enticed by the thump, thump, thumping sound of a basketball as the site begins to load. An animated ball then bounces across the screen and into a basketball net fashioned from the letter "W," the Hall's logo. The crowd cheers, and we are now at the home page (see fig. 1).

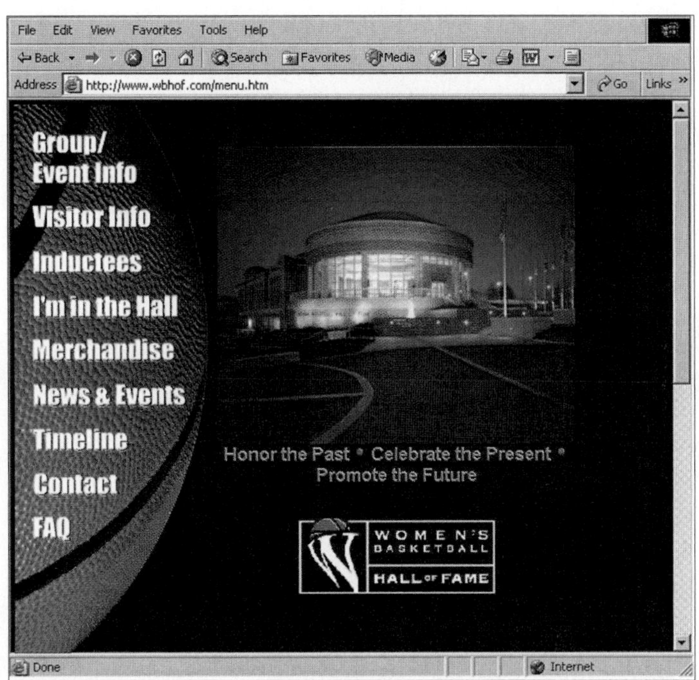

Fig. 1. Women's Basketball Hall of Fame, 2003, 23 June 2003 <http://www.wbhof.com/menu.htm>.

Description (of design)

A simple three-part thematic design in orange and black distinguishes the Hall's Web presence. On the home page, as with its associated pages, the right side of the screen contains an orange basketball-patterned box with links. A distinct "thump" sound indicates that a visitor has clicked on a link. Each of the pages also displays several square photographs and a textbox. The amount of scrolling required varies from screen to screen. Some screens have large amounts of black space at the bottom, and scroll bars allow the viewer to scroll down into black voids. (Of course, Web pages are works in progress, and this one is certain to change. The space left on some screens may indicate that information will be added later.)

Ease of Use

According to Web design experts, images are what separate the true professional Web-page designer from the novice. The expert knows how to efficiently display images that not only look appealing but also load quickly (Munger et al. 85). The colorful photographs at the Women's Basketball Hall of Fame site accomplish both goals.

Exemplification (examples of possible improvements)

Adding cues for easy navigating, such as links that change color or back buttons, would make navigation of this site easier. Having a printer mode option for information pages would save paper and ink. (Currently, the black background with white lettering and numerous images make printing the directions page inefficient.)

Purpose and Audience

Exemplification (examples of goals)

The purpose of this site is to promote the Women's Basketball Hall of Fame as a tourist attraction. Its goals, then, are to persuade people to visit and to provide visitors with ample information to get them there. It is important to note here that the Hall's mission to "Honor the Past, Celebrate the Present, and Promote the Future" of women's basketball is different from its Web page's primary purpose, which is to introduce viewers to specific exhibits and activities.

Definition (of target audience)

The target audience—that is, people most likely to visit the Hall—is basketball players. However, there are numerous photographs of families and seniors having fun on their Hall visit, indicating a wider audience for the site.

Content

From the list of links, visitors can find information pertaining to group visits and special events. Another link provides directions, fees, hours of operation, and a tour of the facility. A link leading to the inductees' page lists, by year, the photographs and names of every person inducted into the Women's Basketball Hall of Fame. The "I'm in the Hall" link takes virtual visitors to personal Web pages created by children on their visit. And, of course, there is the merchandise link, which makes it easy for Web visitors to order official souvenirs. The "News & Events" pages feature the most recent issue of the Hall's newsletter and additional links to special events. A virtual "scrapbook" features approximately thirty pages of prominent people in women's basketball, a "who's who" of visitors. The timeline, also linked from the main page, outlines the first one hundred years of women's basketball beginning with its inception in 1891. The last two links provide contact information and answers to FAQs about the exceptional building and its centerpiece bronze sculpture.

Exemplification (examples of links and features)

Overall, the presentation of the content is very professional; the text is free of grammatical errors and contradictions, does not rely on emotional appeals, and provides complete contact information. Although the content is current, from time to time Web surfers will encounter dead links. The merchandise link, for example, is down more than it

Exemplification (examples of strengths and weaknesses)

is functioning. While there is a pop-up advertising box on the main page, nowhere in this site are visitors required to register or provide personal information. This makes it easy for visitors to come and go as they please.

Comparison and contrast (objectives of site versus mission of museum)

Despite the site's strengths, it could do a good deal more to celebrate women athletes and their history. At present, instead of streaming videogame highlights or freeze frames of powerful athletes in action, we get static poses of inductees (men in suits and women in dresses) and numerous shots of the Hall. The building is a beautiful and fitting place to honor the pioneers of the sport, and it is certainly appropriate to do so, but not if it means eliminating images of women athletes. There is a curious absence of sweat and athleticism, of women actually playing the game.

Another conspicuous absence is a discussion of the social struggles encountered during the hundred-plus years of women's basketball history. Pat Griffin acknowledges in Strong Women, Deep Closets what every woman athlete implicitly knows: "Sport is more than games. As an institution sport serves important social functions in supporting conventional social values" (16). The Women's Basketball Hall of Fame and its Web site aim at the ideological center, often sanitizing controversy and glossing over hard-fought battles for equality and social acceptance.

A quotation by Pat Summitt on the Web site comes closest to placing women's basketball in a social context as she celebrates the Hall while acknowledging the struggle: "It is time women had a place of their own to celebrate the game of women's basketball."

Although the Women's Basketball Hall of Fame Web site, presumably like the museum, is a work in progress and overlooks some critical (although controversial) issues concerning women in basketball (and in sports in general), this site offers an interesting view of the subject and helps its visitors join in the celebration. Conclusion

Works Cited

Griffin, Pat. Strong Women, Deep Closets: Lesbians and Homophobia in Sport. Champaign, IL: Human Kinetics, 1998.

Munger, David, et al. Researching Online. 3rd ed. New York: Longman, 2000.

Summitt, Pat. "In the Hall." Women's Basketball Hall of Fame. 2003. 23 June 2003 <http://www.inthehall.com/>.

Exercise 4

1. Write a review that evaluates a movie or book. Be sure to focus on assessing the quality of the work, not on presenting your personal reaction to it.
2. Write an essay about a purchase you made and later regretted. Be sure to explain how your evaluation of the item you purchased changed.

Chapter 9

Thinking Critically

Frequently Asked Questions

See Ch. 10

As you read and write essays, you should carefully consider the ideas they present. This is especially true in argumentative essays—those that take a stand on a debatable topic. Although some writers try their best to be fair, others are less scrupulous. They attempt to convince readers by using emotionally charged language, by emphasizing certain facts over others, and by intentionally using flawed logic. For this reason, it is particularly important that you apply **critical thinking** strategies when you read, learning to distinguish fact from opinion, evaluate supporting evidence, detect bias, evaluate visuals, and understand the basic principles of inductive and deductive reasoning.

ESL Tip

This chapter outlines ideas about thinking and reading critically that are common in academic settings in the US. In such settings, people read texts with a critical eye, testing the author's claims to see if they seem true. Reading this chapter will help you understand how your instructor expects you to read and evaluate texts.

9a Distinguishing Fact from Opinion

A **fact** is a verifiable statement that something is true or that something occurred. An **opinion** is a personal judgment or belief that can never be substantiated beyond any doubt and is, therefore, debatable.

Fact: Measles is a potentially deadly disease.

Opinion: All children should be vaccinated against measles.

An opinion may be *supported* or *unsupported.*

Unsupported Opinion: All children in Pennsylvania should be vaccinated against measles.

Supported Opinion: Despite the fact that an effective measles vaccine is widely available, several unvaccinated Pennsylvania children have died of measles each year since 1992. States that have instituted vaccination programs have had no deaths in the same time period. For this reason, all children in Pennsylvania should be vaccinated against measles.

As these examples show, supported opinion is more convincing than unsupported opinion. Remember, however, that support can only make a statement more convincing; it cannot turn an opinion into a fact.

Close-up: Supporting Your Opinions

Opinions can be supported with examples, statistics, or expert opinion.

Examples

The American Civil Liberties Union is an organization that has been unfairly characterized as left wing. It is true that it has opposed prayer in the public schools, defended conscientious objectors, and challenged police methods of conducting questioning and searches of suspects. However, it has also backed the antiabortion group Operation Rescue in a police brutality suit and presented a legal brief in support of a Republican politician accused of violating an ethics law.

Statistics

A recent National Institute of Mental Health study concludes that mentally ill people account for more than 30 percent of the

(continued)

Supporting your opinions (continued)

homeless population (Young 27). Because so many homeless people have psychiatric disabilities, the federal government should seriously consider expanding the state mental hospital system.

Expert Opinion

Clearly no young soldier ever really escapes the emotional consequences of war. As William Manchester, noted historian and World War II combat veteran, observes in his essay "Okinawa: The Bloodiest Battle of All," "the invisible wounds remain" (72).

Exercise 1

Some of the following statements are facts; others are opinions. Identify each fact with the letter *F* and each opinion with the letter *O*. Then consider what kind of information, if any, could support each opinion.

1. The incidence of violent crime fell in the first six months of this year.
2. New gun laws and more police officers led to a decrease in crime early in the year.
3. The television rating system uses a system similar to the familiar movie rating codes to let parents know how appropriate a certain show might be for their children.
4. The new television rating system would be better if it gave specifics about the violence, sexual content, and language in rated television programs.
5. Affirmative action laws and policies have helped women and minority group members advance in the workplace.
6. Affirmative action policies have outlived their usefulness.
7. Women who work are better off today than they were twenty years ago.
8. The wage gap between men and women in similar jobs is smaller now than it was twenty years ago.
9. The Charles River and Boston Harbor currently test much lower for common pollutants than they did ten years ago.
10. We do not need to worry about environmental legislation anymore because we have made great advances in cleaning up our environment.

9b Evaluating Supporting Evidence

The examples, statistics, or expert opinions that you use to support your statements are called **evidence.** The more reliable the supporting evidence, the more willing readers will be to accept a

See 10b1

statement. No matter what kind of evidence writers use, however, it must be *accurate*, *sufficient*, *representative*, and *relevant*.

FAQs links

Evidence is likely to be **accurate** if it comes from a trustworthy source. Such a source quotes *exactly* and does not present remarks out of context. It also presents examples, statistics, and expert testimony fairly, drawing them from other reliable sources.

For evidence to be **sufficient,** a writer must present an adequate amount of evidence. It is not enough, for instance, for a writer to cite just one example in an attempt to demonstrate that most poor women do not receive adequate prenatal care. Similarly, the opinions of a single expert, no matter how reputable, are not enough to support this position.

Writers should also select evidence that is **representative** of a fair range of sources and viewpoints; they should not just choose evidence that supports their thesis and ignore evidence that does not. In other words, they should not permit their biases to govern their choice of evidence. For example, a writer who is making the point that Asian immigrants have had great success in achieving professional status in the United States must draw from a range of Asian immigrant groups—Vietnamese, Chinese, Japanese, Indian, and Korean, for example—not just one.

Finally, evidence must be **relevant**—that is, it must apply to the case being discussed. For example, you cannot support the position that the United States should send medical aid to developing nations by citing examples that apply just to our own nation's health-care system.

Exercise 2

Read the following student paragraph, and evaluate its supporting evidence.

The United States is becoming more and more violent every day. I was talking to my friend Gayle, and she mentioned that a guy her roommate knows was attacked at dusk and had his skull crushed by the barrel of a gun. Later she heard that he was in the hospital with a blood clot in his brain. Two friends of mine were walking home from a party when they were attacked by armed men right outside the A-Plus Mini Market. These two examples make it very clear to me how violent our nation is becoming. My English professor, who is in his fifties, remembers a few similar violent incidents occurring when he was growing up, and he was even mugged in London last year. He believes that if more London police carried guns, the city would be safer. Two of the twenty-five people in our class have been the victims of violent crime, and I feel lucky that I am not one of them.

9c Detecting Bias

A **bias** is a tendency to base conclusions on preconceived ideas rather than on evidence. As a critical reader, you should be aware that bias may sometimes lead writers to see what they want to see and therefore to select only that evidence that is consistent with their own biases.

Close-up: Detecting Bias

FAQs links

When you read, look for the following kinds of bias:

- **The Writer's Stated Beliefs** If a writer declares herself to be a strong opponent of childhood vaccinations, this statement should alert you to the possibility that the writer may not present a balanced view of the subject.
- **Sexist or Racist Statements** A writer who assumes all engineers are male or all nurses are female reflects a clear bias. A researcher who assumes certain racial or ethnic groups are intellectually superior to others is also likely to present a biased view.
- **Slanted Language** Some writers use **slanted language**—language that contains value judgments—to influence readers' reactions. For example, a newspaper article that states "The politician gave an impassioned speech" gives one impression; the statement "The politician delivered a diatribe" gives another.
- **Tone** The tone of a piece of writing indicates a writer's attitude toward readers or toward his or her subject. An angry tone might indicate that the writer is overstating his or her case.
- **Choice of Evidence** Frequently, the examples or statistics cited in a piece of writing reveal the writer's bias. For example, a writer may include only examples that support a point and leave out examples that may contradict it.
- **The Writer's Choice of Experts** A writer should cite experts who represent a fair range of opinion. If, for instance, a writer assessing the president's policy on stem-cell research includes only statements by experts who vehemently oppose this procedure, he or she is presenting a biased case.

See 1c

NOTE: Don't forget that your own biases can also affect your response to a text. When you read, it is important to remain aware of your own values and beliefs and to be alert to how they affect your reactions.

Checklist: Detecting Bias

- ☐ What does the writer tell you about his or her background, values, or beliefs?
- ☐ Does the writer make any statements that you consider sexist, racist, or otherwise offensive?
- ☐ Does the writer use slanted language?
- ☐ Does the writer convey bias through tone?
- ☐ Does the writer choose evidence that presents a balanced view of the issue?
- ☐ Does the writer omit pertinent examples?
- ☐ Does the writer cite experts? If so, do they all share the same opinions?
- ☐ Do your reactions reveal biases in your own thinking?

See 42e

Exercise 3

Read the following essay about home schooling, a movement supported by parents who have abandoned traditional schools in favor of teaching their children at home. After evaluating the quality of the writer's supporting evidence, identify her biases, and decide if these biases undercut her argument in any way. Use the questions in the "Detecting Bias" checklist as a guide.

Questioning the Motives of Home-Schooling Parents

America's most famous home-schooling parents at the moment are Andrea Yates and JoAnn McGuckin. Yates allegedly drowned her five children in a Houston suburb. McGuckin was arrested and charged with child neglect in Idaho. Her six kids barricaded themselves in the family's hovel when child-care workers came to remove them.

The intention here is not to smear the parents who instruct 1.5 million mostly normal children at home. But a social phenomenon that isolates children from the outside world deserves closer inspection.

The home-schooling movement runs an active propaganda machine. It portrays its followers in the most flattering terms—as bulwarks against the moral decay found in public, and presumably private, schools. Although now associated with conservative groups, modern home-schooling got its start among left-wing dropouts in the '60s.

Home-schooled students do tend to score above average on standardized tests. The most likely reason, however, is that most of the parents are themselves upper income and well educated. Students from those backgrounds also do well in traditional schools.

Advocates of home-schooling have become a vocal lobbying force in Washington, D.C. Children taught at home may be socially isolated, but the parents have loads of interaction. Membership in the anti-public-education brigade provides much comradeship.

The mouthpiece for the movement, the Home School Legal Defense Association (*www.hslda.org*), posts articles on its Web site with headlines like, "The Clinging Tentacles of Public Education." Trashing the motivations of professional teachers provides much sport.

Perhaps the time has come to question the motives of some home-schooling parents. Are the parents protecting their children from a cesspool of bad values in the outside world? Or are the parents just people who can't get along with others? Are they "taking charge" of their children's education? Or are they taking their children captive?

Yates and McGuckin are, of course, extreme cases and probably demented. But a movement that insists on parents' rights to do as they wish with their children gives cover for the unstable, for narcissists and for child-abusers.

In West Akron, Ohio, reporters would interview Thomas Lavery on how he successfully schooled his five children in their home. The kids all had top grades and fine manners. They recalled how their father loved to strut before the media.

Eventually, however, the police came for Lavery and charged him with nine counts of child endangerment. According to his children, Lavery smashed a daughter over the head with a soda can after she did poorly in a basketball game. Any child who wet a bed would spend the night alone, locked in the garage.

A child who spilled milk had to drop on his or her knees and lick it up from the floor. And in an especially creepy attempt to establish himself as master, Lavery would order his children to damn the name of God.

The best way to maintain the sanctity of a family madhouse is to keep the inmates inside. Allowing children to move about in the world could jeopardize the deal.

In some cases, it might also prevent tragedy. Suppose one of Andrea Yates' children had gone to a school and told a teacher of the mother's spiraling mental state. The teacher could have called a child-welfare officer and five little lives might have been saved.

Putting the horror stories aside, there's something sad about home-schooled children. During the New Hampshire presidential primary race, I attended an event directed at high-school and college students. The students were a lively bunch, circulating around the giant room, debating and arguing. Except for my table.

About four young people and a middle-aged woman were just sitting there. The teenagers were clearly intelligent and well behaved. I tried to chat, but they seemed wary of talking with strangers. The woman proudly informed me that they were her children and home-schooled.

The Home School Legal Defense Association condemns government interference in any parent's vision of how a child might be

> educated. The group's chairman, Michael Farris, says things like, "We just want to say to the government: We are doing a good job, so leave us alone."
>
> Could that be where JoAnn McGuckin found her twisted sense of grievance? "Those are my kids," she said as Idaho removed her children from their filthy home. "The state needs to mind its own business." (Froma Harrop, *Seattle Times*)

9d Evaluating Visuals

Just as you have to think critically about the ideas you read, you also have to think critically about the visuals that accompany these texts. Whether they are photographs, advertisements, or statistical charts and graphs, visuals are often designed to influence readers—for example, to support a cause or to buy a product. And, like other kinds of evidence, visuals can also distort or misrepresent facts and mislead readers.

(1) Misleading Photographs

Almost all photographs that appear in print have been altered in some way. The most common changes involve cropping the edges of a picture to eliminate distracting background objects, re-coloring a background to emphasize subjects in the foreground, and altering the brightness and contrast of an image to enhance its overall quality or to alter its tone and mood. There is a difference, however, between adjusting an image to make it clearer or more appealing and altering an image for the purpose of misrepresenting facts—for example, in advertisements that show "dramatic" before-and-after weight loss results and in tabloids that show pictures "proving" Elvis is still alive. People usually recognize such photographs for what they are—visual fakes that are calculated to entertain or to help sell a product—and do not take them seriously.

Problems arise, however, when an overly zealous editor, reporter, or photographer alters a serious news photograph in order to support a particular point of view or when a scientist alters a photograph to misrepresent scientific data. For example, most people would agree that cropping a photograph of a battle so that it fits within the boundaries of a two-column newspaper article is acceptable. However, cropping the photograph to eliminate wounded civilians on one side of the image—especially when this tactic is used to make a case for or against the war—is more than just misleading; it is dishonest. The same holds true for a researcher who writes a report in which he includes pictures that have been altered to support his hypothesis.

Another questionable tactic is the use of **staged photographs,** visual images that purport to be spontaneous when they are actually posed. Even the hint of staging can discredit a visual image. One of the most famous examples of this concerns the flag-raising photograph at the battle of Iwo Jima during World War II (see Figure 9.1). Photographer Joe Rosenthal's Pulitzer Prize–winning image is perhaps the most famous war photograph ever taken. When it appeared in newspapers on February 25, 1945, it immediately captured the attention of the American public, so much so that it became the model for the Marine Corps monument in Washington, DC. Almost immediately, however, people began to question whether or not the photograph was staged. Rosenthal did not help matters when he seemed to admit to a correspondent that it was. Later, however, he said that he had been referring to a posed shot he took the same day (see Figure 9.2), not the flag-raising picture. Historians now agree that the famous picture was not staged, but this charge haunted Rosenthal his entire life and is still repeated by some as if it were fact.

Figure 9.1 Soldiers raise a flag at the battle of Iwo Jima, February 1945.

Figure 9.2 Soldiers pose before the camera at Iwo Jima, February 1945.

Exercise 4

Compare and contrast the two Iwo Jima photographs. How do various elements of the two images convey the photographer's purpose, tone, and theme? What elements suggest that the second photo is staged?

Exercise 5

Look at the following photograph in its original and cropped form (Figures 9.3 and 9.4). Compare the two representations of the events taking place. How does the cropped image differ from the original image? Do you think cropping misrepresents the photographer's original intention in any significant way?

Figure 9.3 Couple kissing while women argue.

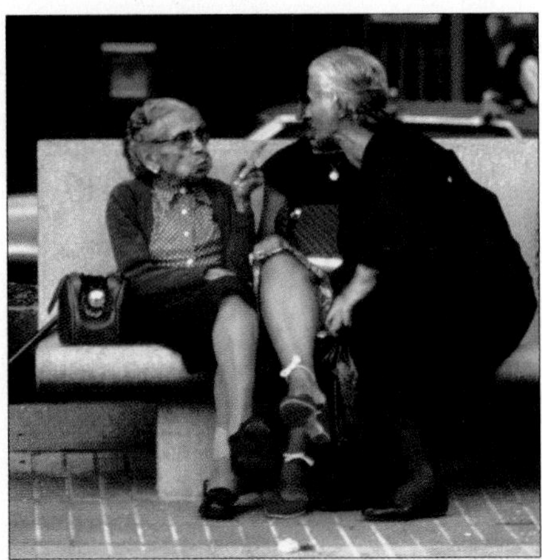

Figure 9.4 Digital alteration of photograph.

http://kirsznermandell.wadsworth.com

Computer Tip: Altering Images

With the advent of desktop digital imaging programs, altering images is no longer something only professionals can do. Programs such as *Adobe Photoshop®* give users access to a wide range of digital image editing techniques. If you do decide to alter an image, however, be careful not to distort or misrepresent it.

(2) Misleading Charts and Graphs

Charts and graphs are effective tools for showing relationships among statistical data in science, business, and other disciplines, where such visuals are often used as supporting evidence. However, charts can skew results and mislead readers when their components (titles, labels, and so on) are manipulated—for example, to show just partial or mislabeled data. Whenever you encounter a chart or graph in a document, be sure to examine it carefully to be certain that visual information is labeled clearly and accurately and that data increments are large enough to be significant.

Consider the potentially misleading nature of the two salary charts on page 171. At first glance, it appears as if the salaries in the "Salaries Up!" chart (Figure 9.5) rose dramatically and those in the "Salaries Stable!" chart (Figure 9.6) remained almost the same. A closer analysis of the two charts, however, reveals that the salaries in the two charts are nearly identical across the six-year period. The data on the two charts seem to differ so dramatically because of the way each chart displays salary increases: in the first chart, salary increases are given in $500 increments; in the second chart, salary increases are given in $5,000 increments. For this reason, a $1,000 increase on the first chart registers quite visibly, whereas on the second chart it hardly shows at all.

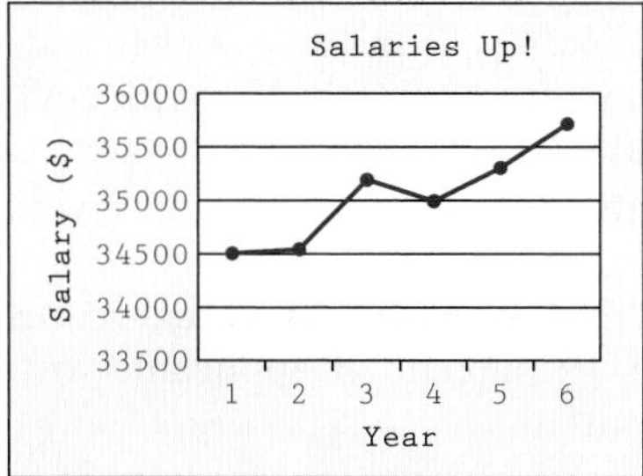

Figure 9.5 Salary chart 1 from the *CPIT Maths2Go* online tutorial.

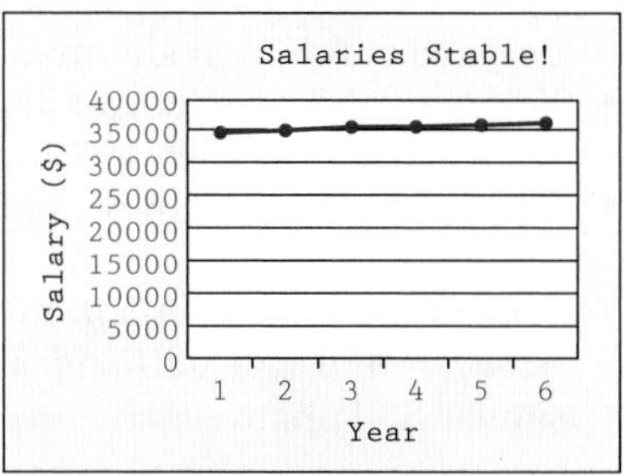

Figure 9.6 Salary chart 2 from the *CPIT Maths2Go* online tutorial.

Exercise 6

Find a chart or graph (in a report or advertisement, for instance) that you think is misleading. Identify the elements that seem to distort the data being portrayed.

9e Understanding Inductive Reasoning

Argumentative essays rely primarily on **logic.** Logical reasoning enables you to construct arguments that reach conclusions in a persuasive and systematic way. Before you can read and evaluate argumentative writing (and write an argumentative essay of your own), it is essential that you understand the basic principles of inductive and deductive reasoning on which arguments are based.

(1) Moving from Specific to General

Inductive reasoning moves from specific facts, observations, or experiences to a general conclusion. Writers use inductive reasoning when they address a skeptical audience that requires a lot of evidence

before it will accept a conclusion. You can see how inductive reasoning operates by studying the following list of specific statements that focus on the relationship between SAT scores and admissions at one liberal arts college.

- The SAT is an admission requirement for all applicants.
- High school grades and rank in class are also examined.
- Nonacademic factors, such as sports, activities, and interests, are taken into account as well.
- Special attention is given to the applications of athletes, minorities, and children of alumni.
- Fewer than 52 percent of applicants for a recent class with SAT verbal scores between 600 and 700 were accepted.
- Fewer than 39 percent of applicants with similar math scores were accepted.
- Approximately 18 percent of applications with SAT verbal scores between 450 and 520 and about 19 percent of applicants with similar SAT math scores were admitted.

After reading the statements above, you can use inductive reasoning to draw the general conclusion that although important, SAT scores are not the one single factor that determines whether or not a student is admitted.

(2) Making Inferences

No matter how much evidence is presented, an inductive conclusion is never certain, only probable. You arrive at an inductive conclusion by making an **inference**, a statement about the unknown based on the known. In order to bridge the gap that exists between your specific observations and your general conclusion, you have to make an **inductive leap.** If you have presented enough specific evidence, this gap will be relatively small and your readers will readily accept your conclusion. If the gap is too big, your readers will accuse you of making a hasty generalization and will not accept your conclusion. Even with the most effective support, absolute certainty is not possible with inductive reasoning. The best you can do is present a convincing case to readers.

See 9h1

For example, suppose a student doing an internship in a state environmental agency is told to propose a way to eliminate the many bottles and cans that litter the state's towns and roadways. The student's reading suggests three possible actions. The state could hire unemployed teenagers to pick up the litter. It could also use brightly colored refuse containers to encourage people to dispose of bottles and cans properly. Finally, the state could require a deposit from all of those who buy beverages in bottles or cans. Further research shows that the first two solutions have had no long-term effect on litter in states that tried them. However, mandatory deposit regulations, along with the outlawing of plastic beverage containers, have significantly decreased the number of bottles and cans in the two states that instituted such measures. Still, because the conditions in the student's state are not exactly the same as those in the states she studied, she must make an inductive leap from the known—the states she studied—to the unknown—the situation in her state. By means of inductive reasoning, the student is able to infer that a mandatory deposit law could be a good solution to the problem. Now, if she supplies enough specific evidence—facts, statistics, and expert opinion—she will be able to convince her readers that her proposal has merit.

Exercise 7

Read the paragraph below, and determine which of the statements that follow can be inferred from the paragraph.

Americans are becoming more ecologically aware with each passing year, but their awareness may be limited. Most people know about the destruction of rain forests in South America, for example, or the vanishing African elephant, but few realize what is going on in their own backyards in the name of progress. Even people who are knowledgeable about such topics as the plight of the wild mustang, the dangers of toxic waste disposal, and acid rain frequently fail to realize either the existence or the importance of "smaller" ecological issues. The wetlands are a good case in point. In recent decades, more than 500,000 acres of wetlands a year have been filled, and it seems unlikely that the future will see any great change. What has happened in recent times is that United States wetlands are filled in one area and "restored" in another area, a practice that is legal according to Section 404 of the Clean Water Act and one that does in fact result in "no net loss" of wetlands. Few see the problems with this. To most, wetlands are mere swamps, and getting rid of swamps is viewed as something positive. In addition, the wetlands typically contain few spectacular species—the sort of glamour animals, such as condors and grizzlies, that easily attract publicity and sympathy. Instead, they contain boring specimens of flora and fauna unlikely to generate great concern among the masses. Yet the delicate balance of the ecosystem is upset by the elimination or "rearrangement" of such marshy areas. True, cosmically speaking, it matters little if one organism (or many) is wiped out. But even obscure subspecies might provide some much-needed product or information in the future. We should not forget that penicillin was made from a lowly mold.

1. The loss of even a single species may be disastrous to the ecosystem of the wetlands.

2. Even though the wetlands are considered swamps, most people are very concerned about their fate.
3. Section 404 of the Clean Water Act is not sufficient to protect the wetlands.
4. Few Americans are concerned about environmental issues.
5. Most people would agree that the destruction of rain forests is worse than the destruction of the wetlands.

9f Understanding Deductive Reasoning

(1) Moving from General to Specific

Deductive reasoning moves from a generalization believed to be true or self-evident to a more specific conclusion. Writers use deductive reasoning when they address an audience that is more likely to be influenced by logic than by evidence. The process of deduction has traditionally been illustrated with a **syllogism,** a three-part set of statements or propositions that includes a **major premise,** a **minor premise,** and a **conclusion.**

Major Premise: All books from that store are new.

Minor Premise: These books are from that store.

Conclusion: Therefore, these books are new.

The major premise of a syllogism makes a general statement that the writer believes to be true. The minor premise presents a specific example of the belief that is stated in the major premise. If the reasoning is sound, the conclusion should follow from the two premises. (Note that these two premises contain all the information expressed in the conclusion; that is, the conclusion introduces no terms that have not already appeared in the major and minor premises.) The advantage of a deductive argument is that if readers accept the premises, they usually grant the conclusion.

Close-up: Using Syllogisms

See Ch. 10

When you write an argument, you can use a syllogism during the planning stage (to test the validity of your points), or you can use it as a revision strategy (to test your logic). In either case, the syllogism enables you to express your deductive argument in its most basic form and to see whether it makes sense.

(2) Constructing Valid Syllogisms

A syllogism is **valid** (or logical) when its conclusion follows from its premises. A syllogism is **true** when it makes accurate claims—that is, when the information it contains is consistent with the facts. To be **sound,** a syllogism must be both valid and true. However, a syllogism may be valid without being true or true without being valid. The following syllogism, for example, is valid but not true.

Syllogism That Is Valid but Not True

Major Premise: All politicians are male.

Minor Premise: Barbara Boxer is a politician.

Conclusion: Therefore, Barbara Boxer is male.

As odd as it may seem, this syllogism is valid. In the major premise, the phrase *all politicians* establishes that the entire class *politicians* is male. After Barbara Boxer is identified as a politician, the conclusion that she is male automatically follows—but, of course, she is not. Because the major premise of this syllogism is not true, no conclusion based on it can be true. Even though the logic of the syllogism is correct, its conclusion is not.

Just as a syllogism can be valid but not true, it can also be true but not valid. In each of the following situations, the structure of the syllogism undercuts its logic.

Syllogism with an Illogical Middle Term A syllogism with an illogical middle term cannot have a valid conclusion. The **middle term** of a syllogism is the term that appears in both the major and minor premises but not in the conclusion. Logic dictates that the middle term of a syllogism must refer to all members of a group.

Invalid Syllogism

Major Premise: All fathers are male.

Minor Premise: Will Smith is a male.

Conclusion: Therefore, Will Smith is a father.

Even though the premises of this syllogism are true, the conclusion is illogical. *Males* is used as the middle term (it appears in both the major and minor premises), but because *male* does not refer to *all males*, it cannot logically function as the middle term. For this reason, the conclusion—"Will Smith is a father"—does not follow, and so the syllogism is invalid.

In the valid syllogism below, only the term *father* can logically function as the middle term because it denotes *all fathers* and appears in both the major and minor premises. For these reasons, the conclusion—"Will Smith is male"—logically follows.

Valid Syllogism

Major Premise: All fathers are male.

Minor Premise: Will Smith is a father.

Conclusion: Therefore, Will Smith is male.

Syllogism with a Term Whose Meaning Shifts A syllogism in which the meaning of a key term shifts cannot have a valid conclusion.

Invalid Syllogism

Major Premise: Only man contemplates the future.

Minor Premise: No woman is a man.

Conclusion: Therefore, no woman contemplates the future.

In the major premise, *man* denotes all human beings. In the minor premise, however, *man* denotes a person who is male. The meaning of each key term in the major premise must remain the same throughout the syllogism, as it does in the following syllogism.

Valid Syllogism

Major Premise: Only human beings contemplate the future.

Minor Premise: No dog is a human being.

Conclusion: Therefore, no dog contemplates the future.

Syllogisms with Negative Premises A syllogism in which *one* of the premises is negative can only have a negative conclusion.

Invalid Syllogism

Major Premise: No person may be denied employment because of a physical disability.

Minor Premise: Deaf persons have a physical disability.

Conclusion: Therefore, a deaf person may be denied employment because of a physical disability.

Because the major premise of the preceding syllogism is negative ("*No* person . . ."), the only conclusion possible is a negative one. ("Therefore, *no* deaf person may be denied employment . . .").

A syllogism in which *both* premises are negative cannot have a valid conclusion.

Invalid Syllogism

Major Premise: Injured workers may not be denied workers' compensation.

Minor Premise: Frank is not an injured worker.

Conclusion: Therefore, Frank may not be denied workers' compensation.

In the preceding syllogism, *both* the major and minor premises are negative. As they now stand, the two premises cannot yield a valid conclusion. (How, for example, can Frank get workers' compensation if he is *not* an injured worker?)

If a syllogism is to yield a valid conclusion, only one of its premises may be negative.

Valid Syllogism

Major Premise: Injured workers may not be denied workers' compensation.

Minor Premise: Frank is an injured worker.

Conclusion: Therefore, Frank may not be denied workers' compensation.

(3) Recognizing Enthymemes

An enthymeme is a syllogism in which one of the premises—often the major premise—is unstated. Enthymemes often occur as sentences containing words that signal conclusions—*therefore*, *consequently*, *for this reason*, *for*, *so*, *since*, or *because*.

Melissa is on the Dean's List; therefore, she is a good student.

The preceding sentence contains the minor premise and the conclusion of a syllogism. The reader must fill in the missing major premise in order to complete the syllogism and see whether or not the reasoning is logical.

Major Premise: All those on the Dean's List are good students.

Minor Premise: Melissa is on the Dean's List.

Conclusion: Therefore, Melissa is a good student.

Political pronouncements frequently take the form of enthymemes: "Because tax cuts help the economy, we should support the president's tax proposals." In such cases, writers leave one or more premises unstated. By keeping their basic assumptions ambiguous or simply assuming that the assumptions are so self-evident that they need not be stated, these writers attempt to influence their audience. Bumper stickers often take this process to extremes, stating just a conclusion ("Eating meat is murder"), leaving readers to supply both the major and minor premises. Careful readers, however, are not so easily fooled.

They supply the missing premise (or premises), and then determine if the resulting syllogism is sound.

Exercise 8

Reread the following two enthymemes.

- Because tax cuts help the economy, we should support the president's tax proposals.
- Eating meat is murder.

Now, supply the missing premises, and determine if the resulting syllogisms are sound—in other words, if they are both valid and true.

Review: Inductive and Deductive Reasoning

Inductive	Deductive
1. Begins with specific observations.	1. Begins with a general statement or proposition.
2. Moves from the specific to the general.	2. Moves from the general to the specific.
3. Conclusion is probable, never certain.	3. Conclusion can be logical or illogical.
4. Progresses by means of inference.	4. Progresses by means of the syllogism.
5. Draws a conclusion about the unknown based on what is known.	5. Draws a conclusion about the known based on what is known.

9g Using Toulmin Logic

Stephen Toulmin, a contemporary philosopher and rhetorician, has formulated another way of analyzing arguments. According to Toulmin, the traditional syllogistic approach, while useful in identifying flaws in logic, is not useful for analyzing arguments that occur in the real world because these arguments tend to be far more complex than a three-part syllogism suggests. To address this shortcoming, Toulmin created a system that enables writers and readers of argument to compose or analyze arguments at a deeper level than the traditional syllogism permits.

According to Toulmin, most arguments contain the following elements: *the claim*, *the qualifiers*, *the support*, *the warrant*, and *the backing*.

Here is an example of how these elements can be used to analyze an argument.

The Toulmin Model of Argument

Claim (the point a writer is trying to prove): College athletes should receive salaries for the time they spend competing in sports.

Qualifiers (words or phrases that limit the claim): College athletes *who participate in programs that bring money into the school* should receive salaries for the time they spend competing in sports.

Support (facts, examples, and expert opinion that support the claim): Colleges and universities make a great deal of money from some of their sports programs.

Warrant (underlying assumption that connects the support with the claim): Athletic scholarships do not fairly compensate student athletes in financially successful programs.

Backing (facts and examples that support the warrant): Studies show that student athletes in major football programs can raise millions of dollars for their schools.

In an argumentative essay, the **claim** is the thesis, an opinion that must be supported with evidence. For example, the claim "College athletes should receive salaries for the time they spend competing in sports" is debatable and could be supported with facts, examples, and expert opinion. (The claim "Many college athletes get athletic scholarships" is a verifiable fact and for that reason is not debatable.) See 10b1

The **qualifiers** are words (*probably*, *sometimes*, *many*, and *few*, for example) or phrases that limit the claim. Qualifiers demonstrate that you have not overstated your claim. They help skeptical readers see that you are reasonable, willing to admit that there are conditions under which your claim does not apply. The more reasonable you appear, the more willing readers will be to accept your argument. In the Toulmin argument above, for example, the qualifier limits the claim by saying that only student athletes who participate in programs that make money for the school (not all student athletes) should receive a salary.

The **support** convinces readers that the claim is worth considering. In the Toulmin argument above, the fact that colleges and universities can make a great deal of money from their sports programs supports the claim that college athletes should receive a salary.

The **warrant** (or **warrants**) is an assumption that readers must accept in order for the argument to succeed. Sometimes a writer will think that a warrant is so obvious (or self-evident) that it need not be stated. In this case, a reader would have to infer the unstated warrant in order to evaluate the argument. At other times, a writer will explicitly state the warrant. Whether the warrant is implied or explicit, you still have to determine if the writer has supplied the **backing,** the facts and examples needed to support the warrant. For example, in the boxed argument on page 179, the underlying assumption is that athletic scholarships do not fairly compensate student athletes. To establish the validity of this assumption, you would have to provide research data to show that sports scholarships do not equitably compensate student athletes (for example, that a wide discrepancy exists between the colleges' profits and the money they spend on athletic scholarships).

Checklist: Evaluating Toulmin Arguments

- ☐ Have you stated your claim? Do you need to qualify your claim to make yourself seem more reasonable?
- ☐ Have you provided enough support? Will readers need more support before they accept your claim?
- ☐ Is your warrant self-evident, or do you need to state it? Have you provided enough backing?

Exercise 9

Read this newspaper editorial carefully.

> A nation succeeds only if the vast majority of its citizens succeed. It therefore stands to reason that with immigrants accounting for about 40 percent of our population growth, the future economic and social success of the United States is bound up with the success of these new Americans. Demography, in a word, is destiny.
>
> This is an important principle to keep in mind as we try to come to grips with the problems and opportunities presented by the flood of legal and illegal immigrants from Mexico and other parts of South and Central America, who now constitute by far our largest immigrant group.
>
> How are we doing in our efforts to assimilate these largely Hispanic newcomers and provide them with a bright future? Some signs are disturbing.
>
> John Garcia, associate professor of political science at the University of Arizona, writing in *International Migration Review*, finds that the average rate of naturalization of Mexican immigrants is one-tenth that of other immigrant naturalization rates. The Select Commission on

Immigration and Refugee Policy made a similar finding. Increasingly, immigrants are separated from everyone else by language, geography, ethnicity and class.

The future success of this country is closely linked to the ability of our immigrants to succeed. Yet 50 percent of our children of Hispanic background do not graduate from high school. Hispanic students score 100 points under the average student on Scholastic Aptitude Test scores. Hispanics have much higher rates of poverty, illiteracy and need for welfare than the national average. This engenders social crisis.

Not all the indicators of assimilation are pessimistic: the success of many Indochinese immigrants has been gratifying. But the warning signs of nonassimilation are increasing and ominous.

America must make sure the melting pot continues to melt: immigrants must become Americans. Seymour Martin Lipset, professor of political science and sociology at the Hoover Institution, Stanford University, observes: "The history of bilingual and bicultural societies that do not assimilate are histories of turmoil, tension and tragedy. Canada, Belgium, Malaysia, Lebanon—all face crises of national existence in which minorities press for autonomy, if not independence. Pakistan and Cyprus have divided. Nigeria suppressed an ethnic rebellion. France faces difficulties with its Basques, Bretons and Corsicans."

The United States is at a crossroads. If it does not consciously move toward greater integration, it will inevitably drift toward more fragmentation. It will either have to do better in assimilating all of the other peoples in its boundaries or it will witness increasing alienation and fragmentation. Cultural divisiveness is not a bedrock upon which a nation can be built. It is inherently unstable.

The nation faces a staggering social agenda. We have not adequately integrated blacks into our economy and society. Our education system is rightly described as "a rising tide of mediocrity." We have the most violent society in the industrial world; we have startlingly high rates of illiteracy, illegitimacy and welfare recipients.

It bespeaks a hubris to madly rush, with these unfinished social agendas, into accepting more immigrants and refugees than all of the rest of the world and then to still hope to keep a common agenda.

America can accept additional immigrants, but we must be sure that they become American. We can be a Joseph's coat of many nations, but we must be unified. One of the common glues that hold us together is language—the English language.

We should be color-blind but linguistically cohesive. We should be a rainbow but not a cacophony. We should welcome different peoples but not adopt different languages. We can teach English through bilingual education, but we should take great care not to become a bilingual society. (Richard D. Lamm, "English Comes First")

A. Answer the following questions about the essay.

1. Former Colorado governor Richard D. Lamm relies on a number of unstated premises about his subject that he expects his audience to accept. What are some of these premises?

2. What kinds of information does Lamm use to support his position?
3. Where does Lamm state his conclusion? Restate the conclusion in your own words.
4. In paragraph 1, Lamm uses deductive reasoning. Express this reasoning as a syllogism.
5. Express the syllogism in paragraph 1 in terms of Toulmin logic.

B. Evaluate the reasoning in the following statements. (If the statement is in the form of an enthymeme, supply the missing term before evaluating it.)

1. All immigrants should speak English. If they do not, they are not real Americans.
2. Richard D. Lamm was born in the United States and grew up in an English-speaking household. Therefore, he has no credibility on the subject of bilingualism.
3. Spanish-speaking immigrants should be required by law to learn English. After all, most eastern European immigrants who came to this country early in the twentieth century learned English.
4. If immigrants do not care enough about our country to learn English, we should not allow them to become citizens.
5. Some immigrants have become financially successful even though they did not learn English. Obviously, then, learning English does not increase an immigrant's chances for success.
6. All Cuban immigrants speak Spanish. Former Secretary of Housing and Urban Development Henry Cisneros speaks Spanish, so he must be a Cuban immigrant.
7. As sociologist Seymour Martin Lipset points out, bilingual societies can be threatened by tension and political unrest. Therefore, it is important that immigrants not be bilingual.

9h Recognizing Logical Fallacies

Fallacies are flawed arguments. A writer who inadvertently uses logical fallacies is not thinking clearly or logically; a writer who intentionally uses them is trying to deceive readers. Learn to recognize fallacies—to challenge them when you read and to avoid them when you write.

ESL Tip

In many cultures, people present arguments in order to persuade others to believe something. However, the rules for constructing such arguments are different in different cultures. In US academic settings, writers are discouraged from using the types of arguments outlined in this section because they are not considered fair.

(1) Hasty Generalization

A **hasty generalization** is a form of improper induction that draws a conclusion based on too little evidence. For example, one disappointing performance by an elected official is not enough to warrant a writer's statement that she will never vote again. Similarly, no one can logically conclude that two bad teachers add up to a bad school or that one or two rejection letters mean that new writers cannot get their work published.

(2) Sweeping Generalization

A **sweeping generalization** is a statement that cannot be adequately supported no matter how much evidence is supplied. For example, **absolute statements,** such as the one that follows, are so sweeping that they allow for no exceptions.

> Everyone should exercise.

Certainly, most people would agree that regular exercise promotes good health. This does not mean, however, that *all* people should exercise. For example, what if a person has a severe heart condition? To avoid making statements that cannot be supported, you should be careful to qualify your statements with words such as *often*, *seldom*, *some*, or *most*.

Stereotypes are sweeping generalizations about the members of a race, religion, gender, nationality, or other group. Because such generalizations are almost never accurate, they undercut the credibility of those who make them.

(3) Equivocation

Equivocation occurs when the meaning of a key word or phrase shifts during an argument.

> It is not in the public interest for the public to lose interest in politics.

Although clever, the shift in meaning of the term *public interest* clouds an important issue.

(4) Non Sequitur (Does Not Follow)

A **non sequitur** occurs when you arrive at a conclusion that does not logically follow from what comes before.

Kim Williams is a lawyer, so she will make a good senator.

See 9f3

This statement is actually an enthymeme, a syllogism that is missing its major premise. In order to analyze this argument, you have to supply the missing major premise: All lawyers make good senators. Because this premise is clearly not true, you cannot proceed deductively from it to the conclusion that Kim Williams will make a good senator.

(5) The Either/Or Fallacy

The **either/or fallacy** occurs when a complex situation is presented as if it has only two sides. If a writer asks whether the policies of the United States toward Latin America are beneficial or harmful, he or she acknowledges only two possibilities, ruling out all others. In fact, the policies of the United States toward some Latin American countries may be beneficial, but US policies toward others may be harmful.

(6) The *Post Hoc* Fallacy (*post hoc, ergo propter hoc*)

Post hoc, ergo propter hoc is Latin for "after this, therefore because of this." The ***post hoc* fallacy** occurs when a writer mistakenly concludes that because one event follows another, the first event *caused* the second. For example, after the United States sold wheat to Russia, the price of wheat rose dramatically. Many people blamed the wheat sale for this rapid increase: one event followed the other closely in time, so people falsely assumed that the first event caused the second. In fact, a complicated series of farm price controls that had been in effect for years caused the increase in wheat prices.

(7) Begging the Question

Begging the question (also known as **circular reasoning**) occurs when a writer states a debatable premise as if it were true. Often this fallacy occurs when a person incorrectly assumes that a proposition is so obvious that it needs no proof.

> Stem-cell research should be banned because nothing good can come from something so inherently evil.

Certainly, the issue of stem-cell research is debatable. What has to be supplied, however, is evidence that stem-cell research is "inherently evil."

(8) False Analogy

See 7d6

Analogies—extended comparisons—enable a writer to explain something unfamiliar by comparing it to something familiar. Skillfully used, an analogy can be quite effective, as when a student illustrates her frustration with the registration process at her college by comparing students to rats in a maze. In an argument, however, an analogy alone proves nothing; it is no substitute for evidence.

A **false analogy** (or **faulty analogy**) assumes that because issues or concepts are similar in some ways, they are similar in other ways. On a television talk show, a psychologist who was asked to explain why people commit crimes gave the following response.

> People commit crimes because they are weak and selfish. They are like pregnant women who know they shouldn't smoke but do so anyway. They have a craving, and they give in to it. The answer is not to punish criminals, but to understand their behavior and to try to change it.

Admittedly, the analogy between criminals and pregnant women who smoke is convincing. However, it oversimplifies the issue. A pregnant woman does not intend to harm her unborn child by smoking; many criminals do intend to harm their victims. To undercut the psychologist's argument, all you need to do is point out the shortcomings of his analogy.

(9) Red Herring

The **red herring** fallacy occurs when a writer changes the subject to distract readers from the issue. Consider the statement, "This company may charge high prices, but it gives a great deal of money to charity each year." The latter issue has nothing to do with the former; still, it may manage to distract readers and lead them away from the real issue.

(10) Argument to Ignorance (*argumentum ad ignorantiam*)

The **argument to ignorance** fallacy occurs when a writer says that something is true because it cannot be proved false or vice versa.

This fallacy occurred during a debate about a policy allowing children who have AIDS to attend public school. A parent asked a doctor, "How can you tell me to send my six-year-old to a school with a child who has AIDS? After all, doctors can't say for sure that my son won't catch AIDS, can they?" In other words, the parent was saying, "My son could contract AIDS from another child in school because you can't prove that he cannot." As persuasive as this line of reasoning can sometimes be, it is logically flawed: no evidence has been presented to support the speaker's conclusion.

(11) The Bandwagon Fallacy

The **bandwagon fallacy** occurs when a writer tries to establish that something is true because everyone believes it is. For example, a newspaper editorial made the statement, "Everyone knows that eating too much candy makes a child hyperactive." Instead of providing evidence to support this claim, the editorial relied on an appeal to go along with the crowd.

(12) Skewed Sample

A **skewed sample** occurs when a statistical sample is collected in such a way that it will lead to one conclusion rather than another. To present accurate results, a statistical sample should be *representative;* that is, it should be typical of the broader population it represents. For example, census questions asked only in English would most likely skew results in favor of English-speaking respondents.

(13) You Also (*tu quoque*)

The **you also** fallacy occurs when a writer argues that a point has no merit because the person making it does not follow his or her own advice. Such an argument is irrelevant because it focuses attention on the person rather than on the issue being debated.

> How can government economists advise Americans to save? Look at how much money the government spent last year.

(14) Argument to the Person (*ad hominem*)

Arguments ***ad hominem*** attack a person rather than an issue. By attacking an opponent, these arguments attempt to turn attention away from the real issues.

That candidate has criticized Congress's commitment to preserving social security. However, she is only forty years old and is a very wealthy woman.

(15) Argument to the People (*ad populum*)

Arguments ***ad populum*** appeal to people's prejudices. A senatorial candidate seeking support in a state whose textile industry has been hurt by foreign competition may allude to "foreigners who are attempting to steal our jobs." By exploiting the prejudices of the audience, the candidate tries to avoid the concrete issues of the campaign.

Checklist: Logical Fallacies

- ☐ **Hasty Generalization** A conclusion based on too little evidence
- ☐ **Sweeping Generalization** A statement that cannot be supported no matter how much evidence is supplied
- ☐ **Equivocation** A shift in the meaning of a key word during an argument
- ☐ **Non Sequitur** A conclusion that does not logically follow from what comes before
- ☐ **Either/Or Fallacy** A complex issue treated as if it has only two sides
- ☐ ***Post Hoc* Fallacy** An unjustified link between cause and effect
- ☐ **Begging the Question** A debatable premise stated as if it were true
- ☐ **False Analogy** An assumption that because things are similar in some ways, they are similar in other ways
- ☐ **Red Herring** A change in subject to distract an audience
- ☐ **Argument to Ignorance** A claim that something is true because it cannot be proved false, or vice versa
- ☐ **Bandwagon Fallacy** An attempt to establish that something is true because everyone believes it is true
- ☐ **Skewed Sample** A statistical sample that favors one population over another
- ☐ **You Also Fallacy** A claim that a position is not valid because the person advocating it does not follow it
- ☐ **Argument to the Person** An attack on the person rather than on the issue
- ☐ **Argument to the People** An appeal to people's prejudices

Exercise 10

Identify the logical fallacies in the following statements. In each case, name the fallacy, and then rewrite the statement to correct the problem.

1. Membership in the Coalition against Pornography has more than quadrupled since the 1990s. Convenience stores in many parts of the country have limited their selection of pornography and, in many cases, taken pornography off the shelves. In 1995, the defense appropriations bill included a ban on the sale of pornography on military installations. The American public clearly believes that pornography has a harmful effect on its audience.
2. With people like Larry Flynt and Hugh Hefner arguing that pornography is harmless, you know that pornography is causing its readers to live immoral lifestyles.
3. The Republican Party and conservative thinkers are all for the free market when the issue is environmental degradation, but they will be the first ones to call for a limit to what can be shown on movies, television, and the Internet.
4. Television is out of control. There is more foul language, sex, and sexual innuendo on television than there has ever been before. The effects of this obscene and pornographic material have been clearly documented in studies that proved that serial killers and other criminals were much more likely to be regular consumers of pornographic materials.
5. We know that television causes children to be more violent. So what can we use to control television? The V-chip, television ratings, and more governmental control of television content will help us reduce violence.
6. Study after study has been completed, and none of the researchers has presented incontrovertible evidence that rap music causes an increase in violent behavior among its listeners.
7. A boy in Idaho set fire to his family's home after watching a television stunt show. From this incident, we can see that television has a negative influence on children's behavior.
8. We want our children to grow up in safe neighborhoods. We would like to see less violence in the schools and on the playgrounds. We would like to be less fearful when we have to go out at night. If we stop polluting our culture with violent images from television and popular music, we can reclaim our communities and our children.
9. Ted Bundy and Richard Ramirez, two of the most violent serial killers ever caught, both used pornography regularly. Pornography caused them to kill women.
10. Some people believe that violence on television affects children and want the government to find ways to limit violence. Others

believe that children are unaffected by the violence they see on television. I do not think violence on television causes children to become violent.

Exercise 11

Read the following excerpt. Identify as many logical fallacies as you can. Then write a letter to the author pointing out the fallacies and explaining how they weaken his argument.

Hunting and eating a free-roaming wild deer is one thing; slaughtering and eating a [wounded] deer is another.

The point . . . is that—despite what our enemies are saying—hunters are just as compassionate as the next fellow. It hurts us to see an animal suffer, and when we can help an animal in need, we go out of our way to do whatever we can.

A case in point is the story . . . about SCI Alaska vice president Dave Campbell's efforts to help a cow moose. That animal had carried a poorly shot arrow in its body for weeks until Campbell saw it and made certain it got help.

Despite how some media handled that story, there is no irony in hunters coming to the rescue of the same species we hunt.

We do it all the time.

A story of hunters showing compassion for an animal is something you'll never see in *The Bunny Huggers' Gazette* (yes, there is such a publication. It's a bimonthly magazine produced on newsprint. According to the publisher's statement, it provides information about vegetarianism, and "organizations, protests, boycotts or legislation on behalf of animal liberation . . .").

Among the protests announced in the June issue of *BHG* are boycotts against the countries of Ireland and Spain, the states and provinces of the Yukon Territory, Alberta, British Columbia, Pennsylvania and Alaska, the companies of American Express, Anheuser-Busch, Bausch & Lomb, Bloomingdale's, Coca-Cola Products, Coors, Gillette, Hartz, L'Oreal, McDonald's, Mellon Bank, Northwest Airlines, Pocono Mountain resorts and a host of others.

Interestingly, BHG tells how a subscribing group, Life Net of Montezuma, New Mexico, has petitioned the US Forest Service to close portions of the San Juan and Rio Grande National Forests between April and November to all entry "to provide as much protection as possible" for grizzly bears that may still exist there. Another subscriber, Predator Project of Bozeman, Montana, is asking that the entire North Cascades region be closed to coyote hunting because gray wolves might be killed by "sportsmen (who) may not be able to tell the difference between a coyote and a wolf."

Although it's not a new idea, another subscriber, Prairie Dog Rescue, is urging persons who are opposed to hunting to apply for limited quota hunting permits because "one permit in peaceful hands means one less opportunity for a hunter to kill."

And if you ever doubted that the vegetarian/animal rights herd is a wacko bunch, then consider the magazine's review of *Human Tissue, A Neglected Experimental Resource.* According to the review, the 24-page essay encourages using human tissues to test "medicines and other substances, any of which would save animals' lives." (Bill Roberts, "The World of Hunting")

Checklist: Thinking Critically

- ☐ Are the writer's points supported primarily by fact or by opinion? Does the writer present opinion as fact?
- ☐ Does the writer offer supporting evidence for his or her statements?
- ☐ What kind of evidence is provided? How convincing is it?
- ☐ Is the evidence accurate? sufficient? representative? relevant?
- ☐ Does the writer display any bias? If so, is the bias revealed through language, tone, or choice of evidence?
- ☐ Does the writer omit pertinent examples?
- ☐ Does the writer present a balanced picture of the issue?
- ☐ Are any alternative viewpoints overlooked?
- ☐ Are any visuals misleading?
- ☐ Are any charts or graphs misleading?
- ☐ Does the writer use valid reasoning?
- ☐ Does the writer use logical fallacies?
- ☐ Does the writer oversimplify complex ideas?
- ☐ Does the writer make reasonable inferences?
- ☐ Does the writer represent the ideas of others accurately? fairly?

Chapter 10

Writing Argumentative Essays

Frequently Asked Questions

For most people, the true test of their critical thinking skills comes when they write an argumentative essay, one that takes a stand on an issue and uses logic and evidence to convince readers. When you write an argument, you follow the same process you use when you write any essay. However, because the purpose of an argument is to convince readers, you need to use some additional strategies to present your ideas to your audience.

10a Planning an Argumentative Essay

(1) Choosing a Debatable Topic

Because an argumentative essay attempts to change the way people think, it must focus on a **debatable topic,** one about which reasonable people may disagree. Factual statements—those about which reasonable people do *not* disagree—are, therefore, not suitable as topics for argument.

> **Fact:** First-year students are not required to purchase a meal plan from the university.
>
> **Debatable Topic:** First-year students *should be* required to purchase a meal plan from the university.

In addition to being debatable, your topic should be one that you know something about. The more information you can provide, the more likely you are to influence your audience. General knowledge is seldom convincing by itself, however, so you will probably have to do some research.

See Pt. 2

Your topic should also be narrow enough so that you can write about it within your page limit. After all, in your argumentative essay, you will have to develop your own ideas and present convincing support while also pointing out the strengths and weaknesses of opposing arguments. If your topic is too broad, you will not be able to treat it in enough detail.

Finally, your topic should be interesting. Keep in mind that some topics—such as "The Need for Gun Control" or "The Fairness of the Death Penalty"—have been discussed and written about so often that you will probably not be able to say anything very interesting about them. Instead of relying on an overused topic, choose one that enables you to contribute something to the debate.

(2) Developing an Argumentative Thesis

After you have chosen a topic, your next step is to state your position in an **argumentative thesis,** one that takes a strong stand. Properly worded, this thesis statement lays the foundation for the rest of your argument.

See 4b

One way to make sure that your thesis statement actually does take a stand is to formulate an **antithesis,** a statement that takes an arguable position that is the opposite of yours. If you can create an antithesis, your thesis statement takes a stand. If you cannot, your statement needs further revision to make it argumentative.

Thesis Statement: Term limits would improve government by bringing people with fresh ideas into office every few years.

Antithesis: Term limits would harm government because elected officials would always be inexperienced.

Close-up: Developing an Argumentative Thesis

To make sure your argumentative thesis is effective, ask the following questions:

- Is your thesis one with which reasonable people would disagree?
- Can you formulate an antithesis?
- Can your thesis be supported by evidence?
- Does your thesis make clear to readers what position you are taking?

Whenever possible, test a tentative thesis statement on classmates—either informally in classroom conversations or formally in peer-review sessions. You may also want to talk to your instructor, do some reading about your topic, or do some exploratory research. Your goal should be to get a grasp of your topic so you can make an informed statement about it.

See 5d2

See 12a

(3) Defining Your Terms

You should always define the key terms you use in your argument; after all, the soundness of an entire argument may hinge on the definition of a word that may mean one thing to one person and another thing to someone else. For example, in the United States, *democratic* elections involve the selection of government officials by popular vote; in other countries, the same term may be used to describe elections in which only one candidate is running or in which all candidates represent the same party. For this reason, if your argument hinges on a key term like *democratic*, you should make sure that your readers know exactly what you mean.

NOTE: In some cases, you may want to use a formal definition in your essay. Instead of quoting from a dictionary, however, you should develop an extended definition that includes examples from your own experience or reading. In this way, your definition can be tailored to the specific issue you are writing about and can provide much more specific information than an all-purpose dictionary definition.

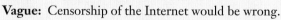

See 7d8

Close-up: Defining Your Terms

Be careful to use precise terms in your thesis statement. Avoid vague and judgmental words, such as *wrong*, *bad*, *good*, *right*, and *immoral*.

Vague: Censorship of the Internet would be wrong.

Clearer: Censorship of the Internet would unfairly limit free speech.

(4) Considering Your Audience

As you plan your essay, keep a specific audience in mind. Are your readers unbiased observers or people deeply concerned about the issue you plan to discuss? Can they be cast in a specific role—concerned parents, victims of discrimination, irate consumers—or are they so diverse that they cannot be categorized? If you cannot be

See 1b

certain who your readers are, you will have to direct your arguments to a general audience.

Always assume a skeptical audience. Even if your readers are sympathetic to your position, you cannot assume that they will accept your ideas without question. Even so, the strategies you use to convince your readers will vary according to your relationship with them. Somewhat sympathetic readers may need to see only that your argument is logical and that your evidence is solid. More skeptical readers may need a good deal of reassurance that you understand their concerns and that you concede some of their points. However, you may never be able to convince hostile readers that your conclusion is valid. The best you can hope for is that these readers will acknowledge the strengths of your argument even if they reject your conclusion.

ESL Tip

If you have not lived in the United States very long, it may be difficult for you to make judgments about what your readers know and believe. Since your instructor is one of your primary readers, consult him or her about this issue.

(5) Refuting Opposing Arguments

As you develop your argument, you should also **refute**—that is, disprove—opposing arguments by showing that they are untrue, unfair, illogical, unimportant, or irrelevant. By refuting an opposing view, you make it less credible to readers. In the following paragraph, a student refutes the argument that Sea World should keep whales in captivity.

> Of course, some will say that Sea World wants to capture only a few whales, as George Will points out in his commentary in Newsweek. Unfortunately, Will downplays the fact that Sea World wants to capture a hundred whales, not just "a few." And, after releasing ninety of these whales, Sea World intends to keep ten for "further work." At hearings in Seattle last week, several noted marine biologists went on record as condemning Sea World's research program.

When an opponent's position is so strong that it cannot be refuted, concede the point, and then discuss its limitations. Martin Luther King Jr. uses this tactic in his "Letter from Birmingham Jail."

You express a great deal of anxiety over our willingness to break laws. This is certainly a legitimate concern. Since we so diligently urge people to obey the Supreme Court's decision of 1954 outlawing segregation in the public schools, at first glance it may seem rather paradoxical for us consciously to break laws. One may well ask: "How can you advocate breaking some laws and obeying others?" The answer lies in the fact that there are two types of laws: just and unjust. I would be the first to advocate obeying just laws. Conversely, one has a moral responsibility to disobey unjust laws. I would agree with St. Augustine that "an unjust law is no law at all."

Concedes point

Discusses its limitations

NOTE: When you acknowledge an opposing view, be careful not to distort or oversimplify it. This tactic, known as creating a **straw man,** can seriously undermine your credibility.

http://kirsznermandell.wadsworth.com

Computer Tip: Refuting Opposing Arguments

As you formulate an argument, you can use your computer to create a table or chart that organizes all the arguments against your position. Using the Table menu in your word-processing application, insert a two-column table. Label the first column "Opposing Arguments" and the second column "Refutations." List the arguments against your position in the first column and your refutations of these arguments in the second column. When you are finished, delete the weakest opposing arguments. When you write your essay, consider only those opposing arguments and refutations that remain: concede the strength of any particularly compelling opposing arguments in the first column; then, use arguments of your own from the second column to refute them.

Exercise 1

Choose one of the following five statements, and list the arguments in favor of it. Then, list the arguments against it. Finally, choose one position (pro or con), and write a paragraph or two supporting it. Be sure to refute the arguments against your position.

1. Public school students who participate in extracurricular activities should have to submit to random drug tests.
2. The federal government should limit the amount of violence shown on television.
3. A couple applying for a marriage license should be required to take an AIDS test.

4. Retirees making more than $50,000 a year should not be eligible for Social Security benefits.
5. Colleges and universities should provide free day care for students' children.

10b Using Evidence Effectively

(1) Supporting Your Argument

Most arguments are built on **assertions**—statements that you make about a debatable topic—backed by evidence—supporting information, in the form of examples, statistics, or expert opinion. If, for instance, you asserted that law-enforcement officials are winning the war against violent crime, you could then support this assertion by referring to a government report stating that violent crime—especially murder—has dramatically decreased during the past decade. This report would be one piece of persuasive evidence.

Only assertions that are *self-evident* ("All human beings are mortal"), *true by definition* (2 + 2 = 4), or *factual* ("The Atlantic Ocean separates England and the United States") need no proof. All other kinds of assertions require support.

NOTE: Remember that you can never prove a thesis conclusively—if you did, there would be no argument. The best you can do is to provide enough evidence to establish a high probability that your thesis is reasonable or valid.

(2) Establishing Credibility

Clear reasoning, compelling evidence, and strong refutations go a long way toward making an argument solid. But these elements in themselves are not sufficient to create a convincing argument. In order to convince readers, you have to satisfy them that you are someone they should listen to—in other words, that you have **credibility.**

Some people, of course, bring credibility with them every time they speak. When a Nobel Prize winner in physics makes a speech about the need to control proliferation of nuclear weapons, we assume that he or she speaks with authority. But most people do not have this kind of credibility. When you write an argument, you must work to establish your credibility by establishing common ground, demonstrating knowledge, maintaining a reasonable tone, and presenting yourself as someone worth listening to.

Establishing Common Ground When you write an argument, it is tempting to go on the attack, emphasizing the differences between your position and those of your opponents. Writers of effective arguments, however, know they can gain a greater advantage by establishing common ground between their opponents and themselves.

Close-up: Using Rogerian Argument

Another way to establish your credibility is to use the techniques of **Rogerian argument,** based on the work of the psychologist Carl Rogers. According to Rogers, you should think of the members of your audience as colleagues with whom you must collaborate to find solutions to problems. Instead of verbally assaulting them, you should emphasize points of agreement. In this way, rather than taking a confrontational stance, you establish common ground and work toward a resolution of the problem you are discussing.

Demonstrating Knowledge Including relevant personal experiences in your argumentative essay can show readers that you know a lot about your subject; demonstrating this kind of knowledge gives you authority. For example, describing what you observed at a National Rifle Association convention can give you authority in an essay arguing for (or against) gun control.

You can also establish credibility by showing you have done research into a subject. By referring to important sources of information and by providing accurate documentation for your information, you show readers that you have done the necessary background reading. Including references to a range of sources—not just one—suggests that you have a balanced knowledge of your subject. However, questionable sources, inaccurate (or missing) documentation, and factual errors can undermine an argument. For many readers, in fact, an undocumented quotation or even an incorrect date can call an entire argument into question.

Maintaining a Reasonable Tone Your tone is almost as important as the information you convey. Talk *to* your readers, not *at* them. If you lecture your readers or appear to talk down to them, you will alienate them. Remember that readers are more likely to respond to a writer who is conciliatory than to one who is strident or insulting.

As you write your essay, use moderate language, and qualify your statements so that they seem reasonable. Try to avoid words and phrases such as *never*, *all*, and *in every case*, which can make your claims seem exaggerated and unrealistic. The statement "Euthanasia is never acceptable," for example, leaves you no room for compromise. A more conciliatory statement might be "In cases of extreme suffering, a patient's desire for death is certainly understandable, but in most cases, the moral, social, and legal implications of euthanasia make it unacceptable."

Presenting Yourself as Someone Worth Listening To When you write an argument, you should make sure you present yourself as someone your readers will want to listen to. Present your argument in positive and forceful terms, and don't apologize for your views. For example, do not rely on phrases—such as "In my opinion" and "It seems to me"—that undercut your credibility. Be consistent, and be careful not to contradict yourself. Finally, limit your use of the first person ("I"), and avoid slang and colloquialisms.

(3) Being Fair

See 9c

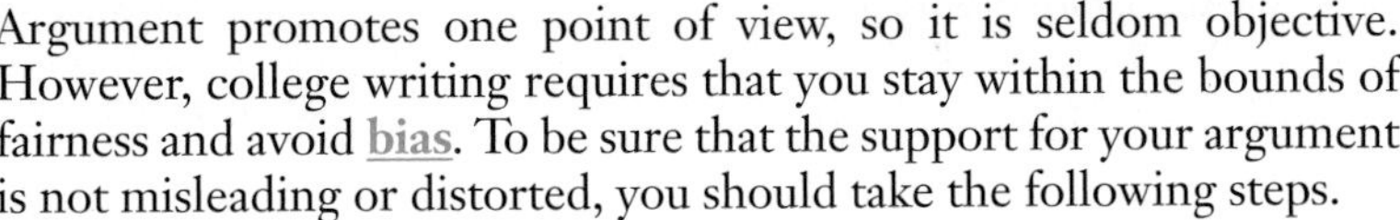

Argument promotes one point of view, so it is seldom objective. However, college writing requires that you stay within the bounds of fairness and avoid bias. To be sure that the support for your argument is not misleading or distorted, you should take the following steps.

Avoid Distorting Evidence Distortion is misrepresentation. Writers sometimes intentionally misrepresent their opponents' views by exaggerating them and then attacking this extreme position. For example, a senator of a northeastern state proposed requiring unmarried mothers receiving welfare to identify their children's fathers and supply information about them. Instead of challenging this proposal on its own merits, a critic distorted the senator's position and attacked it unfairly.

> What is the senator's next idea in his headlong rush to embrace the extreme right-wing position? A program of tattoos for welfare mothers? A badge sewn on to their clothing identifying them as welfare recipients? Creation of colonies in which welfare recipients would be forced to live like lepers? How about an involuntary relocation program into concentration camps?

Avoid Quoting Out of Context A writer or speaker quotes out of context by taking someone's words from their original setting and using them in another. When you select certain statements and ignore others, you can change the meaning of what someone has said or suggested.

> **Mr. N, Township Resident:** I don't know why you are opposing the new highway. According to your own statements, the highway will increase land values and bring more business into the area.
>
> **Ms. L, Township Supervisor:** I think you should look at my statements more carefully. I have a copy of the paper that printed my interview, and what I said was [*reading*]: "The highway will

> increase land values a bit and bring some business to the area. But at what cost? One hundred and fifty families will be displaced, and the highway will divide our township in half." My comments were not meant to support the new highway but to underscore the problems that its construction will cause.

By repeating only some of Ms. L's remarks, Mr. N altered her meaning to suit his purpose. In context, Ms. L's words indicate that although she concedes the highway's few benefits, she believes that its drawbacks outweigh them.

Avoid Slanting When you select only information that supports your case and ignore information that does not, you are guilty of slanting supporting information. Inflammatory language is another form of slanting that creates bias in your writing. For example, a national magazine slanted its information when it described a person accused of a crime as "a hulk of a man who looks as if he could burn out somebody's eyes with a propane torch." Although one-sided presentations frequently appear in tabloids and some popular magazines, you should avoid such distortions in your argumentative essays.

Avoid Using Unfair Appeals Traditionally, writers of arguments use three kinds of appeals to influence readers: **logical appeals** address an audience's sense of reason; **emotional appeals** play on the emotions of a reader; and **ethical appeals** call the reader's attention to the credibility of the writer.

Problems arise when these appeals are used unfairly. For example, writers can use fallacies to fool readers into thinking that a conclusion is logical when it is not. Writers can also employ inappropriate emotional appeals—to prejudice or fear, for example—to influence readers. And finally, writers can unfairly use their credentials in one area of expertise to bolster their stature in another area that they are not qualified to discuss.

See 9h

Checklist: Being Fair

- ☐ Have you distorted your evidence?
- ☐ Have you misrepresented your opponents' views by exaggerating them and then attacking this extreme position?
- ☐ Have you changed the meaning of a statement by focusing on certain words and ignoring others?
- ☐ Have you selected only information that supports your case and ignored information that does not?
- ☐ Have you used inflammatory language calculated to appeal to the emotions or prejudices of your readers?

(4) Using Visuals

See 5b3, 29d

Visuals can add a persuasive dimension to your argumentative essays. Because visual images can have such an immediate impact, they can make a good argumentative essay even more persuasive. In a sense, visuals are another type of evidence that can support your thesis statement. Consider, for example, how the addition of a photograph of a road choked with traffic during rush hour could help you support your assertion that your township should provide more generous subsidies for public transportation. In addition, a graph or chart could easily establish the fact that the local traffic situation has gotten considerably worse over the last decade. (For an example of a visual used in an argumentative essay, see page 206.)

To persuade readers, visuals rely on elements such as figures, language, color, and shading. Consider, for example, the editorial cartoon in Figure 10.1.

Figure 10.1 Cartoon from the *Honolulu Advertiser*.

This cartoon was drawn in response to a United States Supreme Court ruling that upheld the Children's Internet Protection Act, which mandated filters on all Internet computers in public libraries. The goal of this law was to prevent children from accessing sexually explicit material online. This cartoon criticizes the Supreme Court's ruling. Notice that the two figures (one a child and the other an adult) that dominate the cartoon are staring intently at a computer screen. The use of language in the cartoon is limited to the labels "Supreme Court" and "Public Library." Thus, with images and just a very few words, this visual forcefully makes the cartoonist's point: that Americans—even minors—do not need the Supreme Court looking over their shoulders and deciding what information they can access in the library. If you were writing an argument that took the same position as this cartoon, it could certainly help you make your point.

Remember, not all visuals will be appropriate or effective in supporting an argument. In fact, depending on your topic and your audience, certain visuals could discredit your argument. For this reason, when you select visuals, it is always important to remember your purpose and audience and the tone you wish to establish. Just as you would with any other evidence in an argumentative essay, you should evaluate visuals to make sure that they are not taken out of context and that they do not make their points unfairly. See 9d

Checklist: Selecting Visuals

- ☐ What point does the visual make?
- ☐ Does the visual clearly support your argument?
- ☐ In what way do the various elements of the visual reinforce your point?
- ☐ Is the visual aimed at a particular type of audience?
- ☐ Could the visual confuse or distract your readers in any way?
- ☐ Could the visual seem unfair to readers?

Exercise 2

Look at the political cartoon in Figure 10.2.

Figure 10.2 Cartoon from Arizona *Tribune* newspapers.

Use the questions in the checklist on page 201 to help you determine whether or not the cartoon would provide useful evidence in argumentative essays that contain the following statements:

- Because public opinion seems to be turning against the death penalty, it should be abolished as soon as possible.
- If the death penalty is abolished, violent criminals will be more likely to commit violent crimes.
- Because the death penalty seems to be carried out in such an unfair and arbitrary way, it should be abolished as soon as possible.
- Until an exhaustive study of the death penalty can be carried out, state governors should declare a moratorium on capital punishment.
- Although many consider the death penalty to be "cruel and unusual punishment," it is still appropriate for particularly heinous crimes.

Exercise 3

Visit two Web sites that take opposing positions on a controversial topic. What visuals are used on each site, and how are they used to support each site's position?

10c Organizing an Argumentative Essay

In its simplest form, an argument consists of a thesis statement and supporting evidence. However, argumentative essays frequently use inductive and deductive reasoning as well as additional strategies to win audience approval and overcome potential opposition.

Elements of an Argumentative Essay

Introduction

The introduction of your argumentative essay orients your readers to your subject. Here you can show how your subject concerns your audience, establish common ground with your readers, and perhaps explain how your subject has been misunderstood.

Background

In this section, you can briefly present a narrative of past events, an overview of others' opinions on the issue, definitions of key terms, or a review of basic facts.

Thesis Statement

See 4b–c

Your thesis statement can appear anywhere in your argumentative essay. Most often, you present your thesis in your introduction. However, if you are presenting a highly controversial argument—one to which you believe your readers might react negatively—you may postpone stating your thesis until later in your essay, after you have prepared readers to accept it.

Arguments in Support of Your Thesis

Here you present your assertions and the evidence to support them. Most often, you begin with your weakest argument and work up to your strongest. If all your arguments are equally strong, you might begin with those with which your readers are already familiar (and which they are therefore likely to accept) and then move on to relatively unfamiliar ideas.

Refutation of Opposing Arguments

In an argumentative essay, you should summarize and refute the major arguments against your thesis. If you do not address these opposing arguments, doubts about your case will remain in the minds of your readers. If the opposing arguments are relatively weak, refute them after you have made your case. However, if the opposing arguments are strong, concede their strengths and then discuss their limitations before you present your own arguments.

Conclusion

See 7e3

Often, the conclusion restates the major arguments in support of your thesis. Your conclusion can also summarize key points, restate your thesis, remind readers of the weaknesses of opposing arguments, or underscore the logic of your position. Many writers like to end their arguments with a strong last line, such as a quotation or a statement that sums up the argument.

10d Writing and Revising an Argumentative Essay

(1) Writing an Argumentative Essay

The following student essay includes many of the elements discussed in this chapter. The student, Samantha Masterton, was asked to write an argumentative essay on a topic of her choice, drawing her supporting evidence from her own knowledge and experience as well as from other sources.

Masterton 1

Samantha Masterton

Professor Egler

English 102

4 April 2003

The Returning Student: Older Is Definitely Better

Introduction

After graduating from high school, young people must decide what they want to do with the rest of their lives. Many graduates (often without much thought) decide to continue their education uninterrupted, and they go on to college. This group of teenagers makes up what many see as typical first-year college students. Recently, however, this stereotype has been challenged by an influx of older students, including myself, into American colleges and universities. Not only do these students make a valuable contribution to the schools they attend, but they also offer an alternative to young people who go to college simply because they do not know what else to do. A few years off between high school and college can give many—perhaps most—students the life experience they need to appreciate the value of higher education and gain more from it.

Thesis statement

Masterton 2

The college experience of an eighteen-year-old is quite different from that of an older "nontraditional" student. On the one hand, the typical high school graduate is often concerned with things other than cracking books—for example, going to parties, dating, and testing personal limits. On the other hand, older students—those who are twenty-five years of age or older—take seriously the idea of returning to college. Although many high school students do not think twice about whether or not to attend college, older students have much more to consider when they think about returning to college. For example, they must decide how much time they can spend getting their degree and consider the impact attending college will have on their family and their finances.

Background

In the United States, the demographics of college students is changing. According to a 2002 US Department of Education report titled Nontraditional Undergraduates, the percentage of students who could be classified as "nontraditional" has increased over the last decade (see fig. 1). Thus, in spite of the challenges that older students face when they return to school, more and more are choosing to make the effort.

Background (continued)

Most older students return to school with well-defined goals. The US Department of Education's Nontraditional Undergraduates report shows that more than one-third of nontraditional students decided to attend college because it was required by their job,

Argument in support of thesis

Masterton 3

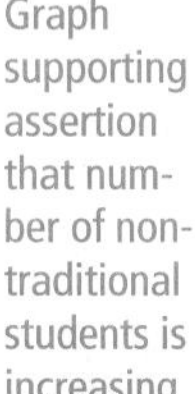

Graph
supporting
assertion
that num-
ber of non-
traditional
students is
increasing

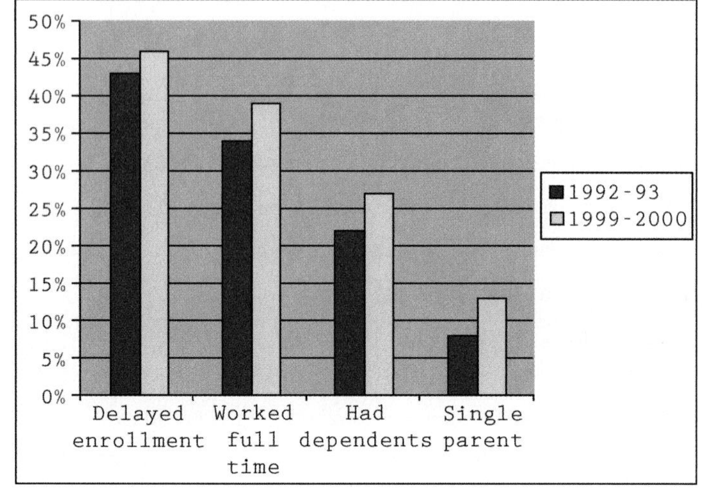

Fig. 1. United States, Dept. of Educ., Office of Educ. Research and Improvement, Natl. Center for Educ. Statistics, Nontraditional Undergraduates (Washington: US Dept. of Educ., 2002) 27 Feb. 2003 <http://nces.ed.gov/pubs2002/2002012.pdf>.

and 87 percent enrolled in order to gain skills (10). Getting a college degree is often a requirement for professional advancement, and older students are therefore more likely to take college seriously. In general, older students enroll in college with a definite course of study in mind. For this reason, they usually take only the classes they need for a particular degree instead of taking many unrelated classes. For older students, college is an extension of work rather than a place to discover what they

Masterton 4

want to be when they graduate. A 2001 study by psychologists Eric R. Landrum, Je Taime Hood, and Jerry M. McAdams concluded, "Nontraditional students seemed to be more appreciative of their opportunities, as indicated by their higher enjoyment of school and appreciation of professors' efforts in the classroom" (744). Clearly defining their goals enables older students to take advantage of the opportunities presented by professors as well as to make use of career offices and other services colleges provide.

The experience adult students have gained in the workplace also gives them advantages in the classroom. Generally, young people just out of high school have not been challenged by real-world situations that include meeting deadlines and setting priorities. Although success in college depends on the ability to set realistic goals and organize time and materials, college itself does little to help students develop these skills. On the contrary, the workplace—where reward and punishment are usually immediate and tangible—is the best place to learn such lessons. Working teaches the basics that are necessary for success: the value of punctuality and attendance, the importance of respect for superiors and colleagues, and the need for establishing priorities and meeting deadlines.

Argument in support of thesis

Older students understand the actual benefits of doing well in school and successfully completing a degree program. Older students I have known very rarely cut lectures or put off studying. This is because older students are often balancing the demands of home and work to attend classes, and they know how important it is to do well. The difficulties of balancing the demands of school, family, and work compel older students to be disciplined and focused—especially concerning their schoolwork. This pays off; older students tend to devote more hours per week to studying and tend to have a higher GPA than younger students do (Landrum, Hood, and McAdams 742-43).

Argument in support of thesis

My experience as an older student has convinced me that many students would benefit from delaying entry into college. Given their greater maturity and experience, older students bring more into the classroom than younger students do. Eighteen-year-olds have been driving for only a year or two, they have just earned the right to vote, and they usually have not lived on their own. They cannot be expected to have formulated definite goals or developed firm ideas about themselves or about the world in which they live. In contrast, older students have generally had a variety of real-life experiences. Most have worked for several years, many have started families. Their years in the "real world" have helped them become more focused and more responsible than they were when they graduated from high school. As a result, they are better prepared for college than

Personal experience used as evidence in support of thesis

Masterton 6

they would have been when they were young. Thus, they not only bring more into the classroom, but they also take more out of it.

Of course, postponing college for a few years is not for everyone. Certainly some teenagers have a definite sense of purpose and maturity well beyond their years, and these individuals would benefit from an early college experience, so that they can get a head start on their careers. Charles Woodward, a law librarian, went to college directly after high school, and for him the experience was positive. "I was serious about learning, and I loved my subject," he said. "I felt fortunate that I knew what I wanted from college and from life." Many younger students, however, are not like Woodward; they graduate from high school without any clear sense of purpose. For this reason, it makes sense for them to postpone college until they are mature enough to benefit from the experience.

Refutation of opposing argument

Granted, some older students have difficulties when they return to college. Because these students have been out of school so long, they may have difficulty studying and adapting to the routines of academic life. As I have seen, though, these problems disappear soon after an initial period of adjustment. Older students quickly get into the swing of things and adapt to college; they even participate in campus life. It is true that many older students find it difficult to balance the needs of their family with

Refutation of opposing argument

college and to cope with the financial burden that tuition and books bring to their family budget. However, this challenge is becoming easier with the growing number of online courses and the availability of distance education, as well as the introduction of governmental programs, such as educational tax credits and grants, to ease the financial burden of returning to school (Agbo 164-65).

Conclusion

All things considered, higher education is often wasted on the young, who are either too immature or too unfocused to take advantage of it. Taking a few years off between high school and college would give these students the breathing room they need to make the most of a college education. The increasing number of older students returning to college seems to indicate that many students are taking this path. According to a US Department of Education report, _Digest of Education Statistics, 2001_, 40 percent of students enrolled in American colleges in 2000 were twenty-five years of age or older. Older students such as these have taken time off to serve in the military, to gain valuable work experience, or to raise a family. Many have traveled, have engaged in informal study, and have taken the time to mature. By the time they get to college, they have defined their goals and made a commitment to achieve them.

Masterton 8

Works-cited list begins new page

Works Cited

Agbo, S. "The United States: Heterogeneity of the Student Body and the Meaning of 'Nontraditional' in U.S. Higher Education." Higher Education and Lifelong Learners: International Perspectives on Change. Eds. Hans G. Schuetze and Maria Slowey. London: Routledge, 2000. 149-69.

Landrum, R. Eric, Je Taime Hood, and Jerry M. McAdams. "Satisfaction with College by Traditional and Nontraditional College Students." Psychological Reports 89 (2001): 740-46.

United States. Dept. of Educ. Office of Educ. Research and Improvement. Natl. Center for Educ. Statistics. Digest of Education Statistics, 2001. Washington: US Dept. of Educ., 2001. 27 Feb. 2003 <http://nces.ed.gov/pubs2002/digest2001/tables/dt174.asp>.

---. ---. Nontraditional Undergraduates. Washington: US Dept. of Educ., 2002. 27 Feb. 2003 <http://nces.ed.gov/pubs2002/2002012.pdf>.

Woodward, Charles B. Personal interview. 21 Mar. 2003.

Two sets of unspaced hyphens indicate that both "United States" and "Dept. of Educ." are repeated from previous entry

(2) Revising an Argumentative Essay

See 5d

When you revise your argumentative essay, you use the same strategies you use for any essay. In addition, you concentrate on some specific concerns, which are listed in the following checklist.

Checklist: Argumentative Essays

- ☐ Is your topic debatable?
- ☐ Does your essay have an argumentative thesis?
- ☐ Have you adequately defined the terms you use in your argument?
- ☐ Have you considered the opinions, attitudes, and values of your audience?
- ☐ Have you summarized and refuted opposing arguments?
- ☐ Have you supported your assertions with evidence?
- ☐ Have you used visuals that strengthen your argument?
- ☐ Have you established your credibility?
- ☐ Have you documented all information that is not your own?
- ☐ Have you been fair?
- ☐ Have you constructed your arguments logically?
- ☐ Have you avoided logical fallacies?
- ☐ Have you provided your readers with enough background information?
- ☐ Have you presented your points clearly and organized them logically?
- ☐ Have you written an interesting introduction and a strong conclusion?

Close-up: Using Transitions in Argumentative Essays

Argumentative essays should include transitional words and phrases to indicate which paragraphs are arguments in support of the thesis, which are refutations of arguments that oppose the thesis, and which are conclusions.

Arguments in support of thesis	Accordingly, because, for example, for instance, in general, given, generally, since
Refutations	Although, admittedly, certainly, despite, granted, in all fairness, naturally, nonetheless, of course
Conclusions	All things considered, as a result, in conclusion, in summary, therefore, thus

Exercise 4

Samantha Masterton deleted the following paragraph from her essay "The Returning Student: Older Is Definitely Better." Do you think Samantha was right to delete it? If it belongs in the essay, where would it go? Does it need any revision?

The dedication of adult students is evident in the varied roles they must play. Many of the adults who return to school are seeking to increase their earning power. They have established themselves in the working world, only to find they cannot advance without more education or a graduate degree. The dual-income family structure enables many of these adults to return to school, but it is unrealistic for them to put their well-established lives on hold while they pursue their education. In addition to the rigors of college, older students are often juggling homes, families, and jobs. However, adult students make up in determination what they lack in time. In contrast, younger students often lack the essential motivation to succeed in school. Teenagers in college often have no clear idea of why they are there and, lacking this sense of purpose, may do poorly even though they have comparatively few outside distractions.

10e Writing Arguments Online

With the prevalence of email, discussion boards, and chat rooms, electronic arguments take place daily on a wide variety of topics. The major difference between these online debates and arguments that appear in print is the way in which information is presented. Writers of print arguments must include background information, explanations, and sometimes visuals as part of the argument itself, but writers of online arguments (such as the one in Figure 10.3 on page 214) can rely on Web links to supplement their discussions with further details or useful resources.

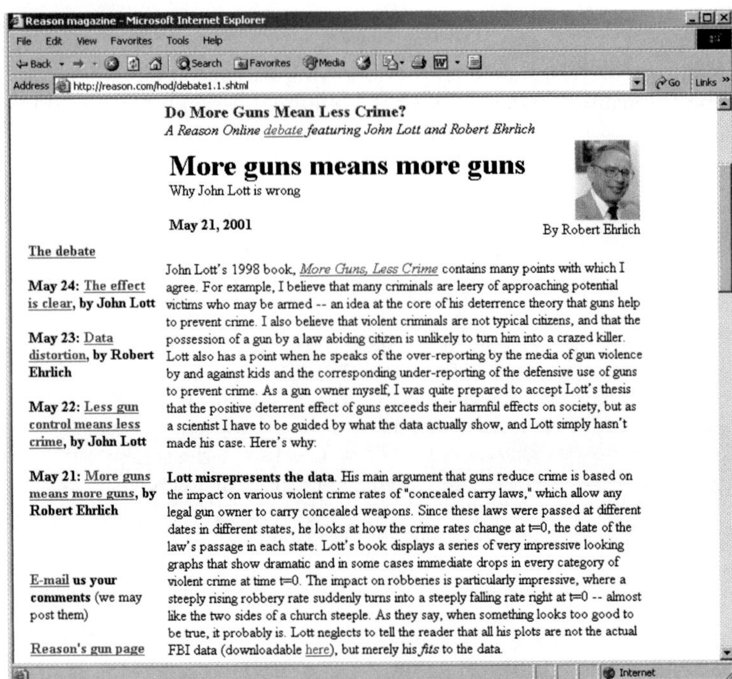

Reason magazine - Microsoft Internet Explorer

File Edit View Favorites Tools Help

Address http://reason.com/hod/debate1.1.shtml

Do More Guns Mean Less Crime?
A Reason Online debate featuring John Lott and Robert Ehrlich

More guns means more guns
Why John Lott is wrong

May 21, 2001 By Robert Ehrlich

The debate

May 24: The effect is clear, **by John Lott**

May 23: Data distortion, **by Robert Ehrlich**

May 22: Less gun control means less crime, **by John Lott**

May 21: More guns means more guns, **by Robert Ehrlich**

E-mail **us your comments** (we may post them)

Reason's gun page

John Lott's 1998 book, *More Guns, Less Crime* contains many points with which I agree. For example, I believe that many criminals are leery of approaching potential victims who may be armed -- an idea at the core of his deterrence theory that guns help to prevent crime. I also believe that violent criminals are not typical citizens, and that the possession of a gun by a law abiding citizen is unlikely to turn him into a crazed killer. Lott also has a point when he speaks of the over-reporting by the media of gun violence by and against kids and the corresponding under-reporting of the defensive use of guns to prevent crime. As a gun owner myself, I was quite prepared to accept Lott's thesis that the positive deterrent effect of guns exceeds their harmful effects on society, but as a scientist I have to be guided by what the data actually show, and Lott simply hasn't made his case. Here's why:

Lott misrepresents the data. His main argument that guns reduce crime is based on the impact on various violent crime rates of "concealed carry laws," which allow any legal gun owner to carry concealed weapons. Since these laws were passed at different dates in different states, he looks at how the crime rates change at t=0, the date of the law's passage in each state. Lott's book displays a series of very impressive looking graphs that show dramatic and in some cases immediate drops in every category of violent crime at time t=0. The impact on robberies is particularly impressive, where a steeply rising robbery rate suddenly turns into a steeply falling rate right at t=0 -- almost like the two sides of a church steeple. As they say, when something looks too good to be true, it probably is. Lott neglects to tell the reader that all his plots are not the actual FBI data (downloadable here), but merely his *fits* to the data.

Figure 10.3 Excerpt from "Do More Guns Mean Less Crime? A *Reason Online* Debate."

If you contribute an argument to a Web site or online discussion group, you should be aware of both the advantages and challenges of writing in an electronic environment. The following checklist presents the issues that you should consider as you draft and revise electronic arguments.

Checklist: Writing Electronic Arguments

- ☐ Follow the basic principles of writing arguments discussed in this chapter.
- ☐ Get to the point quickly, and don't overload readers with excess information.
- ☐ Consider what supplemental information—Web sites, film clips, articles, and so on—you can provide links to.
- ☐ If a debate is taking place through email, discussion groups, or chat rooms, consider the various positions that have been presented. Before writing, ask yourself what new information you have to add to the debate.

- ☐ Consider posting two versions of your argument: a condensed Web-based version for online reading and a longer word-processed version that can be downloaded and read in print form.
- ☐ Before posting an argument to a discussion group, read through the group's list of Frequently Asked Questions (FAQs) to make sure that you do not inadvertently violate any posting guidelines and damage your credibility with the group.
- ☐ Use a balanced, reasonable tone rather than one that is dismissive or potentially insulting.
- ☐ Consider how color, typeface, type size, visuals, and overall design can make your argument clearer.
- ☐ Consider whether to present any information in the form of tables, charts, or graphs.
- ☐ Be sure to edit and proofread. Careful editing for style and tone and proofreading for mechanical errors and typos will help to ensure that the message your argument sends is clear and convincing.

Exercise 5

Look back at the excerpt from *Reason Online* magazine (Figure 10.3). Label the elements of the excerpt (such as its links) that indicate that it is part of an online argument. What do these elements add to the argument? In what way, if any, do they detract from the argument's effectiveness?

Exercise 6

Suppose that you are an editor of a print magazine that is going to publish the argument presented in Exercise 5. Make a list of the specific changes the writer will have to make to the Web version to make his argument suitable for print.

Student Writer at Work

Writing an Argumentative Essay

The following draft was written for a second-semester composition course. Students were told to write about a topic that interested them, focusing on print or electronic media and using their own experience for support. Revise this draft, paying particular attention to the essay's logic, its use of evidence, and the writer's efforts to establish credibility. If you wish, add more examples, including one or more visuals, to support the argument.

Television Violence: Let Us Exercise Our Choice

Television began as what many people thought at the time was a fad. Now, many years later, it is the subject of arguments and controversy. There are even some activist groups who spend all their time protesting television's role in society. The weirdest of these groups are definitely the ones that attack television for being too violent. As far as I am concerned, these people should find better things to do with their time. There is nothing wrong with American television that a little bit of parental supervision would not fix.

The best argument against these protest groups is that television gives people what they want. I am not an expert on the subject, but I do know that the broadcasting industry is a business, a very serious business. Television programming has to give people what they want, or else they won't watch it. This is a fact that many of the so-called experts forget. If the television networks followed the advice of the protestors, they would be out of business within a year.

Another argument against the protest groups is that the First Amendment of the US Constitution guarantees all citizens the right of free speech. I am a citizen, so I should be able to watch whatever I want to. If these protestors do not want to watch violent programs, let them change the channel or turn off their sets. The Founding Fathers realized that an informed citizenry is the best defense against tyranny. Look at some of the countries that control the programs that citizens are able to watch. In Iran and in China, for example, people see only what the government wants them to see. A citizen can be put in prison if he or she is caught watching an illegal program. Is this where our country is heading?

Certainly, American society is too violent. No one can deny this fact, but we cannot blame all the problems of American society on television violence. As far as I know, there is absolutely no proof that the violence people see on television causes them to act violently. Violence in society is probably caused by a number of things—drugs, the proliferation of guns, and unemployment, for example. Before focusing on violence on television, the protestors should address these things. Protestors should also remember that television shows don't kill people; people kill people. Obviously, the protestors are forgetting this important fact.

All things considered, the solution to violence on television is simple: parents should monitor what their children watch. If they don't like what their children are watching, they should change the channel or turn off the television. There is no reason why the majority of television watchers—who are for the most part law-abiding people—should not be able to watch programs they like.

I for one do not want some protester telling me what I can or cannot watch. Moreover, if, by chance, these protesters do succeed in eliminating all violence, the result will be television programming that is boring. Then, television, the vast wasteland, will suddenly be turned into the dull wasteland.

PART 2

Doing Research

Chapter 11

Writing a Research Paper

Frequently Asked Questions

Research is the systematic investigation of a topic outside your own knowledge and experience. However, doing research means more than just reading about other people's ideas. When you undertake a research project, you become involved in a process that requires you to think critically: to evaluate and interpret the ideas explored in your sources and to formulate ideas of your own.

Not so long ago, doing research meant spending long hours in the library flipping through card catalogs, examining heavy reference volumes, and hunting for books on the shelves. Now, technology has dramatically changed the way research is conducted. The wiring of school and community libraries means that today, students and professionals spend a great deal of time in front of a computer, particularly during the exploratory stage of the research process. Still, although the way in which research materials are stored and accessed has changed, the research process itself has not. Whether you are working with **print sources** (books, journals, magazines) or electronic resources (online catalogs, databases, the Internet), in the library or at your home computer, your research will be more efficient if you follow a systematic process such as the one outlined below.

The Research Process

Activity	Date Due	Date Completed
Move from a General Assignment to a Narrow Topic, **11a**	________	________
Map Out a Search Strategy, **11b**	________	________

Activity	Date Due	Date Completed
Do Exploratory Research and Formulate a Research Question, **11c**	______	______
Assemble a Working Bibliography, **11d**	______	______
Develop a Tentative Thesis, **11e**	______	______
Do Focused Research, **11f**	______	______
Take Notes, **11g**	______	______
Fine-Tune Your Thesis, **11h**	______	______
Outline Your Paper, **11i**	______	______
Draft Your Paper, **11j**	______	______
Revise Your Paper, **11k**	______	______
Prepare Your Final Draft, **11l**	______	______

11a Moving from Assignment to Topic

(1) Understanding Your Assignment

Every research paper begins with an assignment. Before you can find a direction for your research, you must be sure you understand the exact requirements of this assignment.

Checklist: Understanding Your Assignment

- ☐ Has your instructor provided a list of possible topics, or are you expected to select a topic on your own?
- ☐ Is your purpose to explain, to persuade, or to do something else?
- ☐ Is your audience your instructor? Your fellow students? Both? Someone else?
- ☐ Can you assume your audience knows a lot (or just a little) about your topic?
- ☐ When is the completed research paper due?
- ☐ About how long should it be?

(continued)

Understanding your assignment (continued)

- ☐ Will you be given a specific research schedule to follow, or are you expected to set your own schedule?
- ☐ Is collaborative work permitted? Is it encouraged? If so, at what stages of the research process?
- ☐ Does your instructor expect you to keep your notes on note cards? In a computer file?
- ☐ Does your instructor expect you to prepare a formal outline?
- ☐ Are instructor–student conferences required?
- ☐ Will your instructor review notes, outlines, or drafts with you at regular intervals?
- ☐ Does your instructor require you to keep a research notebook?
- ☐ What manuscript guidelines and documentation style are you to follow?
- ☐ What help is available to you—from your instructor, other students, experts on your topic, community resources, your library staff?

(2) Choosing a Topic

Once you understand the requirements and scope of your assignment, you need to decide on a topic. In many cases, your instructor will help you choose a topic, either by providing a list of suitable topics or by suggesting a general subject area—for example, a famous trial, an event that happened on the day you were born, a problem on college campuses. Keep in mind, though, that you may still need to narrow your topic to one you can write about: one trial, one event, one problem.

If your instructor prefers that you select a topic on your own, you should consider a number of possible topics and weigh both their suitability for research and your interest in them. You decide on a topic for your research paper in much the same way you decide on a See 3d topic for a short essay: you read, brainstorm, talk to people, and ask questions. Specifically, you talk to friends and family, coworkers, and perhaps your instructor; read magazines and newspapers; take stock of your interests; consider possible topics suggested by your other courses (historical events, scientific developments, and so on); and, of course, browse the Internet.

http://kirsznermandell.wadsworth.com

Computer Tip: Moving from Assignment to Topic

See 13b2

Your search engine's subject guides can be particularly helpful to you as you look for a promising topic for your research or try to narrow a broad subject.

Checklist: Choosing a Research Topic

As you look for a suitable research topic, keep the following guidelines in mind:

- ☐ **Are you genuinely interested in your research topic?** Remember that you will be deeply involved with the topic you select for weeks—perhaps even for an entire semester. If you lose interest in your topic, you are likely to see your research as a tedious chore rather than as an opportunity to discover new information, new associations, and new insights.
- ☐ **Is your topic suitable for research?** Topics limited to your personal experience and those based on value judgments are not suitable for research. For example, "The superiority of Freud's work to Jung's" might sound promising, but no amount of research can establish that one person's work is "better" than another's.
- ☐ **Are the boundaries of your research topic appropriate?** A research topic should be neither too broad nor too narrow. "Julius and Ethel Rosenberg: Atomic Spies or FBI Scapegoats?" is far too broad a topic for a ten-page—or even a hundred-page—treatment, and "One piece of evidence that played a decisive role in establishing the Rosenbergs' guilt" would probably be too narrow for a ten-page research paper. But how one newspaper reported the Rosenbergs' espionage trial or how a particular group of people (government employees or college students, for example) reacted at the time to the couple's 1953 execution would work well.
- ☐ **Can your topic be researched in a library to which you have access?** For instance, the library of an engineering or business school may not have a large collection of books of literary criticism; the library of a small liberal arts college may not have extensive resources for researching technical or medical topics. (Of course, access to the Internet and to specialized subscription databases greatly increases your options.)

(3) Starting a Research Notebook

Keeping a **research notebook,** a combination journal of your reactions and log of your progress, is an important part of the research process. A research notebook maps out your direction and keeps you on track; throughout the research process, it helps you define and redefine the boundaries of your assignment.

In this notebook, you can record lists of things to do, sources to check, leads to follow up on, appointments, possible community contacts, questions to which you would like to find answers, stray ideas, possible thesis statements or titles, and so on. (Be sure to date your entries and to check off and date work completed.)

Some students use a spiral notebook that includes pockets to hold photocopies and computer printouts of downloaded material as well as notes and bibliography cards. Others find a small assignment book is all they need. Still others prefer to use a special computer file as a research notebook. Whatever form your notebook takes, it will be a useful record of what has been done and what is left to do.

Exercise 1

Using your own instructor's guidelines for selecting a research topic, choose a topic for your paper. Then, start a research notebook by entering information about your assignment, schedule, and topic.

11b Mapping Out a Search Strategy

Once you have found a topic to write about, you should plan your **search strategy,** the process you will use to help you locate and evaluate source material. This process reflects the way research works: you begin by doing **exploratory research,** looking at general reference works that give you a broad overview of your topic, and progress to **focused research,** consulting more specialized reference works as well as books and articles (in print or online) on your topic.

The diagram in Figure 11.1 is a general model of a search strategy that you can customize (perhaps with the help of your instructor or reference librarian) to suit the research project you are working on.

11c Doing Exploratory Research and Formulating a Research Question

During **exploratory research,** you develop an overview of your topic, searching the Internet and looking through general reference works such as encyclopedias, bibliographies, and specialized dictionaries (either in print or online). Your goal at this stage is to formulate a **research question,** the question you want your research paper to answer. A research question helps you to decide which sources to seek out, which to examine first, which to examine in depth, and which to skip entirely. (The answer to your research question will be your paper's thesis statement.)

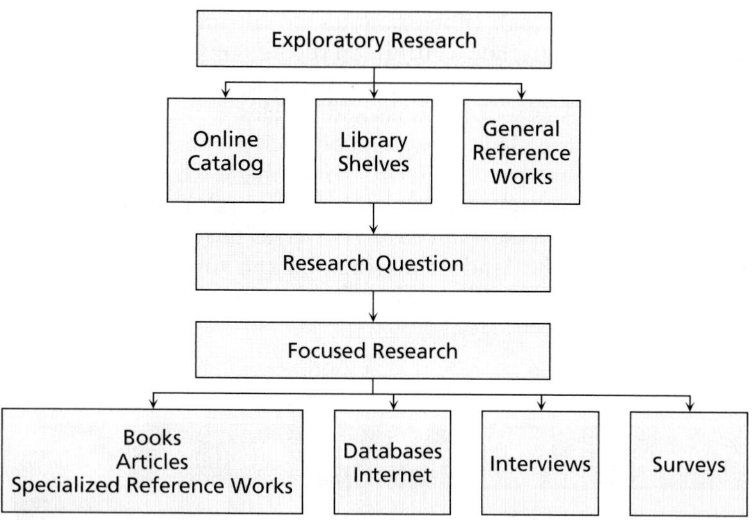

Figure 11.1 Search strategy.

11d Assembling a Working Bibliography

During your exploratory research, you begin to assemble a **working bibliography** for your paper. (This working bibliography will be the basis for your works-cited list, which will include all the sources you cite in your paper.)

See 18a2

Close-up: Assembling a Working Bibliography

As you record bibliographic information for your sources, include the following information:

Book author(s); title (underlined or in italics); call number (for future reference); city of publication; publisher; date of publication; brief evaluation

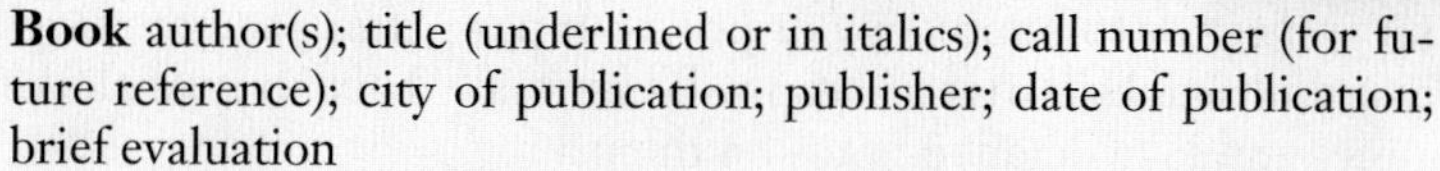

Article author(s); title of article (in quotation marks); title of journal (underlined or in italics); volume number; date; inclusive page numbers; URL (if applicable); date downloaded (if applicable); brief evaluation

As you consider each potential source, keep track of your sources by recording full and accurate bibliographic information in a separate computer file designated "Bibliography" (or, if you prefer, on

individual index cards). (For examples of entries from a student's working bibliography, **see 17d.**) Keep records of interviews (including telephone and email interviews), meetings, lectures, films, and electronic sources as well as books and articles. For each source, include not only basic identifying details—such as the date of an interview, the call number of a library book, the URL of an Internet source and the date you downloaded it, or the author of an article accessed from a database—but also a brief evaluation that includes comments about the kind of information the source contains, the amount of information offered, its relevance to your topic (and, perhaps, its limitations).

http://kirsznermandell.wadsworth.com

Computer Tip: Assembling a Working Bibliography

Various computer software programs can make it easy for you to compile your working bibliography electronically. For example, *WriteNote*, a Web-based research and writing application, enables you to create a personal record of the sources you consult. Later, when you begin writing, you can insert a bibliographic citation from *WriteNote* directly into your *Word* document. *WriteNote* automatically formats the in-text citation and bibliography entry according to one of the many possible documentation styles from which you can choose.

As you go about collecting sources and building your working bibliography, be careful to monitor the quality and relevance of all the materials you examine. Making informed choices early in the research process will save you a lot of time in the long run, so don't collect a large number of sources first and assess their usefulness later. Resist the temptation to check out every book that mentions your subject or to photocopy or print out page after page of marginally useful articles. After all, you will eventually have to read all these sources and take detailed notes on them.

Exercise 2

Consulting Figure 11.1 on page 225, map out a search strategy for your research project (by hand or with your computer). Next, do exploratory research to find a research question for your paper, carefully evaluating the relevance and usefulness of each source. Then, compile your working bibliography. When you have finished, reevaluate your sources and plan additional research if necessary.

11e Developing a Tentative Thesis

Your **tentative thesis** is a preliminary statement of the general idea you think your research will support. This statement, which you will eventually refine into your paper's thesis statement, should answer your research question.

Developing a Tentative Thesis

Subject Area	Topic	Research Question	Tentative Thesis
Issue related to the Internet	Access to the Internet	Do all Americans have equal access to the Internet?	Not all Americans have equal access to the Internet, and this is a potentially serious problem.

Because it suggests the specific direction your research will take as well as the scope and emphasis of your argument, your tentative thesis can help you generate a list of the main points you plan to develop in your paper. This list of points can help you narrow the focus of your research so you can zero in on a few specific categories to explore as you read and take notes.

Listing Your Points

Tentative Thesis: Not all Americans have equal access to the Internet, and this is a potentially serious problem.

- Give background about the Internet; tell why it's important
- Identify groups that don't have access to the Internet
- Explain problems this creates
- Suggest possible solutions

Exercise 3

Following your instructor's guidelines, develop a tentative thesis for your research paper and a tentative list of the points you plan to develop.

11f Doing Focused Research

Once you have decided on a tentative thesis and made a list of the points you plan to explore, you are ready to begin your focused research. When you do **focused research,** you look for the specific information—facts, examples, statistics, definitions, quotations—you need to support your points.

(1) Reading Sources

As you look for information, try to explore as many sources as possible. It makes sense to examine more sources than you actually intend to use so you can proceed even if one or more of your sources turns out to be biased, outdated, unreliable, superficial, or irrelevant—in other words, unusable. You should also make sure that you explore different viewpoints. After all, if you read only those sources that agree on a particular issue, it will be difficult for you to understand the full range of opinion about your topic.

As you explore various sources, quickly evaluate each source's potential usefulness. For example, if your source is a book, skim the table of contents and the index; if your source is a journal article, read the abstract. Then, if an article or a section of a book seems potentially useful, photocopy it for future reference. Similarly, when you find an online source that looks promising, resist the temptation to paste it directly into a section of your paper-in-progress. Instead, print it out (or send it to yourself as an email attachment) so you can evaluate it further later on. (For information on evaluating print and electronic sources, **see 12c.**)

(2) Balancing Primary and Secondary Sources

During your focused research, you will encounter both **primary sources** (original documents and observations) and **secondary sources** (interpretations of original documents and observations).

> **Primary Source:** United States Constitution, Amendment XIV (Ratified July 9, 1868). Section I.
>
> All persons born or naturalized in the United States, and subject to the jurisdiction thereof, are citizens of the United States and the state wherein they reside. No state shall make or enforce any law which shall abridge the privileges or immunities of citizens of the United States; nor shall any state deprive any person of life, liberty, or property, without the process of law; nor deny to any person within its jurisdiction the equal protection of the laws.

Secondary Source: Paula S. Rothenberg, *Racism and Sexism: An Integrated Study.*

> Congress passed the Fourteenth Amendment . . . in July 1868. This amendment, which continues to play a major role in contemporary legal battles over discrimination, includes a number of important provisions. It explicitly extends citizenship to all those born or naturalized in the United States and guarantees all citizens due process and "equal protection" of the law.

For many research projects, primary sources are essential; most research projects, however, rely heavily on secondary sources, which provide scholars' insights and interpretations. Remember, though, that the further you get from the primary source, the more chances exist for inaccuracies caused by misinterpretations or distortions.

Primary and Secondary Sources

Primary Source	**Secondary Source**
Novels, poems, plays, films	Criticism; reviews
Diaries, autobiographies	Biographies
Letters, historical documents, speeches, oral histories	Historical commentaries
Newspaper articles	Editorials
Raw data from questionnaires or interviews	Social science articles; case studies
Observations/experiments	Scientific articles; statistical charts
Photographs, maps, and other visuals	

11g Taking Notes

As you locate information in the library and on the Internet, take notes to create a record of exactly what you found and where you found it.

(1) Recording Source Information

Each piece of information you record in your notes (whether summarized, paraphrased, or quoted from your sources) should be accompanied by a short descriptive heading that indicates its relevance to one of the points you will develop in your paper. Because you will use these headings to guide you as you organize your notes, you should make them as specific as possible. Labeling every note for a paper on the "digital divide" created by the Internet `digital divide` or `Internet`, for example, will not prove very helpful later on. More focused headings—for instance, `dangers of digital divide` or `government's steps to narrow the gap`—will be much more useful.

Also include brief comments that make clear your reasons for recording the information and identify what you think it will contribute to your paper. These comments (enclosed in brackets so you will know they express your own ideas, not those of your source) should establish the purpose of your note—what you think it can explain, support, clarify, describe, or contradict—and perhaps suggest its relationship to other notes or other sources. Any questions you have about the information or its source can also be included in your comment.

Finally, each note should fully and accurately identify the source of the information you are recording. You need not write out the complete citation, but you must include enough information to identify your source. For example, `Gates 499` would be enough to send you back to your working bibliography card or file, where you would be able to find the complete documentation for Henry Louis Gates's essay "One Internet, Two Nations." (If you use more than one source by the same author, you need a more complete reference.)

http://kirsznermandell.wadsworth.com

Computer Tip: Taking Notes

When you take notes, your goal is flexibility: you want to be able to arrange and rearrange information easily and efficiently as your paper takes shape. If you take notes on your computer, type each individual note (accompanied by full source information) under a specific heading rather than listing all information from a single source under the same heading. (Later on, you can move notes around so notes on the same topic are grouped together.) If you take notes by hand, use the time-tested index-card system, taking care to write on only one side of the card and to use a separate index card for each individual note rather than running several notes together on a single card. (For sample student notes, **see 17g.**)

Note-taking software, such as *WriteNote* (see Figure 11.2), can make it easy for you to record and organize information, allowing you to create files in which you store notes (quotations, summaries, paraphrases, your own comments), pictures, or tables; to sort and categorize your material; and even to print out the information in order on computerized note cards.

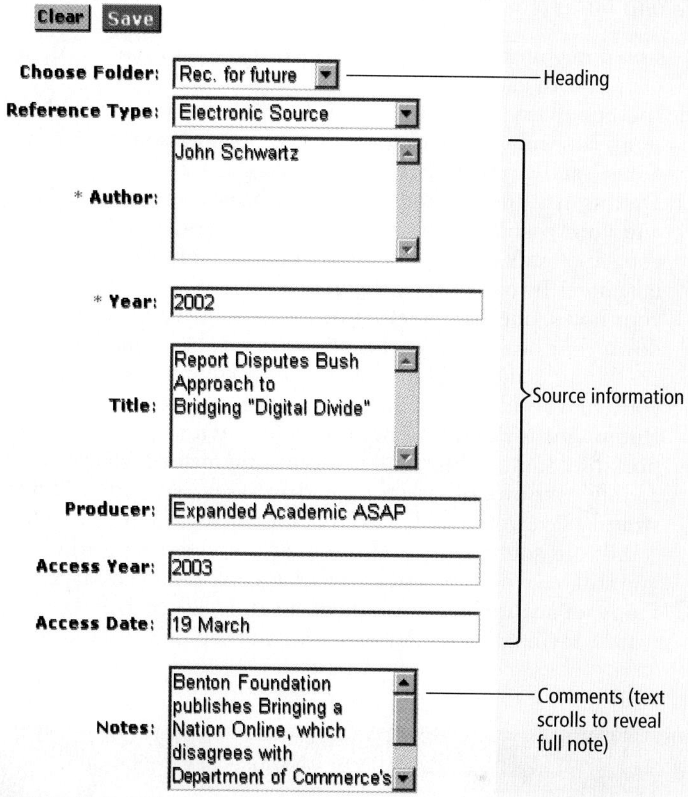

Clear Save

Choose Folder: Rec. for future — Heading

Reference Type: Electronic Source

* Author: John Schwartz

* Year: 2002

Title: Report Disputes Bush Approach to Bridging "Digital Divide"

Producer: Expanded Academic ASAP

Access Year: 2003

Access Date: 19 March

(Author through Access Date: Source information)

Notes: Benton Foundation publishes Bringing a Nation Online, which disagrees with Department of Commerce's — Comments (text scrolls to reveal full note)

Figure 11.2 Creating an electronic source reference and taking notes in *WriteNote*.

NOTE: If you do not have access to note-taking software, type each note under an appropriate heading, and divide notes from one another with extra space or lines. (Take advantage of bold, italics, and underlining to add emphasis where necessary and to help you prioritize information.) Later, you can sort notes into categories as well as add and delete bits of information and experiment with different sequences of ideas.

Checklist: Taking Notes

☐ **Identify the source of each piece of information.** Even if the source is sitting on your bookshelf or

(continued)

Taking notes (continued)

stored in your computer's hard drive, include full source information with each note.

- ☐ **Include everything now that you will need later** to understand your note—names, dates, places, connections with other notes—and to remember why you recorded it.
- ☐ **Distinguish quotations from paraphrases and summaries and your own ideas from those of your sources.** If you copy a source's words, place them in quotation marks. (If you take notes by hand, circle the quotation marks; if you type your notes, put the quotation marks in boldface.) If you write down your own ideas, enclose them in brackets—and, if you are typing, italicize them as well. These techniques will help you avoid accidental plagiarism in your paper.
- ☐ **Put an author's comments into your own words whenever possible,** summarizing and paraphrasing material as well as adding your own observations and analyses. Not only will this strategy save you time later on, but it will also help you understand your sources and evaluate their usefulness now, when you still have time to find alternative sources if necessary.
- ☐ **Copy an author's comments accurately,** using the exact words, spelling, punctuation marks, and capitalization.

See Ch. 16

ESL Tip

If you take notes in English (rather than in your native language), you will probably find it easier to transfer the notes into a draft of your paper. However, you may find it faster and more effective to use your native language when writing your own comments about each note.

(2) Managing Photocopies and Printouts

FAQs links

Much of the information you gather will be in the form of photocopies (of articles, book sections, and so on) and material downloaded or printed out from the Internet. Learning to manage this source information efficiently will save you a lot of time.

First, be careful not to allow the ease of copying and downloading to encourage you to postpone decisions about the usefulness of your sources. Remember, you can easily accumulate so many pages that it will be almost impossible for you to keep track of all your information.

You should also keep in mind that photocopies and printouts are just raw information, not information that has already been interpreted and evaluated. Making copies of sources is only the first step in the process of taking thorough, careful notes. The annotations you make on photocopies and printouts are seldom focused or polished enough to be incorporated directly into your paper; you still have to paraphrase and summarize your source's ideas and make connections among them.

Moreover, photocopies and printouts do not have much flexibility. For example, a single page of text may include information that should be earmarked for several different sections of your paper. This lack of flexibility makes it difficult for you to arrange source material into any meaningful order. Just as you would with any source, you have to transcribe your notes into your computer or onto index cards. These notes will give you the flexibility you need to write your paper.

Remember, you should approach photocopies and material you download or print out just as you approach any other source: as material that you will read, highlight, annotate, and then take notes about.

Close-up: Avoiding Plagiarism

To avoid the possibility of accidental **plagiarism**, be sure to keep all downloaded material in a separate file—not in your notes file. After you read this material and decide how to use it, you can move the notes you take into your notes file (along with full source information).

See Ch. 16

Checklist: Working with Photocopies and Computer Printouts

If you photocopy a source (or print out downloaded material), follow these guidelines.

- ☐ Record full and accurate source information, including the inclusive page numbers, URL, and any other relevant information, on the first page of each copy.
- ☐ Clip or staple together consecutive pages of a single source.
- ☐ Do not copy a source without reminding yourself—*in writing*—why you are doing so. In pencil or on removable

(continued)

Working with photocopies and computer printouts (continued)

self-stick notes, record your initial responses to the source's ideas, jot down cross-references to other works or notes, and highlight important sections.

- ☐ Photocopying can be time consuming and expensive, so try to avoid copying material that is only marginally relevant to your paper.
- ☐ Keep photocopies and printouts in separate files so you will be able to find them when you need them.

Exercise 4

Begin focused research for your paper, reading sources carefully and taking notes as you read. Your notes should include paraphrase, summary, and your own observations and analysis as well as quotations.

11h Fine-Tuning Your Thesis

See 4a–c

After you have finished your focused research and note-taking, you should be ready to refine your tentative thesis into a carefully worded statement that expresses a conclusion your research can support. This thesis statement should be more precise than your tentative thesis, accurately conveying the direction, emphasis, and scope of your paper.

Fine-Tuning Your Thesis

Tentative Thesis	Thesis Statement
`Not all Americans have equal access to the Internet, and this is a potentially serious problem.`	`Although the Internet has changed our lives for the better, it threatens to leave many people behind, creating two distinct classes—those who have access and those who do not.`

If your thesis statement does not express a conclusion your research can support, you will need to revise it. Reviewing your notes carefully, perhaps grouping information in different ways, may help you decide on a more suitable thesis. Or, you may try other techniques—for instance, using your research question as a starting point for additional brainstorming or freewriting.

Exercise 5

Read the following passages. Assume you are writing a research paper on the influences that shaped young writers in the 1920s. What possible thesis statements could be supported by the information in these passages?

1. Yet in spite of their opportunities and their achievements the generation deserved for a long time the adjective [lost] that Gertrude Stein had applied to it. The reasons aren't hard to find. It was lost, first of all, because it was uprooted, schooled away and almost wrenched away from its attachment to any region or tradition. It was lost because its training had prepared it for another world than existed after the war (and because the war prepared it only for travel and excitement). It was lost because it tried to live in exile. It was lost because it accepted no older guides to conduct and because it formed a false picture of society and the writer's place in it. The generation belonged to a period of transition from values already fixed to values that had to be created. (Malcolm Cowley, *Exile's Return*)
2. The 1920s were a time least likely to produce substantial support among intellectuals for any sound, rational, and logical program. Prewar stability and convention were condemned because all evidences of stability seemed illusory and artificial. The very lively and active interest in science was perhaps the decade's most substantial contribution to modern civilization. Yet in this case as well, achievement became a symbol of disorder and a source of disenchantment. (Frederick J. Hoffman, *The 20's*)
3. Societies do not give up old ideals and attitudes easily; the conflicts between the representatives of the older elements of traditional American culture and the prophets of the new day were at times as bitter as they were extensive. Such matters as religion, marriage, and moral standards, as well as the issues over race, prohibition, and immigration were at the heart of the conflict. (Introduction to *The Twenties*, ed. George E. Mowry)

Exercise 6

Carefully read over all the notes you have collected during your focused research, and develop a thesis statement for your paper.

11i Constructing an Outline

Once you have a thesis, you are ready to make an outline to guide you as you write your rough draft.

To make sense out of all the notes you have accumulated, you need to sort and organize them. As you organize and reorganize your notes into categories and subcategories, you will begin to see the ideas in your paper take shape. Your outline will reflect this shape.

A formal outline is different from a list of the main points you tentatively plan to develop in your paper. A **formal outline**—which may be either a topic outline or a sentence outline—includes all the points you will develop. It indicates both the exact order in which you will present your ideas and the relationship between main points and supporting details. (For an example of a student's topic outline, **see 17i.**)

NOTE: The outline you construct at this stage is only a guide for you to follow as you draft your paper; you are likely to change it as you draft and revise. The final outline, which you may be required to hand in with your finished paper, will reflect what you have written and serve as a guide for your readers. (For an example of a formal sentence outline, **see 17i.**)

Checklist: Constructing a Formal Outline

- ☐ Write your thesis statement at the top of the page.
- ☐ Review your notes to make sure each note expresses only one general idea. If this is not the case, recopy any unrelated information, creating a separate note.
- ☐ Check that the heading for each note specifically characterizes that note's information. If it does not, change the heading.
- ☐ Sort your notes according to their headings, keeping a miscellaneous file for notes that do not seem to fit into any category. Irrelevant notes, those unrelated to your paper's thesis, should be set aside (but not discarded).
- ☐ Check your categories for balance. If most of your notes fall into just one or two categories, revise some of your headings to create narrower, more focused categories. If you have only one or two notes in a category, you may need to do additional research or treat that topic only briefly (or not at all).
- ☐ Organize the individual notes within each group, adding more specific subheads to your headings as needed. Arrange your notes in an order that highlights the most important points and subordinates lesser ones.

- ☐ Decide on a logical order in which to discuss your paper's major points.
- ☐ Construct your formal outline, using divisions and subdivisions that correspond to your headings.
- ☐ Review your completed outline to make sure you have not placed too much emphasis on a relatively unimportant idea, ordered ideas illogically, or created sections that overlap with others.

http://kirsznermandell.wadsworth.com

Computer Tip: Outlining

Before you begin writing, create a separate file for each major section of your outline. Then, copy your notes into these files in the order in which you intend to use them. You can print out each file as you need it and use it for a guide as you write.

Exercise 7

Review your notes carefully. Then, sort and group them into categories, and construct a topic outline for your paper.

11j Writing a Rough Draft

When you are ready to write your rough draft, check to be sure you have arranged your notes in the order in which you intend to use them. Follow your outline as you write, using your notes as needed. As you draft, write questions to yourself, and identify points that need further clarification. (You can bracket those ideas or boldface them as you type, or you can write them on self-stick notes as you read the printout of your draft.)

As you move along, leave space for material you plan to add, and bracket phrases or whole sections that you think you may later decide to move or delete. In other words, lay the groundwork for a major revision. Remember that even though you are guided by an outline and notes, you are not bound to follow their content or sequence exactly. As you write, new ideas or new connections among ideas may occur to you. If you find yourself wandering from your thesis or outline, stop to consider whether the departure is justified.

As your draft takes shape, be sure to supply transitions between sentences and paragraphs to indicate how your points are related. To make it easy for you to revise later on, triple-space your draft. Be careful to copy source information fully and accurately on this and every subsequent draft, placing the documentation as close as possible to the material it identifies. (For an excerpt from a student's draft, along with her instructor's comments and her revisions, **see 17k.**)

http://kirsznermandell.wadsworth.com

Computer Tip: Drafting

You can use a split screen or multiple windows to view your notes as you draft your paper. This strategy enables you to copy the material that you need from your notes and then insert it into the text of your paper. (As you copy, be especially careful that you do not unintentionally commit plagiarism.)

(1) Shaping the Parts of the Paper

Like any other essay, a research paper has an introduction, a body, and a conclusion. In your rough draft, as in your outline, you focus on the body of your paper. Do not spend time planning your introduction or conclusion at this stage; your ideas will change as you write, and you will need to revise your opening and closing paragraphs later to reflect those changes.

Introduction In your **introduction,** you identify your topic and establish how you will approach it. Your introduction also includes your thesis statement, which presents the position you will support in the rest of the paper. Sometimes the introductory paragraphs briefly summarize your major supporting points (the major divisions of your outline) in the order in which you will present them. Such a preview of your thesis and support provides a smooth transition into the body of your paper. Your introduction can also present an overview of the problem you will discuss, or it can summarize research already done on your topic. In your rough draft, however, an undeveloped introduction is perfectly acceptable; in fact, your thesis statement alone can serve as a placeholder for the more polished introduction that you will write later.

Body As you draft the **body** of your paper, lead readers through your discussion with strong topic sentences that correspond to the divisions of your outline.

`In the late 1990s, many argued that the Internet had ushered in a new age, one in which instant communication would bring people closer together and eventually eliminate national boundaries.`

You can also use headings if they are a convention of the discipline in which you are writing.

See 29b

`Responses to Digital Divide`

`In response, the government, corporations, nonprofit organizations, and public libraries made efforts to bridge the gap between the "haves" and the "have-nots."`

Even in your rough draft, carefully worded topic sentences and headings will help you keep your discussion under control.

Use different patterns of development to shape the individual sections of your paper, and be sure to connect ideas with clear transitions. If necessary, connect two sections of your paper with a transitional paragraph that shows their relationship.

See 7d

See 7e1

Conclusion The **conclusion** of a research paper often restates your thesis. This is especially important in a long paper because by the time your readers get to the end, they may have lost sight of your paper's main idea. Your conclusion can also include a summary of your key points, a call for action, or perhaps an apt quotation. In your rough draft, however, your concluding paragraph is usually very brief.

See 7e3

(2) Working Source Material into Your Paper

In the body of your paper, you evaluate and interpret your sources, comparing different ideas and assessing conflicting points of view. As a writer, your job is to draw your own conclusions, blending information from various sources into a paper that coherently and forcefully presents your own original viewpoint to your readers.

Be sure to integrate source material smoothly into your paper, clearly and accurately identifying the relationships among various sources (and between those sources' ideas and your own). If two sources present conflicting interpretations, you should be especially careful to use precise language and accurate transitions to make the contrast apparent (for instance, "`Although the Bush administration remains optimistic, some studies suggest . . .`"). When two sources agree, you should make this clear (for example, "`Like Young, McPherson believes . . .`" or "`Department of Commerce statistics confirm Gates's point`"). Such phrasing

See 15d

will provide a context for your own comments and conclusions. If different sources present complementary information about a subject, blend details from the sources carefully, keeping track of which details come from which source.

(3) Integrating Visuals into Your Paper

Photographs, diagrams, graphs, and other visuals can be very useful additions to your research paper because they can provide support for the points you make. You may be able to create a visual on your own (for example, by taking a photograph or creating a bar graph). You may also be able to find an appropriate visual in a book or magazine or in a database that collects images on a wide variety of topics. (For an example of a student's use of an image database, **see 17j3.**)

Exercise 8

Write a rough draft of your paper, being careful to incorporate source material and visuals smoothly and to record source information accurately. Begin drafting with the section for which you have the most material.

11k Revising Your Drafts

You should begin revising by making an outline of your rough draft and comparing it to the outline you made before you began the draft. If you find significant differences, you will have to revise your thesis statement or rewrite sections of your paper. The checklists in 5d5 can guide your revisions of your paper's overall structure and its individual paragraphs, sentences, and words.

As you review your drafts, follow the revision procedures that apply to any paper. In addition, focus on the questions in the following checklist, which apply specifically to research papers.

Checklist: Revising a Research Paper

- ☐ Should you do more research to find support for certain points?
- ☐ Do you need to reorder the major sections of your paper?
- ☐ Should you rearrange the order in which you present your points within those sections?

- ☐ Do you need to add section headings? transitional paragraphs?
- ☐ Have you integrated source material smoothly into your paper? See 15d
- ☐ Have you chosen visuals carefully and integrated them smoothly into your paper?
- ☐ Are quotations blended with paraphrase, summary, and your own observations and reactions?
- ☐ Have you avoided plagiarism by carefully documenting all borrowed ideas? See Ch. 16
- ☐ Have you analyzed and interpreted the ideas of others rather than simply stringing those ideas together?
- ☐ Do your own ideas—not those of your sources—define the focus of your discussion?

If your instructor encourages peer review, take advantage of it. As you move from rough to final draft, you should think more and more about your readers' reactions. Testing out others' reactions to a draft can be extremely helpful.

You will probably take your paper through several drafts, changing different parts of it each time or working on one part over and over again. After revising each draft thoroughly, print out a corrected version and make additional corrections by hand on that draft before typing the next version.

http://kirsznermandell.wadsworth.com

Computer Tip: Revising

When you finish revising your paper, copy the file that contains your working bibliography, and insert it at the end of your paper. Delete any irrelevant entries, and use the bibliographic information to help you compile your works-cited list. (Make sure the format of the entries on your works-cited list conforms to the documentation style you are using.)

Exercise 9

Following the guidelines in 11k and 5b, revise your research paper until you are ready to prepare your final draft.

11l Preparing a Final Draft

Before you print out the final version of your paper, edit and proofread hard copy of your outline and your works-cited list as well as of the paper itself. Next, consider (or reconsider) your paper's title. It should be descriptive enough to tell your readers what your paper is about, and it should create interest in your subject. Your title should also be consistent with the purpose and tone of your paper. (You would hardly want a humorous title for a paper about the death penalty or world hunger.) Finally, your title should be engaging and to the point—and perhaps even provocative. Often, a quotation from one of your sources will suggest a likely title.

See 5e

See 1a,c

When you are satisfied with your title, read your paper through again, proofreading for grammar, spelling, or typing errors you may have missed. Pay particular attention to parenthetical documentation and works-cited entries. (Remember that every error undermines your credibility.) Once you are satisfied that your paper is as accurate as you can make it, print it out one last time. Then, fasten the pages with a paper clip (do not staple the pages or fold the corners together), and hand it in. (For an example of a complete student research paper, along with a sentence outline and a works-cited list, **see 17l.**)

Exercise 10

Prepare a sentence outline and a works-cited list for your research paper. (Sections 5d4 and 6c4 explain and illustrate the specific conventions of sentence outlines; 18a2 illustrates MLA works-cited list format.) Then, edit and proofread your paper, outline, and works-cited list; decide on a title; and type your paper according to the format your instructor requires. Proofread your typed copy carefully before you hand it in.

http://kirsznermandell.wadsworth.com

Computer Tip: Useful Web Sites

A variety of different Web sites may be useful to you as you go through the research process. For an extensive list, see *The Wadsworth Handbook* Web site, http://kirsznermandell.wadsworth.com.

Chapter 12

Doing Library and Field Research

Frequently Asked Questions

A modern, networked college library offers you specialized resources and professional help that you cannot find anywhere else—even on the Internet. In the long run, you will save a great deal of time and effort, as well as gain a deeper understanding of your topic, if you begin your research with a survey of the library's print and electronic resources.

Close-up: Advantages of Using the Library

- Libraries provide access to sources (both print and electronic) that are not available on the "free" Internet and probably never will be.
- Library collections don't disappear or become outdated the way Web sites frequently do.
- Library staff can provide help when you have difficulty finding what you need. When you use the Internet, you're on your own.
- Libraries are organized for efficient information retrieval, with online catalogs and databases that enable you to find relevant resources quickly and easily. When you search the Internet, you may have to sort through hundreds (or thousands) of sites to find a few that are useful.

- Libraries have standards for the selection of material. You have a greater chance of obtaining reliable information when you use library resources than you do if you use the Internet.
- Library resources (both print and electronic) are almost always free to users.

Checklist: Resources Available in the Library

You may think you can find everything you need for your research on the Internet, but this is not true. In fact, your college library offers many additional resources.

- ☐ Books, films, journals, and other material owned or subscribed to by your library
- ☐ Databases covering many years that provide access to print articles (many of them full text) published on all subjects in magazines, newspapers, and peer-reviewed journals
- ☐ Full-text electronic journals available only on a subscription basis
- ☐ Full-text encyclopedias, dictionaries, and other reference works available at no charge that can be accessed through the Web only for a fee
- ☐ Digitized collections of historical documents and primary sources purchased by the library
- ☐ Online research guides and pathfinders created by librarians to help you find sources
- ☐ Lists of recommended Web sites, compiled by librarians, usually arranged by topic or academic subject area

12a Doing Exploratory Research in the Library

College libraries offer you access to the print and electronic sources that you will need for your research. You should begin your exploratory research in the library by consulting general encyclopedias, dictionaries, and bibliographies. (You can also find in the library the many resources you will use during focused research—for example, periodical indexes, articles, and books.)

During exploratory research, your goal is to find a research question for your paper. You can begin this process by searching your col-

lege or university library's **online catalog** to see what kind of information is available about your topic. You can then look at general reference works and consult the library's electronic resources.

Checklist: Before You Start Library Research

- ☐ Know the library's physical layout.
- ☐ Take a tour of the library if one is offered.
- ☐ Familiarize yourself with the library's holdings.
- ☐ Find out if the library has a guide to its resources—both print and electronic.
- ☐ Meet with a librarian if you have questions.
- ☐ Be sure you know the library's hours.
- ☐ Find out if you can access some of the library's resources through your own computer at home or in your dorm room.

(1) Using Online Catalogs

Most college and university libraries—and a growing number of regional and community libraries—have abandoned print catalog systems in favor of **online catalogs**—computer databases that list all the books, articles, and other materials held by the library. (Figure 12.1 on page 246 shows a home page for an online catalog.)

You access an online catalog (as well as other electronic library resources) by using one of the computer terminals located throughout the library and typing in certain words or phrases that enable you to find the information you need. If you have never used an online catalog, ask your reference librarian for help before you begin.

When you search the online catalog for information about your topic, you may conduct either a *keyword search* or a *subject search*. Later on in the research process, when you know more precisely what you are looking for, you can search for a particular book by entering its title, author, or call number.

Conducting a Keyword Search When you carry out a **keyword search,** you enter into the Search box of the online catalog a term or terms associated with your topic. The screen then displays a list of articles that contain those words in their bibliographic citations or abstracts. The more precise your search terms are, the more specific and useful the information you retrieve will be. (Combining keywords with AND, OR, and NOT allows you to narrow or broaden your search. This technique is called conducting a **Boolean search**.)

See 13b3

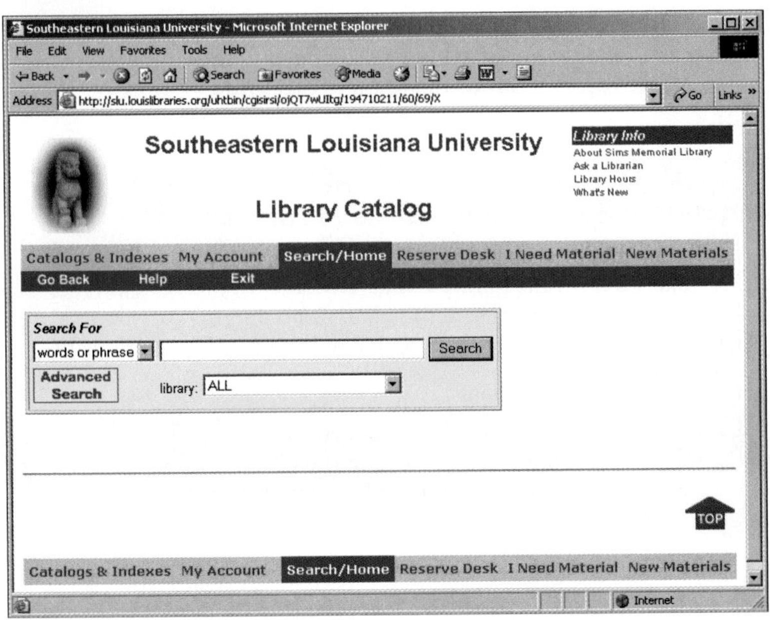

Figure 12.1 Home page of a university library's online catalog.

Checklist: Keyword Dos and Don'ts

When conducting a keyword search, remember the following hints:

- ☐ Use precise, specific keywords to distinguish your topic from similar topics.
- ☐ Enter both singular and plural keywords when appropriate—*printing press* and *printing presses,* for example.
- ☐ Enter both abbreviations and their full-word equivalents (for example, *US* and *United States*).
- ☐ Try variant spellings (for example, *color* and *colour*).
- ☐ Don't use too long a string of keywords. (If you do, you will retrieve large amounts of irrelevant material.)

ESL Tip

You may want to consult with your instructor or a librarian to help you identify keywords relevant to your topic.

Conducting a Subject Search When you carry out a **subject search,** you enter specific subject headings into the online catalog. The subject categories in a library are most often arranged according to headings established in the five-volume manual *Library of Congress Subject Headings*, held at the reference desk of your library. Although it may be possible to guess at a subject heading, your search will be more successful if you consult these volumes to help you identify the exact words you need. (Figure 12.2 shows the results of a search of the subject heading *Music Trade.*)

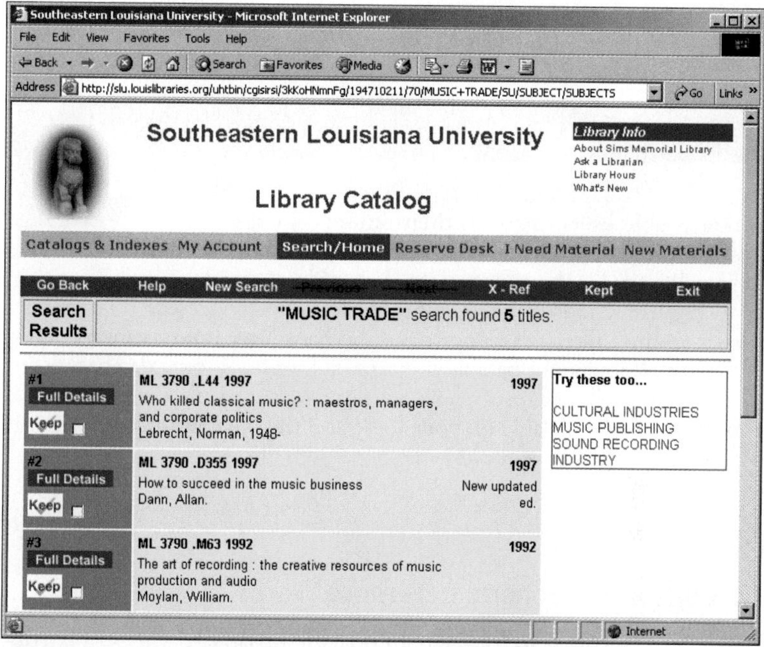

Figure 12.2 Online catalog search results for the subject heading *Music Trade.*

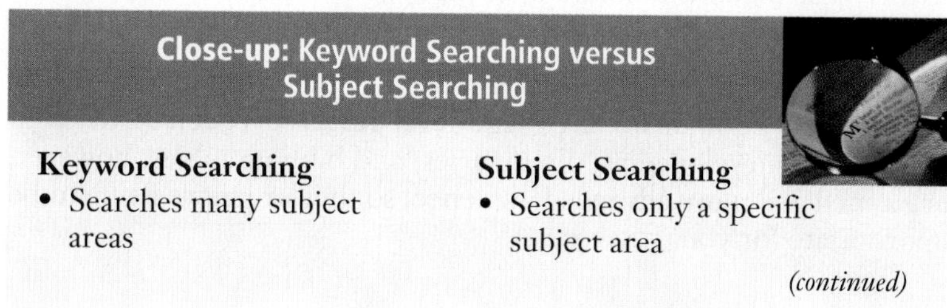

Close-up: Keyword Searching versus Subject Searching

Keyword Searching	Subject Searching
• Searches many subject areas	• Searches only a specific subject area

(continued)

Keyword searching versus subject searching (continued)

Keyword Searching
- Any significant word or phrase can be used
- Retrieves large number of items
- May retrieve many irrelevant items

Subject Searching
- Only the specific words listed in the *Library of Congress Subject Headings* can be used
- Retrieves small number of items
- Retrieves few irrelevant items

http://kirsznermandell.wadsworth.com

Computer Tip: Using Your Library's Web Site

Many college and university libraries have Web sites that enable users to access their online catalogs from a dorm room or from any computer connected to the Internet. Ask at your library for the appropriate Web address and password.

You can also browse the online catalogs of major research libraries, such as the Library of Congress or the New York Public Library. Although you may not be able to access subscription-only databases or indexes, searching a research library's catalog can give you an overview of the sources available on your topic and the bibliographic information you can use to request material via **interlibrary loan**.

(2) Consulting General Reference Works

General reference works, which provide broad overviews of particular subjects, can be helpful when you are doing exploratory research. From these sources, you can learn key facts and specific terminology as well as find dates, places, and people. In addition, general reference works often include bibliographies that you can use later on when you do focused research.

NOTE: Articles in encyclopedias aimed at general readers are usually not detailed enough for a college-level research paper. Articles in specialized encyclopedias, dictionaries, and bibliographies, however, are aimed at a more advanced audience, so they are more likely to be appropriate for your research.

Close-up: General Reference Works

The following kinds of reference works, many of which are available in electronic forms as well as in print, are useful for exploratory research:

General Encyclopedias Many general multivolume encyclopedias are available in electronic format. For example, *The New Encyclopaedia Britannica* is available on CD-ROM and DVD as well as on the World Wide Web at http://www.britannica.com.

Specialized Encyclopedias, Dictionaries, and Bibliographies These specialized reference works contain in-depth articles focusing on a single subject area.

General Bibliographies General bibliographies list books available in a wide variety of fields.

Books in Print An index of authors and titles of books in print in the United States. The *Subject Guide to Books in Print* indexes books according to subject area.

The Bibliographic Index A tool for locating bibliographies.

General Biographical References Biographical reference books provide information about people's lives as well as bibliographic listings.

Living Persons

Who's Who in America Gives concise biographical information about prominent Americans.

Who's Who Collects concise biographical facts about notable British men and women.

Current Biography Includes articles on people of many nationalities.

Deceased Persons

Dictionary of American Biography Considered the best of American biographical dictionaries. Includes articles on over thirteen thousand Americans.

Dictionary of National Biography The most important reference work for British biography.

Webster's Biographical Dictionary Perhaps the most widely used biographical reference work. Includes people from all periods and places.

(3) Using Electronic Resources

Today's libraries have electronic resources that enable you to find a wide variety of sources. The same computer terminals that enable you to access the online catalog may also enable you to access this source material.

Online databases are collections of digital information—citations of books; reports; journal, magazine, and newspaper articles; and so on (and sometimes the articles themselves)—arranged for easy access and retrieval by computer. Different libraries offer different databases and make them available in different ways. Many libraries have implemented Web-based systems that make it easy for them to network their databases (and online catalogs) beyond the library's walls. Some libraries may acquire databases on CD-ROM or DVD, but most subscribe to information service companies, such as DIALOG or Gale, that provide access to hundreds of databases not otherwise available to you. One of your first tasks should be to determine what your library has to offer. Visit your library's Web site, or ask a reference librarian for more information.

Once you have searched the databases and found the right information, you can print out bibliographic citations, **abstracts** (short summaries), or even full text. In some cases, you may be able to download the information to disk.

General and Specialized Subscription Databases Some databases, called **bibliographic databases,** include references to articles published in magazines and scholarly journals and may also be available in print. They provide information about each article but do not usually include the full text of the article itself. (**Full-text** databases include the entire text of articles, online encyclopedias, or other works.) These databases are **proprietary,** which means that libraries must subscribe to them in order to make them available to students and faculty. Licensing and copyright agreements generally restrict the use of these subscription databases; they are not available from outside the library to those who are not affiliated with the school.

Some library databases for articles cover many subject areas (*Expanded Academic ASAP* or *LexisNexis Academic Universe*, for example); others cover one subject area in great detail (*PsycINFO* or *Sociological Abstracts*, for example). The choices available to you may seem overwhelming at first. Assuming that your library offers a variety of databases (some libraries subscribe to hundreds), how do you know which ones will be best for your research topic? One strategy is to begin by searching a general database that includes full-text articles and then move on to a more specialized database that covers your subject in more detail. The specialized databases are more likely to include scholarly and professional journal articles, but they are also less likely to include the full text. They will, however, include abstracts that can help you determine the usefulness of an article. If you are in doubt about which databases would be most useful to you, be sure to ask a librarian for suggestions. (Figure 12.3 shows a partial list of databases to which a library subscribes; Figure 12.4 on page 252 shows a printout from a library subscription database.)

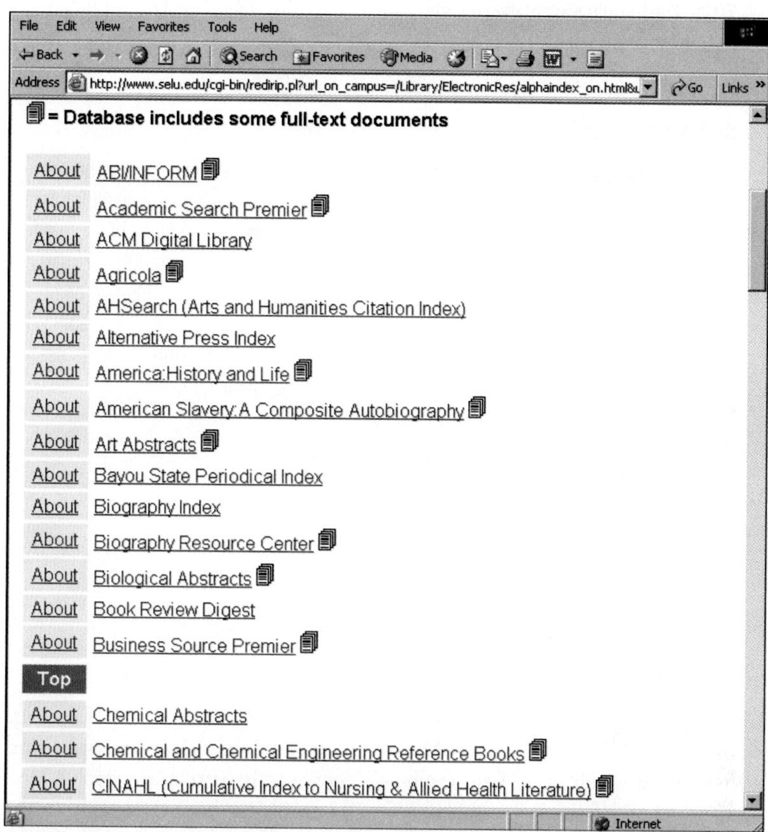

Figure 12.3 Partial list of databases to which a library subscribes.

Searching Databases There are two ways to search library databases for information on a topic: by subject headings and by keyword(s). **Subject headings** are taken from a list of terms recognized by that database. Sometimes it is easy to choose a subject heading, but sometimes, it is harder to choose an appropriate term. For example, what do you call older people? Are they senior citizens? elderly? the aged? (Some databases provide a print or online thesaurus to help you pick subject headings.)

The other option is **keyword searching**, which allows you to type in any significant term likely to be found in the title, subject headings, abstract, or (if the full text is available) text of an article. Keyword searching also allows you to link terms using **boolean**

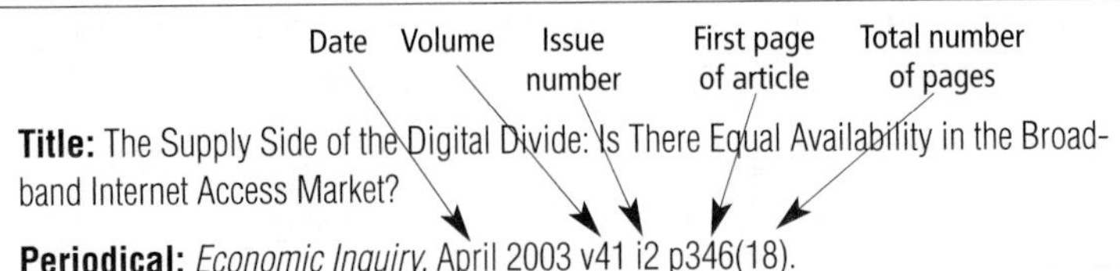

Title: The Supply Side of the Digital Divide: Is There Equal Availability in the Broadband Internet Access Market?

Periodical: *Economic Inquiry,* April 2003 v41 i2 p346(18).

Author: James E. Prieger

Author's Abstract: The newest dimension of the digital divide is access to broadband (high-speed) Internet service. Using comprehensive US data covering all forms of access technology (chiefly DSL and cable modem), I look for evidence of unequal broadband availability in areas with high concentrations of poor, minority, or rural households. There is little evidence of unequal availability based on income or on black or Hispanic concentration. There is mixed evidence concerning availability based on Native American or Asian concentration. Other findings: Rural location decreases availability; market size, education, Spanish language use, commuting distance, and Bell presence increase availability. (JEL L96, J78, L51)

Subjects: Digital Divide (Technology) = Demographic Aspects

Internet = Usage

Features: tables; figures

Figure 12.4 Library subscription database printout.

operators (AND, OR, NOT). For example, *elderly* AND *abuse* would retrieve only articles that mention both elderly people and abuse; *elderly* OR *aged* OR *senior citizens* would retrieve articles that mention any of these terms. Keyword searching is particularly helpful when you need to narrow or expand the focus of your search.

Both subject heading and keyword searches are useful ways to find articles on your topic. The most important thing is to be persistent. One good article often leads to another because abstracts and text may suggest other terms you can use. References and footnotes may suggest additional sources as well. Figure 12.5 shows a search page from a library subscription database.)

CD-ROMs and DVDs Many of the subscription databases available online are also available on CD-ROM or DVD. In some cases, libraries subscribe to a CD-ROM or DVD service or database the same way they do to a printed index or journal and receive updates periodically. In other cases, reference books available in print—for example, *The Oxford English Dictionary* and *The Encyclopaedia Britannica*—are also published on CD-ROMs or DVDs. Many libraries offer individual workstations where CD-ROMs or DVDs can be loaded

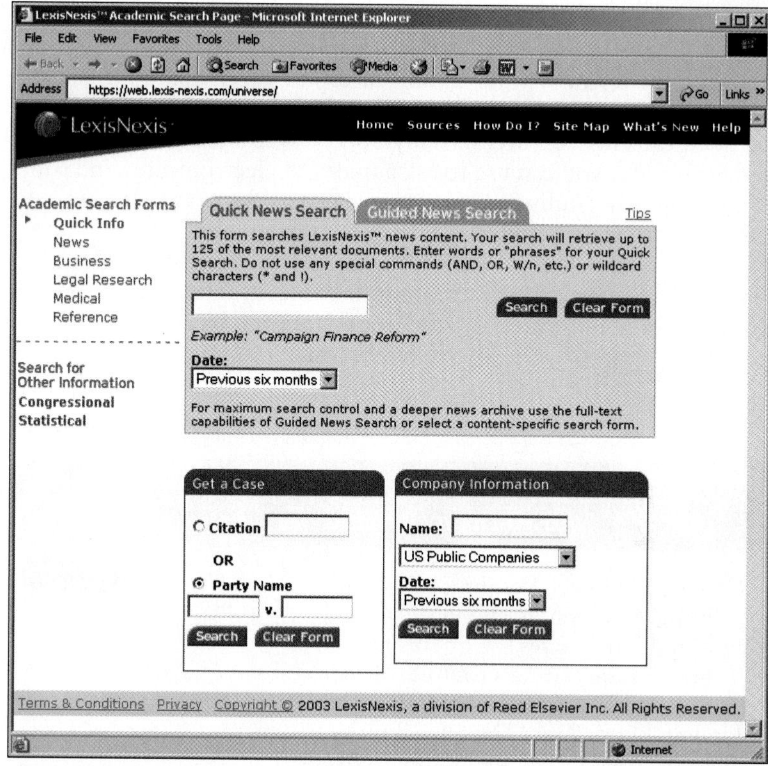

Figure 12.5 Search page from *LexisNexis Academic Universe*, a library subscription database.

and the information can be viewed and printed out. Increasingly, however, CD-ROMs and DVDs are being phased out in favor of password-protected Web-based systems.

12b Doing Focused Library Research

Once you have completed your exploratory research and formulated your research question, it is time to move to focused research. During **focused research,** you examine the specialized reference works, books, and articles devoted specifically to your topic. At this stage, you may also need to make use of the special services that many college libraries provide.

If your library has a Web site (and most libraries do), you may find it enables you to access to more than just the library catalog or the various periodicals to which it subscribes. In fact, many library Web sites are gateways to a vast amount of information, including research guides on a wide variety of topics; electronic journals and newspapers to which the library subscribes; and links to recommended Internet resources. Many library Web sites also include online forms that you can use to ask a question electronically, and some even include an online chat service that enables you to access a librarian from your home or residence hall computer.

Some of the library Web sites you can visit are listed below, but remember to check your own library's Web site and to ask at the reference desk about available resources. You may be surprised to discover how "wired" your library has become.

http://kirsznermandell.wadsworth.com

Computer Tip: Web Resources for Focused Library Research

General Reference Resources (Carnegie-Mellon U.)
    http://eserver.org/reference/
How to Find Articles (U. of Toronto)
    http://library.scar.utoronto.ca/Bladen_Library/Research101/findart.htm
Finding Books (U. of Dayton Libraries—some restrictions)
    http://www.udayton.edu/~library/daynet
Internet Public Library—Newspapers
    http://aristotle.ipl.org/cgi-bin/reading/news.out.pl
Internet Public Library—Magazines
    http://aristotle.ipl.org/reading/serials/
Primary vs. Secondary Sources (U. of Toronto)
    http://library.scar.utoronto.ca/Bladen_Library/Research101/primary.htm
Library Catalogs—Terminology
    http://www.nucat.library.nwu.edu
Library Catalogs—Dewey Decimal System
    http://www.oclc.org/fp/

(1) Consulting Specialized Reference Works

During your exploratory research, you used general reference works to help you narrow your topic and formulate your research question. Now, you can access specialized works to find facts, examples, statistics, definitions, and expert opinion.

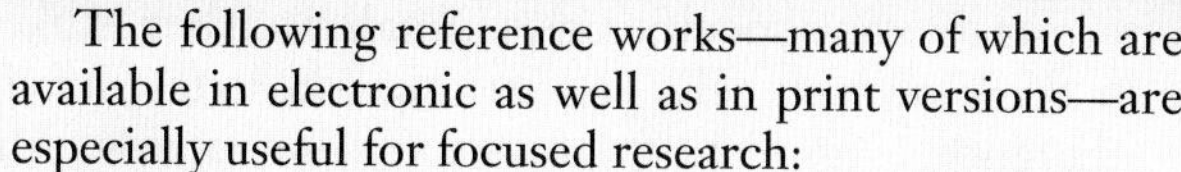

Close-up: Specialized Reference Works

The following reference works—many of which are available in electronic as well as in print versions—are especially useful for focused research:

Unabridged Dictionaries **Unabridged dictionaries,** such as the *Oxford English Dictionary*, are comprehensive works that give detailed information about words.

Special Dictionaries These dictionaries focus on such topics as usage, synonyms, slang and idioms, etymologies, and foreign terms; some focus on specific disciplines, such as accounting or law.

Yearbooks and Almanacs A **yearbook** is an annual publication that updates factual and statistical information already published in a reference source. An **almanac** provides lists, charts, and statistics about a wide variety of subjects.

World Almanac Includes statistics about government, population, sports, and many other subjects. Published annually since 1868.

Information Please Almanac Includes information unavailable in the *World Almanac*. Published annually since 1947.

Facts on File Covering 1940 to the present, this work offers digests of important news stories from metropolitan newspapers.

Editorials on File Reprints important editorials from American and Canadian newspapers.

Statistical Abstract of the United States Summarizes the statistics gathered by the US government. Published annually.

Atlases An **atlas** contains maps and charts as well as historical, cultural, political, and economic information.

National Geographic Atlas of the World (National Geographic Society) The most up-to-date atlas available.

Rand McNally Cosmopolitan World Atlas A modern and extremely legible medium-sized atlas.

We the People: An Atlas of America's Ethnic Diversity Presents information about specific ethnic groups. Maps show immigration routes and settlement patterns.

Quotation Books A **quotation book** contains numerous quotations on a wide variety of subjects. Such quotations can be useful for your paper's introductory and concluding paragraphs.

Bartlett's Familiar Quotations Quotations are arranged chronologically by author.

The Home Book of Quotations Quotations are arranged by subject. An author index and a keyword index are also included.

(2) Consulting Books

The online catalog gives you the information you need—specifically, the call numbers—for locating specific titles. A **call number** is like a book's address in the library: it tells you exactly where to find the book you are looking for. (Figure 12.6 shows an online catalog entry for a book.)

File Edit View Favorites Tools Help

Back Search Favorites Media

Address http://utdirect.utexas.edu/lib/utnetcat/full.WBX?search_type=FL&search_text=NORRIS%2C+PIPP Go Links

UTNetCAT Search Results

THE GENERAL LIBRARIES • THE UNIVERSITY OF TEXAS AT AUSTIN

New Search Title (omit initial article) Search

FULL DISPLAY

AUTHOR:
Norris, Pippa

TITLE:
Digital divide : civic engagement, information poverty, and the Internet worldwide / Pippa Norris.

PUBLISHED:
Cambridge ; New York : Cambridge University Press, 2001.

DESCRIPTION:
xv, 303 p. : ill. ; 24 cm.

SERIES:
Communication, society, and politics

NOTES:
Includes bibliographical references (p. 273-285) and index.

SUBJECTS:
Digital divide.
Internet--Political aspects.
Internet--Social aspects.
Political participation--Computer network resources.

ISBN:
0521807514 (hb.)
0521002230 (pb.)

OCLC NUMBER:
46359519

Done Internet

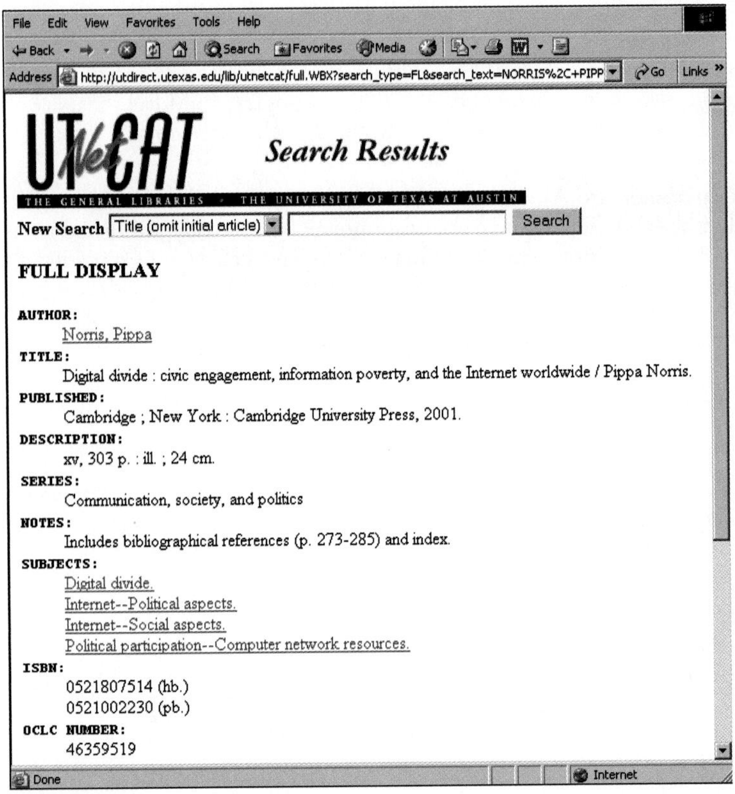

Figure 12.6 Online catalog entry for a book.

Once you become familiar with the physical layout of the library and the classification system your library uses, you should find it quite simple to locate the books you need.

Close-up: Library Materials

The Circulating Collection

- Books (hardback and paperback)—novels, essay collections, biographies, and so on

- Periodicals—newspapers, magazines, and journals
- CDs, audiotapes, and videotapes—music, films, speeches, and so on
- Large-print books and Books-on-Tape

The Reference Collection

- Dictionaries, encyclopedias, handbooks, and atlases that provide facts and background information
- Bibliographies and indexes that tell you what source material is available for the subject you are researching
- Special subject guides that help you find detailed information quickly

The Dewey Decimal Classification System Some public libraries, as well as some smaller college libraries, arrange books according to the **Dewey Decimal Classification System** (DDC). This organizational system arranges all holdings in the library into ten broad areas and then assigns them numbers.

Close-up: Dewey Decimal Subject Numbers

000–099	General knowledge
100–199	Philosophy
200–299	Religion
300–399	Social sciences
400–499	Language
500–599	Pure sciences
600–699	Technology (applied sciences)
700–799	Fine arts
800–899	Literature
900–999	History

This means that if you are working on a science-related topic, browsing through the books on the 500 shelves may help you find useful information about your topic.

The Library of Congress Classification System The books on the shelves of your college library are most likely arranged according to the **Library of Congress Classification System**. Because the library of Congress in Washington, DC, contains almost every book ever published in the United States, it uses a flexible system of classification that can accommodate an ever-growing base of information. Once you understand this classification system, you can browse through your library's shelves with a sense of what material is there and where it is located.

Close-up: Library of Congress Classification System

A	General works
B	Philosophy, psychology, and religion
C–F	History
G	Geography, anthropology, recreation
H	Social science
J	Political science
K	Law
L	Education
M	Music
N	Fine arts
P	Language and literature
Q	Science
R	Medicine
S	Agriculture
T	Technology
U	Military science
V	Naval science
Z	Bibliography and library sciences

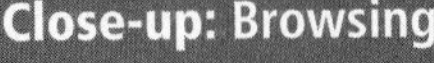

Close-up: Browsing

When you locate a book in the library, take some time to browse. Libraries shelve books according to general subject areas—philosophy, history, political science, and so on. If you browse in the general area of the book you located, you just may find other books that are relevant to your topic.

Checklist: Tracking Down a Missing Book

Problem

Book has been checked out of library.

Book is not in library's collection.

Possible Solution

- ☐ Consult person at circulation desk.
- ☐ Check other nearby libraries.
- ☐ Ask instructor if he or she owns a copy.
- ☐ Arrange for interlibrary loan (if time permits).

Problem	Possible Solution
Journal is not in library's collection/article is ripped out of journal.	☐ Arrange for interlibrary loan (if time permits). ☐ Check to see whether article is available in a full-text database. ☐ Ask librarian whether article has been reprinted as part of a collection.

(3) Consulting Articles

A **periodical** is a newspaper, magazine, scholarly journal, or other publication published at regular intervals (weekly, monthly, or quarterly). Articles in scholarly journals can be the best, most reliable sources you can find on a subject; they provide current information and are written by experts on the topic. And, because these journals focus on a particular subject area, they can provide in-depth analysis.

FAQs links

NOTE: You cannot access most scholarly journals on the free Internet. Although you may occasionally find individual articles on the Internet, the easiest and most reliable way to access scholarly journals is through one of the databases in your college library.

Periodical indexes are databases that list articles from a selected group of magazines, newspapers, or scholarly journals. These databases may be available in bound volumes, on microfilm or microfiche, and on CD-ROM or DVD; however, most libraries now offer them online. These databases are updated frequently and provide the most current information available.

Close-up: Frequently Used Subscription Databases

Choosing the right periodical index for your research is important. Each database, whether print or electronic, has a different focus and indexes different magazines or journals. Some include only citations; others include the full text of articles. Some cover many subjects or disciplines; others cover one subject or discipline in great detail. Some include only fairly recent articles; others go back many years. Some focus on news-reporting sources and popular magazines; others include only articles from scholarly and professional journals.

Using a database that is not appropriate for your topic leads to wasted time and frustration. For example, searching a database that

(continued)

Frequently used subscription databases (continued)

focuses on the humanities will not help you much if you are looking for information on a business topic, such as *corporate crime.*

The following subscription databases are found in most academic libraries. (Be sure to check your library's Web site or ask a librarian about those available to you.)

General Indexes	**Description**
Ebscohost	Database system for thousands of periodical articles on many subjects
Expanded Academic ASAP	A largely full-text database covering all subjects in thousands of magazines and scholarly journals
FirstSearch	Full-text articles from many popular and scholarly periodicals
LexisNexis Academic Universe	Includes full-text articles from national, international, and local newspapers. Also includes large legal and business sections.
Readers' Guide to Periodical Literature	Index to popular periodicals.

Specialized Indexes	**Description**
Dow Jones Interactive	Full text of articles from US newspapers and trade journals
ERIC	Largest database of education-related journal articles and reports in the world
General BusinessFile ASAP	A full-text database covering business topics
PubMed (MEDLINE)	Covers articles in medical journals. Some may be available in full text.
PsycINFO	Covers psychology and related fields
Sociological Abstracts	Covers the social sciences

(4) Finding Primary and Secondary Sources

See 11f2

Primary sources give firsthand accounts of topics or events. They include diaries, letters, speeches, manuscripts, memoirs, autobiographies, records of governments or organizations, newspaper articles, and even books written at the time an event occurred. Primary sources also include photographs, maps, films, tape recordings, novels, short stories, poems, or plays.

Checklist: Finding Primary Sources

- ☐ Do a keyword search of your online catalog. Use keywords that combine your topic with additional terms that describe the format of the primary source—for example, *slaves* AND *narratives.*
- ☐ See if the online catalog lists any bibliographies that might include primary sources. For example, a bibliography on an author might list works *by* the author (primary sources) as well as works *about* the author (secondary sources).
- ☐ Check with a reference librarian to see if your library subscribes to any databases that contain full-text primary sources.
- ☐ Check with a reference librarian to see if your library houses government publications that may include primary sources.
- ☐ Check with a reference librarian to see if your library houses any manuscripts.
- ☐ Use the Internet to find digitized collections of primary source materials—for example, documents that relate to US history, transcripts of television shows, or video clips.

Secondary sources are accounts or interpretations of topics or events. In many cases, their purpose is to interpret or analyze primary sources. Secondary sources include textbooks, literary criticism, and encyclopedias. See 11f2

Checklist: Finding Secondary Sources

- ☐ Search your library's online catalog for books. Combine a term that describes your topic with terms such as *interpretation*, *criticism*, or *bibliography*.
- ☐ Search the library's subscription databases for articles in scholarly journals, popular magazines, and newspapers that discuss the causes, effects, and interpretation of events.
- ☐ Check the notes, bibliographies, and works-cited lists at the end of books and articles.
- ☐ Do a keyword search on the Internet—but be sure to critically evaluate any information you find.

(5) Using Special Library Resources

As you do focused research, ask a librarian for help if you plan to use any of the library's special services or collections.

Close-up: Special Library Resources

The following resources are available in most academic libraries:

- **Interlibrary Loans** Your library may be part of a library system that allows loans of books from one location to another. If this is the case, a loan of a book usually takes no more than a day or two. However, be sure to check with your librarian. If the loan takes longer, you may not be able to take advantage of this service unless you initiate the loan early in your research.
- **Special Collections** Your library may house special collections of books, manuscripts, or documents. (In addition, churches, ethnic societies, historical trusts, and museums sometimes have material that you cannot find anywhere else.)
- **Vertical File** The vertical file includes pamphlets from a variety of organizations and interest groups, newspaper clippings, and other material collected by librarians because of its relevance to the research interests of your college's population.
- **Government Documents** Federal, state, and local governments publish a variety of print and electronic materials, ranging from consumer information to detailed statistical reports. A large university library may have a separate government documents area with its own catalog or index. The *Monthly Catalog of U.S. Government Publications* may be located either there or among the indexes in the reference area.

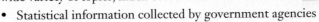

Close-up: Finding Government Publications

The US Government publishes information on a wide variety of topics, much of it accessible on the Web.

- Statistical information collected by government agencies
- Reports issued by government agencies such as the Environmental Protection Agency, the Department of Education, and NASA
- Primary research collections in the National Archives, presidential libraries, and the four national libraries
- US Supreme Court decisions
- Information about members of Congress and other government officials
- Legislation
- Presidential papers, political speeches, treaties, and US patents

NOTE: A good Web site for locating government publications is http://www.firstgov.gov. This Web site is a **gateway** (a site designed to be a starting point, complete with links, search tools, and information) to materials published by the US government.

Exercise 1

Which library research sources would you consult to find the following information?

1. A discussion of Monica Ali's novel *Brick Lane* (2003)
2. A government publication about how to heat your home with solar energy
3. Biographical information about the American anthropologist Margaret Mead
4. Books about Margaret Mead and her work
5. Organizational literature about what is being done to prevent the killing of wolves in North America
6. Information about the theories of Albert Einstein
7. Current information about the tobacco lobby
8. The address at which to contact Edward P. Jones, an American writer
9. Whether your college library has *The Human Use of Human Beings* by Norbert Wiener
10. Current information about AmeriCorps

12c Evaluating Print and Electronic Sources

Whenever you find a source (print or electronic), take the time to **evaluate** it—to assess its usefulness and its reliability. To determine the usefulness of a library source, ask the following questions:

1. **Does the source treat your topic in enough detail?** To be useful, the source should treat your topic in detail. Skim a book's table of contents and index for references to your topic. To be of any real help, a book should include a section or chapter on your topic, not simply a footnote or brief reference. For articles, either read the abstract or skim the entire article for key facts, looking closely at section headings, information set in boldface

type, and topic sentences. An article should have your topic as its central subject (or at least one of its main concerns).

2. **Is the source current?** The date of publication tells you whether the information in a book or article is up to date. A source's currency is particularly important for scientific and technological subjects, but even in the humanities, new discoveries and new ways of thinking lead scholars to reevaluate and modify their ideas. Be sure to check with your instructor to see if he or she prefers sources that have been published after a particular date.
3. **Is the source respected?** A contemporary review of a source can help you make this assessment. *Book Review Digest*, available in the reference section of your library, lists popular books that have been reviewed in at least three newspapers or magazines and includes excerpts from representative reviews. Book reviews are also available from the *New York Times Book Review*'s Web site, http://www.nytimes.com/books, which includes the text of book reviews that the newspaper has published since 1997.
4. **Is the source reliable?** Is a piece of writing largely fact or unsubstantiated opinion? Does the author support his or her conclusions? Does the author include documentation? Is the supporting information balanced? Is the author objective, or does he or she have a particular agenda to advance? Is the author associated with a special-interest group that may affect his or her view of the issue? Compare a few statements with a neutral source—a textbook or an encyclopedia, for instance—to see whether an author seems to be slanting facts.

In general, **scholarly publications**—books and journals aimed at an audience of expert readers—are more respected and reliable than **popular publications**—books, magazines, and newspapers aimed at an audience of general readers. However, assuming they are current, written by reputable authors, and documented, articles from some popular publications may be appropriate for your research. Remember, though, that many popular publications do not adhere to the same rigorous standards as scholarly publications do. For example, although some popular periodicals (such as *Atlantic Monthly* and *Harper's*) generally contain articles that are reliable and carefully researched, other periodicals may not. In addition, although scholarly books and articles go through a long process of peer review before they are published, popular publications often do not. For these reasons, before you use information from popular sources, such as *Newsweek* or *Sports Illustrated*, check with your instructor.

Close-up: Scholarly versus Popular Publications

Scholarly Publications	Popular Publications
Scholarly publications report the results of research.	Popular publications entertain and inform.
Scholarly publications are frequently published by a university press or have some connection with a university or academic organization.	Popular publications are published by commercial presses.
Scholarly publications are **refereed;** that is, an editorial board or group of expert reviewers determines what will be published.	Popular publications are usually not refereed.
Scholarly publications are usually written by someone who is a recognized authority in the field about which he or she is writing.	Popular publications may be written by experts in a particular field, but more often they are written by freelance or staff writers.
Scholarly publications are written for a scholarly audience, so they often use technical vocabulary and include challenging content.	Popular publications are written for general readers, so they usually use an accessible vocabulary and do not offer challenging content.
Scholarly publications nearly always contain extensive documentation as well as a bibliography of works consulted.	Popular publications rarely cite sources or use documentation.
Scholarly publications are published primarily because they make a contribution to a particular field of study.	Popular publications are published primarily to make a profit.

Exercise 2

Read the following paragraphs carefully, paying close attention to the information provided about their sources and authors as well as to their content. Decide which sources would be most useful and reliable in supporting the thesis "Winning the right to vote has (or has not) significantly changed the role of women in national politics." Which sources, if any, should be disregarded? Which would you examine first? Why?

1. Almost forty years after the adoption of the Nineteenth Amendment, a number of promised or threatened events have failed to materialize. The millennium has not arrived, but neither has the country's social fabric been destroyed. Nor have women organized a political party to elect only women candidates to public office. . . . Instead, women have shown the same tendency to divide along orthodox party lines as male voters. (Eleanor Flexner, *Century of Struggle*, Atheneum, 1968. *A scholarly treatment of women's roles in America since the Mayflower, this book was well reviewed by historians.*)
2. Woman has been the great unpaid laborer of the world, and although within the last two decades a vast number of new employments have been opened to her, statistics prove that in the great majority of these, she is not paid according to the value of the work done, but according to sex. The opening of all industries to women, and the wage question as connected with her, are the most subtle and profound questions of political economy, closely interwoven with the rights of self-government. (Susan B. Anthony; first appeared in Vol. I of *The History of Woman Suffrage;* reprinted in *Voices from Women's Liberation*, ed. Leslie B. Tanner, NAL, 1970. *An important figure in the battle for women's suffrage, Susan B. Anthony* [1820–1906] *also lectured and wrote on abolition and temperance.*)
3. Women . . . have never been prepared to assume responsibility; we have never been prepared to make demands upon ourselves; we have never been taught to expect the development of what is best in ourselves because no one has ever expected *anything* of us—or for us. Because no one has ever had any intention of turning over any serious work to us. (Vivian Gornick, "The Next Great Moment in History Is Ours," *Village Voice*, 1969. *The Voice is a liberal New York City weekly.*)
4. With women as half the country's elected representatives, and a woman President once in a while, the country's machismo problems would be greatly reduced. The old-fashioned idea that manhood depends on violence and victory is, after all, an important part of our troubles. . . . I'm not saying that women leaders would eliminate violence. We are not more moral than men; we are only uncorrupted by power so far. When we do acquire power, we might turn out to have an equal impulse toward aggression. (Gloria Steinem, "What It Would Be Like If Women Win," *Time*, 1970. *Steinem, a well-known feminist and journalist, is one of the founders of* Ms. *magazine.*)

5. Nineteen eighty-two was the year that time ran out for the proposed equal rights amendment. Eleanor Smeal, president of the National Organization for Women, the group that headed the intense 10-year struggle for the ERA, conceded defeat on June 24. Only 24 words in all, the ERA read simply: "Equality of rights under the law shall not be denied or abridged by the United States or by any state on account of sex." Two major opinion polls had reported just weeks before the ERA's defeat that a majority of Americans continued to favor the amendment. (June Foley, "Women 1982: The Year That Time Ran Out," *The World Almanac & Book of Facts*, 1983.)
6. When you think about it, right-wing victories have almost always depended on *turning on* the conservative minority, and *turning off* everybody else. This was done categorically by denying suffrage to black men and to women of all races; physically, by implementing poll taxes and literacy tests; and procedurally, by creating barriers that still make registration and voting a more daunting task here than in any other democracy. It's interesting that the psychological turnoff—the idea that politics is a dirty game, and voting doesn't matter—began to be pushed just as the 1960s civil rights movement was showing the nation that voting could be meaningful. (Gloria Steinem, "Voting as Rebellion," *Ms.* Sept./Oct. 1996.)
7. It won't happen this year. But the next chance at the White House is only four years away, and more women than you might think are already laying the groundwork for their own presidential bids. Bolstered by changing public attitudes, women in politics no longer assume that the Oval Office will always be a male bastion. In 1936, when George Gallup first asked people whether they would "vote for a woman for president if she qualified in every other respect," 65 percent said they would not. Back then, women were only slightly more open to the idea than men. Things are far different today. A recent poll shows that 90 percent of Americans, men included, say they could support a woman for president. (Eleanor Clift and Tom Brazaitis, *Madam President*, ©2000 by Eleanor Clift and Tom Brazaitis by Scribner. *The authors profile the women who they say are positioning themselves to be president.*)

12d Doing Field Research

In addition to the research you do in the library and on the Internet, some projects may require you to conduct an interview or to carry out a survey.

Close-up: Electronic Research Tools

When you think of conducting an interview or survey, you may think that all you need are a pencil and notepad—or, in the case of an interview, a cassette recorder. Although these are still necessary tools, you may require additional equipment. For example, you might consider using digital video and audio recorders, as well as digital cameras, all of which allow for direct upload to your computer.

(1) Conducting an Interview

An **interview** often gives you material that you cannot get by any other means—for instance, biographical information, a firsthand account of an event, or the opinions of an expert.

http://kirsznermandell.wadsworth.com

Computer Tip: Conducting an Email Interview

Using email to conduct an interview can save you a great deal of time. Before you send your questions, make sure the person is willing to cooperate. If the person agrees, send a short list of specific questions. After you have received the answers, send a response thanking the person for his or her cooperation.

The kinds of questions you ask in an interview depend on the information you want. **Open-ended questions**—questions designed to elicit general information—allow a respondent great flexibility in answering: "*Do you think students today are motivated? Why or why not?*" **Closed-ended questions**—questions intended to elicit specific information—enable you to zero in on a particular detail about a subject: "*How much money did the government's cost-cutting programs actually save?*"

Checklist: Conducting an Interview

- ☐ Always make an appointment.
- ☐ Prepare a list of specific questions tailored to the subject matter and the time limit of your interview.

- ☐ Do background reading about your topic. (Do not ask for information that you can easily find elsewhere.)
- ☐ Have paper and a pen with you. If you want to record the interview, get your subject's permission in advance.
- ☐ Allow the person you are interviewing to complete an answer before you ask another question.
- ☐ Take notes, but continue to pay attention as you do so.
- ☐ Pay attention to the reactions of your interview subject.
- ☐ Be willing to depart from your prepared list of questions to ask follow-up questions.
- ☐ At the end of the interview, thank your subject for his or her time and cooperation.
- ☐ Send a brief note of thanks.

(2) Conducting a Survey

If you are examining a contemporary social, psychological, or economic issue—the level of satisfaction on your college campus, for instance—a **survey** of attitudes or opinions could be indispensable. Begin by identifying the group of people you will poll. This group can be a **convenient sample**—for example, people in your chemistry lecture—or a **random sample**—names chosen from a telephone directory, for instance. When you choose a sample, you must have enough respondents to convince readers that your sample is *significant.* If you poll ten people in your French class about an issue of college policy, and your university has ten thousand students, you cannot expect your readers to be convinced by your results.

You should also be sure your questions are worded clearly and designed to elicit the information you wish to get. For example, short-answer or multiple-choice questions elicit specific responses that can be easily quantified. Paragraph-length responses, however, can be difficult to quantify. Also, be sure that you do not ask so many questions that respondents lose interest and stop answering. Finally, be careful not to ask biased or leading questions.

If your population is your fellow students, you can slip questionnaires under their doors in the residence hall, or you can distribute them in class, if your instructor permits. If your questionnaire is brief, allow respondents a specific amount of time, and collect the forms yourself. If filling out forms on the spot will take too much time, request that responses be returned to you or placed in a box set up in a central location. (Questions and responses can also be exchanged by email.)

Determining exactly what your results tell you is challenging and sometimes unpredictable. For example, even though only 20 percent of your respondents may be fraternity members, the fact that nearly all fraternity members in your sample favor restrictions on hazing would be an unexpected and significant finding.

Checklist: Conducting a Survey

- ☐ Determine what you want to know.
- ☐ Select your sample.
- ☐ Design your questions.
- ☐ Distribute the questionnaires.
- ☐ Collect the questionnaires.
- ☐ Analyze the responses.
- ☐ Decide how to use the results in your paper.

Chapter 13

Doing Internet Research

Frequently Asked Questions

If I use the Internet, do I still have to go to the library? (p. 272)

What can I do to make my Web search more productive? (p. 278)

How do I choose the right search engine? (p. 278)

13a Understanding the Internet

The **Internet** is a vast system of networks that links millions of computers. Because of its size and diversity, the Internet allows people from all over the world to communicate quickly and easily.

Furthermore, because it is inexpensive to publish text, pictures, and sound online (via the Internet), businesses, government agencies, libraries, and universities are able to make available vast amounts of information: years' worth of newspaper articles, hundreds of thousands of pages of scientific or technical papers, government reports, images of all the paintings in a museum, virtual tours of historically significant buildings or sites—even an entire library of literature.

Close-up: Resources Available on the Internet

- Breaking news from a variety of news outlets
- Stock market quotes, sports, and other topics of current, popular interest
- Photographs, image files, and television and radio broadcasts
- Information disseminated by organizations, professional associations, and individuals
- Digitized collections of historical documents and primary sources
- Recent publications of the US and state governments and their agencies
- Some reference sources, such as online dictionaries, encyclopedias, phone books, and style manuals
- Current issues of some newspapers, magazines, and journals
- Complete texts of books (usually those published before 1920)

As you might imagine, the various components of the Internet have revolutionized the way scholars and students conduct research. Even with all its advantages, however, the Internet does not give you access to the high-quality print and electronic resources found in a typical college library. For this reason, you should consider the Internet to be a supplement to your library research, not a substitute for it.

Close-up: Limitations of Internet Research

FAQs links

- Many important and useful publications are available only in print or through the library's subscription databases and not on the Internet.
- An Internet search can yield far more information (most of it irrelevant to your topic) than you can reasonably handle or properly evaluate. The information in your college library will almost always be more focused and more useful than much of what you will find on the Internet.
- The information you see on an Internet site—unlike information in your library's subscription databases—may not be there when you try to access it at a later time. (For this reason, MLA recommends that you print out all Internet documents you use in your research.)
- Anyone can publish on the Internet, so sites can vary greatly in quality. Because librarians screen the material in your college library, it is likely to meet academic standards of reliability. (Even so, you still have to evaluate any information before you use it in a paper.) See 12c
- Although the authorship and affiliation of Internet documents can often be difficult or impossible to determine, this is not usually the case with the sources in your college library.

13b Using the World Wide Web for Research

When most people refer to the Internet, they actually mean the **World Wide Web,** which is just a part of the Internet. (**See 13c** for other components of the Internet that you can use in your research.) The Web relies on **hypertext links,** keywords highlighted in blue (and often underlined). By clicking your mouse on these links, you can move easily from one **Web page** (a single document) to another or from one **Web site** (a collection of Web pages) to another.

To carry out a Web search, you need a **Web browser,** a tool that enables you to view information on the Web. Two of the most popular browsers—*Microsoft Internet Explorer* and *Netscape Navigator*—display the full range of text, photos, sound, and video available in Web documents. (Most new computers come with one or both of these browsers already installed.)

NOTE: Other Web browsers include *Mozilla* and *Safari* (for the Mac). In addition, some browsers are designed especially for users with disabilities. (Figure 13.1 shows a screen from a Web browser that uses screen magnification and audio.)

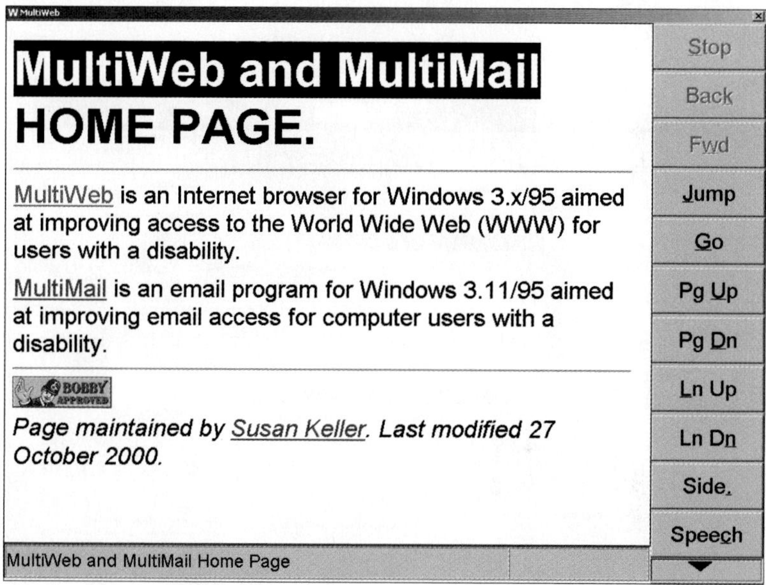

Figure 13.1 ***MultiWeb*** **browser.**

Once you are connected to the Internet, you use your browser to access a **search engine,** a program that searches for and retrieves documents available on the Internet.

There are three ways to use search engines to find the information you want: *entering an electronic address, using subject guides,* and *doing a keyword search.*

(1) Entering an Electronic Address

The most basic way to access information on the Web is to go directly to a specific electronic address, called a **URL** (uniform resource locator). Search engines and Web browsers display a dialog box that enables you to enter the URL of a particular Web site. You may also type the URL directly into the Location text field on your browser's **home page** (the page you see when you open your browser). (Figure 13.2 shows a dialog box and a location field.) Once you type in a URL and click on Open or Search (or hit Enter or the return key), you will be connected to the Web site you want. Make sure to type the URL exactly as it appears—without adding spaces or adding or deleting punctuation marks. Remember that omitting just a single letter or punctuation mark will send you to the wrong site—or to no site at all.

Figure 13.2 Entering an address in *Netscape Navigator*.

Close-up: What to Do If You Cannot Connect

If you cannot connect to the Web site that you want, do not give up. There are several strategies that you can use to help you connect.

- Wait a short period of time, and try again. If a Web site is extremely busy, it may block users.
- Make sure that you have typed in the URL correctly.

- If the URL is very long, delete a section of the end of the URL—from slash to slash—and try again.
- Try using just the base URL—the part that ends with *.com* or *.gov*. If this abbreviated URL does not take you where you want to go, you have an incorrect address.
- If you are following a link from one document to another and cannot connect, type the URL of the link into the location field of your search engine, and try again.

http://kirsznermandell.wadsworth.com

Computer Tip: Understanding URLs

The first section of a URL indicates the type of file being accessed. In the address http://www.google.com/images, *http* indicates that the file is in hypertext transfer protocol. After the colon and the two slashes is the name of the host site where the file is stored (www.google.com). The *www* tells the user that the Web site is on the World Wide Web, *google* is the domain name, and *com* shows that this is a commercial institution. Following this section is the directory path to the file (*images*).

For links to Web sites for exploratory and focused research, go to http://kirsznermandell.wadsworth.com ▶ *The Wadsworth Handbook* ▶ Chapter 13 ▶ Web Sites for Exploratory and Focused Research.

(2) Using Subject Guides

You can also use subject guides to help you locate information. Some search engines, such as *Yahoo!*, *About.com*, and *Look Smart*, contain a **subject guide**—a list of general categories (*Arts*, *Business*, *Computers*, and so on) from which you can choose. (Figure 13.3 on page 276 shows the home page of a search engine with a subject guide.) Each of these categories will lead you to a more specific list of categories and subcategories until, eventually, you get to the topic you want. For example, clicking on *Society* would lead you to *Activism* and then to *Animal Rights* and eventually to an article concerning cruelty to animals on factory farms. Although using subject guides is a time-consuming strategy for finding specific information, it can be an excellent tool during exploratory research, when you want to find or narrow a topic.

(3) Doing a Keyword Search

Finally, you can locate information by doing a **keyword search.** You do this by entering a keyword (or words) into your search engine's

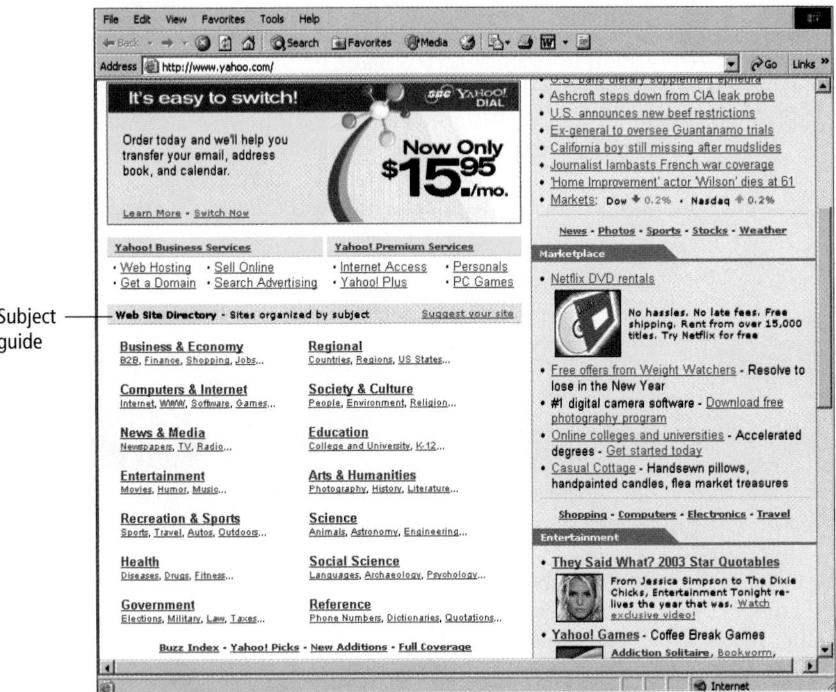

Figure 13.3 ***Yahoo!*** **home page with subject guide.**

search field. (Figure 13.4 shows a search engine's keyword search page.) The search engine will identify any site in its database on which the keyword (or words) you have typed appear. (These sites are called **hits.**) If, for example, you simply type *Civil War* (say, in hope of finding information on Fort Sumter during the Civil War), the search engine will generate an enormous list of hits—well over a million. This list will likely include, along with sites that might be relevant to your research, the Civil War Reenactors home page as well as sites that focus on Civil War music.

Because searching this way is inefficient and time consuming, you need to *focus* your search by using **search operators,** words and symbols that tell a search engine how to interpret your keywords. One way to focus your search is to put quotation marks around your search term (type *"Fort Sumter"* rather than *Fort Sumter*). This will direct the search engine to locate only documents containing this phrase.

Another way to focus your search is to carry out a **Boolean search,** combining keywords with AND, OR, NOT (typed in all capital letters), or a plus or minus sign to eliminate irrelevant hits

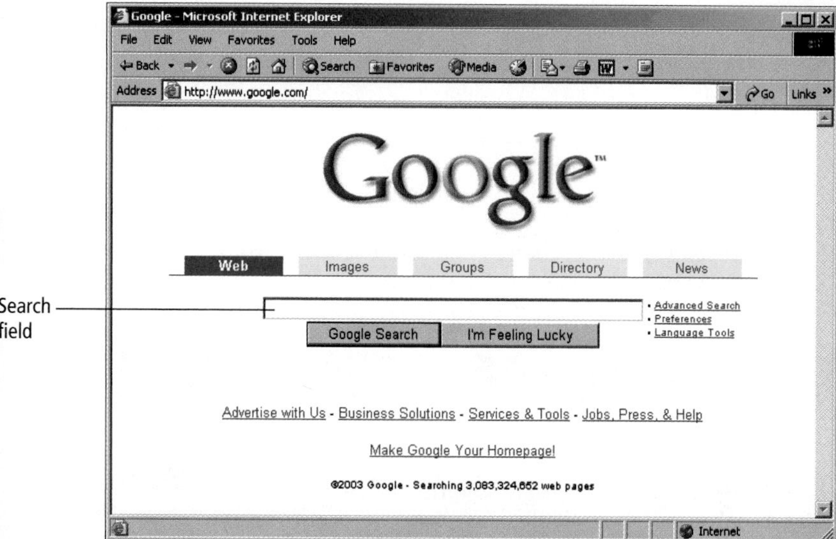

Figure 13.4 ***Google*** **keyword search page.**

from your search. (To do this type of search, you may have to select a search engine's Advanced Search option.) For example, to find Web pages that focus on the battle of Fort Sumter in the Civil War, type *Civil War* AND *Fort Sumter.* If you do, your search will yield only items that contain *both* terms. (If you typed in *Civil War* OR *Fort Sumter,* your search will yield items that contain *either* term.) Some search engines allow you to search using three or more keywords—*Civil War* AND *Fort Sumter* NOT *national monument,* for example. In this case, your search would yield items that contained both the terms *Civil War* and *Fort Sumter,* but not the term *national monument.* By limiting your search in this way, you would just get items that discussed Fort Sumter and the Civil War and eliminate items that discussed Fort Sumter's current use as a national monument. Focusing your search in this way enables you to avoid irrelevant Web pages.

http://kirsznermandell.wadsworth.com

Computer Tip: Using Search Operators

" " (quotation marks) Use quotation marks to search for a specific phrase: *"Baltimore Economy"*

AND Use AND to search for sites that contain both words: *Baltimore* AND *Economy*

(continued)

Using search operators (continued)

OR Use OR to search for sites that contain either word: *Baltimore* OR *Economy*

NOT Use NOT to exclude the word that comes after the NOT: *Baltimore* AND *Economy* NOT *Agriculture*

+ (plus sign) Use a plus sign to include the word that comes after it: *Baltimore* + *Economy*

– (minus sign) Use a minus sign to exclude the word that comes after it: *Baltimore* + *Economy* – *Agriculture*

Checklist: Getting the Most from Your Web Search

If you get too many hits:

- ☐ Read the Help screens; look for search tips specific to the search engine. Be sure you know how to search for an exact phrase.
- ☐ Use more specific terms.
- ☐ Combine search terms to narrow your search (use AND or + between terms).
- ☐ Scan the first screen of hits; they are probably the most relevant.
- ☐ Look for sites sponsored by the government, educational institutions, or professional organizations; they are probably the most reliable.

If you get too few hits:

- ☐ Check the library's subscription databases or online catalog instead. The topic may be one for which you are not likely to get high-quality results on the Web (literary criticism, for example).
- ☐ Check for spelling or typing errors.
- ☐ Try a broader search term that includes your topic.
- ☐ Think of other words or phrases that describe your topic.
- ☐ Try a different search engine or subject directory.
- ☐ Ask for help from your instructor or at the library's reference desk.

(4) Finding the Right Search Engine

Some search engines are more user-friendly than others; some allow for more sophisticated searching functions; some are updated more frequently; and some are more comprehensive than others. As you try out various search engines, you will probably settle on a favorite that you will turn to first whenever you need to find information.

Popular Search Engines

AllTheWeb (www.alltheweb.com): This excellent search engine provides comprehensive coverage of the Web. Many users think that this search engine is as good as *Google*. In addition to generating Web page results, *AllTheWeb* has the ability to search for news stories, pictures, video clips, MP3s, and FTP files.

AltaVista (www.altavista.com): Good, precise engine for focused searches. Fast and easy to use.

Ask Jeeves (www.ask.com): Good beginner's site. Allows you to narrow your search by asking questions, such as *Are dogs smarter than pigs?*

Excite (www.excite.com): Good for general topics. Because it searches over 250 million Web sites, you often get more information than you need.

Go (http://infoseek.go.com): Enables you to access information in a directory of reviewed sites, news stories, and Usenet groups.

Google (www.google.com): One of the best search engines available. Accesses a large database that includes both text and graphics. It is easy to navigate, and searches usually yield a high percentage of useful hits.

HotBot (www.hotbot.com): Excellent, fast search engine for locating specific information. Good search options allow you to fine-tune your searches.

Lycos (www.lycos.com): Enables you to search for specific media (graphics, for example). A somewhat small index of Web pages.

Teoma (www.teoma.com): Teoma is a search engine owned by *Ask Jeeves.* Although it has a smaller index of the Web than *Google* and *AllTheWeb,* it is very effective when it comes to answering questions. It contains a Refine feature that offers suggested topics to explore after you do a search. It also has a Resources section of results that will point you to linked resources about various topics.

WebCrawler (www.webcrawler.com): Good for beginners. Easy to use.

Yahoo! (www.yahoo.com): Good for exploratory research. Enables you to search using either subject headings or keywords. Searches its own indexes as well as the Web.

Because even the best search engines search only a fraction of what is on the Web, if you use only one search engine, you will most likely miss much valuable information. It is therefore a good idea to repeat each search with several different search engines or to use one of the **metasearch** or **metacrawler** engines that uses several search engines simultaneously. (Figure 13.5 shows a meta-search engine.)

NOTE: It is a good idea to begin a search by checking your library's Web site for a list of recommended Web sites, arranged by topic.

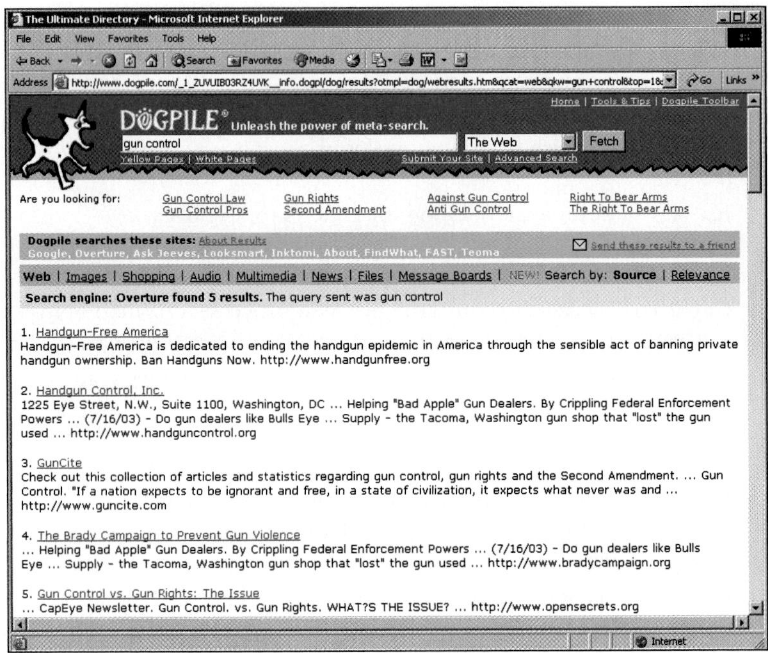

Figure 13.5 Search results for "gun control" in *Dogpile* metasearch engine.

http://kirsznermandell.wadsworth.com

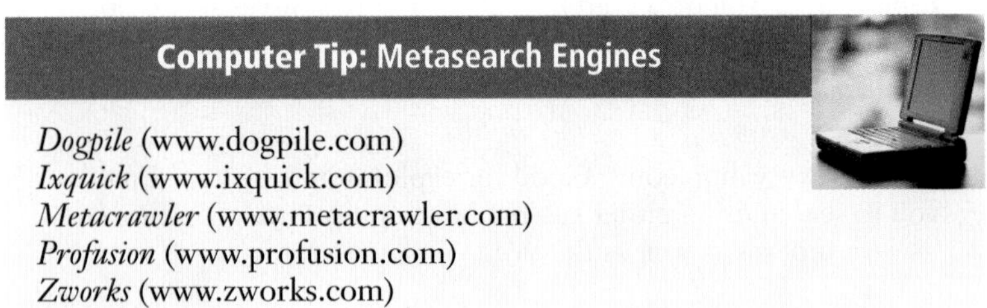

Computer Tip: Metasearch Engines

Dogpile (www.dogpile.com)
Ixquick (www.ixquick.com)
Metacrawler (www.metacrawler.com)
Profusion (www.profusion.com)
Zworks (www.zworks.com)

In addition to the popular general-purpose search engines and metasites, there are also numerous search engines devoted entirely to specific subject areas, such as literature, business, sports, and women's issues. Hundreds of such specialized search engines are indexed at

Allsearchengines.com (www.allsearchengines.com). These sites are especially useful during focused research, when you are looking for in-depth information about your topic.

http://kirsznermandell.wadsworth.com

Computer Tip: Specialized Search Engines

Voice of the Shuttle (humanities search engine)
http://vos.ucsb.edu/

Pilot-Search.com (literary search engine)
http://www.pilot-search.com/

FedWorld (US government database and report search engine)
http://www.fedworld.gov/

HealthFinder (health, nutrition, and diseases information for consumers)
http://www.healthfinder.gov/default.htm

The Internet Movie Database (search engine and database for film facts, reviews, and so on)
http://www.imdb.com

SportQuest (sports search engine)
http://www.sportquest.com/

FindLaw (legal search engine)
http://www.findlaw.com/

NOTE: *Search Engine Watch* at www.searchenginewatch.com maintains an extensive, comprehensive, and up-to-date list of the latest search engines. Not only does this site list search engines by category, but it also reviews them.

Checklist: Tips for Effective Searching

- ☐ **Choose your keywords carefully.** A search engine is only as good as the keywords you use. Use quotation marks and Boolean search operators to make your searches more productive. Review the Computer Tip box on pages 277–78 before you use any search engine.
- ☐ **Include enough terms.** If you are looking for information on housing, for example, search for several different variations of your keyword: *housing, houses, house buyer, buying houses,*

(continued)

Tips for effective searching (continued)

residential real estate, and so on. Some search engines, like *Infoseek*,automatically search plurals; others do not. Some, like *AltaVista*, automatically search variants of your keyword; others require you to think of the variants by yourself.

- ☐ **Choose the right search engine.** No one all-purpose search site exists. Make sure you review the tips for choosing a search engine on pages 278–81.
- ☐ **Use more than one search engine.** Because different search engines index different sites, try several. If one does not yield results after a few tries, switch to another. Also, do not forget to do a metasearch with a search engine like *Metacrawler.*
- ☐ **Add useful sites to your bookmarks or favorites list.** Whenever you find a particularly useful Web site, **bookmark** it by selecting this option on the menu bar of your browser (with some browsers, such as *Internet Explorer,* this option is called *Favorites*). If you add a site to your bookmark list, you can return to the site whenever you want to by opening the Bookmark menu and selecting it.

NOTE: Your Internet browser has a History feature that enables you to retrace the sites you visited during a particular period of time (which you specify). By using this feature, you can recall URLs that you may have forgotten to bookmark or sites that you cannot remember how you accessed. (You can find out how to access and customize your browser's History feature by consulting your browser's Help screen.)

13c Using Other Internet Tools

In addition to the World Wide Web, the Internet contains a number of other components that you can use to help you gather information for your research.

(1) Using Email

Email can be useful as you do research because it enables you to exchange ideas with classmates, ask questions of your instructors, and even conduct long-distance interviews. You can follow email links in

Web documents, and you can also transfer word-processing documents or other files (as email attachments) from one computer to another.

NOTE: If possible, send files as **email attachments.** The alternative—copying and pasting word-processing files directly into an email—frequently results in a loss of formatting. This can cause problems in documents such as works-cited pages, résumés, and outlines, making them impossible to read.

(2) Using Listservs

Listservs (sometimes called **discussion lists**), electronic mailing lists to which you must subscribe, enable you to communicate with groups of people interested in particular topics. (Many schools and even individual courses have their own listservs.) Individuals in a listserv send emails to a main email address, and these messages are routed to all members of the group. Some listserv subscribers may be experts who can answer your queries. Keep in mind, however, that you must evaluate any information you get from a listserv before you use it in your research.

(3) Using Newsgroups

Like listservs, **newsgroups** are discussion groups. Unlike listserv messages, which are sent to you as email, newsgroup messages are collected on the **Usenet** system, a global collection of news servers, where anyone can access them. In a sense, newsgroups function as gigantic bulletin boards where users post messages that others can read and respond to. Thus, newsgroups can provide specific information as well as suggestions about where to look for further information. Just as you would with a listserv, you should evaluate information you get from a newsgroup before you use it.

(4) Using FTP and Telnet

At one time, Internet users needed special software to access telnet and FTP. Now they can be accessed with most programs that access the Web.

FTP (file transfer protocol) enables you to transfer documents at high speed from one computer on the Internet to another. With FTP, you can get the full text of books and articles as well as pictures. The most common use for FTP is for downloading updates from computer software manufacturers.

Computer Tip: Compression Tools

Because many FTP files and folders are compressed for quicker download and are transferred in nonreadable form, you need a program to uncompress them to make them readable. Often, these compression utilities are freeware or shareware. Compressed files are usually referred to as *zipped* files, and suffixes such as *.zip* or *.rar* designate their file type.

Telnet is a program that enables you to make a connection via telephone to another computer on the Internet. With telnet, you can download anything from another host computer.

(5) Using MUDS, MOOS, IRCS, and Instant Messaging

With emails and listservs, there is a delay between the time a message is sent and the time it is received. **MUDS, MOOS, IRCS,** and **instant messaging** enable you to send and receive messages in real time. In other words, communication is **synchronous;** that is, messages are sent and received as they are typed. Synchronous communication programs are being used more and more in college settings—for class discussions, online workshops, and collaborative projects.

Checklist: Observing Netiquette

Netiquette refers to the guidelines that responsible users of the Internet should follow. When you use the Internet, especially email and synchronous communication, keep the following guidelines in mind.

- ☐ **Avoid shouting.** All-uppercase letters indicate that a person is SHOUTING. This can be distracting and irritating.
- ☐ **Watch your tone.** Make sure you send the message you actually intend to convey. What may sound humorous to you may seem sarcastic or impolite to someone else.
- ☐ **Be careful what you write.** Remember, anything you put in writing will be instantly sent to the address or addresses you have designated. Once you hit Send, it may be too late to call back your message. For this reason, treat an email message or a posting as you would a written letter. Take the

time to proofread and to consider carefully what you have written.

- ☐ **Respect the privacy of others.** Do not forward or post a message that you have received unless you have permission from the sender to do so.
- ☐ **Do not flame.** When you **flame,** you send an insulting electronic message. This tactic is both immature and counterproductive.
- ☐ **Make sure you use the correct electronic address.** Be certain that your message goes to the right person. Nothing is more embarrassing than sending a communication to the wrong address.
- ☐ **Use your computer facility ethically and responsibly.** Do not use computers in public labs for personal communications or for entertainment. This is a misuse of the facility, and it ties up equipment that others may be waiting to use.

Chapter 14

Evaluating Web Sites

Frequently Asked Questions

What does a Web site's URL tell me about its purpose? (p. 287)
How can I determine if an anonymous Web source is legitimate? (p. 290)
What should I keep in mind about a Web site's graphic design? (p. 294)

Web sites vary greatly in quality and reliability. Because it is so easy for anyone to operate a Web site and thereby publish anything, regardless of quality, critical evaluation of Web-based material is more important than evaluation of more traditional sources of information, such as books and journal articles.

Sources you find on the Web (and on the Internet in general) may present theories, rumors, hearsay, speculation, or even intentional misrepresentations as fact. Sometimes it is difficult to distinguish such questionable information from legitimate material because you do not know your source as well as you might know a reputable journal or magazine. To complicate matters further, unscrupulous individuals can (and sometimes do) represent themselves as respected authorities with impressive credentials, even using the names of other people, and make claims that seem credible but are not.

The proliferation of Web-based information has led to another disturbing problem. Many Web sites freely "borrow" material from other Web sites or from print sources without acknowledging these sources or documenting the information. If you inadvertently use "borrowed" information from one of these sites, you will be guilty of

See Ch. 16

plagiarism.

Determining the quality of a Web site is crucial if you plan to use it as a source for your research. If you are using a Web site for personal information or entertainment, it is probably enough just to be aware of what is legal and what is illegal (for example, you should not download copyrighted material, such as software or music, illegally posted on a Web site). However, if you are using the Internet to locate appropriate sources for a research project, you need to be much more careful. To evaluate a Web site, you must look closely at its *purpose*, *content*, and *format*.

14a Determining a Web Site's Purpose

In general terms, Web pages may be designed to inform, to persuade, or simply to entertain. More specifically, a site's purpose may be anything from advocating a political position to selling merchandise to disseminating news—or even promoting a person's private agenda. To assess a site's objectivity and reliability, you need to know its purpose. For example, you would hardly trust a fast-food chain's Web site to present an objective discussion of the role fast food plays in childhood obesity.

Close-up: Understanding URLs

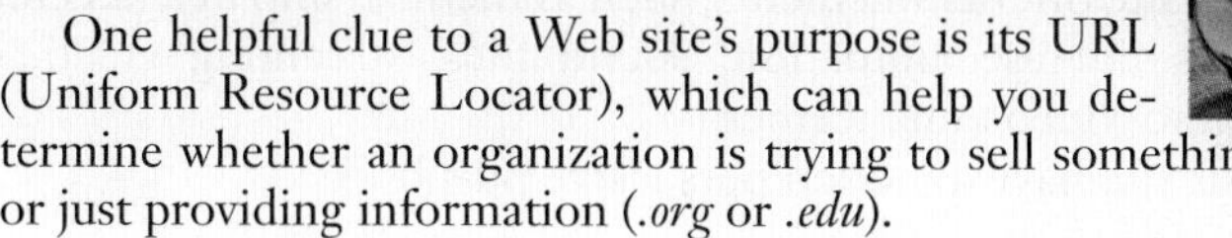

One helpful clue to a Web site's purpose is its URL (Uniform Resource Locator), which can help you determine whether an organization is trying to sell something (*.com*) or just providing information (*.org* or *.edu*).

.org = Organization
.com = Business
.edu = Educational institution
.gov = Government
.mil = Military
.net = Network
.xx = Two-letter country code, such as .us or .uk

FAQs

You can use the following six categories and the accompanying questions to help you determine a Web site's purpose.

Advocacy **Advocacy sites** support a cause or position and are usually sponsored by organizations (for profit or nonprofit) whose purpose is to influence public opinion. These sites may represent a large corporation, such as a national political party or candidate, or a special-interest group, such as the National Rifle Association or the Sierra Club. The URLs of these sites are most likely to end in *.org*.

- Does this site solicit membership and/or money?
- Is this site calling for a particular action?
- Does this site include a policy statement?

Business/Marketing These sites are maintained by commercial enterprises attempting to promote or sell products or services. The businesses may exist entirely online, or they may be affiliated with bricks-and-mortar stores or catalog businesses. The URLs of these sites will most likely end in *.com.*

- Does this site sell goods or services?
- Does this site request demographic information for marketing purposes?
- Does this site take online orders?
- Does this site offer a catalog?

Entertainment These sites are designed to entertain—for example, through humor, the arts, or music. Some sites exist purely for entertainment, while others may combine entertainment with marketing a product or advocating a viewpoint. The URLs of these sites will have a variety of endings.

- Does this site offer games or activities?
- Does this site offer enticements, such as membership in a fan club?
- Does this site use animation, sound files, streaming video, or other audio-video enhancements?
- Does this site have a hidden persuasive purpose?

Information/Reference These sites present factual information—for example, in online encyclopedias or almanacs. Remember, though, that some of these sites may also be marketing a product or service. The URLs of these sites most likely end in *.edu* or *.gov*, but some end in *.com.*

- Is the information conveyed in the form of tables, statistics, glossaries, or other accepted methods of presenting factual data?
- Does a recognized organization, government agency, or educational institution maintain the site?
- Can the source of the information in the site be verified?

News These sites provide up-to-the-minute local, national, or international news. Some are affiliated with the print or broadcast media, but others exist only online. The URLs of these sites are likely to end in *.com.*

- Is the organization responsible for this information a recognized news outlet?
- Does the site clearly separate news from editorial comment?

Personal Sites maintained by individuals may be published independently or be affiliated with larger institutions. The URLs of these sites will frequently contain a mark called a tilde (~).

- Is the site's content primarily personal opinion?
- Is the creator of the site anonymous?
- Does an institution or organization sponsor the site?

Exercise 1

Examine the following home page for the Mothers Against Drunk Driving Web site (Figure 14.1). Determine which purpose—advocacy, business/marketing, entertainment, information/reference, news, or personal—the site serves. Does it serve more than one purpose?

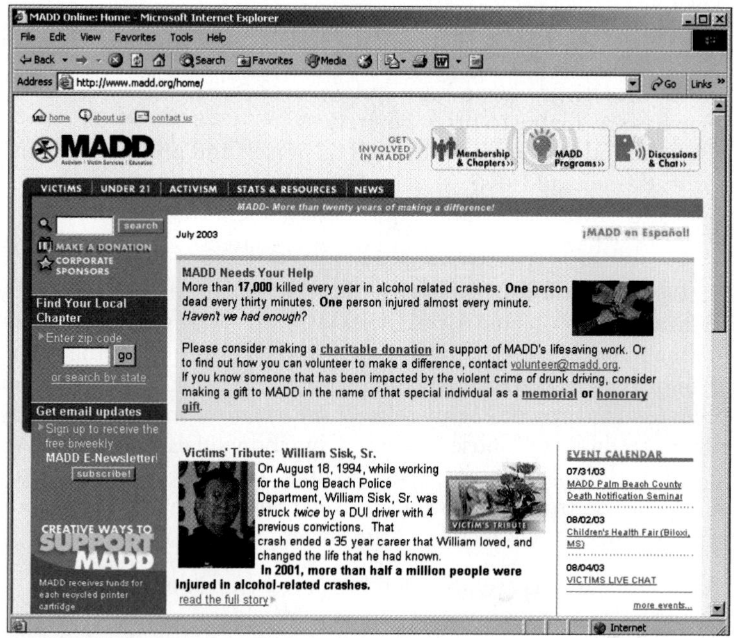

Figure 14.1 MADD home page.

Exercise 2

Work in a small group to select a controversial issue or topic of interest. Then, search your topic on the Internet. Select three to five Web sites on this topic, and determine each site's purpose.

14b Evaluating a Web Site's Content

Once you have determined the purpose of a Web site, you should closely examine its content. If the site exists primarily to entertain, market goods and services, advocate a particular viewpoint, or provide personal information, you should immediately be on the alert for possible biases or other problems. Even if the site appears to be informational, you will still have to evaluate its content in terms of *accuracy*, *credibility*, *objectivity*, *currency*, *coverage* or *scope*, and *stability*.

Accuracy **Accuracy** refers to the reliability of the material itself and to the use of proper documentation. Keep in mind that factual errors should cause you to question the reliability of the material you are reading.

- Is the text free of errors in sentence structure, usage, and grammar?
- Does the site provide a list of references?
- Are links available to other references?
- Has the author identified himself or herself and provided an email or traditional address?
- Does the author encourage questions and comments?
- Can information be verified in other resources?

Credibility **Credibility** refers to the credentials of the person or organization responsible for the site. Web sites vary greatly in quality and reliability. Those operated by well-known institutions (the Smithsonian or the US Department of Health and Human Services, for example) tend to provide highly reliable information and therefore have built-in credibility. Those operated by individuals (personal Web pages, for example) are often less reliable. Before using information that you access from a Web site, consider the credibility of the sponsoring organization as well as of the author of the material.

- What credentials are provided for the author or authors?
- Is the author an authority in his or her field?
- Does the site claim to be **refereed?** In other words, does an editorial board or a group of experts determine what material appears on the Web site, or is this an individual decision?
- Does the sponsoring organization exist apart from its Web presence?
- Does the site display a corporate logo? If so, is this corporation a legitimate one?
- Can you determine how long the Web site has existed?

Checklist: Determining the Legitimacy of an Anonymous Web Source

FAQs link

When a Web source is anonymous, you have to take special measures to determine its legitimacy. The following strategies can help you get the information you need to assess the legitimacy of an anonymous source.

- ☐ **Post a query.** If you get information from a newsgroup or a listserv, ask others in the group what they know about the source and its author.
- ☐ **Follow the links.** Follow the hypertext links in a document to other documents. If the links take you to legitimate sources, you know that the author is aware of these sources of information.
- ☐ **Do a keyword search.** Do a search using the name of the organization or the article as keywords. Other documents (or citations in other works) may identify the author, and this will help you assess the legitimacy of your source.

Objectivity **Objectivity** refers to the degree to which a Web site exhibits bias. Some Web sites make no secret of their biases. They openly advocate a particular point of view or action, or they are clearly trying to sell something. The biases of other Web sites may be harder to identify. For example, a Web site may present itself as a source of factual information when it is actually advocating a specific point of view. You need to determine a site's biases before you use material as a resource for academic work.

- Does advertising appear in the text?
- Does a corporation, political organization, or special-interest group sponsor the site?
- Does the site provide links to sites with a political purpose?
- Does the site have an expressed policy concerning the advertising that it exhibits?
- Does the site express a particular viewpoint?

Currency **Currency** refers to how up to date a Web site is. The easiest way to assess a site's currency is to determine when it was last updated. Keep in mind, however, that even if the date on the site is current, the information that the site includes may not be.

- Is the most recent update available?
- Are all the links to other sites still functioning?
- Is the actual information on the page up to date?
- Does the site clearly identify the date it was created and revised?

Coverage or Scope **Coverage,** or **scope,** refers to the comprehensiveness of the information on a Web site. More is not necessarily better, but the information provided by some sites may be scanty or incomplete. Others may provide information that is no more than common knowledge. Still others may present discussions aimed at a targeted audience, such as high school students, and therefore may not be suitable for college-level research.

- Does the site provide wide coverage of the subject matter?
- Does the site provide in-depth coverage?
- Does the site provide information that is not available elsewhere?
- Does the site identify a target audience, particularly by age or grade level? Does the target audience suggest the site is appropriate for your research needs?

Stability **Stability** means that the site is being maintained and that it will be around when you want to access it again. If you use a Web site that is here today and gone tomorrow, it will be difficult for readers to check your sources or for you to obtain updated information. For this reason, you should print and keep copies of all material from Web sites that you use in your papers.

- Is the site updated regularly?
- Has the site been active for a long period of time?
- Is an organization or institution committed to financing and maintaining the site?

Exercise 3

Examine the following home page for the *Washington Post* Web site (Figure 14.2). Use the criteria discussed in 14b to evaluate its content in terms of accuracy, credibility, objectivity, currency, coverage or scope, and stability.

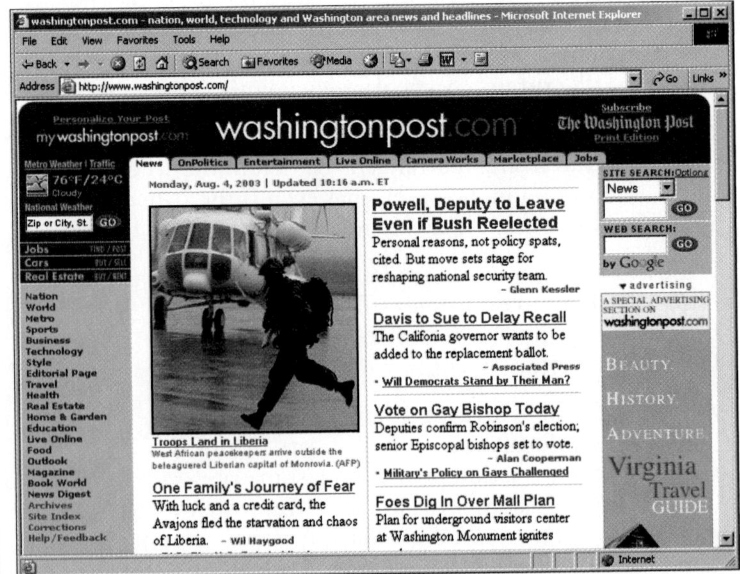

Figure 14.2 The *Washington Post* home page.

Exercise 4

Study the two Web pages shown in Figures 14.3 and 14.4. Use the criteria outlined in 14a to evaluate their purposes. Then, use the criteria in 14b to evaluate their content. Finally, write a paragraph in which you compare the two sites.

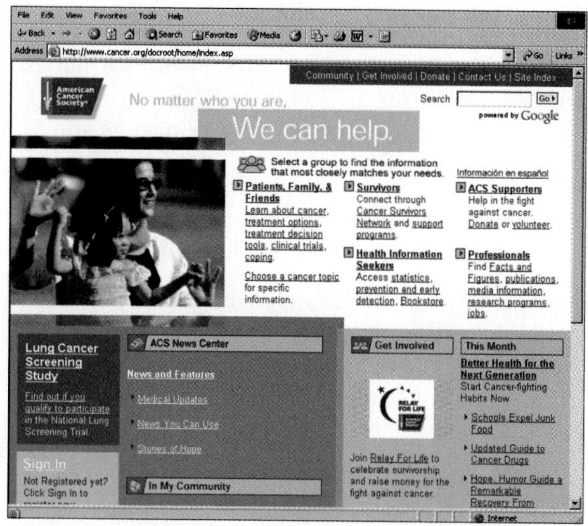

Figure 14.3 American Cancer Society home page.

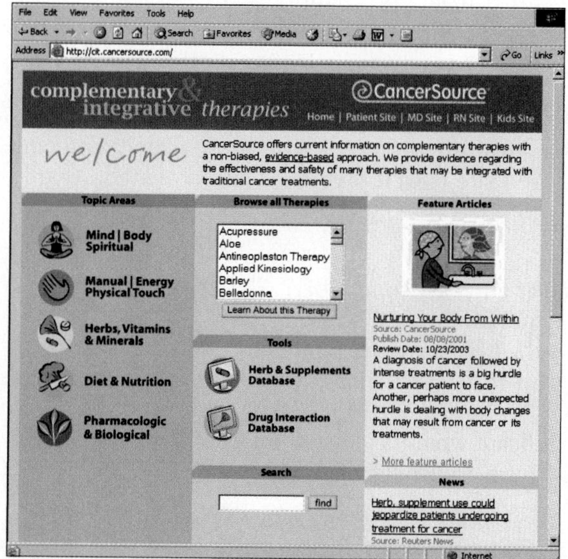

Figure 14.4 CancerSource Complementary & Integrative Therapies home page.

14c Evaluating a Web Site's Format

Format refers to the way text and graphics are arranged on the page. A sloppy, haphazard format should alert you to the possibility that the information on the site is suspect. Likewise, a site that overwhelms viewers with graphics should cause you to wonder if the graphics are a substitute for content. For this reason, format is an important criterion for evaluating a Web site. When you judge a Web site on the basis of format, pay careful attention to its *organization*, *graphic design*, and *ease of navigation*.

Organization **Organization** refers to the way information is structured—with headings, subheadings, hypertext links, and so on.

- Does the home page provide all the major headings you need to move easily to the other Web pages?
- Are links clearly and logically worded?
- Can you easily find what you want?

Graphic Design Graphic design refers to the artwork as well as the visual arrangement of text.

FAQs links

- Does the artwork serve a purpose, or is it purely ornamental?
- Is the home page free of clutter?
- Is advertising distinct from information?
- Are pages linked visually through color, logos, or other layout features?

Ease of Navigation **Navigation** refers to your progress as you move through a Web site from the home page to more deeply embedded information. If a Web site is well organized and designed, it will be easy to navigate.

- Is there a site map?
- Are the links clear and easy to identify?
- Does the site require a minimum of scrolling?
- Do the links lead where they claim to lead?
- Do the links lead to pages that are complete rather than under construction?
- Does the site indicate what its icons represent?
- Do links alert you to especially large files?

Exercise 5

Examine the home page for the Library of Congress Web site (Figure 14.5). Use the criteria in 14c to evaluate its format in terms of organization, graphic design, and ease of navigation.

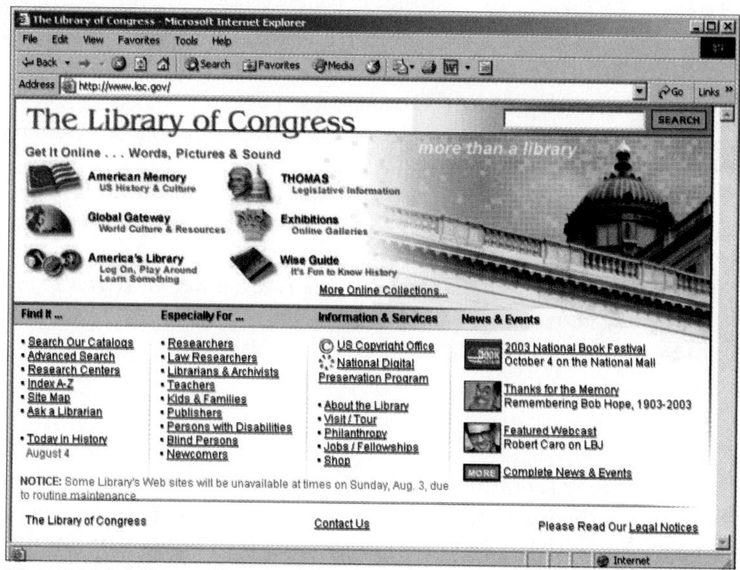

Figure 14.5 Library of Congress home page.

Exercise 6

Compare the Web-based version of a newspaper to its print counterpart, applying the criteria explained in this chapter to help you evaluate their comparative effectiveness in terms of organization, graphic design, and ease of navigation. (You can find links to hundreds of newspapers at www.newspapers.com.)

Chapter 15

Summarizing, Paraphrasing, Quoting, and Synthesizing Sources

Frequently Asked Questions

See 11g

See 15d3

Although it may seem like a good strategy, copying down the words of a source is the least efficient way of taking notes. Experienced researchers know that a better strategy is to take notes that combine summary and paraphrase with direct quotation. By doing so, they make sure they understand both the material and its relevance to their research. This, in turn, makes it possible for them to synthesize sources, combining borrowed material with their own original ideas in a coherent piece of writing.

15a Writing a Summary

A **summary** is a brief restatement, *in your own words*, of the main idea of a passage or an article. When you write a summary, you condense the author's ideas into a few concise sentences. A summary is always much shorter than the original because it omits the examples, asides, analogies, and rhetorical strategies that writers use to add emphasis and interest.

When you summarize, use your own words, not the exact language or phrasing of your source. If you think it is necessary to reproduce a distinctive word or phrase, place it in quotation marks; otherwise, you will be committing plagiarism. Remember that your summary should accurately represent the author's ideas and should

See Ch. 16

include only the ideas of your source, not your own interpretations or opinions. Finally, be sure to document all quoted words and paraphrases as well as the summary itself.

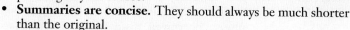

Close-up: Summaries

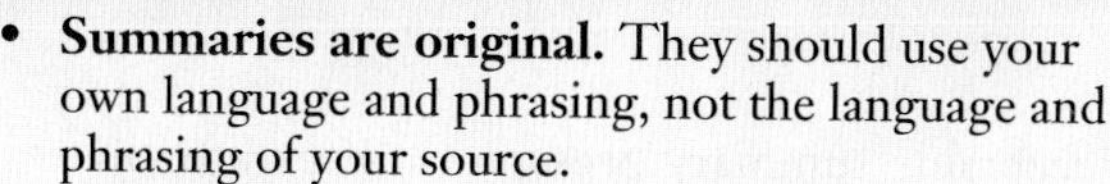

- **Summaries are original.** They should use your own language and phrasing, not the language and phrasing of your source.
- **Summaries are concise.** They should always be much shorter than the original.
- **Summaries are accurate.** They should precisely express the main idea of your source.
- **Summaries are objective.** They should not include your opinions.
- **Summaries are complete.** They should reflect the entire source, not just one part of it.

Compare the following three passages. The first is an original source; the second, an acceptable summary; and the third, an unacceptable summary.

Original Source:

Today, the First Amendment faces challenges from groups who seek to limit expressions of racism and bigotry. A growing number of legislatures have passed rules against "hate speech"—[speech] that is offensive on the basis of race, ethnicity, gender, or sexual orientation. The rules are intended to promote respect for all people and protect the targets of hurtful words, gestures, or actions.

Legal experts fear these rules may wind up diminishing the rights of all citizens. "The bedrock principle [of our society] is that government may never suppress free speech simply because it goes against what the community would like to hear," says Nadine Strossen, president of the American Civil Liberties Union and professor of constitutional law at New York University Law School. In recent years, for example, the courts have upheld the right of neo-Nazis to march in Jewish neighborhoods; protected cross-burning as a form of free expression; and allowed protesters to burn the American flag. The offensive, ugly, distasteful, or repugnant nature of expression is not reason enough to ban it, courts have said.

But advocates of limits on hate speech note that certain kinds of expression fall outside of First Amendment protection. Courts have ruled that "fighting words"—words intended to provoke immediate violence—or speech that creates a clear and present danger are not protected forms of expression. As the classic argument goes, freedom of speech does not give you the right to yell "Fire!" in a crowded theater. (Sudo, Phil. "Freedom of Hate Speech?" *Scholastic Update* 124.14 [1992]: 17–20)

Acceptable Summary: The right to freedom of speech, guaranteed by the First Amendment, is becoming more difficult to defend. Some people think that stronger laws against the use of "hate speech" weaken the First Amendment. But others argue that some kinds of speech remain exempt from this protection (Sudo 17).

The preceding acceptable summary presents an accurate, objective overview of the original without using its exact language or phrasing. (The one distinctive phrase borrowed from the source is placed within quotation marks.)

Compare the acceptable summary with the following unacceptable summary. Notice that the unacceptable summary uses words and phrases from the original without placing them in quotation marks. This use constitutes plagiarism. In addition, the unacceptable summary expresses the writer's opinion ("Other people have the sense to realize . . .").

See Ch. 16

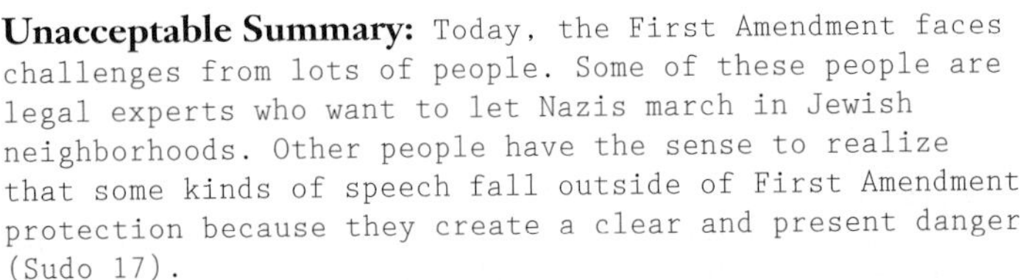

Unacceptable Summary: Today, the First Amendment faces challenges from lots of people. Some of these people are legal experts who want to let Nazis march in Jewish neighborhoods. Other people have the sense to realize that some kinds of speech fall outside of First Amendment protection because they create a clear and present danger (Sudo 17).

Checklist: Writing a Summary

- ☐ Reread your source until you understand it.
- ☐ Write a one-sentence restatement of the main idea.
- ☐ Write your summary, using the one-sentence restatement as your topic sentence. Use your own words and phrasing, not those of your source. Include quotation marks where necessary.
- ☐ Add appropriate documentation.

15b Writing a Paraphrase

A summary conveys just the main idea of a source; a **paraphrase** gives a *detailed* restatement of a source's important ideas in their entirety. It not only indicates the source's main points, but it also reflects its order, tone, and emphasis. Consequently, a paraphrase can sometimes be as long as the source itself.

When you paraphrase, make certain that you use your own words, except when you want to quote to give readers a sense of the original. If you do include quotations, circle the quotation marks in your notes so that you will not forget to document them later. Try not to look at the source as you write, use language and syntax that come naturally to you, and avoid duplicating the wording or sentence structure of the original. Whenever possible, use synonyms that accurately convey the meaning of the original word or phrase. If you cannot think of a synonym for an important term, quote—but remember to document all direct quotations from your source as well as the entire paraphrase. Finally, be sure that your paraphrase reflects only the ideas of your source—not your analysis or interpretation of those ideas.

Close-up: Paraphrases

- **Paraphrases are original.** They should use your original language and phrasing, not the language and phrasing of your source.
- **Paraphrases are accurate.** They should precisely reflect both the ideas and the emphasis of your source.
- **Paraphrases are objective.** They should not include your opinions.
- **Paraphrases are complete.** They should include all the important ideas in your source.

Following are an original passage, an acceptable paraphrase, and an unacceptable paraphrase.

Original Passage:

When you play a video game, you enter into the world of the programmers who made it. You have to do more than identify with a character on a screen. You must act for it. Identification through action has a special kind of hold. Like playing a sport, it puts people into a highly focused and highly charged state of mind. For many people, what is being pursued in the video game is not just a score, but an altered state.

The pilot of a race car does not dare to take . . . attention off the road. The imperative of total concentration is part of the high. Video games demand the same level of attention. They can give people the feeling of being close to the edge because, as in a dangerous situation, there is no time for rest and the consequences of wandering attention [are] dire. With pinball, a false move can be recuperated. The machine can be shaken, the ball repositioned. In a video game, the program has no tolerance for error, no margin for safety. Players experience their every movement as instantly translated into game action. The game is relentless in its demand that all other time stop and in its demand that the player take full responsibility for every act, a point that players often sum up [with] the phrase "One false move and you're dead." (Turkle, Sherry. *The Second Self: Computers and the Human Spirit.* New York: Simon & Schuster, 1984. 83–84.)

Acceptable Paraphrase: The programmer defines the reality of the video game. The game forces a player to merge with the character who is part of the game. The character becomes an extension of the player, who determines how he or she will think and act. According to Turkle, like sports, video games put a player into a very intense "altered state" of mind that is the most important part of the activity (83).

The total involvement they demand is what attracts many people to video games. These games can simulate the thrill of participating in a dangerous activity without any of the risks. There is no time for rest and no opportunity to correct errors of judgment. Unlike video games, pinball games are forgiving. A player can—within certain limits—manipulate a pinball game to correct minor mistakes. With video games, however, every move has immediate consequences. The game forces a player to adapt to its rules and to act carefully. One mistake can cause the death of the character on the screen and the end of the game (Turkle 83-84).

Although the preceding acceptable paraphrase follows the order and emphasis of the original—and even quotes a key phrase—its wording and sentence structure are very different from those of the source. Still, it conveys the key ideas of the source and maintains an objective tone.

The following unacceptable paraphrase simply echoes the phrasing and syntax of the original, borrowing words and expressions without enclosing them in quotation marks. This constitutes plagiarism. In addition, the paraphrase digresses into a discussion of the writer's own views about the relative merits of pinball and video games ("That is why I like . . .").

See Ch. 16

Unacceptable Paraphrase: Playing a video game, you enter into a new world—one the programmer of the game made. You can't just play a video game; you have to identify with it. Your mind goes to a new level, and you are put into a highly focused state of mind.

Just as you would if you were driving a race car or piloting a plane, you must not let your mind wander. Video games demand complete attention. But the sense that at any time you could make one false move and lose is their attraction—at least for me. That is why I like video games more than pinball. Pinball is just too easy. You can always recover. By shaking the machine or quickly operating the flippers, you can save the ball. Video games, however, are not so easy to control. Usually, one slip and you're dead (Turkle 83-84).

ESL Tip

If you find yourself imitating a writer's sentence structure and vocabulary, try reading the passage you want to paraphrase and then putting it aside and thinking about it. Then, try to write down the ideas you remember without looking back at the original text.

Checklist: Writing a Paraphrase

- ☐ Reread your source until you understand it.
- ☐ Write your paraphrase, following the order, tone, and emphasis of the original and making sure that you do not use the words or phrasing of the original without enclosing the borrowed material within quotation marks.
- ☐ Add appropriate documentation.

15c Quoting Sources

When you **quote,** you copy an author's statements exactly as they appear in a source, word for word and punctuation mark for punctuation mark, enclosing the borrowed material in quotation marks. As a rule, you should not quote extensively in a research paper. Numerous quotations interrupt the flow of your discussion and give readers the impression that your paper is just a collection of other people's ideas.

Checklist: When to Quote

- ☐ Quote when a source's wording or phrasing is so distinctive that a summary or paraphrase would diminish its impact.

(continued)

When to quote (continued)

- ☐ Quote when a source's words—particularly those of a recognized expert on your subject—will lend authority to your presentation.
- ☐ Quote when an author's words are so concise that paraphrasing would create a long, clumsy, or incoherent phrase or would change the meaning of the original.
- ☐ Quote when you plan to disagree with a source. Using a source's exact words helps convince readers you are being fair.

NOTE: Remember to document all quotations that you use in your paper.

Exercise 1

Choose a debatable issue from the following list.

- Illegal immigrants' rights to free public education
- Helmet requirements for motorcycle riders
- Community service requirements for college students
- Making English the official language of the United States
- Requiring every citizen to carry a national identification card
- A constitutional amendment prohibiting the defacing of the American flag

Write a one-sentence summary of your own position on the issue; then, interview a classmate and write a one-sentence summary of his or her position on the same issue. Be sure each sentence includes the reasons that support the position. Next, locate a source that discusses your issue, and write a paraphrase of the writer's position, quoting a few distinctive phrases. Finally, write a single sentence that compares and contrasts the three positions.

Exercise 2

Assume that in preparation for a paper on the effects of the rise of the suburbs, you read the following paragraph from the book *Great Expectations: America and the Baby Boom Generation* by Landon Y. Jones. Reread the paragraph, and write a brief summary. Then, paraphrase the paragraph, quoting only those words and phrases you consider especially distinctive.

> As an internal migration, the settling of the suburbs was phenomenal. In the twenty years from 1950 to 1970, the population of the suburbs doubled from 36 million to 72 million. No less than 83 percent of

the total population growth in the United States during the 1950s was in the suburbs, which were growing fifteen times faster than any other segment of the country. As people packed and moved, the national mobility rate leaped by 50 percent. The only other comparable influx was the wave of European immigrants to the United States around the turn of the century. But as *Fortune* pointed out, more people moved to the suburbs every year than had ever arrived on Ellis Island.

15d Integrating Source Material into Your Writing

Weave paraphrases, summaries, and quotations smoothly into your discussion, adding your own analysis or explanation to increase coherence and to show the relevance of your source material to the points you are making.

Close-up: Integrating Source Material into Your Writing

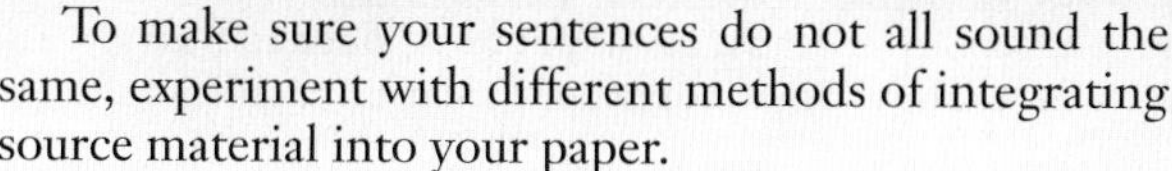

To make sure your sentences do not all sound the same, experiment with different methods of integrating source material into your paper.

- Vary the verbs you use to introduce a source's words or ideas (instead of repeating *says*).

acknowledges	discloses	implies
suggests	observes	notes
concludes	believes	comments
insists	explains	claims
predicts	summarizes	illustrates
reports	finds	proposes
warns	concurs	speculates
admits	affirms	indicates

- Vary the placement of the **identifying tag** (the phrase that identifies the source), putting it in the middle or at the end of the quoted material instead of always at the beginning.

Quotation with Identifying Tag in Middle: "A serious problem confronting Amish society from the viewpoint of the Amish themselves," observes Hostetler, "is the threat of absorption into mass society through the values promoted in the public school system" (193).

Paraphrase with Identifying Tag at End: The Amish are also concerned about their children's exposure to the public school system's values, notes Hostetler (193).

(1) Integrating Quotations

Be sure to work quotations smoothly into your sentences. Quotations should never be awkwardly dropped into your paper, leaving the relationship between the quoted words and your point unclear. Instead, use a brief introductory remark to provide a context for the quotation, and quote only those words you need to make your point.

Acceptable: For the Amish, the public school system is a problem because it represents "the threat of absorption into mass society" (Hostetler 193).

Unacceptable: For the Amish, the public school system represents a problem. "A serious problem confronting Amish society from the viewpoint of the Amish themselves is the threat of absorption into mass society through the values promoted in the public school system" (Hostetler 193).

Whenever possible, use an **identifying tag** to introduce the source of the quotation.

Identifying Tag: As John Hostetler points out, the Amish see the public school system as a problem because it represents "the threat of absorption into mass society" (193).

Close-up: Punctuating Identifying Tags

Whether or not to use a comma with an identifying tag depends on where you place the tag in the sentence. If the identifying tag immediately precedes a quotation, use a comma. If the identifying tag does not immediately precede a quotation, do not use a comma.

As Hostetler points out, "The Amish are successful in maintaining group identity" (56).

Hostetler points out that the Amish frequently "use severe sanctions to preserve their values" (56).

Never use a comma after *that*.

Hostetler says that/ Amish society is "defined by religion" (76).

Substitutions or Additions within Quotations Indicate changes or additions that you make to a quotation by enclosing your changes in brackets.

Original Quotation: "Immediately after her wedding, she and her husband followed tradition and went to visit almost everyone who attended the wedding" (Hostetler 122).

Quotation Revised to Make Verb Tenses Consistent: Nowhere is the Amish dedication to tradition more obvious than in the events surrounding marriage. Right after the wedding celebration, the Amish bride and groom "visit almost everyone who [has] attended the wedding" (Hostetler 122).

Quotation Revised to Supply an Antecedent for a Pronoun: "Immediately after her wedding, [Sarah] and her husband followed tradition and went to visit almost everyone who attended the wedding" (Hostetler 122).

Quotation Revised to Change an Uppercase to a Lowercase Letter: The strength of the Amish community is illustrated by the fact that "[i]mmediately after her wedding, she and her husband followed tradition and went to visit almost everyone who attended the wedding" (Hostetler 122).

Omissions within Quotations When you delete unnecessary or irrelevant words, substitute an ellipsis (three spaced periods) for the deleted words.

Original Quotation: "Not only have the Amish built and staffed their own elementary and vocational schools, but they have gradually organized on local, state, and national levels to cope with the task of educating their children" (Hostetler 206).

Quotation Revised to Eliminate Unnecessary Words: "Not only have the Amish built and staffed their own elementary and vocational schools, but they have gradually organized . . . to cope with the task of educating their children" (Hostetler 206).

Close-up: Omissions within Quotations

Be sure you do not misrepresent or distort the meaning of quoted material when you shorten it. For example, do not say, "the Amish have managed to maintain . . . their culture" when the original quotation is "the Amish have managed to maintain *parts of* their culture."

NOTE: If the passage you are quoting already contains ellipses, MLA style requires that you place brackets around any ellipses you add.

Long Quotations Set off a quotation of more than four typed lines of prose (or more than three lines of poetry) by indenting it one inch (ten spaces) from the margin. Double-space, and do not use quotation marks. If you are quoting a single paragraph, do not indent the first line. If you are quoting more than one paragraph, indent the first line of each complete paragraph an additional one-quarter inch (three spaces). Integrate the quotation into your paper by introducing it with a complete sentence followed by a colon. Place parenthetical documentation one space after the end punctuation.

> According to Hostetler, the Amish were not always hostile to public education:
>
> > The one-room rural elementary school served the Amish community well in a number of ways. As long as it was a public school, it stood midway between the Amish community and the world. Its influence was tolerable, depending upon the degree of influence the Amish were able to bring to the situation. (196)

(2) Integrating Paraphrases and Summaries

Introduce your paraphrases and summaries with identifying tags, and end them with appropriate documentation. By doing so, you make certain that your readers are able to differentiate your own ideas from those of your sources.

Correct (Identifying Tag Differentiates Ideas of Source from Ideas of Writer): Art can be used to uncover many problems that children have at home, in school, or with their friends. For this reason, many therapists use art therapy extensively. According to William Alschuler in *Art and Self-Image*, children's views of themselves in society are often reflected by their art style. For example, a cramped, crowded art style using only a portion of the paper shows a child's limited role (260).

Misleading (Ideas of Source Blend with Ideas of Writer): Art can be used to uncover many problems that children have at home, in school, or with their friends. For this reason, many therapists use art therapy extensively. Children's views of themselves in society are often reflected by their art style. For example, a cramped, crowded art style using only a portion of the paper shows their limited role (Alschuler 260).

Exercise 3

Look back at the summary and paraphrase what you wrote for Exercise 2. Write three possible identifying tags for each, varying the verbs you use for attribution and the placement of the identifying tag. Be sure to include appropriate documentation at the end of each passage.

(3) Synthesizing Sources

When you write a **synthesis,** you use paraphrase, summary, and quotation to combine material from two or more sources, along with your own ideas, in order to express an original viewpoint. (In this sense, an entire research paper is a synthesis.) You begin synthesizing material by comparing your sources and determining how they are alike and different, where they agree and disagree, and whether they reach the same conclusions. As you identify connections between one source and another or between a source and your own ideas, you develop your own perspective on your subject. It is this viewpoint, summarized in a thesis statement (in the case of an entire paper) or in a topic sentence (in the case of a paragraph), that becomes the focus of your synthesis.

As you write your synthesis, make your points one at a time, and use material from your sources to support these points. Be certain you use identifying tags as well as the transitional words and phrases that your readers will need to follow your discussion. Finally, remember that your ideas, not the ideas of your sources, should be central to your discussion.

The following synthesis was written by a student as part of a research paper.

> Computers have already changed our lives. They carry out (at incredible speed) many of the everyday tasks that make our way of life possible. For example, computer billing, with all its faults, makes modern business possible, and without computers we would not have access to the telephone services or television reception that we take for granted. But computers are more than fast calculators. According to one computer expert, they are well on their way to learning, creating, and someday even thinking (Raphael 21). Another computer expert, Douglas Hofstadter, agrees, saying that someday a computer will have both "will . . . and consciousness" (423). It seems likely, then, that as a result of the computer, our culture will change profoundly (Turkle 15).

Exercise 4

Write a paragraph that synthesizes the three positions you worked with in Exercise 1. (If you like, you may use the sentence comparing the three positions, drafted in response to Exercise 1, as your topic sentence.)

Chapter 16

Avoiding Plagiarism

16a Defining Plagiarism

Plagiarism occurs when you present another person's ideas or words as if they were your own. In this case, you not only cheat yourself by losing an opportunity to learn, but you also cheat your instructors and your fellow students by undercutting the trust and intellectual honesty that is necessary if education is to take place.

Most plagiarism that occurs is **unintentional plagiarism**—for example, inadvertently pasting a quoted passage from a downloaded file directly into a paper and forgetting to include the quotation marks and documentation. Even noted scholars have been known to make mistakes when working with sources. But there is a difference between an honest mistake and **intentional plagiarism**—for example, copying sentences from a journal article or submitting a paper that someone else has written. The penalties for unintentional plagiarism may sometimes be severe, but intentional plagiarism is almost always dealt with harshly: students who intentionally plagiarize can receive a failing grade for the paper (or the course) or even be expelled from school. Outside of academia, intentional plagiarism is also taken seriously. In recent years, a *New York Times* reporter was fired when he admitted to committing plagiarism, and another reporter had her Pulitzer Prize revoked for fabricating information.

The availability on the Web of information that can be downloaded and copied has increased the likelihood of accidental plagiarism. In fact, the freewheeling appropriation and circulation of information that routinely takes place on the Web may give the false impression that this material does not need to be documented. (Students sometimes cut and paste pictures, graphs, and even words and sentences from the Web into their papers without realizing that they are plagiarizing.) Whether they appear in print or in electronic form, however, the words and ideas of others must be properly documented.

http://kirsznermandell.wadsworth.com

Computer Tip: Avoiding Plagiarism

The same technology that has made plagiarism easier to commit has also made it easier to detect. By doing a *Google* search, an instructor can quickly find the source of a phrase that has been plagiarized from a Web site. Other products search subscription databases and identify plagiarized passages in student papers. *InSite* is a Web-based application that compares, word for word, the information contained on the Web and in *InfoTrac*® *College Edition* (a subscription database) with passages in student papers. This makes it possible for students to use *InSite* to search their own drafts for unintentionally plagiarized material before submitting final papers to their instructors. Figure 16.1 shows the results of an *InSite* Originality Report indicating that certain parts of a paper have been plagiarized.

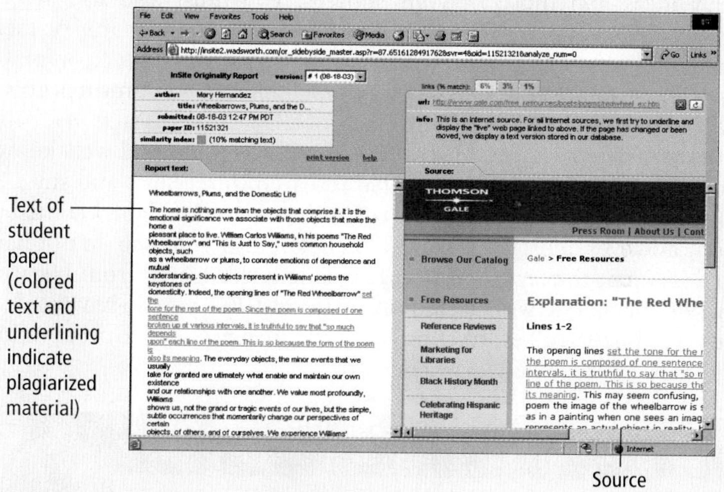

Figure 16.1 ***InSite* Originality Report.**

16b Avoiding Unintentional Plagiarism

The most common cause of unintentional plagiarism is sloppy research habits. To avoid this problem, start your research paper early, choose a topic that interests you, and understand that the skills you learn now will help you in other courses as well as after you graduate. Do not cut and paste text from a Web site or full-text database directly into your paper. Never use sources that you have not actually read or invent sources that do not exist. If you paraphrase, do so correctly by following the examples in 16c; changing a few words here and there is not enough.

ESL Tip

Because writing in a second language can be difficult, you may be tempted to closely follow the syntax and word choice of your sources. Be aware, however, that your instructors consider this plagiarism. If you are having difficulty expressing the ideas of a source in your own words, talk to your instructor (or to a writing center tutor), who can help you avoid plagiarism and the penalties that go with it.

See Pt. 3

In addition to taking careful notes and distinguishing between your ideas and those of your sources, you must also use proper documentation. In general, you must document any words or ideas that you borrow from your sources (whether print or electronic). Of course, certain items need not be documented: **common knowledge** (information every reader probably knows), facts available from a variety of reference sources, familiar sayings and well-known quotations, and your own original research (interviews and surveys, for example). Information that is another writer's original contribution, however, must be acknowledged. So, although you do not have to document the fact that John F. Kennedy graduated from Harvard in 1940 or that he was elected president in 1960, you do have to document a historian's evaluation of his presidency. The best rule to follow is if you have doubts, document.

Close-up: Avoiding Two Special Kinds of Plagiarism

In general, you should not submit a paper to one course that you have already received a grade for in another course. If you intend to substantially rework the paper, however, you may be able to use it—but be sure to get permission from both course instructors.

Collaborative work presents another problem. If you participate in a collaborative research project, make sure that you clearly identify the sections that each person worked on and that you get guidelines from your instructor for documenting collaborative work.

16c Revising to Eliminate Plagiarism

You can avoid plagiarism by using documentation whenever it is required and by adhering to the following guidelines.

(1) Enclose Borrowed Words in Quotation Marks

Original: Historically, only a handful of families have dominated the fireworks industry in the West. Details such as chemical recipes and mixing procedures were cloaked in secrecy and passed down from one generation to the next. . . . One effect of familial secretiveness is that, until recent decades, basic pyrotechnic research was rarely performed, and even when it was, the results were not generally reported in scientific journals. (Conkling, John A. "Pyrotechnics." *Scientific American* July 1990: 96)

Plagiarism: John A. Conkling points out that until recently, little scientific research was done on the chemical properties of fireworks, and when it was, the results were not generally reported in scientific journals (96).

Even though the writer documents the source of his information, he uses the source's exact words without placing them in quotation marks.

Correct (Borrowed Words in Quotation Marks): John A. Conkling points out that until recently, little scientific research was done on the chemical properties of fireworks, and when it was, "the results were generally not reported in scientific journals" (96).

Correct (Paraphrase): John A. Conkling points out that the little research conducted on the chemical composition of fireworks was seldom reported in the scientific literature (96).

http://kirsznermandell.wadsworth.com

Computer Tip: Plagiarism and Internet Sources

Any time you download text from the Internet, you run the risk of committing unintentional plagiarism. To avoid the possibility of plagiarism, follow these guidelines:

(continued)

Plagiarism and Internet sources (continued)

- Download information into individual files so that you can keep track of your sources.
- Do not simply cut and paste blocks of downloaded text into your paper; summarize or paraphrase this material first.
- If you record the exact words of your source, enclose them in quotation marks.
- Whether your information is from emails, online discussion groups, listservs, or Web sites, give proper credit by providing appropriate documentation.
- Always document figures, tables, charts, and graphs obtained from the Internet or from any other electronic source.

(2) Do Not Imitate a Source's Syntax and Phrasing

Original: Let's be clear: this wish for politically correct casting goes only one way, the way designed to redress the injuries of centuries. When Pat Carroll, who is a woman, plays Falstaff, who is not, casting is considered a stroke of brilliance. When Josette Simon, who is black, plays Maggie in *After the Fall*, a part Arthur Miller patterned after Marilyn Monroe and which has traditionally been played not by white women, but by blonde white women, it is hailed as a breakthrough.

But when the pendulum moves the other way, the actors' union balks. (Quindlen, Anna. "Error, Stage Left." *New York Times* 12 Aug. 1990, sec. 1: 21)

Plagiarism: Let us be honest. The desire for politically appropriate casting goes in only one direction, the direction intended to make up for the damage done over hundreds of years. When Pat Carroll, a female, is cast as Falstaff, a male, the decision is a brilliant one. When Josette Simon, a black woman, is cast as Maggie in *After the Fall*, a role that Arthur Miller based on Marilyn Monroe and that has usually been played by a woman who is not only white but also blonde, it is considered a major advance.

But when the shoe is on the other foot, the actors' union resists (Quindlen 21).

Although this writer does not use the exact words of her source, she closely imitates the original's syntax and phrasing, simply substituting synonyms for the author's words.

Correct (Paraphrase; One Distinctive Phrase Placed in Quotation Marks): According to Anna Quindlen, the actors' union supports "politically correct casting" (21) only when it means casting a woman or minority group member in a role created for a male or a Caucasian. Thus, it is acceptable for actress Pat Carroll to play Falstaff or for black actress Josette Simon to play Marilyn Monroe; in fact, casting decisions such as these are praised. But when it comes to casting a Caucasian in a role intended for an African American, Asian, or Hispanic, the union objects (21).

NOTE: Although the parenthetical documentation at the end identifies the passage's source, the quotation requires separate documentation.

(3) Document Statistics Obtained from a Source

Although many people assume that statistics are common knowledge, they are usually the result of original research and must therefore be documented. Moreover, providing the source of the statistics helps readers to assess their reliability.

Correct: According to one study, male drivers between the ages of sixteen and twenty-four accounted for the majority of accidents. Of 303 accidents recorded almost one half took place before the drivers were legally allowed to drive at eighteen (Schuman et al. 1027).

(4) Differentiate Your Words and Ideas from Those of the Source

Original: At some colleges and universities traditional survey courses of world and English literature . . . have been scrapped or diluted. At others they are in peril. At still others they will be. What replaces them is sometimes a mere option of electives, sometimes "multicultural" courses introducing material from Third World cultures and thinning out an already thin sampling of Western writings, and sometimes courses geared especially to issues of class, race, and gender. Given the notorious lethargy of academic decision-making, there has probably been more clamor than change; but if there's enough clamor, there will be change. (Howe, Irving. "The Value of the Canon." *The New Republic* 2 Feb. 1991: 40–47)

Plagiarism: Debates about expanding the literary canon take place at many colleges and universities across the United States. At many universities, the Western literature survey courses have been edged out by courses that emphasize minority concerns. These courses are "thinning out an already thin sampling of Western writings" in favor of courses geared especially to issues of "class, race, and gender" (Howe 40).

Because the writer does not differentiate his ideas from those of his source, it appears that only the quotations in the last sentence are borrowed when, in fact, the first sentence also owes a debt to the original. The writer should have clearly identified the boundaries of the borrowed material by introducing it with an identifying tag and ending with documentation. (Note that a quotation *always* requires separate documentation.)

Correct: Debates about expanding the literary canon take place at many colleges and universities across the United States. According to critic Irving Howe, at many universities the Western literature survey courses have been edged out by courses that emphasize minority concerns (41). These courses, says Howe, are "thinning out an already thin sampling of Western writings" in favor of "courses geared especially to issues of class, race, and gender" (40).

Checklist: Avoiding Plagiarism

- ☐ **Take careful notes.** Be sure you have recorded information from your sources carefully and accurately.
- ☐ **In your notes, clearly identify borrowed material.** In handwritten notes, put all words borrowed from your sources inside circled quotation marks, and enclose your own comments within brackets. If you are taking notes on a computer, boldface all quotation marks.
- ☐ **In your paper, differentiate your ideas from those of your sources** by clearly introducing borrowed material with an identifying tag and by following it with documentation.
- ☐ **Enclose all direct quotations** used in your paper within quotation marks.
- ☐ **Review all paraphrases and summaries** in your paper to make certain they are in your own words and that any distinctive words and phrases from a source are quoted.
- ☐ **Document all quoted material and all paraphrases and summaries** of your sources.
- ☐ **Document all information** that is open to dispute or that is not common knowledge.
- ☐ **Document all opinions, conclusions, figures, tables, statistics, graphs, and charts** taken from a source.
- ☐ **Never submit the work of another person as your own.** Do not buy a paper from an online paper mill or use a paper given to you by a friend. In addition, do not include in your paper passages that have been written by a friend, relative, or writing tutor.

Exercise

The following student paragraph uses material from three sources, but its author has neglected to cite them. After reading the paragraph and the three sources that follow it, identify the material that has been quoted directly from a source. Compare the wording to the original for accuracy, and insert quotation marks where necessary, making sure the quoted passages fit smoothly into the paragraph. Differentiate the ideas of the student from those of each of the three sources by using identifying tags to introduce any quotations. (If you think the student did not need to quote a passage, paraphrase it instead.) Finally, add parenthetical documentation for each piece of information that requires it.

Student Paragraph

Oral history is an important way of capturing certain aspects of the past that might otherwise be lost. While history books relate the stories of great men and great events, rarely do they include the experiences of ordinary people—slaves, concentration camp survivors, and the illiterate, for example. By providing information about the people and emotions of the past, oral history makes sense of the present and gives a glimpse of the likely future. But because any particular rendition of a life history relies heavily on personal memory, great care must be taken to evaluate and explain the context of an oral history. Like any other historical account, oral history is just one of many possible versions of an individual's past.

Source 1

Oral history relies heavily on memory, a notoriously malleable entity; people remake the past in light of present concerns and knowledge. Yet not all memories are false, and oral history gives us testimony that might otherwise be lost—stories of slaves, of concentration camp survivors, of the illiterate and the obscure, of the legion "ordinary people" who rarely find their way into the history books. Oral history gives us the human element, the thoughts and emotions and confusions that lie beneath the calm surface of written documents. Even when people remake the past because memories are faulty or unbearable, we can learn much about the ways in which the past affects the present. (Freedman, Jean R. "Never Underestimate the Power of a Bus: My Journey to Oral History." *Oral History Review* 29.2 [2002]: 30.)

Source 2

[There is a] widely held view that history belongs to great men and great events, not ordinary people or ordinary life. Yet we know that "ordinary" people in our local districts have important stories to tell. . . . Local histories tell us, on the one hand, that things were done differently in the past, but on the other hand, that in essence people and emotions were much the same. We need to learn from the past to make sense of the present, and get a glimpse of the likely future. (Gregg, Alison. "Planning and Managing an Oral History Collection." *Aplis* 13.4 [Dec. 2000]: 174.)

Source 3

One aspect of oral history . . . concerns the way in which any particular rendition of a life history is a product of the personal present. It is well-recognized that chronicles of the past are invariably a product of the present, so that different "presents" inspire different versions of the past. Just as all historical accounts—the very questions posed or the interpretive framework imposed—are informed by the historian's present, so, too, is a life history structured by both the interviewer's and the narrator's present. . . . [O]ral history cannot be treated as a source of some narrative truth, but rather as one of many possible versions of an individual's past. . . . [and] the stories told in an oral history are not simply the source of explanation, but rather require explanation. (Honig, Emily. "Getting to the Source: Striking Lives: Oral History and the Politics of Memory." *Journal of Women's History* 9.1 [1997]: 139.)

Chapter 17

Doing Research: A Case Study

Frequently Asked Questions

Kimberly Larsen Romney, a student in a second-semester composition class, was given the following assignment.

> Write a ten- to fifteen-page research paper that takes a position on any issue related to the Internet. Keep a research notebook that traces your progress.

The research paper was to be a full-semester project, so Kimberly had fourteen weeks in which to research and write the paper. This chapter shows her progress, reproducing computer screens that record her comments about various stages of the project as well as showing some examples of her research activities.

Kimberly's instructor, Professor Linda Wilson, required regular conferences at which she reviewed students' progress and checked their research notebooks; a segment of the assignment was due at each meeting. At various points in the process, Professor Wilson required students to participate in peer review, and she told students to use a variety of print, electronic, and nonlibrary sources, particularly Internet sources, and to incorporate visuals into their papers. With these general guidelines in mind, Kimberly began to think about her assignment.

17a Moving from Assignment to Topic

(1) Understanding the Assignment

Professor Wilson gave our English class an assignment today. By the end of the semester, we have to hand in a ten- to fifteen-page paper on a controversial issue related to the Internet. We're supposed to explain the issue and present our position. At the end of next week, Professor Wilson will meet with each student in the class to help us decide on a search strategy. In two weeks, we have to turn in an outline of our paper and meet with Professor Wilson again so she can make comments and suggestions. The final paper has to use MLA documentation.

(2) Choosing a Topic

Last semester, I wrote a personal essay about my difficulties using computers and the Internet when I arrived at college. In class, we'd read an essay by Henry Louis Gates Jr. that confirmed what I thought: not everyone feels comfortable using computers and the Internet. Gates says that the Internet threatens to create two societies—one that is tapped into the digital economy and one that is not, and he refers to this problem as the "digital divide." For this paper, I'd like to expand the paper I wrote for my first-semester composition course and talk more broadly about the digital divide. I asked my comp professor if I could, and she gave me permission. (I'll check with Professor Wilson too.)

I've been thinking about how far I've come in terms of improving my computer skills. I feel much more proficient using word-processing programs and using the Internet for research. For that reason, I think this paper will be much better than the one I wrote last semester.

(3) Starting a Research Notebook

I'm setting up a file on my computer called "Digital Divide," and I plan to keep all the documents I create for my paper here, including a *Word* document I'm calling "Research Notebook." When I wrote my paper last semester, I kept a journal on my computer and found it really useful. Today, I outlined my schedule and listed a few potential sources to check.

17b Mapping Out a Search Strategy

Today, I met with Professor Wilson to discuss my search strategy. After she approved my topic, she suggested I start by familiarizing myself with the history of the Internet, going to the Internet itself for this information. Once I understand the Internet and its history, I can use our school library's resources, such as online indexes and subscription databases and the online catalog, to find specific information. Professor Wilson suggested that I use the keywords "digital divide" when I search for sources.

17c Doing Exploratory Research and Formulating a Research Question

(1) Doing Exploratory Research

Today, I started researching. First, I did a preliminary search using my favorite Internet search engine, *Google*, at http://www.google.com. I typed in the keywords *digital divide* and got over 840,000 hits.

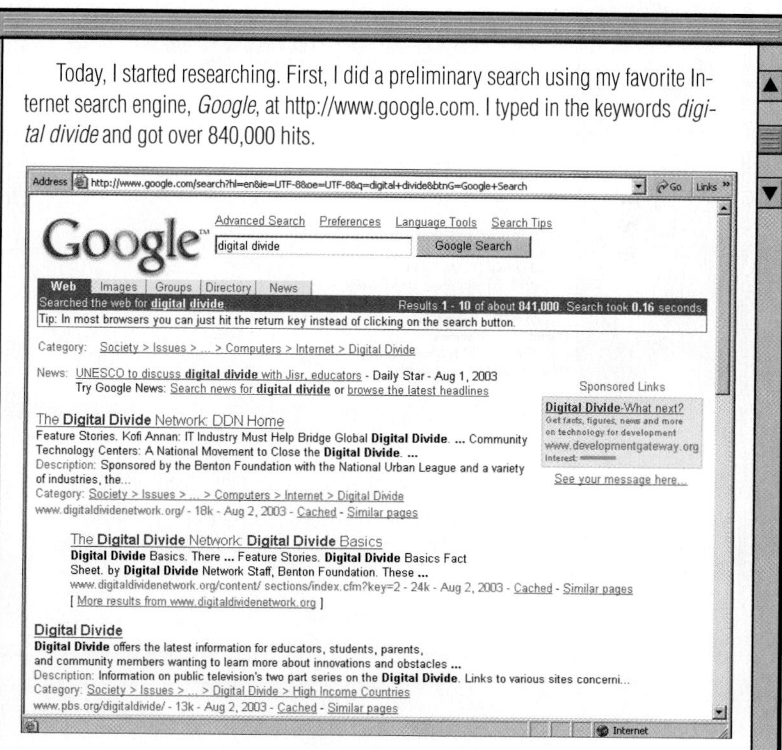

I really like *Google* because it does its own search within my search and lists the Web sites in order of relevance. This way, I only have to look at the first ten to twenty sites because I already know that these are the most relevant ones for my topic. Through this search I found *The Digital Divide Network,* which is a Web site that posts information and articles about research and public programs aimed at bridging the digital divide. A report published by the Benton Foundation, *Bringing a Nation Online,* is posted here, and it looks really helpful. It refers to another report published by the federal government called *A Nation Online.* When I went back to *Google* and typed in the keywords *A Nation Online,* I was able to find this report too.

I next decided to try an online database. One of my favorites is *InfoTrac College Edition,* which came with my handbook; it contains millions of abstracts and full-text articles.

InfoTrac College Edition allows me to search the subject guide, and it lets me search with keywords. I found the subject guide helpful because it showed me what kinds of articles talk about the digital divide (newspapers or periodicals) and because it broke down the different subject categories, which helped me focus my research.

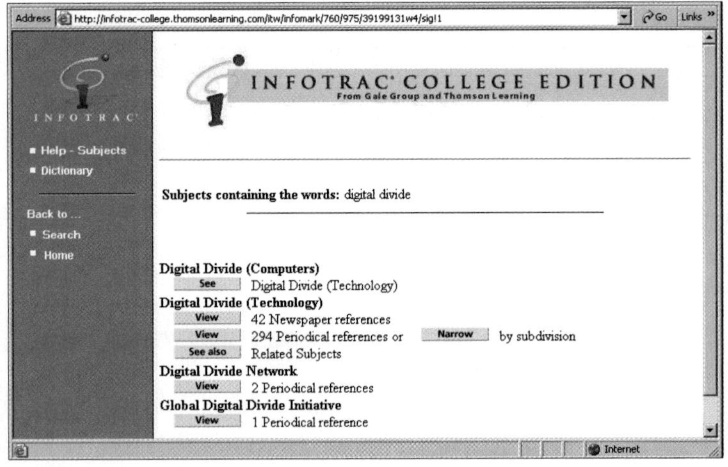

To see if I was missing anything, I decided to see what the library had to offer. I used a subscription database called *Expanded Academic ASAP,* which works much like Internet search engines. I just typed in keywords and found some new articles related to my topic.

University of Texas at Austin
Expanded Academic ASAP Plus ingenta

Keyword search (in title, citation, abstract): digital divide

Citations 1 to 20 (of 844)

Mark all items on this page

Mark **The Digital Divide and Managing Workforce Diversity: A Commentary.** D.L. Ford Jr, G.L. Whaley.
Applied Psychology: An International Review July 2003 v52 i3 p476(10)
Abstract

Mark **UN chief urges business leaders to help bridge global digital divide.**
Xinhua News Agency June 18, 2003 p1008169h5553 (226 words)
Text

Mark **Spanning the ; digital divide.** (UK's Get Started campaign)
Computer Weekly June 17, 2003 p32 (1753 words)
Text

Mark **The Digital-Asset Divide -- Content-management Interwoven vendor went shopping to catch up to rivals in digital assets.** Tony Kontzer.
InformationWeek June 9, 2003 p53 (339 words)
Text

Mark **Sustainable Internet access for the rural poor? Elements of an emerging Indian model.** J. James.
Futures June 2003 v35 i5 p461(12)
Abstract

Mark **Digital divide and purchase intention: Why demographic psychology matters.** S.H. Akhter.
Journal of Economic Psychology June 2003 v24 i3 p321(7)
Abstract

Finally, I looked in the online catalog. By doing a subject keyword search with the term *digital divide,* I was able to find a couple of books related to my topic.

(2) Formulating a Research Question

After researching my topic for a few days, I was able to decide on my research question: How widespread is the “digital divide,” and what problems does it cause?

17d Assembling a Working Bibliography

I've been keeping track of all the potential sources I come across. I can keep two windows open on my computer, so I keep my Internet browser and my *Word* document open at the same time. This way, I can write down a brief evaluation that

includes the kind and amount of information in the source, its relevance to my topic, and its limitations while I review the source. I've titled this document "Sources," and I plan to email an updated copy to Professor Wilson as an attachment so that she can check my sources and make sure I'm on the right track.

I've also been doing research at the library. When I go to the library, I take a set of index cards with me. As I review each source, I write down the author, the title, the publication information, and a quick evaluation of the source on a card. When I get home, I transfer this information to my "Sources" document.

Research Activity: Assembling a Working Bibliography (in Computer File)

Author: CBS AP
Title: "Digital Divide Debated"
Publication Information: http://www.cbsnews.com/stories/2002/05/30/tech/main510589.shtml
May 30, 2002
Accessed March 2, 2003
Evaluation: Reports on Bush administration's argument that the digital divide is no longer a significant problem. Cites the findings of the February 2002 Commerce report.

Research Activity: Assembling a Working Bibliography (on Index Card)

Norris, Pippa — Author

Digital Divide: Civic Engagement, Information Poverty, and the Internet Worldwide — Title

Cambridge: Cambridge UP, 2001 — Publication information

A book about the digital divide that explains its history and its relationship to economics and class. — Evaluation

17e Developing a Tentative Thesis

I've done a lot of research and have decided on a tentative thesis that I think my sources can help me support: Not all Americans have equal access to the Internet, and this is potentially a serious problem.

17f Doing Focused Research

(1) Reading Sources

To make sure I get everything I can out of each source, I first skim it and then go back and reread it, highlighting the key points. As I read, I ask myself which parts of the information are fact and which are the opinion of the author. This is difficult to do, so I sometimes have to read the information two or three times. Because I know I might find later that some of my sources aren't useful, I'm trying to locate as many sources as I can.

(2) Evaluating Sources

As I gather new sources, I evaluate them according to Professor Wilson's guidelines. (She referred me to section 12c in my handbook.) For my print sources, I sometimes ask a reference librarian or Professor Wilson whether an author is credible. I also consider how current a source is. I'm trying to find sources no more than a couple of years old (except for sources of background about the Internet). I'm also discarding sources that are mostly opinion. One that I want to keep is an interview with one of my former high school teachers, who can give me reliable information for my section on how public schools are making efforts to provide people with Internet access.

17g Taking Notes

When I take notes on sources I've photocopied or downloaded, or on books I've borrowed from the library, I use my computer. I use lines to separate individual notes on the page so I can move them around later on, and I write source information on every note. At the top of each note, I write a heading to identify the part of my paper where I might use the information. I reread the notes as I type, adding in brackets any questions or comments I think of.

Research Activity: Taking Notes (in Computer File)

Short heading — Source

Problems of digital divide — Rangel-King, *Houston Chronicle*, 12/6/01

Note (quotation)

"African-Americans make up only 11 percent of the information technology workforce and account for less than 1 percent of the doctorate level computer science degrees conferred, according to a recent study performed by Data Source Associates."

Efforts to close gap — Rangel-King, *Houston Chronicle*, 12/6/01

Note (paraphrase)

Houston-based Association of Minority Information Technology Professionals (AMITP) works to close digital divide by providing networking opportunities to African Americans in technology industry. [How successful have they been? How many members?]

Comment

Recommendations for the future — Rangel-King, *Houston Chronicle*, 12/6/01

Note (summary)

Schools need IT professionals to work as mentors to both students and teachers in inner-city schools. [Good idea—but how will schools find these mentors?]

Comment

For sources I read in the library, I use index cards. I take the cards with me to the library, and when I get home, I enter my notes into *Microsoft Word*, along with my comments and source information. I circle quotation marks so I'll remember these words come from a source.

Research Activity: Taking Notes (on Index Card)

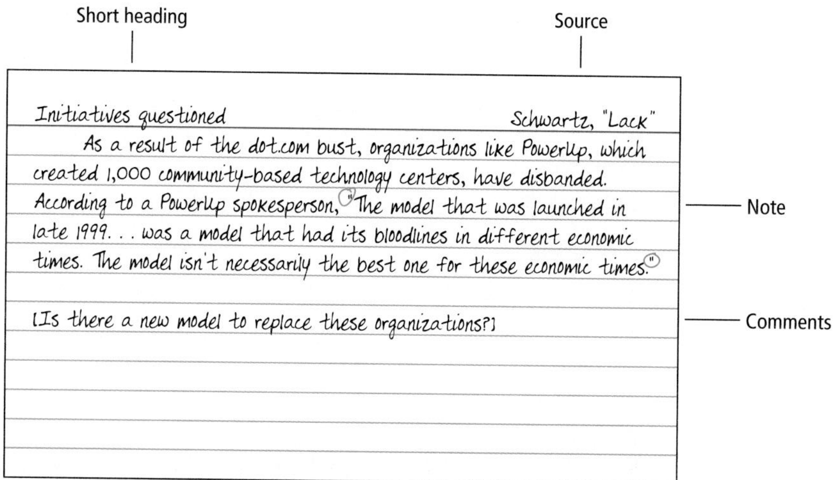

Initiatives questioned — Schwartz, "Lack"

As a result of the dot.com bust, organizations like PowerUp, which created 1,000 community-based technology centers, have disbanded. According to a PowerUp spokesperson, "The model that was launched in late 1999. . . was a model that had its bloodlines in different economic times. The model isn't necessarily the best one for these economic times."

[Is there a new model to replace these organizations?]

17h Fine-Tuning the Thesis

When I reread all my notes, I revised my tentative thesis so that it could clearly communicate the position I planned to take on the issue. My final thesis is more specific than my tentative thesis was: Although the Internet has changed our world for the better, it threatens to leave many people behind, creating two distinct classes—those who have access and those who do not.

17i Constructing a Formal Outline

Today, I wrote my outline. Professor Wilson told us that constructing a topic outline now would help us when we wrote our rough draft later, so I gathered all my notes together and started arranging them into categories based on my headings. I came up with six main categories, representing the most important topics I want to cover, and I managed to fit each of my notes into one of these categories. I'll meet with Professor Wilson tomorrow to go over the outline. If it's okay, I can start to draft my paper.

Research Activity: Constructing a Formal (Topic) Outline

Thesis statement: Although the Internet has changed our lives for the better, it threatens to leave many people behind, creating two distinct classes—those who have access and those who do not.

I. History of the Internet
   A. ARPANET
   B. Expansion (1972)
   C. HTML
II. Internet during the 1990s
   A. Empowering tool
   B. Source of knowledge and prosperity
III. Problems of digital divide
   A. Lack of access by many groups
   B. Educational and economic disadvantages
   C. Widening gap
IV. Efforts by government and others to close gap
   A. Community Technology Centers Program
   B. Commerce Department's Technology Opportunities Program
   C. Bill and Melinda Gates Foundation
   D. The Digital Divide Network and The Civil Rights Forum
V. Initiatives questioned
   A. Bush administration's view
   B. Worsening economy
   C. Challenges by minority groups
VI. Recommendations for the future
   A. Improve access to technology, especially the Internet
   B. Redefine "digital divide" to make it more inclusive
   C. Continue federal funding

17j Writing a Rough Draft

(1) Shaping the Parts of the Paper

I've discussed my outline with Professor Wilson, and we made a few changes. Now, I'm ready to start writing my rough draft.

In my introduction, I'm going to explain the importance of understanding technology in today's society; this will allow me to bring up the digital divide.

In the body of the paper, I plan to start with the history of the Internet and briefly discuss its benefits. Then, I'll discuss the digital divide and what people, organizations, and public officials have done to try to bridge the divide. Finally, I'll talk about current opinions regarding the digital divide.

In my conclusion, I'll summarize my ideas and restate my thesis.

(2) Working Source Material into the Paper

One of the most difficult challenges I've faced is integrating my research into my paper. I've tried to show how each of my sources supports my thesis, and I've also tried to connect sources to one another. For example, I discuss the *Bringing a Nation Online* report and then talk about the *New York Times* piece by John Schwartz that examines this report.

(3) Working Visuals into the Paper

I wanted to find a couple of visuals to incorporate into my paper. I found a great graph from the *A Nation Online* report, but I also wanted to find a picture. I was especially interested in finding a visual that could support my discussion of programs aimed at closing the digital divide. A librarian told me that a good place to look for visuals is on the *Google* image search engine at http://images.google.com. When I did my search using the keywords *digital divide,* I got over 3,000 hits, so I knew I needed a narrower focus. One of the nonprofit initiatives that interested me most was PowerUp. This program was hit hard by the dot.com bust and was closing its doors after only a few years of operation. So I did an image search using the keywords *digital divide PowerUp* and found a photo that showed how PowerUp had helped one of the poorer Austin, Texas, neighborhoods by building a computer center there.

Address http://images.google.com/imgres?imgurl=tspweb02.tsp.utexas.edu/webarchive/02-14-01/Images/21401easttech.b.maloney.jp Go Links
Google This is the image: tspweb02.tsp.utexas.edu/.../ 21401easttech.b.maloney.jpg
Remove Frame
Back to Results
Image has been scaled down. See full-size image.
This image may be subject to copyright.
Below is the image in its original context on the page: tspweb02.tsp.utexas.edu/webarchive/ 02-14-01/SectionSL.html
State & Local
World & Nation
Sports
Opinion
Entertainment
Classifieds
Advertising Rates
Archives
AP News
Contact Us
'E-team' provides local youth with lessons in technology
PowerUp program aims to close digital divide in East Austin
By Shelley Doggett
Daily Texan Staff
A new computer facility for East Austin middle-school students officially opened its doors Tuesday with the help of the Austin Area Urban League and AOL Time
More State & Local Stories
* MADD lobbies at Capitol in support of bills
* 'E-team' provides local youth with lessons in technology
Internet

17k Revising Drafts

When I finished my rough draft, I sent my paper to Professor Wilson as an email attachment. She looked over my paper and used the Comment feature in *Microsoft Word* to make suggestions. After I read her comments, I made the specific revisions she suggested.

Rough Draft with Instructor's Comments (Excerpt)

The Education Department's Community Technology Centers Program (CTC) helped finance computer activity centers for students and adults. Also, the Department of Commerce's Technology Opportunities Program (TOP) provided money and services to organizations that needed more technology to operate efficiently. One recipient was America's Second Harvest.

Comment: What did this organization do, and from what source did you get this information? See 15a.

The Bill and Melinda Gates Foundation, for example, has provided libraries across the country with funding that allows them to purchase computers and connect them to the Internet (Egan) **[Add page number?]**. The Digital Divide Network is a Web site that posts stories about the digital divide from a variety of perspectives. By posting information on the Web site that they created, the site's sponsor hopes to raise awareness of the problems that the digital divide causes. The Civil Rights Forum is a Web site that focuses on the digital divide. This site says that their goal is to "bring civil rights organizations and community groups into the debate over the future of our media environment." **[Add source]** Recently, however, many of those initiatives have been questioned for a variety of reasons. Many people, for example, argue that the digital divide is no longer a significant problem. In 2001, a phone survey of more than 350,000 Americans conducted by the company Media Audit determined that 44 percent of African-American households were accessing the Internet, "an increase of over 41 percent over the last three years." Further, the company found that Latino households were also increasingly accessing the Internet. In fact, 42 percent of Latino households were using the Internet in 2001 (Roach). In February 2002, the Department of Commerce published its annual digital divide report. Using the most recent US Census data, the report argues that from 1998 to 2001 . . .

Comment: You need a transition sentence before this one to show that this paragraph is about a new idea. See 7b6.

Comment: Wordy. See 36a.

Comment: Pronoun-antecedent agreement. See 48b.

Comment: This should begin a new paragraph. See 7a.

Comment: Incorrect pronoun reference. See 46c.

Comment: Who said this? See 15c.

Revision

The Education Department's Community Technology Centers Program (CTC) helped finance computer activity centers for students and adults. Also, the Department of Commerce's Technology Opportunities Program (TOP) provided money and services to organizations that needed more technology to operate efficiently. One recipient was America's Second Harvest, which used the funds to track donations to its national network of food banks (Schwartz, "Report").

Nonprofit organizations also worked to bridge the digital divide. The Bill and Melinda Gates Foundation, for example, has provided libraries across the country with funding that allows them to purchase computers and connect them to the Internet (Egan). The Digital Divide Network is a Web site that posts stories about the digital divide from a variety of perspectives. By posting information, the site's sponsor hopes to raise awareness of the problems that the digital divide causes. Similarly, The Civil Rights Forum is a Web site that focuses on the digital divide from the perspective of minorities and people of color. This site says that its goal is to "bring civil rights organizations and community groups into the debate over the future of our media environment."

Recently, however, many of these initiatives have been questioned for a variety of reasons. Many people, for example, argue that the digital divide is no longer a significant problem. In 2001, a phone survey of more than 350,000 Americans conducted by the company Media Audit determined that 44 percent of African-American households were accessing the Internet, "an increase of over 41 percent over the last three years" (Roach). Further, the company found that Latino households were also increasingly accessing the Internet. In fact, 42 percent of Latino households were using the Internet in 2001 (Roach). In February 2002, the Department of Commerce published its annual digital divide report. Using the most recent US Census data, the report argues that from 1998 to 2001 . . .

When I finished my rough draft, I made a writing center appointment so I could go over my draft with a tutor. Having another person review my draft was a big help. For example, the tutor suggested that adding statistics to certain sections of my paper would strengthen it. (I took her advice, and I added a bar graph too.)

I also emailed my draft to two of my friends and asked them to read it and provide feedback. They each typed their comments in a different color so it was easy to see who wrote what.

Peer Review (Excerpt)

You need a transition sentence here! Ditto, this is really awk.☺ A recent article Tell us the name and where this came from. observes that many African-American and other minority groups argue that digital divide rhetoric might actually stereotype minorities. The article says that digital divide rhetoric "could discourage businesses or academics from creating content or services tailored for minority communities—ultimately making the digital divide a self-fulfilling prophecy." Do you need a p. #? By talking as if there is a digital divide, many scholars and leaders in the African-American community fear that this idea will be accepted as a fact rather than a condition. Tara L. McPherson says Use a stronger word—*asserts, claims,* etc. Wilson doesn't like us to keep using "says." ☺ that "the idea of challenging the digital divide is not about denying its existence. But it is to ensure that the focus on the digital divide doesn't naturalize a kind of exclusion of investment." I think you're supposed to have the author's last name here.

My classmates made some good suggestions. I considered each comment and then made the necessary changes. Suggestions regarding MLA documentation were easy to fix. I just looked in Chapter 18 in the handbook and made corrections accordingly. The most difficult change I had to make was adding a transition sentence to the paragraph—a sentence that would connect this paragraph to the one before it and also summarize what this paragraph was about.

Revision with Track Changes

In other cases, the groups targeted by digital divide programs argue that they might do more harm than good. A recent article in the *Chronicle of Higher Education* observes that many African-American and other minority groups argue that digital divide rhetoric might actually stereotype minorities. The article says that digital divide rhetoric "could discourage businesses or academics from creating content or services tailored for minority communities—ultimately making the digital divide a self-fulfilling prophecy" (Young). By talking as if there is a digital divide, many scholars and leaders in the African-American community fear that this idea will be accepted as a fact rather than a condition. Tara L. McPherson ~~says~~ argues that "the idea of challenging the digital divide is not about denying its existence. But it is to ensure that the focus on the digital divide doesn't naturalize a kind of exclusion of investment~~.~~" (qtd. in Young).

17l Preparing a Final Draft

Professor Wilson required us to write a sentence outline and to include it with our paper and also to include a title page (even though MLA does not require one). I've written sentence outlines before, and they're usually very helpful. Writing this last outline helped me see how each idea connected to the next. It made me feel much more comfortable with my final draft. So now I've finally finished my paper, and I'm ready to hand it in.

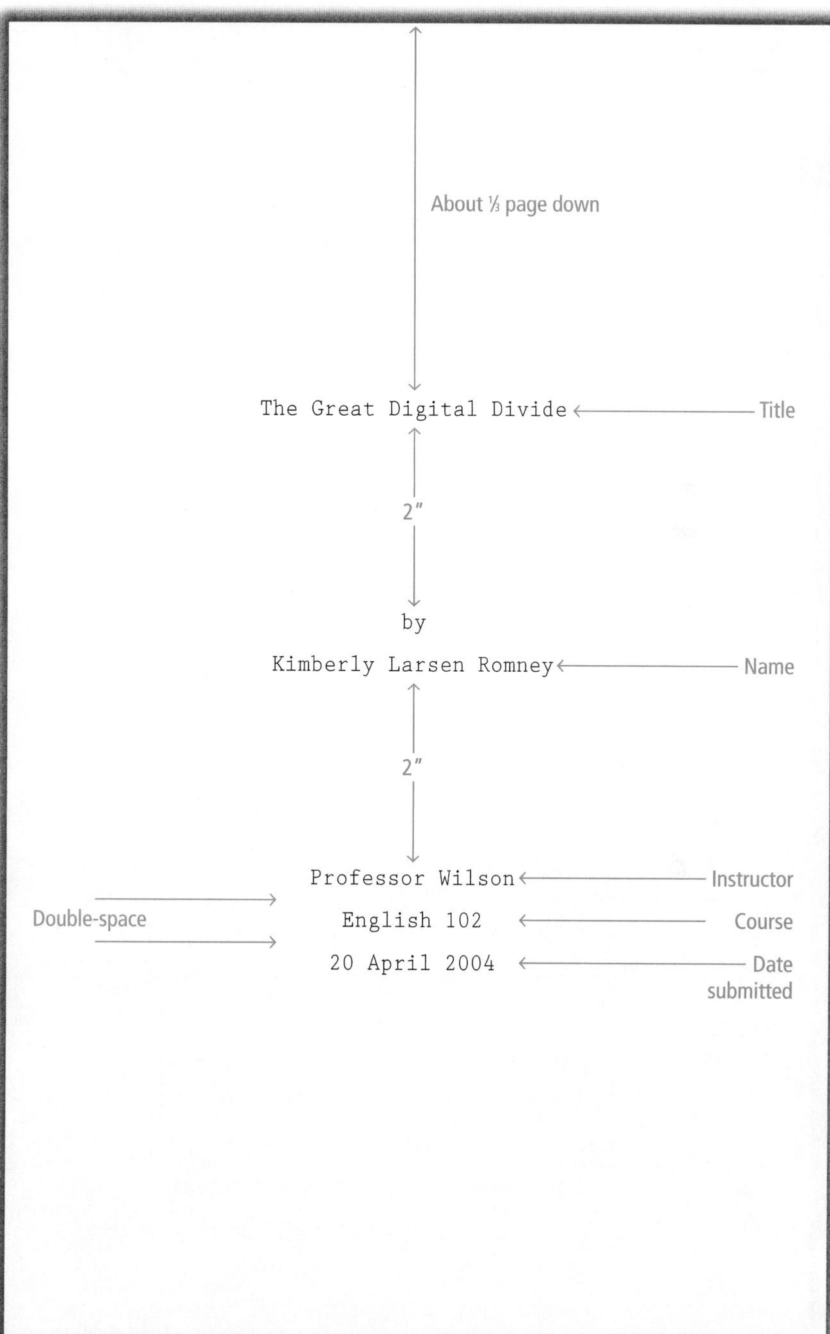
About ⅓ page down
The Great Digital Divide
Title
2″
by
Kimberly Larsen Romney
Name
2″
Professor Wilson
Instructor
Double-space
English 102
Course
20 April 2004
Date submitted

Lowercase roman numerals used for outline pages

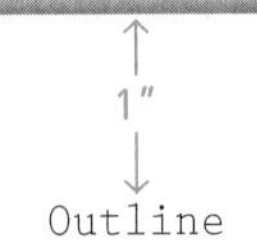

Romney i

Outline

Thesis statement: Although the Internet has changed our lives for the better, it threatens to leave many people behind, creating two distinct classes—those who have access and those who do not.

I. The Internet's popularity has soared in recent years, but it has existed for more than thirty years.
   A. The Internet began in 1969 as ARPANET, a communication system designed to survive nuclear attacks.
   B. It was expanded in 1972 into a system of interconnected networks.
   C. In the 1990s, HTML was created to allow information on the Internet to be displayed graphically.

II. In the late 1990s, many argued that the Internet had ushered in a new age.
   A. Former Vice President Al Gore saw the Internet as an empowering tool.
   B. Gore believed the Internet would bring knowledge and prosperity to the entire world.

III. Others questioned the benefits of the Internet.
   A. They argued that the Internet was out of reach for many Americans.
      1. Low-income and minority households were less likely than others to have computers.

Romney ii

2. For minorities, Internet content was as much of a problem as economics.

B. They argued that those without Internet access had difficulties at school, trouble obtaining jobs, and fewer opportunities to save money and time as consumers.

C. They argued that the Internet was widening the economic and social divide that already separated Americans.

IV. In response, the government, corporations, nonprofit organizations, and public libraries made efforts to bridge the gap between the "haves" and "have-nots."

A. The federal government has launched programs like the Community Technology Centers Program (CTC), which helps finance computer activity centers for students and adults.

B. The Department of Commerce's Technology Opportunities Program (TOP) provided money and services to organizations that needed a technology boost.

C. The Bill and Melinda Gates Foundation funded libraries trying to provide patrons with Internet access.

D. Nonprofit organizations sponsor Web sites like The Digital Divide Network and The Civil Rights Forum, which continue to raise public awareness on a global scale.

Romney iii

V. Recently, however, the need for many of these initiatives has been questioned.
   A. Recent surveys have found that the Internet is being used by minorities and the impoverished.
      1. A Media Audit phone survey found an increase in Internet use among minorities.
      2. A Department of Commerce report also found an increase in Internet access.
      3. The Bush administration argues that the digital divide is no longer a problem and wants to discontinue federal funding to programs like CTC and TOP.
   B. Since the dot.com bust, many companies have discontinued funding for programs like PowerUp, which aimed to broaden Internet access.
   C. Some groups targeted by digital divide programs argue that they might do more harm than good.

VI. While the digital divide may be narrowing, problems remain.
   A. The poor, the elderly, the disabled, and minorities still have difficulty accessing the Internet.
   B. The digital divide applies not just to Internet access, but to access to technology in general.

Romney iv

1. Technological illiteracy presents obstacles to voting.
2. African Americans are not well represented in technology fields.
3. Children in rural areas lack access to technology.

VII. Clearly, much still needs to be done.

A. The Internet must be made available to the widest possible audience.
B. Training must be provided to people unfamiliar with the new technology.
C. The most likely "have-nots" must be targeted.

FAQs links

1"

½"

Romney 1

1"

The Great Digital Divide ⟵ Center title

Indent 5 spaces (or ½") ⟶ Today, a basic understanding of computers ← Double-space ← and how to use them is necessary for success. For this reason, those who are unfamiliar with modern digital technology find themselves at a great disadvantage when it comes to education and employment. One of the most exciting digital technologies available is the information superhighway—better known as the Internet. The Internet, with its accompanying software and services, is rapidly changing the way we access and see information. Clearly, the Internet offers great promise, but some argue that it is creating many problems as well. Although the Internet has changed our lives for the better, it threatens to leave many people behind, creating two distinct classes—those who have access and those who do not.

1" ⟷ 1" ⟷

Thesis statement

¶s 2–4 present background on history of the Internet, summarizing information from two sources

The Internet's popularity has soared in recent years, but the Internet has existed for more than thirty years. It began in 1969 under the name ARPANET (ARPA stood for Advanced Research Projects Agency, which was part of the United States Department of Defense). During the Cold War, the United States government allocated funds to establish a communication system that would function even if part of it were destroyed. The first ARPANET system consisted of just four connected computers, but by 1972, fifty universities and research facilities (all

1"

Student's last name and page number on every page (including the first)

Romney 2

doing research for the military) were linked (Norris 26-32).

Beginning in 1972, researchers decided to expand the scope of this project. They wanted to find a way to increase the number of computers that could be on ARPANET. Researchers established a collection of protocols called TCP/IP (Transmission Control Protocol/Internet Protocol). The conversion to TCP/IP, completed in 1983, allowed ARPANET to connect all the new networks (UNIX, USENET, and BITNET, for example) that had come into existence since 1972. This new system was given the name "Internet" (Kristula).

Finally, in the 1990s, a computer language called HTML (HyperText Markup Language) was created to allow information on the Internet to be displayed graphically. Whereas the older networks on the Internet looked like typed pages, HTML displayed information in a more visually stimulating format. This advance gave rise to the World Wide Web, which allowed users to access text, graphics, sound, and even video while moving from one site to another simply by clicking on a hypertext link. This in turn made the Internet more accessible and aroused unprecedented interest in the new digital technology (Kristula).

In the late 1990s, many argued that the Internet had ushered in a new age, one in which instant

Romney 3

Material from Internet source, introduced by author's name, does not include a parenthetical reference with a paragraph or page number because this information was not provided in the electronic text

communication would bring people closer together and eventually eliminate national boundaries. In "Building a Global Community," former Vice President Al Gore took this optimistic view, seeing the Internet as a means "to deepen and extend our oldest and most cherished global values: rising standards of living and literacy, an ever-widening circle of freedom, and individual empowerment." Gore went on to say that he could envision the day when we would "extend our knowledge and our prosperity to our most isolated inner cities, to the barrios, the favelas, the colonias, and our most remote rural villages."

Parenthetical documentation refers to material accessed from a Web site

Others, however, argued that for many people the benefits of the Internet were not nearly this obvious or far-reaching. They maintained that the Internet was creating what many have called a "digital divide" (Civil Rights Forum), which excludes a large percentage of the poor, elderly, disabled, and members of many minority groups from current technological advancements. A survey conducted by the US Department of Commerce in 1999 showed that people with higher annual household incomes and whites were more likely to own computers than minorities and people from low-income households. Approximately 80 percent of households with incomes of $75,000 or above had computers, compared to 16 percent of households earning $10,000-$15,000. The

Romney 4

survey also found that in households with incomes between $15,000 and $34,999, only 23 percent of African-American and 26 percent of Hispanic households had computers, compared to 47 percent of white households (US Dept. of Commerce).

While the Department of Commerce study suggested that financial circumstances were responsible for the "digital divide," the gap in computer ownership across incomes indicated that other factors might be contributing to the disparity. In a 1999 New York Times op-ed article, Henry Louis Gates Jr. argued that bridging the digital divide would "require more than cheap PC's"; it would "involve content" (500).[1] African Americans were not interested in the Internet, Gates wrote, because the content rarely appealed to them. Gates compared the lack of interest in the Internet with the history of African Americans' relationship to the recording industry: "Blacks began to respond to this new medium only when mainstream companies like Columbia Records introduced so-called race records, blues and jazz discs aimed at a nascent African American market" (501). Gates believed that Web sites that address the needs of African Americans could play the same role that race records did for the music industry. Ignoring the race problem, Gates warned, would lead to a form of cyber-segregation that would devastate the African-American community (501).

¶ synthesizes information from a Commerce Department study and a newspaper article

Superscript number identifies content note

Romney 5

Student's original conclusions; no documentation necessary

It was clear to many that people without Internet access had difficulty at school, trouble obtaining jobs, and fewer opportunities to save money and time as consumers. They also lacked access to educational materials and to jobs posted on the Internet. With access to only a portion of available goods and services, people who were offline did not have the advantages that people who were online could routinely get. The Internet was clearly widening the economic and social divide that already separated people in this country.

In response, the government, corporations, nonprofit organizations, and public libraries made efforts to bridge the gap between the "haves" and "have-nots." For example, the Education Department's Community Technology Centers Program (CTC) helped finance computer activity centers for students and adults. Also, the Department of Commerce's Technology Opportunities Program (TOP) provided money and services to organizations that needed more technology to operate efficiently. One recipient was America's Second Harvest, which used the funds to track donations to its national network of food banks (Schwartz, "Report").

Parenthetical documentation includes abbreviated title when two or more works by the same author are cited

Nonprofit organizations also worked to bridge the digital divide. The Bill and Melinda Gates Foundation, for example, has provided libraries across the country with funding that allows them to

Romney 6

purchase computers and connect to the Internet (Egan). Nonprofit organizations also sponsor Web sites. The Digital Divide Network is a Web site that posts stories about the digital divide from a variety of perspectives. By posting information, the site's sponsor hopes to raise awareness of the problems that the digital divide causes. Similarly, The Civil Rights Forum is a Web site that focuses on the digital divide from the perspective of minorities and people of color. This site says that its goal is to "bring civil rights organizations and community groups into the debate over the future of our media environment."

Recently, however, the need for many of these initiatives has been questioned for a variety of reasons. Some people, for example, argue that the digital divide is no longer a significant problem. In 2001, a phone survey of more than 350,000 Americans conducted by the company Media Audit determined that 44 percent of African-American households were accessing the Internet, "an increase of over 41 percent over the last three years" (Roach). Further, the company found that Latino households were also increasingly accessing the Internet. In fact, 42 percent of Latino households were using the Internet in 2001 (Roach). In February 2002, the US Department of Commerce published its annual digital divide report. Using the most recent US Census data, the

Romney 7

report argues that from 1998 to 2001, Internet access in homes increased significantly. Moreover, as illustrated in fig. 1, computer use by young people between the ages of 3 and 24 rose dramatically between 1998 and 2001.

Arguing that significant strides have been made to bridge the digital divide, the Bush administration believes that programs like CTC and TOP are no longer needed ("Digital Divide Debated"). At the same time, as the result of the dot.com bust, private industry

Graph summarizes relevant data. Source information is typed directly below the figure. This information does not appear in the works-cited list because the source is not used elsewhere in the paper.

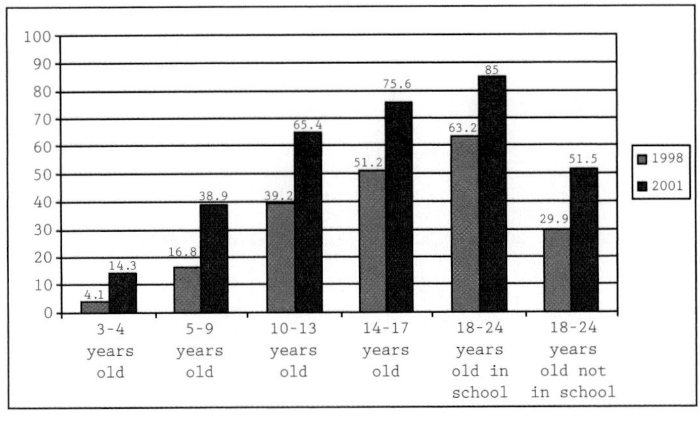

Fig. 1. United States, Dept. of Commerce, Economics and Statistics Admin., Natl. Telecommunications and Information Admin., A Nation Online: How Americans Are Expanding Their Use of the Internet (Washington, DC: US Dept. of Commerce, 2002) 43, 22 Feb. 2004 <http://www.ntia.doc.gov/ntiahome/dn/anationonline2.pdf>.

Romney 8

has withdrawn some support for efforts to bridge the digital divide. One organization, called PowerUp, worked with corporations to create community-based technology centers like the one in Austin, Texas, pictured in fig 2. In places like Austin, PowerUp worked to establish a computer center in the city's impoverished neighborhood by collaborating with AOL Time Warner and the Austin Urban League (Doggett). Despite its initial success, the organization was

Fig. 2. Austin's former mayor, Kirk Watson, poses with AOL Time Warner Cable Vice President for Public Affairs, Lidia Argraz, and PowerUp representatives, Shelley Doggett. "'E-Team' Provides Local Youth with Lessons in Technology," The Daily Texan Online 14 Feb. 2001, 3 Mar. 2004 <http://www.dailytexanonline.com/>.

Romney 9

hard hit by an economic downturn. According to a PowerUp spokesperson, "The model that was launched in late 1999 . . . was a model that had its bloodlines in different economic times. The model isn't necessarily the best one for these economic times" (Schwartz, "Lack"). In 2002, PowerUp closed its offices, leaving the community centers they created to find funding on their own.

Ellipses indicate that the student has deleted words from the quotation

In other cases, the groups targeted by digital divide programs argue that they might do more harm than good. A recent article in the Chronicle of Higher Education observes that many African American and other minority groups argue that digital divide rhetoric might actually stereotype minorities. The article says that digital divide rhetoric "could discourage businesses or academics from creating content or services tailored for minority communities—ultimately making the digital divide a self-fulfilling prophecy" (Young). Many scholars and leaders in the African-American community fear that a focus on the digital divide will lead to its being seen as a fact to be accepted rather than as a problem to be solved. Tara L. McPherson agrees, arguing that "the idea of challenging the digital divide is not about denying its existence. But it is to ensure that the focus on the digital divide doesn't naturalize a kind of exclusion of investment" (qtd. in Young).

"Qtd. in" indicates that McPherson's comments were quoted in Young's article.

Romney 10

Despite the appearance that the digital divide is closing and the claims that digital divide rhetoric may actually be counterproductive, many public officials and private interest groups continue to voice their concerns that gaps in technological literacy and availability remain a problem among many populations and communities. In fact, a 2002 report published by the Benton Foundation disagrees with the US Department of Commerce's findings. This report, <u>Bringing a Nation Online: The Importance of Federal Leadership</u>, contends that federal funding is key in continuing to bring more people into the digital age. While the Department of Commerce report maintains that most people have access to computers in their homes, <u>Bringing a Nation Online</u> uses the same statistics to argue that many people continue to have difficulty accessing the Internet. The authors found that 75 percent of people with household incomes less than $15,000 and 66 percent with incomes between $15,000 and $35,000 are not yet using the Internet (Benton Foundation). Wealthier Americans, however, have significantly greater access to the Internet. Of the Americans with incomes of $50,000-$75,000 a year, 67.3 percent use the Internet (Benton Foundation). Thus, the authors strongly disagree with the Bush administration's recommendation to cut programs like the Department of Commerce's Technology

Romney 11

Opportunities Program and the Community Technology Centers Program:

Quotation of more than four lines is typed as a block, indented ten spaces (or 1"), and double-spaced, with no quotation marks. Parenthetical documentation is placed one space after end punctuation.

> TOP and CTC are important engines of digital opportunity. They are emblematic of the importance of federal leadership in the effort to bridge the digital divide. Federal leadership brings the power of information to underserved communities. A federal retreat from that leadership role would undermine innovative efforts to bring digital opportunity to underserved communities and jeopardize many successful community programs. Rather than walking away from the investment, the federal government should build upon the success of these programs to bring digital opportunity to the entire nation. (Benton Foundation)

Other evidence also suggests that the digital divide is not only a problem of Internet access, but a problem of access to technology in general. The election reform bill of 2001, for example, allocated billions of dollars to create better voting technology in poor and minority areas. William Kennard observes that in areas where punch card machines were used, voters were seven times more likely to have their ballots discarded than in areas that used other types of ballots. For this reason, minorities and the poor are not only disconnected

Romney 12

from technology, "they are also disconnected from our democracy" (Kennard). Similarly, a Houston Chronicle article refers to the small number of African Americans working in the information technology field, citing a study by a company called Data Source Associates that found that African Americans make up only 11 percent of workers in technology fields (Rangel-King).[2]

Superscript number identifies content note

It is not only minorities and the impoverished who are affected by the digital divide. Many people know that children in inner-city schools lack access to computer technology and to the Internet, but few know that children attending schools in rural areas are also at risk. Vicky Wellborn, a high school English teacher in a small town, reports that her school only recently instituted a computer literacy program. As they ordered computers, the instructors realized that one of their biggest challenges would be training themselves. Although the computer literacy program has been helpful to many students, the difficulties of teaching an unfamiliar subject continue to challenge teachers at the school (Wellborn).

Although many strides have been made in closing the gap between those who have access to the Internet and technology and those who do not, problems and new challenges remain. Steps must be taken to solve these problems. First, we must continue efforts to make the

Romney 13

Conclusion recommends solutions for problem of "digital divide." Because ¶ introduces no new material (it summarizes material already discussed and presents student's original conclusions), no documentation is necessary.

Internet available to the widest possible audience. We must also ensure that the rhetoric surrounding the term digital divide is used to close this gap, not to create a new one by establishing or reinforcing stereotypes about minorities. A broader definition of what the digital divide is might help us to see that it has the potential to marginalize many groups of people—the poor, the elderly, the disabled, and rural schoolchildren, for example—not just members of minority groups. On a practical level, the federal government should continue to fund programs that increase access to computer technology in general, and to the Internet in particular. Unless we take steps to make these resources available to all, we will quickly become two separate and unequal societies: one "plugged-in" and privileged and one "unplugged" and marginalized.

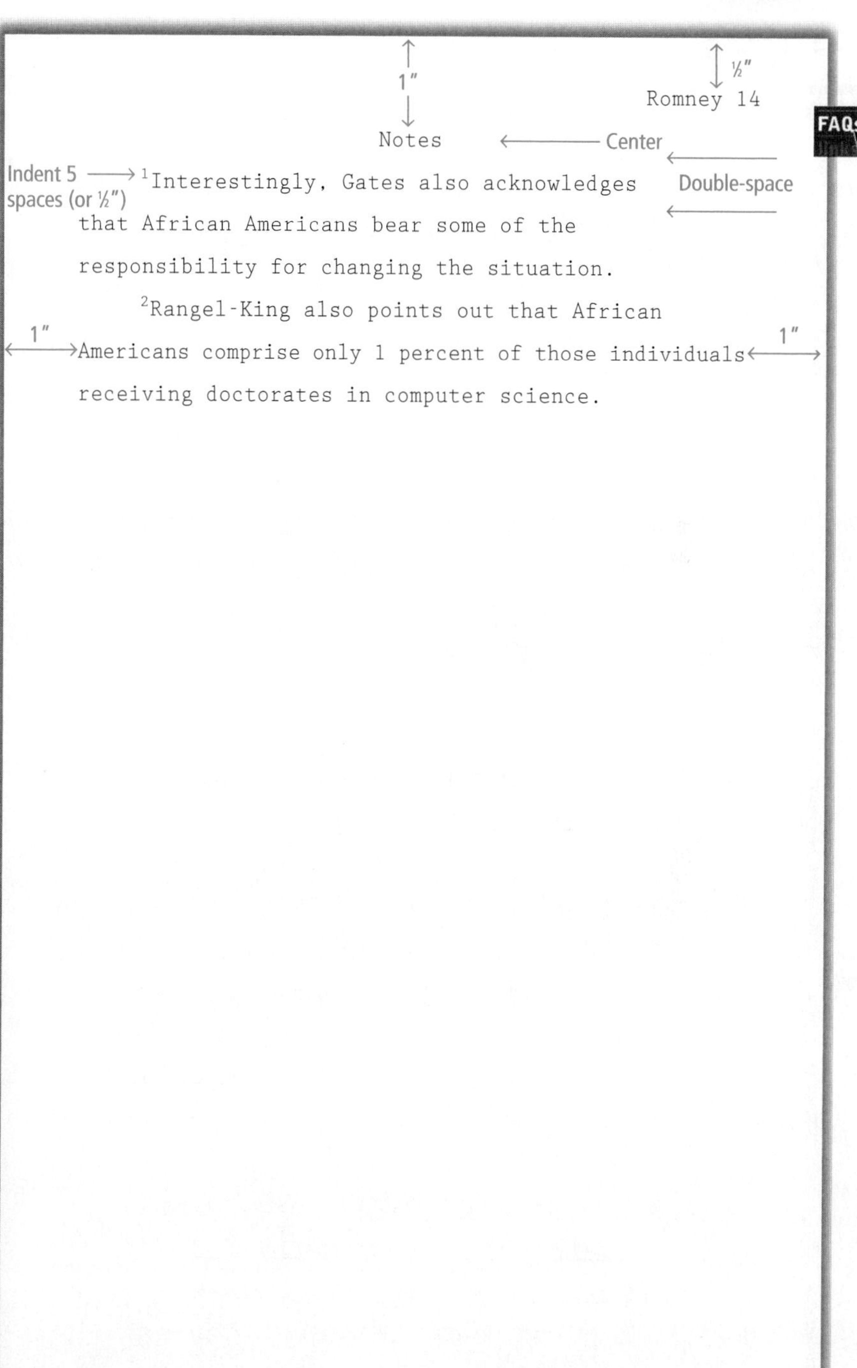
1"
½"
Romney 14
Notes
Center
FAQs
Indent 5 spaces (or ½")
Double-space
[1]Interestingly, Gates also acknowledges that African Americans bear some of the responsibility for changing the situation.
[2]Rangel-King also points out that African Americans comprise only 1 percent of those individuals receiving doctorates in computer science.
1"
1"

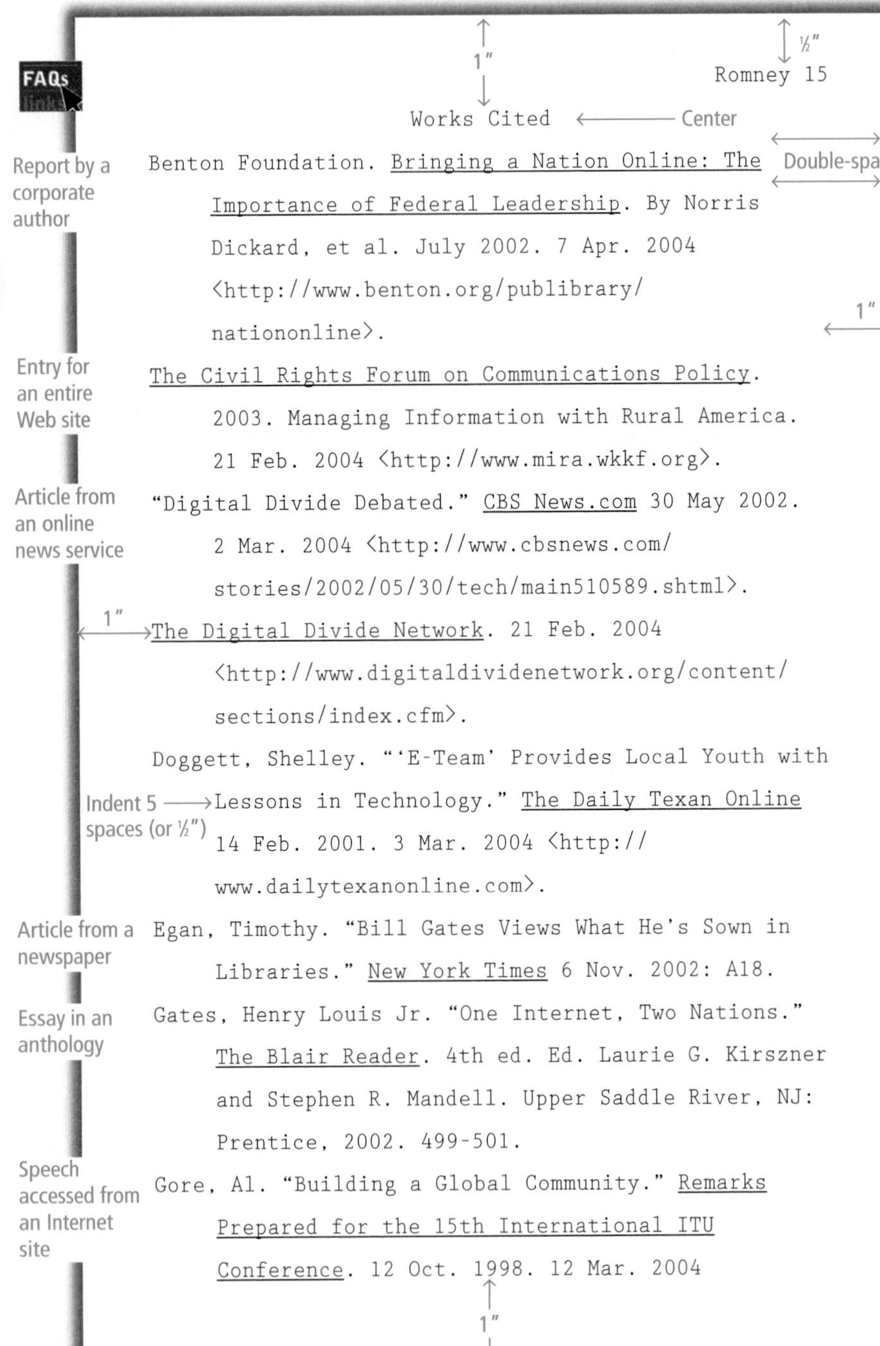

Works Cited

Benton Foundation. Bringing a Nation Online: The Importance of Federal Leadership. By Norris Dickard, et al. July 2002. 7 Apr. 2004 <http://www.benton.org/publibrary/nationonline>.

The Civil Rights Forum on Communications Policy. 2003. Managing Information with Rural America. 21 Feb. 2004 <http://www.mira.wkkf.org>.

"Digital Divide Debated." CBS News.com 30 May 2002. 2 Mar. 2004 <http://www.cbsnews.com/stories/2002/05/30/tech/main510589.shtml>.

The Digital Divide Network. 21 Feb. 2004 <http://www.digitaldividenetwork.org/content/sections/index.cfm>.

Doggett, Shelley. "'E-Team' Provides Local Youth with Lessons in Technology." The Daily Texan Online 14 Feb. 2001. 3 Mar. 2004 <http://www.dailytexanonline.com>.

Egan, Timothy. "Bill Gates Views What He's Sown in Libraries." New York Times 6 Nov. 2002: A18.

Gates, Henry Louis Jr. "One Internet, Two Nations." The Blair Reader. 4th ed. Ed. Laurie G. Kirszner and Stephen R. Mandell. Upper Saddle River, NJ: Prentice, 2002. 499-501.

Gore, Al. "Building a Global Community." Remarks Prepared for the 15th International ITU Conference. 12 Oct. 1998. 12 Mar. 2004

Romney 16

<http://clinton3.nara.gov/WH/EOP/OVP/speeches/itu.html>.

Kennard, William E. "Democracy's Digital Divide." Christian Science Monitor 7 Mar. 2002. Academic Universe: News. LexisNexis. U of Texas Lib. System, TX. 17 Mar. 2004 <http://web.lexis-nexis.com>.

Kristula, Dave. "The History of the Internet." Davesite.com. Aug. 2001. 19 Feb. 2004 <http://www.davesite.com/webstation/net-history.shtml>.

Norris, Pippa. Digital Divide: Civic Engagement, Information Poverty, and the Internet Worldwide. Cambridge: Cambridge UP, 2001.

Rangel-King, Kristi. "Tech Group Aims to Close 'Digital Divide.'" Houston Chronicle 6 Dec. 2001. Academic Universe: News. LexisNexis. U of Texas Lib. System, TX. 12 Mar. 2004 <http://web.lexis-nexis.com>.

Roach, Ronald. "More Minority Households Gain Internet Access." Black Issues in Higher Education 5 July 2001. InfoTrac College Edition. InfoTrac. 21 Mar. 2004 <http://infotrac.thomsonlearning.com>.

Schwartz, John. "A Lack of Money Forces Computer Initiative to Close." New York Times 30 Oct. 2002. Expanded Academic ASAP. Gale Group Databases. U of Texas Lib. System, TX. 20 Mar. 2004 <http://www.galegroup.com>.

Newspaper article accessed from a library subscription database

Document from a Web site

Book with one author

Romney 17

Three unspaced hyphens used instead of repeating author's name

Government document accessed from the Internet

---. "Report Disputes Bush Approach to Bridging 'Digital Divide.'" New York Times 11 July 2002. Expanded Academic ASAP. Gale Group Databases. U of Texas Lib. System, TX. 19 Mar. 2004 <http://www.galegroup.com>.

United States. Dept. of Commerce. Economics and Statistics Admin. Natl. Telecommunications and Information Admin. Falling through the Net: Defining the Digital Divide: A Report on the Telecommunications and Information Technology Gap in America. Washington: GPO, 1999. 20 Mar. 2004 <http://www.ntia.doc.gov/ntiahome/fttn99/FTTN.pdf>.

Wellborn, Vicky. "Re: Computer Literacy." Email to the author. 23 Sept. 2003.

Young, Jeffrey. "Does 'Digital Divide' Rhetoric Do More Harm Than Good?" Chronicle of Higher Education 9 Nov. 2004. 20 Mar. 2004 <http://www.chronicle.com>.

STUDENT WRITER AT WORK

Synthesizing Sources

The following excerpt from an essay written for a media studies course does not use sources. After reading the excerpt below and the six quotations that follow it, decide which quotations would be useful in supporting the writer's points. Then, insert the letter that corresponds to each quotation you select where you think it best fits. You may discard any material that does not provide useful support.

Gender and Sexuality in the Media

Gender and sexuality expectations and norms in our society are portrayed weekly through the characters on the television show Dawson's Creek, a program about a group of young adults who struggle to find their way through life. Gender and sexuality are very important in this series, yet the series does not (with one notable exception) challenge society's assumptions about what "normal" male and female behavior is and what it is not.

The men in Dawson's Creek seem predominantly concerned with "masculine" issues, such as high social status and professional success. For example, one of the main characters, Pacey, changes his job in an attempt to become more masculine. Pacey works as a cook until his older brother and a few male friends encourage him to find a more masculine profession. After following their advice, Pacey lands a job as a salesman for a local corporation. When he and his friends plan to attend a social function with Pacey's colleagues, they make a bet to see who will bring the most attractive female date. Pacey's participation in this bet (along with his new job, which he considers manlier than his previous job), reinforces his masculinity. Excessive competitiveness—especially when it involves showing off a female at a social function—is a stereotypical norm of males. The woman is treated as a possession, as something the man has won through battle.

The women in Dawson's Creek seem to be concerned largely with "feminine" issues, such as dress, appearance, and men. For example, the women dress in revealing clothing and spend a lot of time on their appearance to attract men. Their dating patterns do not challenge society's norms. On one occasion, a man in her class asks Jen out on a date. The date picks her up at home, opens doors for her, pays for everything, and is generally very attentive. In this example, it is the female as much as the male who upholds traditional patriarchal expectations since Jen seems to expect this kind of treatment, perhaps accepting it as her due simply because she is a woman. In this case, the male is expected to take charge and the female to go along with his direction: as long as the woman looks good, nobody is supposed to complain.

This kind of adherence to gender role expectations is, however, violated by the character of Jack, a homosexual male, who challenges societal assumptions about gender and sexuality. First, Jack joins a fraternity on his college campus, subverting the stereotype that fraternity men are straight and proud of it. While fraternity men are often labeled as rough and tough, acting in very masculine ways, Jack does not conform to this stereotype and is not concerned with partying or with having sex with women. Moreover, Jack talks about his feelings with his friends, violating the usual preconception that only women, not men, talk about their feelings.

Source 1

Cancian, Francesca M. "The Feminization of Love." *Gendered Intimacies.* Chicago: U of Chicago P, 1986. 29-42.

Quotation A

"Women are more open to sharing their feelings than men are."

Quotation B

"Men seem to separate sex and love while women connect them, but paradoxically, sexual intercourse seems to be the most meaningful way of giving and receiving love for many men."

Source 2

Laner, Mary Riege, and Nicole A. Ventrone. "Dating Scripts Revisited." *Journal of Family Issues* 21.4 (May 2000): 76-91.

Quotation C

"Culturally scripted notions about dating behaviors have remained the same over the past few decades."

Quotation D

"Men and women appear to know these dating scripts for themselves and for their partners, making first dates highly predictable."

Source 3

Lorber, Judith. "Believing Is Seeing." *Paradoxes of Gender*. New Haven, CT: Yale UP, 1994. 16-29.

Quotation E

"The differences between men and women are meaningless until social practices transform them."

Quotation F

"Bodies differ in many ways physiologically, but they are completely transformed by social practices to fit into the salient categories of a society, the most pervasive of which are 'female' and 'male' and 'women' and 'men.' "

PART 3

Documentation Styles

DIRECTORY OF MLA PARENTHETICAL REFERENCES

DIRECTORY OF MLA WORKS-CITED LIST ENTRIES

Print Sources

Entries for Books

Authors

Editions, Multivolume Works, Forewords, Translations

Parts of Books

Search

Electronic Sources

Entries from Internet Sites

Internet-Specific Sources

Books, Articles, Reviews, Letters, and Reference Works on the Internet

Paintings, Photographs, Cartoons, and Maps on the Internet

Entries from Subscription Services

Journal Articles, Magazine Articles, and News Services from Subscription Services

Chapter 18
MLA Documentation Style

Frequently Asked Questions

MLA

Documentation, the formal acknowledgment of the sources you use in your paper, enables your readers to judge the quality and originality of your work. This chapter explains and illustrates the documentation style recommended by the Modern Language Association (MLA). Chapter 19 discusses the documentation style of the American Psychological Association (APA); Chapter 20 gives an overview of the formats recommended by *The Chicago Manual of Style* (Chicago); and Chapter 21 presents the formats recommended by the Council of Science Editors (CSE) as well as a list of style manuals recommended by organizations in other disciplines.

18a Using MLA Style*

MLA style is required by many teachers of English and other languages as well as by teachers in other humanities disciplines. This method of documentation has three parts: *parenthetical references in the body of the paper* (also known as *in-text citations*), *a works-cited list*, and *content notes.*

(1) Parenthetical References in the Text

MLA documentation uses **parenthetical references** in the body of the paper keyed to a works-cited list at the end of the paper. A typical

*MLA documentation style follows the guidelines set in the *MLA Handbook for Writers of Research Papers*, 6th ed. New York: MLA, 2003.

parenthetical reference consists of the author's last name and a page number.

```
The colony's religious and political freedom appealed to
many idealists in Europe (Ripley 132).
```

Close-up: Placing Parenthetical References

To make sure each parenthetical reference in your paper clearly refers to the information it documents, follow these guidelines.

- Place documentation after each quotation as well as at the end of each passage of paraphrase or summary. Avoid using a single parenthetical reference to cover several pieces of information from a variety of different sources.
- Place documentation so that it will not interrupt your discussion—ideally, at the end of a sentence.
- To differentiate your ideas from those of your sources, place an identifying tag before, and documentation after, each piece of borrowed material.

See 15d

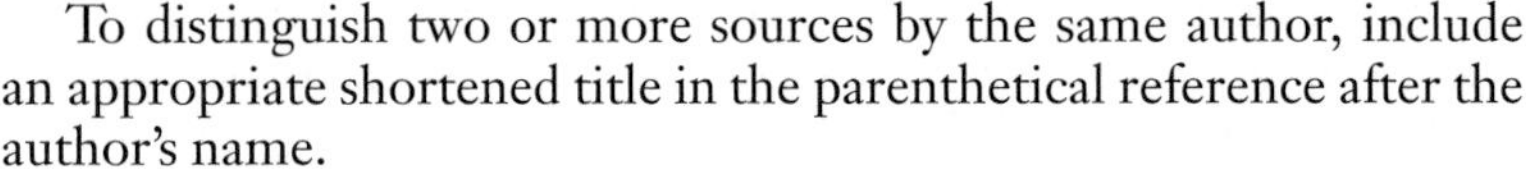

To distinguish two or more sources by the same author, include an appropriate shortened title in the parenthetical reference after the author's name.

```
Penn emphasized his religious motivation (Kelley, William
Penn 116).
```

If you state the author's name or the title of the work in your discussion, do not include it in the parenthetical reference.

```
Penn's political motivation is discussed by Joseph J.
Kelley in Pennsylvania, The Colonial Years, 1681-1776
(44).
```

Close-up: Punctuating with MLA Parenthetical References

Paraphrases and Summaries Parenthetical references are placed *before* the sentence's end punctuation.

```
Penn's writings epitomize seventeenth-century
religious thought (Dengler and Curtis 72).
```

Quotations Run In with the Text Parenthetical references are placed *after* the quotation but *before* the end punctuation.

```
As Ross says, "Penn followed his conscience in all
matters" (127).

According to Williams, "Penn's utopian vision was
informed by his Quaker beliefs . . ." (72).
```

Quotations Set Off from the Text When you quote more than four lines of prose or more than three lines of poetry, parenthetical references are placed one space after the end punctuation.

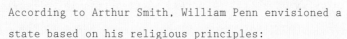

```
According to Arthur Smith, William Penn envisioned a
state based on his religious principles:

        Pennsylvania would be a commonwealth in
        which all individuals would follow God's
        truth and develop according to God's law.
        For Penn, this concept of government was
        self-evident. It would be a mistake to see
        Pennsylvania as anything but an expression
        of Penn's religious beliefs. (314)
```

SAMPLE MLA PARENTHETICAL REFERENCES

1. A Work by a Single Author

```
Fairy tales reflect the emotions and fears of children
(Bettelheim 23).
```

2. A Work by Two or Three Authors

```
The conventions of the ancient Greek theater reflect the
culture in which they developed (Watson and McKernie 17).

With the advent of behaviorism, psychology began a new
phase of inquiry (Cowen, Barbo, and Crum 31-34).
```

3. A Work by More Than Three Authors

List only the first author, followed by `et al.` ("and others").

```
The European powers believed they could change the
fundamentals of Muslim existence (Bull et al. 395).
```

4. A Work in Multiple Volumes

If you list more than one volume of a multivolume work in your works-cited list, include the appropriate volume and page number (separated by a colon followed by a space).

```
The French Revolution had a great influence on William
Blake (Raine 1: 52-53).
```

5. A Work without a Listed Author

Use a shortened version of the title in the parenthetical reference, beginning with the word by which it is alphabetized in the works-cited list.

```
In spite of political unrest, Soviet television remained
fairly conservative, ignoring all challenges to the
system ("Soviet" 3).
```

6. A Work That Is One Page Long

Do not include a page reference for a one-page article.

```
Sixty percent of Arab Americans work in white-collar jobs
(El-Badru).
```

7. An Indirect Source

If you must use a statement by one author that is quoted in the work of another author, indicate that the material is from an indirect source with the abbreviation `qtd. in` ("quoted in").

```
Wagner stated that myth and history stood before him
"with opposing claims" (qtd. in Thomas 65).
```

8. More Than One Work

Cite each work as you normally would, separating one from the other with a semicolon.

```
The Brooklyn Bridge has been used as a subject by many
American artists (McCullough 144; Tashjian 58).
```

NOTE: Long parenthetical references distract readers. Whenever possible, present them as content notes.

9. A Literary Work

When citing a work of prose, it is often helpful to include more than the author's name and the page number in the parenthetical citation. Follow the page number with a semicolon, and then add any additional information that might be necessary.

```
In Moby Dick, Melville refers to a whaling expedition
funded by Louis XIV of France (151; ch. 24).
```

Parenthetical references to poetry do not include page numbers. In parenthetical references to long poems, cite division and line numbers, separating them with a period.

> In the <u>Aeneid</u>, Virgil describes the ships as cleaving the "green woods reflected in the calm water" (8.124).

(In this citation, the reference is to book 8, line 124 of the *Aeneid.*)

When citing short poems, identify the poet and the poem in the text of the paper and use line numbers in the citation.

> In "A Song in the Front Yard," Brooks says, "I've stayed in the front yard all my life / I want a peek at the back" (lines 1-2).

NOTE: When citing lines of a poem, include the word `line` (or `lines`) in the first parenthetical reference; use just numbers in subsequent references.

In citing plays, include the act, scene, and line numbers (in arabic numerals), separated by periods; titles of well-known literary works are often abbreviated (<u>Mac</u>. 2.2.14-16). In biblical citations, include both chapter and the verse; titles of books of the Bible may also be abbreviated. (Gen. 5.12).

10. An Entire Work

When citing an entire work, include the author's name and the work's title in the text of your paper rather than in a parenthetical reference.

> Herbert Gans's <u>The Urban Villagers</u> is a study of an Italian-American neighborhood in Boston.

11. Two or More Authors with the Same Last Name

To distinguish authors with the same last name, include their initials in the parenthetical references.

> Recent increases in crime have caused thousands of urban homeowners to install alarms (L. Cooper, 115). Some of these alarms use sophisticated sensors that were developed by the army (D. Cooper, 76).

12. A Government Document or a Corporate Author

Cite such works using the organization's name followed by the page number (American Automobile Association 34). You can avoid long parenthetical references by working the organization's name into your paper.

According to the President's Commission for the Study of Ethical Problems in Medicine and Biomedical and Behavioral Research, the issues relating to euthanasia are complicated (76).

13. An Electronic Source

If a reference to an electronic source includes paragraph numbers rather than page numbers, use the abbreviation par. or pars. followed by the paragraph number or numbers.

The earliest type of movie censorship came in the form of licensing fees, and in Deer River, Minnesota, "a licensing fee of $200 was deemed not excessive for a town of 1000" (Ernst, par. 20).

If the electronic source has no page or paragraph numbers, try to cite the work in your discussion rather than in a parenthetical reference. By consulting your works-cited list, readers will be able to determine that the source is electronic and may therefore not have page numbers.

In her article "Limited Horizons," Lynne Cheney says that schools do best when students read literature not for practical information but for its insights into the human condition.

(2) Works-Cited List

The **works-cited list,** which appears at the end of your paper, gives publication information for all the research materials you cite. (If your instructor tells you to list all the sources you read, whether you actually cited them or not, give this list the title Works Consulted.) Double-space within and between entries on the list, and indent the second and subsequent lines of each entry one-half inch (five spaces). Items on the list should be arranged alphabetically. (**See 18b** for manuscript guidelines.)

SAMPLE MLA WORKS-CITED LIST ENTRIES

Print Sources

Entries for Books

Book citations include the author's name; book title (underlined); and publication information (place, publisher, date). Capitalize all major words of the title except articles, coordinating conjunctions, prepositions, and the *to* of an infinitive (unless such a word is the first or last word of the title or subtitle). Do not underline the period that follows a book's title.

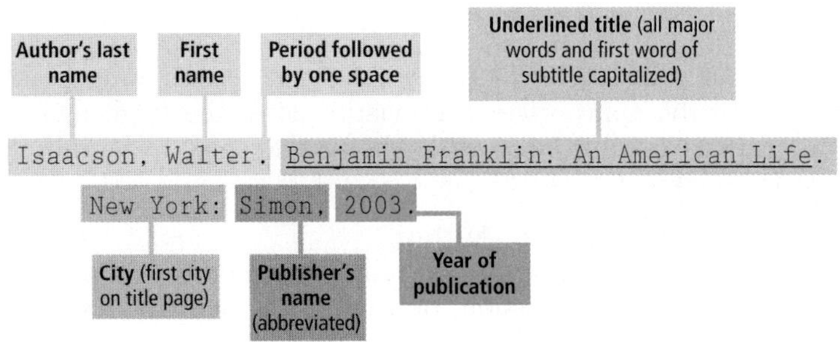

Authors

1. A Book by One Author

Use a short form of the publisher's name; *Alfred A. Knopf, Inc.*, for example, is shortened to *Knopf*, and *Oxford University Press* becomes *Oxford UP.*

Bettelheim, Bruno. <u>The Uses of Enchantment: The Meaning and Importance of Fairy Tales</u>. New York: Knopf, 1976.

2. A Book by Two or Three Authors

List the first author last name first. List subsequent authors first name first in the order in which they appear on the title page.

Watson, Jack, and Grant McKernie. <u>A Cultural History of the Theater</u>. New York: Longman, 1993.

3. A Book by More Than Three Authors

You may either list the first author only, followed by `et al.` ("and others"), or you may include all the authors in the order in which they appear on the title pages.

Bull, Henry, et al. <u>The Near East</u>. New York: Oxford UP, 1990.

Bull, Henry, George Carr, Kim Hoffman, and Gordon Forbes. <u>The Near East</u>. New York: Oxford UP, 1990.

4. Two or More Books by the Same Author

List books by the same author in alphabetical order by title. After the first entry, use three unspaced hyphens followed by a period in place of the author's name.

Thomas, Lewis. The Lives of a Cell: Notes of a Biology Watcher. New York: Viking, 1974.

---. The Medusa and the Snail: More Notes of a Biology Watcher. New York: Viking, 1979.

If the author is the editor or translator of the second entry, place a comma and the appropriate abbreviation after the hyphens (---, ed.). See entry 6 for more on edited books and entry 13 for more on translated books.

5. A Book by a Corporate Author

A book is cited by its corporate author when individual members of the association, commission, or committee that produced it are not identified on the title page.

American Automobile Association. Western Canada and Alaska. Heathrow, FL: AAA Publishing, 1999.

Editions, Multivolume Works, Forewords, Translations

6. An Edited Book

An edited book is a work prepared for publication by a person other than the author. If your focus is on the *author's* work, begin your citation with the author's name. After the title, include the abbreviation Ed. ("Edited by") followed by the name of the editor or editors.

Bartram, William. The Travels of William Bartram. Ed. Mark Van Doren. New York: Dover, 1955.

If your focus is on the *editor's* work, begin your citation with the editor's name followed by the abbreviation ed. ("editor") if there is one editor or eds. ("editors") if there is more than one. After the title, give the author's name preceded by the word By.

Van Doren, Mark, ed. The Travels of William Bartram. By William Bartram. New York: Dover, 1955.

7. A Subsequent Edition of a Book

When citing an edition other than the first, indicate the edition number that appears on the work's title page.

Gans, Herbert J. The Urban Villagers. 2nd ed. New York: Free, 1982.

8. A Republished Book

Include the original publication date after the title of a republished book—for example, a paperback version of a hardcover book.

Wharton, Edith. The House of Mirth. 1905. New York: Scribner's, 1975.

9. A Book in a Series

If the title page indicates that the book is a part of a series, include the series name, neither underlined nor enclosed in quotation marks, and the series number, followed by a period, before the publication information.

Davis, Bertram H. Thomas Percy. Twayne's English Authors Ser. 313. Boston: Twayne, 1981.

10. A Multivolume Work

When all volumes of a multivolume work have the same title, include the number of the volume you are using.

Raine, Kathleen. Blake and Tradition. Vol. 1. Princeton: Princeton UP, 1968.

When you use two or more volumes, cite the entire work.

Raine, Kathleen. Blake and Tradition. 2 vols. Princeton: Princeton UP, 1968.

If the volume you are using has an individual title, you may cite the title without mentioning any other volumes.

Durant, Will, and Ariel Durant. The Age of Napoleon. New York: Simon, 1975.

If you wish, however, you may include supplemental information such as the number of the volume, the title of the entire work, the total number of volumes, and the inclusive publication dates.

11. The Foreword, Preface, or Afterword of a Book

Taylor, Telford. Preface. Less Than Slaves. By Benjamin B. Ferencz. Cambridge: Harvard UP, 1979. xiii-xxii.

12. A Book with a Title within Its Title

If the book you are citing contains a title that is normally underlined to indicate italics (a novel, play, or long poem, for example), do *not* underline the interior title.

Knoll, Robert E., ed. Storm over The Waste Land. Chicago: Scott, 1964.

If the book you are citing contains a title that is normally enclosed within quotation marks, keep the quotation marks.

Herzog, Alan, ed. Twentieth Century Interpretations of "To a Skylark." Englewood Cliffs: Prentice, 1975.

13. A Translation

García Márquez, Gabriel. One Hundred Years of Solitude. Trans. Gregory Rabassa. New York: Avon, 1991.

Parts of Books

14. A Short Story, Play, or Poem in an Anthology

Chopin, Kate. "The Storm." Literature: Reading, Reacting, Writing. Ed. Laurie G. Kirszner and Stephen R. Mandell. 5th ed. Boston: Wadsworth, 2004. 176-79.

Shakespeare, William. Othello, The Moor of Venice. Shakespeare: Six Plays and the Sonnets. Ed. Thomas Marc Parrott and Edward Hubler. New York: Scribner's, 1956. 145-91.

See entry 17 for guidelines about how to cite more than one work from the same anthology.

15. A Short Story, Play, Poem, or Essay in a Collection of an Author's Work

Walcott, Derek. "Nearing La Guaira." Selected Poems. New York: Farrar, 1964. 47-48.

16. An Essay in an Anthology

Even if you cite only one page of the essay in your paper, supply inclusive page numbers for the entire essay.

Lloyd, G. E. R. "Science and Mathematics." The Legacy of Greece. Ed. Moses I. Finley. New York: Oxford UP, 1981. 256-300.

17. More Than One Work from the Same Anthology

List each work from the same anthology separately, followed by a cross-reference to the entire anthology. List complete publication information for the anthology itself.

Bolgar, Robert R. "The Greek Legacy." Finley 429-72.

Finley, Moses I., ed. The Legacy of Greece. New York: Oxford UP, 1981.

Williams, Bernard. "Philosophy." Finley 202-55.

18. An Article in a Reference Book (Signed/Unsigned)

For a signed article, begin with the author's name. For unfamiliar reference books, include full publication information.

Drabble, Margaret. "Expressionism." The Oxford Companion to English Literature. 5th ed. New York: Oxford UP, 1985.

If the article is unsigned, begin with the title. For familiar reference books, do not include publication information.

"Cubism." The Encyclopedia Americana. 1994 ed.

NOTE: You may omit page numbers if the reference book lists entries alphabetically.

If you are listing one definition among several from a dictionary, include the abbreviation Def. ("Definition") along with the letter or number that corresponds to the definition.

"Justice." Def. 2b. The Concise Oxford Dictionary. 10th ed. 1999.

Dissertations, Pamphlets, Government Publications

19. A Dissertation (Published/Unpublished)

Cite a published dissertation the same way you would cite a book, but add relevant dissertation information before the publication information. For dissertations published by University Microfilms International (UMI), include the order number at the end of the entry.

Peterson, Shawn. Loving Mothers and Lost Daughters: Images of Female Kinship Relations in Selected Novels of Toni Morrison. Diss. U of Oregon, 1993. Ann Arbor: UMI, 1994. ATT 9322935.

NOTE: University Microfilms, which publishes most of the dissertations in the United States, also publishes in CD-ROM. For the proper format for citing CD-ROMs, see entries 77 and 78.

Use quotation marks for the title of an unpublished dissertation.

Romero, Yolanda Garcia. "The American Frontier Experience in Twentieth-Century Northwest Texas." Diss. Texas Tech U, 1993.

20. A Pamphlet

If no author is listed, begin with the underlined title.

Existing Light Photography. Rochester: Kodak, 1989.

21. A Government Publication

If the publication has no listed author, begin with the name of the government followed by the name of the agency; you may use an abbreviation if its meaning is clear: United States. Cong. Senate.

United States. Office of Consumer Affairs. 2003 Consumer's Resource Handbook. Washington: GPO, 2003.

When citing two or more publications by the same government, use three unspaced hyphens in place of the name for the second and subsequent entries. If you also cite more than one work from the same agency of that government, use an additional set of unspaced hyphens in place of the agency name.

United States. FAA. Passenger Airline Safety in the Twenty-First Century. Washington: GPO, 2003.

---. ---. Recycled Air in Passenger Airline Cabins. Washington: GPO, 2002.

Entries for Articles

Article citations include the author's name; the title of the article (in quotation marks); the title of the periodical (underlined); the month (abbreviated except for May, June, and July) and the year; and the pages on which the full article appears, without the abbreviations *p.* or *pp.*

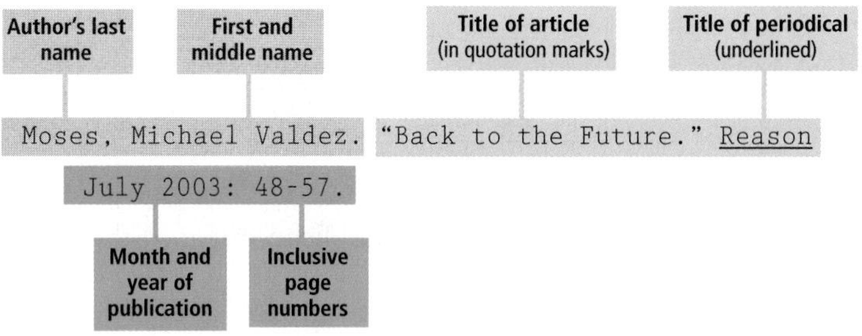

Scholarly Journals

22. An Article in a Scholarly Journal with Continuous Pagination through an Annual Volume

For an article in a journal with continuous pagination—for example, one in which an issue ends on page 172 and the next issue begins with page 173—include the volume number, followed by the date of publication (in parentheses). Follow the publication date with a colon, a space, and the inclusive page numbers.

Huntington, John. "Science Fiction and the Future." College English 37 (1975): 340-58.

23. An Article in a Scholarly Journal with Separate Pagination in Each Issue

For a journal in which each issue begins with page 1, include the volume number, a period, and the issue number.

Sipes, R. G. "War, Sports, and Aggression: An Empirical Test of Two Rival Theories." American Anthropologist 4.2 (1973): 65-84.

Magazines and Newspapers

24. An Article in a Weekly Magazine (Signed/Unsigned)

For signed articles, start with the author, last name first. In dates, the day precedes the month.

Traub, James. "The Hearts and Minds of City College." New Yorker 7 June 1993: 42-53.

For unsigned articles, start with the title of the article.

"Solzhenitsyn: A Candle in the Wind." Time 23 Mar. 1970: 70.

25. An Article in a Monthly Magazine

Roll, Lori. "Careers in Engineering." Working Woman Nov. 1982: 62.

26. An Article That Does Not Appear on Consecutive Pages

When, for example, an article begins on page 120 and then skips to page 186, include only the first page number and a plus sign.

Griska, Linda. "Stress and Job Performance." Psychology Today Nov.-Dec. 1995: 120+.

27. An Article in a Newspaper (Signed/Unsigned)

Oates, Joyce Carol. "When Characters from the Page Are Made Flesh on the Screen." New York Times 23 Mar. 1986, late ed.: C1+.

"Soviet Television." Los Angeles Times 13 Dec. 1990, sec. 2: 3+.

NOTE: Omit the article *the* from the title of a newspaper even if the actual title includes the article.

28. An Editorial in a Newspaper

"Tough Cops, Not Brutal Cops." Editorial. New York Times 5 May 1994, late ed.: A26.

29. A Letter to the Editor of a Newspaper

Chang, Paula. Letter. Philadelphia Inquirer 10 Dec. 2003, suburban ed.: A17.

30. A Book Review in a Newspaper

Fox-Genovese, Elizabeth. "Big Mess on Campus." Rev. of Illiberal Education: The Politics of Race and Sex on Campus, by Dinesh D'Souza. Washington Post 15 Apr. 1991, ntnl. weekly ed.: 32.

31. An Article with a Title within Its Title

If the article you are citing contains a title that is normally enclosed within quotation marks, use single quotation marks for the interior title.

Nash, Robert. "About 'The Emperor of Ice Cream.'" Perspectives 7 (1954): 122-24.

If the article you are citing contains a title that is normally underlined to indicate italics, underline it in your works-cited entry.

Leicester, H. Marshall, Jr. "The Art of Impersonation: A General Prologue to The Canterbury Tales." PMLA 95 (1980): 213-24.

Entries for Other Miscellaneous Print and Nonprint Sources

Lectures and Interviews

32. A Lecture

Sandman, Peter. "Communicating Scientific Information." Communications Seminar, Dept. of Humanities and Communications. Drexel U, 26 Oct. 1999.

33. A Personal Interview

West, Cornel. Personal interview. 28 Dec. 2002.

Tannen, Deborah. Telephone interview. 8 June 2003.

34. A Published Interview

Stavros, George. "An Interview with Gwendolyn Brooks." Contemporary Literature 11.1 (Winter 1970): 1-20.

Letters

35. A Personal Letter

Tan, Amy. Letter to the author. 7 Apr. 2001.

36. A Letter Published in a Collection

Joyce, James. "Letter to Louis Gillet." 20 Aug. 1931. James Joyce. By Richard Ellmann. New York: Oxford UP, 1965. 631.

37. A Letter in a Library's Archives

Stieglitz, Alfred. Letter to Paul Rosenberg. 5 Sept. 1923. Stieglitz Archive. Yale, New Haven.

Films, Videotapes, Radio and Television Programs, Recordings

38. A Film

Include the title of the film (underlined), the distributor, and the date, along with other information of use to readers, such as the names of the performers, the director, and the writer.

Citizen Kane. Dir. Orson Welles. Perf. Welles, Joseph Cotten, Dorothy Comingore, and Agnes Moorehead. RKO, 1941.

If you are focusing on the contribution of a particular person, begin with that person's name.

Welles, Orson, dir. Citizen Kane. Perf. Welles, Joseph Cotten, Dorothy Comingore, and Agnes Moorehead. RKO, 1941.

39. A Videotape, DVD, or Laser Disc

Cite a videotape, DVD (digital videodisc), or laser disc like a film, but include the medium before the name of the distributor.

Miller, Arthur. Interview. The Crucible. Dir. William Schiff. Videocassette. The Mosaic Group, 1987.

40. A Radio or Television Program

"Prime Suspect 3." By Lynda La Plante. Perf. Helen Mirren. Mystery! PBS. WNET, New York. 28 Apr. 1994.

41. A Recording

List the composer, conductor, or performer (whichever you are focusing on), followed by the title (and, when citing jacket notes, a description of the material), manufacturer, and year of issue.

Boubill, Alain, and Claude-Michel Schönberg. Miss Saigon. Perf. Lea Salonga, Claire Moore, and Jonathan Pryce. Cond. Martin Koch. Geffen, 1989.

Marley, Bob. "Crisis." Lyrics. Bob Marley and the Wailers. Kava Island Records, 1978.

Paintings, Photographs, Cartoons, Advertisements

42. A Painting

Hopper, Edward. Railroad Sunset. 1929. Whitney Museum of American Art, New York.

43. A Photograph

Cite a photograph in a museum's collection in the same way you cite a painting.

Stieglitz, Alfred. The Steerage. Los Angeles County Museum of Art.

To cite a personal photograph, begin with a descriptive title (neither underlined nor set within quotation marks), followed by the place the photograph was taken, the photographer, and the date.

Rittenhouse Square, Philadelphia. Personal photograph by author. 6 May 2003.

44. A Cartoon or Comic Strip

Trudeau, Garry. "Doonesbury." Comic strip. Philadelphia Inquirer 19 July 1999, late ed.: E13.

45. An Advertisement

Microsoft. Advertisement. National Review 28 June 1999: 11.

Electronic Sources

Entries from Internet Sites

The documentation style for Internet sources presented here conforms to the most recent guidelines published in the *MLA Handbook for Writers of Research Papers* (6th ed.) and found online at <http://www.mla.org>. (If your instructor prefers that you use **Columbia Online Style** for citing electronic sources, see pages 390–93.)

MLA style recognizes that full source information for Internet sources is not always available. Include in your citation whatever information you can reasonably obtain: the title of the Internet site (underlined); the version number of the source (if applicable); the date of electronic publication (or update); the number or range of pages, paragraphs, or sections (if available); the name of any institution or sponsor; the date of access to the source; and the URL. Figure 18.1 shows where to find the information needed for documenting an electronic source.

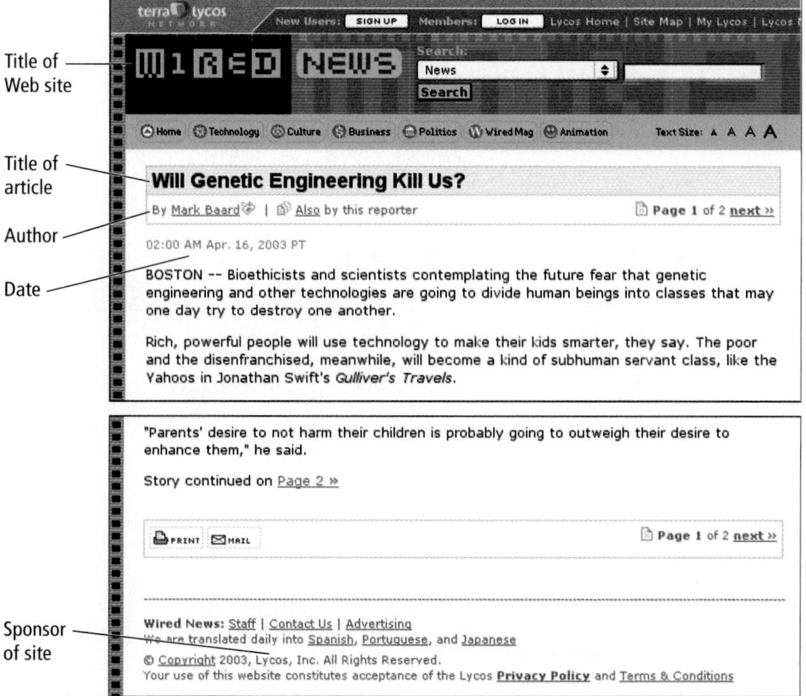

Figure 18.1 Part of an online article showing the location of the information needed for documentation.

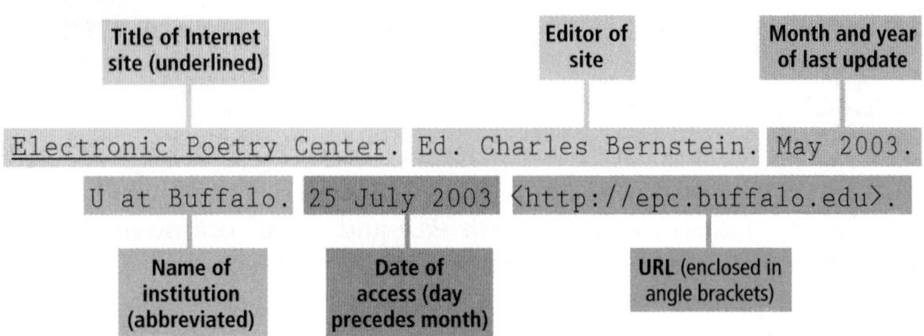

MLA requires that you enclose the electronic address (URL) within angle brackets to distinguish the address from the punctuation in the rest of the citation. If a URL will not fit on a line, the computer will carry the entire URL over to the next line. If you prefer to divide the URL, divide it after a slash. (Do not insert a hyphen.) If it is excessively long, give just the URL of the site's search page. Readers can then access the document by entering the author's name or the source's title.

Internet-Specific Sources

46. An Entire Web Site

Philadelphia Writers Project. Ed. Miriam Kotzen Green. May 1998. Drexel U. 12 June 2001 <http://www.Drexel.edu/letrs/wwp>.

47. A Document within a Web Site

"D Day: June 7th, 1944." The History Channel Online. 1999. History Channel. 7 June 2002 <http://historychannel.com/thisday/today/997690.html>.

48. A Home Page for a Course

Mulry, David. Composition and Literature. Course home page. Jan. 2003-Apr. 2003. Dept. of English, Odessa College. 6 Apr. 2003 <http:// www.odessa.edu/dept/english/dmulryEnglish_1302.html>.

49. A Personal Home Page

Gainor, Charles. Home page. 22 July 2003. 10 Nov. 2003 <http://www.chass.utoronto.ca:9094/~char>.

50. A Linked Site

If you get information from a linked site—that is, if you connect from one site to another—include the title of the document you cite (followed by its date) and the abbreviation `Lkd.` (followed by the original site from which you accessed your document). Follow this with the date of access and the URL.

Schnell, Eric H. Writing for the Web: A Primer for Librarians. Vers. 11. Jan. 2003. Lkd. OWL at Purdue U. 24 July 2003 <http://owl.english.purdue.edu/internet/resources/writetech.html#web>.

51. A Radio Program Accessed from an Internet Archive

Edwards, Bob. "Country Music's First Family." Morning Edition. 16 July 2002. NPR Archives. 2 Oct. 2002 <http://www.npr.org/programs/morning/index.html>.

52. An Email

Adkins, Camille. Email to the author. 28 June 2001.

53. An Online Posting (Newsgroup or Online Forum)

Gilford, Mary. "Dog Heroes in Children's Literature." Online posting. 17 Mar. 1999. 12 Apr. 1999 <news:alt.animals.dogs>.

Schiller, Stephen. "Paper Cost and Publishing Costs." Online posting. 24 Apr. 1999. 11 May 1999. Book Forum. 17 May 1999 <www.nytimes.com/webin/webx?13A^41356.ee765e/0>.

54. A Synchronous Communication (MOO or MUD)

MOOs (multiuser domain, object oriented) and MUDs (multiuser domain) are Internet programs that enable users to communicate in real time. To cite a communication obtained on a MOO or a MUD, give the name (or names) of the writer(s), a description of the event, the date of the event, the forum (LinguaMOO, for example), the date of access, and the URL (starting with `telnet://`).

Guitar, Gwen. Online discussion of Cathy in Emily Brontë's Wuthering Heights. 17 Mar. 1999. LinguaMOO. 17 Mar. 1999 <telnet://lingua.utdallas.edu:8888>.

Books, Articles, Reviews, Letters, and Reference Works on the Internet

55. A Book

Douglass, Frederick. My Bondage and My Freedom. Boston, 1855. 8 June 2000 <gopher://gopher.vt.edu:10024/22/178/3>.

56. An Article in a Scholarly Journal

When you cite information from an electronic source that has a print version, include the publication information for the printed source, the number of pages or paragraphs (if available), and the date you accessed it.

Dekoven, Marianne. "Utopias Limited: Post-Sixties and Postmodern American Fiction." Modern Fiction Studies 41.1 (1995): 13 pp. 17 Mar. 1999 <http://muse.jhu.edu/journals/mfs.v041/41.1dwkovwn.html>.

57. An Article in a Magazine

Weiser, Jay. "The Tyranny of Informality." Time 26 Feb. 1996. 1 Mar. 2002 <http://www.enews.com/magazines.tnr/current/022696.3.html>.

58. An Article in a Newspaper

Lohr, Steve. "Microsoft Goes to Court." New York Times on the Web 19 Oct. 1998. 29 Apr. 1999 <http://www.nytimes.com/web/docroot/library.ciber/week/1019business.html>.

59. An Article in a Newsletter

"Unprecedented Cutbacks in History of Science Funding." AIP Center for History of Physics 27.2 (Fall 1995). 26 Feb. 1996 <http://www.aip.org/history/fall95.html>.

60. A Review

Ebert, Roger. Rev. of Star Wars: Episode I—The Phantom Menace, dir. George Lucas. Chicago Sun-Times Online 8 June 2000. 22 June 2000 <http://www.suntimes.com/output/ebert1/08show.html>.

61. A Letter to the Editor

Chen-Cheng, Henry H. Letter. New York Times on the Web 19 July 1999. 19 July 1999 <http://www.nytimes.com/hr/mo/day/letters/ichen-cheng.html>.

62. An Article in an Encyclopedia

Include the article's title, the title of the database (underlined), the version number, the date of electronic publication, the sponsor, and the date of access as well as the URL.

"Hawthorne, Nathaniel." Encyclopaedia Britannica Online. 2002. Encyclopaedia Britannica. 16 May 2002 <http://www.search.eb.com>.

63. A Government Publication

Cite an online government publication the same way you would a print version; end with the information required for an electronic source.

United States. Dept. of Justice. Bureau of Justice Statistics. Violence against Women: Estimates from the Redesigned National Crime Victimization Survey. Jan. 1995. 10 July 2003 <www.ojp.usdoj.gov/bjs/020131.pdf>.

Paintings, Photographs, Cartoons, and Maps on the Internet

64. A Painting

Seurat, Georges-Pierre. Evening, Honfleur. 1886. Museum of Mod. Art, New York. 8 Jan. 2004 <http://www.moma.org/collection/depts/paint_sculpt/blowups/paint_sculpt_002.html>.

65. A Photograph

Brady, Mathew. Ulysses S. Grant 1822-1885. Mathew Brady's National Portrait Gallery. 2 Oct. 2002 <http://www.npg.si.edu/exh/brady/gallery/56gal.html>.

66. A Cartoon

Stossel, Sage. "Star Wars: The Next Generation." Cartoon. Atlantic Unbound 2 Oct. 2002. 14 Nov. 2002 <http://www.theatlantic.com/unbound/sage/ss990519.htm>.

67. A Map

"Philadelphia, Pennsylvania." Map. U.S. Gazetteer. US Census Bureau. 17 July 2000 <http://www.census.gov/cgi-bin/gazetteer>.

Close-up: Internet Sources

WARNING: Using information from Internet sources—especially newsgroups and online forums—is risky. Contributors are not necessarily experts, and frequently they are incorrect and misinformed. Unless you can be certain the information you are obtaining from these sources is reliable, do not use it. You can check the reliability of an Internet source by consulting Chapter 14 or by asking your instructor or reference librarian for guidance.

Entries from Subscription Services

Subscription services can be divided into those to which you subscribe (**personal subscription services**), such as America Online, and those to which your library subscribes (**library subscription services**), such as Gale Group Databases, LexisNexis, and ProQuest Direct.

To cite information from a **personal subscription service,** include the name of the database (underlined) as well as the name of the subscription service. If the personal subscription service provides a URL for a specific document, follow the examples in entries 46–54. Personal subscription services usually supply information without a URL, however. If the subscription service enables you to use a keyword to access material, type `Keyword` followed by a colon and the keyword (after the date of access).

"Kafka, Franz." Compton's Encyclopedia Online. Vers. 3.1. 2000. America Online. 8 June 2003. Keyword: Compton's.

If instead of using a keyword you follow a series of topic labels, type the word `Path` followed by a colon and then the sequence of topics (separated by semicolons) you followed to get to the material.

"Elizabeth Adams." History Resources. 11 Nov. 2002. America Online. 28 Apr. 2002. Path: Research; Biography; Women in Science; Biographies.

To cite information from a **library subscription service,** supply the publishing information (including page numbers, if available) followed by the underlined name of the database (if known), the name of the subscription service, the library at which you accessed the database, the date of access, and the URL of the service's home page.

Luckenbill, Trent. "Environmental Litigation: Down the Endless Corridor." Environment 8 June 2001: 34-42. ABI/INFORM Global. ProQuest Direct. Drexel U Lib., Philadelphia, PA. 12 Oct. 2001 <http://www.umi.com/proquest>.

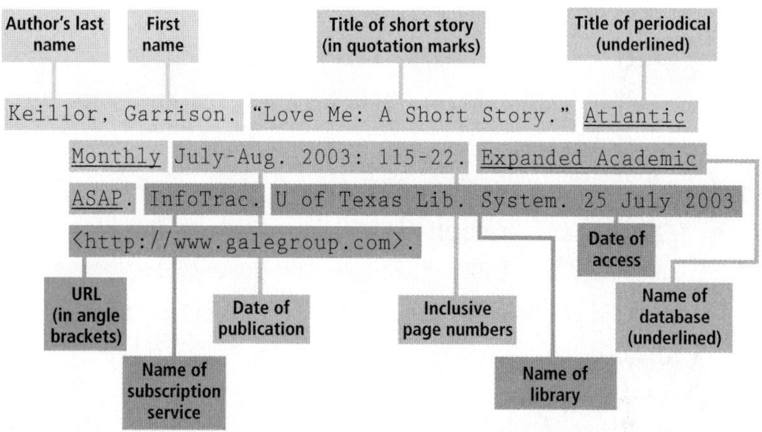

Journal Articles, Magazine Articles, and News Services from Subscription Services

68. A Scholarly Journal Article with Separate Pagination in Each Issue

Schaefer, Richard J. "Editing Strategies in Television News Documentaries." Journal of Communication 47.4 (1997): 69-89. InfoTrac OneFile Plus. Gale Group Databases. Augusta R. Kolwyck Lib., Chattanooga, TN. 2 Oct. 2002 <http://library.cstcc.cc.tn.us/ref3.shtml>.

NOTE: Along with the name of the library, you may include the city and state if you think they would be of use.

69. A Scholarly Journal Article with Continuous Pagination Throughout an Annual Volume

Hudson, Nicholas. "Samuel Johnson, Urban Culture, and the Geography of Postfire London." <u>Studies in English Literature</u> 42 (2002): 557-80. <u>MasterFILE Premier</u>. EBSCOhost. Augusta R. Kolwyck Lib., Chattanooga, TN. 15 Sept. 2003 <http://library.cstcc.cc.tn.us/ref3.shtml>.

70. A Monthly Magazine Article

Livermore, Beth. "Meteorites on Ice." <u>Astronomy</u> July 1993: 54-58. <u>Expanded Academic ASAP Plus</u>. Gale Group Databases. Augusta R. Kolwyck Lib., Chattanooga, TN. 12 Nov. 2003 <http://library.cstcc.cc.tn.us/ref3.shtml>.

Wright, Karen. "The Clot Thickens." <u>Discover</u> Dec. 1999. <u>MasterFILE Premier</u>. EBSCOhost. Augusta R. Kolwyck Lib., Chattanooga, TN. 10 Oct. 2003 <http://library.cstcc.cc.tn.us/ref3.shtml>.

71. A News Service

Ryan, Desmond. "Some Background on the Battle of Gettysburg." <u>Knight Ridder/Tribune News Service</u> 7 Oct. 1993. <u>InfoTrac OneFile Plus</u>. Gale Group Databases. Augusta R. Kolwyck Lib., Chattanooga, TN. 16 Nov. 2003 <http://infotrac.galegroup.com/menu>.

72. A News Wire

"General Dwight D. Eisenhower's Official WW II Diaries Discovered." <u>US Newswire</u> 20 Nov. 2001. <u>InfoTrac OneFile Plus</u>. Gale Group Databases. Augusta R. Kolwyck Lib., Chattanooga, TN. 20 Jan. 2003 <http://library.cstcc.cc.tn.us/ref3.shtml>.

73. A Newspaper Article

Meyer, Greg. "Answering Questions about the West Nile Virus." <u>Dayton Daily News</u> 11 July 2002: Z3-7.

Academic Universe News. LexisNexis. Augusta R. Kolwyck Lib., Chattanooga, TN. 17 Feb. 2003 <http://library.cstcc.cc.tn.us/ref3.shtml>.

Reference Works and Pamphlets from Subscription Services

74. A Reference Book Article

Laird, Judith. "Geoffrey Chaucer." Cyclopedia of World Authors. 1997 ed. MagillOnLiterature. EBSCOhost. Augusta R. Kolwyck Lib., Chattanooga, TN. 14 Sept. 2003 <http://library.cstcc.cc.tn.us/ref3.shtml>.

75. A Dictionary Definition

"Migraine." Mosby's Medical, Nursing, and Allied Health Dictionary. 1998 ed. Health Reference Center. Gale Group Databases. Augusta R. Kolwyck Lib., Chattanooga, TN. 16 Apr. 2003 <http://library.cstcc.cc.tn.us/ref3.shtml>.

76. A Pamphlet

National Institute of Diabetes and Digestive and Kidney Diseases. Prevent Diabetes Problems: Keep Your Eyes Healthy. Pamphlet. 1 May 2000. Health Reference Center Academic. Gale Group Databases. Augusta R. Kolwyck Lib., Chattanooga, TN. 2 Oct. 2002 <http://library.cstcc.cc.tn.us/ref3.shtml>.

Other Electronic Sources

DVDs and CD-ROMs

77. A Nonperiodical Publication on DVD, CD-ROM, or Diskette Database

Cite a nonperiodical publication on DVD, CD-ROM, or diskette the same way you would cite a book, but also include a description of the medium of publication.

"Windhover." The Oxford English Dictionary. 2nd ed. DVD. Oxford: Oxford UP, 2001.

"Whitman, Walt." DiskLit: America Authors. CD-ROM. Boston: Hall, 2000.

78. A Periodical Publication on a DVD or CD-ROM Database

Zurbach, Kate. "The Linguistic Roots of Three Terms." Linguistic Quarterly 37 (1994): 12-47. InfoTrac: Magazine Index Plus. CD-ROM. Information Access. Jan. 2001.

Close-up: Columbia Online Style

Columbia Online Style (COS) was developed to accommodate the wide variety of sources that are available in an electronic environment. For this reason, some instructors prefer their students to use COS humanities style instead of MLA style when they document electronic sources. Remember that the MLA does not recognize COS, so be sure to check with your instructor before you use it.

Format

Author's Last Name, First Name. "Title of Document." *Title of Complete Work* [if applicable]. Version or File Number [if applicable]. Document date or date of last revision [if different from access date]. Protocol and address, access path or directories (Access date).

NOTE: Like MLA style, Columbia Online Style requires a double-space within and between entries. However, Columbia Online Style uses italics where MLA requires underlining. In addition, angle brackets are not used in COS.

1. A World Wide Web Site

Sandy, Adam. "Roller Coaster History." Coney Island History. 2001. http://www.ultimaterollercoaster.com/coasters/history/history-coney.html (12 Nov. 2001).

NOTE: If the Web site lists no author, include the name of the group, organization, corporation, news service, or governmental agency in place of the author's name.

2. An Article from a News Service

Associated Press. "Toledo Jeep Workers Approve New Contract." *Auto.com* 3 Oct. 2002. http://www.auto.com/industry/iwirc3_20021003.htm (27 June 2003).

3. A Work by a Group or Organization

Shark Research Institute. "Landmark Victories to Protect Two Species of Giant Sharks." 18 Nov. 2002. http://www.sharks.org/news/11.18.02.html (27 June 2003).

4. A Corporate Home Page

McDonald's. "McDonald's." http://www.mcdonalds.com (28 May 2003).

5. An Online Journal Article

Dekoven, Marianne. "Utopias Unlimited: Post Sixties and Postmodern American Fiction." *Modern Fiction Studies*. 41:1 (1995). http://muse.jhu.edu/journals/mfs.v041/41.1dwkovwn.html (17 Mar. 1999).

6. A Previously Published Article or Document

Include the original publication information before the title of the archive site, the URL, and the date of access.

Weinberg, Robert A. "Of Clones and Clowns." *The Atlantic Monthly* 289.6 (June 2002): 54. *The Atlantic Online*. http://www.theatlantic.com/issues/2002/06/weinberg.htm (15 June 2003).

7. An Online Magazine

Walker, Rob. "Is the Stock Market in Denial?" *Slate* 15 Nov. 2001. http://slate.msn.com/?id-2058732 (19 Nov. 2001).

(continued)

Columbia online style (continued)

8. An Online News Service or Online Newspaper

McGirk, Tim. "Deep Loyalties, Ancient Hatreds." *Time.com*. 12 Nov. 2001. http://www.time.com/time/magazine/article/0,9171,1101011119-183964,00.html (19 Nov. 2001).

9. Email, Listservs, and Newsgroups

Goren, Seth. "Joke of the Week." Personal email (14 Nov. 2001).

Friedlander, Sandy. "Computer Collaboration in the Writing Classroom." *Alliance for Computers and Writing Listserv*. acw-l@unicorn.acs.ttu.edu (17 June 2000).

Provizor, Norman. "Jazz in the 1990s." 2 Mar. 2000. alt.music.jazz (5 Mar. 2000).

10. A Gopher Site

Douglass, Stephen. "Can Computers Think?" *Journal of Experimental and Artificial Intelligence* (1999). gopher://gopher.liv.ac.uk:80/00/phil/philos-12-files/searle.harnad (7 Aug. 2000).

11. An FTP Site

Johnson, Cassandra. "Cleaning Up Hypertext Links." 3 Dec. 2000. ftp://ftp.daedalus.com/pub/CCCC95/johnson (14 Oct. 2001).

12. A Telnet Site

Rigg, Doreen. "Lesson Plan for Teaching about the Hubble Telescope." *Space News*. 11 Oct. 2000. telnet://spacelink.msfc.nasa.gov.guest (2 Dec. 2000).

13. A Synchronous Communication Site

Guitar, Gwen. "Update." *DaMOO.* telnet://damoo.csun.edu:7777 (4 Dec. 1996).

14. An Online Reference Source

Kevles, D. J. "Human Genome Project." *Columbia Encyclopedia.* 6th ed. NY: Columbia UP, 2001. *America Online.* Reference Desk/Encyclopedias/Columbia Encyclopedia (17 Nov. 2001).

15. Electronic Publications and Online Databases

Cinbac, James. "Wishing Won't Do It: Baby Boomers Save for Retirement." Business Week, 1 Apr. 2000: 50. *InfoTrac SearchBank.* File #9606273898 (12 Aug. 2000).

16. Software Programs and Video Games

Mac Washer. Vers. 2.1. St. Louis: Webroot Software, 2000.

Abuse. Vers. 3.2. Chicago: Bungie Software Products, 1996.

(3) Content Notes

Content notes—multiple bibliographical citations or other material that does not fit smoothly into the text—are indicated by a **superscript** (raised numeral) in the paper. Notes can appear either as footnotes at the bottom of the page or as endnotes on a separate sheet entitled Notes (or Note, if there is only one endnote), placed after the last page of the paper and before the works-cited list. Content notes are double-spaced within and between entries. The first line is indented one-half inch (5 spaces), and subsequent lines are typed flush left.

For Multiple Citations

In the Paper

Many researchers emphasize the necessity of having dying patients share their experiences.[1]

In the Note

[1]Kübler-Ross 27; Stinnette 43; Poston 70; Cohen and Cohen 31-34; Burke 1: 91-95.

For Other Material

In the Paper

The massacre during World War I is an event the survivors could not easily forget.[2]

In the Note

[2]For a firsthand account of these events, see Bedoukian 178-81.

Exercise

The following notes identify sources used in a paper on censorship and the Internet. Following the proper format for MLA parenthetical documentation, create a parenthetical reference for each source, and then create a works-cited list, arranging the sources in the proper order. (If your instructor requires a different method of documentation, use that style instead.)

1. Page 72 in a book called Banned in the USA by Herbert N. Foerstel. The book has 231 pages and was published in a second edition in 2002 by Greenwood Press, located in Westport, Connecticut. The author's name appears in the text of your paper.
2. A statement made by Esther Dyson in her keynote address at the Newspapers 1996 Conference. Her statement is quoted in an article by Jodi B. Cohen called Fighting Online Censorship. The speech has not been printed in any other source. The article is in the April 13, 1996, edition of the weekly business journal Editor & Publisher. Dyson's quotation appears on page 44. The article begins on page 44 and continues on page 60. Dyson's name is mentioned in the text of your paper.
3. If You Don't Love It, Leave It, an essay by Esther Dyson in the New York Times Magazine, July 15, 1995, on pages 26 and 27. Your quotation comes from the second page of the essay. No author's name is mentioned in the text of your paper.
4. An essay by Nat Hentoff titled Speech Should Not Be Limited on pages 22–26 of the book Censorship: Opposing Viewpoints, edited by Terry O'Neill. The book is published by Greenhaven Press in St. Paul, Minnesota. The publication year is 1985. The quotation you have used is from page 24, and the author is mentioned in the text of your paper.

5. An essay on the Internet called A Parent's Guide to Supervising a Child's Online and Internet Experiences. The document is by Robert Cannon, Esq., and you have Version 2.0 of the essay, which was updated May 10, 2002. Though the essay prints out on four pages, the pages are not numbered. In your paper, you summarize information from the second and third pages of the document. You accessed the information on January 20, 2003, from *Expanded Academic ASAP Plus* through your library's subscription service, Gale Group Databases.

18b MLA Manuscript Guidelines

Although MLA papers do not usually include abstracts, internal headings, tables, or graphs, this situation is changing. If you want to use any of these elements in your paper, be sure to check with your instructor.

The guidelines in the following checklists are based on the latest version of the *MLA Handbook for Writers of Research Papers.*

Checklist: Typing Your Paper

When typing your paper, use the student paper in 18c as your model.

- ☐ Type your paper with a one-inch margin at the top and bottom and on both sides. Double-space your paper throughout.
- ☐ Type your name, your instructor's name, the course title, and the date on separate lines against the upper-left margin. Double-space, center, and type the title. Double-space again, and begin typing the text of the paper.

  NOTE: MLA does not recommend a title page. If your instructor requires one, ask for guidelines, or use the format illustrated in 17l.
- ☐ Capitalize all important words in your title, but not prepositions, articles, coordinating conjunctions, or the *to* in infinitives (unless they begin or end the title or subtitle). Do not underline your title or enclose it in quotation marks. Never put a period after the title, even if it is a sentence.
- ☐ Set off more than four lines of prose or more than three lines of poetry by indenting the whole quotation one inch (or 10 spaces). If you quote a single paragraph or part of a paragraph,

(continued)

Typing your paper (continued)

do not indent the first line beyond one inch. If you quote two or more paragraphs, indent the first line of each paragraph an additional quarter inch. (If the first sentence does not begin a paragraph, do not indent it. Indent the first line only in successive paragraphs.)

- ☐ Number all pages of your paper consecutively—including the first—in the upper right-hand corner, one-half inch from the top, flush right. Type your name followed by a space before the page number on every page.
- ☐ If you use source material in your paper, follow MLA documentation style.

See 18a

Checklist: Using Visuals

See 5b3, 29d

- ☐ Insert visuals into the text as close as possible to where they are discussed.
- ☐ Label each table with the word `Table` followed by an arabic numeral (for instance, `Table 1`). Double-space, and type a descriptive caption, with the first line flush left with the left-hand margin; indent subsequent lines one-quarter inch. Capitalize the caption as if it were a title. (Both the table number and descriptive caption should appear above the table.) Type the word `Source` below the table, followed by a colon and all source information. Type the first line of the source note flush with the left-hand margin; indent subsequent lines one-quarter inch.
- ☐ Label other types of visual material—graphs, charts, photographs, clip art, drawings, and so on—`Fig.` (Figure) followed by an arabic numeral (for example, `Fig. 2`). Type each label and a title or caption on the same line, followed by source information, directly below the visual. Type all lines flush with the left-hand margin.
- ☐ Label musical illustrations `Ex.` (Example) followed by an arabic numeral and a title or caption. Type all lines flush with the left-hand margin, directly below the illustration. When typing captions for visuals other than tables, capitalize only the first word, proper nouns, or other titles.
- ☐ Do not include the source of the visual in the works-cited list unless you use other material from that source elsewhere in the paper.

Checklist: Preparing the MLA Works-Cited List

See 18a3

- ☐ Begin the works-cited list on a new page after the last page of text or content notes, numbered as the next page of the paper.
- ☐ Center the title `Works Cited` one inch from the top of the page. Double-space between the title and the first entry.
- ☐ Each entry on the works-cited list has three divisions: author, title, and publication information. Separate divisions with a period and one space.
- ☐ List entries alphabetically, last name first. Use the author's full name as it appears on the title page. If a source has no listed author, alphabetize it by the first word of the title (not counting the article).
- ☐ Type the first line of each entry flush with the left-hand margin; indent subsequent lines five spaces (or one-half inch).
- ☐ Double-space within and between entries.
- ☐ Enclose URLs in angle brackets. If a URL carries over to the next line, break the URL after a slash; do not insert a hyphen. If your word-processing program automatically converts URLs to hotlinks, turn off this feature. (You can do this with *Microsoft Word* by opening the AutoCorrect function under the Tools menu, and then selecting AutoFormat.)

18c Sample MLA-Style Research Paper

This paper was written by Roger Rouland, a student in an introductory art history class. The instructor gave students six weeks to write an eight- to ten-page paper on any school or movement of art. During the semester they had discussed "outsider art" and viewed the works of several outsider artists, and Roger decided to explore the works of one such artist further in a paper. The paper includes MLA-style in-text citations, a notes page, a works-cited list, and two visuals.

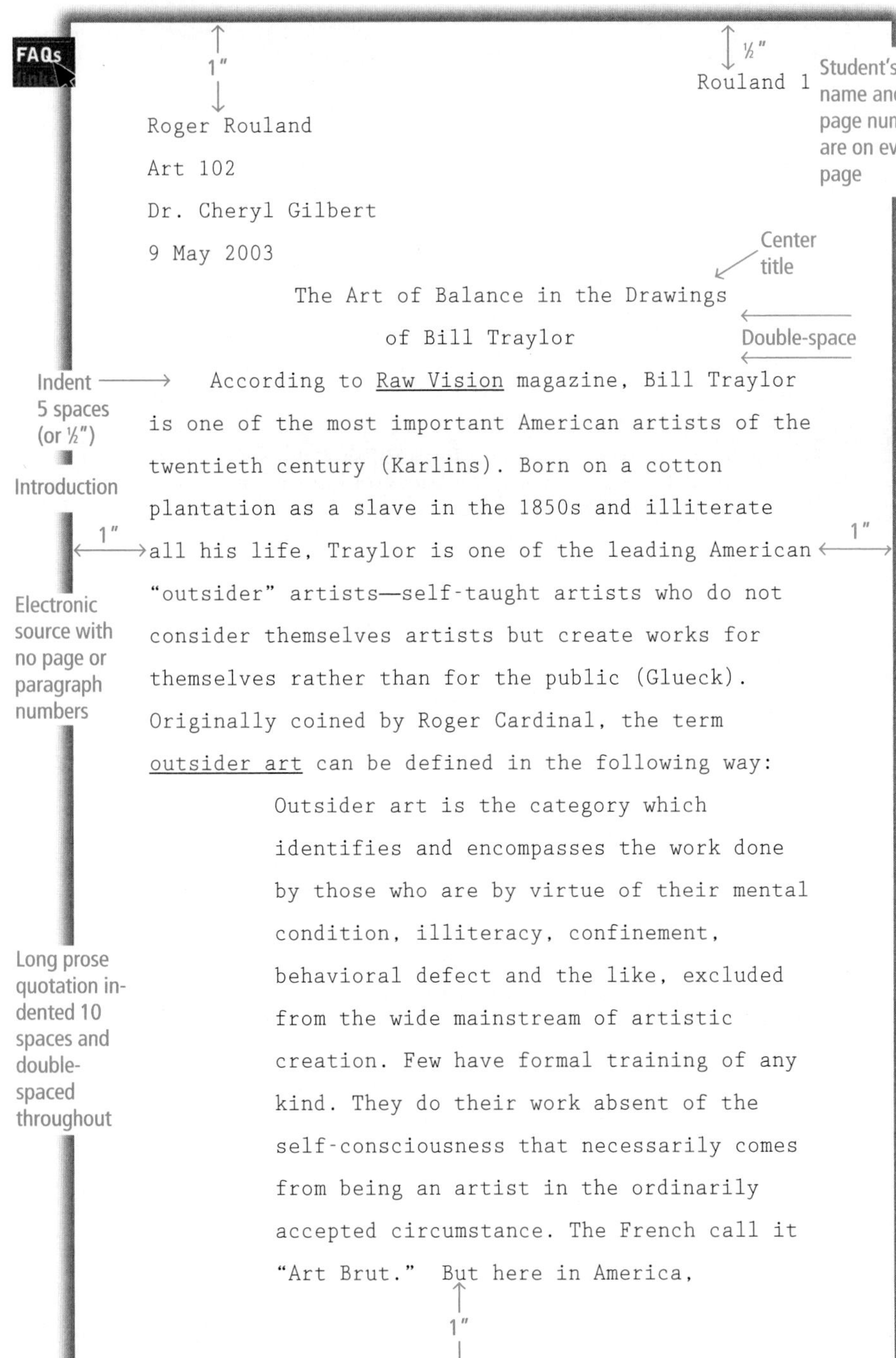
FAQs links
1"
½"
Rouland 1
Student's name and page number are on every page
Roger Rouland
Art 102
Dr. Cheryl Gilbert
9 May 2003
Center title
The Art of Balance in the Drawings
of Bill Traylor
Double-space
Indent 5 spaces (or ½")
According to Raw Vision magazine, Bill Traylor is one of the most important American artists of the twentieth century (Karlins). Born on a cotton plantation as a slave in the 1850s and illiterate all his life, Traylor is one of the leading American "outsider" artists—self-taught artists who do not consider themselves artists but create works for themselves rather than for the public (Glueck). Originally coined by Roger Cardinal, the term outsider art can be defined in the following way:
Introduction
1"
1"
Electronic source with no page or paragraph numbers
Outsider art is the category which identifies and encompasses the work done by those who are by virtue of their mental condition, illiteracy, confinement, behavioral defect and the like, excluded from the wide mainstream of artistic creation. Few have formal training of any kind. They do their work absent of the self-consciousness that necessarily comes from being an artist in the ordinarily accepted circumstance. The French call it "Art Brut." But here in America,
Long prose quotation indented 10 spaces and double-spaced throughout
1"

Rouland 2

> "Outsider Art" also refers to the work done by the poor, illiterate, and self-taught African Americans whose artistic product is not the result of a controlling mental or behavioral factor but of their untaught and impoverished social conditions. (Louis-Dreyfus iv)

As a Southern African-American man with few resources and little formal training, Traylor fits the definition of an outsider artist whose works are defined by the hardships he faced.

In 1939, at the age of eighty-five, Traylor began a short but prolific period of creativity, and in less than four years, he produced about fifteen hundred drawings based on his memories of rural life and his observations of city street life (Porter). Although critics have observed that "balance—how something stands upright—is a constant preoccupation in Traylor's inventions" (Morrin 32), they have generally ignored Traylor's use of various sticklike objects or appendages (including wooden legs, canes, crutches, umbrellas, guns, and pointing figures) to express this theme. In fact, these objects or appendages often convey the misfortunes, arrogance, and prejudice Traylor endured during his long life.

"Porter" citation has no page number because article was accessed from the Internet

Thesis statement

After the Civil War, Traylor continued to work as a farmhand and sharecropper on the plantation on

Rouland 3

Shortened title included in parenthetical reference because more than one work by Kurzmeyer is cited

Superscript number indicates content note

which he was born; he later married and fathered more than a dozen children (Kurzmeyer, "The Life" 171-72). Sometime between 1935 and 1939, Traylor left the plantation and settled in Montgomery. After rheumatism forced him to give up a job at a Montgomery shoe factory, Traylor began receiving welfare checks (Kurzmeyer, "The Life" 173). By 1939, he was walking with two canes (Lyons 32), sleeping in the back of a funeral parlor, and spending his days on Monroe Street. There he would sit with a board on his lap for an easel, with his back to a boarded-up pool-hall door (Shannon, "Traylor's Triumph" 62). On the day he started drawing, Traylor was discovered by the white artist Charles Shannon, who began bringing him art supplies (Shannon, Bill Traylor).[1] Traylor used the colored pencils, brushes, and show-card paint but ignored the poster board Shannon brought, opting instead to use weathered cardboard (Shannon, "Traylor's Triumph" 62).

Between 1940 and 1942, Shannon arranged two small exhibitions of Traylor's work (Kurzmeyer, "The Life" 174-75), but at that time, the art world was more interested in abstract expressionism than in realistic representations. Traylor died a relatively unknown artist in 1949. In the 1970s, though, Shannon, who had saved all of Traylor's work from the 1939-42 period, began cataloging and publicizing Traylor's work. Traylor's posthumous big break came

Rouland 4

with the 1982 exhibit Black Folk Art in America, 1930-1980 (Shannon, "Traylor's Triumph" 88). Traylor was the star of the show, which, "almost overnight, sparked a market feeding frenzy, especially for Traylor" (Tully 121). Traylor's popularity quickly grew through outsider art shows and large one-man exhibits (Perez-Pena 1). Today, Traylor's work is considered part of the American twentieth-century art canon although the term outsider art continues to be used to describe his work.

Paragraph synthesizes information from four different sources

Traylor drew using his own "flat style," which he invented because he did not know how to create three-dimensional objects (Lyons 28). A common motif Traylor used in balancing his flat elements was the sticklike appendages and objects carried by or attached to human figures. In Self-Portrait, for instance, a lone man is depicted walking toward the right. He wears a top hat with two wide bills pointing left and right. He has a long nose pointed downward and a wide elongated chin that, like the nose, is pointed forward but downward. The man's upper body is brown, his boots are gray, and his pants are deep blue, a color characteristic of Traylor's work (Patton 109). The man's arms are bent at right angles, and he holds canes pointed downward at slight right angles. The two canes are the keys to the balance in this work, and they are also the symbols of the character's hardship.

Rouland 5

Reference is to figure in the text of the paper

In <u>Self-Portrait</u> and in drawings such as <u>One-Legged Man with Crutch and Cane</u>, artificial appendages bring balance to the drawings and to the figures themselves. In other drawings, whether intentional or not, sticks held by persons seem to indicate differences in social status and vanity. In <u>Man on Crutch and Woman with Umbrella</u> (see fig. 1), for example, Traylor contrasts a woman who carries a petite umbrella that does not reach to the ground and a one-legged man who needs a crutch for support.

Source information is typed directly below the figure. Because this source is not used elsewhere in the paper, it does not appear in the works-cited list.

Fig. 1. Bill Traylor, <u>Man on Crutch and Woman with Umbrella</u>, Smithsonian American Museum of Art, Washington, DC.

Rouland 6

The woman carries the umbrella for show while the man uses the crutch out of necessity. The woman's head is also slightly tilted, while one hand rests on her hip. Meanwhile, her head is pulled back from the man, who holds a finger out as if lecturing while pointing upward with a finger from his other hand. In this case, the man on a crutch obviously (and literally) has the upper hand while the woman of some social standing appears to be intimidated by the man talking to her.

The two figures in <u>Man on Crutch and Woman with Umbrella</u> also are arranged so that although they are basically eye to eye, the woman's feet are below the shorter man's foot and crutch, with the crutch essentially level with the woman's knees. The woman's feet nearly touch the bottom of the cardboard surface while the man's hat almost touches the top. There is a slight space above the woman's head and a bit larger space below the man's feet. Filling in and balancing this larger space is Traylor's signature,[2] running below and between the toe of the man's shoe and base of his crutch. This placement of the artist's signature suggests that someone is speaking who has something important (if not confrontational) to say to the upper-crust woman. In other words, although Traylor probably still had both legs when he drew this picture,[3] it seems fairly certain he would have identified more

Superscript numbers indicate content notes

Rouland 7

with the man who needed a cane and crutch to walk than with the woman who carried an umbrella for show.

In Traylor's more abstract works, sticklike appendages also play an important role in indicating social position. In House with Figures (see fig. 2), a large black man with a long slender nose and prominent chin is the focal point. The man stands on top of a house, holds a hammer in his right hand and a chicken in his left, and has apparently knocked a man off the roof of the house.

Fig. 2. Bill Traylor, House with Figures, High Museum of Art, Atlanta.

Source information is typed directly below the figure. Because this source is not used elsewhere in the paper, it does not appear in the works-cited list.

Rouland 8

In several respects, the man on the house resembles the figure in <u>Self-Portrait</u>: he has a large top hat with tilted brim, a long pointed nose, and a large wide chin.

In <u>House with Figures</u>, a white woman in a red dress stands behind the man on the house and whips him. The scene seems to suggest Traylor's days on the plantation and his involvement with chicken thieves. The woman, with the face outlined but not shaded, is typical of Traylor's portrayal of whites (Lyons 32). Among the other figures in this busy picture are a man flying from the roof, a black woman pointing up toward the roof, and two other black men, one hiding beneath the house and another sitting comfortably inside smoking a pipe.

Whether through his own volition or spurred by the whip of the white woman, the man on the roof is the only one who is taking an active role in saving the chickens and chasing away the thief. It is noteworthy that he holds a tool, a hammer, as opposed to the whip of the white woman or the pipe of the black man. Traylor seems to suggest that the man on the roof is the one responsible for saving the chicken although he is likely not the one responsible for the thief's nearly getting away with a crime; that responsibility would seem to fall on the man hiding beneath the house or the man inside smoking. Still, the man on the roof is the one receiving

This paragraph contains the student's original ideas, so no documentation is needed

Rouland 9

the whipping. Not only does the picture appear autobiographical, but it also uses sticklike appendages to point the viewer to the action and suggest a theme. In his own life, Traylor was often victimized because of his color and social position; in spite of this, however, he sees himself as remaining above it all, behaving heroically in the face of prejudice and adversity.

Conclusion summarizes student's evaluation of Traylor's work

Traylor's works reflect his attitude toward life and show how he was ultimately able to transcend the limits of his personal experience. In several important works, he makes use of sticklike constructions to distinguish figures and to bring geometric balance to his human figures and to the drawings in which they appear. This recurring motif is important because it focuses attention on people of high social standing who were responsible for the hardships, arrogance, prejudice, and perhaps violence that Traylor experienced. In this way, Traylor uses "his drawings to understand and define conflicts with which he [is] familiar" (Kurzmeyer, "Plow and Pencil" 24), and he does so in a way that "provides an outlet for the restricted and oppressed existence of African Americans between the post-reconstruction and the post-war civil rights eras" (Sims 93).

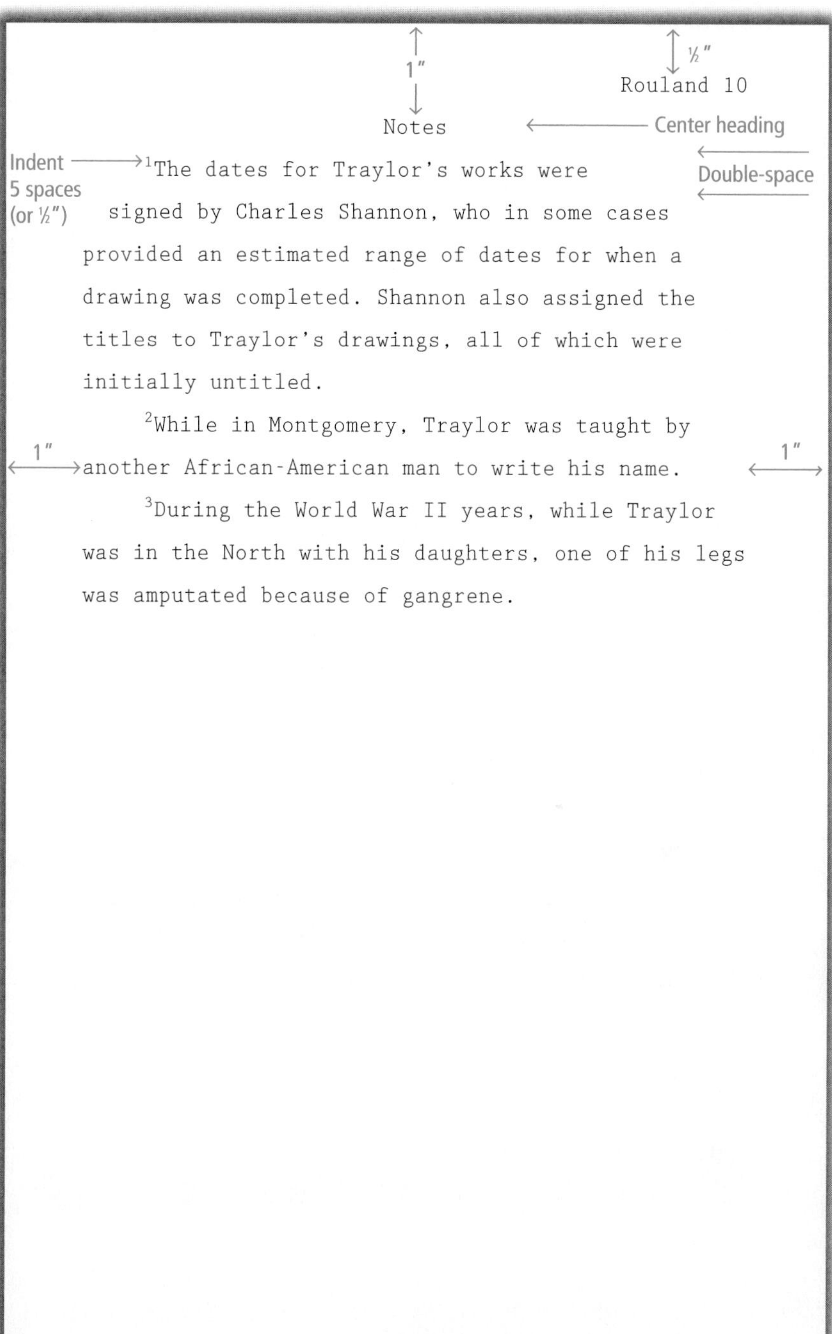
1"
½"
Rouland 10
Notes
Center heading
Indent 5 spaces (or ½")
Double-space
[1]The dates for Traylor's works were signed by Charles Shannon, who in some cases provided an estimated range of dates for when a drawing was completed. Shannon also assigned the titles to Traylor's drawings, all of which were initially untitled.
[2]While in Montgomery, Traylor was taught by another African-American man to write his name.
1"
1"
[3]During the World War II years, while Traylor was in the North with his daughters, one of his legs was amputated because of gangrene.

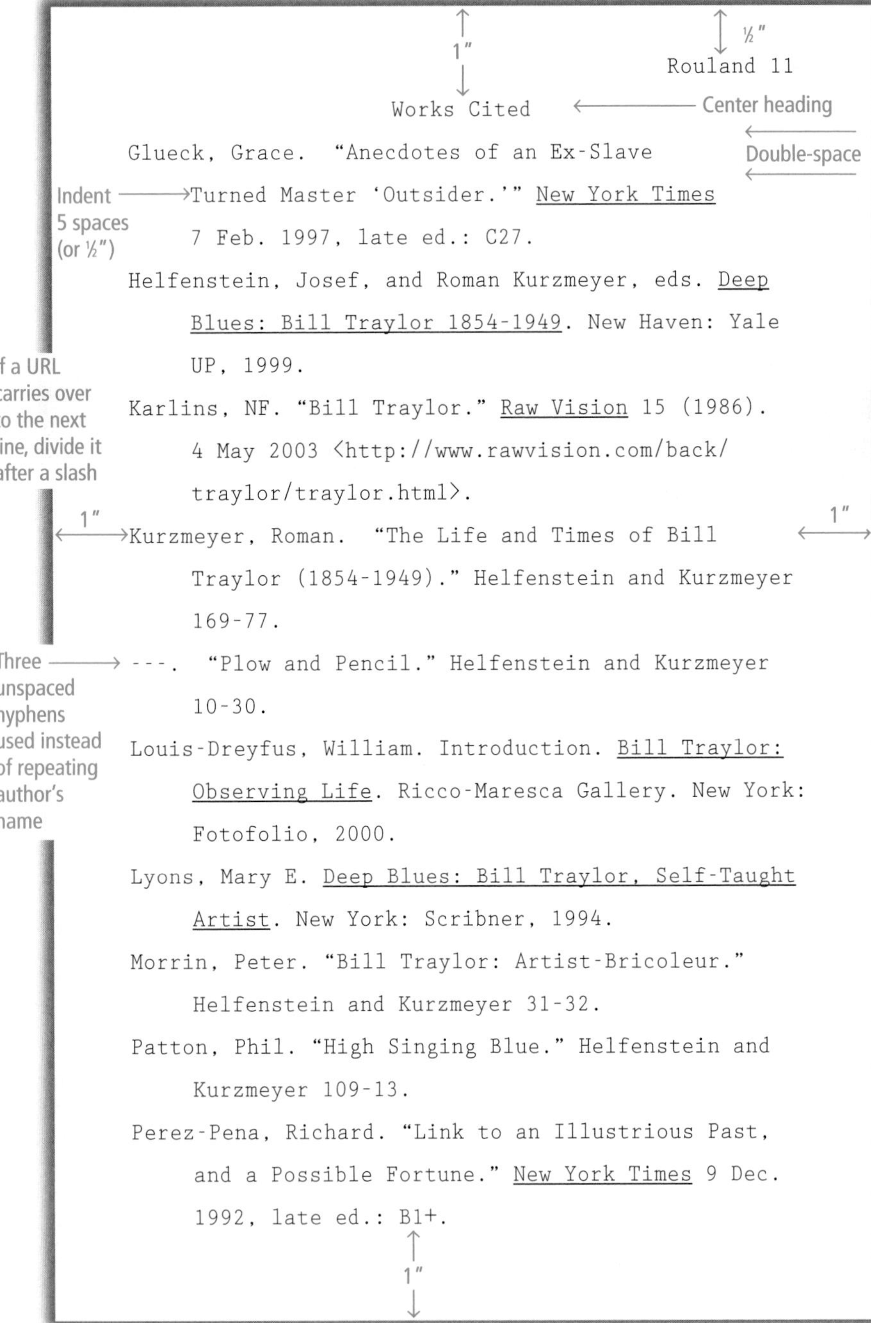

1"
½"
Rouland 11
Works Cited
Center heading
Double-space
Glueck, Grace. "Anecdotes of an Ex-Slave
Indent 5 spaces (or ½")
Turned Master 'Outsider.'" New York Times
7 Feb. 1997, late ed.: C27.
Helfenstein, Josef, and Roman Kurzmeyer, eds. Deep
Blues: Bill Traylor 1854-1949. New Haven: Yale
UP, 1999.
If a URL carries over to the next line, divide it after a slash
Karlins, NF. "Bill Traylor." Raw Vision 15 (1986).
4 May 2003 <http://www.rawvision.com/back/
traylor/traylor.html>.
1"
Kurzmeyer, Roman. "The Life and Times of Bill
1"
Traylor (1854-1949)." Helfenstein and Kurzmeyer
169-77.
Three unspaced hyphens used instead of repeating author's name
---. "Plow and Pencil." Helfenstein and Kurzmeyer
10-30.
Louis-Dreyfus, William. Introduction. Bill Traylor:
Observing Life. Ricco-Maresca Gallery. New York:
Fotofolio, 2000.
Lyons, Mary E. Deep Blues: Bill Traylor, Self-Taught
Artist. New York: Scribner, 1994.
Morrin, Peter. "Bill Traylor: Artist-Bricoleur."
Helfenstein and Kurzmeyer 31-32.
Patton, Phil. "High Singing Blue." Helfenstein and
Kurzmeyer 109-13.
Perez-Pena, Richard. "Link to an Illustrious Past,
and a Possible Fortune." New York Times 9 Dec.
1992, late ed.: B1+.
1"

Rouland 12

Porter, Ann. "Outsider Art Comes In." *Vermont Quarterly Online Magazine*. Summer 1999. U of Vermont. 3 May 2003 <http://universitycommunications.uvm.edu/vq/vqsummer/outsider.html>.

Shannon, Charles. "Bill Traylor's Triumph." *Arts and Antiques* 5.1 (1988): 61-88.

---. Introduction. *Bill Traylor: 1854-1947*. New York: Hirschl, 1986.

Sims, Lowery Stokes. "Bill Traylor: Inside the Outsider." Helfenstein and Kurzmeyer 92-95.

Tully, Judd. "Outside, Inside, or Somewhere In-Between?" *ARTnews* 95.5 (1996): 118-21.

DIRECTORY OF APA IN-TEXT CITATIONS

DIRECTORY OF APA REFERENCE LIST ENTRIES

Print Sources

Entries for Books

Authors

Editions, Multivolume Works, Forewords

Parts of Books

Government Reports

Entries for Articles

Scholarly Journals

Chapter 19

APA Documentation Style

Frequently Asked Questions

19a Using APA Style

APA style* is used extensively in the social sciences in disciplines such as psychology, sociology, and economics. APA documentation has three parts: *in-text citations*, a *reference list*, and optional *content footnotes.*

(1) In-Text Citations

APA documentation uses short in-text citations in the body of the paper. These citations are keyed to an alphabetical list of references that follows the paper. A typical in-text citation consists of the author's last name (followed by a comma) and the year of publication in parentheses immediately after the author's name.

```
Many people exhibit symptoms of depression after the
death of a pet (Russo, 2000).
```

If the author's name appears in the introductory phrase, the in-text citation includes just the year of publication.

```
According to Russo (2000), many people exhibit symptoms
of depression after the death of a pet.
```

Note that you may include the author's name and the date either in the introductory phrase or in parentheses at the end of the borrowed material.

When quoting directly, also include the page number in parentheses after the quotation.

---

*APA documentation style follows the guidelines set in the *Publication Manual of the American Psychological Association*, 5th ed. Washington, DC: APA, 2001.

According to Weston (1996), children from one-parent homes read at "a significantly lower level than those from two-parent homes" (p. 58).

NOTE: A long quotation (forty words or more) is not set in quotation marks. It is set as a block, and the entire quotation is double-spaced and indented five to seven spaces (or one-half inch) from the left margin. The citation is placed in parentheses one space after the final punctuation.

SAMPLE APA IN-TEXT CITATIONS

1. A Work by a Single Author

Many college students suffer from sleep deprivation (Anton, 1999).

2. A Work by Two Authors

There is growing concern over the use of psychological testing in elementary schools (Albright & Glennon, 1982).

3. A Work by Three to Five Authors

If a work has more than two but fewer than six authors, mention all names in the first reference; in subsequent references in the same paragraph, cite only the first author followed by et al. ("and others"). When the reference appears in later paragraphs, include the year.

First Reference

(Sparks, Wilson, & Hewitt, 2001)

Subsequent References in the Same Paragraph

(Sparks et al.)

Reference in Later Paragraphs

(Sparks et al., 2001)

4. A Work by Six or More Authors

When a work has six or more authors, cite the name of the first author followed by et al. and the year in all references.

(Miller et al., 1995)

Close-up: Citing Works by Multiple Authors

When referring to multiple authors in your discussion, join the last two names with and.

According to Rosen, Wolfe, and Ziff (1988). . . .

(continued)

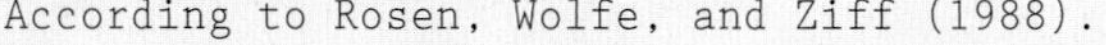

Citing works by multiple authors (continued)

In-text citations, however, require an **ampersand.**

```
(Rosen, Wolfe, & Ziff, 1988)
```

5. Works by Authors with the Same Last Name

If your reference list includes works by two or more authors with the same last name, use each author's initials in all in-text citations.

```
F. Bor (2001) and S. D. Bor (2000) concluded that . . .
```

6. A Work by a Corporate Author

If the name of a corporate author is long, abbreviate it after the first citation.

First Reference

```
(National Institute of Mental Health [NIMH], 2001)
```

Subsequent Reference

```
(NIMH, 2001)
```

7. A Work with No Listed Author

If a work has no listed author, cite the first two or three words of the title and the year. Use quotation marks around titles of periodical articles and chapters of books; use italics for titles of books, periodicals, brochures, reports, and the like.

```
("New Immigration," 2000)
```

8. A Personal Communication

Cite letters, memos, telephone conversations, personal interviews, emails, messages from electronic bulletin boards, and so on only in the text—*not* in the reference list.

```
(R. Takaki, personal communication, October 17, 2001)
```

9. An Indirect Source

```
Cogan and Howe offer very different interpretations of
the problem (cited in Swenson, 2000).
```

10. A Specific Part of a Source

Use abbreviations for the words *page* (p.), *pages* (pp.), *chapter* (chap.), and *section* (sec.).

```
These theories have an interesting history (Lee, 1966,
chap. 2).
```

11. An Electronic Source

For an electronic source that does not show page numbers, use the paragraph number preceded by a ¶ symbol or the abbreviation `para.`

```
Conversation at the dinner table is an example of a
family ritual (Kulp, 2001, ¶ 3).
```

In the case of an electronic source that has neither page numbers nor paragraph numbers, cite a heading in the source and the number of the paragraph (following the heading) in which the material is located.

```
Healthy eating is a never-ending series of free choices
(Shapiro, 2001, Introduction section, para. 2).
```

If the source has no headings, you may not be able to specify an exact location.

12. Two or More Works within the Same Parenthetical Reference

List works by different authors in alphabetical order, separated by semicolons.

```
This theory is supported by several studies (Barson &
Roth, 1995; Rose, 2001; Tedesco, 2002).
```

List works by the same author or authors in order of date of publication, with the earliest date first.

```
This theory is supported by several studies (Rhodes &
Dollek, 2000, 2002, 2003).
```

For works by the same author published in the same year, designate the work whose title comes first alphabetically *a*, the one whose title comes next *b*, and so on; repeat the year in each citation.

```
This theory is supported by several studies (Shapiro,
2003a, 2003b).
```

13. A Table

If you use a table from a source, give credit to the author in a note at the bottom of the table. Do not include this information in the reference list.

Note. From "Predictors of Employment and Earnings Among JOBS Participants," by P. A. Neenan and D. K. Orthner, 1996, *Social Work Research, 20* (4), p. 233.

(2) Reference List

The **reference list** gives the publication information for all the sources you cite. It should appear at the end of your paper on a new numbered page titled `References` (or `Bibliography` if you are listing all the works you consulted, whether or not you cited them in your paper). Entries on the reference list should be arranged alphabetically. Double-space within and between reference list entries, and indent the second and subsequent lines of each entry one-half inch (five spaces). (**See 19b** for manuscript guidelines.)

SAMPLE APA REFERENCE LIST ENTRIES

Print Sources

Entries for Books

Book citations include the author's name; the year of publication (in parentheses); the book title (italicized); and publication information. Capitalize only the first word of the title and subtitle and any proper nouns. Include any additional necessary information—edition, report number, or volume number, for example—in parentheses after the title.

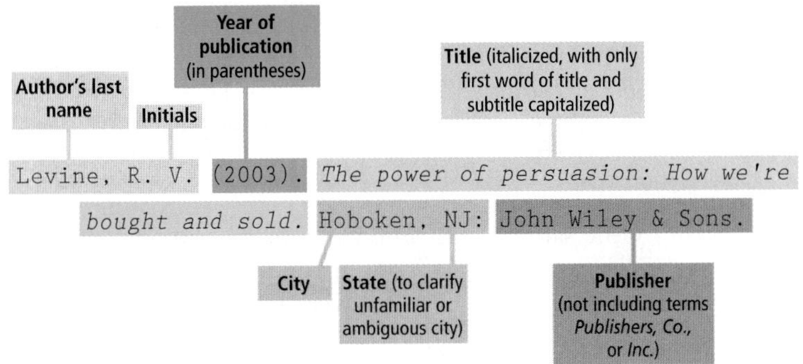

1. A Book with One Author

Use a short form of the publisher's name. Write out the names of associations, corporations, and university presses. Include the words `Book` and `Press`, but do not include terms such as `Publishers`, `Co.`, or `Inc.`

> Maslow, A. H. (1974). *Toward a psychology of being.* Princeton: Van Nostrand.

2. A Book with More Than One Author

List up to six authors—by last name and initials. For more than six authors, add `et al.` after the sixth name.

Wolfinger, D., Knable, P., Richards, H. L., & Silberger, R. (1990). *The chronically unemployed.* New York: Berman Press.

3. A Book with No Listed Author or Editor

Writing with a computer. (2000). Philadelphia: Drexel Press.

4. A Book with a Corporate Author

When the author and the publisher are the same, include the word `Author` at the end of the citation instead of repeating the publisher's name.

League of Women Voters of the United States. (2001). *Local league handbook.* Washington, DC: Author.

Editions, Multivolume Works, Forewords

5. An Edited Book

Lewin, K., Lippitt, R., & White, R. K. (Eds.). (1985). *Social learning and imitation.* New York: Basic Books.

6. A Work in Several Volumes

Jones, P. R., & Williams, T. C. (Eds.). (1990–1993). *Handbook of therapy* (Vols. 1-2). Princeton: Princeton University Press.

7. The Foreword, Preface, or Afterword of a Book

Taylor, T. (1979). Preface. In B. B. Ferencz, *Less than slaves* (pp. ii–ix). Cambridge: Harvard University Press.

Parts of Books

8. A Selection from an Anthology

Give inclusive page numbers preceded by `pp.` (in parentheses) after the title of the anthology. The title of the selection is not enclosed in quotation marks.

Lorde, A. (1984). Age, race, and class. In P. S. Rothenberg (Ed.), *Racism and sexism: An integrated study* (pp. 352–360). New York: St. Martin's Press.

NOTE: If you cite two or more selections from the same anthology, give the full citation for the anthology in each entry.

9. An Article in a Reference Book

Edwards, P. (Ed.). (1987). Determinism. In *The encyclopedia of philosophy* (Vol. 2, pp. 359–373). New York: Macmillan.

Government Reports

10. A Government Report

National Institute of Mental Health. (1987). *Motion pictures and violence: A summary report of research* (DHHS Publication No. ADM 91-22187). Washington, DC: U.S. Government Printing Office.

Entries for Articles

Article citations include the author's name; the date of publication (in parentheses); the title of the article; the title of the periodical (italicized); the volume number (italicized); the issue number, if any (in parentheses); and the inclusive page numbers (including all digits). Capitalize only the first word of the article's title and subtitle. Do not underline or italicize the title of the article or enclose it in quotation marks. Give the periodical title in full, and capitalize all words except articles, prepositions, and conjunctions of fewer than four letters. Use p. or pp. when referring to page numbers in newspapers, but omit this abbreviation when referring to page numbers in journals and popular magazines.

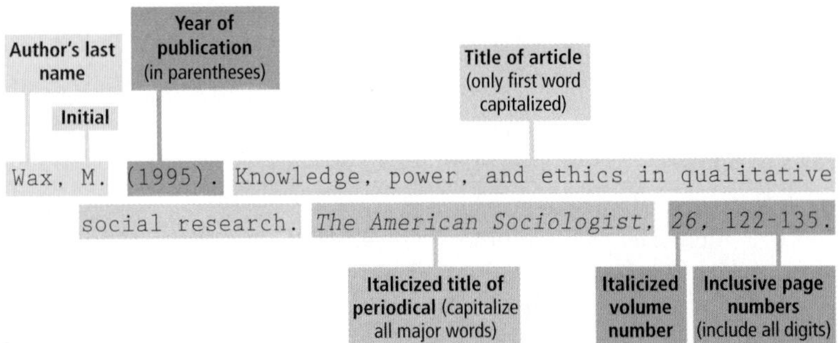

Scholarly Journals

11. An Article in a Scholarly Journal with Continuous Pagination through an Annual Volume

Miller, W. (1969). Violent crimes in city gangs. *Journal of Social Issues, 27,* 581–593.

12. An Article in a Scholarly Journal with Separate Pagination in Each Issue

Williams, S., & Cohen, L. R. (1984). Child stress in early learning situations. *American Psychologist, 21*(10), 1–28.

Magazines and Newspapers

13. A Magazine Article

McCurdy, H. G. (1983, June). Brain mechanisms and intelligence. *Psychology Today, 46,* 61–63.

14. A Newspaper Article

If an article appears on nonconsecutive pages, give all page numbers, separated by commas (for example, A1, A14). If the article appears on consecutive pages, indicate the full range of pages (for example, A7-A9).

James, W. R. (1993, November 16). The uninsured and health care. *Wall Street Journal,* pp. A1, A14.

15. A Letter to the Editor of a Newspaper

Williams, P. (2000, July 19). Self-fulfilling stereotypes [Letter to the editor]. *Los Angeles Times,* p. A22.

Entries for Miscellaneous Print Sources

Letters

16. A Personal Letter

References to unpublished personal letters, like references to all other personal communications, should be included only in the text of the paper, not in the reference list.

17. A Published Letter

Joyce, J. (1931). Letter to Louis Gillet. In Richard Ellmann, *James Joyce* (p. 631). New York: Oxford University Press.

Entries for Other Sources

Television Broadcasts, Films, CDs, Audiocassette Recordings, Computer Software

18. A Television Broadcast

Murphy J. (Executive Producer). (2002, March 4). *The CBS evening news* [Television broadcast]. New York: Columbia Broadcasting Service.

19. A Television Series

Sorkin, A., Schlamme, T., & Wells, J. (Executive Producers). (2002). *The west wing* [Television series]. Los Angeles: Warner Bros. Television.

20. A Film

Spielberg, S. (Director). (1994). *Schindler's list* [Motion picture]. United States: Universal.

21. A CD Recording

Marley, B. (1977). Waiting in vain. On *Exodus* [CD]. New York: Island Records.

22. An Audiocassette Recording

Skinner, B. F. (Speaker). (1972). *Skinner on Skinnerism* (Cassette Recording). Hollywood, CA: Center for Cassette Studies.

23. Computer Software

Sharp, S. (1995). Career Selection Tests (Version 5.0) [Computer software]. Chico, CA: Avocation Software.

Electronic Sources

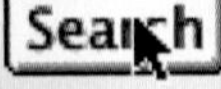

APA guidelines for documenting electronic sources focus on Web sources, which often do not include all the bibliographic information that print sources do. For example, Web sources may not include page numbers or a place of publication. At a minimum, a Web citation should have a title, a date (the date of publication, update, or retrieval), and an electronic address (URL). If possible, also include the author(s) of a source. When you need to break the URL at the end of a line, break it after a slash or before a period (do not add a hyphen). Do not add a period at the end of the URL. (Current guidelines for electronic sources can be found on the APA Web site at www.apa.org.)

Entries from Internet Sites

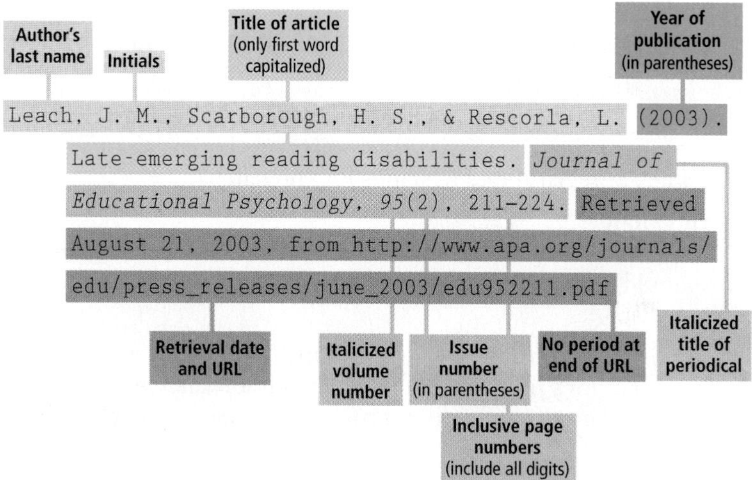

Internet-Specific Sources

24. An Internet Article Based on a Print Source

If you have seen the article only in electronic format, include the phrase `Electronic version` in brackets after the title.

Winston, E. L. (2000). The role of art therapy in treating chronically depressed patients [Electronic version]. *Journal of Bibliographic Research, 5*, 54–72.

NOTE: If you have reason to believe the article you retrieved is different from the print version, add the date you retrieved it and the URL.

25. An Article in an Internet-Only Journal

Hornaday, J., & Bunker, C. (2001). The nature of the entrepreneur. *Personal Psychology, 23*, Article 2353b. Retrieved November 21, 2001, from http://journals.apa.org/volume23/pre002353b.html

26. A Document from a University Web Site

Beck, E. (1997, July). *The good, the bad & the ugly: Or, why it's a good idea to evaluate web sources.* Retrieved January 7, 2002, from New Mexico State University Library Web site: http://lib.nmsu.edu/instruction/evalcrit.html

27. A Web Document (No Author Identified, No Date)

The stratocaster appreciation page. (n.d.). Retrieved July 27, 2002, from http://members.tripod.com/~AFH/

NOTE: The abbreviation n.d. stands for "no date."

28. An Email

As with all other personal communication, references to personal email should be included only in the text of your paper, not in the reference list.

29. A Message Posted to a Newsgroup

List the author's full name—or, if that is not available, the screen name. In brackets after the title, provide information that will help readers access the message.

Shapiro, R. (2001, April 4). Chat rooms and interpersonal communication [Msg 7]. Message posted to news://sci.psychology.communication

30. A Searchable Database

Nowroozi, C. (1992). What you lose when you miss sleep. *Nation's Business,* 80(9), 73-77. Retrieved April 22, 2001, from Expanded Academic ASAP database.

Abstracts, Newspaper Articles

31. An Abstract

Guinot, A., & Peterson, B. R. (1995). *Forgetfulness and partial cognition* (Drexel University Cognitive Research Report No. 21). Abstract retrieved December 4, 2001, from http://www.Drexel.edu/~guinot/deltarule-abstract.html

32. An Article in a Daily Newspaper

Farrell, P. D. (1997, March 23). New high-tech stresses hit traders and investors on the information superhighway. *Wall Street Journal.* Retrieved April 4, 1999, from http://wall-street.news.com/ forecasts/stress/stress.html

(3) Content Footnotes

APA format permits content notes, indicated by **superscripts** (raised numerals) in the text. The notes are listed on a separate numbered page, titled `Footnotes`, following the appendixes (or after the reference list if there are no appendixes). Double-space all notes, indenting the first line of each note five to seven spaces (or one-half inch) and beginning subsequent lines flush left. Number the notes with superscripts that correspond to the numbers in your text.

19b APA Manuscript Guidelines

Social science papers have internal headings (internal sections including an introduction (not titled), `Method`, `Results`, and `Discussion`). Each section of a social science paper is a complete unit with a beginning and an end so it can be read separately and still make sense out of context. The body of the paper may include charts, graphs, maps, photographs, flowcharts, or tables.

The following guidelines are based on the latest version of the *Publication Manual of the American Psychological Association.*

Checklist: Typing Your Paper

When typing your paper, use the student paper in 19c as your model.

- ☐ Leave one-inch margins at the top and bottom and on both sides. Double-space your paper throughout.
- ☐ Indent the first line of every paragraph and the first line of every content footnote five to seven spaces (or one-half inch) from the left-hand margin.
- ☐ Set off a **long quotation** (more than forty words) in a block format by indenting the entire quotation five to seven spaces (or one-half inch) from the left-hand margin.
- ☐ Number all pages consecutively. Each page should include a **page header** (an abbreviated title) and a page number typed one-half inch from the top and one inch from the right-hand

(continued)

Typing your paper (continued)

edge of the page. Leave five spaces (or one-half inch) between the page header and the page number.

See 29b

- ☐ Center and type major headings with uppercase and lowercase letters. Place minor headings flush left, typed with uppercase and lowercase letters and italicized.

See 29c

- ☐ Format items in a series as a numbered list.
- ☐ Arrange the pages of the paper in the following order:
  - Title page (page 1) includes a page header, **running head,** title, and **byline** (your name)
  - Abstract (page 2)
  - Text of paper (beginning on page 3)
  - Reference List (new page)
  - Appendixes (start each on a new page)
  - Content footnotes (new page)
- ☐ If you use source material in your paper, citations should be consistent with APA documentation style.

See 19a

http://kirsznermandell.wadsworth.com

Computer Tip: Document Formatting

Several document formatting options in your word-processing program can help you format your research paper according to APA style. For example, you can use the Header/Footer option to place the appropriate words consistently at the top right of your paper. To use this tool, select the View menu and scroll down to Header/Footer (see Figure 19.1).

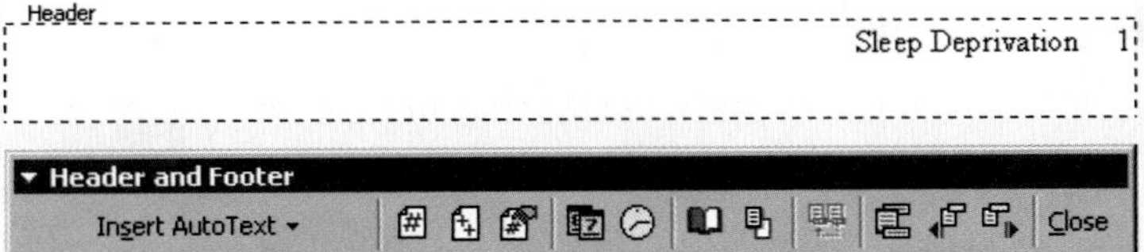

Figure 19.1 ***Microsoft Word*** **Header menu.**

Checklist: Using Visuals

APA distinguishes between two types of visuals: **tables** and **figures** (charts, graphs, photographs, and diagrams). In manuscripts not intended for publication, tables and figures are included in the text. A short table or figure should appear on the page where it is discussed; a long table or figure should be placed on a separate page just after the page where it is discussed.

- ☐ Number all **tables** consecutively. Each table should have a label and a title. The label consists of the word `Table` (not in italics), along with an arabic numeral, typed flush left above the table.
- ☐ Double-space and type a brief explanatory title for each table (in italics) flush left below the label. Capitalize the first letters of principal words of the title.

  Table 7

  Frequency of Negative Responses of Dorm Students to

  Questions Concerning Alcohol Consumption

- ☐ Number all **figures** consecutively. Each figure should have a label and a caption. The label consists of the word `Figure` (typed flush left below the figure) followed by the figure number (both in italics).
- ☐ The caption explains the figure and serves as a title. Double-space the caption, but do not italicize it. Capitalize only the first word, and end the caption with a period. The caption follows the label (on the same line).

  Figure 1. Duration of responses measured in seconds.

NOTE: If you use a table or figure from an outside source, include full source information in a note at the bottom of the table. This information does not appear in your reference list.

Checklist: Preparing the APA Reference List

- ☐ Begin the reference list on a new page after the last page of text or content footnotes, numbered as the next page of the paper. See 19a3
- ☐ Center the title `References` at the top of the page.
- ☐ List the items on the reference list alphabetically (with author's last name first).
- ☐ Type the first line of each entry at the left-hand margin. Indent subsequent lines five to seven spaces (or one-half inch).
- ☐ Separate the major divisions of each entry with a period and one space.
- ☐ Double-space the reference list within and between entries.

Checklist: Arranging Entries in the APA Reference List

- ☐ Single-author entries precede multiple-author entries that begin with the same name.

  Field, S. (1987)
  Field, S., & Levitt, M. P. (1984)

- ☐ Entries by the same author or authors are arranged according to date of publication, starting with the earliest date.

  Ruthenberg, H., & Rubin, R. (1985)
  Ruthenberg, H., & Rubin, R. (1987)

- ☐ Entries with the same author or authors and date of publication are arranged alphabetically according to title. Lowercase letters (*a*, *b*, *c*, and so on) that indicate the order of publication are placed within parentheses.

  Wolk, E. M. (1996a). Analysis . . .
  Wolk, E. M. (1996b). Hormonal . . .

19c Sample APA-Style Research Paper

The following student paper, “Sleep Deprivation in College Students,” uses APA documentation style. It includes a title page, an abstract, a reference list, a table, and two figures (a photograph and a bar graph).

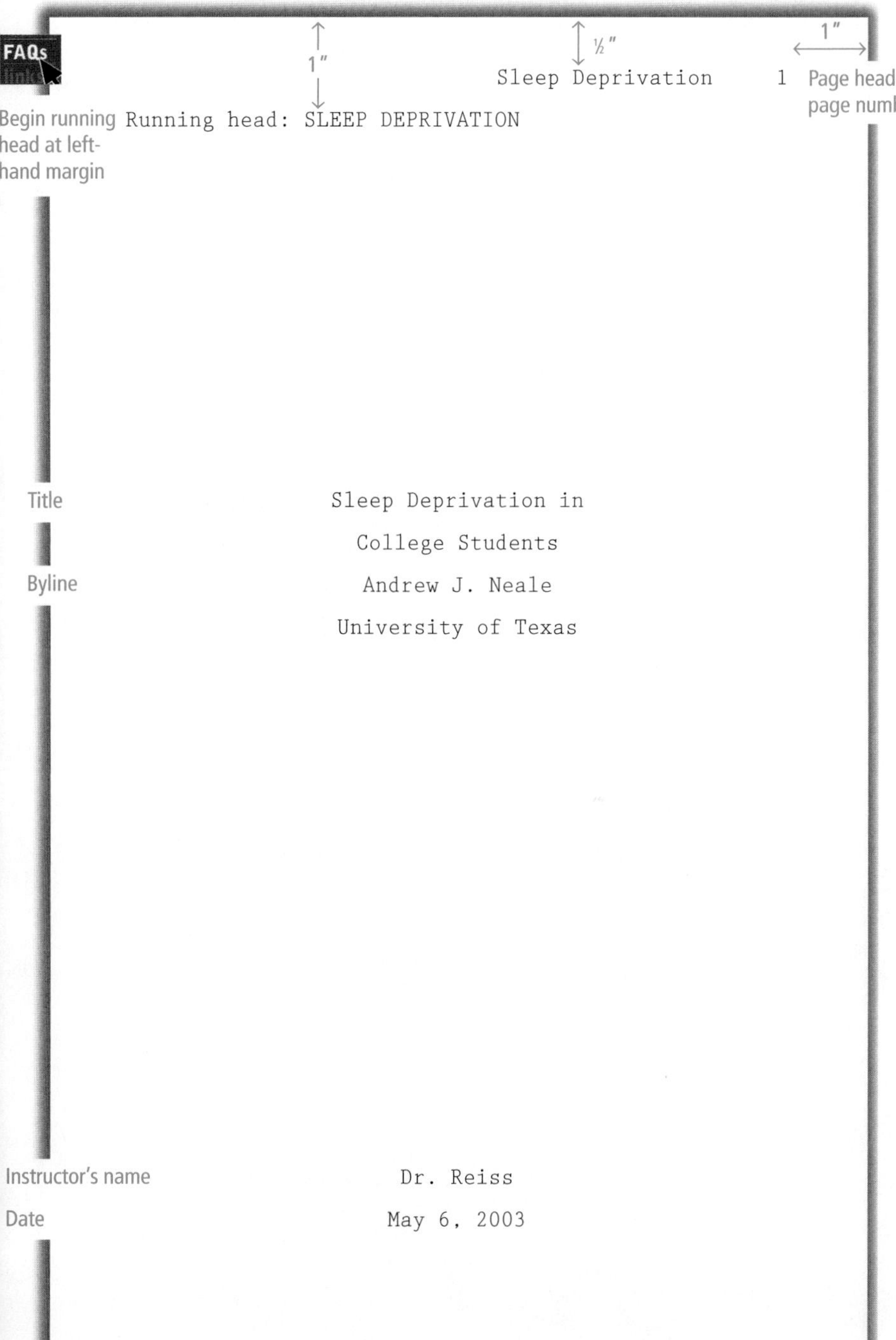
FAQs
1″
½″
1″
Sleep Deprivation 1
Page header, page number
Begin running head at left-hand margin
Running head: SLEEP DEPRIVATION
Title
Sleep Deprivation in
College Students
Byline
Andrew J. Neale
University of Texas
Instructor's name
Dr. Reiss
Date
May 6, 2003

1"

Sleep Deprivation 2

Page header and number on every page

Center

Abstract

A survey of 50 first-year college students in an introductory biology class was conducted. The survey consisted of 5 questions regarding the causes and results of sleep deprivation and specifically addressed the students' study methods and the grades they received on the fall midterm. The study's hypothesis was that although students believe that forgoing sleep to study will yield better grades, sleep deprivation actually causes a decrease in performance. In support of this hypothesis, 43% of the students who received either an A or a B on the fall midterm deprived themselves of sleep in order to cram for the test, whereas 90% of those who received a C or a D were sleep deprived.

Abstract typed as a single paragraph in block format

1"

Sleep Deprivation 3

Full title (centered) → Sleep Deprivation in College Students

Double-space

For many college students, sleep is a luxury that they feel they cannot afford. Bombarded with tests and assignments and limited by a 24-hour day, students often attempt to make up time by forgoing sleep. Ironically, students may actually impair their scholastic performance by failing to get adequate sleep. According to several psychological and medical studies, sleep deprivation can lead to memory loss and health problems, both of which are more likely to harm a student's academic performance than to help it.

Introduction

Thesis statement

1" 1"

Sleep is often overlooked as an essential component of a healthy lifestyle. Millions of Americans wake up daily to alarm clocks because their bodies have not gotten a sufficient amount of sleep. This indicates that for many people, sleep is viewed as a luxury rather than a necessity. As National Sleep Foundation Executive Director Richard L. Gelula observes, "Some of the problems we face as a society—from road rage to obesity—may be linked to lack of sleep or poor sleep" (National Sleep Foundation, 2002, ¶ 3). In fact, according to the National Sleep Foundation, "excessive sleepiness is associated with reduced short-term memory and learning ability, negative mood, inconsistent performance, poor productivity and loss of some forms of behavioral control" (2000, ¶ 2).

Literature review (¶s 2–7)

Quotation requires its own documentation and a page number. A ¶ number is used for Internet sources.

1"

Sleep Deprivation 4

Figure placed on page where it is discussed

Label, caption, and full source information

Figure 1. Student sleeping on his backpack. *Note.* Retrieved from http://www.indexstock .com/store/Chubby.asp?ImageNumber=577914,n.d.

Focus shifts to student sleep deprivation

Figure 1 introduced and discussed

Sleep deprivation is particularly common among college students, many of whom maintain busy lifestyles and are required to memorize a great deal of material before their exams. As Figure 1 demonstrates, it is common for college students to take a quick catnap between classes or fall asleep while studying in the library because they are sleep deprived. Approximately 44% of young adults experience daytime sleepiness at least a few days a month (National Sleep Foundation, 2002). Many students face daytime sleepiness on the day of an exam because they stayed up all night studying. These students believe that if they read and review immediately before taking a test—even though this usually means losing sleep—they will remember more information and thus get better grades. However, this is not the case.

A study conducted by professors Mary Carskadon at Brown University in Providence, Rhode Island, and Amy Wolfson at the College of the Holy Cross in Worcester, Massachusetts, showed that high school students who got adequate sleep were more likely to do well in their classes (Carpenter, 2001). According to their study of the correlation between grades and sleep, students who went to bed earlier on both weeknights and weekends earned mainly A's and B's. The students who received D's and F's averaged about 35 minutes less sleep per day than the high achievers (cited in Carpenter). Apparently, then, sleep is essential to high academic achievement.

Student uses past tense when discussing other researchers' studies

cited in indicates an indirect source

Once students reach college and have the freedom to set their own schedules, however, many believe that sleep is expendable. For example, students believe that if they use the time they would normally sleep to study, they will do better on exams. A recent survey of 144 undergraduate students in introductory psychology classes contradicted this assumption. According to this study, long sleepers, or those individuals who slept 9 or more hours out of a 24-hour day, had significantly higher grade point averages (GPAs) than short sleepers, or individuals who slept less than 7 hours out of a 24-hour day. Therefore, contrary to the belief of many college students, more sleep is often required to achieve a high GPA (Kelly, Kelly, & Clanton, 2001).

Many students believe that sleep deprivation is not the cause of their poor performance, but rather that a host of other factors might be to blame. A study in the *Journal of American College Health* tested the effect that several factors have on a student's performance in school, as measured by students' GPAs. Some of the factors considered included exercise, sleep, nutritional habits, social support, time management techniques, stress management techniques, and spiritual health (Trockel, Barnes, & Egget, 2000). The most significant correlation discovered in the study was between GPA and the sleep habits of students. Sleep deprivation had a more negative impact on GPAs than any other factor did (Trockel et al.).

First reference includes all three authors; *et al.* replaces second and third authors in subsequent reference in same paragraph

Despite these findings, numerous students continue to believe that they will be able to remember more material if they do not sleep at all before an exam. They fear that sleeping will interfere with their ability to retain information. Pilcher & Walters (1997), however, showed that sleep deprivation actually impaired learning skills. In this study, one group of students was sleep-deprived, while the other got 8 hours of sleep before the exam. Each group estimated how well they had performed on the exam. The students who were sleep-deprived believed their performance on the test was better than did those who were not sleep-deprived, but actually the performance of the sleep-deprived students was significantly worse than that of those who got 8 hours of sleep prior to the test (Pilcher & Walters, 1997, cited in Bubolz, Brown, & Soper, 2001). This study confirms that sleep deprivation harms cognitive performance and reveals that many students believe that the less sleep they get, the better they will do.

A survey of students in an introductory biology class at the University of Texas demonstrated the effects of sleep deprivation on scholastic performance and supported the hypothesis that despite students' beliefs, forgoing sleep does not lead to better test scores.

Student uses past tense when discussing his own research study

Method

To ascertain the causes and results of sleep deprivation, a study of the relationship between sleep and test performance was conducted. A survey of 50 first-year college students in an introductory biology class was completed, and their performance on the fall midterm was analyzed.

Each student was asked to complete a survey composed of the following five questions about their sleep patterns and their performance on the fall midterm.

List is indented ½" (5 to 7 spaces) and treated as long block quotation

1. Did you deprive yourself of sleep when studying for the fall midterm?
2. Do you regularly deprive yourself of sleep when studying for an exam?
3. What was your grade on the exam?
4. Do you feel your performance was helped or harmed by the amount of sleep you had?
5. Will you deprive yourself of sleep when you study for the final exam?

To maintain confidentiality, the students were not asked to put their names on the survey. Also, to determine whether the students answered question 3 accurately, the group grade distribution from the surveys was compared to the number of A's, B's, C's, and D's shown in the instructor's record of the test results. The two frequency distributions were identical.

Results

Analysis of the survey data indicated a significant difference between the grades of students who were sleep deprived and the grades of those who were not. The results of the survey are presented in Table 1.

Table 1 introduced

Table 1

Label

Results of Survey of Students in University of Texas Introduction to Biology Class Examining the Relationship between Sleep Deprivation and Academic Performance

Brief explanatory title

Grade Totals	Sleep-Deprived	Not Sleep-Deprived	Usually Sleep-Deprived	Improved	Harmed	Continue Sleep Deprivation?
A = 10	4	6	1	4	0	4
B = 20	9	11	8	8	1	8
C = 10	10	0	6	5	4	7
D = 10	8	2	2	1	3	2
Total	31	19	17	18	8	21

The grades in the class were curved so that out of 50 students, 10 received A's, 20 received B's, 10 received C's, and 10 received D's. For the purposes of this survey, an A or B on the exam indicates that the student performed well. A grade of C or D on the exam is considered a poor grade.

Of the 50 students in the class, 31 (or 62%) said they deprived themselves of sleep when studying for the fall midterm. Of these students, 17 (or 34%) of the class answered yes to the second question, reporting they regularly deprive themselves of sleep before an exam.

Statistical findings in table reported

Of the 31 students who said they deprived themselves of sleep when studying for the fall midterm, only 4 earned A's, and the majority of the A's in the class were received by those students who were not sleep-deprived. Even more significant was the fact that of the 4 students who were sleep-deprived and got A's, only one student claimed usually to be sleep-deprived on the day of an exam. Thus, assuming the students who earn A's in a class do well in general, it is possible that sleep deprivation did not help or harm these students' grades. Not surprisingly, of the 4 students who received A's and were sleep-deprived, all said they would continue to use sleep deprivation to enable them to study for longer hours.

The majority of those who used sleep deprivation in an effort to obtain a higher grade received B's and C's on the exam. A total of 20 students earned a grade of B on the exam. Of those students, only nine, or 18% of the class, said they were deprived of sleep when they took the test.

Students who said they were sleep-deprived when they took the exam received the majority of the poor grades. Ten students got C's on the midterm, and of these 10 students, 100% said they were sleep-deprived when they took their test. Of the 10 students (20% of the class) who got D's, 8 said they were sleep deprived. Figure 2 shows the significant relation that was found between poor grades on the exam and sleep deprivation.

Figure 2 introduced

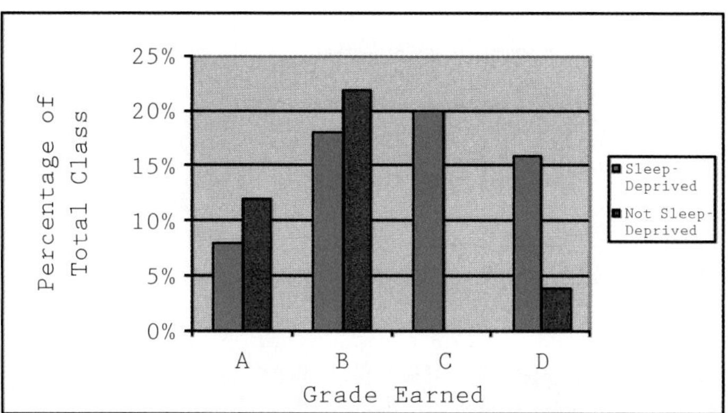

Figure 2. Results of survey of students in University of Texas introduction to biology class examining the relationship between sleep deprivation and academic performance.

Label

Caption

No source information needed for student's original graph

Discussion

For many students, sleep is viewed as a luxury rather than as a necessity. Particularly during the exam period, students use the hours in which they would normally sleep to study. However, this method does not seem to be effective. The survey discussed here reveals a clear correlation between sleep deprivation and lower exam scores. In fact, the majority of students who performed well on the exam, earning either an A or a B, were not deprived of sleep. Therefore, students who choose studying over sleep should rethink their approach and consider that sleep deprivation may actually lead to impaired academic performance.

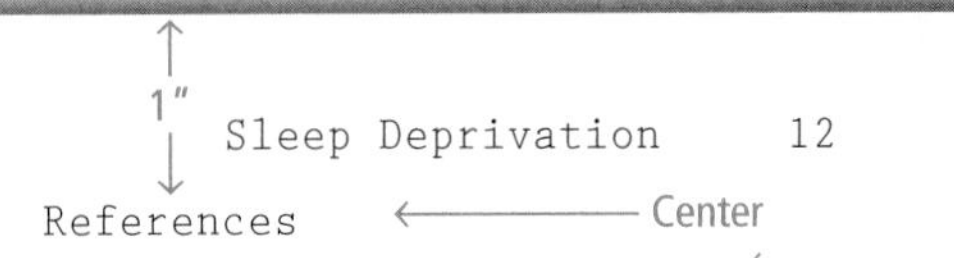

References ← Center

← Double-space

Bubolz, W., Brown, F., & Soper, B. (2001). Sleep habits and patterns of college students: A preliminary study. *Journal of American College Health, 50,* 131–135.

Carpenter, S. (2001). Sleep deprivation may be undermining teen health. *Monitor on Psychology, 32*(9). Retrieved March 9, 2003, from http://www.apa.org/monitor/oct01/sleepteen.html

Kelly, W. E., Kelly, K. E., & Clanton, R. C. (2001). The relationship between sleep length and grade-point average among college students. *College Student Journal, 35*(1), 84–90.

National Sleep Foundation. (2000). *Adolescent sleep needs and patterns: Research report and resource guide.* Retrieved March 16, 2003, from http://www.sleepfoundation.org/publications/sleep_and_teens_report1.pdf

National Sleep Foundation. (2002, April). *Epidemic of daytime sleepiness linked to increased feelings of anger, stress, and pessimism.* Retrieved March 14, 2003, from http://www.sleepfoundation.org/nsaw/pk_pollresultsmood.html

Trockel, M., Barnes, M., & Egget, D. (2000). Health-related variables and academic performance among first-year college students: Implications for sleep and other behaviors. *Journal of American College Health, 49,* 125–131.

Indent → 5 spaces (or ½")

Entries listed in alphabetical order

DIRECTORY OF CHICAGO-STYLE ENDNOTES AND BIBLIOGRAPHY ENTRIES

Print Sources

Chapter 20

Chicago Documentation Style

Frequently Asked Questions

20a Using Chicago Style

The Chicago Manual of Style is used in history and in some social science and humanities disciplines. **Chicago style*** has two parts: *notes at the end of the paper* (**endnotes**) and *a list of bibliographic citations.* (Chicago style encourages the use of endnotes, but it allows the use of footnotes at the bottom of the page.)

(1) Endnotes and Footnotes

The notes format calls for a **superscript** (raised numeral) in the text after source material you have either quoted or referred to. This numeral, placed after all punctuation marks except dashes, corresponds to the numeral that accompanies the note.

Endnote and Footnote Format: Chicago Style

In the Text

```
By November of 1942, the Allies had proof that the Nazis
were engaged in the systematic killing of Jews.[1]
```

---

*Chicago-style documentation follows the guidelines set in *The Chicago Manual of Style*, 15th ed. Chicago: University of Chicago Press, 2003. The manuscript guidelines and sample research paper at the end of this chapter follow guidelines set in Kate L. Turabian's *A Manual for Writers of Term Papers, Theses, and Dissertations*, 6th ed. Chicago: University of Chicago Press, 1993. Turabian style, which is based on Chicago style, addresses formatting concerns specific to college writers.

In the Note

1. David S. Wyman, *The Abandonment of the Jews: America and the Holocaust 1941–1945* (New York: Pantheon Books, 1984), 65.

(2) Bibliography

In addition to the heading Bibliography, Chicago style allows Selected Bibliography, Works Cited, and References. Bibliography entries are arranged alphabetically. Double-space within and between entries.

SAMPLE CHICAGO-STYLE ENDNOTES AND BIBLIOGRAPHY ENTRIES

Print Sources

Entries for Books

Capitalize the first, last, and all major words of titles and subtitles. Chicago style recommends the use of italics for titles, but underlining to indicate italics is also acceptable.

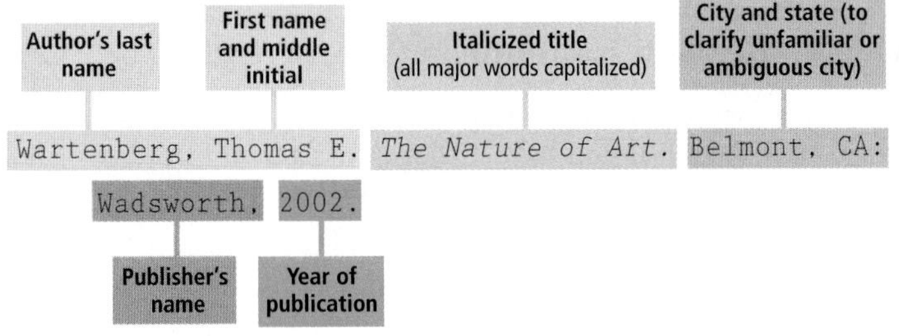

Authors

1. A Book by One Author

Endnote

1. Robert Dallek, *An Unfinished Life: John F. Kennedy 1917–1963.* (New York: Little Brown, 2003), 213.

Bibliography

Dallek, Robert, *An Unfinished Life: John F. Kennedy 1917–1963* New York. Little Brown, 2003.

2. A Book by Two or Three Authors

Endnote

Two Authors

2. Jack Watson and Grant McKerney, *A Cultural History of the Theater* (New York: Longman, 1993), 137.

Three Authors

2. Nathan Caplan, John K. Whitmore, and Marcella H. Choy, *The Boat People and Achievement in America: A Study of Economic and Educational Success* (Ann Arbor: University of Michigan Press, 1990), 51.

Bibliography

Two Authors

Watson, Jack, and Grant McKerney. *A Cultural History of the Theater.* New York: Longman, 1993.

Three Authors

Caplan, Nathan, John K. Whitmore, and Marcella H. Choy. *The Boat People and Achievement in America: A Study of Economic and Educational Success.* Ann Arbor: University of Michigan Press, 1990.

3. A Book by More Than Three Authors

Endnote

Chicago style favors and others rather than et al. in endnotes.

3. Robert E. Spiller and others, eds., *Literary History of the United States* (New York: Macmillan, 1953), 24.

Bibliography

All authors' names are listed in the bibliography.

Spiller, Robert E., Willard Thorp, Thomas H. Johnson, and Henry Seidel Canby, eds. *Literary History of the United States.* New York: Macmillan, 1953.

4. A Book by a Corporate Author

If the title page of a publication issued by an organization does not identify a person as the author, the organization is listed as the author, even if its name is repeated in the title, in the series title, or as the publisher.

Endnote

4. National Geographic Society, *National Parks of the United States*, 3rd ed. (Washington, DC: National Geographic Society, 1997), 77.

Bibliography

National Geographic Society. *National Parks of the United States.* 3rd ed. Washington, DC: National Geographic Society, 1997.

Editions, Multivolume Works

5. An Edited Book

Endnote

5. William Bartram, *The Travels of William Bartram*, ed. Mark Van Doren (New York: Dover Press, 1955), 85.

Bibliography

Bartram, William. *The Travels of William Bartram.* Edited by Mark Van Doren. New York: Dover Press, 1955.

6. A Subsequent Edition of a Book

Endnote

6. Laurie G. Kirszner and Stephen R. Mandell, *The Wadsworth Handbook*, 7th ed. (Boston: Wadsworth, 2005), 52.

Bibliography

Kirszner, Laurie G., and Stephen R. Mandell. *The Wadsworth Handbook.* 7th ed. Boston: Wadsworth, 2005.

7. A Multivolume Work

Endnote

7. Kathleen Raine, *Blake and Tradition* (Princeton, NJ: Princeton University Press, 1968), 1:143.

Bibliography

Raine, Kathleen. *Blake and Tradition.* Vol. 1. Princeton, NJ: Princeton University Press, 1968.

Parts of Books

8. A Chapter in a Book

Endnote

8. Peter Kidson, "Architecture and City Planning," in *The Legacy of Greece*, ed. M. I. Finley (New York: Oxford University Press, 1981), 379.

Bibliography

Kidson, Peter. "Architecture and City Planning." *In The Legacy of Greece*, edited by M. I. Finley, 376–400. New York: Oxford University Press, 1981.

9. An Essay in an Anthology
Endnote

9. G. E. R. Lloyd, "Science and Mathematics," in *The Legacy of Greece*, ed. Moses Finley (New York: Oxford University Press, 1981), 270.

Bibliography

Lloyd, G. E. R. "Science and Mathematics." In *The Legacy of Greece*, edited by Moses Finley, 256–300. New York: Oxford University Press, 1981.

Religious Works

10. A Religious Work

References to religious works (such as the Bible) are usually confined to the text or notes and not listed in the bibliography. In citing the Bible, include the book (abbreviated), the chapter (followed by a colon), and the verse numbers. Identify the version, but do not include a page number.

Endnote

10. Phil. 1:9–11 (King James Version).

Entries for Articles

Scholarly Journals

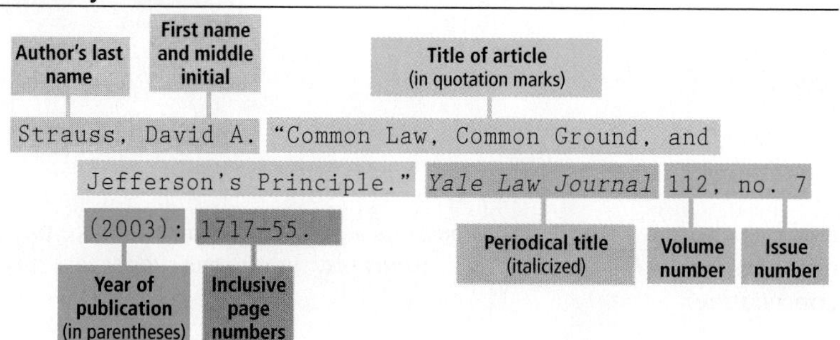

11. An Article in a Scholarly Journal with Continuous Pagination through an Annual Volume

Endnote

11. John Huntington, "Science Fiction and the Future," *College English* 37 (Fall 1975): 341.

Bibliography

Huntington, John. "Science Fiction and the Future." *College English* 37 (Fall 1975): 340–58.

12. An Article in a Scholarly Journal with Separate Pagination in Each Issue

Endnote

12. R. G. Sipes, "War, Sports, and Aggression: An Empirical Test of Two Rival Theories," *American Anthropologist* 4, no. 2 (1973): 80.

Bibliography

Sipes, R. G. "War, Sports, and Aggression: An Empirical Test of Two Rival Theories." *American Anthropologist* 4, no. 2 (1973): 65–84.

Magazines and Newspapers

13. An Article in a Weekly Magazine (Signed/Unsigned)

Endnote

Signed

13. Pico Iyer, "A Mum for All Seasons," *Time*, April 8, 2002, 51.

Unsigned

13. "Burst Bubble," *NewScientist*, July 27, 2002, 24.

Bibliography

Signed

Iyer, Pico. "A Mum for All Seasons." *Time*, April 8, 2002.

NOTE: Although the endnote specifies a page number, inclusive page numbers are omitted in the bibliography when the pages are not consecutive.

Unsigned

"Burst Bubble." *NewScientist*, July 27, 2002, 24–25.

14. An Article in a Monthly Magazine (Signed/Unsigned)

Endnote

Signed

14. Tad Suzuki, "Reflecting Light on Photo Realism," *American Artist*, March 2002, 47.

Unsigned

14. "Repowering the U.S. with Clean Energy Development," *BioCycle*, July 2002.

Bibliography

Signed

Suzuki, Tad. "Reflecting Light on Photo Realism." *American Artist*, March 2002, 46–51.

Unsigned

"Repowering the U.S. with Clean Energy Development." *BioCycle*, July 2002, 14.

15. An Article in a Newspaper (Signed/Unsigned)

Endnote

Because the pagination of newspapers can change from edition to edition, Chicago recommends against giving page numbers for newspaper articles.

Signed

15. Francis X. Clines, "Civil War Relics Draw Visitors, and Con Artists," *New York Times*, August 4, 2002, national edition, sec. A.

Unsigned

15. "Feds Lead Way in Long-Term Care," *Atlanta Journal-Constitution*, July 21, 2002, sec. E.

Bibliography

Signed

Clines, Francis X. "Civil War Relics Draw Visitors, and Con Artists." *New York Times*, August 4, 2002, national edition, sec. A.

Unsigned

"Feds Lead Way in Long-Term Care." *Atlanta Journal-Constitution*, July 21, 2002, sec. E.

NOTE: Omit the article *the* from the newspaper's title. Include a city name in the title, even if it is not part of the actual title.

Entries for Miscellaneous Print and Nonprint Sources

Interviews

16. A Personal Interview

Endnote

16. Cornel West, interview by author, tape recording, June 8, 2003.

Bibliography

Personal interviews are not listed in the bibliography.

17. A Published Interview

Endnote

17. Gwendolyn Brooks, interview by George Stavros, *Contemporary Literature* 11, no. 1 (Winter 1970): 12.

Bibliography

Brooks, Gwendolyn. Interview by George Stavros. *Contemporary Literature* 11, no. 1 (Winter 1970): 1–20.

Letters, Government Documents

18. A Personal Letter

Endnote

18. Julia Alvarez, letter to the author, April 10, 2002.

Bibliography

Personal letters are not listed in the bibliography.

19. A Government Document

Endnote

19. U.S. Department of Transportation, *The Future of High-Speed Trains in the United States: Special Study, 2001* (Washington, DC: GPO, 2002), 203.

Bibliography

U.S. Department of Transportation. *The Future of High-Speed Trains in the United States: Special Study, 2001.* Washington, DC: GPO, 2002.

Videotapes, DVDs, and Recordings

20. A Videotape or DVD

Endnote

20. *Interview with Arthur Miller*, dir. William Schiff, 17 min., The Mosaic Group, 1987, videocassette.

Bibliography

Interview with Arthur Miller. Directed by William Schiff. 17 min. The Mosaic Group, 1987. Videocassette.

21. A Recording

Endnote

21. Bob Marley, "Crisis," *Bob Marley and the Wailers*, Kava Island Records 423 095-3, compact disc.

Bibliography

Marley, Bob. "Crisis." *Bob Marley and the Wailers.* Kava Island Records 423 095-3. Compact disc.

Electronic Sources

Search

Internet citations for electronic sources include the author's name; the title of the document (enclosed in quotation marks); the publication date (or, if no date is available, the abbreviation n.d.); the URL; and the date of access (in parentheses). The following examples illustrate the formats for endnotes and bibliographic entries.

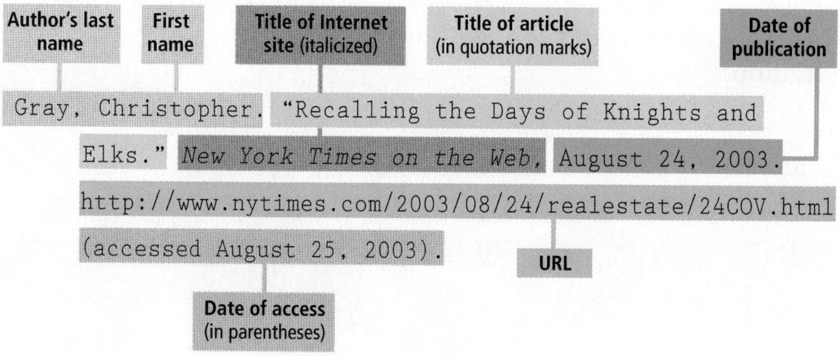

Author's last name | First name | Title of Internet site (italicized) | Title of article (in quotation marks) | Date of publication

Gray, Christopher. "Recalling the Days of Knights and Elks." *New York Times on the Web*, August 24, 2003. http://www.nytimes.com/2003/08/24/realestate/24COV.html (accessed August 25, 2003).

URL | Date of access (in parentheses)

Entries from Internet Sites

Internet-Specific Sources

22. An Article in an Online Journal

Endnote

22. Robert F. Brooks, "Communication as the Foundation of Distance Education," *Kairos: A Journal of Rhetoric, Technology, and Pedagogy* 7, no. 2 (2002), http://english.ttu.edu/kairos/index.html (accessed March 20, 2002).

Bibliography

Brooks, Robert F. "Communication as the Foundation of Distance Education." *Kairos: A Journal of Rhetoric, Technology, and Pedagogy* 7, no. 2 (2002). http://english.ttu.edu/kairos/index.html (accessed March 20, 2002).

23. An Article in an Online Magazine

Endnote

23. Steven Levy, "I Was a Wi-Fi Freeloader," *Newsweek*, October 9, 2002, http://www.msnbc.com/news/816606.asp (accessed January 9, 2004).

Bibliography

Levy, Steven. "I Was a Wi-Fi Freeloader." *Newsweek*, October 9, 2002. http://www.msnbc.com/news/816606.asp (accessed January 9, 2004).

24. An Article in an Online Newspaper

Endnote

24. William J. Broad, "Piece by Piece, the Civil War *Monitor* Is Pulled from the Atlantic's Depths," *New York Times on the Web*, July 18, 2002, http://query.nytimes.com/search/advanced (accessed June 15, 2004).

Bibliography

Broad, William J. "Piece by Piece, the Civil War *Monitor* Is Pulled from the Atlantic's Depths." *New York Times on the Web*, July 18, 2002. http://query.nytimes.com/search/advanced (accessed June 15, 2004).

25. A Web Site or Home Page

Endnote

25. David Perdue, "Dickens's Journalistic Career," *David Perdue's Charles Dickens Page*, September 24, 2002, http://www.fidnet.com/~dap1955/dickens (accessed September 10, 2003).

Bibliography

Perdue, David. "Dickens's Journalistic Career." *David Perdue's Charles Dickens Page*. September 24, 2002. http://www.fidnet.com/~dap1955/dickens (accessed September 10, 2003).

26. An Email Message

Do not include the author's email address after his or her name.

Endnote

26. Meg Halverson, "Scuba Report," personal email, April 2, 2004.

Bibliography

Email messages are not listed in the bibliography.

27. A Listserv Message

Include the name of the list and the date of the individual posting. Include the listserv address after the date of publication.

Endnote

27. Dave Shirlaw, email to Underwater Archeology discussion list, September 6, 2002, http://lists.asu.edu/archives/sub-arch.html (May 12, 2002).

Bibliography

Listserv messages are not listed in the bibliography.

Entries from Subscription Services

Documents from a Database

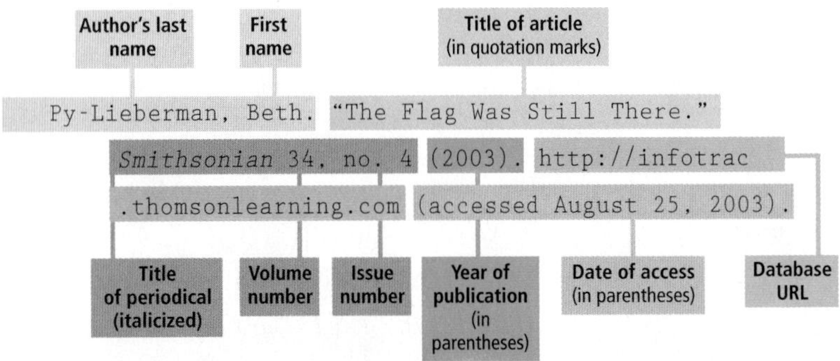

28. A Scholarly Journal Article from a Database

Include as much publication information as you can. Always give the URL of the service's main entrance; the date of access (in parentheses) is optional.

Endnote

28. Richard J. Schaefer, "Editing Strategies in Television Documentaries," *Journal of Communication* 47, no. 4 (1997): 80, http://www.galegroup.com/onefile (accessed October 2, 2003).

Bibliography

Schaefer, Richard J. "Editing Strategies in Television Documentaries." *Journal of Communication* 47, no. 4 (1997):80. http://www.galegroup.com/onefile (accessed October 2, 2003).

Close-up: Subsequent References to the Same Work

In the first reference to a work, use the full citation; in subsequent references to the same work, list only the author's last name, followed by a comma, an abbreviated title, then a comma, and a page number.

First Note on Espinoza

1. J. M. Espinoza, *The First Expedition of Vargas in New Mexico, 1692* (Albuquerque: University of New Mexico Press, 1949), 10–12.

Subsequent Note

5. Espinoza, *First Expedition*, 29.

NOTE: *The Chicago Manual of Style* allows the use of the abbreviation *ibid.* ("in the same place") for subsequent references to the same work as long as there are no intervening references. *Ibid.* takes the place of the author's name and the work's title—but not the page number.

First Note on Espinoza

1. J. M. Espinoza, *The First Expedition of Vargas in New Mexico, 1692* (Albuquerque: University of New Mexico Press, 1949), 10–12.

Subsequent Note

2. Ibid., 23.

Keep in mind, however, that the use of *Ibid.* is giving way to the use of the author's last name and the page number for subsequent references to the same work.

20b Chicago-Style Manuscript Guidelines

Checklist: Typing Your Paper

When you type your paper, use the student paper in 20c as your model.

- ☐ On the title page, include the full title of your paper as well as your name. Also include the course title, the instructor's name, and the date. Each element on the title page is considered a major heading and should appear in full capitals.
- ☐ Type your paper with a one-inch margin at the top, at the bottom, and on both sides.
- ☐ Double-space your paper throughout.

(continued)

Typing your paper (continued)

- ☐ Indent the first line of each paragraph five spaces. Set off a long prose quotation (ten or more typed lines or more than one paragraph) from the text by indenting the entire quotation one-half inch from the left-hand margin. Do not use quotation marks. If the quotation is a full paragraph, include the paragraph indentation.
- ☐ Number all pages consecutively at the top of the page, with the number either centered or flush right. Page numbers should appear at a consistent distance (at least three-fourths of an inch) from the top edge. The title page is not numbered; the first full page of the paper is numbered page 1.
- ☐ Use superscript numbers to indicate in-text citations. Type superscript numbers at the end of cited material (quotations, paraphrases, or summaries). Leave no space between the superscript number and the preceding letter or punctuation mark. The note number should be placed at the end of a sentence (or at the end of a clause). The number should come after any punctuation mark except for a dash, which it precedes.
- ☐ When you cite source material in your paper, use Chicago documentation style.

See 20a

Checklist: Using Visuals

According to *The Chicago Manual of Style*, there are two types of visuals: **tables** and **figures** (or **illustrations**), including charts, graphs, photographs, maps, and diagrams.

Tables

- ☐ Give each **table** a label and an arabic number (`TABLE 1`, `TABLE 2`, and so on).
- ☐ Give each table a descriptive title in the form of a sentence. Place the title after the table number.
- ☐ Place both the label and title above the table.
- ☐ Place source information below the table, introduced by the word *Source*. (If there is more than one source, begin with *Sources*.)

Source: David E. Fisher and Marshall Jon Fisher, *Tube: The Invention of Television* (Washington, DC: Counterpoint Press, 1996), 185.

If the sources are listed in the bibliography, use a shortened form.

`Source: Fisher and Fisher 1996.`

Figures

- ☐ Give each **figure** a label, an arabic number, and a caption. The label `Figure` may be abbreviated `Fig.` (`Figure 1`, `Fig. 1`).
- ☐ Place both the label and caption below the figure, on the same line.
- ☐ Place source information in parentheses at the end of the title or caption.

```
Fig. 1. Television and its influence on young
children. (Photograph from ABC Photos.)
```

Checklist: Preparing Chicago-Style Endnotes

FAQs

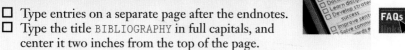

- ☐ Begin the endnotes on a new page after the last page of the paper and preceding the bibliography.
- ☐ Type the title `NOTES` in full capitals and center it two inches from the top of the page.
- ☐ Number the page on which the endnotes appear as the next page of the paper.
- ☐ Type and number notes in the order in which they appear in the paper, beginning with number 1.
- ☐ Type the note number on (not above) the line, followed by a period and one space.
- ☐ Indent the first line of each note one-half inch (or five spaces); type subsequent lines flush with the left-hand margin.
- ☐ Double-space within and between entries.
- ☐ Break URLs after slashes, before punctuation marks, and before or after the symbols = and &.

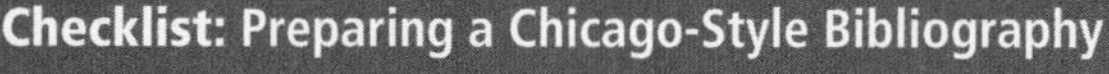

Checklist: Preparing a Chicago-Style Bibliography

- ☐ Type entries on a separate page after the endnotes.
- ☐ Type the title `BIBLIOGRAPHY` in full capitals, and center it two inches from the top of the page.
- ☐ List entries alphabetically according to the author's last name.
- ☐ Type the first line of each entry flush with the left-hand margin. Indent subsequent lines one-half inch (five spaces).
- ☐ Double-space within and between entries.

20c Sample Chicago-Style Research Paper

The following student paper, "The Flu of 1918 and the Potential for Future Pandemics," was written for a history course. It uses Chicago-style documentation and includes a title page, a notes page, and a bibliography.

Title page is not numbered

THE FLU OF 1918 AND THE POTENTIAL FOR

FUTURE PANDEMICS

BY

RITA LIN

Title is centered and followed by name

AMERICAN HISTORY 301

Course title

DR. WALTER HIGH

Instructor's name

MARCH 5, 2003

Date

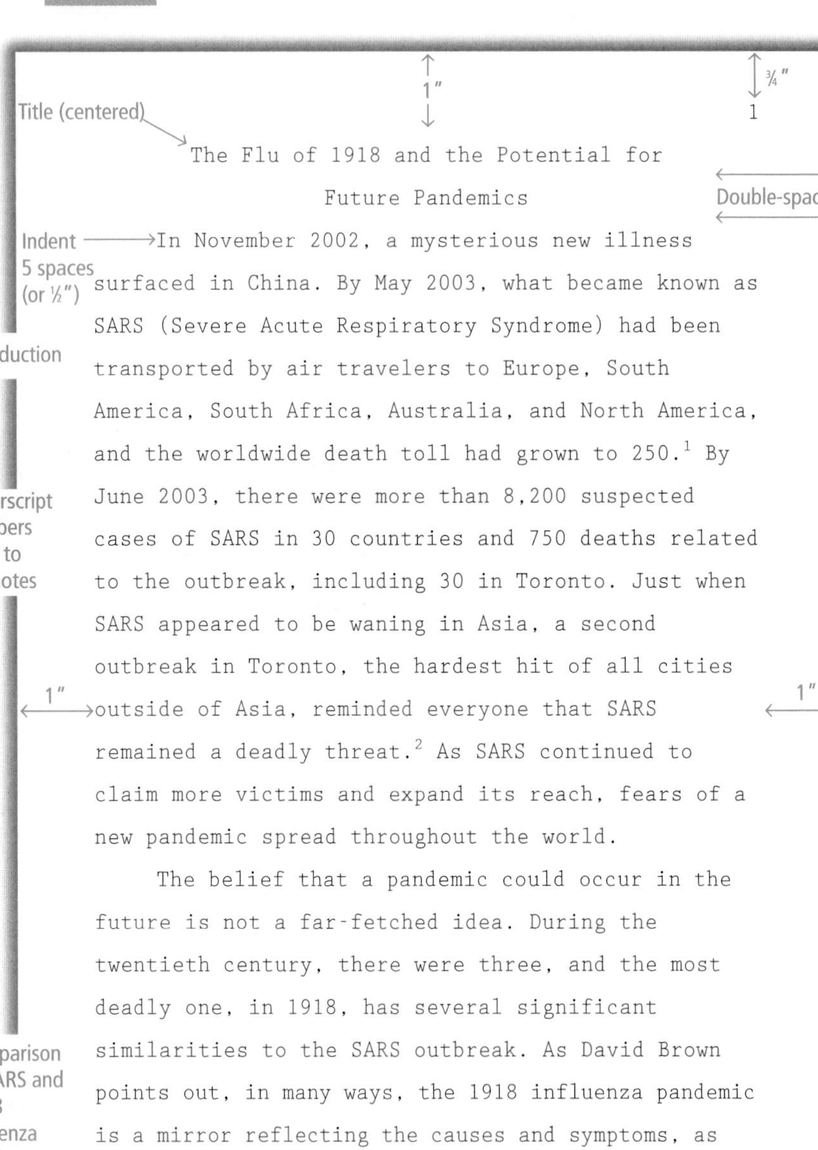

1"
¾"
1
Title (centered)
The Flu of 1918 and the Potential for
Future Pandemics
Double-space
Indent 5 spaces (or ½")
In November 2002, a mysterious new illness surfaced in China. By May 2003, what became known as SARS (Severe Acute Respiratory Syndrome) had been transported by air travelers to Europe, South America, South Africa, Australia, and North America, and the worldwide death toll had grown to 250.[1] By June 2003, there were more than 8,200 suspected cases of SARS in 30 countries and 750 deaths related to the outbreak, including 30 in Toronto. Just when SARS appeared to be waning in Asia, a second outbreak in Toronto, the hardest hit of all cities outside of Asia, reminded everyone that SARS remained a deadly threat.[2] As SARS continued to claim more victims and expand its reach, fears of a new pandemic spread throughout the world.
Introduction
Superscript numbers refer to endnotes
1"
1"
The belief that a pandemic could occur in the future is not a far-fetched idea. During the twentieth century, there were three, and the most deadly one, in 1918, has several significant similarities to the SARS outbreak. As David Brown points out, in many ways, the 1918 influenza pandemic is a mirror reflecting the causes and symptoms, as well as the future potential, of SARS. Both are caused by a virus, result in respiratory illness, and spread through casual contact and coughing. Outbreaks for both are often traced to one
Comparison of SARS and 1918 influenza pandemic
1"

individual, quarantine is the major weapon against the spread of both, and both likely arose from mutated animal viruses. Moreover, as Brown observes, the greatest fear regarding SARS is that it will become so widespread that transmission chains will be undetectable, and health officials will be helpless to restrain outbreaks. Such was the case with the 1918 influenza, which also began mysteriously in China and was transported around the globe (at that time by World War I military ships). By the time the flu lost its power in the spring of 1919, in a year's time it had killed more than 50 million people worldwide[3]—more than twice as many as those who died during the four and a half years of World War I. Thus, if SARS is a reflection of the potential for a future flu pandemic—and experts believe it is—the international community needs to acknowledge the danger, accelerate its research, and develop an extensive virus-surveillance system.

Thesis statement

Clearly, the 1918 flu was different from anything ever known to Americans. Among the peculiarities of the pandemic was its origin and cause. In the spring of 1918, the virus, in relatively mild form, mysteriously appeared on a Kansas military base. After apparently dying out, the flu returned to the United States in late August. At that point, the influenza was no ordinary flu; it "struck with incredible speed, often killing a

History of 1918 pandemic

Bracket indicates that comma was added by student writer

victim within hours of contact[,] . . . so fast that such infections rarely had time to set in."[4] Unlike previous strains, the 1918 flu struck healthy young people.

The initial spring outbreak in the United States, confined primarily to military bases, was largely ignored by public officials and the press because the nation's attention was focused on the war overseas. As a result, little was done to prepare for the deadly fall and winter to come. During the summer, though, the flu made the circuit of European battlefields and circled the globe. Meanwhile, while the United States remained unusually healthy, the country was sending hundreds of thousands of soldiers overseas, where they had unprecedented contact with the world's peoples. During the late summer, the influenza virus mutated, most likely in Brest, France. There, and at two other port cities—Freetown, Sierra Leone, and Boston—during "the last week of August, a savagely lethal Spanish influenza exploded to life. . . . At the end of a calm summer, influenza returned to America—now in its most virulent form."[5]

After coming ashore in Boston with returning soldiers, the 1918 influenza quickly spread to civilian populations, progressing down the eastern seaboard and across the country within six weeks.[6] In Philadelphia, one of the hardest hit cities, the

4

History of 1918 flu epidemic, continued

outbreak occurred in early October, just 5 days after crowds gathered at a major bond rally.[7] During the remaining days of that month, nearly 11,000 residents of the city died. Along with cities, military bases continued to be a major area of infection,[8] leading to naval base quarantines in places like San Francisco. In late September, San Francisco thought it was safe and lifted the quarantines, but in mid-October, following a series of parades, community sings, and public bond drives, a major outbreak of the flu occurred there.

Such was the pattern for the spread of infection in the United States, where nearly 675,000 people died of the flu, with major urban outbreaks often made worse (if not directly caused) by the war effort at home and its related public displays of patriotism. Troops overseas, or on the seas, fared no better than those at home. About 621,000 deployed American soldiers became ill with influenza before the Armistice was signed on November 11, 1918.[9] In an unusual coincidence, the flu in the United States began waning about the same time as the peace accord was finalized, although a third spring wave hit some cities, such as San Francisco.

Effects of 1918 flu epidemic

After the fact, the scope of the 1918 pandemic appears astounding; it dwarfs the first six months of SARS. Considering differences in population, outside the United States the 1918 flu death toll was

5

equally (if not more) staggering: 228,000 Britons; 225,000 Germans; 375,000 Italians; and 450,000 Russians died. The highest death rate occurred on the Indian subcontinent, where more than 12 million perished in October 1918, "a month of disease unparalleled in the history of human civilization."[10] Across the globe, the flu touched nearly every inhabited area except the St. Lawrence seaway, the Pribilof islands in the Bering Sea, the northern coast of Iceland, and American Samoa. (The latter two locations successfully carried out travel bans and refused to accept unauthorized landings to their regions.) There was little else to be done although quarantines in nonisland countries did not in general work well.[11]

Analysis of 1918 flu epidemic

The major problem was the public response, which was lethargic at best and in many respects exacerbated the potential for the spread of influenza. First, there was initial public denial in numerous cities where officials believed the flu would not reach them. Perhaps worse, President Woodrow Wilson was unduly silent on the flu and, if anything, set a poor example. In an act that appeared to defy the flu's power, in October 1918 he led a parade of 25,000 people "through the streets of flu-ridden New York," and "[m]any, following the lead of the President himself, continued to prioritize Liberty Loan rallies, parades, and 'patriotic sings,' despite the obvious threat to public health."[12] American newspapers likewise said little about the flu. Moreover, there was no public health structure in place to deal with a pandemic, and what public warnings were given were not always understood or heeded by people, particularly the large populations of foreign-speaking immigrants in major cities.[13] Health workers were hampered in their efforts because physicians did not know what they were fighting.[14] Scientists believed that the flu was caused by bacteria and were unable to create an effective vaccine since this belief was wrong.[15]

Current status of the flu

Even after the influenza disappeared as mysteriously as it had come, nearly everything about the flu's origins and the source of its power remained unknown. In the decade that followed, the field of virology was born, and in 1933 the influenza virus was isolated for the first time. Today, three basic types of flu virus—A, B, and C—are recognized. Almost every winter, A and B spawn minor epidemics, causing about 25,000 deaths annually in the United States. A flu shot can prevent most types of A and B influenza, but only when vaccines are designed to combat known strains of flu. Unfortunately, flu viruses can mutate in two ways: through antigenic *drift*, in which small changes occur in the virus, producing strains not recognizable by human immune systems, and through

7

antigenic *shift.* When such an antigenic shift occurs, the result is "a new influenza . . . that most people have little or no protection against."[16] Pandemics, like that of 1918, occur when such a new flu virus appears.

Current information about the 1918 flu virus

It was not until the twenty-first century that virologists truly began unlocking some of the secrets behind the 1918 pandemic. In 2001, Australian researchers discovered that the 1918 flu virus's "genes came from two different sources, then combined to form a super-virulent strain of the flu."[17] Most likely, researchers deduced, the 1918 flu strain was "an unusual recombination of pig and human flu genes" and did not involve birds as previously theorized.[18] Then, in 2002, American scientists literally constructed a flu virus resembling the 1918 strain and discovered that existing drugs could be used to curb the spread of a virus similar to the 1918 influenza. Moreover, parts of the 1918 virus's DNA, discovered in preserved tissue samples, are now being studied. As a result, the "chemical spelling" of some of the more virulent genes from the flu has been found.[19] The entire DNA makeup of the 1918 flu virus remains elusive, however.

Alfred W. Crosby Jr., a preeminent pandemic historian, said in a phone interview that these research successes are impressive, but we still do

8

not know some very important things, such as how the virus killed so many, particularly its young victims. "It's like knowing that the murderer had a blue suit with brass buttons, but what does a blue suit with brass buttons have to do with murder?" Crosby says in the interview.[20] In other words, only part of the mystery of the 1918 pandemic has been solved.

Quotation is from a phone interview, so no page number is given

Experts fear that the 1918 flu virus could return or that a similar deadly virus could arise.[21] Some thought that such a fear was going to be realized in early 2003 when a new outbreak of the 1997 Hong Kong bird flu resurfaced in China, spawning fears of a new pandemic, but widespread bird flu never materialized that spring.[22] What did materialize in March, though, was SARS.

While some "researchers have concluded that SARS will not mimic the 1918 influenza pandemic, given its relatively slow spread," they do not expect SARS to disappear altogether in the summer of 2003.[23] As a matter of fact, Crosby sees a similarity in the rise of SARS and the 1918 flu, both of which materialized in America in the spring. Crosby notes in the interview that "health officials fear what may happen next fall and winter [2003–04] if the virus goes through the same sequence" and reappears in a more deadly and infectious form.[24]

Discussion of SARS outbreak

Meanwhile, influenza experts like Crosby are convinced that a virus as deadly as the 1918 flu will

9

create a pandemic in the near future. Crosby explains in the interview that what is needed is "money for an international public health infrastructure to be ready for another pandemic. We need money for better international surveillance of diseases. We need to quickly know when a new virus arrives because we need to come up with vaccines and then produce them and get them to the public in time."[25]

Conclusion

Whether a pandemic will occur in the future is not in doubt; what is in question is whether the world will be prepared, and the answer lies with the international community. As Alfred Crosby explains, "There will be another pandemic. We're overdue and waiting for all hell to bust loose." In the meantime, health workers hope that government officials realize the need to fund and expedite research before a pandemic strikes. If governments do not realize this need, we already know "the worst-case scenario . . . is not theoretical. It happened 85 years ago when . . . at least 50 million people died."[26]

10

NOTES

Indent 5 spaces (or ½") Double-space

1. Nancy Shute, "SARS Hits Home," *U.S. News & World Report*, May 5, 2003, 42.

2. "Canada Waits for SARS News as Asia Under Control," *Sydney Morning Herald on the Web*, June 2, 2003, http://www.smh.com.au/text/articles/2003/06/01/1054406076596.htm (accessed June 6, 2003).

Endnotes listed in order in which they appear in the paper

3. David Brown, "A Grim Reminder in SARS Fight: In 1918, Spanish Flu Swept the Globe, Killing Millions," *MSNBC News Online*, June 4, 2003, http://www.msnbc.com/news/921901.asp (accessed June 6, 2003).

4. Doug Rekenthaler, "The Flu Pandemic of 1918: Is a Repeat Performance Likely?—Part 1 of 2," *Disaster Relief: New Stories*, February 22, 1999, http://www.disasterrelief.org/Disasters/990219Flu/ (accessed March 9, 2003).

5. Lynette Iezzoni, *Influenza 1918: The Worst Epidemic in American History* (New York: TV Books, 1999), 40.

6. "1918 Influenza Timeline," *Influenza 1918*, 1999, http://www.pbs.org/wgbh/amex/influenza/timeline/index.html (accessed March 9, 2003).

7. Iezonni, *Influenza 1918*, 131–132.

8. Brown, "Grim Reminder."

9. Iezonni, *Influenza 1918*, 88–89.

10. Ibid, 204.

Second and subsequent references to the same source include author's last name, shortened title, and page number(s).

Ibid. is used for a subsequent reference to the same source when there are no intervening references.

11

11. Brown, "Grim Reminder."

12. Iezonni, *Influenza 1918*, 60.

13. Alfred W. Crosby Jr., *America's Forgotten Pandemic: The Influenza of 1918* (New York: Cambridge University Press, 1989), 67.

14. Ibid. 96.

15. Iezonni, *Influenza 1918*, 108.

16. Daren Dandurant, "Virus Changes Can Make Flu a Slippery Foe to Combat," *MSNBC News Online*, January 17, 2003, http://www.msnbc.com/local/sco/m8052.asp (accessed March 30, 2003).

17. Kristen Philipkoski, "Science Tracks Influenza Genes," *Wired News*, September 6, 2001, http://www.wired.com/news/medtech/0,1286,46608,00.html (accessed March 30, 2003).

18. Becky Ham, "The Genetic Genesis of a Killer Flu," *MSNBC News Online*, September 6, 2001, http://www.msnbc.com/news/624982.asp (accessed March 30, 2003).

19. Robert Cooke, "Drugs vs. the Bug of 1918: Virus' Deadly Code Is Unlocked to Test Strategies to Fight It," *Newsday*, October 1, 2002, 49.

20. Alfred W. Crosby, Jr., phone interview by the author, June 9, 2003.

21. Cooke, "Drugs vs. the Bug," 49.

22. "Global Killers: Invisible Threat of Mutant Bugs," *The Scotsman*, March 17, 2003, 6.

12

23. John Dodge, “Written in the SARS,” *Bio-IT World*, May 2003, http://www.bio-itworld.com/news/050903_report2510.html (accessed June 6, 2003).

24. Crosby, interview.

25. Ibid.

26. Brown, “Grim Reminder.”

First line of each entry is flush with the left-hand margin; subsequent lines are indented 5 spaces

Entries are listed alphabetically according to the author's last name

2"

13

Center → BIBLIOGRAPHY

Double-space

"1918 Influenza Timeline." *Influenza 1918*, 1999. http://www.pbs.org/wgbh/amex/influenza/timeline/index.html (accessed March 9, 2003).

Billings, Molly. "The Influenza Pandemic of 1918." *Human Virology at Stanford: Interesting Viral Web Pages*, June 1997. http://www.stanford.edu/group/virus/uda/index.html (accessed March 17, 2003).

Brown, David. "A Grim Reminder in SARS Fight: In 1918, Spanish Flu Swept the Globe, Killing Millions." *MSNBC News Online*, June 4, 2003. http://www.msnbc.com/news/921901.asp (accessed June 6, 2003).

"Canada Waits for SARS News as Asia Under Control." *Sydney Morning Herald on the Web*, June 2, 2003. http://www.smh.com.au/text/articles/2003/06/01/1054406076596.htm (accessed June 6, 2003).

Cooke, Robert. "Drugs vs. the Bug of 1918: Virus' Deadly Code Is Unlocked to Test Strategies to Fight It." *Newsday*, October 1, 2002.

Crosby, Alfred W., Jr. *America's Forgotten Pandemic: The Influenza of 1918*. New York: Cambridge University Press, 1989.

Dandurant, Daren. "Virus Changes Can Make Flu a Slippery Foe to Combat." *MSNBC News Online*,

14

January 17, 2003. http://www.msnbc.com/local/sco/m8052.asp (accessed March 30, 2003).

Dodge, John. "Written in the SARS." *Bio-IT World,* May 2003. http://www.bio-itworld.com/news/050903_report2510.html (accessed June 6, 2003).

"Global Killers: Invisible Threat of Mutant Bugs." *The Scotsman,* March 17, 2003.

Ham, Becky. "The Genetic Genesis of a Killer Flu." *MSNBC News Online,* September 6, 2001. http://www.msnbc.com/news/624982asp (accessed March 30, 2003).

Iezzoni, Lynette. *Influenza 1918: The Worst Epidemic in American History.* New York: TV Books, 1999.

Philipkoski, Kristen. "Science Tracks Influenza Genes." *Wired News,* September 6, 2001. http://www.wired.com/news/medtech/0,1286,46608,00.html (accessed March 30, 2003).

Rekenthaler, Doug. "The Flu Pandemic of 1918: Is a Repeat Performance Likely?—Part 1 of 2." *Disaster Relief: New Stories,* February 22, 1999. http://www.disasterrelief.org/Disasters/990219Flu (accessed March 9, 2003).

Shute, Nancy. "SARS Hits Home." *U.S. News & World Report,* May 5, 2003, 38–44.

DIRECTORY OF CSE REFERENCE LIST ENTRIES

Print Sources

Entries for Books

Entries for Articles

Entries for Miscellaneous Print and Nonprint Sources

Electronic Sources

Entries from Internet Sites

Chapter 21

CSE (Formerly CBE) and Other Documentation Styles

Frequently Asked Questions

21a Using CSE Style*

CSE style,* recommended by the Council of Science Editors (CSE), is used in biology, zoology, physiology, anatomy, and genetics. CSE style has two parts—*documentation in the text* and a *reference list.*

(1) Documentation in the Text

CSE style recommends two documentation formats: *citation-sequence format* and *name-year format.*

Citation-Sequence Format The **citation-sequence format** calls for either **superscripts** (raised numbers) in the text of the paper (the preferred form) or numbers inserted parenthetically in the text of the paper.

> One study[1] has demonstrated the effect of low dissolved oxygen.

These numbers correspond to a list of references at the end of the paper. When the writer refers to more than one source in a single note, the numbers are separated by a hyphen if they are in sequence and by a comma if they are not.

> Some studies[2-3] dispute this claim.
>
> Other studies[3,6] support these findings.

---

*CSE style follows the guidelines set in the style manual of the Council of Biology Editors: *Scientific Style and Format: The CBE Manual for Authors, Editors, and Publishers*, 6th ed. New York: Cambridge UP, 1994. The Council of Biology Editors has changed its name to the Council of Science Editors.

Name-Year Format The **name-year format** calls for the author's name and the year of publication to be inserted parenthetically in the text. If the author's name is used to introduce the source material, only the date of publication is needed in the parenthetical citation.

```
A great deal of heat is often generated during this
process (McGinness 1999).
According to McGinness, a great deal of heat is often
generated during this process (1999).
```

When two or more works are cited in the same parentheses, the sources are arranged chronologically (from earliest to latest) and separated by semicolons.

```
Epidemics can be avoided by taking tissue cultures
(Domb 1998) and by intervention with antibiotics
(Baldwin and Rigby 1984; Martin and others 1992; Cording
1998).
```

NOTE: The citation *Baldwin and Rigby 1984* refers to a work by two authors; the citation *Martin and others 1992* refers to a work by three or more authors.

(2) Reference List

The format of the reference list depends on the documentation format you use. If you use the name-year documentation format, your reference list will resemble the reference list for an APA paper. If you use the citation-sequence documentation style, your sources will be listed by number, in the order in which they appear in your paper, on a `References` page. Double-space within and between entries. Type the number flush left, followed by a period and one space. Align the second and subsequent lines with the first letter of the author's last name.

SAMPLE CSE CITATION-SEQUENCE REFERENCE LIST ENTRIES

Print Sources

Entries for Books

List the author or authors with last name followed by a space but not a comma. Then, list the initial or initials (unspaced) that represent the first and middle names (followed by a period); the title (not underlined, and with only the first word capitalized); the place of publication; the full name of the publisher (followed by a semicolon); the year (followed by a period); and the total number of pages (including back matter, such as the index).

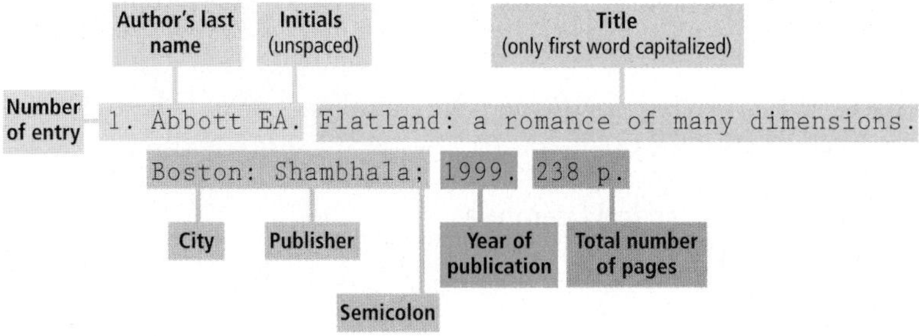

Authors

1. A Book with One Author

```
1. Hawking SW. Brief history of time: from the big bang
   to black holes. New York: Bantam; 1995. 198 p.
```

NOTE: No period separates the initials that represent the author's first and middle names.

2. Book with More Than One Author

```
2. Horner JR, Gorman J. Digging dinosaurs. New York:
   Workman; 1988. 210 p.
```

Editions

3. An Edited Book

```
3. Goldfarb TD, editor. Taking sides: clashing views on
   controversial environmental issues. 2nd ed. Guilford
   (CT): Dushkin; 1987, 323 p.
```

NOTE: The name of the publisher's state, province, or country can be added within parentheses to clarify the location. The two-letter postal service abbreviation can be used for the state or province.

Parts of Books

4. A Chapter or Other Part of a Book with a Separate Title but with the Same Author

```
4. Asimov I. Exploring the earth and cosmos: the growth
   and future of human knowledge. New York: Crown; 1984.
   Part III, The horizons of matter; p 245-94.
```

NOTE: No period follows the `p` when it precedes a page number.

5. A Chapter or Other Part of a Book with a Different Author

5. Gingerich O. Hints for beginning observers. In: Mallas JH, Kreimer E, editors. The Messier album: an observer's handbook. Cambridge: Cambridge Univ Pr; 1978: p 194-5.

NOTE: When giving inclusive page numbers, give only the nonrepeated digits—for example, 197-8 (*not* 197-198).

Religious Works, Classical Literature

6. Religious Work

General Reference

6. The Bible. Philippians 1:9-11.

Specific Reference

6. The New Jerusalem Bible. Garden City (NY): Doubleday; 1985. Luke 15:11-32. p 1715-6.

7. Classical Literature

General Reference

7. The Odyssey. 17:319-32.

Specific Reference

7. Homer. Odyssey; Book 17:319-32. In: Lombardo S, translator and editor. The essential Homer: selections from the Iliad and the Odyssey. Indianapolis: Hackett; 2000. p 391-2.

Entries for Articles

List the author or authors (last name first); the title of the article (not in quotation marks, and with only the first word capitalized); the abbreviated name of the journal (with all major words capitalized, but not italicized or underlined); the year (followed by a semicolon); the volume number (followed by a colon); and inclusive page numbers. No spaces separate the year, the volume, and the page numbers. Month names longer than three letters are abbreviated to their first three letters.

Scholarly Journals

8. An Article in a Journal Paginated by Issue

8. Sarmiento JL, Gruber N. Sinks for anthropogenic carbon. Phy Today 2002;55(8):30-6.

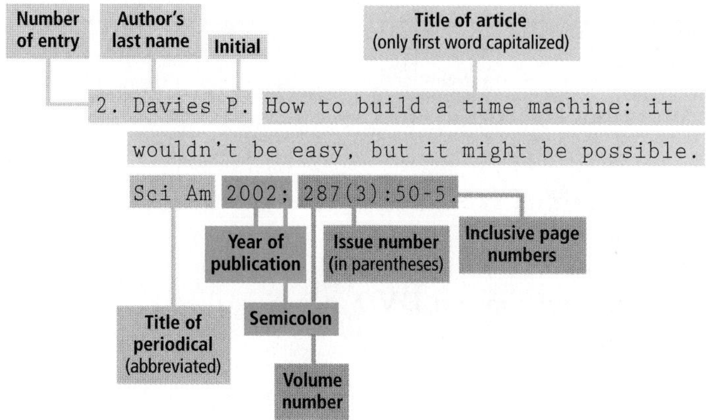

9. An Article in a Journal with Continuous Pagination

9. Brazil K, Krueger P. Patterns of family adaptation to childhood asthma. J Pediatric Nursing 2002;17:167-73.

Omit the month (and day for weeklies) and issue number for journals with continuous pagination in volumes.

Magazines and Newspapers

10. A Magazine Article (Signed/Unsigned)

Signed

10. Nadis S. Using lasers to detect E.T. Astronomy 2002 Sep:44-9.

Unsigned

10. [Anonymous]. Brown dwarf glows with radio waves. Astronomy 2001 Jun:28.

11. A Newspaper Article (Signed/Unsigned)

Signed

11. Husted B. Don't wiggle out of untangling computer wires. Atlanta Journal-Constitution 2002 Jul 21;Sect Q1(col 1).

Unsigned

11. [Anonymous]. Scientists find gene tied to cancer risk. New York Times 2002 Apr 22;Sect A:18(col 6).

Entries for Miscellaneous Print and Nonprint Sources

Films, Videotapes, Recordings, Maps

12. An Audiocassette

12. Ascent of man [audiocassette]. Bronowski J. New York: Jeffrey Norton Pub; 1974. 1 audiocassette: 2-track, 55 min.

13. A Film, Videotape, or DVD

13. Women in science [videocassette]. Stoneberger B, Clark R, editor, American Society for Microbiology, producer. Madison (WI): Hawkhill; 1998. 1 videocassette: 42 min, sound, color, 1/2 in. Accompanied by: 1 guide.

14. A Map

A Sheet Map

14. Amazonia: a world resource at risk [ecological map]. Washington: Nat Geographic Soc; 1992. 1 sheet.

A Map in an Atlas

14. Central Africa [political map]. In: Hammond citation world atlas. Maplewood (NJ): Hammond; 1996. p 114-5. Color, scale 1:13,800,000.

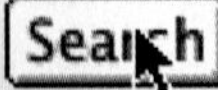

Electronic Sources

Entries from Internet Sites

Internet-Specific Sources

15. An Online Book

15. Bohm D. Causality and chance in modern physics [monograph online]. Philadelphia: Univ of Pennsylvania Pr; 1999. Available from: http://www.netlibrary.com/ebook_info.asp?product_id517169 via the INTERNET. Accessed 2002 Aug 17.

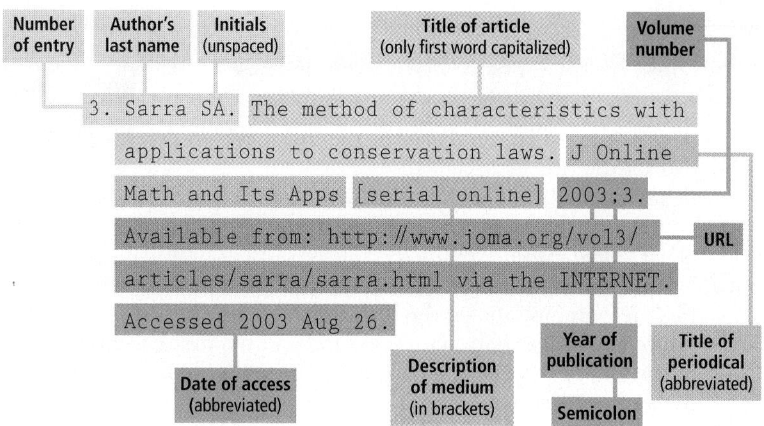

16. An Online Journal

16. Lasko P. The *Drosophila melanogaster* genome: translation factors and RNA binding proteins. J Cell Biol [serial online] 2000;150(2):F51-6. Available from: http://www.jcb.org/search.dtl via the INTERNET. Accessed 2002 Aug 15.

21b CSE Manuscript Guidelines

Checklist: Typing Your Paper

When you type your paper, use the student paper in 21c as your model.

- ☐ Type your name, the course, and the date flush left one inch from the top of the first page.
- ☐ If required, include an **abstract** (a 250-word summary of the paper) on a separate page following the title page.
- ☐ Double-space throughout.
- ☐ Insert tables and figures in the body of the paper. Number tables and figures in separate sequences (`Table 1, Table 2; Figure 1, Figure 2`; and so on).
- ☐ Number pages consecutively in the upper right-hand corner; include a shortened title above the page number.
- ☐ When you cite source material in your paper, follow CSE documentation style.

See 21a

Checklist: Preparing the CSE Reference List

- ☐ Begin the reference list on a new page after the last page of the paper, numbered as the next page.
- ☐ Center the title `References`, `Literature Cited`, or `References Cited` about one inch from the top of the page.
- ☐ List the entries in the order in which they first appear in the paper, *not alphabetically*.
- ☐ Number the entries consecutively; type the note numbers flush left on (not above) the line, followed by a period.
- ☐ Leave two spaces between the period and the first letter of the entry; align subsequent lines directly beneath the first letter of the author's last name.
- ☐ Double-space within and between entries.

21c Sample CSE-Style Research Paper

The following student paper explores the dangers of global warming for humans and wildlife. The paper cites seven sources and displays one graph, illustrating the CSE citation-sequence format.

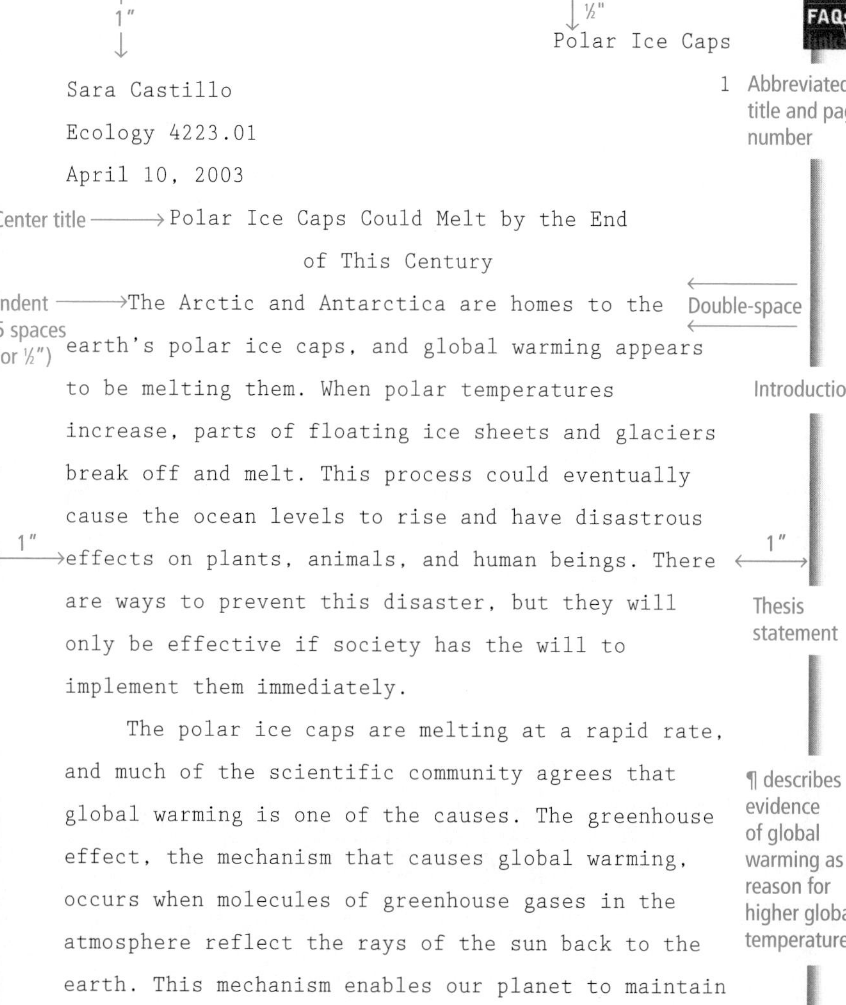

Polar Ice Caps 1

Sara Castillo

Ecology 4223.01

April 10, 2003

Polar Ice Caps Could Melt by the End of This Century

The Arctic and Antarctica are homes to the earth's polar ice caps, and global warming appears to be melting them. When polar temperatures increase, parts of floating ice sheets and glaciers break off and melt. This process could eventually cause the ocean levels to rise and have disastrous effects on plants, animals, and human beings. There are ways to prevent this disaster, but they will only be effective if society has the will to implement them immediately.

The polar ice caps are melting at a rapid rate, and much of the scientific community agrees that global warming is one of the causes. The greenhouse effect, the mechanism that causes global warming, occurs when molecules of greenhouse gases in the atmosphere reflect the rays of the sun back to the earth. This mechanism enables our planet to maintain a temperature adequate for life. However, as the concentration of greenhouse gases in the atmosphere increases, more heat from the sun is retained, and the temperature of the earth rises.[1]

Greenhouse gases include carbon dioxide (CO_2), methane, and nitrous oxide.[2] Since the beginning

Polar Ice Caps

2

of the industrial revolution in the late 1800s, people have been burning fossil fuels that create CO_2.[3] This CO_2 has led to an increase in the greenhouse effect and has contributed to the global warming that is melting the polar ice caps. As Figure 1 shows, the surface temperature of the earth has increased by about 1 degree Celsius (1.8 degrees Fahrenheit) since the 1850s. Some scientists have

Figure 1 introduced

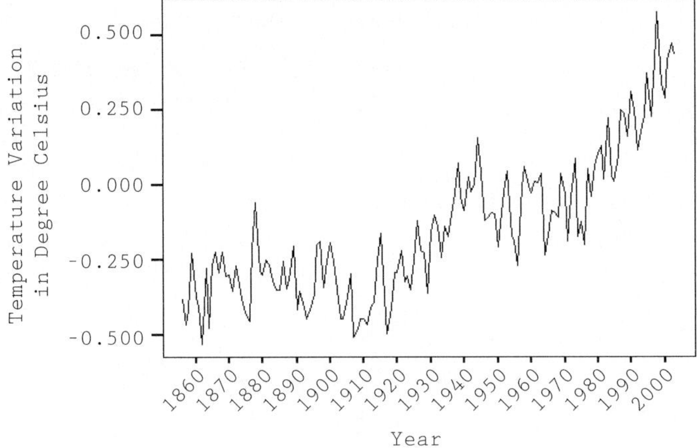

Figure placed close to where it is discussed

Figure 1 Global temperature variation from the average during the base period 1961-1990 (adapted from Climatic research unit: data: temperature 2003). Available from: http://www.cru.uea.ac.uk/cru/data/temperature/ via the INTERNET. Accessed 2003 Mar 11.

Label, caption, and full source information

Polar Ice Caps

3

predicted that temperatures will increase even further.

It is easy to see the effects of global warming. For example, the Pine Island Glacier in Antarctica was depleted at a rate of 1.6 meters per year between 1992 and 1999. This type of melting is very likely to increase the fresh water that drains into the oceans each year, thus increasing ocean levels.[4] The large ice cap that covers the North Pole in the Arctic Ocean may be gone by 2100, according to a recent NASA study. Also according to NASA, between 1978 and 2000, 1.2 million square kilometers of what was previously thought to be a permanent summer ice cap melted.[5]

¶ presents evidence that ice caps are melting

Portions of the ice caps have always melted during the summer months, resulting in slightly elevated sea levels. During the winter months, the water refreezes into a glacier or floating ice sheet. However, summers are becoming warmer, so more ice is melting. At the same time, less of the melted ice is refreezing back into the ice caps. This results in a cycle of melting and refreezing in which sea ice is more vulnerable to melting the next summer.[5] Because of this cycle, the Arctic and Antarctica are slowly losing their ice caps.

Another reason for the melting ice caps is the Pacific Decadal Oscillation (PDO), a weather pattern

¶ explains other possible reasons for ice caps melting

Next two ¶s describe likely consequences of global warming

that persists for 20 to 30 years and is most powerful in the North Pacific/North American sector. The PDO weather pattern was responsible for a cool spell between 1946 and 1977 and a warm spell from 1977 to the mid-1990s.[6] This cool-warm pattern resulted in the melting not only of the Arctic poles but also of the polar ice in the Antarctic. The mechanism that causes this weather pattern is unknown, which makes it hard to predict the next cycle of warming and cooling.

If ocean temperatures increase and the ice caps melt as predicted, there will be disastrous effects, and wildlife will be the first to suffer. Polar bears may become endangered by the melting of ice caps because their habitats and food sources may be damaged or destroyed.[3] Some fish may not be able to adapt to the warm waters caused by global warming and may also become endangered or even extinct. For example, salmon have adapted to a narrow range of cold temperatures in the ocean, and the warming of the seas may force them to leave their home in the North Pacific Ocean.[3] Animals in Antarctica may suffer as well. For example, Adélie penguins will have trouble surviving because the melting ice drifts and rising seas will cause their habitat to shrink, and the penguins will have to compete for scarce resources, such as adequate nesting sites.[7]

As the ice caps continue to melt, human beings may also suffer. If the oceans rise, they will flood coastlines and make certain parts of the world uninhabitable. Recently, the inhabitants of the Nilandu Atoll were forced to relocate because of rising sea levels. Some experts believe global warming contributed to this situation.[1] The countries that will be most affected by the increase in sea level are in Asia (because of the Indus River) and Africa (because of the Nile River). If the water level in the Indus or the Nile rises significantly, nearby low-lying lands will be flooded. In the United States, Hawaii, as well as Florida, California, and other coastal states will also be jeopardized by flooding.[1] About 37% of the earth's population could be displaced due to the rising sea levels. This flooding could lead to the erosion of coastlines and coastal property. Even more threatening is the possibility of a salt-water intrusion that would contaminate the freshwater wells people use for drinking.[3] The rising temperatures could also endanger terrestrial plants and animals that cannot adapt fast enough.

There are several things that can be done now to alleviate the problem of global warming. One is to limit the use of fossil fuels, which would decrease the amount of carbon dioxide in the

¶ proposes possible solutions

atmosphere. Automobile makers are already selling "hybrid" cars that use both gasoline and electricity and that get over 50 miles to a gallon. In addition, in his State of the Union address, President Bush proposed government funding for the development of a hydrogen-powered car. An even more important step would be for the industrialized nations of the world to agree to reduce their use of fossil fuels and to provide developing countries with energy alternatives. Also, all industrialized nations should offer money and equipment to developing nations to help them reduce their use of fossil fuels.[3] Populations can also begin to use alternative fuels such as sun, wind, and water to make the energy needed to power homes and cars.

Summary

If people continue to use large amounts of fossil fuels, the temperature of the earth will continue to rise. The result will be the melting of the polar ice caps into the Arctic and Antarctic Oceans. If the ice caps do melt, rising ocean levels will most likely have disastrous effects on both animal and human life. Steps can and must be taken to slow down and perhaps eliminate the factors that cause global warming. Alternative fuels for automobiles and renewable sources of electricity would be a good place to start taking that first step toward solving this terrible problem.

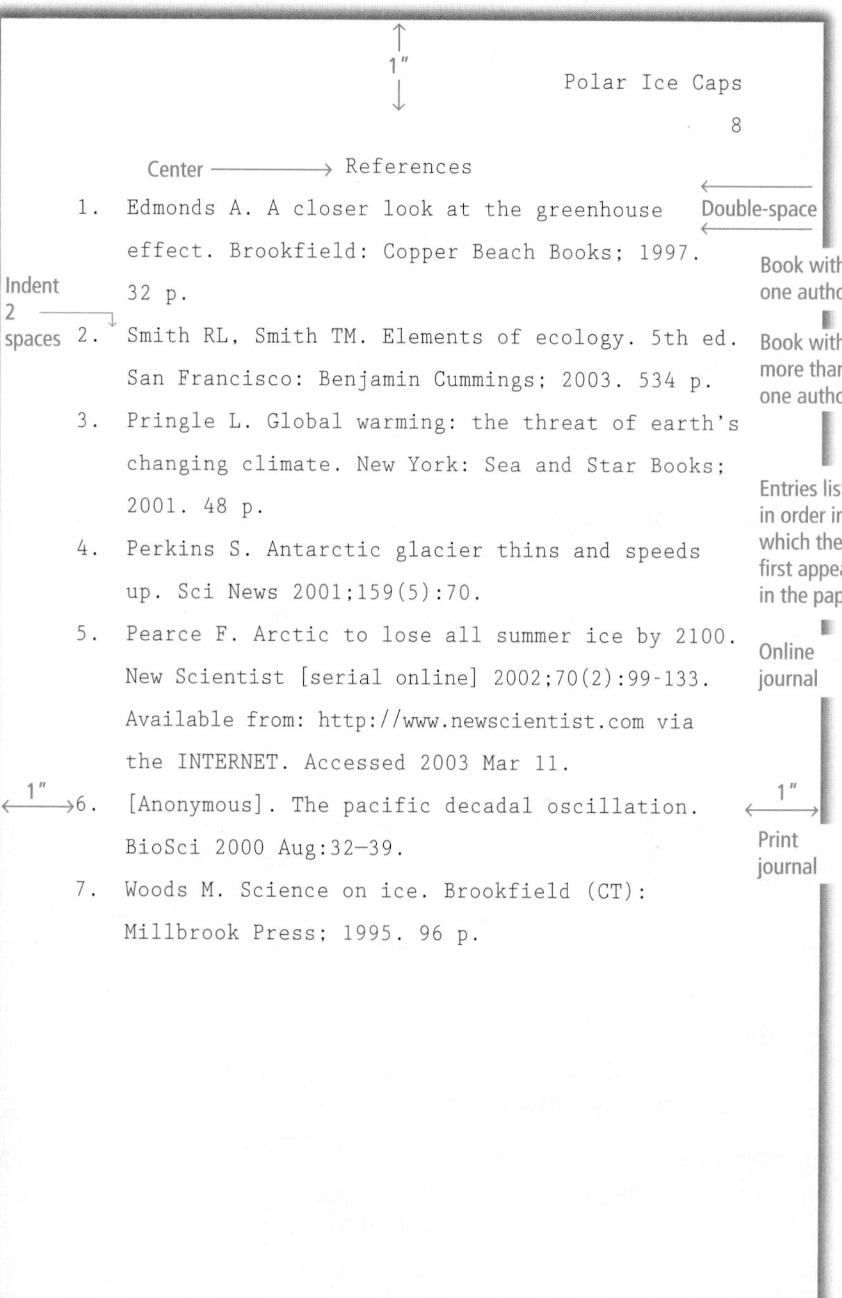

1. Edmonds A. A closer look at the greenhouse effect. Brookfield: Copper Beach Books; 1997. 32 p.
2. Smith RL, Smith TM. Elements of ecology. 5th ed. San Francisco: Benjamin Cummings; 2003. 534 p.
3. Pringle L. Global warming: the threat of earth's changing climate. New York: Sea and Star Books; 2001. 48 p.
4. Perkins S. Antarctic glacier thins and speeds up. Sci News 2001;159(5):70.
5. Pearce F. Arctic to lose all summer ice by 2100. New Scientist [serial online] 2002;70(2):99-133. Available from: http://www.newscientist.com via the INTERNET. Accessed 2003 Mar 11.
6. [Anonymous]. The pacific decadal oscillation. BioSci 2000 Aug:32–39.
7. Woods M. Science on ice. Brookfield (CT): Millbrook Press; 1995. 96 p.

21d Using Other Documentation Styles

The following style manuals describe documentation formats and manuscript guidelines used in various fields.

Chemistry

Dodd, Janet S. American Chemical Society. *The ACS Guide: A Manual for Authors and Editors.* 2nd ed. Washington: Amer. Chemical Soc., 1997.

Geology

United States Geological Survey. *Suggestions to Authors of the Reports of the United States Geological Survey.* 7th ed. Washington: GPO, 1991.

Government Documents

Garner, Diane L. *The Complete Guide to Citing Government Information Resources: A Manual for Writers and Librarians.* Rev. ed. Bethesda: Congressional Information Service, 1993.

United States Government Printing Office. *Style Manual.* Washington: GPO, 2000.

Journalism

Goldstein, Norm, ed. *Associated Press Stylebook and Briefing on Media Law.* 35th ed. New York: Associated P, 2000.

Law

The Bluebook: A Uniform System of Citation. Comp. Editors of *Columbia Law Review* et al. 16th ed. Cambridge: Harvard Law Rev. Assn., 1996.

Mathematics

American Mathematical Society. *AMS Author Handbook.* Providence: Amer. Mathematical Soc., 1998.

Medicine

Iverson, Cheryl. *Manual of Style: A Guide for Authors and Editors.* 9th ed. Chicago: Amer. Medical Assn., 1997.

Music

Holman, D. Kirn, ed. *Writing about Music: A Style Sheet from the Editors of 19th-Century Music.* Berkeley: U California P, 1988.

Physics

American Institute of Physics. *AIP Style Manual.* 5th ed. New York: Am. Inst. of Physics, 1995.

Scientific and Technical Writing

Rubens, Philip, ed. *Science and Technical Writing: A Manual of Style.* 2nd ed. New York: Routledge, 2001.

STUDENT WRITER AT WORK

Using MLA Documentation Style

The following draft of an essay was written for an introductory literature class. The student writer focuses on "Harlem," Langston Hughes's famous poem, and includes several quotations from the primary source, the poem itself. However, she has not yet added quotations and paraphrases from secondary sources.

At the end of the draft, you will find several quotations from secondary sources along with complete citation information for each source. First, incorporate one quotation (or a paraphrase of a quotation) smoothly into each paragraph, adding a few words of introduction to identify the source and to supply the context. Then, add a parenthetical citation for each quotation or paraphrase you incorporate, using MLA format. Finally, expand the works-cited list to include all the sources you used.

¶1 Langston Hughes's poem "Harlem" speaks about the gap between the expectations of African Americans who migrated north and the reality of racism. This gulf, clearly shown in everything from living conditions to educational opportunities, often led to pent-up frustration that could later come back to haunt victims and persecutors alike. The speaker of the poem asks readers to consider the ways in which different people might express or repress such frustration. The imagery the speaker uses helps to convey the impact of lost dreams on the psyche of an oppressed people.

¶2 It is crucial to discuss what dreams Southern black people had before analyzing why and how those dreams were not realized. For a short time, when World War I inspired many African Americans to move north, such dreams seemed attainable, plausible, and within the grasp of anyone who dared to leave the South. For example, the dream of a fair wage seemed tantalizingly close.

The poem's speaker calls attention to the fact that ¶3 these people have been reduced by the dominant society into something less than human. In asking whether the dream now has a "stink like rotten meat" (line 6), the speaker suggests not only that the African-American people are still perceived as animals, as they were during their enslavement, but also that they are figuratively dead: their spirits have been worn down to the point where they no longer are able to hold on to their dreams. The speaker then asks whether the dream will "crust and sugar over— / like a syrupy sweet?" (7-8). These lines conjure up images of the sweet glory and almost candy-high exuberance of fleeing the South and reaching the North. However, as the short-lived feeling of being treated humanely quickly recedes, the dreamer faces the reality that such visions have grown stale. Segregation and lack of opportunity make the dreams rot. These lines also refer to the dashed hopes of older African-American migrants: the heavy crust is like a heavy load, which in time coats over the sweetness of youth and its dreams.

In the end, the speaker concludes that the dream may ¶4 soon be over. Older black migrants have gone north and lived through the nightmare of poor jobs at low pay. However, a young person carrying such a yoke might not sag, might someday throw it off in rage and frustration, and this is the danger that Hughes foreshadows in his poem: that one day all of this repression of African Americans will come back and explode. The poem's last line hints at the coming of change and sends a clear message that it will not be long before black Americans rise up and begin demanding changes, refusing to let go of the dream. In this powerful poem, Hughes is warning readers about the powder keg that is the state of race relations in his America.

Work Cited

Hughes, Langston. "Harlem." In The Collected Poems of Langston Hughes. Ed. Arnold Rampersad. New York: Vintage, 1994.

Source Material for Paragraph 1

"African-American History: The Harlem Renaissance." *Africana.* 7 Sept 2003. 25 Mar 2003 <http://www.africana.com/archive/articles/tt_387.asp>.

"During a phenomenon known as the Great Migration, hundreds of thousands of black Americans moved from an economically depressed rural South to industrial cities of the North to take advantage of the employment opportunities created by World War I."

"The literature would follow in the 1920s by describing the reality of black life in America and the struggle for racial identity."

De Santis, Christopher C., ed. Langston Hughes and the Chicago Defender: Essays on Race, Politics, and Culture, 1942-62. Chicago: U Illinois P, 1995. 8.

"What we are doing is writing and speaking about—and working for—freedom and democracy as a reality—not as a shadow."

Source Material for Paragraph 2

"African-American History: The Harlem Renaissance." *Africana.* 7 Sept 2003. 25 Mar 2003 <http://www.africana.com/archive/articles/tt_387.asp>.

"During the 1910s a new political agenda advocating racial equality arose in the African American community, particularly in its growing middle class."

"For thousands of blacks around the world, the Harlem Renaissance was proof that the white race did not hold a monopoly on literature and culture."

De Santis, Christopher C., ed. Langston Hughes and the Chicago Defender: Essays on Race, Politics, and Culture, 1942-62. Chicago: U Illinois P, 1995. 8.

Should "we not believe in the American dream, too—or is that dream just for white folks?"

Source Material for Paragraph 3

"African-American History: The Harlem Renaissance." *Africana.* 7 Sept 2003. 25 Mar 2003 <http://www.africana.com/archive/articles/tt_387.asp>.

"What united participants was their sense of taking part in a common endeavor and their commitment to giving artistic expression to the African American experience."

Source Material for Paragraph 4

De Santis, Christopher C., ed. Langston Hughes and the Chicago Defender: Essays on Race, Politics, and Culture, 1942-62. Chicago: U Illinois P, 1995. 8.

"The Negro people of America today are not threatening to fight and kill white Americans in order to get their rights."

PART 4

Writing in the Disciplines

Writing in the Disciplines

All instructors, regardless of academic discipline, have certain expectations when they read a paper. They expect to see standard English, correct grammar and spelling, clear thinking, and accurate documentation of sources. In addition, they expect to see logical organization, convincing support, and careful editing. Despite these similarities, however, instructors in various disciplines have different

Humanities

Disciplines	Assignments	Style and Format
Languages Literature Philosophy History Linguistics Religion Art history Music	Response essay Summary essay Annotated bibliography Bibliographic essay Analysis essay	*Style* Specialized vocabulary Direct quotations *Format* Little use of internal headings or visuals

Social Sciences

Disciplines	Assignments	Style and Format
Anthropology Psychology Economics Business Education Sociology Political science Social work Criminal justice	Personal experience essay Book review Case study Annotated bibliography Review of research essay Proposal	*Style* Specialized vocabulary, including statistical terminology *Format* Internal headings Visuals (graphs, maps, flowcharts, photographs) Numerical data (in tabular form)

Natural and Applied Sciences

Disciplines	Assignments	Style and Format
Natural Sciences Biology Chemistry Physics Astronomy Geology Mathematics *Applied Sciences* Engineering Computer science Nursing Pharmacy	Laboratory report Observation/essay Literature survey Abstract Biographical essay	*Style* Frequent use of passive voice Few direct quotations *Format* Internal headings Tables, graphs, and illustrations (exact formats vary)

expectations about a paper—for example, they expect different documentation styles and different specialized vocabularies. To a large extent, then, learning to write in a particular discipline involves learning the conventions that scholars in that field have agreed to follow. Part 4 discusses the conventions specific to humanities, social science, and natural and applied science disciplines.

Documentation	Research Methods and Sources
English, languages, philosophy: MLA History, art history: Chicago	Library sources (print and electronic) Interviews Observations (museums, concerts) Oral history Internet

Documentation	Research Methods and Sources
APA	Library sources (print and electronic) Surveys Observations (behavior of groups and individuals) Internet

Documentation	Research Methods and Sources
Biology: CSE Other scientific disciplines use a variety of different documentation styles; **see 21d**	Library sources (print and electronic) Observations Experiments Surveys Internet

Chapter 22

Writing in the Humanities

Frequently Asked Questions

The **humanities** include art, drama, film, history, languages, literature, music, philosophy, and religion. In these disciplines, research often involves analyzing or interpreting a primary source—a literary work, a historical document, a musical composition, or a painting or piece of sculpture—or making connections between one work and another. Scholars in humanities disciplines may also cite secondary sources—commentaries on primary sources—to support their points or develop new interpretations.

See 11f2, 12b4

22a Understanding Purpose, Audience, and Tone

Writing assignments in the humanities—in subjects such as literature, philosophy, ethnic studies, and art history—may be formal or informal. While formal writing may require you to use academic discourse and MLA documentation style and format, informal writing assignments may require no more than your personal responses to your reading and observations. Each of these two types of writing has a distinct purpose and tone.

See Ch. 18

Informal writing assignments may have a variety of names: journals, responses, or daily logs, for example. The purpose of this type of writing is generally to encourage reflection. For this reason, it is acceptable for you to use a relatively conversational, even colloquial, style and to use the first person (*I*). Often, your instructor will specify an audience: your classmates, the instructor, or someone else. Sometimes, you may be asked to share these personal writings via the World Wide Web, perhaps by posting weekly responses to a class Web page or class discussion list. At other times, you may keep these writings entirely personal—for example, in a journal that reflects on your learning throughout a semester.

More **formal** writing assignments—bibliographic essays, literary analyses, research papers, and so on—often require that you summarize, analyze, or evaluate print and electronic sources and synthesize information from a variety of sources. Because the purpose of a formal writing assignment is often to persuade an audience to accept a particular point of view or position, such assignments require a more objective tone and a higher level of diction than informal assignments do.

22b Writing Assignments

(1) Response Essay

In some humanities disciplines (particularly literature, music, and art), you may be asked to write a **response essay,** an informal reaction to a literary work, a painting, a dance performance, or a concert. This kind of assignment requires you to write a first-person account of your feelings and to explore the factors that influenced your reactions.

ESL Tip

Depending on your cultural background, you may not have much experience with personal writing in a school setting. However, when you write a response essay, your instructor expects you to write about *your own reactions* rather than writing a general description of the subject of your essay.

Assignment (World Music)

In preparation for writing an informal response to a musical production on campus, attend one of the performances offered by the Music and Drama Department during the upcoming month. Take notes as you watch and listen to the performance. Then, write an informal essay that communicates your response to the performance. What was memorable or remarkable? How did the audience react at particular moments? How did you feel as you were watching and listening, and then how did you feel when the performance was over?

Sample Response Essay (Excerpt)

Chu's cello recital last Sunday night was the first time I've ever been to a classical music recital. I didn't want to go; in fact, so I wouldn't have to go alone, I convinced my roommate to come to the concert with me by first taking her out for pizza. Despite my reservations, I really enjoyed the concert. The music was more varied than I expected, and a lot of the tunes have been running through my head ever since. Believe it or not, I might even go out and buy the CD!

When I first arrived, I saw that the people in the audience were pretty much who I expected to see at a classical music recital, including quite a few faculty I recognized. (I'm sure they were shocked to see me there.) The audience was quiet as they waited for Chu's entrance; everyone just kind of sat looking at the darkened stage, which contained a very large grand piano and a cello. When Chu came on stage, the applause was almost deafening. I hadn't realized he was so famous. The audience quieted down in expectation when he sat down and picked up his bow. The first item on the program was a solo titled <u>Allegretto Minimoso</u>. I have to admit, once he started to play, I didn't even notice what was going on in the audience anymore. His music made me think of tall cliffs towering over the ocean under a bright sky during a storm. I was hooked from the first moment.

(2) Summary Essay

See Ch. 27

Instructors in the humanities may ask you to write summaries to show that you have read and understood assigned material. Summary is often used in essay exams.

Assignment (European Philosophers)

To demonstrate your understanding of the readings in this course, write a summary of Louis Althusser's chapter on Ideological State Apparatus, which discusses one of the most important concepts of European Marxism. Your summary, which should be two to three pages long, should reflect the main ideas of the chapter and include the most important examples Althusser provides. Be sure to include the chapter's title and author in your first paragraph along with a sentence that states the main point of the article.

You are not required to include a works-cited list with this essay; however, be sure to provide correct in-text citations, following MLA guidelines, for any quotations or paraphrases you use.

Sample Summary Essay (Excerpt)

In "Ideology and Ideological State Apparatuses," Louis Althusser develops a general theory that defines ideology in a broad sense while explaining its role in promulgating the class system. He sees ideology as existing outside of history, as having an unchanging structure (128) and as therefore predictable in its effect. Althusser claims that ideology, whether it is political, religious, ethical, or economic, forms "imaginary" boxes, or varying "world outlooks" (130), which frame individuals' efforts to honestly assess their own living conditions. Ideology reels us in by asserting that we are free-thinking individuals, stringing us along while simultaneously stripping us of autonomy.

Althusser sees ideology as an ongoing cultural set of practices involving all classes who use it to define their relationship to their living conditions. Ideology creates subjects by hailing them, or "interpellating" (161) them, in every communicative act. It names, acknowledges, and therefore empowers the subject as a person of free will; it also creates in that subject an agent who willingly cedes autonomy, submitting freely to commandments from the Subject (capital S) of the ideology. The subject willingly follows the practices and rituals associated with the Subject while reflecting and reinforcing the ideology in private social and economic relations.

(3) Annotated Bibliography and Bibliographic Essay

See 12c

If you are writing a research paper that includes many sources, your instructor may ask you to prepare an **annotated bibliography**—a list of sources (accompanied by full source information) followed by summary and evaluation—and a bibliographic essay that discusses the sources and their relevance to your research.

Assignment (Nineteenth-Century American Literature)

Your reading and research work for this course will culminate in a bibliographic essay that explores an issue presented in one of the primary texts we have read. For example, you may wish to explore nineteenth-century notions of colonialism or a poet's responses to the Civil War. Select one of the assigned primary readings (one novel, one collection of poetry, or one collection of short stories or essays by a single writer) for this project.

You will be required to prepare an annotated bibliography (due Week 6) of secondary sources (critical scholarly sources, such as literary journals and monographs). Each annotation should include a complete MLA-style citation of the source, a short paragraph summarizing the main points of the source, and a short paragraph evaluating the usefulness of the source to your own research.

You will then be required to compose a bibliographic essay (due Week 10) that discusses the sources you have selected. Do not simply describe or summarize your sources; synthesize, compare, and contrast the sources, developing your own argument throughout your essay. Be sure to include paraphrases and quotations from your sources, and include a works-cited list.

Sample Annotated Bibliography (Excerpt)

Lutes, Jean Marie. "Cultivating Domesticity: Labor Reform and the Literary Culture of the Lowell Mill Girls." Works and Days 22.11 (1993): 7-27. In this article, Lutes shows how the young women working in the Lowell Mills in the 1840s used their limited leisure time to educate themselves. They formed reading groups, arranged and attended lectures on historical and anthropological topics, took an active interest in religion, and also participated in political movements such as the abolition of slavery. Lutes explains that the women did this not just for intellectual stimulation, but also to make themselves into better future wives and mothers. Lutes also shows the irony of the fact that women campaigned against slavery while remaining in jobs that were dependent on the production of cotton by slaves, and she makes clear the irony of their gaining independence through their jobs while still hoping to enter traditional marriages.

This article really helped me to think about the ironies contained in the Lowell women's writings: they thought they were improving things for themselves, their families, and their communities, but really nothing was changing.

Sample Bibliographic Essay

The women mill operatives of Lowell, Massachusetts, produced a variety of writings in different genres that portray the ways in which they negotiated their everyday urban experiences in their boardinghouses and on the factory production line. While their descriptions of daily life in the mill town can be read as a story of their journey to financial independence, these writings also reveal the women's collective coming of political age. The Lowell Offering, first published in 1840, was a "monthly magazine, thirty pages long, priced at six and one-quarter cents an issue" (Eisler 33) that began as a corporately owned concern but later was bought, run, and edited by two women who were both former mill operatives. While the publishers of the Offering focused on presenting the working women's own creations, <u>The Factory Girl's Garland</u>, also begun in 1840 (only to fold less than one year later), was more of a "liberal reformist paper [that] spoke paternalistically in favor of the mill women, and at times even preached at them" (Vogel 791). Jean Marie Lutes explains that some labor reformists among the operatives found the "sentimental tales, romantic stories, and poetic rhyme" of the <u>Offering</u> too "neutral," accusing it of having "neglected the operative as a working being" (8). Therefore, they chose to represent their concerns through the <u>Voice of Industry</u>, a newspaper whose "case for reform," Lutes argues, was only made possible through the preliminary cultural work performed by the less critical <u>Offering</u>: while the <u>Voice</u> explicitly called for recognition of working class women's rights, it was the <u>Offering</u> that "initiate[d] the discourse of female working-class culture" (9). These periodicals demonstrate various ways in which the operatives were initiating change for white working-class women through both their physical and their literary labors.

However, as they attempted—through their writings—to establish their claims to independence, they had to work against the dominant ideology of dependent femininity that was manifested not only in most men's writing but also in the majority of writings by the few published women of the day.

The women's overseers at work were male, while their boardinghouse landladies reported to the male owners of the mills: "in these ways, the manufacturers thought to transfer the patriarchal structure of the women's country backgrounds into the factory setting. They hoped that the women would be cooperative and uncomplaining workers—just as, it seemed, they were obedient daughters" (Vogel 789).

So, while they may have found a brand of independence that was perhaps not experienced by working-class women before then, it was decidedly not independence from patriarchal supervision. In their writing, too, they were constrained by patriarchy: the popular Offering was instigated and owned by men, and although the Voice was owned and operated by female mill employees, it, too, fed "the nation's fascination with the 'culture' of the Lowell mill girls [that] satisfied the corporate need to control public perception of female workers" (Lutes 9). Each of these publications succeeded in making heard a brand of feminism, but in the end, that "feminism" was little more than a reproduction of the dominant white, republican patriarchy.

Works Cited

Eisler, Benita. The Lowell Offering: Writings by New England Mill Women (1840-1845). New York: Norton, 1998.

Lutes, Jean Marie. "Cultivating Domesticity: Labor Reform and the Literary Culture of the Lowell Mill Girls." Works and Days 22.11 (1993): 7-27.

Vogel, Lise. "Their Own Work: Two Documents from the Nineteenth-Century Labor Movement." Signs: Journal of Women in Culture and Society 1.3 (1976): 787-802.

(4) Analysis Essay

Analysis essays are common in various humanities disciplines. (For examples of literary analyses, **see Chapter 23;** for an example of an art history analysis, **see 18c**.)

Assignment (Advanced Composition)

Research a current ad campaign for a specific product, service, or cause. Select a poster, billboard, or other visual from the campaign, and write a persuasive ad analysis. In your essay, examine the ad's purpose, target audience, and overall message. Describe how the ad's various elements (words and images) work together to reach the intended audience, and explain who benefits from the ad's message, and how.

Sample Analysis Essay (Excerpt)

The Teen Action Board, a nonprofit group of Massachusetts high school students, recently launched a multimedia campaign aimed at helping to prevent teen dating abuse. The "See It and Stop It!" campaign has produced a number of posters as well as radio and television ads to alert teens to the prevalence and danger of dating abuse in America. One poster entitled "He Calls Her" (see fig. 1) shows a young woman named Angela, whose boyfriend smothers her with repeated phone calls. This ad illustrates the techniques the campaign uses to call attention to the subtler forms of dating abuse that many teens, particularly females, encounter.

The "He Calls Her" poster uses words and images to convey the campaign's overall message: that the effects of dating abuse are clear, even when the signs of abuse are not. The central image of a despondent Angela holding her cell phone, framed on one side with more snapshots of Angela and her phone, shows the reality of a suffocating relationship. The repetition of the phrase "He calls her" reinforces the constancy of the abuse. In addition, the "cut-and-paste" design of the ad—including the hastily taped edges of the creased photos, the prominent text seemingly made from a label-maker, and the smaller, ransom-note-style slogan and logo—conveys the harsh reality and pressing urgency of teen dating abuse.

The ad establishes a contrast between a healthy relationship ("He calls her") and an unhealthy one ("He calls her 50 times a day") and implores its teen audience

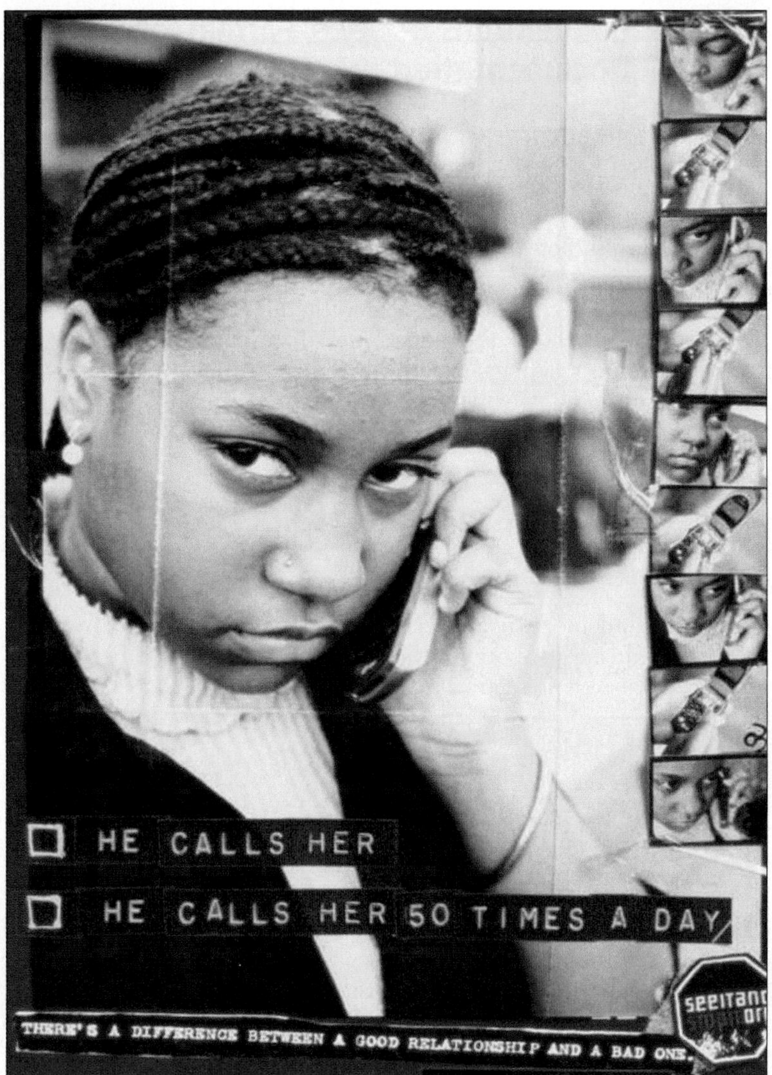

Fig. 1. "See It and Stop It!" campaign poster, The Advertising Council, 2003, 26 Feb. 2004 <http://www.adcouncil.org/pdf/teenaction_print_hecallsher.pdf>.

to take a stand against abuse. The concluding plea to "speak up against abuse" urges the audience to recognize abuse and to do something about it.

22c Conventions of Style, Format, and Documentation

(1) Style and Format

Each humanities discipline has its own specialized vocabulary. You should use the terms used in the field, but be careful not to overuse technical terminology. You can use the first person (*I*) when you are expressing your own reactions and convictions—for example, in a response essay. In other situations, avoid the first person.

Although papers in the humanities do not usually include abstracts, internal headings, tables, or graphs, this situation is changing. Be sure you know what your instructor expects.

NOTE: When you write papers about literature, follow the special conventions that apply to literary analysis.

(2) Documentation

Literature and modern and classical language scholars, as well as scholars in music and sometimes art history, use MLA documentation style; history scholars use Chicago style.

22d Avoiding Plagiarism

Humanities sources are usually books and journal articles, so plagiarism is often the result of inaccurate summary and paraphrase, failure to use quotation marks where they are required, and confusion between your ideas and those of your sources.

Whenever you use sources, you must be careful to document them. In this way, you acknowledge the work of others who influenced your ideas or contributed to your conclusions. Take accurate notes, avoid cutting and pasting chunks of information into your paper, and whenever you quote, summarize, or paraphrase, do so honestly. Document ideas as well as words, no matter where they come from. "Borrowing" without acknowledgment is plagiarism, and the penalties for plagiarism can be severe. (You do not have to document **common knowledge.** If you have any questions about what constitutes common knowledge in your humanities discipline, be sure to check with your instructor.)

22e Using Visuals and Technology

The humanities include a range of disciplines that rely on visual and multimedia texts as well as printed ones. As a result, you are likely to have a great deal of flexibility and creativity in determining what visual media to include in your papers and research projects as well as in choosing a format in which to produce your work. For example, while a response essay for a literature course may focus on a written work, a response essay for an art history, music appreciation, or theater course will likely focus on a visual image in your textbook or on the Web (or in a gallery or museum); on an audio recording on CD or in concert; or even on a theatrical performance or a film or television dramatization. Following the guidelines of copyright and fair use, you may be able to include an image or brief audio excerpt—or even a digital video clip of a live or televised performance—in your project. Similarly, if a review essay you write focuses on film, television, or theater, it may be possible for you to include media clips—or, in some cases, hyperlinks to files and Internet resources that provide a more detailed picture of the event you are reviewing.

22f Research Sources

Each discipline within the humanities has its own methodology, so it is important to know not only the sources or tools that are used by scholars in that field, but also the way students and scholars conduct research. In literature, for example, scholars may analyze, explain, or interpret the text of a poem, short story, or novel, or the work of a particular author. They study the text itself, but often they also look in books and journal articles for evidence that will support their conclusions. They use the tools of their discipline: library resources (online catalogs, specialized databases, periodical indexes, bibliographies, and so on) and Internet resources to locate that evidence. In other humanities disciplines—such as history—specialized databases, periodical indexes, reference works, and Web sites also exist. But primary sources, such as narratives, letters, diaries, or other original documents, also provide important evidence in historical research.

In some cases, you may be asked to provide your own analysis, interpretation, or criticism of an original text, work of art, or musical composition, without regard to what has already been written about it. More often, however, you will be asked to use secondary sources

to reinforce your conclusions, especially where you are an undergraduate student.

Doing library research in the humanities does not usually require that you know what the latest thinking is about a particular work, author, artwork, musical composition, idea, or theory. Older books and journal articles may be as valuable as recent ones. When you begin your research, you can consult the *Humanities Index*, a general resource that lists articles from more than two hundred scholarly journals in such areas as history, language, literary criticism, philosophy, and religion. It is available in print—with entries arranged alphabetically in yearly volumes according to author and subject—and in electronic form.

Many specialized sources are also available for each humanities discipline. They include databases that cover the literature of that discipline and other sources that provide background information about people, creative works, literary or artistic movements, or historical time periods. Some of these specialized sources will be found in your library's reference collection; others may be available online.

Close-up: Finding Additional Sources

Reading the lists of works cited at the ends of books, chapters, or journal articles may help you to identify other relevant sources. Reference works also frequently include lists of sources for further reading. Annotated bibliographies can help you distinguish the useful from the irrelevant sources.

(1) Reference Books

Library research is an important part of study in many humanities disciplines. When you begin your research in any subject area, the *Humanities Index* is one general source you can use. Another excellent index available in print and as a computer-searchable database is the *Arts and Humanities Citation Index*. Following is a list of reference books for specific humanities disciplines:

Art

Art Abstracts/Art Index
Artwords: A Glossary of Contemporary Art Theory
Bibliography of the History of Art
Contemporary Artists
Dictionary of Art
Dictionary of Women Artists

Encyclopedia of Aesthetics
Encyclopedia of Comparative Iconography: Themes Depicted in Works of Art
Encyclopedia of World Art
Index to Art Reproductions in Books
New Dictionary of Modern Sculpture
Oxford Companion to Western Art
Praeger Encyclopedia of Art
Thames and Hudson Dictionary of Art and Artists
Who Was Who in American Art

Drama

Cambridge Guide to Theatre
Contemporary Theatre, Film, and Television
Continuum Companion to Twentieth Century Theatre
Crown Guide to the World's Great Plays from Ancient Greece to Rome
Dictionary of the Performing Arts
Guide to Critical Reviews
International Dictionary of Theatre
McGraw-Hill Encyclopedia of World Drama
Modern World Drama: An Encyclopedia
New York Times Theatre Reviews
Oxford Encyclopedia of Theatre and Performance
The Performing Arts: A Guide to the Reference Literature
Play Index
World Encyclopedia of Contemporary Theatre

Film

Film Comment
The Film Encyclopedia
Film Review Annual
Guide to Critical Reviews
International Dictionary of Film and Filmmakers
International Index to Film Periodicals
International Index to Multimedia Information
Magill's Survey of Cinema
The Motion Picture Guide
The Movie List Book: A Reference Guide to Film Themes, Settings, and Series
New Biographical Dictionary of Film
New York Times Film Reviews
Oxford History of World Cinema
Variety Film Reviews

History

America: History and Life
Cambridge Ancient History
Cambridge Medieval History
Companion to British History
CRIS (Combined Retrospective Index to Journals in History)
Dictionary of American Biography (DAB)

Dictionary of American History
Dictionary of the Middle Ages
Dictionary of National Biography (DNB)
Encyclopedia of Africa South of the Sahara
Encyclopedia of Latin American History and Culture
Encyclopedia of the Renaissance
Encyclopedia of Urban America: The Cities and Suburbs
Encyclopedia of the Vietnam War
Growing Up in America
Guide to Historical Literature (AHA)
Handbook to Life in Ancient Greece
Harvard Guide to American History
Historical Abstracts
History of the Internet: A Chronology
Medieval England: An Encyclopedia
New Cambridge Modern History
Reader's Guide to Military History
Women in World History

Language and Literature

Annual Bibliography of English Language and Literature (ABELL)
Biography Index
Book Review Digest
Book Review Index
British Writers
Cassell's Encyclopedia of World Literature
Children's Literature Review
Contemporary Authors
Current Biography
Dictionary of Languages
Dictionary of Literary Biography
Dictionary of Modern American Usage
Encyclopedia of the Essay
Encyclopedia of Folklore and Literature
Encyclopedia of Latin American Literature
Encyclopedia of the Novel
Essay and General Literature Index
European Writers
Language and Language Behavior Abstracts (LLBA)
Literary History of the United States (LHUS)
Literature Online
Literature Resource Center
MLA International Bibliography
Native American Literatures
New Princeton Encyclopedia of Poetry and Poetics
Oxford Companion to American Literature
Oxford Companion to Classical Literature
Oxford Companion to English Literature
Oxford English Dictionary

Reference Guide to Short Fiction
Salem Press Critical Surveys of Poetry, Fiction, Long Fiction, and Drama
Twentieth Century Authors
World Literature Criticism
World of Poets

Music

Baker's Biographical Dictionary of 20th Century Classical Musicians
Encyclopedia of Popular Music
Garland Encyclopedia of World Music
International Dictionary of Black Composers
International Index to Music Periodicals
Music Article Guide
Music Index
Music Reference and Research Materials
New Grove Dictionary of Jazz
New Grove Dictionary of Music and Musicians
New Harvard Dictionary of Music
New Oxford Companion to Music
Popular Musicians
RILM Abstracts of Music Literature
Rolling Stone Encyclopedia of Rock and Roll

Philosophy

Cambridge Dictionary of Philosophy
Concise Encyclopedia of Western Philosophy and Philosophers
Dictionary of the History of Ideas
Encyclopedia of Asian Philosophy
Encyclopedia of the Enlightenment
Encyclopedia of Philosophy
Masterpieces of World Philosophy in Summary Form
Modern Philosophy: An Introduction and Survey
Oxford Companion to Philosophy
Philosopher's Index
Routledge Encyclopedia of Philosophy

Religion

Cambridge Companion to the Bible
Encyclopedia of Christianity
Encyclopedia of Ethics
Encyclopedia Judaica
Encyclopedia of Religion
Encyclopedia of Women and World Religion
HarperCollins Dictionary of Religion
Hutchinson Encyclopedia of Living Faiths
New Catholic Encyclopedia
New Encyclopedia of Islam
New Encyclopedia of Judaism
Oxford Dictionary of the Christian Church

Oxford Dictionary of Religion
Oxford History of Islam
Religion Index

(2) Databases for Computer Searches

Some of the most helpful databases for humanities disciplines include *Arts and Humanities Citation Index; Art Abstracts/Art Index; MLA International Bibliography; Religion Index; Philosopher's Index, Essay and General Literature Index; Art Bibliographies Modern; America: History and Life; Historical Abstracts; Language and Language Behavior Abstracts (LLBA); and RILM Abstracts of Music Literature.* Ask a reference librarian about the availability of these and other databases in your library.

(3) Web Sites

For links to Web sites for specific humanities disciplines, go to http://kirsznermandell.wadsworth.com ▶ *The Wadsworth Handbook* ▶ Chapter 22 ▶ Humanities Web Sites.

(4) Other Sources of Information

Research in the humanities is not limited to print and electronic resources. For example, historians may do interviews and archival work or consult records collected in town halls, churches, or courthouses; art historians visit museums and galleries; and music scholars attend concerts.

See 12d

In addition, nonprint sources, such as interviews and surveys, can be important resources for a paper in any humanities discipline.

Chapter 23

Writing about Literature

Frequently Asked Questions

How do I find the real meaning of a literary work? (p. 515)
Do I put a title in quotation marks, or do I underline it? (p. 517)

23a Reading Literature

When you read a literary work about which you plan to write, use the same critical thinking skills and active reading strategies you apply to other works you read: preview the work, and highlight it to identify key ideas and cues to meaning; then, annotate it carefully.

As you read and take notes, focus on the special concerns of literary analysis, considering elements like a short story's plot, a poem's rhyme or meter, or a play's characters. Look for *patterns,* related groups of words, images, or ideas that run through a work. Look for *anomalies,* unusual forms, unique uses of language, unexpected actions by characters, or unusual treatments of topics. Finally, look for *connections,* links with other literary works, with historical events, or with biographical information.

Close-up: Reading Literature

When you read a work of literature, keep in mind that you do not read to magically discover the one correct meaning the writer has hidden between the lines. The "meaning" of a literary work is created by the interaction between a text and its readers. Do not assume, however, that a work can mean whatever you want it to mean; ultimately, your interpretation must be consistent with the stylistic signals, thematic suggestions, and patterns of imagery in the text.

23b Writing about Literature

When you have finished your reading and annotating, brainstorm to discover a topic to write about; then, organize your material. As you arrange related material into categories, you will begin to see a structure for your paper. At this point, you are ready to start drafting your essay.

When you write about literature, your goal is to make a point and support it with appropriate references to the work under discussion or to related works or secondary sources. As you write, you observe the conventions of literary criticism, which has its own specialized vocabulary and formats. You also respond to discipline-specific assignments. For instance, you may be asked to **analyze** a work, to take it apart and consider one or more of its elements—perhaps the plot or characters in a story or the use of language in a poem. Or, you may be asked to **interpret** a work, to try to explore its possible meanings. Less often, you may be called on to **evaluate** a work, to judge its strengths and weaknesses.

More specifically, you may be asked to trace the critical or popular reception to a work; to compare two works by a single writer (or by two different writers); or to consider the relationship between a work of literature and a literary movement or historical period. You may also be asked to analyze a character's motives or the relationship between two characters, or to comment on a story's setting or tone. In any case, understanding exactly what you are expected to do will make your writing task easier.

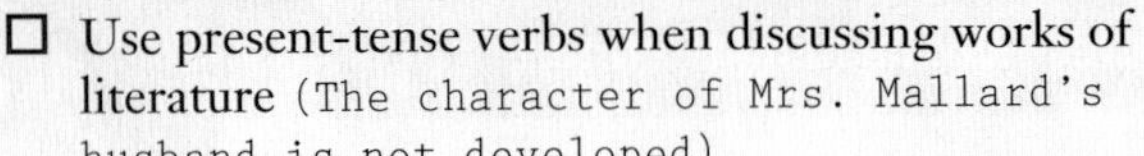

Checklist: Writing about Literature

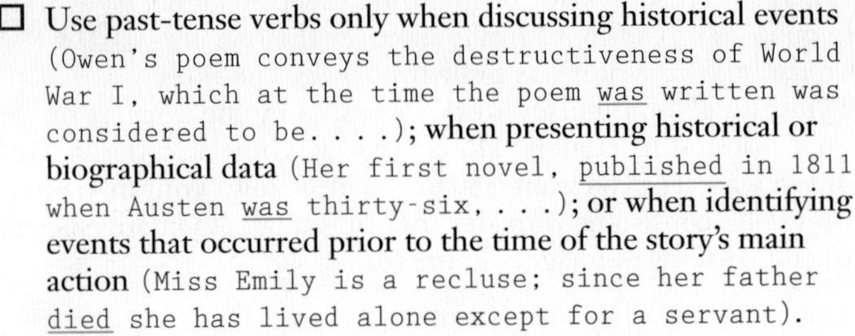

- ☐ Use present-tense verbs when discussing works of literature (`The character of Mrs. Mallard's husband is not developed`).
- ☐ Use past-tense verbs only when discussing historical events (`Owen's poem conveys the destructiveness of World War I, which at the time the poem was written was considered to be. . . .`); when presenting historical or biographical data (`Her first novel, published in 1811 when Austen was thirty-six, . . .`); or when identifying events that occurred prior to the time of the story's main action (`Miss Emily is a recluse; since her father died she has lived alone except for a servant`).

- ☐ Support all points with specific, concrete examples from the work you are discussing, briefly summarizing key events, quoting dialogue or description, describing characters or setting, or paraphrasing ideas.
- ☐ Combine paraphrase, summary, and quotation with your own interpretations, weaving quotations smoothly into your paper **(see Ch. 15)**.
- ☐ Be careful to acknowledge all sources, including the literary work or works under discussion. Introduce the words or ideas of others with a reference to the source, and follow borrowed material with appropriate parenthetical documentation. Be sure you have quoted accurately and enclosed the words of others in quotation marks.
- ☐ Use parenthetical documentation **(see 18a1)**, and include a works-cited list **(see 18a2)** in accordance with MLA documentation style.
- ☐ When citing a part of a short story or novel, supply the page number (`168`). For a poem, give the line numbers (`2-4`). For a classic verse play, include act, scene, and line numbers (`1.4.29-31`). For other plays, supply act and/or scene numbers. (When quoting more than four lines of prose or more than three lines of poetry, be sure to follow the guidelines outlined in 54b.)
- ☐ Avoid subjective expressions like *I feel, I believe, it seems to me,* and *in my opinion.* These weaken your paper by suggesting that its ideas are "only" your opinion and have no validity in themselves.
- ☐ Avoid unnecessary plot summary. Your goal is to draw a conclusion about one or more works and to support that conclusion with pertinent details. If a plot development supports a point you wish to make, a *brief* summary is acceptable, but plot summary is no substitute for analysis.
- ☐ Use literary terms accurately. For example, be careful not to confuse *narrator* or *speaker* with *writer* (feelings or opinions expressed by a narrator or character do not necessarily represent those of the writer). You should not say, "In the poem's last stanza, *Frost* expresses his indecision," when you mean the poem's *speaker* is indecisive.

  For a glossary of literary terms, go to http://kirsznermandell.wadsworth.com ▶ *The Wadsworth Handbook* ▶ Chapter 23 ▶ Literary Terms, or *The Wadsworth Handbook* Animated CD-ROM ▶ Resources ▶ Chapter 23 ▶ Literary Terms.
- ☐ Underline titles of books and plays **(see 57a)**; enclose titles of short stories and poems within quotation marks **(see 54c)**. Book-length poems are treated as long works, and titles should be underlined.

23c Writing about Fiction

When you write a **literary analysis** of a work of fiction, you follow the same process you use when you write any paper about literature. However, you concentrate on elements—such as plot, character, setting, and point of view—central to works of fiction.

Checklist: Writing about Fiction

- ☐ **Plot** What happens in the story? What conflicts can you identify? Are they resolved? In what order are the events arranged? Why are they arranged in this way?
- ☐ **Character** Who is the protagonist? The antagonist? What role do minor characters play? What are each character's most striking traits? Does the protagonist grow and change during the story? Are the characters portrayed sympathetically? How do characters interact with one another? What motivates the characters?
- ☐ **Setting** Where and when is the story set? How does the setting influence the plot? How does it affect the characters?
- ☐ **Point of View** Is the story told by an anonymous third-person narrator or by a character who uses first-person (*I* or *we*) point of view? Is the first-person narrator trustworthy? Is the narrator a participant in the action or just a witness to the story's events? How would a different point of view change the story?
- ☐ **Style, Tone, and Language** Is the style simple or complex? Is the tone intimate or distant? What kind of imagery is used? Is the level of diction formal or informal?
- ☐ **Theme** What central theme or themes does the story explore?

Carla Watts, a student in an introductory literature course, was asked to select a short story from the literature anthology her class was using and to write an essay about it, basing her analysis solely on her own reactions to the story, not on literary criticism. The following story, written in 1983 by Gary Gildner, is the one she decided to write about. (Carla's essay appears on pages 525–29.)

Sleepy Time Gal

In the small town in northern Michigan where my father lived as a young man, he had an Italian friend who worked in a restaurant. I will call his friend Phil. Phil's job in the restaurant was as ordinary as you can imagine—from making coffee in the morning to sweeping up at night. But what was not ordinary about Phil was his piano playing. On Saturday nights my father and Phil and their girlfriends would drive ten or fifteen miles to a roadhouse by a lake where they would drink beer from schooners and dance and Phil would play an old beat-up piano. He could play any song you named, my father said, but the song everyone waited for was the one he wrote, which he would always play at the end before they left to go back to the town. And everyone knew of course that he had written the song for his girl, who was as pretty as she was rich. Her father was the banker in their town, and he was a tough old German, and he didn't like Phil going around with his daughter.

My father, when he told the story, which was not often, would tell it in an offhand way and emphasize the Depression and not having much, instead of the important parts. I will try to tell it the way he did, if I can.

So they would go to the roadhouse by the lake, and finally Phil would play his song, and everyone would say, Phil, that's a great song, you could make a lot of money from it. But Phil would only shake his head and smile and look at his girl. I have to break in here and say that my father, a gentle but practical man, was not inclined to emphasize the part about Phil looking at his girl. It was my mother who said the girl would rest her head on Phil's shoulder while he played, and that he got the idea for the song from the pretty way she looked when she got sleepy. My mother was not part of the story, but she had heard it when she and my father were younger and therefore had that information. I would like to intrude further and add something about Phil writing the song, maybe show him whistling the tune and going over the words slowly and carefully to get the best ones, while peeling onions or potatoes in the restaurant; but my father is already driving them home from the roadhouse, and saying how patched up his tires were, and how his car's engine was a gingerbread of parts from different makes, and some parts were his own invention as well. And my mother is saying that the old German had made his daughter promise not to get involved with any man until after college, and they couldn't be late. Also my mother likes the sad parts and is eager to get to their last night before the girl goes away to college.

So they all went out to the roadhouse, and it was sad. The women got tears in their eyes when Phil played her song, my mother said. My father said that Phil spent his week's pay on a new shirt and tie, the first tie he

continued

continued from the previous page

ever owned, and people kidded him. Somebody piped up and said, Phil, you ought to take that song down to Bay City—which was like saying New York City to them, only more realistic—and sell it and take the money and go to college too. Which was not meant to be cruel, but that was the result because Phil had never even got to high school. But you can see people were trying to cheer him up, my mother said.

Well, she'd come home for Thanksgiving and Christmas and Easter and they'd all sneak out to the roadhouse and drink beer from schooners and dance and everything would be like always. And of course there were the summers. And everyone knew Phil and the girl would get married after she made good her promise to her father because you could see it in their eyes when he sat at the old beat-up piano and played her song.

That last part about their eyes was not, of course, in my father's telling, but I couldn't help putting it in there even though I know it is making some of you impatient. Remember that this happened many years ago in the woods by a lake in northern Michigan, before television. I wish I could put more in, especially about the song and how it felt to Phil to sing it and how the girl felt when hearing it and knowing it was hers, but I've already intruded too much in a simple story that isn't even mine.

Well, here's the kicker part. Probably by now many of you have guessed that one vacation near the end she doesn't come home to see Phil, because she meets some guy at college who is good-looking and as rich as she is and, because her father knew about Phil all along and was pressuring her into forgetting about him, she gives in to this new guy and goes to his hometown during the vacation and falls in love with him. That's how the people in town figured it, because after she graduates they turn up, already married, and right away he takes over the old German's bank—and buys a new Pontiac at the place where my father is the mechanic and pays cash for it. The paying cash always made my father pause and shake his head and mention again that times were tough, but here comes this guy in a spiffy white shirt (with French cuffs, my mother said) and pays the full price in cash.

And this made my father shake his head too: Phil took the song down to Bay City and sold it for twenty-five dollars, the only money he ever got for it. It was the same song we'd just heard on the radio and which reminded my father of the story I just told you. What happened to Phil? Well, he stayed in Bay City and got a job managing a movie theater. My father saw him there after the Depression when he was on his way to Detroit to work for Ford. He stopped and Phil gave him a box of popcorn. The song he wrote for the girl has sold many millions of records, and if I told you the name of it you could probably sing it, or at least whistle the tune. I wonder what the girl thinks when she hears it. Oh yes, my father met Phil's wife too. She worked in the movie theater with him, selling tickets and cleaning the carpet after the show with one of those sweepers you push. She was also big and loud and nothing like the other one, my mother said.

Carla began by reading the story through quickly. Then, she reread it more carefully, highlighting and annotating as she read.

Highlighting and Annotating

When do events take place?

In the small town in northern Michigan where my father lived as a young man, he had an Italian friend who worked in a restaurant. I will call his friend Phil. Phil's job in the restaurant was as ordinary as you can imagine—from making coffee in the morning to sweeping up at night. But what was not ordinary about Phil was his piano playing. On Saturday nights my father and Phil and the girlfriends would drive ten or fifteen miles to a roadhouse by a lake where they would drink beer from schooners and dance and Phil would play an old beat-up piano. He could play any song you named, my father said, but the song everyone waited for was the one he wrote, which he would always play at the end before they left to go back to the town. And everyone knew of course that he had written the song for his girl, who was as pretty as she was rich. Her father was the banker in their town, and he was a tough old German, and he didn't like Phil going around with his daughter.

Sat. nights = special—dancing, beer, etc.

?

Sounds like fairy tale

My father, when he told the story, which was not often, would tell it in an offhand way and emphasize the Depression and not having much, instead of the important parts.* I will try to tell it the way he did, if I can.

Carla's next task was to brainstorm to find ideas. As she searched for a topic for her essay, she found it helpful to brainstorm separately on plot, character, setting, point of view, tone and style, and theme to see which suggested the most promising possibilities.

Brainstorming Notes

Plot

Flashback — narrator remembers story father told.
Story: Phil loved rich banker's daughter, wrote song for her, girl married someone else, Phil sold song for $25.00, married another woman.
Ordinary, predictable story of "star-crossed lovers" from different backgrounds ("Probably by now many of you have guessed . . ."), but what actually happened isn't important.

Character

Phil — Italian, never went to high school, ordinary job in restaurant, extraordinary piano player.
Girl — no name, pretty, rich, educated
Narrator — ?
Mother — romantic
Father — mechanic; gentle, practical

Setting

"small town in northern Michigan"
Past — when narrator's father was a young man
In woods — near lake
Roadhouse — dancing, drinking, beat-up piano

Point of View

Narrator tells story to reader, but there's a story inside the story.
Father tells his story, mother qualifies his version (she's "not part of the story" but has heard it), narrator tells how they told it.
Point of view keeps shifting — characters compete to tell the story ("I would like to intrude further . . .").
Father's version: stresses Depression, hard times
Mother's version: stresses relationship, "sad parts"
Readers encouraged to find own point of view; narrator of story addresses readers.
Three characters invent and reinvent and embellish story each time they tell it.

Tone and Style

Conversational style — narrator talks to reader ("Well, here's the kicker part.")
Like a fairy tale (girl = "as pretty as she was rich"; father = "a gentle but practical man")
Casual speech, contractions: "Well," "some guy," etc.

Theme

Which is "real" story?
Subject of Phil's story = missed chances, failure.
Subject of narrator's story = the past?
Values of different characters?
Conflict between real events and memory?

When Carla looked over her brainstorming notes, she saw at once that character and point of view suggested the most interesting possibilities for her paper. Still, she found herself unwilling to start drafting her essay until she could find out more about the story's title, which she thought must be significant. When her instructor told her that the title was the name of an actual song, she was easily able to find the song's lyrics on the Internet. She recorded her reactions to this information in a journal entry.

Journal Entry

"Sleepy Time Gal" = name of song
*Mother says Phil got inspiration for song from the way his girl looked when she got sleepy. **Does title of story refer to girl or to song? ***
Song = fantasy about the perfect married life that should follow the evenings of dancing: in a "cottage" the wife will be happy cooking and sewing for her husband and will end her evenings early. She'll be happy to forget about dancing and be a stay-at-home wife.
Maybe lyrics describe what Phil wants and never gets?

At this point, Carla decided to make an informal outline by arranging some of the most useful material from her brainstorming notes, journal entry, and annotations into categories. She gave these categories headings that corresponded to the three versions of Phil's story presented in "Sleepy Time Gal," and she added related supporting details as they occurred to her.

Informal Outline

Three Versions of Phil's Story

Mother's Version

"Likes the sad parts" and the details of the romance: the way the father made the daughter promise not to get involved with a man until she finished college, the way the women got tears in their eyes when Phil played his song.
Remembers girl's husband had French cuffs.
Remembers Phil's wife = "big and loud."
Notes people were trying to cheer Phil up.
Remembers girl resting head on Phil's shoulder, and how he got idea for song.

Father's Version

Depression/money: mentions Phil's patched tires and engine, how he spent a week's pay on new clothes, how girl's husband pays cash for a new Pontiac.
"Times were tough"

Narrator's Version

Facts of story — but wants to add more about Phil's process of writing song (because he, like Phil, = artist?), more about romance ("you could see it in their eyes"). Wants to embellish story.
("I wish I could put more in . . .")

Carla's notes and lists eventually suggested a thesis statement for her paper.

Thesis statement: Sleepy Time Gal is a story that is not about the "gal" of the title or about the man the narrator calls Phil but rather about the different viewpoints of its three narrators.

Guided by this tentative thesis statement, Carla went on to write and revise her paper, following the process detailed in Chapters 3–5. The final draft of Carla's paper follows. Annotations have been added to identify the conventions that apply to writing essays about works of fiction. (Note that because all students in the class selected stories from the same text, Carla's instructor did not require a works-cited list.)

Watts 1

Carla Watts

Professor Sierra

English 1001

12 March 2004

Whose Story?

Midway through Gary Gildner's short story "Sleepy Time Gal," the narrator acknowledges, "I've already intruded too much in a simple story that isn't even mine" (215). But whose story is "Sleepy Time Gal"? It is presented as the tale of Phil, an ordinary young man of modest means who falls in love with a rich young woman, writes a song for her, and loses both the woman and the song, as well as the fame and fortune the song could have brought him, apparently because he is unwilling to fight for either. But actually, "Sleepy Time Gal" is not Phil's story, and it is not the story of the girl he loves; the story belongs to the three characters who compete to tell it.

Title of short story is in quotation marks

Parenthetical documentation identifies page on which quotation appears

Thesis statement

The story these characters tell is a simple one; it is also familiar. Phil is a young man with an ordinary job. He has little education and no real prospects of doing anything beyond working in a restaurant doing menial jobs. He is in love with a girl whose father is a rich banker, a girl who goes to college. Phil has no more chance of marrying the girl than he has of becoming educated or becoming a millionaire. He has written a song for her, but he

Brief plot summary is combined with interpretation

Watts 2

is doomed to sell the rights to it for twenty-five dollars. Phil may be a man with dreams and expectations that go beyond the small Michigan town and the roadhouse, but he does not seem to be willing to struggle to make his dreams come true. Ironically, he never achieves the happy married life his song describes; his dreams remain just dreams, and he settles for life in the dream world of a movie theater.

Father's perspective

Past tense used to identify events that occurred before story's main action

The character who seems to be the author of Phil's story is the narrator's father: he is the only one who knew Phil and witnessed the story's events, and he has told it again and again to his family. But the story he tells reveals more than just what happened to Phil; it says a lot about his own life, too. The father is a mechanic who eventually leaves his small Michigan town for Detroit. As the narrator observes, he is "a gentle but practical man" (214). We can assume he has seen some hard times; he sees Phil's story only in the context of the times, and "times were tough" (216). The narrator says, "My father, when he told the story, . . . would tell it in an offhand way and emphasize the Depression and not having much, instead of the important parts" (214). In the father's version, seemingly minor details are important: Phil's often-mended car engine, "a gingerbread of parts from different makes" (215),

Ellipsis indicates student has omitted words from quotation

Watts 3

and incidents like how Phil spent a week's pay on a new shirt and tie, "the first tie he ever owned" (215), and how the girl's husband paid cash for a new Pontiac. These details are important to the father because they have to do with money. He sees Phil's story as more about a particular time (the Depression era) than about particular people. Whenever he hears Phil's song on the radio, he remembers that time.

Mother's perspective

The narrator's mother, however, sees Phil's story as a romantic, timeless story of hopelessly doomed lovers. She did not witness the story's events, but she has heard the story often. According to the narrator, she "likes the sad parts and is eager to get to their last night before the girl goes away to college" (215). She remembers how the women in the roadhouse got tears in their eyes when Phil played the song he wrote. The mother's selective memory helps to characterize her as somewhat romantic and sentimental, interested in people and their relationships (the way the girl's father made her promise to avoid romantic entanglements until after college; the way Phil's friends tried to cheer him up) and in visual details (the way the girl rested her head on Phil's shoulder; the French cuffs on her husband's shirt). In the interaction between the characters, she sees drama and even tragedy. The sentimental story of

Point is supported by specific references to story

Watts 4

lost love appeals to her just as the story of lost opportunity appeals to the father.

Narrator's perspective

The narrator knows the story only through his father's telling and retelling of it, and he says, "I will try to tell it the way he did, if I can" (214). But this is impossible because as he tells the story, he embellishes it, and he makes it his own. He is the one who communicates the story to readers, and he ultimately decides what to include and what to leave out. His story reflects both his parents' points of view: the focus on both characters and events, both romance and history. In telling Phil's story, he tells the story of a time, re-creating a Depression-era struggle of a man who could have made it big but wound up a failure; however, he also recounts a story about people, a romantic, sentimentalized story of lost love. And, at the same time, he tells a story about his own parents.

Narrator's perspective continued

The narrator, like Phil, is creative; he needs to convey the facts of the story, but he must struggle to resist the temptation to add to them—to add more about how Phil went about writing the song, "maybe show him whistling the tune and going over the words slowly and carefully to get the best ones" (214-15), and to add more about the romance itself. The narrator is clearly embellishing the story—for instance, when he says everyone knew Phil and the girl would get married because "you could see it in

Watts 5

their eyes" (215), he admits that this detail is not in his father's version of the story—but he is careful to identify his own contributions, explaining, "I couldn't help putting it in there" (215). The narrator cannot help wondering about the parts his father did not tell, and he struggles to avoid rewriting the story to include them. Sometimes he cannot help himself, and he apologizes for his lapses with a phrase like "I have to break in here . . ." (214). But, for the most part, the narrator knows his place, knows it is not really his story to tell: "I wish I could put more in, especially about the song and how it felt to Phil to sing it and how the girl felt when hearing it and knowing it was hers, but I've already intruded too much in a simple story that isn't even mine" (215).

Conclusion reinforces thesis

Phil's story is, as the narrator acknowledges, a simple one, almost a cliché. But Gary Gildner's story, "Sleepy Time Gal," is more complex. In it, three characters create and re-create a story of love and loss, ambition and failure, all contributing the details they feel should be stressed. In the process, they reveal something about themselves and about their own hopes and dreams.

23d Writing about Poetry

When you write a paper about poetry, you follow the same process discussed in 23c. However, you concentrate on the elements poets use to create and enrich their work—for example, voice, form, sound, meter, language, and tone.

Checklist: Writing about Poetry

- ☐ **Voice** Who is the poem's speaker? What is the speaker's attitude toward the poem's subject? How would you characterize the speaker's tone?
- ☐ **Word Choice and Word Order** What words seem important? Why? What does each word say? What does it suggest? Are any words repeated? Why? Is the poem's diction formal or informal? Is the arrangement of words conventional or unconventional?
- ☐ **Imagery** What images are used in the poem? To what senses (sight, sound, smell, taste, or touch) do they appeal? Is one central image important? Why? Is there a pattern of related images?
- ☐ **Figures of Speech** Does the poet use simile? metaphor? personification? What do figures of speech contribute to the poem?
- ☐ **Sound** Does the poem include rhyme? Where? Does it have regular meter (that is, a regular pattern of stressed and unstressed syllables)? Does the poem include repeated consonant or vowel sounds? What do these elements contribute to the poem?
- ☐ **Form** Is the poem written in **open form** (with no definite pattern of line length, rhyme, or meter) or in **closed form** (conforming to a pattern)? Why do you think this kind of form is used?
- ☐ **Theme** What central theme or themes does the poem explore?

ESL Tip

You may find English-language poetry difficult to understand, but you should know that even native English speakers may have trouble understanding poetry because of the special ways in which poets use words. Do your best, and remember that as a person who speaks more than one language, you may have a greater sensitivity to language than people who speak only one language.

Daniel Johanssen, a student in an introductory literature course, wrote an essay about Delmore Schwartz's 1959 poem "The True-Blue American." Daniel's essay appears on pages 533–35; annotations highlight some conventions of writing about poetry. (Note that because all students in the class selected poems from the same text, Daniel's instructor did not require a works-cited list.)

The True-Blue American

Jeremiah Dickson was a true-blue American,
For he was a little boy who understood America, for he felt that he must
Think about *everything*; because that's *all* there is to think about,
Knowing immediately the intimacy of truth and comedy,
Knowing intuitively how a sense of humor was a necessity
For one and for all who live in America. Thus, natively, and
Naturally when on an April Sunday in an ice cream parlor Jeremiah
Was requested to choose between a chocolate sundae and a banana split
He answered unhesitatingly, having no need to think of it
Being a true-blue American, determined to continue as he began:
Rejecting the either-or of Kierkegaard,[1] and many another European;
Refusing to accept alternatives, refusing to believe the choice of between;
Rejecting selection; denying dilemma; electing absolute affirmation:
knowing
in his breast
The infinite and the gold
Of the endless frontier, the deathless West.

---

[1]Søren Kierkegaard (1813–1855)—Danish philosopher who greatly influenced twentieth-century existentialism. *Either-Or* (1841) is one of his best-known works.

continued

continued from the previous page

"Both: I will have them both!" declared this true-blue American
In Cambridge, Massachusetts, on an April Sunday, instructed
By the great department stores, by the Five-and-Ten,
Taught by Christmas, by the circus, by the vulgarity and grandeur of Niagara Falls and the Grand Canyon,
Tutored by the grandeur, vulgarity, and infinite appetite gratified and
Shining in the darkness, of the light
On Saturdays at the double bills of the moon pictures,
The consummation of the advertisements of the imagination of the light
Which is as it was—the infinite belief in infinite hope—
of Columbus, Barnum, Edison, and Jeremiah Dickson.

Johanssen 1

Daniel Johanssen

Professor Stang

English 1001

8 April 2004

Irony in "The True-Blue American"

The poem "The True-Blue American," by Delmore Schwartz, is not as simple and direct as its title suggests. In fact, the title is extremely ironic. At first, the poem seems patriotic, but actually the flag-waving strengthens the speaker's criticism. Even though the poem seems to support and celebrate America, it is actually a bitter critique of the negative aspects of American culture.

According to the speaker, the primary problem with America is that its citizens falsely believe themselves to be authorities on everything. The following lines introduce the theme of the "know-it-all" American: "For he was a little boy who understood America, for he felt that he must / Think about <u>everything</u>; because that's <u>all</u> there is to think about" (lines 2-3). This theme is developed later in a series of parallel phrases that seem to celebrate the value of immediate intuitive knowledge and a refusal to accept or to believe anything other than what is American (4-6).

Americans are ambitious and determined, but these qualities are not seen in the poem as virtues. According to the speaker, Americans reject

Title of poem is in quotation marks

Thesis statement

Slash separating lines of poetry (space before and after slash)

Parenthetical documentation indicates line numbers (the word *line* or *lines* is included only in the first reference)

Johanssen 2

sophisticated "European" concepts like doubt and choices and alternatives and instead insist on "absolute affirmation" (13)—simple solutions to complex problems. This unwillingness to compromise translates into stubbornness and materialistic greed. This tendency is illustrated by the boy's asking for <u>both</u> a chocolate sundae <u>and</u> a banana split at the ice cream parlor—not "either-or" (11). Americans are characterized as pioneers who want it all, who will stop at nothing to achieve "The infinite and the gold / Of the endless frontier, the deathless West" (16-17). For the speaker, the pioneers and their "endless frontier" are not noble or self-sacrificing; they are like greedy little boys at an ice cream parlor.

According to the speaker, the greed and materialism of America began as grandeur but ultimately became mere vulgarity. Similarly, the "true-blue American" is not born a vulgar parody of grandeur; he learns it from his true-blue fellows:

More than 3 lines of poetry are set off from text. Quotation is indented 1" or 10 spaces from left margin; no quotation marks are used. Documentation is placed one space after final punctuation.

instructed
By the great department stores, by the
   Five-and-Ten,
Taught by Christmas, by the circus, by the
     vulgarity and grandeur of Niagara
     Falls and the Grand Canyon,
Tutored by the grandeur, vulgarity,
       and infinite appetite
       gratified. . . . (19-23)

Johanssen 3

Among the "tutors" the speaker lists are such American institutions as department stores and national monuments. Within these institutions, grandeur and vulgarity coexist; in a sense, they are one and the same.

The speaker's negativity climaxes in the phrase "Shining in the darkness, of the light" (24). This paradoxical statement suggests that negative truths are hidden beneath America's glamorous surface. All the grand and illustrious things of which Americans are so proud are personified by Jeremiah Dickson, the spoiled brat in the ice cream parlor.

Conclusion reinforces thesis

Like America, Jeremiah has unlimited potential. He has native intuition, curiosity, courage, and a pioneer spirit. Unfortunately, however, both America and Jeremiah Dickson are limited by their willingness to be led by others, by their greed and impatience, and by their preference for quick, easy, unambiguous answers rather than careful philosophical analysis. Regardless of his—and America's—potential, Jeremiah Dickson is doomed to be hypnotized and seduced by glittering superficialities, light without substance, and to settle for the "double bills of the moon pictures" (25) rather than the enduring truths of a philosopher like Kierkegaard.

23e Writing about Drama

When you write a paper about a play, you focus on the special conventions of drama. For example, you might consider not just the play's plot and characters but also its staging.

Checklist: Writing about Drama

- ☐ **Plot** What happens in the play? What conflicts are developed? How are they resolved? Are there any subplots? What events, if any, occur offstage?
- ☐ **Character** Who are the major characters? The minor characters? What relationships exist among them? What are their most distinctive traits? What do we learn about characters from their words and actions? from the play's stage directions? from what other characters tell us? Does the main character change or grow during the course of the play? What motivates the characters?
- ☐ **Staging** When and where is the play set? How do the scenery, props, costumes, lighting, and music work together to establish this setting? What else do these elements contribute to the play?
- ☐ **Theme** What central theme or themes does the play explore?

Kimberly Allison, a student in an introductory literature class, was assigned to write a short paper on one element—plot, character, staging, or theme—in a one-act play. She chose to write about the characters in Susan Glaspell's 1916 play *Trifles*. Her completed paper, annotated to highlight some conventions of writing about drama, appears on pages 537–42. (Note that because all students in the class selected plays from the same text, Kimberly's instructor did not require a works-cited list.)

Allison 1

Kimberly Allison

English 1013

Professor Johnson

1 March 2004

Desperate Measures:

Acts of Defiance in Trifles

Susan Glaspell wrote her best-known play, Trifles, in 1916, at a time when women were beginning to challenge their socially defined roles, realizing that their identities as wives and domestics kept them in a subordinate position in society. Because women were demanding more autonomy, traditional institutions such as marriage, which confined women to the home and made them mere extensions of their husbands, were beginning to be reexamined.

Opening sentence identifies author and work (play title is underlined)

Introduction places play in historical context

As a married woman, Glaspell was evidently touched by these concerns, perhaps because when she wrote Trifles she was at the mercy of her husband's wishes and encountered barriers in pursuing her career. But for whatever reason, Glaspell chose as the play's protagonist a married woman, Minnie Foster (Mrs. Wright), who has challenged society's expectations in a very extreme way: by murdering her husband. Minnie's defiant act has occurred before the action begins, and as the play unfolds, two women, Mrs. Peters and Mrs. Hale, piece together the details of the situation surrounding the murder. As the events unfold, however, it becomes clear that

Allison 2

Thesis statement

the focus of <u>Trifles</u> is not on who killed John Wright, but on the themes of the subordinate role of women, the confinement of the wife in the home, and the experiences all women share; through these themes, Glaspell shows her audience the desperate measures women had to take to achieve autonomy.

Topic sentence identifies first point paper will discuss: women's subordinate role

The subordinate role of women, particularly Minnie's role in her marriage, becomes evident in the first few minutes of the play when Mr. Hale observes that the victim, John Wright, had little concern for his wife's opinions: "I didn't know as what his wife wanted made much difference to John" (1164). Here Mr. Hale suggests that Minnie was powerless against the wishes of her husband. Indeed, as these characters imply, all Minnie's acts and thoughts were controlled by her husband; Minnie had power only in her kitchen. Mrs. Peters and Mrs. Hale understand this situation because their own behavior is controlled by their husbands. Therefore, when Sheriff Peters mocks Minnie's concern about her preserves, saying, "Well, can you beat the women! Held for murder and worrying about her preserves" (1166), he is, in a sense, condemning the women for worrying about domestic matters rather than about the murder that has been committed. Indeed, the sheriff's comment suggests that he assumes women's lives are trivial, an assumption that pervades the thoughts and speech of all three men.

Allison 3

Mrs. Peters and Mrs. Hale are similar to Minnie in another way as well: throughout the play, they are confined to the kitchen of the Wrights' house, while their husbands enter and exit the house at will. This scenario mirrors Minnie's daily life, as she remained in the home while her husband went to work and into town. The two women are aware of Minnie's isolation: "Not having children makes less work—but it makes a quiet house, and Wright out to work all day, and no company when he did come in" (1171). Beginning to identify with Minnie's loneliness, Mrs. Peters and Mrs. Hale recognize that, busy in their own homes, they have, in fact, participated in isolating and confining Minnie. Mrs. Hale declares, "I wish I had come over once in a while! That was a crime! That was a crime! Who's going to punish that? . . . I might have known she needed help!" (1173).

Topic sentence introduces second point paper will discuss: women's confinement

Soon the two women discover that Minnie's only connection to the outside world was her bird, the symbol of her confinement; Minnie was a caged bird who was kept from singing and communicating with others because of her restrictive husband. And piecing together the evidence—the disorderly kitchen, the poorly stitched quilt pieces, and the dead canary—the women come to believe that John Wright broke the bird's neck just as he had broken Minnie's spirit. Now, Mrs. Peters and Mrs. Hale see

Transitional paragraph discusses women's observations and conclusions

Allison 4

the connection between the dead canary and Minnie's situation. The stage directions describe the moment when the women become aware of the truth: "Their eyes meet," and they share "A look of growing comprehension, of horror" (1172).

Topic sentence introduces third point paper will discuss: commonality of women's experiences

Through their observations and discussions in Mrs. Wright's kitchen, Mrs. Hale and Mrs. Peters come to understand the commonality of women's experiences. Mrs. Hale speaks for both of them when she says, "I know how things can be—for women. . . . We all go through the same things—it's all just a different kind of the same thing" (1173). And, once the two women recognize the experiences they share, they begin to understand that they must join together in order to challenge a male-oriented society; although their experiences may seem trivial to the men, the "trifles" of their lives are significant to them. They realize that Minnie's independence and identity were crushed by her husband and that their own husbands see women's lives as trivial and unimportant as well. This realization leads them to commit an act as defiant as the one that has gotten Minnie into trouble: they conceal the evidence of Minnie's guilt from their husbands and from the law.

Significantly, Mrs. Peters does acknowledge that "the law is the law," but she also seems to believe that because Mr. Wright treated his wife badly, Minnie is justified in killing him. The women

Allison 5

also realize, however, that for men the law is black and white and that an all-male jury will not take into account the extenuating circumstances that prompted Minnie to kill her husband. And even if Minnie were allowed to communicate to the all-male court the emotional abuses she has suffered, the law would undoubtedly view her experience as trivial.

Nevertheless, because Mrs. Hale and Mrs. Peters empathize with Minnie's condition, they suppress the evidence they find, enduring their husbands' condescension rather than standing up to them. Through this desperate, defiant action, the women attempt to break through the boundaries of their social role, just as Minnie has done. Although Minnie is imprisoned for her crime, she has freed herself; and, although Mrs. Peters and Mrs. Hale conceal their insights about Minnie's motives, fearing the men will laugh at them, these women are really challenging society and freeing themselves as well.

Conclusion places play in historical context

In Trifles, Susan Glaspell addresses many of the problems shared by early twentieth-century women, including their subordinate status and their confinement in the home. In order to emphasize the pervasiveness of these problems, and the desperate measures women had to take to break out of their restrictive social roles, Glaspell does more than focus on the plight of the woman who has ended her

Allison 6

isolation and loneliness by committing a heinous crime against society. By illustrating the differences between male and female experience, she shows how men define the roles of women and how women can challenge these roles in search of their own significance in society and their eventual independence.

Chapter 24

Writing in the Social Sciences

Frequently Asked Questions

What kinds of assignments can I expect in the social sciences? (p. 544)

What documentation styles are used in the social sciences? (p. 553)

What research sources will I use in my social sciences courses? (p. 554)

The **social sciences** include anthropology, business, criminal justice, economics, education, political science, psychology, social work, and sociology. When you approach an assignment in the social sciences, your purpose is often to study the behavior of individuals or groups. You may be seeking to understand causes; predict results; define a policy, habit, or trend; or analyze a problem. Before you can approach a problem in the social sciences, you must develop a **hypothesis,** an educated guess about what you believe your research will suggest. Then, you can gather the data that will either prove or disprove that hypothesis. Data may be quantitative or qualitative. **Quantitative data** are numerical—the "countable" results of surveys and polls. **Qualitative data** are less exact and more descriptive—the results of interviews or observations, for example.

24a Understanding Purpose, Audience, and Tone

Like writing assignments in the humanities, writing assignments in the social sciences can be informal or formal. Informal writing assignments ask you to record your personal observations and reactions. More formal writing assignments require you to analyze and synthesize data. Each of these types of assignments has its own characteristic style and tone.

Informal writing assignments encourage you to examine ideas, phenomena, and data in the world around you. One example of an informal writing assignment is a personal experience essay, in which you are asked to relate your own observations of an event or an experience. Because you are being asked for your personal reactions, it is acceptable to use the first person (*I*) as well as a conversational tone.

Formal writing assignments—such as case studies, research essays, and proposals—use an objective tone and a technical vocabulary. These assignments often require you to examine similarities and differences between what you have observed and what you have read or to evaluate terms and concepts from your course readings and lectures. While writing in the social sciences tends to be informative, it may also be persuasive; for example, although a research proposal describes your planned research, it is written to persuade readers to support your work.

See 8b–c

Sometimes your instructor will define an audience for your assignment—your classmates, a supervisor of a social services agency, or a public official, for example—but sometimes you have to come up with your own or assume that you are addressing a general audience of readers in your field. (If you are working in a group, you may distribute your assignment by email or by means of a listserv.)

Close-up: Using the Passive Voice

Unlike writers in the humanities, writers in the social sciences often use the passive voice. The passive voice enables these writers to avoid the first person and to present their research in objective terms.

See 47d

24b Writing Assignments

(1) Personal Experience Essay

In some social science disciplines (particularly psychology, education, and sociology), you may be asked to write an informal **personal experience essay** that reports on a field trip or a site visit or even an interview with a professional working in the field. In this kind of assignment, you record specific details about an event. For example, students in an education class might record their observations of a class of hearing-impaired students, and students in a sociology class might write about their visit to a state correctional facility.

Assignment (Anthropology: Service Learning)

Describe your first visit to your field-learning site. How did you feel as you made your way there? What expectations did you have? Record your initial impressions of the site: How did you feel as you were walking in? What were the first things you noticed? What surprises did you have?

Sample Personal Experience Essay (Excerpt)

I walked from Main Street to River and finally onto the two-lane gravel street of Park, where I could see from the distance the dogs running around their pens at the Humane Society. As I walked by the fenced cages, I saw the need in the dogs' eyes, and from that moment, I knew that my interaction with them would be beneficial for me as well as for them. I walked slowly up to the main office, not sure what to expect. At home, I volunteered at a daycare center, but this was my first time working with animals.

Working with animals was my first choice for the service-learning part of this course. I have loved animals ever since I was a child. Animals don't judge, so they are the best companions. However, normally I interact with the pets in people's homes, so I was not accustomed to the behaviors of the affection-starved animals that I encountered at the Humane Society. Each animal has its own sad story of being abandoned or lost. Each has its own personality traits as well. On my first day at the Humane Society, I met Barney, a dog with an interesting personality. He had a bright blue collar around his neck and was full of energy. During our thirty-minute walk, he purposely walked around me and tangled me up in his leash. He repeated this "game" as often as I would allow him to, and he reacted well to affection. Because he didn't seem to be hand-shy, I concluded that his owner had not abused him. Barney and I have already formed a close bond.

(2) Book Review

Instructors in the social sciences may ask you to write a book review. A **book review** should include enough summary to familiarize your audience with the book's content. It should also include your evaluation of the book and your analysis of its contribution to the discipline. Be sure to include the author, date, and title of the book in your first paragraph.

Assignment (Political Science)

Who: Your audience for this assignment is your class research group.

What: Write a book review, summarizing the content and commenting on the usefulness to the field, of Steven Kelman's *Making Public Policy: A Hopeful View of American Government.*

When: Due next Tuesday.

Where: For your weekly group meeting.

Why: This book will be one of your sources for your group research project. Reviews will be evaluated according to how well they demonstrate your understanding of the book, the insights they provide into your research topic, and how well they are written.

Sample Book Review (Excerpt)

Kelman next examines the Presidency. In this section, he explores the relationship between the Presidency and the bureaucracy. Rather than dividing the Executive and the bureaucracy into the Senior Executive Service and the Civil Service, Kelman limits his discussion to the Executive Office of the President (EOP) and direct political appointments.

Kelman's observations concerning the importance of organizational structure, ground rules, and operating tradition are important. Particularly significant is how organizational characteristics affect the flow of debate, information, and decision making as well as how these characteristics eliminate certain issues from consideration. For example, when a congressional committee debates legislation, the consequences of different organizational structures become visible and are subject to debate and change. When a committee chair excludes an issue from debate, however, the different organizational structures never become visible. According to Kelman, political decision makers may not even be conscious of the exclusion.

Kelman never draws a clear distinction between public spirit and public involvement, two key concepts in his book. At first, Kelman defines public spirit negatively—that is, public spirit is the absence of self-interest in political decision making. Later, he confuses public spirit with public involvement. Perhaps this confusion occurs because Kelman believes the structural mechanisms that promote public involvement also promote public spirit.

(3) Case Study

Social science courses, especially psychology, sociology, and anthropology, frequently require you to write **case studies** in which you are asked to describe, analyze, and solve problems involving human and institutional interactions. Case studies are usually informative rather than persuasive, describing a problem and suggesting solutions or treatments.

In political science, case studies can examine foreign policy negotiations or analyze such issues as government infringement on civil liberties. In psychology, social work, and educational psychology, the case study typically focuses on an individual and his or her interaction with peers or with agency professionals.

Assignment (Psychology of the Family)

Write a formal case study of the family that you have been studying.

Sample Case Study

Family Profile

The Newberg family consists of Tom and Tina and their children David (8), Angela (6), and Cristina (4).

Problem

Tom has been laid off from his automobile production-line job. Tina is not employed outside the home. They have a mortgage on their home as well as $6,000 in credit card debt.

The loss of income when Tom was laid off from his job caused a change in the economic status of the Newberg family. Initially, Tom and Tina tended to have a negative attitude toward their situation and were not resourceful. Tom tried to maintain the traditional family structure, wanting to be the sole provider, while Tina continued to stay at home with their children. Both Tom and Tina seemed to see no solution to their problems and saw no way to alleviate their financial difficulties. Both were habitual smokers, and this habit increased their expenses even more.

Observations

Tom spent so much time looking for a job that he had little time with his family—especially the children. At first, Tina borrowed money from her parents to try to start a door-to-door beauty products business. When this failed, she found a job driving a delivery truck, but it was only part time. Tom and Tina's financial situation put severe strain on the family. Even so, the couple made no plans about where the family would go if they lost their house; they just kept hoping things would improve.

Discussion

Even when both the Newbergs managed to get full-time jobs, they were unable to achieve the lifestyle they wanted. Image is very important to Tom and Tina: they had to look like a traditional family in order to have self-esteem. This is especially important to Tom. The prognosis for the Newberg family, even though they now have a regular income, is not promising unless they learn to cooperate, to set goals as a family, and to share responsibilities. Both debt counseling and family counseling are strongly recommended.

(4) Annotated Bibliography and Review-of-Research Essay

Social science instructors may ask you to assemble your research sources into an **annotated bibliography** that provides a paragraph of summary and evaluation for each source. You may also be asked to write a **review-of-research essay** (sometimes called a **review of literature essay**), in which you discuss the entries in your annotated bibliography. The review-of-research essay is often part of a social science research paper. By commenting on recent scholarship on a particular topic, you demonstrate knowledge of the topic as well as an understanding of different critical approaches to that topic.

Assignment (Sociology)

> Research an issue of your choice, one that interests you and that has a significant impact on particular populations in your state. Then, compile an annotated bibliography of at least six sources. Finally, write a review-of-research essay that would be useful to professionals in the field.

Sample Annotated Bibliography (Excerpt)

Adams, J. R. (2002). Farm bill funding boosts FMNP. National Association of Farmers' Market Nutrition Programs. Retrieved September 25, 2002, from http://www.nafmnp.org. This article provides current information on the Farmers' Market Nutrition Program (FMNP), with particular reference to its legislative appropriation status. The 2002 Food Security and Rural Investment Act restored funding for the Women, Infants, and Children (WIC) Program, which had previously been cut by half. However, the future for these programs is still not certain, as the administration has not yet made any allocation for the current fiscal year. The author stresses the need for continued lobbying to keep FMNP and WIC programs alive.

Sample Review-of-Research Essay (Excerpt)

At least two separate constituencies are concerned with maintaining the Farmers' Market Nutrition Program: farmers who can benefit from the increased sales and marketing, and consumers who receive the goods from the farmers. J. R. Adams (2002) discusses the efforts farmers and lobbyists have made in securing funding for the program, stressing recent victories in obtaining government funding. For example, even though funding had originally been cut by half from the previous year in the projected budget for 2002, this shortfall was corrected, and the program's funding was sustained at the same level as it stood in 2001 (Rosen, 2002). Farmers stand to benefit from this program, and from the similar Seniors Farmers' Market Nutrition Program (SFMNP), through their increased sales to government-funded markets. Similarly, as S. Z. Greenberg et al. (2001) point out, these programs not only create a potential new market for farmers' products but also may benefit from private grants to supplement government funding.

(5) Proposal

A **proposal,** often the first stage of a research project, can clarify and focus a project's direction and goals. In a proposal, you define your research project and make a convincing case for it.

Assignment (Psychology of Substance Abuse)

Write a proposal to solve a problem associated with alcohol abuse. Your proposal should include a cover page, an executive summary, a statement of the problem, a statement of your objectives, a description of your methods, a review of relevant literature (including careful documentation of your sources), and a budget and timeline projection, along with your own conclusions and recommendations for solving the problem. Each source you use, including Web sites, journal articles, monographs, or interviews, should be carefully documented according to APA style.

Sample Proposal (Excerpt)

Statement of the Problem

The physiological effects of alcohol can impair a person's normal functioning. The severity of effects is dependent on an individual's Blood Alcohol Concentration (BAC), which itself is determined by the individual's weight, speed of alcohol consumption, and amount of alcohol consumed. If an individual's BAC is higher than .08, he or she can be charged with Driving Under the Influence (DUI). As Figure 1 illustrates, the number of DUIs in Frewsdale is high, with 1067 DUI charges in the past 5 years. Of course, this number reflects only the individuals who were actually caught; the number of people driving with a BAC higher than .08 is probably much higher, as shown by our survey of Frewsdale University students, in

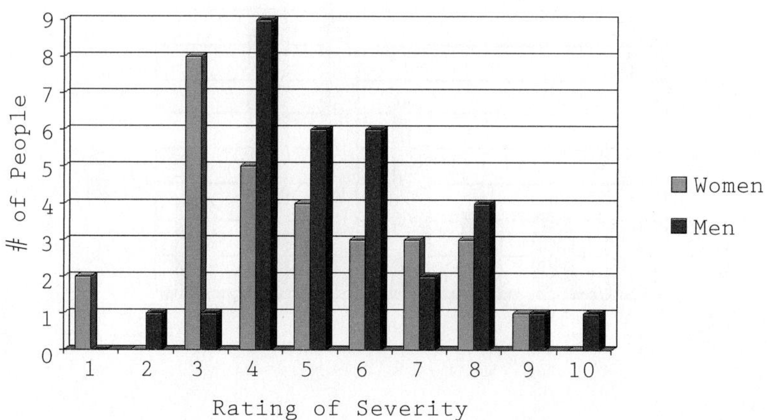

Figure 1. Drunk driving in Frewsdale.

which more than 80% of respondents—none of whom had ever received a DUI charge—indicated that they had seen or that they knew somebody who had driven drunk.

The entire community of Frewsdale would benefit from a program that would get drunk drivers off the road. An alternative transportation method available to people who have been drinking would greatly reduce the number of DUIs in Frewsdale. Furthermore, such a program would reduce the number of people who walk home alone late at night and potentially put themselves at risk.

We propose a safe-ride program for the city, aimed primarily at providing a free ride home on weekends (when people most frequently go out, as Figure 2 shows) for college students and other residents who have been drinking.

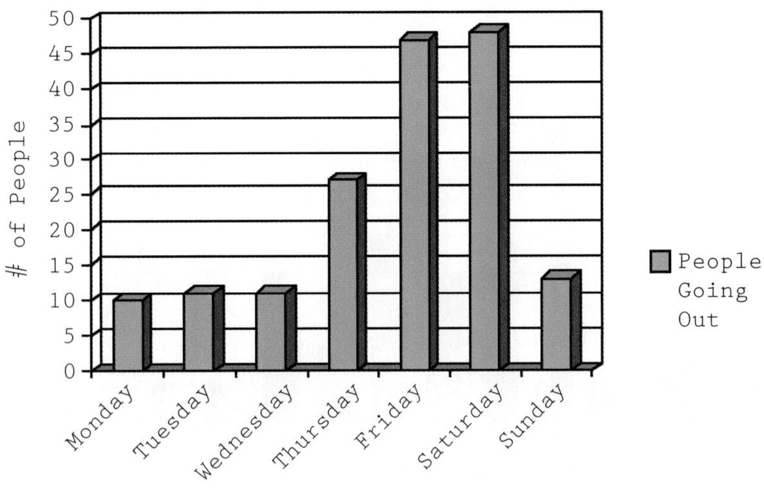

Figure 2. Nights people go out in Frewsdale.

24c Conventions of Style, Format, and Documentation

(1) Style and Format

Like other disciplines, social science uses a technical vocabulary. Because you are addressing specialists, you should use the specialized vocabulary of the discipline and, when you discuss charts and tables, you should use statistical terms, such as *mean*, *percentage*, and *chi square*. Keep in mind, however, that you should use plain English to explain what percentages, means, and standard deviations signify in terms of your analysis.

A social science research paper often follows a specific format. For example, APA manuscript guidelines require a title page that includes a **running head,** a title, and a **byline** (your name, school, and so on). Every page of the paper, including the title page, should have a **page header,** an abbreviated title and page number printed at the top. Social science papers also include **internal headings** (for example, *Method*, *Results*, *Background of Problem*, *Description of Problem*, *Solutions*, and *Conclusion*). Each section of a social science paper is a complete unit with a beginning and an end so that it can be read separately, out of context, and still make sense. The body of the paper may present and discuss graphs, maps, photographs, flowcharts, or tables.

See 19b

(2) Documentation

Many of the journals in the various social science disciplines use APA documentation style.

See Ch. 19

24d Avoiding Plagiarism

See Ch. 16

When writing in the social sciences, it is important to avoid plagiarism by correctly documenting the data, words, and ideas of others that you use in your paper. In addition, social scientists are bound by other ethical considerations regarding the treatment of research subjects, the protection of privacy, and the granting of credit to those who have made substantial contributions to a research project.

24e Using Visuals and Technology

Because of the many types of documents social scientists write and the varied methods of data collection, visuals and technology play an important role in all phases of the writing process.

In the data collection stage of a project, field research (for example, for a personal experience essay or a case study) may involve more than transcribing information into print. Digital cameras may play an important role in capturing important interactions among subjects, and both digital video and digital audio recorders can assist in the transcription of interviews. These devices connect easily to a computer and allow writers to include both images and audio files in various social science projects.

See 12d1

In addition, a range of software available for both the PC and Macintosh—for example, *Adobe Photoshop* for image editing, Apple's *I-Movie* for video editing, and *Sound Forge and Peak* for sound editing—can help with data representation. These programs are quite useful in helping you select and edit most image, video, or audio data for Web or print delivery. Other useful software applications include statistical packages such as *SAS* and *SPSS*, which analyze quantitative data.

Various types of writing in the social sciences have specific style and formatting conventions that require attention to document design. For example, the use of tables and charts to present the statistical results of survey data is common. In addition, the general formatting of documents requires the use of headings and subheadings, spacing, and other stylistic elements, such as boldface and italics. Familiarizing yourself with the various menus in your word-processing program that allow you to create and edit tables and charts, as well as with spreadsheet programs like *Microsoft Excel*, will help you in the writing and document design process in the social sciences.

See Ch. 29

24f Research Sources

Although library research is an important component of social science research, students, professionals, and scholars also engage in field research. In **library research,** social scientists consult print and electronic versions of compilations of statistics, government documents, and newspaper articles, in addition to scholarly books and articles. In **field research,** social scientists conduct interviews and

See 12d

surveys and observe individuals and groups. Because so much of their data are quantitative, social scientists must know how to analyze statistics and how to read and interpret tables.

Social scientists also must be able to analyze or evaluate the work of others in their fields. They may conduct literature reviews to discover what research has already been done, or they may analyze research reports. Social scientists are particularly interested in case studies and published reports of surveys, opinion polls, interviews, experiments, and observations that may be useful in proving or disproving a theory.

Unlike researchers in the humanities, who are not always limited to the most recent information available, social scientists are required to base their studies on the most current thinking surrounding a topic. Statistics *must* be up to date. For this reason, although books may be useful for gathering background information and putting a topic in context, for the most current information, researchers turn to electronic databases to locate recent scholarly journal articles and government publications.

Some excellent databases and print indexes cover the literature of the social sciences. *Social Sciences Citation Index* is available in print and as a database titled *Web of Science*. Other databases and indexes cover specific disciplines within the social sciences. In addition to databases, the Internet may be very helpful to social scientists who are looking for government information, including census data, statistics, congressional reports, laws, and reports issued by government agencies.

See Ch. 13

If you are unsure about using the online catalog or databases to find appropriate books, government publications, statistics, or journal articles, ask for help in the reference department of your library.

(1) Reference Books

The following reference sources, many of which are available on CD-ROM, DVD, or online as well as in print, are useful in a variety of social science disciplines.

Anthropology

Abstracts in Anthropology
Anthropological Literature
Companion Encyclopedia of Anthropology: Humanity, Culture and Social Life
Countries and Their Cultures
Dictionary of Anthropology
Encyclopedia of Cultural Anthropology
Encyclopedia of World Cultures
International Bibliography of Social and Cultural Anthropology
Worldmark Encyclopedia of Cultures and Daily Life

Business and Economics

ABI Inform
Accounting and Tax Index
Advertising Age Encyclopedia of Advertising
Business Information Sources
Business Periodicals Index
Dictionary of Economics
Directory of Business Information Resources
Encyclopedia of Banking and Finance
Encyclopedia of Business
Encyclopedia of Management
Gale Encyclopedia of U.S. Economic History
Handbook of North American Industry: NAFTA and the Economies of Its Members
International Encyclopedia of the Stock Market
Journal of Economic Literature
McGraw-Hill Dictionary of Modern Economics
Personnel Management Abstracts
Rand McNally Commercial Atlas and Marketing Guide
Wall Street Journal Index

Criminal Justice

American Justice
Capital Punishment: A Bibliography
Criminal Justice Abstracts
Criminal Justice Research in Libraries and on the Internet
Criminology, Penology, and Police Science Abstracts
Dictionary of Criminal Justice
Encyclopedia of American Prisons
Encyclopedia of Capital Punishment in the United States
Encyclopedia of Crime and Justice
Encyclopedia of Crime and Punishment
Encyclopedia of International Terrorism
Encyclopedia of World Crime
Violence in America

Education

Current Index to Journals in Education
Dictionary of Education
Digest of Education Statistics
Education Index
Encyclopedia of American Education
Encyclopedia of Educational Research
Encyclopedia of Special Education
Historical Dictionary of Women's Education in the United States
Multicultural Education in the United States
Resources in Education

Review of Research in Education
Yearbook of the National Society for the Study of Education

Ethnic Studies

African American Encyclopedia
American Statistics Index
Bibliografia Chicana: A Guide to Information Sources
CQ Researcher
Dictionary of Mexican American History
Encyclopedia of Black America
Ethnic Studies in the United States: A Guide to Research
Gale Encyclopedia of Native American Tribes
Handbook of North American Indians
Harvard Encyclopedia of American Ethnic Groups
Human Resources Abstracts
Index to International Statistics
International Bibliography of the Social Sciences
International Encyclopedia of the Social and Behavioral Sciences
Native American Women
Population Index
Public Affairs Information Service (PAIS)
Reference Encyclopedia of the American Indian
Reference Library of Black America
Social Sciences Citation Index
Social Sciences Index
Statistical Abstract of the United States
Statistical Abstract of the World
Statistical Reference Index (SRI)
Women's Studies: A Guide to Information Sources

Political Science and Law

ABC Political Science
American Political Dictionary
Black's Law Dictionary
CIS Index (Congressional Information Service)
CRIS: Combined Retrospective Index to Journals in Political Science
Dictionary of Modern Politics
Dictionary of Political Thought
Encyclopedia of the American Constitution
Encyclopedia of Constitutional Amendments, Proposed Amendments and Amending
Encyclopedia of European Social History
Encyclopedia of Modern World Politics
Encyclopedia of the Third World
Encyclopedia of the United Nations and International Agreements
Encyclopedia of U.S. Foreign Relations
Europa World Year Book
Foreign Affairs Bibliography

Index to Legal Periodicals
International Encyclopedia of Public Policy and Administration
International Political Science Abstracts
ISLA (International Services on Latin America)
Landmark Decisions of the United States Supreme Court
Worldmark Encyclopedia of the Nations

Psychology

Biographical Dictionary of Psychology
Blackwell Dictionary of Cognitive Psychology
Companion Encyclopedia of Psychology
Corsini Encyclopedia of Psychology and Behavioral Science
Dictionary of Psychology
Encyclopedia of Cognitive Science
Encyclopedia of Human Behavior
Encyclopedia of Mental Health
Encyclopedia of Psychology
International Encyclopedia of Psychiatry, Psychology, Psychoanalysis and Neurology
Psychological Abstracts
Psychology Basics

Sociology and Social Work

Critical Dictionary of Sociology
Encyclopedia of Family Life
Encyclopedia of Feminist Theories
Encyclopedia of Social Work
Encyclopedia of Sociology
Encyclopedia of Women and Gender
Handbook of Sociology
Human Resources Abstracts
Sage Family Studies Abstracts
Sociological Abstracts
Statistical Handbook on Poverty in the Developing World
Women's Studies Abstracts

(2) Government Documents

Government documents are important resources for social scientists because they contain complete and up-to-date facts and figures on a wide variety of subjects. Government documents can be located through the *Monthly Catalog*, which contains the list of documents (in print, microfiche, and electronic form) published each month. Other useful indexes include *The Congressional Information Service Index*, *The American Statistics Index*, and *The Index to U.S. Government Periodicals*. (**See 12b5** for more on locating government documents.)

(3) Newspaper Articles

Newspaper articles are particularly good resources for research subjects in political science, economics, and business. Useful sources of information from newspapers are *NewsBank*, *National Newspaper Index*, and *LexisNexis Academic Universe*. Some major newspapers also publish indexes to their contents.

(4) Databases for Computer Searches

Some of the more widely used databases for social science disciplines are *Cendata; General BusinessFile ASAP; Social Sciences Citation Index; Social Sciences Index; PsycINFO; ERIC; Sociological Abstracts; Information Science Abstracts; PAIS International; Population Bibliography; EconLit; ABI/INFORM; Management Contents; LexisNexis Academic Universe;* and *Facts on File.*

Ask a reference librarian about the availability of these and other databases in your library.

(5) Web Sites

For links to Web sites for specific social sciences disciplines, go to http://kirsznermandell.wadsworth.com ▶ *The Wadsworth Handbook* ▶ Chapter 24 ▶ Social Sciences Web Sites.

(6) Other Sources of Information

See 12d

Interviews, surveys, and observations of the behavior of various groups and individuals are important nonlibrary sources for social science research. Sometimes an assignment may ask you to use your classmates as subjects for surveys or interviews. For example, in a political science class, your instructor may ask you to interview a sample of college students and classify them as conservative, liberal, or moderate. You may be asked to poll each group to find out college students' attitudes on such issues as the death penalty, affirmative action, or the problems of the homeless. If you were writing a paper on educational programs for the mentally gifted, in addition to library research you might observe two classes—one of gifted students and one of average students. You might also interview students, teachers, or parents. Similarly, research in psychology and social work may rely on your observations of clients and their families.

Chapter 25

Writing in the Natural and Applied Sciences

Frequently Asked Questions

25a Understanding Purpose, Audience, and Tone

Writing assignments in the natural and applied sciences—for example, in courses in biology, chemistry, geology, astronomy, mathematics, physics, engineering, nursing, and computer science—will usually use a formal, objective tone and follow documentation guidelines such as those published by the Council of Science Editors (CSE). Although science writing is primarily concerned with accurately reporting observations and experimental data, it may also be persuasive. Most scientific writing is aimed at readers who are familiar with the technical language and writing conventions of a particular scientific discipline, but occasionally it may be aimed at general readers. Its express purpose is to report empirical data (data that are obtained by observations and experiments), and it uses the **scientific method.**

Close-up: The Scientific Method

The **scientific method** relies on empirical data to explain and solve problems. After using secondary sources to research a problem, you gather and interpret information by following these steps.

1. Propose a **hypothesis** that makes a claim about the cause and effect of the problem.
2. Plan a research design and methodology.

3. Carry out the experiment, recording observations and data.
4. Analyze the results of the experiment, carefully comparing the initial hypothesis with the actual results.
5. Make recommendations for further experiments.

25b Writing Assignments

(1) Laboratory Report

One of the most frequently assigned writing tasks in the sciences is the laboratory report, which is divided into sections that reflect the stages of the scientific method. However, not every section will be necessary for every experiment, and some experiments may call for additional components, such as an abstract or reference list. In addition, lab experiments may include tables, charts, graphs, and illustrations. The exact format for a lab report is usually defined by the course's lab manual.

A **lab report** is an explanation of a process. Because its purpose is to enable readers to understand a complex series of tasks, it must present stages clearly and completely, in exact chronological order, and illustrate the purpose of each step. In addition, a lab report must provide descriptions of the equipment used in an experiment.

See 7d4

Assignment (Chemistry)

Write a lab report that summarizes your laboratory findings. Include sections that outline your purpose, equipment, procedures, results, and conclusions.

Sample Laboratory Report

Purpose

The purpose of this lab experiment is to determine the iron content of an unknown mixture containing an iron salt by titration with potassium permanganate solution.

Equation to find % of Fe: $5Fe^{2+} + MnO_{4^-} + 8H^+ = 5Fe^{3+} + Mn^{2+} + 4H_2O$

Equipment

Equipment includes two 60 ml beakers, a graduated cylinder, a scale, 600 ml of distilled water, 2 grams of

H_2SO_4, 5 grams of $KMnO_4$, 100 ml of $H_2C_2O_4 \cdot 2H_2O$, and a Bunsen burner.

Procedure

1) A $KMnO_4$ solution was prepared by dissolving 1.5 grams of $KMnO_4$ in 500 ml of distilled water.

2) Two samples $H_2C_2O_4 \cdot 2H_2O$ of about 0.2 grams each were weighed.

3) Each sample was dissolved in 60 ml of H_2O and 30 ml of H_2SO_4 in a 250 ml beaker.

4) The mixture was heated to 80°C and titrated slowly with $KMnO_4$ until the mixture turned pink.

5) The procedure was repeated twice.

Results

Percentage of iron: 1st run = 12.51 ml

2nd run = 11.2 ml

Conclusions

Calculation for % of iron

$$\frac{12.5 \text{ ml} \times .0894 \text{ M}}{100 \text{ ml}/1} \times \frac{5 \text{ moles Fe}}{1 \text{ mole } MnO_4} \times \frac{55.85 \text{ g/mol}}{.5 \text{ g}} \times 100 =$$

$$\frac{66.11}{500} = 13.22\% \text{ Fe}$$

(2) Observation Essay

Some science instructors may ask you to write about and analyze your own observations of the natural world. This is one of the few assignments in the natural and applied sciences in which you will be encouraged to use the first person (*I*). In this type of essay, you first record your observations in detail (using scientific terminology where necessary) and then provide scientific analysis of the phenomena you describe.

Assignment (Ecology)

Write an article for a local environmentalists' magazine in which you describe a place that has significant emotional meaning for you and discuss the environmental impact of human beings on the place you are describing.

Sample Observation Essay (Excerpt)

Several times each year when my brother and I were young, my mother took us camping at Lake Wenatchee. Across the lake from our campground was Dirty Face Mountain.

Lake Wenatchee, part of Alpine Lakes, is in the Wenatchee National Forest, where over 700 small, freshwater lakes are scattered throughout the central Cascade region. The average annual precipitation is 40 inches; this rainfall accounts for the mixed conifers—Douglas firs, grand firs, and cedars—that thrive there. The rain-shadow effect also causes the soils in the region to be rich in organic materials as well as basalt, pumice, and volcanic ash. However, human activity—clear-cutting of old growth forest, damming of rivers, and fire suppression—is altering the area's natural ecology. These activities lead to a build-up of debris, a higher number of forest fires, severe soil erosion, and the endangerment of local species of animals and fish.

One image of Dirty Face summarizes all the problems that human incursion is causing to the land around the mountain. While climbing one stretch of a barely distinguishable trail, I noticed a very large area on the side of the mountain that had no trees. It was an ugly patch of bare, dry ground. At the time, I did not understand the purpose of cutting down all of those trees. I was too young to realize the ecological damage that the clear-cutting could have on the land around Dirty Face. Because the terrain is sloped, clear-cutting the trees causes extreme soil erosion, including mudslides. Because it also destroys animal habitats, many species of owl, woodpecker, and squirrel will soon be added to the Endangered Species list.

Although clearing the land may be necessary for building new homes, for producing fuel and paper, and for developing agriculture, the trees are being cut faster than they are being replaced. We should all question whether the goods being produced are worth more than the oxygen that the trees produce when alive. Before it is too late, we must assess the probable results that the clear-cutting of so many trees will produce.

(3) Literature Survey

Literature surveys are common in the sciences, often appearing as a section of a proposal or as part of a research paper. A **literature survey** summarizes a number of studies and sometimes compares and contrasts them. By doing so, the literature survey provides a theoretical context for the paper's discussion.

A literature survey should have a formal and objective tone and be aimed at readers who are experts in your field. The purpose of a literature survey is to give these readers a comprehensive overview of a range of scholarly publications about your subject. Although you may touch on the history of your topic, your primary focus should be on the most current research available.

Assignment (Biology)

Research an aspect of plant biology and write up your findings in a formal article that contains the following sections: Abstract, Introduction, Literature Survey, Materials, Methods, Results, Discussion, Conclusions, Reference List, and Appendix (if necessary). This should be a formal paper, free from grammatical and mechanical errors.

Sample Literature Survey (Excerpt)

The cell *Myxococcus xanthus* responds to starvation by initiating a cycle that culminates with the cell forming spore-filled fruiting bodies. This developmental cycle, which is dependent upon changes in gene expression, ensures cell sporulation at the appropriate time and place. Thousands of cells are affected by this process. Recent studies strongly suggest that NtrC-like activators are a crucial component of the complex regulatory controls of

M. xanthus' developmental program. Twelve NtrC activators were found to be most important in the process.[1] These findings led to further research that examined the specific developmental moments at which NtrC proteins activate specific sets of genes throughout the process.[2] In addition, Garza and others[3] identified two inductive components of the early part of the developmental process.

References

1. Gorski L, Kaiser D. Targeted mutagenesis of σ^{54} activator proteins in *Myxococcus xanthus.* J of Bacteriol 1998;180:5896-5905.
2. Keseler IM, Kaiser D. An early A-signal-dependent gene in *Myxococcus xanthus* has a σ^{54}-like promoter. J of Bacteriol 1995;177:4638-44.
3. Garza AG, Pollack JS, Harris BZ, Lee A, Keseler IM, Licking EF, Singer M. SdeK is required for early fruiting body development in *Myxococcus xanthus.* J of Bacteriol 1998;180:4628-37.

(4) Abstract

An **abstract**—a concise summary of a technical article—is a standard part of many assignments in the natural sciences. In addition, many scientific indexes include abstracts so that researchers can determine whether an article is of use to them. In the natural sciences, the purpose of an abstract is to inform readers about the goals, methods, and results of the original article.

Close-up: Abstracts

There are two kinds of abstracts:

1. An **indicative abstract** gives a general overview of an article. Its purpose is to help readers decide whether they want (or need) to read the original article.

(continued)

Abstracts (continued)

2. An **informative abstract,** which contains more specific and technical details than an indicative abstract, provides readers with detailed and specific information. Readers can often obtain essential information from an informative abstract without actually reading the article itself.

You begin writing an abstract after you have finished writing your paper. When writing an abstract, follow the organization of your paper, devoting a sentence or two to each of its major sections. State the purpose, the method of research, results, and conclusions in the order in which they appear in the paper, but include only essential information. Keep in mind that abstracts in the sciences do not use quotations or paraphrases.

The following abstract was written as part of the assignment on page 564.

Sample Abstract

This project used Wisconsin Fast Plants to determine the effect of gibberellic acid on plants. Gibberellic acid is a growth hormone that stimulates a plant to grow taller by elongation of internode length. The research tested the hypothesis that plants that are treated with gibberellic acid will grow taller than plants that are untreated, and the internode length on treated plants will be longer than that on untreated plants. Results supported this hypothesis: the internode length on treated plants was longer than that on untreated plants. Furthermore, even the dwarf plants that were treated with gibberellic acid grew longer, reaching almost the same height as the control standard plants by the last day of measurement. Therefore, the results of this experiment indicate that gibberellic acid can stimulate the growth of plants by elongation of internode length, though not by internode number.

(5) Biographical Essay

In a science or math course, an instructor may ask you to research and write an essay about a historical figure. When writing your essay, try to relate the information you find about your subject to the work you have been doing in the course: for example, how do Mendel's ideas about genetics connect to your work on heredity, or how have Copernicus's theories about the solar system influenced the way astronomy is studied today?

Assignment (Geometry)

Select a well-known historical figure in geometry whose life and work we have discussed in class, and find out as much as possible about that person's work. Then, write a biographical essay in which you present his or her contributions to geometry and discuss how these ideas relate to what you have studied in this course. Use only information learned in this course (no outside sources).

Sample Biographical Essay (Excerpt)

Jean-Victor Poncelet was born in Metz, northeastern France, in July 1788. He studied calculus with Gaspard Monge at the École Polytechnique and then joined the army as a lieutenant of engineers, following Napoleon to Russia. While he was a prisoner of war in Saratoff on the River Volga, he began researching projective geometry, investigating the projective properties of figures later in his great work *Trailé des Propriétés Projectives des Figures*.

Projective geometry is a branch of geometry concerned with properties of geometric figures that retain their character. The basic elements of projective geometry are points, lines, and planes, and the following statements are assumed: (1) two points lie in a unique line; (2) three points not on the same line determine a plane; (3) two lines in a plane intersect in a point; (4) two planes intersect in a line; and (5) three planes not containing the same line intersect in a point. The concept of parallel does not exist in projective geometry because any pair of distinct lines intersects in a point, and if these lines are parallel in the sense of Euclidean geometry, then their point of intersection is at infinity. The project plane is the plane that includes the ideal line or line at infinity, consisting of all such ideal points.

25c Conventions of Style, Format, and Documentation

(1) Style and Format

Because writing in the sciences focuses on the experiment, not on those conducting the experiment, writers often use the passive voice. For example, in a lab report, you would say, "The mixture was heated for forty-five minutes" rather than "I heated the mixture for forty-five minutes." Another stylistic convention concerns verb tense: a conclusion or a statement of generally accepted fact should be in the present tense ("Objects in motion *tend* to stay in motion"); a summary of a study, however, should be in the past tense ("Watson and Crick *discovered* the structure of DNA"). Finally, note that direct quotations are seldom used in scientific papers.

Because you are writing to inform or persuade other scientists, you should write clearly and concisely. Remember to use technical terms only when they are necessary to convey your meaning. Too many terms can make your paper difficult to understand—even for scientists familiar with your discipline. (Sometimes a scientific paper will include a glossary that lists and defines terms that may be unfamiliar to readers.)

Visuals are an important part of scientific papers. Be careful to place tables as close to your discussion of them as possible and to number and label any type of illustration or diagram so you can refer to it in your text. Keep in mind that each scientific discipline prescribes formats for tables and other visuals and the way they are to be presented. Therefore, you cannot use a single format for all your scientific writing.

See 29d

Remember that different scientific journals follow different conventions of style and use different paper formats and documentation styles. For example, although the *CBE Manual* governs the overall presentation of papers in biology, the *Journal of Immunology* might have a format different from that of the *Journal of Parasitology*. (The *CBE Manual* lists the different journals that use their own paper formats.) Your instructor may ask you to prepare your paper according to the style sheet of a journal to which you could submit your work. Although publication may seem a remote possibility to you, following a style sheet reminds you that writing in the sciences involves writing for a specific audience.

You should also learn the various abbreviations by which journals are referred to in the reference sections of science papers. For example, *The American Journal of Physiology* is abbreviated "Amer J Physiol," and *The Journal of Physiological Chemistry* is abbreviated "J of Physiol Chemistry." (Note that in CSE style, the abbreviated forms of journal titles are *not* underlined in the reference list.)

(2) Documentation

Documentation style varies from one scientific discipline to another; even within a given discipline, documentation style may vary from one journal to another. For this reason, ask your instructor which documentation style is required. Many disciplines in the sciences use a number-reference format. For instance, electrical engineers use the format of the Institute for Electronics and Electrical Engineers, chemists use the format of the American Chemical Society, and mathematicians use the format of the American Mathematical Society.

25d Avoiding Plagiarism

In the sciences, it is especially important to acknowledge the work of others who contributed to your research results. If many people contribute to a research project, the work of each one must be properly cited. Falsifying data or using the experimental results, computer codes, chemical formulas, graphs, images, ideas, or words of others without proper acknowledgment is particularly serious because it undermines the integrity of your work.

If you need more information about what constitutes plagiarism in the sciences or how to cite the work of individual collaborators in a research report, be sure to check with your instructor.

25e Using Visuals and Technology

During the prewriting and drafting stages of your writing, much of your work will involve representing data visually—for example, compiling tables or flow charts. (Your word processor's drawing tools can help you design the visuals you need.) During the drafting process, these visuals can help you organize information and keep track of complex cause-and-effect relationships.

You can also use your computer to help you organize your notes into files that correspond to the typical sections of a document—for example, Abstract, Introduction, Methods, Results, and References. Later on, you can expand each section and combine sections to form the final version of your document.

More than in other disciplines, research and writing in the natural and applied sciences are done collaboratively. Multiple authors for lab reports, research reports, and grants are common, and a number of electronic strategies—for example, the Comment and Track Changes features in a word processor, email, online real-time discussion, and file storage on a local network or shared computer—can make this collaborative process easier.

25f Research Sources

Although much scientific research takes place in the laboratory or in the natural world, it is also important that scientists know how to do library research. Literature surveys allow scientists to discover what research has already been done; they can then conduct meaningful experiments that build upon that research, prove or disprove a theory, or solve a problem. Scientists then explain the process so that others can reproduce their results, communicate their findings, and add to the body of scientific knowledge. Much of this research is collaborative. It is not uncommon for a group of students (or a student and faculty member) to work on different aspects of a research problem in the laboratory or in the library and then jointly report on the results.

As in the social sciences, it is vital for scientists to have the most recent information available. Books may provide background information, define terms, and assess what has been discovered in the past, but scholarly journal articles, conference proceedings, technical reports, and research reports are essential for locating the most up-to-date and relevant literature.

Some of the largest and most comprehensive databases are those that cover the journal literature of the sciences. *Science Citation Index* covers all the natural and applied sciences. Others cover specific disciplines: *PubMed* (medicine), *Biological Abstracts* (biology), and *Chemical Abstracts* (chemistry) are examples of specialized databases that are also available in print.

Close-up: Using Scientific Databases

Some science databases are complex and difficult to use. If you need help, ask for assistance at your library's reference desk.

(1) Reference Books

Because scientists are interested in the number of times and the variety of sources in which a study is cited, they frequently consult the *Science Citation Index*. The following reference sources, many of which are available on DVD, on CD-ROM, in online databases, or in print, are used in various science disciplines.

Chemistry

Analytical Abstracts
Chemical Abstracts
Comprehensive Natural Products Chemistry
Concise Encyclopedia of Biochemistry and Molecular Biology
Dictionary of Organic Compounds
Facts on File Dictionary of Chemistry
History and Use of Our Earth's Chemical Elements: A Reference
How to Find Chemical Information: A Guide for Practicing Chemists
Information Sources in Chemistry
Kirk-Othmer Encyclopedia of Chemical Technology
McGraw-Hill Encyclopedia of Chemistry
World of Chemistry

Computer Science

Dictionary of Computer Science, Engineering, and Technology
Encyclopedia of Computer Science
Encyclopedia of Computers and Computing History

Earth Sciences

Abstracts of North American Geology
Annotated Bibliography of Economic Geology
Bibliography and Index of Geology
Encyclopedia of Atmospheric Sciences
Encyclopedia of Prehistory
Encyclopedia of Weather and Climate
Geological Abstracts
Geophysical Abstracts
Guide to USGS Publications
Macmillan Encyclopedia of Earth Sciences
Oxford Companion to the Earth
Weather America

Engineering

Applied Mechanics Reviews
Applied Science and Technology Index
Chemical Engineers' Condensed Encyclopedia of Process Equipment
Encyclopedia of Materials: Science and Technology
Engineering Index
Government Reports Announcements and Index (NTIS)
Handbook of Mechanical Engineering Calculations
Macmillan Encyclopedia of Energy
Marks' Standard Handbook for Mechanical Engineers
Pollution Abstracts
Selected Water Resources Abstracts
Standard Handbook of Environmental Engineering
Wiley Encyclopedia of Electrical and Electronics Engineering

General Science

American Men and Women of Science
Applied Science and Technology Index
Biographical Directory of Women in Science
CRC Handbook of Chemistry and Physics
Dictionary of Scientific Biography
Gale Encyclopedia of Science
General Science Index
Instruments of Science: An Historical Encyclopedia
McGraw-Hill Encyclopedia of Science and Technology
The Nobel Scientists: A Biographical Encyclopedia
Reader's Guide to the History of Science
Reference Sources in Science, Engineering, Medicine, and Agriculture
Science and Its Times
Sciences of the Earth: An Encyclopedia of Events, People, and Phenomena
Scientific American Science Desk Reference
Scientific and Technical Information Sources
Van Nostrand's Scientific Encyclopedia

Life Sciences

Bibliography of Agriculture
Biological Abstracts
Biological and Agricultural Index
Biology Digest
Concise Encyclopedia of Biochemistry and Molecular Biology
Cumulative Index to Nursing and Allied Health Literature
Dictionary of Genetics
Encyclopedia of Biodiversity
Encyclopedia of Bioethics
Encyclopedia of Endangered Species
Encyclopedia of Evolution
Encyclopedia of Genetics

Encyclopedia of Public Health
Environment Abstracts Annual
Gale Encyclopedia of Medicine
Grzimek's Animal Life Encyclopedia
Hospital Literature Index
Index Medicus
International Dictionary of Medicine and Biology
Smithsonian Book of North American Mammals
Zoological Record

Mathematics

Computer and Control Abstracts
CRC Concise Encyclopedia of Mathematics
CRC Standard Mathematical Tables and Formulae
Current Index to Statistics
Encyclopedia of Mathematics
Encyclopedia of Statistical Sciences
Encyclopedic Dictionary of Mathematics
Mathematical Reviews
Notable Mathematicians: From Ancient Times to the Present
Notable Women in Mathematics: A Biographical Dictionary
Penguin Desk Encyclopedia of Science and Mathematics
Recognizing Excellence in the Mathematical Sciences: An International Compilation of Awards, Prizes, and Recipients

Physics and Astronomy

Cambridge Astronomy Dictionary
Compact NASA Atlas of the Solar System
CRC Handbook of Chemistry and Physics
Dictionary of Physics
Encyclopedia of Astronomy and Astrophysics
Encyclopedia of the Atomic Age
Encyclopedia of Chemical Physics and Physical Chemistry
Handbook of Physical Quantities
History of Astronomy: An Encyclopedia
Information Sources in Physics
Macmillan Encyclopedia of Physics
Physics Abstracts
Q is for Quantum: An Encyclopedia of Particle Physics
Solid State and Superconductivity Abstracts

(2) Databases for Computer Searches

Helpful databases for research in the sciences include: *BIOSIS; Agricola; Aquatic Sciences and Fisheries Abstracts; Columbia Earthscape; CAB Abstracts; CINAHL; Compendex; NTIS; Inspec; PubMed; MATHSCI; Life Sciences Collection; GEOREF; Chemical Abstracts; Environmental Sciences and Pollution Management Abstracts; Science Citation Index; Wildlife and Ecology Studies Worldwide; GEOBASE; OceanBase;* and *Zoological*

Record Online. Check with a reference librarian about the availability of these and other databases in your library.

(3) Web Sites

For links to Web sites for specific natural and applied sciences disciplines, go to http://kirsznermandell.wadsworth.com ▶ *The Wadsworth Handbook* ▶ Chapter 25 ▶ Natural and Applied Sciences Web Sites.

(4) Other Sources of Information

Opportunities for hands-on research outside the library vary widely because of the many ways in which scientists can gather information. In agronomy, for example, researchers collect soil samples; in toxicology, they test air or water quality. In marine biology, they might conduct research in a particular aquatic environment, and in chemistry, they conduct experiments to identify an unknown substance. Scientists also conduct surveys: epidemiologists study the spread of communicable diseases, and cancer researchers question populations to determine how environmental or dietary factors influence the likelihood of contracting cancer. Finally, the Internet is an important source of up-to-date scientific information. In fact, scientists have used the Internet for years to communicate and share information about their research.

STUDENT WRITER AT WORK

Writing about Literature

In the following excerpt from an introductory literature paper comparing two poems, the student writer has not observed all the conventions of writing about literature. Read the excerpt carefully, and then use the Writing about Literature checklist on pages 516–17 to help you identify and correct the student writer's errors.

Poets Sylvia Plath and Ted Hughes were married in 1956, and each later wrote a poem about their wedding. In A Pink Wool Knitted Dress (1996), Hughes spoke hopefully about his wedding day, describing his bride as "transfigured. / So slender and new . . ." (40-41). In contrast, Plath's earlier poem, Wreath for a Bridal (1956), conveyed less optimistic feelings, and the poet's voice is dark and depressed. Clearly, the two poets have very different views of their wedding day. For example, both Plath and Hughes described the setting of the wedding, but they did so in very different tones. Plath used many painful images. "Crouched daylong in cloisters of stinging nettle / They lie, cut-grass assaulting each separate sense" (7-8). Here, Plath described the feeling of being trapped in a small and painful place with poison stinging and assaulting her. In my opinion, this is not an image that the average woman would associate with her wedding day. In contrast, the initial image that Hughes presented—one of purity and peacefulness—seems more appropriate to me. Here the poet says, "Before anything had smudged anything / You stood at the altar" (2-3). Hughes depicted a scene of freshness and unspoiled natural beauty, while Plath spoke of the painful, trapped feeling that marriage brought to her. This and other differences in these two poems suggest that Plath and Hughes had different views of their marriage as well as of their wedding day.

PART 5

Developing Strategies for Academic Success

Chapter 26

Ten Habits of Successful Students

Frequently Asked Questions

What tools can I use to help me manage my time? (p. 578)
What is the best way to study? (p. 580)
What college services can help me? (p. 586)

As you have probably already observed, the students who are most successful in school are not always the brightest students. In fact, successful students have *learned* to be successful: they have developed specific strategies for success, and they apply those strategies to their education. If you take the time, you can learn the habits of successful students and apply them to your own college education—and, later on, to your career.

26a Learn to Manage Your Time Effectively

College makes many demands on your time. It is hard, especially at first, to balance studying, course work, family life, friendships, and a job. But if you don't take control of your schedule, it will take control of you; if you don't learn to manage your time, you will always be behind, struggling to catch up.

Fortunately, there are two tools that can help you manage your time: a **personal organizer** and a **monthly calendar.** Of course, simply buying an organizer and a calendar will not solve your time-management problems—you have to use them effectively and regularly.

Carry your organizer with you at all times, and post your calendar in a prominent place (perhaps above your desk or next to your phone). Remember to record *in both places* school-related deadlines, appointments, and reminders (every due date, study group meeting, conference appointment, and exam) and outside responsibilities, such as work hours and medical appointments. Be sure to record tasks and dates as soon as you learn of them; if you don't write something down immediately, you are likely to forget it. (If you make an entry in your organizer while you are in class, be sure to copy it onto calendar when you get back from school.)

You can also use your organizer to help you plan a study schedule, as illustrated in Figure 26.1. You do this by blocking out times to study or to complete assignment-related tasks—such as a library database search for a research paper—in addition to appointments and deadlines. (It is a good idea to make these entries in pencil so you can adjust your schedule as new responsibilities arise.) If you have a study schedule, you will be less likely to procrastinate—and therefore less likely to become overwhelmed.

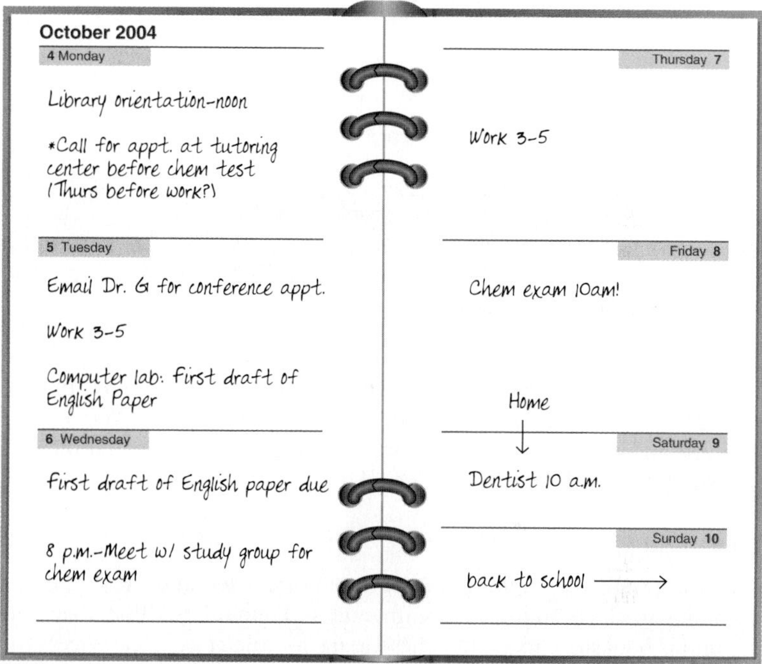

Figure 26.1 Sample organizer pages for one week.

http://kirsznermandell.wadsworth.com

Computer Tip: Using Electronic Organizers

If you prefer, you can keep your schedule on your computer (or even on your cell phone). For example, *Microsoft Outlook* enables you to set up a calendar/organizer in day-, week-, or month-at-a-glance formats (see Figure 26.2). Once you have set up your calendar and organizer pages, you can easily add and delete entries, move appointments and reminders from one day to another, and print out pages.

(continued)

Using electronic organizers (continued)

Calendar . October 04-October 10

Monday, October 04
12:00pm 1:00pm Library orientation

Thursday, October 07
3:00pm 5:00pm Work

Tuesday, October 05
3:00pm 5:00pm Work

Friday, October 08
Home
10:00am 11:00am Chem exam!

Wednesday, October 06
8:00pm 9:30pm Meet w/study group for chem. exam

Saturday, October 09
Home
10:00am 11:00am Dentist

Sunday, October 10
Home
12:00pm Back to school

September 2004 | October 2004

Due Date	TaskPad
Mon 9/8/2004	Call for appt. at tutoring center ...
Tue 9/9/2004	Computer lab: First draft of Engl...
Tue 9/9/2004	Email Dr. G for conference appt.
Wed 9/10/2004	First draft of English paper due

Figure 26.2 ***Microsoft Outlook*** **calendar page.**

Remember: your college years can be a very stressful time, but although some degree of stress is inevitable, it can be kept in check. If you are an organized person, you will be better able to handle the pressures of a college workload.

Exercise 1

Buy a monthly calendar and a personal organizer, and fill in the upcoming week's deadlines, appointments, and reminders. (Note that your campus bookstore may offer these items for sale at reduced prices—or even distribute them at no cost.) Bring both the calendar and the organizer to class, and exchange them with another student's. Are your classmate's entries similar to yours? How do you account for any major differences you notice? Do you have too many entries? too few? Edit your calendar and organizer pages to reflect any new insights you have gained from this exercise. Then, add graphic elements (underlining, boxes, and so on) to highlight particularly important items.

26b Put Studying First

To be a successful student, you need to understand that studying is something you do *regularly*, not right before an exam. You also need to know that studying does not mean just memorizing facts; it also means reading, rereading, and discussing ideas until you understand them.

To make studying a regular part of your day, set up a study space that includes everything you need (supplies, good light, a comfortable chair) and does not include anything you do not need (clutter, distractions). Then, set up a tentative study schedule. Try to designate at least two hours each day to complete assignments due right away, to work on those due later on, and to reread class notes. When you have exams and papers, you can adjust your schedule accordingly.

Close-up: Understanding Your Learning Style

See 2a2–3

Some students prefer to study alone; others prefer to study in groups. Some students learn best from reading material, highlighting and annotating extensively or even recopying their notes. Still others are **aural learners,** who learn most effectively by listening to instructors or other students (or to taped lectures), or **visual learners,** who understand concepts best when they can see (or draw) images. Understanding what kind of learner you are will help you achieve your goals as a student.

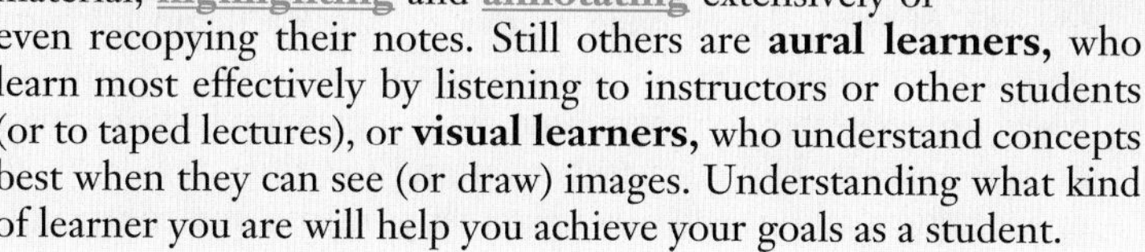

Successful students often form study groups, and this is a strategy you should use whenever you can—particularly in a course you find challenging. A study group of four or five students who meet regularly (not just the night before an exam) can make studying more focused and effective as well as less stressful. By discussing concepts with your classmates, you can try out your ideas and get feedback, clarify complex concepts, and formulate questions for your instructor.

Checklist: Doing Collaborative Work

Working collaboratively—in a study group, for example—requires some degree of organization. To get the most out of collaborative work, you need to set some ground rules for the group you are working with.

- ☐ Meet regularly.
- ☐ Decide in advance who will be responsible for particular tasks.
- ☐ Set deadlines.

(continued)

Doing collaborative work (continued)

- ☐ Listen when someone else is speaking.
- ☐ Don't reject other people's ideas and suggestions without considering them very carefully.
- ☐ Have one person take notes to keep a record of the group's activities.
- ☐ Take stock of problems and progress at regular intervals.
- ☐ Be mindful of other students' learning styles and special needs.

Exercise 2

1. Set up a study space in your home or your dorm room, and then draw a diagram of this space.
2. Plan a tentative study schedule for the next two weeks.
3. Set up a study group of at least three students to review material for one of your classes once or twice a week. (Begin by getting phone numbers and email addresses from everyone in your proposed group.) After your first exam, write a paragraph evaluating the group's success. Did all members attend meetings regularly, keep up with the readings and other class assignments, and contribute to the group's discussions? Consider changing the group's size, membership, schedule, or routine to help you solve any problems you observe.

26c Be Sure You Understand School and Course Requirements

To succeed in school, you need to know what is expected of you—and, if you are not sure, to ask.

When you first arrived at school, you probably received a variety of orientation materials—a student handbook, library handouts, and so on—that set forth the rules and policies of your school. Read these documents carefully (if you have not already done so), and be sure you understand what is expected of you. If you do not understand, ask your peer counselor or your adviser for clarification.

You also need to know the specific requirements of each course you take. In a sense, education is a series of contracts between you and your instructors, and each course syllabus explains the terms of a particular contract. In a syllabus, you learn an instructor's policies about attendance and lateness, assignments and deadlines, plagiarism, and classroom etiquette. In addition, a syllabus may explain penalties for late assignments or missed quizzes, explain how assignments are graded, tell how much each assignment is worth, or note additional requirements, such as field work or group projects. Requirements vary significantly from course to course, so read each syllabus (as well as any supplementary handouts) carefully.

ESL Tip

If you did not attend high school in the United States, some of your instructors' class policies and procedures may seem strange to you. To learn more about the way US college classes are run, read the syllabus for each of your courses and talk to your instructors about your concerns. You may also find it helpful to talk to older students with cultural backgrounds similar to your own; they can tell you what aspects of US classroom culture were particularly surprising to them and give you advice about how to cope.

As the semester progresses, your instructors will probably give you additional information about their expectations. For example, before an exam you will be told what material will be covered, how much time you will have to complete the test, and whether you will be expected to write an essay or fill in an answer sheet that will be graded electronically. When a paper is assigned, you may be given specific information about its content, length, and due date as well as about its format (font size, line spacing, and margin width, for example). If your instructor does not give you this information, make sure you find out what is expected of you.

Close-up: Creating a Portfolio

Some instructors may require that you submit a **portfolio,** a collection of your classwork in print or electronic form. Portfolios may be reviewed and graded at the end of the term or at regular intervals throughout the term. If your instructor requires you to assemble a portfolio of written work, be sure to find out exactly what material is to be included (for example, only the final draft or earlier drafts as well?) and what format is required for each assignment.

Exercise 3

Review all the course materials you have been given so far in one of your classes. Make a list of ten important questions that are answered in these handouts (for example, "What is the date of the midterm exam?" or "Are late papers always penalized?"). Then, give your list of questions to a classmate, and use your handouts to help you answer your classmate's list of questions. If you are unable to answer some of the questions on this list, be sure to find out the answers from your instructor.

26d Be an Active Learner in the Classroom

Education is not about sitting passively in class and waiting for information and ideas to be given to you. It is up to you to be an active participant in your own education.

First, take as many small classes as you can. These classes enable you to interact with other students and with your instructor. If a large course has recitation sections, be sure to attend these regularly, even if they are not required. Also, be sure to take as many classes as possible that require writing. Good writing skills are essential to your success as a student (and as a college graduate entering the workforce), and you will need all the practice you can get.

Take responsibility for your education by attending class regularly and arriving on time. Listen attentively, and take careful, complete notes. (Try to review these notes later with other students to make sure you have not missed anything important.) Do your homework on time, and keep up with the reading. When you read an assignment, use active reading techniques, interacting with the text instead of just looking at what is on the page. If you have time, read beyond the assignment, looking on the Internet and in books, magazines, and newspapers for related information.

See Ch 2a

As important as it is to listen and take notes in class, it is just as important (particularly in small classes and recitations) to participate in class discussions: to ask and answer questions, volunteer opinions, and give helpful feedback to other students. By participating in such discussions, you learn more about the subject matter being discussed, and you also learn to consider other points of view, to test your ideas, and to respect the ideas of others.

ESL Tip

Especially in small classes, US instructors usually expect students to participate in class discussion. If you feel nervous about speaking up in class, you might start by expressing your support of a classmate's opinion.

Exercise 4

1. Working in a group of three or four students, brainstorm to devise some additional active learning strategies.
2. Consulting your class notes if necessary, work with your group to develop a list of four or five questions you could ask your instructor in order to get additional information about the topics covered in the previous day's class. (Be sure to phrase the questions so they do not elicit simple yes or no answers.)

26e Be an Active Learner Outside the Classroom

Taking an active role in your education is also important outside the classroom. Do not be afraid to approach your instructors; take advantage of their office hours, and keep in touch with them by email. Get to know your major adviser well, and be sure he or she knows who you are and where your academic interests lie. Make appointments, ask questions, and explore possible solutions to problems: this is how you learn.

ESL Tip

Visiting your instructors during office hours is a good idea. These visits give you a chance to ask questions about your course assignments and lectures, and they can also help you establish relationships with your instructors. Such relationships will be helpful in the future if you have a problem with a course or need a letter of recommendation. In many cases, you can visit your instructors during their office hours without an appointment. Check your course syllabi to find out when office hours are and whether or not appointments are required.

Another way to become an active learner is to become part of your school community. Read your school newspaper, check the Web site regularly, join clubs, and apply for internships. This participation can help you develop new interests and friendships as well as enhance your education.

Close-up: Finding Internships

Many businesses, nonprofit organizations, and government agencies offer internships (paid or unpaid) to qualified students. These internships, which can last for a summer, a single term, or an entire academic year, give students the opportunity to learn about a particular career or field of study while earning college credit. Internships may also offer the chance to experience life in another part of the country—or in another part of the world. If your school does not have an office that coordinates internships, ask your academic adviser, a reference librarian, or your career services personnel for help.

Finally, participate in the life of your community outside your school. Take service learning courses, if they are offered at your school, or volunteer at a local school or social agency. As successful students know, education is more than just attending classes.

Exercise 5

1. If you do not already have your instructors' and advisers' email addresses in your email address book, enter them now, along with their office phone numbers. (If you own a cell phone, enter the numbers in your phone book.)
2. Make a list of the extracurricular activities you participate in at school. Next, list three activities you would *like* to participate in. For each of these three activities, list all the benefits you might expect to gain from participating. Then, write a sentence explaining how you can become involved.
3. In a paragraph, describe your ideal internship—one that would not only prepare you for your chosen career but would also be enjoyable and perhaps even exciting.

26f Take Advantage of College Services

Colleges and universities offer students a wide variety of support services. Most students will need help of one kind or another at some point during their college careers; if help is available, it makes sense to use it.

For example, if you are struggling with a particular course, you can go to the tutoring service offered by your school's academic support center or by an individual department. Often, the tutors are students who have done well in the course, and their perspective will be very helpful. If you need help with writing or revising a paper, you can make an appointment with the writing lab, where tutors will give you advice (but will *not* rewrite or edit your paper for you). If you are having trouble deciding on what courses to take or what to major in, you can see your academic adviser. If you are having trouble adjusting to college life, your peer counselor or (if you live in a dorm) your resident adviser may be able to help you. Finally, if you have a personal or family problem you would rather not discuss with another student, you can make an appointment at your school's counseling center, where you can get advice from professionals who understand student problems.

ESL Tip

Many ESL students find using the writing lab (sometimes called a writing center) very helpful. Most writing labs provide assistance with assignments for any course, and they often assist with writing job application letters and résumés. Tutors can provide you with help in brainstorming for topics or ideas for your paper; planning your paper's organization; drafting various sections of your paper; and revising, editing, and proofreading. Many writing labs have tutors who specialize in working with ESL students.

Many other services are available—for example, at your school's computer center, job placement service, and financial aid office. Your academic adviser or instructors can tell you where to find the help you need, but it is up to you to make the appointment.

Exercise 6

Working with another student, draw a simple map of your school's campus that identifies the location (or locations) of each of the following college services:

- Tutoring center
- Writing lab
- Computer lab
- Academic advising
- Counseling center

- Student health center
- Your major's department offices
- Career services office
- Financial aid office
- Bookstore
- Parking lots

26g Use the Library

As more and more material becomes available on the Internet, you may begin to think of your college library as outdated or even obsolete. But learning to use the library is an important part of your education.

The library has a lot to offer. First, the library can provide a quiet place to study—something you may need if you have a large family or noisy roommates. The library also contains materials that cannot be found online—rare books, special collections, audiovisual materials—as well as electronic databases that contain material you will not find on the free Internet.

Finally, the library is the place where you have access to the experience and expert knowledge of your school's reference librarians. These professionals can answer questions, guide your research, and point you to sources that you might never have found on your own.

Exercise 7

Visit your school library. Arrange for a library assistant to give you a tour and to introduce you to the library's print and electronic resources. Ask questions, take notes, and be sure to take copies of handouts about the library's hours and services. Also, find out the names of the reference librarians who work with students in the courses you are taking. In class, compare notes with other students; if you still have questions about how to use the library, ask your instructor where to go for additional help.

26h Use Technology

Today, technological competence is essential to success in college. For this reason, it makes sense to develop good word-processing skills and to be comfortable with the Internet. You should also know how to send and receive email from your university account as well as how to attach files to your email. Beyond the basics, you should learn how to manage the files you download, how to evaluate Web sites, and how to use the electronic resources of your library. You might also find it helpful to know how to scan documents (containing images as well as text) and how to paste these files into your documents.

See Ch. 14

If you do not have these skills, you need to locate campus services that will help you get them. Workshops and online tutorials may be available through your school library or campus computing services, and individual assistance on software and hardware use is available in computer labs.

http://kirsznermandell.wadsworth.com

Computer Tip: Emailing Your Instructor

If you use email to contact your instructor, be aware that the same etiquette you would use in a face-to-face setting applies online. You can enhance your credibility by including a specific request or question in the subject line, by addressing your instructor in the same way he or she prefers to be addressed in the classroom, and by including your name at the end of the email, particularly when your email address does not clearly indicate your identity. Finally, be sure to check your message for grammatical and mechanical errors.

Part of being technologically savvy in college involves being aware of the online services your campus has to offer. For example, many campuses rely on customizable information-management systems called **portals.** Not unlike commercial services, such as Yahoo! or America Online, a portal (see Figure 26.3) requires you to log in with a user ID and password to access services such as locating and contacting your academic adviser and viewing your class schedule and grades.

In addition to these online services, many campuses have course management software, such as *WebCT* or *Blackboard,* that allows instructors to create a Web-based component to their courses. This can include posting the syllabus and copies of lectures in HTML, word-processed, or *PowerPoint* form; creating online quizzes and exams; requiring virtual class discussion on bulletin boards and in chat rooms; and requiring students to submit all coursework electronically through email attachments or through digital drop boxes.

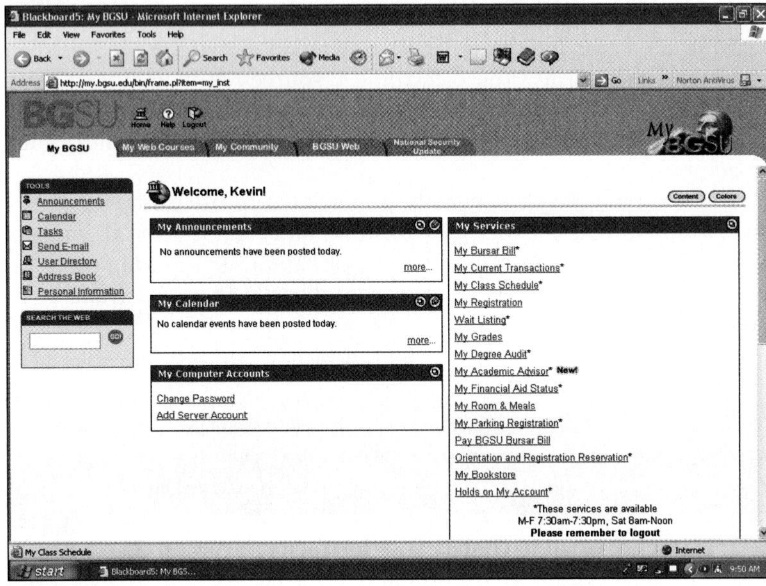

Figure 26.3 Portal at Bowling Green State University.

If your course has an online component, (or if it is a true distance course where you do not meet face to face), it is important to manage your time in the same way you would for a traditional course. This includes regularly logging in to the course to check for announcements and ongoing class discussions; spending the same amount of time on virtual activities as you would on face-to-face activities; and devoting specific periods of time to the course by blocking out time on your calendar and personal organizer for this purpose.

Finally, you need to know not only how to use technology to enhance a project—for example, how to use *PowerPoint* for an oral presentation or *Excel* to make a table—but also *when* to use technology (and when not to).

Exercise 8

1. Compare your computer skills with those of a classmate. Are your skills roughly equivalent, or is one of you considerably more proficient or more confident? How do you account for any differences?
2. What computer skill would you most like to acquire? Write a paragraph explaining why you want to learn this skill and how you believe it will help you. Then, find out (from an instructor, the computer lab, or a more computer-savvy classmate) exactly how and where you can learn that skill.

26i Make Contacts—and Use Them

One of the most important things you can do for yourself is to make academic and professional contacts that you can use during college and after you graduate.

Your first contacts are your classmates. Be sure you have the names, phone numbers, and email addresses of at least two students in each of your classes. These contacts will be useful to you if you miss class, if you need help understanding your notes, or if you want to start a study group.

You should also build relationships with students with whom you participate in college activities, such as the college newspaper or the tutoring center. These people are likely to share your goals and interests, and so you may want to get feedback from them as you move on to choose a major, consider further education, and make career choices.

Finally, develop relationships with your instructors, particularly those in your major area of study. One of the things cited most often in studies of successful students is the importance of **mentors,** experienced individuals whose advice you trust. Long after you leave college, you will find these contacts useful. Keep in touch; it will pay off.

Close-up: Finding Mentors

The most obvious way to locate a mentor is to develop a relationship with an instructor you admire, perhaps taking several courses with him or her. Alternatively, you can develop a close professional relationship with a supervisor at work or in an internship. You should also consider the advantages of working for one of your professors—as a research assistant, in a work-study job, or even as a babysitter or petsitter. A professor who knows you well will be likely to take a special interest in your education and in your career.

Exercise 9

1. Identify a potential mentor, and write a letter that you could send to that person. In your letter, explain why you would like to work in his or her field and ask for advice about how to achieve your goals.
2. Write a profile of your ideal mentor. What personal qualities, education, experience, and professional status should this person have?

How would you expect this person to help you? (Consider your short-term as well as your long-term goals, and consider the personal, educational, and employment decisions you would need to make in order to achieve these goals.)

26j Be a Lifelong Learner

Your education should not stop when you graduate from college, and this is something you should be aware of from the first day you set foot on campus. To be a successful student, you need to be a lifelong learner.

Get in the habit of reading newspapers; know what is happening in the world outside school. Talk to people outside the college community so that you don't forget there are issues that have nothing to do with courses and grades. Never miss an opportunity to learn: try to get in the habit of attending plays and concerts sponsored by your school or community and lectures offered at your local library or bookstore.

And think about the life you will lead after college. Think about who you want to be and what you have to do to get there. This is what successful students do.

Exercise 10

1. Find an article in a newspaper that has direct bearing on your school or your field of study. Write a one-paragraph summary of this article. (If you prefer, you can write an analysis of a relevant photograph.)
2. Study the classified ads in a newspaper, and find two advertisements: one for a job for which you believe you qualify right now, and one for your "dream job." (If you cannot locate appropriate ads, write them yourself.)

3. Write your résumé.

Checklist: Becoming a Successful Student

- ☐ Do you have a personal organizer? a calendar? Do you use them regularly?
- ☐ Have you set up a comfortable study space?
- ☐ Have you made a study schedule?

- ☐ Have you joined a study group?
- ☐ Have you read your course syllabi and orientation materials carefully?
- ☐ Are you attending classes regularly and keeping up with your assignments?
- ☐ Do you take advantage of your instructors' office hours?
- ☐ Do you participate in class?
- ☐ Do you participate in college life?
- ☐ Do you know where to get help if you need it?
- ☐ Do you know how to use your college library? Do you use it?
- ☐ Are you satisfied with your level of technological expertise? Do you know where to get additional instruction?
- ☐ Are you trying to make contacts and find mentors?
- ☐ Do you see yourself as a lifelong learner?

Close-up: Ten Habits to Avoid

1. **Procrastination** No matter how tempting it is to postpone studying for a test, writing a paper, making a writing lab appointment, or setting up a meeting with your adviser, you should not procrastinate. To make sure you have enough time to complete a task, you need to find time whenever you can—between classes, at lunch, even while riding on public transportation. If you delay, your responsibilities will eventually catch up to you.
2. **Lateness** To avoid penalties that will hurt your grades, you should hand in assignments on time. You should also do everything you can to take an exam on the day it is given. (Some instructors give a more difficult make-up exam to those who miss a scheduled test.) Finally, try to complete all your semester's coursework on time; request an Incomplete grade only in an emergency.
3. **Cuts** Even if an instructor allows you a certain number of cuts, you should not miss class unless you absolutely have to. If you do miss a class, don't email your instructor and ask, "Did I miss anything?" (The answer to this question is, "Of course you did"; it is your responsibility to find out—by asking classmates and consulting the syllabus—what you missed and to make it up.)
4. **Poor Communication** Regular communication with your course instructors (as well as with lab assistants and recitation

(continued)

Ten habits to avoid (continued)

instructors) is vital to your success in college. Good communication will ensure that you understand what is expected of you and know how to achieve it.

5. **Focus on Grades** Focusing on your grades instead of on your education is a poor strategy for academic success. Instead of asking your instructors (or even yourself), "What do I have to do to get an A in this course?" ask, "How can I improve my understanding of the material?" or "What can I do better?"
6. **Poor Health Habits** Take care of yourself. Eat healthy, regular meals; exercise when you can; avoid drugs and alcohol. If you smoke, stop; if you don't smoke, don't start.
7. **Poor Sleep Habits** Resist the temptation to study (or party) all night. Try to go to sleep and wake up at about the same time each day rather than staying up late and sleeping until noon on the weekends. If you tend to oversleep on school or work days, set two alarms (one of them across the room so that you will have to get out of bed to turn it off). As a last resort, request a wake-up call from a friend.
8. **Inappropriate Behavior** To be a successful student, you need to show proper decorum in the classroom and in instructor conferences. Be polite and respectful, listen when others speak, and don't interrupt. In class, remove your hat, raise your hand when you want to speak, and watch your language. In email, observe the rules of netiquette.

See 13c

9. **Negative Attitudes** Try not to see one poor grade or negative instructor comment as the beginning of a trend that spells failure. Listen to criticism, learn from your mistakes, and take steps to improve.
10. **Overscheduling** College is hard work, but it doesn't have to be torture. Don't sign up for more courses than you can handle or take on more projects than you can reasonably hope to complete, and don't work so many hours at your job that you have no time to study. Take breaks when you need to; schedule some downtime, and use it. Make friends, make time for yourself, reward yourself when you deserve it—and have fun.

Chapter 27

Writing Essay Exams

Frequently Asked Questions

Taking exams is a skill, one you have been developing throughout your life as a student. Although both short-answer and essay exams require you to study, to recall what you know, and to budget your time carefully as you write your answers, only essay questions ask you to synthesize information and to arrange ideas in a series of clear, logically connected sentences and paragraphs. To write an essay examination, or even a paragraph-length answer, you must do more than memorize facts; you must see the relationships among them. In other words, you must think critically about your subject.

Close-up: Writing In-Class Essays

Many of the strategies that can help you write strong responses to essay exams can also help you plan, write, and revise other kinds of in-class essays.

If you are asked to write an in-class essay, follow the steps outlined in this chapter, and be sure you understand exactly what you are being asked to do and how much time you have in which to do it. Keep in mind, however, that in-class essays, unlike essay exams, may be evaluated on their style and structure as well as on their content. This means, for example, that they should have fully developed introductory and concluding paragraphs.

ESL Tip

Writing essay exam answers can be especially stressful because you have a short amount of time to write a thoughtful, accurate, and well-organized essay, using acceptable grammar and mechanics. One way to make this process easier is to have a clear plan before you begin writing. First, decide what information you want to include in your answer and how you want to organize it, and then make an informal outline of your ideas to guide you as you write.

27a Planning an Essay Exam Answer

Because you are under time pressure during an exam, you may be tempted to skip the planning and revision stages of the writing process. But if you write in a frenzy and hand in your exam without a second glance, you are likely to produce a disorganized or even incoherent answer. With careful planning and editing, you can write an answer that demonstrates your understanding of the material.

(1) Review Your Material

Be sure you know beforehand the scope and format of the exam. How much of your text and class notes will be covered—the entire semester's work or only the material presented since the last test? Will you have to answer every question, or will you be able to choose among alternatives? Will the exam be composed entirely of fill-in, multiple-choice, or true/false questions, or will it call for sentence-, paragraph-, or essay-length answers? Will the exam test your ability to recall specific facts, or will it require you to demonstrate your understanding of the course material by drawing conclusions?

All exams challenge you to recall and express in writing what you already know—what you have read, what you have heard in class, what you have reviewed in your notes. Before you take any exam, then, you must study: reread your text and class notes, highlight key points, and perhaps outline particularly important sections of your notes.

Different kinds of exams, however, require different strategies. When you prepare for a short-answer exam, you may memorize facts without analyzing their relationship to one another or their relationship to a body of knowledge as a whole: the definition of *pointillism*, the date of Queen Victoria's death, the formula for a quadratic equation, three reasons for the fall of Rome, two examples of conditioned reflexes, four features of a feudal economy, six steps in the process of synthesizing Vitamin C. When you prepare for an essay exam, however, you must do more than remember bits of information; you must also make connections among ideas.

When you are sure you know what to expect, see if you can anticipate the essay questions your instructor might ask. Try out likely questions on classmates, and see whether you can do some collaborative brainstorming to outline answers to possible questions. If you have time, you might even practice answering one or two in writing.

(2) Consider Your Audience and Purpose

The audience for an exam is the instructor who prepared it. As you read the questions, think about what your instructor has emphasized in class. Keep in mind that your purpose is to demonstrate that you understand the material, not to make clever remarks or introduce irrelevant information. Also, make every effort to use the vocabulary of the particular academic discipline and to follow any discipline-specific stylistic conventions your instructor has discussed.

(3) Read through the Entire Exam

Before you begin to write, read the questions carefully to determine your priorities and your strategy. First, be sure that your copy of the test is complete and that you understand exactly what each question requires. If you need clarification, ask your instructor or proctor for help. Then, plan carefully, deciding how much time you should devote to answering each question. Often, the point value of each question or the number of questions on the exam indicates how much time you should spend on each answer. If an essay question is worth fifty out of one hundred points, for example, you will probably have to spend at least half (and perhaps more) of your time planning, writing, and proofreading your answer.

Next, decide where to start. Responding first to questions whose answers you are sure of is usually a good strategy. This tactic ensures that you will not become bogged down in a question that baffles you, left with too little time to write a strong answer to a question that you understand well. Moreover, starting with the questions that you are sure of can help build your confidence.

(4) Read Each Question Carefully

To write an effective answer, you need to understand the question. As you read any essay question, you may find it helpful to underline key words and important terms.

Sociology: Distinguish among Social Darwinism, instinct theory, and sociobiology, giving examples of each.

Music: Explain how Milton Babbitt used the computer to expand Schoenberg's twelve-tone method.

Philosophy: Define existentialism and identify three influential existentialist works, explaining why they are important.

Look carefully at the wording of each question. If the question calls for a comparison and contrast of two styles of management, a description or analysis of one style, no matter how comprehensive, will not be acceptable. If the question asks for causes and effects, a discussion of causes alone will not do.

Close-up: Key Words in Exam Questions

Pay careful attention to the words used in exam questions.

- Explain
- Compare
- Contrast
- Trace
- Evaluate
- Discuss
- Clarify
- Relate
- Justify
- Analyze
- Interpret
- Describe
- Classify
- Identify
- Illustrate
- Define
- Support
- Summarize

The wording of the question suggests what you should emphasize. For instance, an American history instructor would expect very different answers to the following two exam questions:

- Give a detailed explanation of the major causes of the Great Depression, noting briefly some of the effects of the economic collapse on the United States.
- Give a detailed summary of the effects of the Great Depression on the United States, briefly discussing the major causes of the economic collapse.

Although the preceding questions look alike, the first calls for an essay that stresses *causes*, whereas the second calls for one that stresses *effects*.

ESL Tip

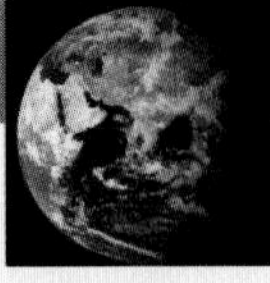

If you don't understand a word or a part of an essay question, ask your instructor for clarification.

(5) Brainstorm to Find Ideas

Once you think you understand the question, you need to find something to say. Begin by **brainstorming,** quickly listing all the relevant ideas you can remember. Then, identify the most important points on your list, and delete the others. A quick review of the exam question and your supporting ideas should lead you toward a workable thesis for your essay answer.

27b Shaping an Essay Exam Answer

Like an essay, an effective exam answer has a definite structure.

(1) Stating a Thesis

Often, you can rephrase the exam question as a thesis statement. For example, the American history exam question "Give a detailed summary of the effects of the Great Depression on the United States, briefly discussing the major causes of the economic collapse" suggests the following thesis statement.

Effective Thesis Statement: The Great Depression, caused by the American government's economic policies, had major political, economic, and social effects on the United States.

An effective thesis statement addresses all aspects of the question but highlights only relevant concerns. The following thesis statements are not effective.

Vague Thesis Statement: The Great Depression, caused largely by profligate spending patterns, had a number of very important results.

Incomplete Thesis Statement: The Great Depression caused major upheaval in the United States.

Irrelevant Thesis Statement: The Great Depression, caused largely by America's poor response to the 1929 stock market crash, had more important consequences than World War II did.

(2) Making an Informal Outline

Because time is limited, you should plan your answer before you write it. Therefore, once you have decided on a suitable thesis, you should make an informal outline of your major points.

On the inside cover of your exam book, or on its last sheet, list your supporting points in the order in which you plan to discuss them. Once you have completed your outline, check it against the exam question to make certain it covers everything the question calls for—and *only* what the question calls for.

An informal outline for an answer to the American history question introduced earlier ("Give a detailed summary of the effects of the Great Depression on the United States, briefly discussing the major causes of the economic collapse") might look like this.

```
    Thesis Statement: The Great Depression, caused by the
American government's economic policies, had major political,
economic, and social effects on the United States.
    Supporting Points:
      Causes
      American economic policies: income poorly distributed,
      factories expanded too much, more goods produced than
      could be purchased.
      Effects
      1. Economic situation worsened—farmers, businesses,
         workers, and stock market all affected.
      2. Roosevelt elected—closed banks, worked with Congress to
         enact emergency measures.
      3. Reform—TVA, AAA, NIRA, etc.
      4. Social Security Act, WPA, PWA
```

27c Writing and Revising an Essay Exam Answer

Referring to your outline, you can now begin to draft your answer. Don't bother crafting an elaborate or unusual **introduction;** your time is precious, and so is your reader's. A simple statement of your thesis that summarizes your answer is your best introductory strategy: this approach is efficient, and it reminds you to address the question directly.

To develop the **body** of the essay, follow your outline point by point, using clear topic sentences and transitions to indicate your progression and to help your instructor see that you are answering the question in full. Such signals, along with parallel sentence structure and repeated key words, make your answer easy to follow.

The most effective **conclusion** for an essay examination is a clear, simple restatement of the thesis or a summary of the essay's main points.

Although essay answers should be complete and detailed, they should not contain irrelevant material. Every unnecessary fact or opinion increases your chance of error, so don't repeat yourself or volunteer unrequested information, and don't express your own feelings or opinions unless such information is specifically asked for. In addition, be sure to support all your general statements with specific examples.

Finally, be sure to leave enough time to revise what you have written. As you reread, try to view your answer objectively. Is your thesis statement clearly worded? Does your essay support your thesis and answer the question? Are your facts correct, and are your ideas presented in a logical order? Review your topic sentences and transitions; check sentence structure and word choice, spelling and punctuation. If a sentence—or even a whole paragraph—seems irrelevant, cross it out. If you suddenly remember something you want to add, you can insert a few additional words with a caret (^). Neatly insert a longer addition at the end of your answer, box it, and label it so your instructor will know where it belongs.

ESL Tip

Because of time pressure, you will probably not be able to write in-class essay exam answers that are as polished as your out-of-class writing. Still, you should do your best to convey your ideas as clearly as you can. Especially in classes outside of the English department, instructors are usually more concerned with the accuracy of the content of your answers than with your writing style. Therefore, instead of wasting time searching for the "perfect" words or phrases, use words and grammatical constructions that are familiar to you. After you have written an answer that you feel is accurate, well developed, and well organized, you can use any remaining time to check your grammar and mechanics.

The one-hour essay answer that appears below follows the outline on page 600. Notice how the student restates the question in her thesis statement and keeps the question in focus by repeating key words like *cause*, *effect*, *result*, *response*, and *impact*.

Effective Essay Exam Answer

Question: Give a detailed summary of the effects of the Great Depression on the United States, briefly discussing the major causes of the economic collapse.

Introduction—thesis statement rephrases exam question

The Great Depression, caused by the American government's economic policies, had major political, economic, and social effects on the United States.

Policies leading to Depression (¶ 2 summarizes causes)

The Depression was precipitated by the stock market crash of October 1929, but its actual causes were more subtle: they lay in the US government's economic policies. First, personal income was not well distributed. Although production rose during the 1920s, the farmers and other workers got too little of the profits; instead, a disproportionate amount of income went to the richest 5 percent of the population. The tax policies at this time made inequalities in income even worse. A good deal of income also went into development of new manufacturing plants. This expansion stimulated the economy but encouraged the production of more goods than consumers could purchase. Finally, during the economic boom of the 1920s, the government did not attempt to limit speculation or impose regulations on the securities market; it also did little to help build up farmers' buying power. Even after the crash began, the government made mistakes: instead of trying to address the country's deflationary economy, the government focused on keeping the budget balanced and making sure the United States adhered to the gold standard.

Transition from causes to effects

The Depression, devastating to millions of individuals, had a tremendous impact on the nation as a whole. Its political, economic, and social consequences were great.

Between October 1929 and Roosevelt's inauguration on March 4, 1932, the economic situation grew worse. Businesses were going bankrupt, banks were failing, and stock prices were falling. Farm prices fell drastically, and hungry farmers were forced to burn their corn to heat their homes. There was massive unemployment, with millions of workers jobless and humiliated, losing skills and self-respect. President Hoover's Reconstruction Finance Corporation made loans available to banks, railroads, and businesses, but Hoover thought state and local funds (not the federal government) should finance public works programs and relief. Confidence in the president declined as the country's economic situation worsened.

Early effects (¶s 4–8 summarize important results in chronological order)

One result of the Depression was the election of Franklin Delano Roosevelt. By the time of his inauguration, most American banks had closed, thirteen million workers were unemployed, and millions of farmers were threatened by foreclosure. Roosevelt's response was immediate: two days after he took office, he closed all the remaining banks and took steps to support the stronger ones with loans and to prevent the weaker ones from reopening. During the first hundred days of his administration, he kept Congress in special session. Under his leadership, Congress enacted emergency measures designed to provide "Relief, Recovery, and Reform."

Additional effects: Roosevelt's emergency measures

In response to the problems caused by the Depression, Roosevelt set up agencies to reform some of the conditions that had helped to cause the Depression in the first place. The Tennessee Valley Authority, created in May 1933, was one of these. Its purposes were to control floods by building new dams and improving old ones and to provide cheap, plentiful electricity. The TVA improved the standard of living of area farmers and drove down the price of power all over the country. The Agricultural Adjustment Administration, created the same

Additional effects: Roosevelt's reform measures

month as the TVA, provided for taxes on basic commodities, with the tax revenues used to subsidize farmers to produce less. This reform measure caused prices to rise.

Additional effects: NIRA, other laws, and so on

Another response to the problems of the Depression was the National Industrial Recovery Act. This act established the National Recovery Administration, an agency that set minimum wages and maximum hours for workers and set limits on production and prices. Other laws passed by Congress between 1935 and 1940 strengthened federal regulation of power, interstate commerce, and air traffic. Roosevelt also changed the federal tax structure to redistribute American income.

Additional effects: Social Security, WPA, and so on

One of the most important results of the Depression was the Social Security Act of 1935, which established unemployment insurance and provided financial aid for the blind and disabled and for dependent children and their mothers. The Works Progress Administration (WPA) gave jobs to over two million workers, who built public buildings, roads, streets, bridges, and sewers. The WPA also employed artists, musicians, actors, and writers. The Public Works Administration (PWA) cleared slums and created public housing. In the National Labor Relations Act (1935), workers received a guarantee of government protection for their unions against unfair labor practices by management.

Conclusion—restatement of thesis

As a result of the economic collapse known as the Great Depression, Americans saw their government take responsibility for providing immediate relief, for helping the economy recover, and for taking steps to ensure that the situation would not be repeated. The economic, political, and social impact of the laws passed during the 1930s is still with us, helping to keep our government and our economy stable.

Notice that in her answer the student does not include any irrelevant material: she does not, for example, describe the conditions of people's lives in detail, blame anyone in particular, discuss the president's friends and enemies, or consider parallel events in other countries. She covers only what the question asks for. Notice, too, how topic sentences ("One result of the Depression . . ."; "In response to the problems caused by the Depression . . ."; "One of the most important results of the Depression . . .") keep the primary purpose of the discussion in focus and guide her instructor through the essay.

A well-planned essay like the preceding one is not easy to write. Consider the following ineffective answer to the same question.

Ineffective Essay Exam Answer

The Great Depression is generally considered to have begun with the stock market crash of October 1929 and to have lasted until the defense buildup for World War II. It was a terrible time for millions of Americans, who were not used to being hungry or out of work. Perhaps the worst economic disaster in our history, the Depression left its scars on millions of once-proud workers and farmers who found themselves reduced to poverty. We all have heard stories of businessmen committing suicide when their investments failed, of people selling apples on the street, and of farmers and their families leaving the Dust Bowl in desperate search of work. My own grandfather, laid off from his job, had to support my grandmother and their four children on what he could make from odd carpentry jobs. This was the Depression at its worst.

No clear thesis; vague, subjective impressions of the Depression

What else did the Depression produce? One result of the Depression was the election of Franklin Delano Roosevelt. Roosevelt immediately closed all banks. Then Congress set up the Federal Emergency Relief

Administration, the Civilian Conservation Corps, the Farm Credit Administration, and the Home Owners' Loan Corporation. The Reconstruction Finance Corporation and the Civil Works Administration were two other agencies designed to provide "Relief, Recovery, and Reform." All these agencies helped Roosevelt in his efforts to lead the nation to recovery while providing relief and reform.

Gratuitous summary

Along with these emergency measures, Roosevelt set out to reform some of the conditions he felt were responsible for the economic collapse. Accordingly, he created the Tennessee Valley Authority (TVA) to control floods and provide electricity in the Tennessee Valley. The Agricultural Adjustment Agency levied taxes and got the farmers to grow less, causing prices to rise. Thus, these agencies, the TVA and the AAA, helped to ease things for the farmers.

Unsupported generalization

The National Industrial Recovery Act established the National Recovery Administration, which was designed to help workers. It established minimum wages and maximum hours, both of which made conditions better for workers. Other important agencies included the Federal Power Commission, the Interstate Commerce Commission, the Maritime Commission, and the Civil Aeronautics Authority. Changes in the tax structure at about this time made the tax system fairer and eliminated some inequities. Roosevelt, working smoothly with his cabinet and with Congress, took many important steps to ease the nation's economic burden.

Why were these agencies important? What did they do?

Digression: discussion of Roosevelt is irrelevant

Despite the fact that he was handicapped by polio, Roosevelt was a dynamic president. His fireside chats, which millions of Americans heard on the radio every week, helped to reassure Americans that things would be fine. This increased his popularity. But he had

```
problems too. Not everyone agreed with him. Private
electric companies opposed the TVA, big business
disagreed with his support of labor unions, the rich
did not like the way he restructured the tax system,
and many people saw him as dangerously radical. Still,
he was one of the most popular presidents ever.
 —Social Security Act: unemployment insurance, aid
  to blind and disabled and children
 —WPA: built public projects
 —PWA: public housing
 —National Labor Relations Act: strengthened labor
  unions
```

Undeveloped information

This essay only indirectly answers the exam question. It devotes too much space to unnecessary elements: an emotional introduction, needlessly repeated words and phrases, gratuitous summaries, and unsupported generalizations. Without a thesis statement to guide her, the writer slips into a discussion of only the immediate impact of the Depression and never discusses its causes or long-term effects. Although the body paragraphs do provide the names of many agencies created by the Roosevelt administration, they do not explain the purpose of most of them. Consequently, the student seems to consider the formation of the agencies, not their contributions, to be the Depression's most significant result.

Because the student took a time-consuming detour to discuss Roosevelt, she had to list some points at the end of the essay without discussing them fully; moreover, she was left with no time to sum up her main points, even in a one-sentence conclusion. Although it is better to include undeveloped information than to skip it altogether, an undeveloped list has shortcomings. Many instructors will not give credit if you do not write out your answer in full. More important, you cannot effectively show logical or causal relationships in a list.

27d Writing Paragraph-Length Essay Exam Answers

Some essay questions ask for a paragraph-length answer, not a full essay. A paragraph should be just that: not one or two sentences, not a list of points, not more than one paragraph.

A paragraph-length answer should be unified by a clear topic sentence. Just as an essay answer begins with a thesis statement, a paragraph answer opens with a topic sentence that summarizes what the paragraph will cover. You should generally phrase this sentence so that it echoes the wording of the exam question. The paragraph should also be coherent—that is, its statements should be linked by transitions that move the reader along. Finally, the paragraph should be well developed, with enough relevant detail to convince your reader that you know what you are talking about.

Effective Paragraph-Length Exam Answer

Question: In one paragraph, define the term *management by objectives*, give an example of how it works, and briefly discuss an advantage of this approach.

Definition — As defined by Horngren, management by objectives is an approach by which a manager and his or her superior together formulate goals, and plans by which they can achieve these goals, for a forthcoming period. Example — For example, a manager and a superior can formulate a responsibility accounting budget, and the manager's performance can then be measured according to how well he or she meets the objectives defined by the budget. Advantage — The advantage of this approach is that the goals set are attainable because they are not formulated in a vacuum. Rather, the objectives are based on what the entire team reasonably expects to accomplish. As a result, the burden of responsibility is shifted from the superior to the team: the goal itself defines all the steps needed for its completion.

In this answer, key phrases ("As *defined* by . . ."; "For *example* . . ."; "The *advantage* of this approach . . .") clearly identify the various parts of the question being addressed. The writer includes just what the question asks for, and no more. His use of the wording of the question helps make the paragraph orderly, coherent, and emphatic.

The student who wrote the following response may know what *management by objectives* is, but his paragraph sounds more like a casual explanation to a friend than an answer to an exam question.

Ineffective Paragraph-Length Exam Answer

Management by objectives is when managers and their bosses get together to formulate their goals. This is a good system of management because it cuts down on hard feelings between managers and their superiors. Because they set the goals together, they can make sure they're attainable by considering all possible influences, constraints, and so on, that might occur. This way neither the manager nor the superior gets all the blame when things go wrong.

Sketchy, casual definition

No example given

Vague

Remember, no response to an exam question will be effective unless you take the time to read the question carefully, plan your response, and outline your answer before you begin to write. It is always a good idea to use the wording of the question in your answer and to reread your answer to make sure it explicitly answers the question.

Chapter 28

Writing for the Workplace

Frequently Asked Questions

Work is often a part of the college experience, with many students having part-time jobs, internships, work-study positions, or cooperative education experiences. The skills that you develop in these activities frequently are transferable to the employment that you will have after you graduate. For this reason, it is important that you learn how to write for the workplace.

28a Writing Business Letters

Business letters should be brief and to the point, with important information placed early in the letter. Be concise, avoid digressions, and try to sound as natural as possible.

The first paragraph of your letter should introduce your subject and mention any pertinent previous correspondence. (Note that paragraphs in business letters are not indented.) The body of your letter should present the information readers need in order to understand your points. (If your ideas are complicated, present your points in a bulleted or numbered list.) Your conclusion should reinforce your message.

See 29c

Single-space within paragraphs, and double-space between paragraphs. Proofread carefully to make sure there are no errors in spelling or punctuation. Most often business letters use **block format,** with all parts of the letter aligned with the left-hand margin.

FAQs

Sample Letter: Block Format

6732 Wyncote Avenue
Houston, TX 77004
May 3, 2003

Heading

Mr. William S. Price Jr., Director
Division of Archives and History
Department of Cultural Resources
109 East Jones Street
Raleigh, NC 27611

Inside address

Dear Mr. Price:

Salutation (followed by a colon)

Thank you for sending me the material I requested about pirates in colonial North Carolina.

Both the pamphlets and the bibliography were extremely useful for my research. Without your help, I am sure my paper would not have been so well received.

I have enclosed a copy of my paper, and I would appreciate any comments you may have. Again, thank you for your time and trouble.

Body

Sincerely yours,

Complimentary close

Kevin Wolk

Written signature

Kevin Wolk

Typed signature

cc: Dr. N. Provisor, Professor of History

Copy sent

Enc.: Research paper

Additional data

28b Writing Letters of Application

Like all business letters, letters of application should be short and focused. When you apply for employment, your primary objective is to obtain an interview. The **letter of application** summarizes your qualifications for a specific position.

Begin your letter of application by identifying the job you are applying for and stating where you heard about it—in a newspaper, in a professional journal, on a Web site, or from your school's job placement service, for example. Be sure to include the date of the advertisement and the exact title of the position. End your introduction with a statement that expresses your ability to do the job.

In the body of your letter, provide the information that will convince your reader of your qualifications—for example, relevant courses you have taken and pertinent job experience. Be sure to address any specific points mentioned in the advertisement. Above all, emphasize your strengths, and explain how they relate to the specific job for which you are applying.

Conclude by saying that you have enclosed your résumé and stating that you are available for an interview, noting any dates on which you will not be available. (Be sure to include your phone number and your email address.)

Checklist: Letters of Application

- ☐ Does the first paragraph of the letter identify the job for which you are applying, mention where you heard about it, and state that you want to be considered?
- ☐ Does the body of the letter explain why you are qualified for the job?
- ☐ Does the concluding paragraph refer to your résumé, request an interview, and give your phone number and your email address?
- ☐ Does the letter look professional?

http://kirsznermandell.wadsworth.com

Computer Tip: Letter Templates

The various templates found within your word-processing program can help you structure your letters (as well as résumés, memos, faxes, and brochures). The professional letter template in *Microsoft Word*, for example, helps you position and space addresses and salutations (see Figure 28.1). Although such letter templates prompt you to include certain kinds of information in your documents, it is up to you to decide exactly what information you need to write a clear, concise, and effective letter.

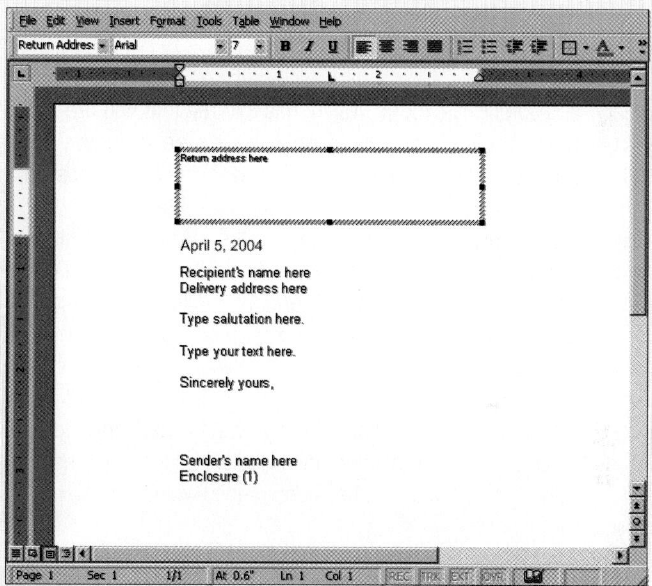

Figure 28.1 ***Microsoft Word*** **professional letter template.**

Sample Letter of Application

Heading

246 Hillside Drive
Urbana, IL 61801
October 20, 2003
Kr237@metropolis.105.com

Inside address

Mr. Maurice Snyder, Personnel Director
Guilford, Fox, and Morris
22 Hamilton Street
Urbana, IL 61822

Salutation

Dear Mr. Snyder:

Body

My college advisor, Dr. Raymond Walsh, has told me that you are interested in hiring a part-time accounting assistant. I believe that my academic background and my work experience qualify me for this position.

I am presently a junior accounting major at the University of Illinois. During the past year, I have taken courses in taxation, trusts, and business law. I am also proficient in <u>Lotus</u> and <u>ClarisWorks</u>. Last spring, I gained practical accounting experience by working in our department's tax clinic.

Double-space →

After I graduate, I hope to get a master's degree in taxation and then return to the Urbana area. I believe that my experience in taxation as well as my familiarity with the local business community would enable me to contribute to your firm.

Single-space →

I have enclosed a résumé for your examination. I will be available for an interview any time after midterm examinations, which end October 25. I look forward to hearing from you.

Complimentary close

Sincerely yours,

Written signature

Sandra Kraft

Typed signature

Sandra Kraft

Additional data

Enc.: Résumé

Close-up: Writing Follow-Up Letters

After you have been interviewed, you should send a letter to the person (or persons) who interviewed you (see Figure 28.2). First, thank your interviewer for taking the time to see you. Then, briefly summarize your qualifications and your interest in the position. Because so few applicants write follow-up letters, such letters can have a very positive effect on those who receive them.

Dear Mr. Snyder:

Thank you for interviewing me last week for the internship position and for showing me your offices. Your computer department was very impressive, and the information I obtained there has helped me focus my career goals.

I especially enjoyed seeing how you use computers to track your clients' tax liabilities. The conversation I had with the employees in the computer department confirmed my belief that Guilford, Fox, and Morris would be an excellent place to work. I hope to see all of you again this summer.

Sincerely,

Sandra Kraft

Sandra Kraft

Figure 28.2 Sample follow-up letter.

Exercise 1

Look through the employment advertisements in your local newspaper or in the files of your college placement service. Choose one job, and write a letter of application in which you summarize your achievements and discuss your qualifications for the position.

28c Designing Print Résumés

A résumé lists relevant information about your education, your job experience, your goals, and your personal interests.

ESL Tip

You may wish to indicate your visa status and your language skills on your résumé. When describing honors received in another country that may not be familiar to potential employers, it is wise to provide explanatory information. For example, you might indicate what percentage of graduates receive the honor you have been awarded.

NOTE: In some countries, job applicants list information about their age and marital status in their job application materials. However, in the United States, this is usually not done because employers are not legally allowed to discriminate on the basis of such factors.

There is no single correct format for a résumé. You may decide to arrange your résumé in **chronological order** (see page 618), listing your education and work experience in sequence (beginning with the most recent) or in **emphatic order** (see page 619) beginning with the material that will be of most interest to an employer (for example, important skills). Whatever a résumé's arrangement, it should be brief—one page is usually sufficient for an undergraduate—easy to read, clear and emphatic, logically organized, and completely free of errors.

Checklist: Components of a Résumé

- ☐ The **heading** includes your name, school address, home address, telephone number, and email address.
- ☐ A statement of your **career objective** (optional), placed at the top of the page, identifies your professional goals.
- ☐ The **education section** includes the schools you have attended, starting with the most recent one and moving back in time. (After graduation from college, do not list your high school unless you have a compelling reason to do so—for instance, if it is nationally recognized for its academic standards or it has an active alumni network in your field.)
- ☐ The **summary of work experience** generally starts with your most recent job and moves backward in time.

- ☐ The **background** or **interests section** lists your most important (or most relevant) special interest and community activities.
- ☐ The **honors section** lists academic achievements and awards.
- ☐ The **references section** lists the full names and addresses of at least three references. If your résumé is already one full page long, a line saying that your references will be sent upon request is sufficient.

http://kirsznermandell.wadsworth.com

Computer Tip: Résumé Templates

Just as they can help you format professional letters, the various templates found within your word-processing program can help you design your résumé (see Figure 28.3). Keep in mind, however, that an effective résumé requires more than just a clear format. Although templates make the task of formatting easier, you must provide the details that will lead a prospective employer to conclude that you are a strong candidate for a job.

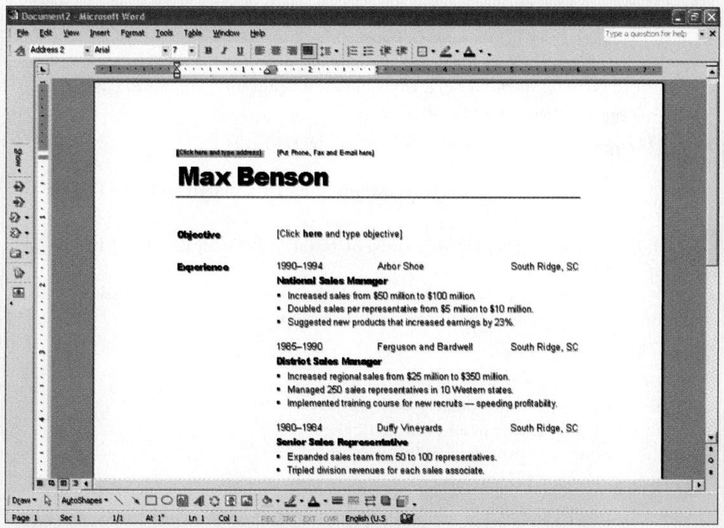

Figure 28.3 ***Microsoft Word*** **résumé template.**

Sample Résumé: Chronological Order

KAREN L. OLSON

SCHOOL
3812 Hamilton St. Apt. 18
Philadelphia, PA 19104
215-382-0831
olsont@dunm.ocs.drexel.edu

HOME
110 Ascot Ct.
Harmony, PA 16037
412-452-2944

EDUCATION

DREXEL UNIVERSITY, Philadelphia, PA 19104
Bachelor of Science in Graphic Design
Anticipated Graduation: June 2004
Cumulative Grade Point Average: 3.2 on a 4.0 scale

COMPUTER SKILLS AND COURSE WORK

HARDWARE
Familiar with both Macintosh and PC systems

SOFTWARE
Adobe Illustrator, Photoshop, and *Type Align; QuarkXPress; CorelDRAW; Micrografx Designer*

COURSES
Corporate Identity, Environmental Graphics, Typography, Photography, Painting and Printmaking, Sculpture, Computer Imaging, Art History

EMPLOYMENT EXPERIENCE

UNISYS CORPORATION, Blue Bell, PA 19124
June–September 2001, Cooperative Education
Graphic Designer. Designed interior pages as well as covers for target marketing brochures. Created various logos and spot art designed for use on interoffice memos and departmental publications.

CHARMING SHOPPES, ING, Bensalem, PA 19020
June-December 2000, Cooperative Education
Graphic Designer/Fashion Illustrator, Created graphics for future placement on garments. Did some textile designing. Drew flat illustrations of garments to scale in computer. Prepared presentation boards.

THE TRIANGLE, Drexel University, Philadelphia, PA 19104
January 2001–present
Graphics Editor. Design all display advertisements submitted to Drexel's student newspaper.

DESIGN AND IMAGING STUDIO, Drexel University, Philadelphia, PA 19104
October 1999–June 2001
Monitor. Supervised computer activity in studio. Answered telephone. Assisted other graphic design students in using computer programs.

ACTIVITIES AND AWARDS

The Triangle, Graphics Editor: 2000–present
Kappa Omicron Nu Honor Society, vice president: 1999–present
Dean's List: spring 1998, fall and winter 1999
Graphics Group, vice president: 1999–present

REFERENCES AND PORTFOLIO

Available upon request.

Sample Résumé: Emphatic Order

Michael D. Fuller

SCHOOL
27 College Avenue
University of Maryland
College Park, MD 20742
(301) 357-0732
mful532@aol.com

HOME
1203 Hampton Road
Joppa, MD 21085
(301) 877-1437

Restaurant Experience

McDonald's Restaurant, Pikesville, MD. Cook.
Prepared hamburgers. Acted as assistant manager for two weeks while manager was on vacation. Supervised employees, helped prepare payroll and work schedules. Was named employee of the month. Summer 2000.

University of Maryland, College Park, MD. Cafeteria busboy.
Cleaned tables, set up cafeteria, and prepared hot trays. September 2001–May 2002.

Other Work Experience

University of Maryland Library, College Park, MD. Reference assistant. Filed, sorted, typed, shelved, and catalogued. Earnings offset college expenses. September 2000–May 2001.

Education

University of Maryland, College Park, MD (sophomore).
Biology major, Expected date of graduation: June 2004.
Forest Park High School, Baltimore, MD.

Interests

Member of University Debating Society.
Tutor in University's Academic Enrichment Program.

References

Mr. Arthur Sanducci, Manager
McDonald's Restaurant
5712 Avery Road
Pikesville, MD 22513

Mr. William Czernick, Manager
Cafeteria
University of Maryland
College Park, MD 20742

Ms. Stephanie Young, Librarian
Library
University of Maryland
College Park, MD 20742

Close-up: Résumé Style

Use strong action verbs to describe your duties, responsibilities, and accomplishments.

accomplished	achieved	supervised
communicated	collaborated	instructed
completed	implemented	proposed
performed	organized	trained

NOTE: Use past tense for past positions and present tense for current positions.

28d Designing Electronic Résumés

Presently, the majority of résumés are still submitted on paper, but electronic résumés—scannable and Web-based—are gaining in popularity, and many experts believe the paper résumé will soon be a thing of the past.

(1) Scannable Résumés

Many employers request scannable résumés that they can download into a database for future reference. If you have to prepare such a résumé, keep in mind that scanners will not pick up columns, bullets, or italics and that shaded or colored paper will make your résumé difficult to scan.

NOTE: If you are sending your résumé as an email attachment to be downloaded into a database, use the guidelines discussed here. If it will be stored as a print document, follow the guidelines in 28c.

Whereas in a print résumé you use specific action verbs (*edited company newsletter*) to describe your accomplishments, in a scannable résumé you also use key nouns (*editor*) that can be entered into a company database. These words will help employers find your résumé when they carry out a keyword search for applicants with certain skills. To facilitate a keyword search, applicants often include a Keyword section on their résumé. For example, if you wanted to emphasize your computer skills, you would include keywords such as *WordPerfect*, *FileMaker Pro*, and *PowerPoint*.

Sample Résumé: Scannable

Constantine G. Doukakis
2000 Clover Lane
Fort Worth, TX 76107

Phone: (817) 735-9120
Email: Douk@aol.com

Employment Objective: Entry-level position in an organization that will enable me to use my academic knowledge and the skills that I learned in my work experience.

Education:

University of Texas at Arlington, Bachelor of Science in Civil Engineering, June 2000. Major: Structural Engineering. Graduated Magna Cum Laude. Overall GPA: 3.754 on a 4.0 base.

Scholastic Honors and Awards:

Member of Phi Eta Sigma First-Year Academic Honor Society, Chi Epsilon Civil Engineering Academic Society, Tau Beta Pi Engineering Academic Society, Golden Key National Honor Society.

Jack Woolf Memorial Scholarship for Outstanding Academic Performance.

Cooperative Employment Experience:

Dallas-Fort Worth International Airport, Tarrant County, TX, Dec. 1998 to June 1999. Assistant Engineer. Supervised and inspected airfield paving, drainage, and utility projects as well as terminal building renovations. Performed on-site and laboratory soil tests. Prepared concrete samples for load testing.

Dallas-Fort Worth International Airport, Tarrant County, TX, Jan. 1999 to June 1999. Draftsperson in Design Office. Prepared contract drawings and updated base plans as well as designed and estimated costs for small construction projects.

Johnson County Electric Cooperative, Clebume, TX, Jan. 1998 to June 1998. Junior Engineer in Plant Dept. of Maintenance and Construction Division. Inspected and supervised in-plant construction. Devised solutions to construction problems. Estimated costs of materials for small construction projects. Presented historical data relating to the function of the department.

Key Words:

Organizational and leadership skills. Written and oral communication skills, C++, IBM, Macintosh, DOS, Windows 2000, and Mac OS. Word, Excel, FileMakerPro, PowerPoint, WordPerfect, Internet client software. Computer model development. Technical editor.

(2) Web-Based Résumés

See Ch. 30

It is becoming common to have a version of your résumé posted on a personal Web site. Usually, a Web-based résumé is an alternative to a print résumé that you have mailed or a scannable version that you have submitted to a database or as an email attachment. Figure 28.4 shows a Web-based version of a student's résumé. The student has also included on her Web site a PDF (portable document format) version of her résumé that is available for downloading and printing (see Figure 28.5).

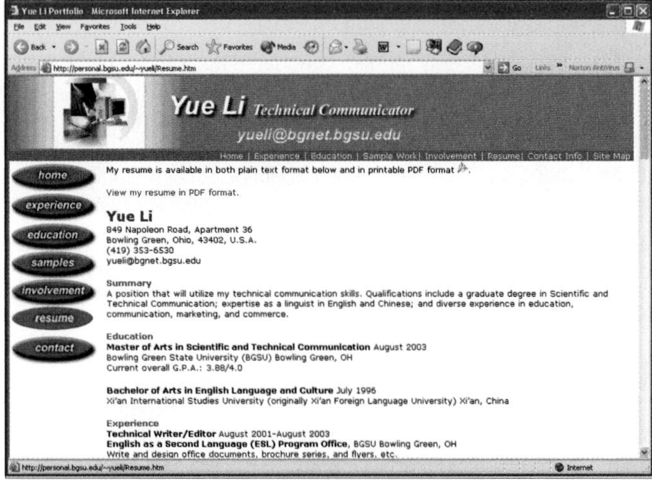

Yue Li Technical Communicator
yueli@bgnet.bgsu.edu

Home | Experience | Education | Sample Work | Involvement | Resume | Contact Info | Site Map

home · experience · education · samples · involvement · resume · contact

My resume is available in both plain text format below and in printable PDF format.

View my resume in PDF format.

Yue Li
849 Napoleon Road, Apartment 36
Bowling Green, Ohio, 43402, U.S.A.
(419) 353-6530
yueli@bgnet.bgsu.edu

Summary
A position that will utilize my technical communication skills. Qualifications include a graduate degree in Scientific and Technical Communication; expertise as a linguist in English and Chinese; and diverse experience in education, communication, marketing, and commerce.

Education
Master of Arts in Scientific and Technical Communication August 2003
Bowling Green State University (BGSU) Bowling Green, OH
Current overall G.P.A.: 3.88/4.0

Bachelor of Arts in English Language and Culture July 1996
Xi'an International Studies University (originally Xi'an Foreign Language University) Xi'an, China

Experience
Technical Writer/Editor August 2001-August 2003
English as a Second Language (ESL) Program Office, BGSU Bowling Green, OH
Write and design office documents, brochure series, and flyers, etc.

Figure 28.4 Sample student Web-based résumé.

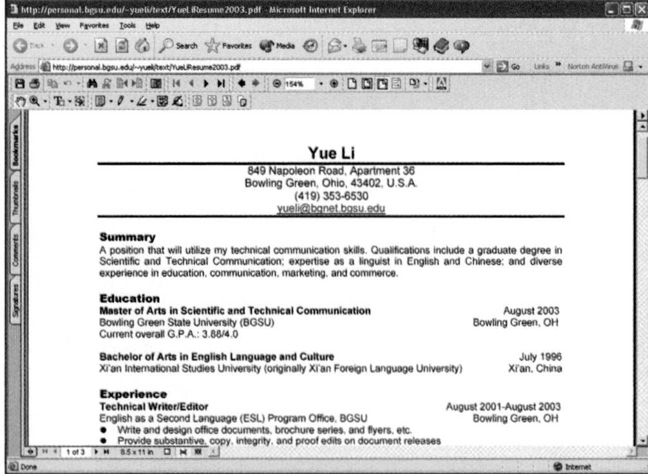

Yue Li
849 Napoleon Road, Apartment 36
Bowling Green, Ohio, 43402, U.S.A.
(419) 353-6530
yueli@bgnet.bgsu.edu

Summary
A position that will utilize my technical communication skills. Qualifications include a graduate degree in Scientific and Technical Communication; expertise as a linguist in English and Chinese; and diverse experience in education, communication, marketing, and commerce.

Education
Master of Arts in Scientific and Technical Communication August 2003
Bowling Green State University (BGSU) Bowling Green, OH
Current overall G.P.A.: 3.88/4.0

Bachelor of Arts in English Language and Culture July 1996
Xi'an International Studies University (originally Xi'an Foreign Language University) Xi'an, China

Experience
Technical Writer/Editor August 2001-August 2003
English as a Second Language (ESL) Program Office, BGSU Bowling Green, OH
- Write and design office documents, brochure series, and flyers, etc.
- Provide substantive, copy, integrity, and proof edits on document releases

Figure 28.5 Sample student PDF résumé.

http://kirsznermandell.wadsworth.com

Computer Tip: PDF Résumés

A PDF résumé allows you to maintain the original design of your word-processed résumé file, including the use of boldface and italic type, bullets, and horizontal rules. Another advantage of this type of résumé is that anyone can view and print a PDF file with the free, downloadable *Adobe Acrobat Reader* (http://www.adobe.com/products/acrobat/readermain.html).

Close-up: Electronic Portfolios

Many disciplines are moving toward **electronic portfolios,** Web-based collections of materials that represent a job applicant's skills and abilities (see Figure 28.6). Prospective employers can select the items in the portfolio of most interest to them, perhaps following up on a reference in a cover letter or a link in an electronic résumé. Portfolios may also include personal statements, writing samples, and even video or audio clips.

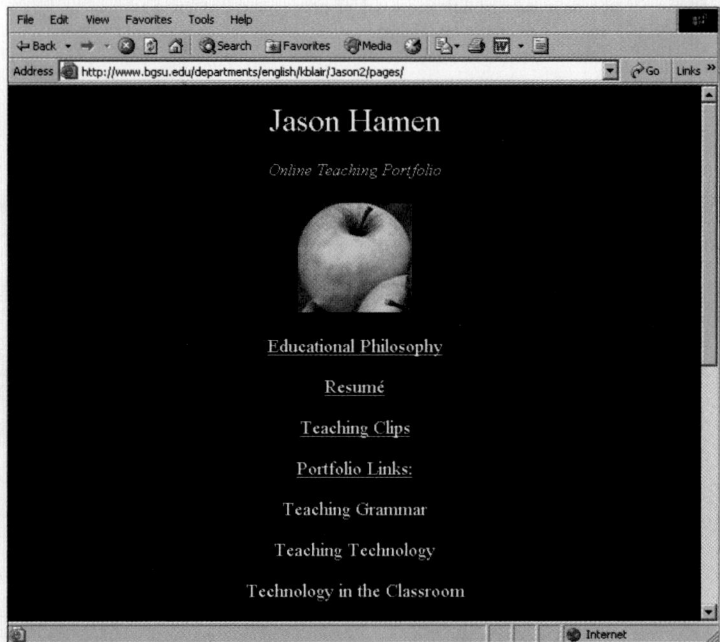

Figure 28.6 Home page for an electronic portfolio.

Exercise 2

Prepare two versions of your résumé—one print and the other scannable—that you could include with the letter of application you wrote for Exercise 1. How are these two résumés alike? How are they different?

28e Writing Memos

See 1a

Memos communicate information within an organization. A memo can be short or long, depending on its purpose.

Begin your memo with a purpose statement that presents your reason for writing it. Follow this statement with a background section that gives readers the information they will need to understand the current situation. Then, in the body of your memo, present your support, the detailed information that supports the main point of your memo. If your memo is short, use bulleted or numbered lists to emphasize information. If it is long—more than two or three paragraphs—use headings to designate the various sections of the memo (*Summary*, *Background*, *Benefits*, and so on). End your memo with a statement of your conclusions and recommendations.

Sample Memo

TO: Ina Ellen, Senior Counselor
FROM: Kim Williams, Student Tutor Supervisor
SUBJECT: Construction of a Tutoring Center
DATE: November 10, 2003

Opening component

This memo proposes the establishment of a tutoring center in the Office of Student Affairs.

Purpose statement

BACKGROUND

Under the present system, tutors must work with students at a number of facilities scattered across the university campus. As a result, tutors waste a lot of time running from one facility to another and are often late for appointments.

NEW FACILITY

Body

I propose that we establish a tutoring facility adjacent to the Office of Student Affairs. The two empty classrooms next to the office, presently used for storage of office furniture, would be ideal for this use. We could furnish these offices with the desks and file cabinets already stored in these rooms.

BENEFITS

The benefits of this facility would be the centralizing of the tutoring services and the proximity of the facility to the Office of Student Affairs. The tutoring facility could also use the secretarial services of the Office of Student Affairs.

Conclusion

RECOMMENDATIONS

To implement this project we would need to do the following:

1. Clean up and paint rooms 331 and 333
2. Use folding partitions to divide each room into five single-desk offices
3. Use stored office equipment to furnish the center

I am certain these changes would do much to improve the tutoring service. I look forward to discussing this matter with you in more detail.

28f Writing Emails and Sending Faxes

(1) Writing Emails

In many workplaces, virtually all internal (and some external) communications are transmitted as email. Although personal email tends to be quite informal, business email should observe the conventions of standard written communication.

Checklist: Writing Emails

The following guidelines can help you communicate effectively in an electronic environment:

- ☐ Write in complete sentences. Avoid the slang, imprecise diction, and abbreviations that are commonplace in personal email.
- ☐ Use an appropriate tone. Address readers with respect, just as you would in a standard business letter.
- ☐ Include a subject line that clearly identifies your content. If your subject line is vague, your email may be deleted without being read.
- ☐ Make your message as short as possible. Because most emails are read on the screen, long discussions are difficult to follow.
- ☐ Use short paragraphs, and leave an extra space between paragraphs.
- ☐ Use lists and internal headings to make your message easier to read and understand. (Keep in mind, however, that your recipient may not be able to view certain formatting elements, such as boldface, italics, and indentation.)
- ☐ Take the time to edit your email, and delete excess words and phrases.
- ☐ Proofread carefully before sending your email. Look for errors in grammar, spelling, and punctuation.
- ☐ Make sure that your list of recipients is accurate and that you do not send your email to unintended recipients.
- ☐ Do not send your email until you are absolutely certain your message says exactly what you want it to say.
- ☐ Do not forward an email unless you have the permission of the sender.
- ☐ Watch what you write. Always remember that email written at work is the property of the employer, who has the legal right to access it, even without your permission.

(2) Sending Faxes

In spite of the prevalence of email, businesses still routinely send and receive many faxes. Forms that need signatures, papers that cannot easily be digitized, copies of printed documents, and print communications that must be sent immediately all are transmitted by fax.

Close-up: Sending Messages by Fax

Remember that faxes are often received not by an individual but at a central location, so include a cover sheet that contains the recipient's name and title, the data, the company and department, the fax and telephone numbers, and the total number of pages faxed. In addition, supply your own name and telephone and fax numbers. (It is also a good idea to call ahead to alert the addressee that a fax is coming.)

Close-up: Using Voice Mail

Like email, voice mail can present challenges. The following tips will help you deliver a voice-mail message clearly and effectively.

- **Organize your message before you deliver it.** Long, meandering, or repetitive messages will frustrate listeners.
- **Begin your message with your name and affiliation as well as the date and time of your call.**
- **State the subject of your message first.** Then, fill in the details.
- **Speak slowly.** Many experts advise people to speak much more slowly than they would in normal conversation.
- **Speak clearly.** Enunciate your words precisely so a listener will understand your message the first time. Be sure to spell your name.
- **Give your phone number twice—once at the beginning and again at the end of your message.** No one wants to replay a long voice-mail message just to get a phone number.

Chapter 29

Designing Effective Documents

Frequently Asked Questions

What is document design? (p. 628)
When I list points, should I use bullets, or should I use numbers? (p. 634)
When should I use visuals in my paper? (p. 636)

The term **document design** denotes the principles that help you determine how to design a piece of written work—a research paper, report, or Web page, for example—so that it communicates its ideas clearly and effectively. A well-designed document has a visual format that emphasizes key ideas and is easy on the eye. Although formatting conventions—for example, how tables and charts are constructed and how information is arranged on a title page—may differ from discipline to discipline, all well-designed documents share the same general characteristics: an effective format, clear headings, useful lists, and helpful visuals.

29a Creating an Effective Visual Format

An effective document contains visual cues that help readers find, read, and interpret information on a page. For example, wide margins can give a page a balanced, uncluttered appearance; white space can break up a long discussion; and distinctive type size and typeface can make a word or phrase stand out on a page.

(1) Margins

Margins frame a page and keep it from looking overcrowded. Because long lines of text can overwhelm readers and make a document difficult to read, a page should have margins of at least one inch all around. If the material you are writing about is highly technical or unusually difficult, use wider margins (one and a half inches). Keep in mind, however, that various disciplines may have different requirements for margins and that even those requirements may differ from assignment to assignment. Before you prepare a document, consult the appropriate style sheet.

Except for documents such as flyers and brochures, where you might want to isolate blocks of text for emphasis, you should **justify** (uniformly align, except for paragraph indentations) the left-hand margin. You can either leave a ragged edge on the right, or you can justify your text so all the words are aligned evenly along the right margin. (A ragged edge is often preferable because it varies the visual landscape of your text, making it easier to read.)

(2) White Space

White space is the area of a page that is intentionally left blank. Used effectively, white space can isolate material and thereby focus a reader's attention on it. You can use white space around a block of text—a paragraph or a section, for example—or around visuals such as charts, graphs, and photographs. White space can eliminate clutter, break a discussion into manageable components, and help readers process information more easily.

http://kirsznermandell.wadsworth.com

Computer Tip: Borders, Horizontal Rules, and Shading

Most word-processing programs enable you to create borders, horizontal rules, and shaded areas of text. Border and shading options are usually found under the Format menu of your word-processing program. With these features, you can select line style, thickness, and color and adjust white space, boxed text, and the degree of shading.

(3) Color

While white space is important in breaking up material on the page, **color** (when used in moderation) can help to emphasize and clarify information while making it visually appealing. In addition to using color to emphasize information, you can use it to distinguish certain types of information—for example, titles can be one color and subheadings can be another, complementary color. Remember, however, that too many colors can confuse readers and detract from your visual emphasis. Many software applications, including *Microsoft Word* and *PowerPoint*, contain design templates (such as the one in Figure 29.1) that make it easy for you to choose a color scheme or to create your own.

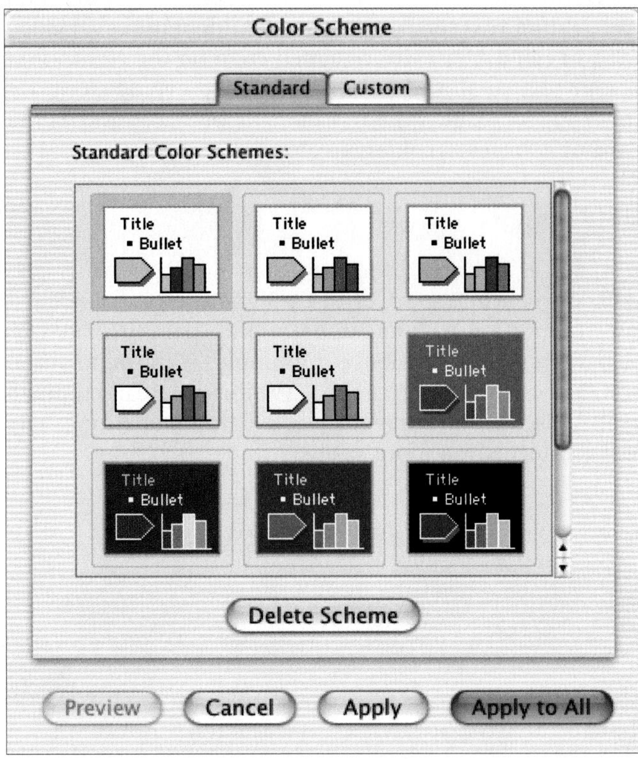

Figure 29.1 ***Microsoft PowerPoint*** **Color Scheme menu.**

(4) Typeface and Type Size

Your computer gives you a wide variety of typefaces and type sizes (measured in **points**) from which to choose. **Typefaces** are distinctively designed sets of letters, numbers, and punctuation marks. The typeface you choose should be suitable for your purpose and audience. In your academic writing, avoid fancy or elaborate typefaces—script or old English, for example—that call attention to themselves and distract readers. Instead, select a typeface that is simple and direct—Courier, Times New Roman, or Arial, for example. In nonacademic documents—such as Web pages and flyers—decorative typefaces may be used to help you emphasize a point or attract a reader's attention.

You also have a wide variety of **type sizes** available to you. For most of your academic papers, you will use a 10- or 12-point type (headings will sometimes be larger). Documents such as advertisements, brochures, and Web pages, however, may use a variety of type sizes. (Keep in mind that point size alone is not a reliable guide for size. For instance, 12-point type in **Chicago** is much larger than 12-point type in Courier or Arial Condensed Light.)

Close-up: Serif and Sans Serif Typefaces

Typefaces can be classified into two general groups: *serif* and *sans serif*. **Serif** typefaces are those that have curved lines at the ends of letters. Popular serif fonts include Times, Courier, and Palatino. Considered easy to read, serif fonts are used in long print documents, such as books, newspapers, and reports. **Sans serif** typefaces are those that have no curved extensions. Typical sans serif fonts include Helvetica and Arial. Because of their bold, modern appearance, sans serif fonts are often used for headings and titles; for visual aids in oral presentations; and for short electronic documents, such as Web pages.

(5) Line Spacing

Line spacing refers to the amount of space between the lines of a document. If the lines are too far apart, the text will seem to lack cohesion; if the lines are too close together, the text will appear crowded and be difficult to read. The type of writing you do may determine line spacing: the paragraphs of business letters, memos, and some reports are usually single-spaced and separated by a double space, but the paragraphs of academic papers are usually double-spaced.

29b Using Headings

Used effectively, headings act as signals that help readers process information, and they also break up a text, making it inviting and easy to read. Different academic disciplines have different requirements concerning headings. For this reason, you should consult the appropriate style manual before inserting headings in a paper.

Close-up: Uses of Headings

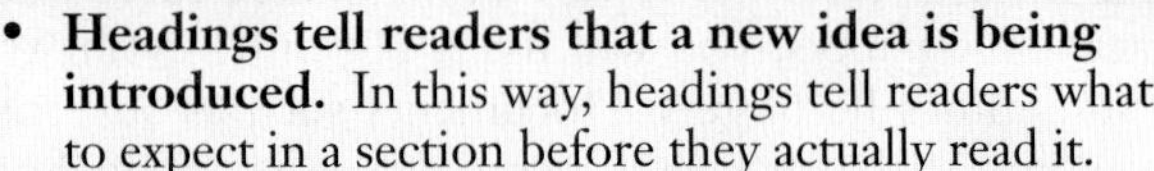

- **Headings tell readers that a new idea is being introduced.** In this way, headings tell readers what to expect in a section before they actually read it.
- **Headings emphasize key ideas.** By isolating an idea from the text around it, headings help readers identify important information.
- **Headings indicate how information is organized in a text.** Headings use various typefaces and type sizes (as well as indentation) to indicate the relative importance of ideas. For example, the most important information in a text will be set off as first-level headings and have the same typeface and type size. The next most important information will be set off as second-level headings, also with the same typeface and type size.

(1) Number of Headings

The number of headings you use depends on the document. A long, complicated document will need more headings than a shorter, less complicated one. Keep in mind that too few headings may not be of much use, but too many headings will make your document look like an outline.

(2) Phrasing

See 40a

Headings should be brief, informative, and to the point. They can be single words—*Summary* or *Introduction*, for example—or they can be phrases (always stated in parallel terms): *Traditional Family Patterns, Alternate Family Patterns, Modern Family Patterns*. Finally, headings can be questions (*How Do You Choose a Major?*) or statements (*Choose Your Major Carefully*).

(3) Indentation

Indenting is one way of distinguishing one level of heading from another. The more important a heading is, the closer it is to the left-hand margin: first-level headings are justified left, second-level headings are indented five spaces, and third-level headings are indented another two or three spaces. Headings and subheadings may also be *centered*, placed *flush left*, or *run into the text*.

(4) Typographical Emphasis

You can emphasize important words in headings by using **boldface,** *italics,* or ALL CAPITAL LETTERS. Used in moderation, these distinctive typefaces make a text easier to read. Used excessively, however, they slow readers down.

(5) Consistency

Headings at the same level should have the same format—the same typeface, type size, spacing, and color. In addition, if one first-level heading is boldfaced and centered, all other first-level headings must be boldfaced and centered. Using consistent patterns reinforces the connection between content and ideas and makes a document easier to understand.

NOTE: Never separate a heading from the text that goes with it: if a heading is at the bottom of one page and the text that goes with it is on the next page, move the heading onto the next page so readers can see the heading and the text together.

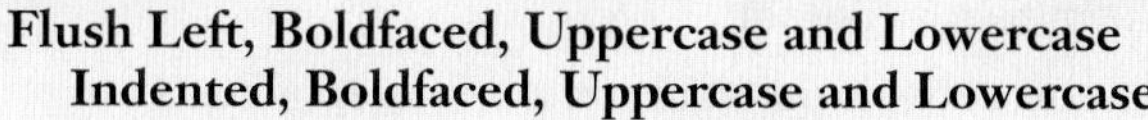

Flush Left, Boldfaced, Uppercase and Lowercase

Indented, Boldfaced, Uppercase and Lowercase

Indented, italicized, lowercase; run into the text at the beginning of a paragraph; ends with a period.

Or

Centered, Boldfaced, Uppercase and Lowercase

Flush Left, Underlined, Uppercase and Lowercase

Indented, underlined, lowercase; run into the text at the beginning of a paragraph; ends with a period.

Or

ALL CAPITAL LETTERS, CENTERED

29c Constructing Lists

By breaking long discussions into a series of key ideas, a list makes information easier to understand. By isolating individual pieces of information this way and by providing visual cues (such as bullets or numbers), a list directs readers to important information on a page.

Checklist: Constructing Effective Lists

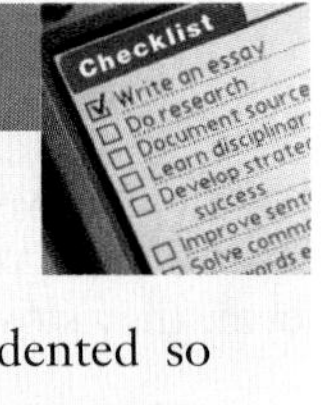

When constructing lists, you should follow these guidelines.

☐ **Indent each item.** Each item on a list should be indented so that it stands out from the text around it.

☐ **Set off items with numbers or bullets.** Use **bullets** when items are not organized according to any particular sequence or priority (the members of a club, for example). Use **numbers** when you want to indicate that items are organized according to a sequence (the steps in a process, for example) or priority (the things a company should do to decrease spending, for example).

☐ **Introduce a list with a complete sentence.** Do not simply drop a list into a document; introduce it with a complete sentence (followed by a colon) that tells readers what the list contains and why you are including it in your discussion.

☐ **Use parallel structure.** Lists are easiest to read when all items are parallel and about the same length.

A number of factors can cause high unemployment:

- a decrease in consumer spending
- a decrease in factory orders
- a decrease in factory output

☐ **Punctuate correctly.** If the items on a list are fragments (as they are in the previous example), begin each item with a lowercase letter, and do not end it with a period. However, if the items on a list are complete sentences (as they are in the example below), begin each item with a capital letter and end it with a period.

Here are the three steps we must take to reduce our spending:

1. We must cut our workforce by 10 percent.
2. We must use less-expensive vendors.
3. We must decrease overtime payments.

Figure 29.2 shows a page from a student's report that incorporates some of the effective design elements discussed in 29a–c. Notice that the use of different typefaces and type sizes contribute to the document's overall readability.

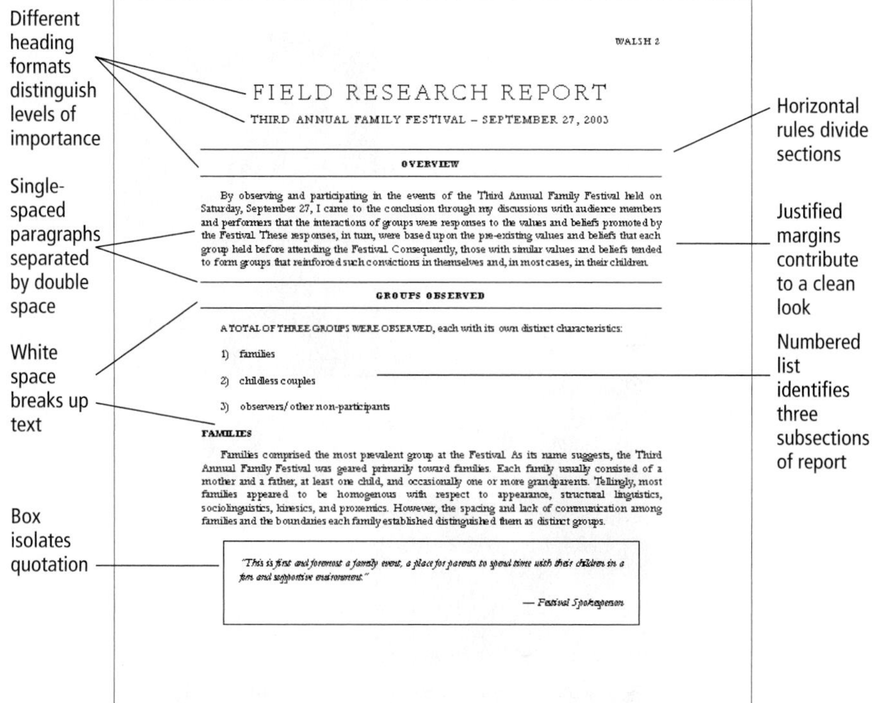

WALSH 2

FIELD RESEARCH REPORT

THIRD ANNUAL FAMILY FESTIVAL – SEPTEMBER 27, 2003

OVERVIEW

By observing and participating in the events of the Third Annual Family Festival held on Saturday, September 27, I came to the conclusion through my discussions with audience members and performers that the interactions of groups were responses to the values and beliefs promoted by the Festival. These responses, in turn, were based upon the pre-existing values and beliefs that each group held before attending the Festival. Consequently, those with similar values and beliefs tended to form groups that reinforced such convictions in themselves and, in most cases, in their children.

GROUPS OBSERVED

A TOTAL OF THREE GROUPS WERE OBSERVED, each with its own distinct characteristics:

1) families

2) childless couples

3) observers/other non-participants

FAMILIES

Families comprised the most prevalent group at the Festival. As its name suggests, the Third Annual Family Festival was geared primarily toward families. Each family usually consisted of a mother and a father, at least one child, and occasionally one or more grandparents. Tellingly, most families appeared to be homogenous with respect to appearance, structural linguistics, sociolinguistics, kinesics, and proxemics. However, the spacing and lack of communication among families and the boundaries each family established distinguished them as distinct groups.

"This is first and foremost a family event, a place for parents to spend time with their children in a fun and supportive environment."

— Festival Spokesperson

Figure 29.2 A well-designed page from a student's report.

Exercise 1

Look at the advertisement in Figure 29.3 on page 636, noting its organization, format, and design. How does the ad make use of margins, white space, typeface and type size, line spacing, and other document design features to emphasize important elements of the text? Can any design elements be improved?

Exercise 2

Select two different documents—for example, a page from a procedure manual and an invitation, or a report and a flyer. Then, make a list of the design elements each document contains. Finally, evaluate the relative effectiveness of the two documents, given their intended audiences.

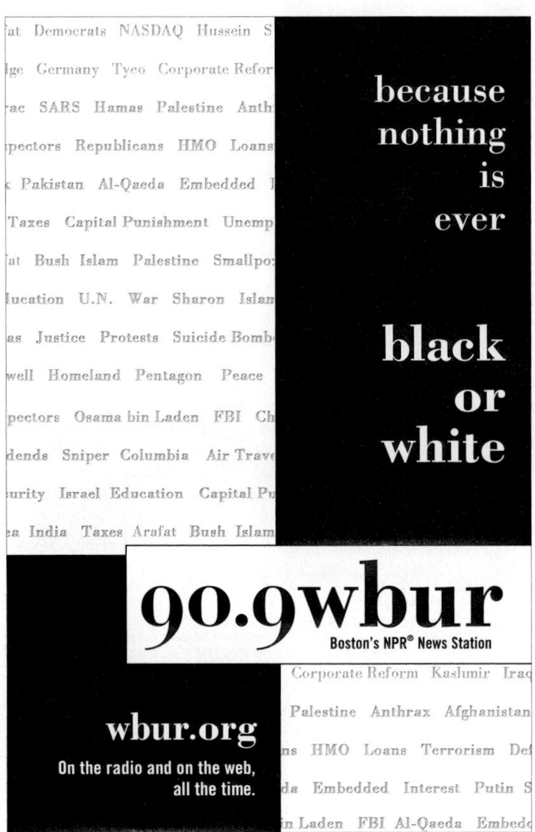

Figure 29.3 Print advertisement for a radio station.

29d Using Visuals

FAQs links

Visuals, such as tables, graphs, diagrams, and photographs, can help you convey complex ideas that are difficult to communicate with words and can also help you attract readers' attention.

You can create your own tables and graphs by using applications in software packages like *Excel*, *Lotus*, or *Word*. In addition, many stand-alone graphics software packages enable you to create complex charts, tables, and graphs that contain three-dimensional effects. You can also photocopy or scan diagrams and photographs from a print source or download them from the Internet or from CD-ROMs or DVDs. Remember, however, that if you use a visual from a source, you must use appropriate documentation.

See Pt. 3

Close-up: Visuals and Copyright

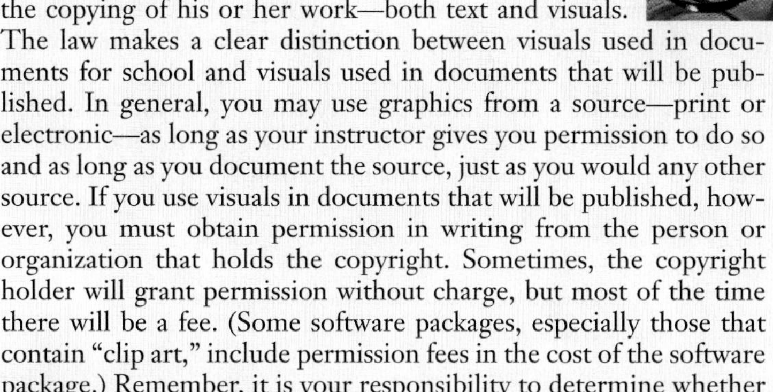

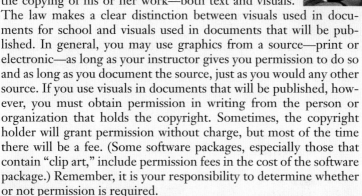

Copyright gives an author the legal right to control the copying of his or her work—both text and visuals. The law makes a clear distinction between visuals used in documents for school and visuals used in documents that will be published. In general, you may use graphics from a source—print or electronic—as long as your instructor gives you permission to do so and as long as you document the source, just as you would any other source. If you use visuals in documents that will be published, however, you must obtain permission in writing from the person or organization that holds the copyright. Sometimes, the copyright holder will grant permission without charge, but most of the time there will be a fee. (Some software packages, especially those that contain "clip art," include permission fees in the cost of the software package.) Remember, it is your responsibility to determine whether or not permission is required.

http://kirsznermandell.wadsworth.com

Computer Tip: Formatting Visuals

Most software applications have tools that enable you to format visuals you have added to your documents (see Figure 29.4). Simply double-click the visual you have inserted into your document to open a format box that enables you to adjust the visual's color, size, and layout.

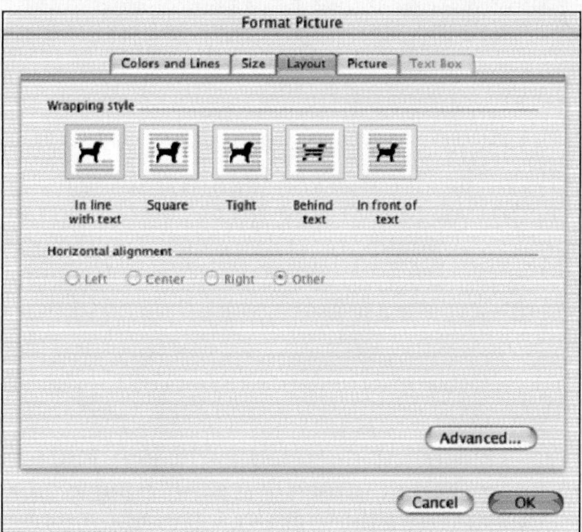

Figure 29.4 ***Microsoft Word*** **Format Picture menu.**

(1) Tables

Tables present data in a condensed, visual format—arranged in rows and columns. Tables may contain numerical data, text, or a combination of the two. When you plan your table, make sure you include only the data that you will need; discard information that is too detailed or difficult to understand. Keep in mind that tables may distract readers, so include only those necessary to support your discussion. (The table in Figure 29.5 reports the student writer's original research and therefore needs no documentation.)

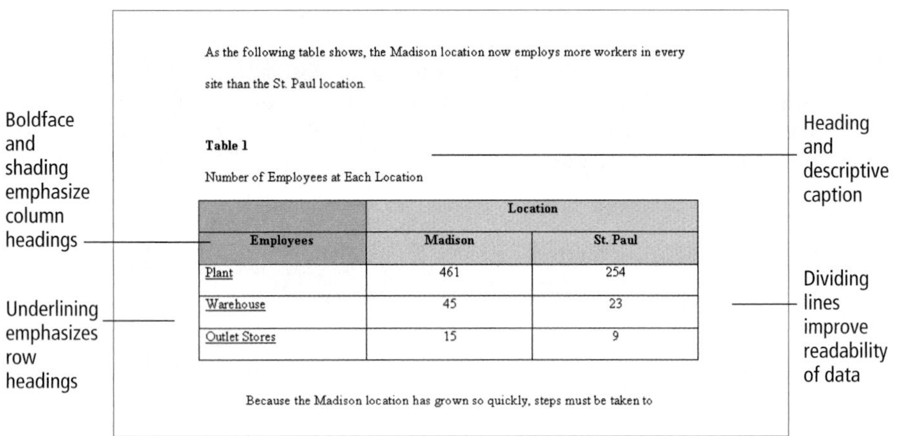

As the following table shows, the Madison location now employs more workers in every site than the St. Paul location.

Table 1

Number of Employees at Each Location

	Location	
Employees	**Madison**	**St. Paul**
Plant	461	254
Warehouse	45	23
Outlet Stores	15	9

Because the Madison location has grown so quickly, steps must be taken to

Figure 29.5 Sample table from a student paper.

(2) Graphs

Like tables, graphs present data in visual form. Whereas tables may present specific numerical data, graphs convey the general pattern or trend that the data suggest. Because graphs tend to be more general (and therefore less accurate) than tables, they are frequently accompanied by tables. Figure 29.6 is an example of a bar graph showing data from a source.

(3) Diagrams

A diagram calls readers' attention to specific details of a mechanism or object. Diagrams are often used in scientific and technical writing to clarify concepts that are difficult to explain in words. Figure 29.7, which illustrates the sections of an orchestra, serves a similar purpose in a music education paper.

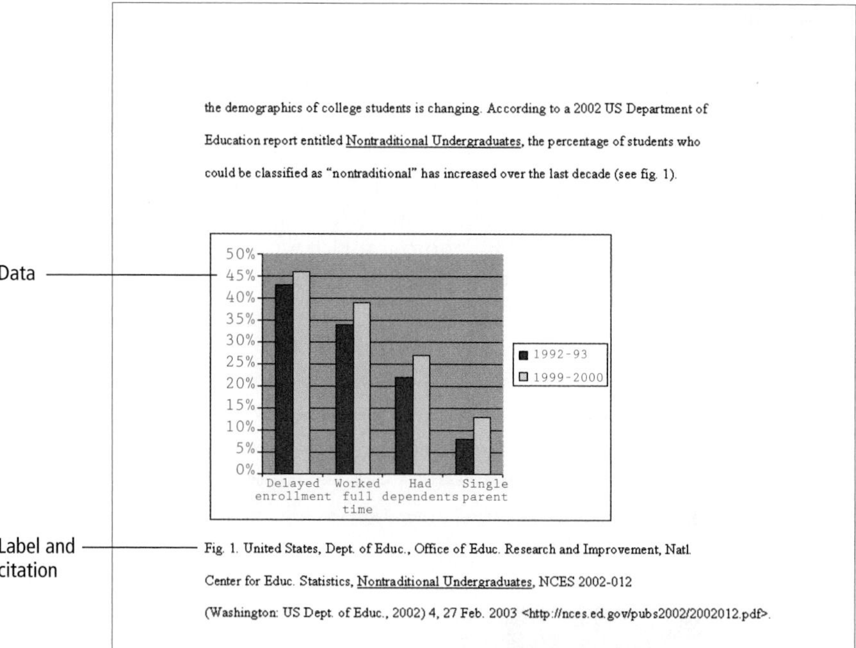

the demographics of college students is changing. According to a 2002 US Department of Education report entitled Nontraditional Undergraduates, the percentage of students who could be classified as "nontraditional" has increased over the last decade (see fig. 1).

Fig. 1. United States, Dept. of Educ., Office of Educ. Research and Improvement, Natl. Center for Educ. Statistics, Nontraditional Undergraduates, NCES 2002-012 (Washington: US Dept. of Educ., 2002) 4, 27 Feb. 2003 <http://nces.ed.gov/pubs2002/2002012.pdf>.

Figure 29.6 Sample graph from a student paper.

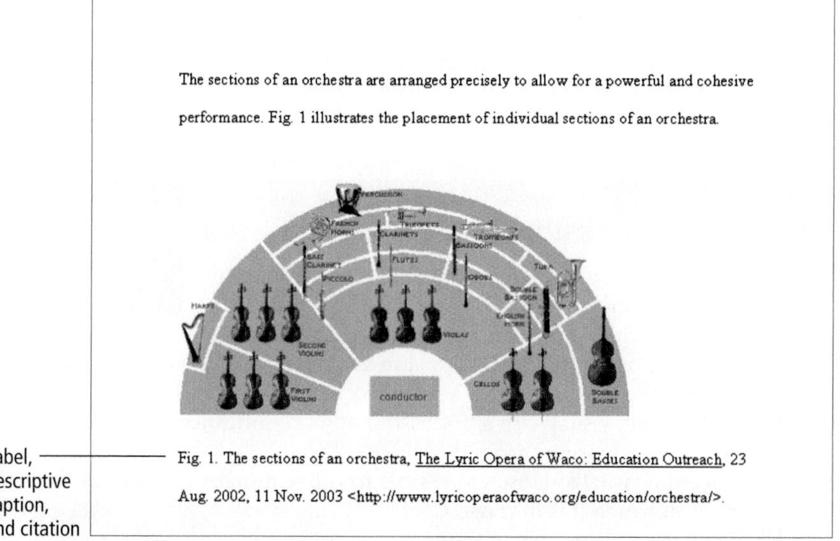

The sections of an orchestra are arranged precisely to allow for a powerful and cohesive performance. Fig. 1 illustrates the placement of individual sections of an orchestra.

Fig. 1. The sections of an orchestra, The Lyric Opera of Waco: Education Outreach, 23 Aug. 2002, 11 Nov. 2003 <http://www.lyricoperaofwaco.org/education/orchestra/>.

Figure 29.7 Sample diagram from a student paper.

(4) Photographs

Photographs enable you to show exactly what something or someone looks like—an animal in its natural habitat, a work of fine art, or an actor in costume, for example. Although computer technology that enables you to paste photographs directly into a text is widely available, you should use it with restraint. Not every photograph will support or enhance your written text; in fact, an irrelevant photograph will distract readers. The photograph of a wooded trail in Figure 29.8 illustrates the student writer's description.

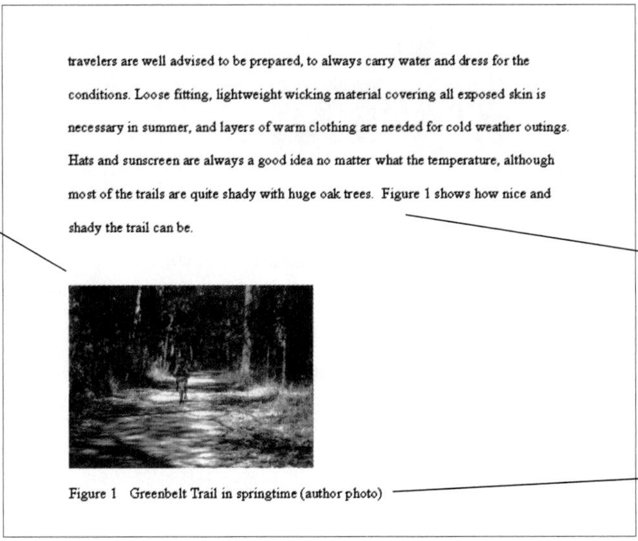

travelers are well advised to be prepared, to always carry water and dress for the conditions. Loose fitting, lightweight wicking material covering all exposed skin is necessary in summer, and layers of warm clothing are needed for cold weather outings. Hats and sunscreen are always a good idea no matter what the temperature, although most of the trails are quite shady with huge oak trees. Figure 1 shows how nice and shady the trail can be.

Figure 1 Greenbelt Trail in springtime (author photo)

Photo sized and placed appropriately within text with consistent white space above and below

Reference to photo provides context

Label and descriptive caption

Figure 29.8 Sample photograph from a student paper.

Checklist: Using Visuals

- ☐ Use a visual only when it contributes something important to the discussion, not for embellishment.
- ☐ Use the visual in the text only if you plan to discuss it in your paper (place the visual in an appendix if you do not).
- ☐ Introduce each visual with a complete sentence.
- ☐ Follow each visual with a discussion of its significance.
- ☐ Leave wide margins around each visual.
- ☐ Place the visual as close as possible to the section of your document in which it is discussed.
- ☐ Label each visual appropriately.
- ☐ Document each visual borrowed from a source.

Exercise 3

Analyze the chart in Figure 29.9, noting the visual elements that are used to convey the billing costs of material, labor, and equipment on a construction project. Summarize the data in a brief paragraph. Then, list the advantages and disadvantages of presenting the data visually as opposed to verbally.

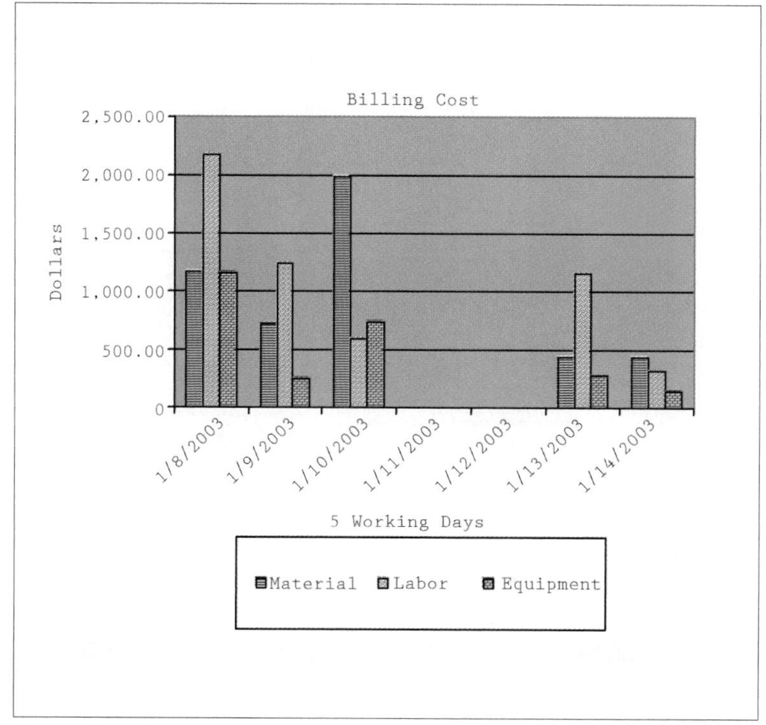

Figure 29.9 Billing cost chart.

29e Using Desktop Publishing

During your college career, you may be asked to use your computer for **desktop publishing**—using graphics as well as words to produce documents. For example, you may produce a brochure or newsletter for a student organization to which you belong or as a service learning project for a course you are taking (Figure 29.10 shows a sample student brochure). Brochures and newsletters are frequently aimed at consumers of a product or service or at members of an organization. These documents may be informative, persuasive, or both.

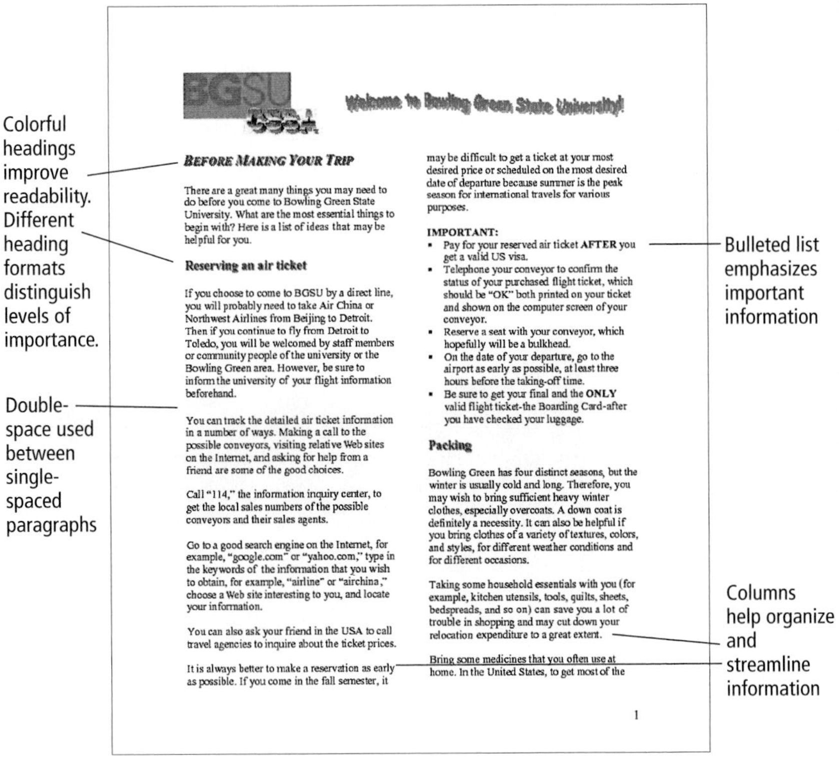

Colorful headings improve readability. Different heading formats distinguish levels of importance.

Double-space used between single-spaced paragraphs

Bulleted list emphasizes important information

Columns help organize and streamline information

BGSU

Welcome to Bowling Green State University!

BEFORE MAKING YOUR TRIP

There are a great many things you may need to do before you come to Bowling Green State University. What are the most essential things to begin with? Here is a list of ideas that may be helpful for you.

Reserving an air ticket

If you choose to come to BGSU by a direct line, you will probably need to take Air China or Northwest Airlines from Beijing to Detroit. Then if you continue to fly from Detroit to Toledo, you will be welcomed by staff members or community people of the university or the Bowling Green area. However, be sure to inform the university of your flight information beforehand.

You can track the detailed air ticket information in a number of ways. Making a call to the possible conveyors, visiting relative Web sites on the Internet, and asking for help from a friend are some of the good choices.

Call "114," the information inquiry center, to get the local sales numbers of the possible conveyors and their sales agents.

Go to a good search engine on the Internet, for example, "google.com" or "yahoo.com," type in the keywords of the information that you wish to obtain, for example, "airline" or "airchina," choose a Web site interesting to you, and locate your information.

You can also ask your friend in the USA to call travel agencies to inquire about the ticket prices.

It is always better to make a reservation as early as possible. If you come in the fall semester, it may be difficult to get a ticket at your most desired price or scheduled on the most desired date of departure because summer is the peak season for international travels for various purposes.

IMPORTANT:

- Pay for your reserved air ticket **AFTER** you get a valid US visa.
- Telephone your conveyor to confirm the status of your purchased flight ticket, which should be "OK" both printed on your ticket and shown on the computer screen of your conveyor.
- Reserve a seat with your conveyor, which hopefully will be a bulkhead.
- On the date of your departure, go to the airport as early as possible, at least three hours before the taking-off time.
- Be sure to get your final and the **ONLY** valid flight ticket-the Boarding Card-after you have checked your luggage.

Packing

Bowling Green has four distinct seasons, but the winter is usually cold and long. Therefore, you may wish to bring sufficient heavy winter clothes, especially overcoats. A down coat is definitely a necessity. It can also be helpful if you bring clothes of a variety of textures, colors, and styles, for different weather conditions and for different occasions.

Taking some household essentials with you (for example, kitchen utensils, tools, quilts, sheets, bedspreads, and so on) can save you a lot of trouble in shopping and may cut down your relocation expenditure to a great extent.

Bring some medicines that you often use at home. In the United States, to get most of the

1

Figure 29.10 Sample student brochure.

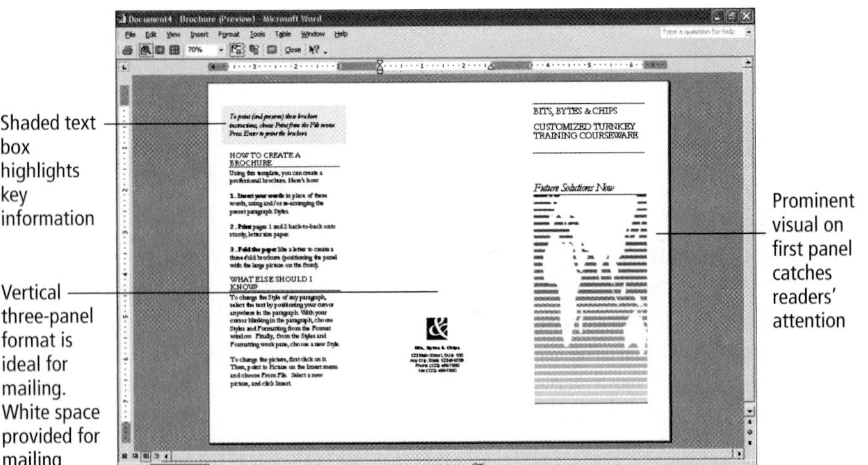

Figure 29.11 ***Microsoft Word*** **brochure template.**

Most word-processing programs, such as *Microsoft Word*, contain templates (see Figure 29.11, for example) that can help you design your newsletter or brochure. With these templates, you can select layout, color scheme, and typeface as well as document dimensions and paper size.

For more options, you can use one of the many desktop publishing software packages that are commercially available. *Microsoft Publisher*, like *Microsoft Word*, provides templates for a range of document types. More advanced desktop publishing programs include *Adobe PageMaker* and *QuarkXPress*, both of which are used extensively in business and industry.

Exercise 4

Develop a promotional document for an organization on campus. Before you begin the document-design process, interview someone affiliated with the organization to determine the type of information you will need, the format in which the information should be delivered, and the image the organization wishes to project to the campus community.

Chapter 30

Designing Web Sites

Frequently Asked Questions

At some point in your college career, you may be asked to create a Web page or even a full Web site—for example, as a course assignment or as a way of marketing your job skills. Like other documents, Web pages follow the conventions of document design. Because so much of the content is meant to be read directly online, your choices of text, color, and navigation strategy are especially important.

Close-up: Components of a Web Page

A **personal home page** usually contains information about how to contact the author, along with a brief biography. A home page can also be the first page of a **Web site,** a group of related Web pages about a personal, professional, or academic topic. In this case, the home page contains **links**—highlighted words, images, or URLs—that allow users to move from one page to another or to another Web site.

30a Planning Your Web Site

When you plan your Web site, you should consider your purpose, audience, and tone, just as you would when planning a print document. In addition, of course, you should consider what content to include. Finally, just as an essay or research paper may have a set page limit, your own Web site may have size and file-type limitations.

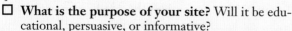

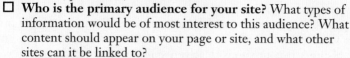

Checklist: Planning Your Web Site

When planning your site, ask yourself the following questions:

- ☐ **What is the purpose of your site?** Will it be educational, persuasive, or informative?
- ☐ **Who is the primary audience for your site?** What types of information would be of most interest to this audience? What content should appear on your page or site, and what other sites can it be linked to?
- ☐ **What information will you include on your site?** What information will appear on your home page? What information will appear on other pages of the Web site?
- ☐ **What mood do you want your site to convey?** What colors and fonts should you use to help you convey this mood?

(1) Outlining

Before you create your Web site, you should consider how your Web pages will relate to one another. Beginning with the home page, users will navigate from one part of your Web site to another. For this reason, your home page should provide an overview of your site and give users a clear sense of the material the site contains.

You should start planning your Web site by considering how its pages will be organized. One way to do this is to list the information on your Web site under headings or categories, just as you would if you were making an informal outline. Later on, you can use this list to create a **site map** (see Figure 30.1), a feature that helps users of large Web sites locate and link to relevant content.

See 4d

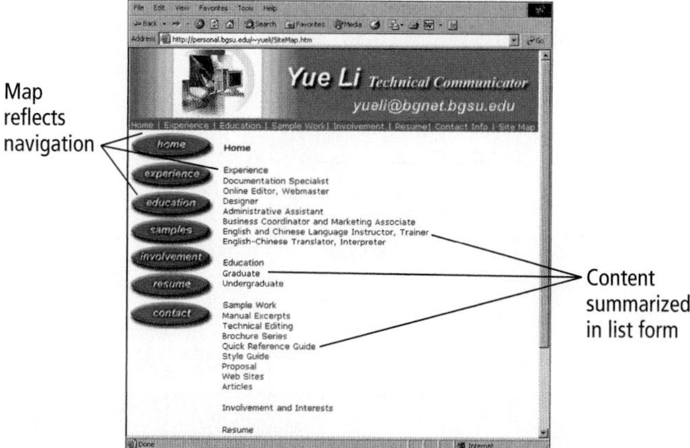

Figure 30.1 Sample site map for a student's Web portfolio.

(2) Storyboarding

Another way to plan your Web site is to storyboard, using 3″ × 5″ index cards to represent the various elements of your Web site and moving these cards around until you arrive at an arrangement that makes sense. If your Web site is relatively simple, you can arrange pages so that one page leads sequentially to the next. For example, your personal Web site could begin with a home page, then progress to a page that presents your interest in sports, then to one that presents your volunteer work, and then, finally, to one that presents your résumé. If your site is relatively complicated, however, you will have to group pages together in order of importance or in order of their relevance to a particular category. (See Figures 30.2 and 30.3 for examples of a linear and a nonlinear storyboard.)

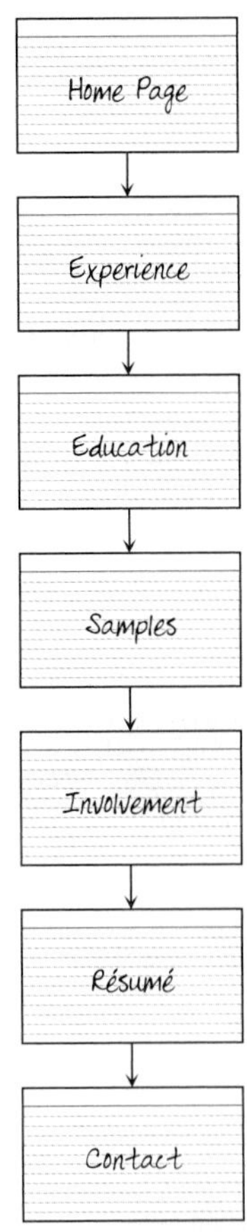

Figure 30.2 Linear storyboard.

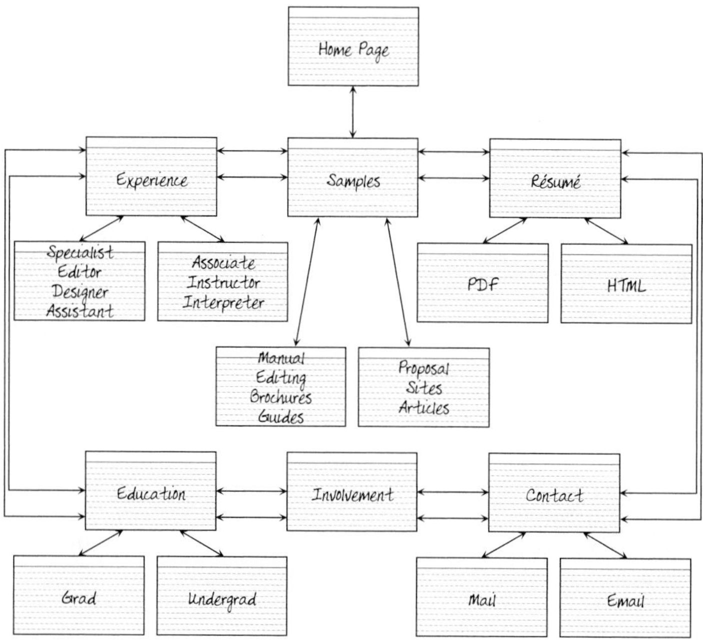

Figure 30.3 Nonlinear storyboard.

Exercise 1

Select three Web sites: one personal, one academic (such as your university's site), and one professional or organizational (such as that of the American Cancer Society). How do these sites differ in purpose, audience, and tone? How are these differences reflected in the designs of each site?

30b Creating Your Web Site

Once you have planned your Web site, you will need to select a method for creating the site itself. Essentially, there are three ways to create pages within your Web site: you can use Web authoring software packages; you can use Web tools within your word-processing program; or you can create a page from scratch by using **HTML** (hypertext markup language), the programming language used to convert standard documents into World Wide Web hypertext documents.

- **Web Authoring Packages** Many Web authoring packages—for example, *Macromedia Dreamweaver* and *Microsoft FrontPage*—will automatically translate your pages into HTML. The advantage of an authoring package is that you do not have to have a working knowledge of HTML in order to develop your site. Some of these packages even make certain interactive functions—such as navigation bars, forms, or media effects—easier to implement.

- **Web Tools within Your Word-Processing Program** Most word processors have an option under the File menu or the Save menu that automatically saves word-processed documents as HTML documents suitable for Web delivery. Although this option is appropriate for a single document, such as your résumé, it does not have the features you will need to create an entire Web site. For example, you cannot insert navigation buttons or include columns and tables that will transfer to the Web.
- **Text Editors that Allow Coding "By Hand"** If you have advanced knowledge of HTML, this is a good option. Text editors, including *Simple Text* for the Mac and *Notepad* for the PC, enable you to control all elements of your Web site design. The major drawback of using a text editor is that HTML coding can be confusing, and some special effects require complicated codes.

Exercise 2

Explore the Web tools within your word-processing program. What options do you have for creating individual Web pages?

30c Selecting and Inserting Visuals

You can find visuals for your Web site by looking for other sites on the Web that make visuals available for others to use. You can usually find them with your search engine—*Google*, for example, has an image directory at http://images.google.com that you can search. You can also create and upload visuals yourself by using either a digital camera or a scanner. Once a visual has been created and saved electronically, you can use a graphics package such as *Adobe Photoshop* to adjust the visual's size, contrast, or color scheme; to crop the image; or to add text (see Figure 30.4). Other visual options include creating your own banners and backgrounds with special colors and textures.

Once you have edited a visual, you must save it in one of two standard formats for the Web: JPG (for photographic images containing a wide range of colors) or GIF (for graphic files with fewer colors, line art, and text).

Close-up: Determining Visual File Format and Size

Before inserting a visual into a Web page, check the visual's size by clicking once on the file icon for the visual so that it is highlighted. Then, select Properties from the file menu. A small window will appear with information about the file's format and size. Anything over 50k (kilobytes) is likely to take too much time to load.

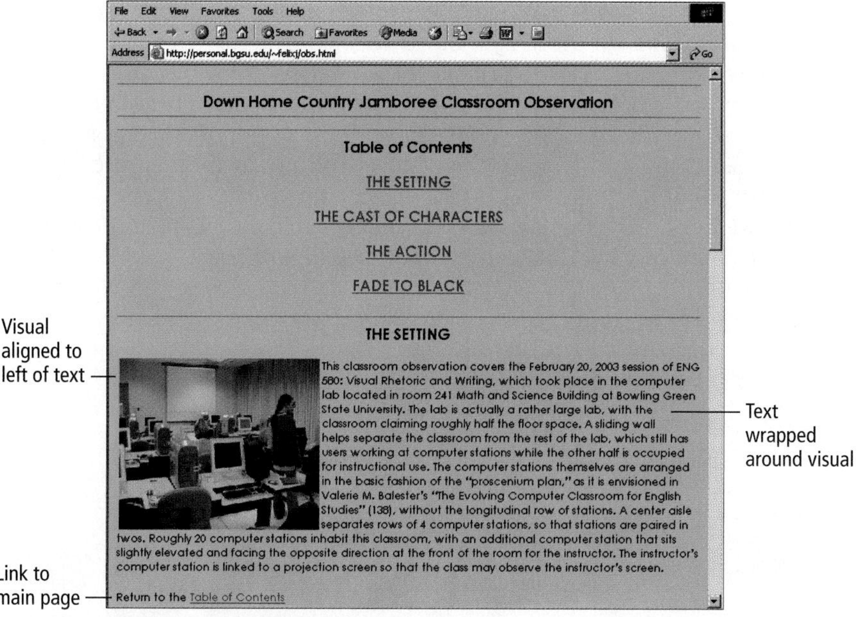

Figure 30.4 Sample Web page with visual.

Exercise 3

Select a visual you could include on a personal Web site. If you have access to *Netscape Composer* or another Web authoring package, practice inserting and aligning the visual near some text and adjusting its height and width in relation to the text. How well does the visual thematically and visually correspond to your written content and overall visual design? What alterations can you make to the visual before you reinsert it? What changes in size and alignment should you make once the visual is reinserted on the page?

30d Planning Navigation

Web sites use a number of design features to make navigation easier. As you create the pages of your Web site, you should consider the following options for helping readers navigate your site.

- **Splash Pages** Many Web designers include a splash page on their Web sites. A splash page, such as the one shown in Figure 30.5, is usually more visual than textual, usually containing only limited background information and navigation features, such as links to the site's content. Its purpose is to create interest and draw users into the site. A more detailed overview of the site appears on another page that serves as the true home page.
- **Navigation Text, Buttons, and Bars** Navigation text, buttons, bars, or other graphic icons, such as arrows or pictures, enable readers to move from one page of a Web site to another (see Figure 30.6).
- **Anchors** Anchors (or **relative links**) enable readers to jump from one part of a Web page to another (see Figure 30.6).

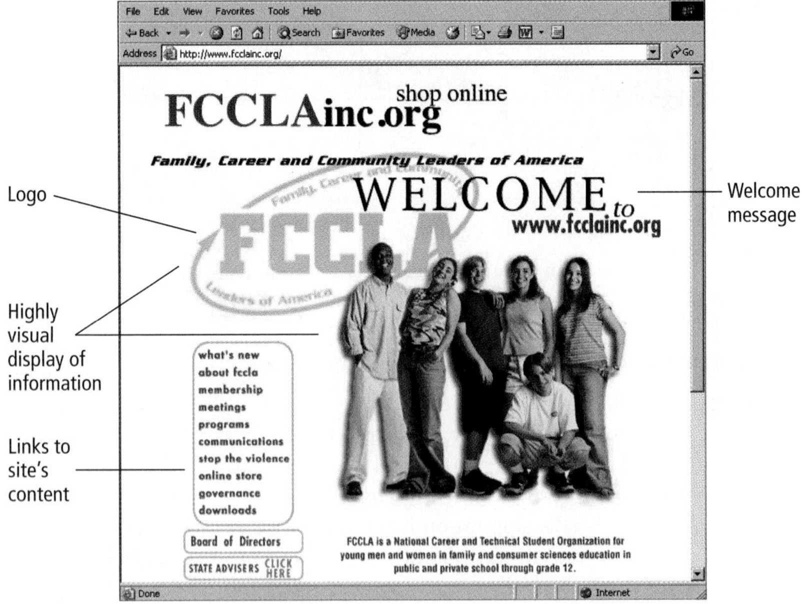

Figure 30.5 Sample splash page.

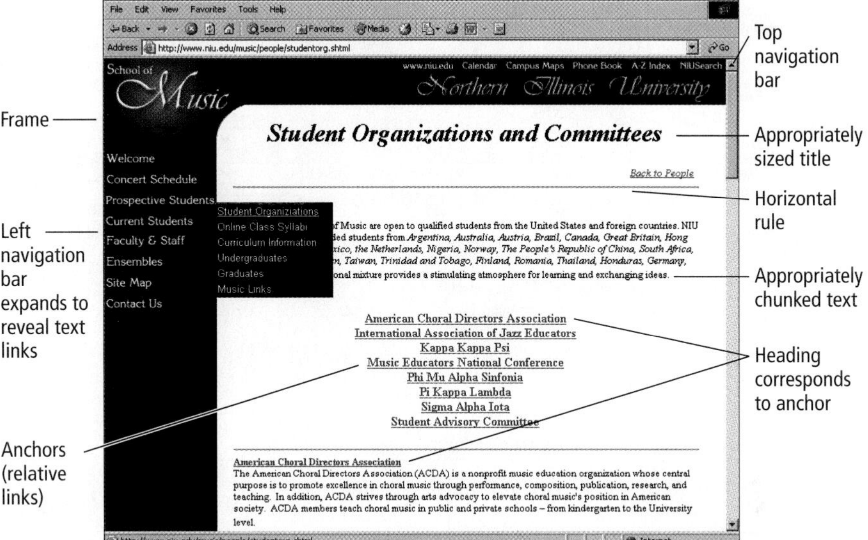

Figure 30.6 Sample Web page with navigation links, anchors, and frames.

- **Horizontal Rules** Horizontal rules divide sections and parts of a page (see Figure 30.6). You can use colored or patterned rules that coordinate with the color scheme of the Web site.
- **Chunking or Clustering** Chunking or clustering means placing related items of text close to one another (see Figures 30.4 and 30.6). This technique cuts down on scrolling and helps users read content easily on the screen. By surrounding clusters of information with white space, you can create separate "screens" of content.
- **Frames** Like tables, frames organize text and graphics. Unlike tables, however, frames enable you to divide a single Web page into multiple windows (see Figure 30.6).
- **Text Formatting Features** Like printed texts, Web texts follow the principles of document design, using design elements such as single-spaced text, headings, subheadings, and bulleted lists, as well as boldface and italics to emphasize points. (Underlining is usually not used in Web texts because readers might mistake underlined text for a hyperlink.)

- **Style Sheets** A style sheet enables you to set in advance the standard features of your site—including font, size, and color for different heading levels and text (see Figure 30.7). In this way, you not only save time, but you also create a consistent visual format throughout your Web site.

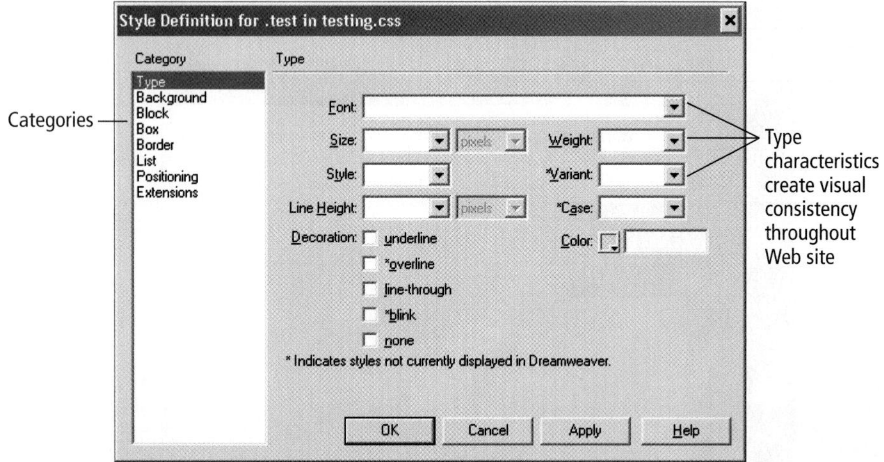

Figure 30.7 ***Macromedia Dreamweaver*** **style sheet option.**

- **Tables** Tables within a Web site enable you to place text and graphics in exact positions on a page. By selecting the number of columns and rows, you can create "cells" to be filled with text, graphics, or both (see Figure 30.8). If you set the table border width to zero, the table itself will not be visible on the screen, but the "cells" will still be there to control the layout.

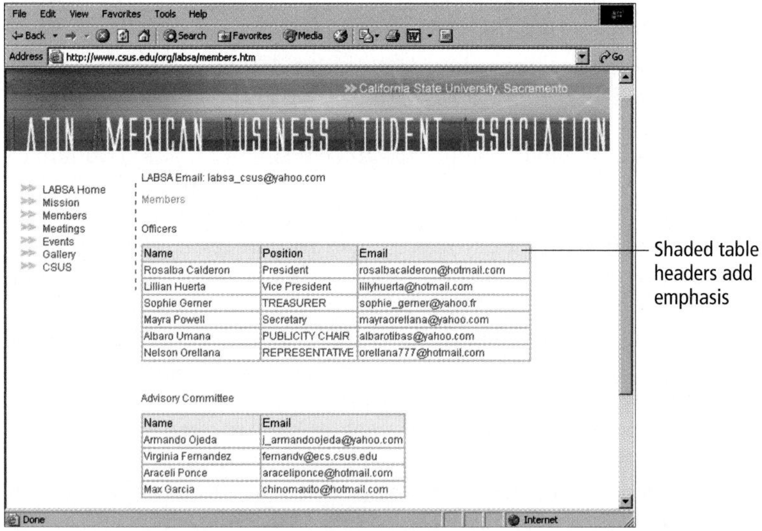

Figure 30.8 Sample Web page with tables.

Checklist: Designing Effective Web Pages

- ☐ Use the same type size and typeface for equivalent information. Keep headings and body text consistent throughout your site.
- ☐ Select sans serif fonts, which are easily readable online. Typical sans serif fonts include Arial, Helvetica, and Tahoma.
- ☐ Select images that reinforce your theme or argument. Do not let style substitute for content.
- ☐ Use text, buttons, and bars to facilitate navigation.
- ☐ Use special multimedia effects in moderation. Animation, video, and audio are distracting if they are not consistent with your site's purpose.
- ☐ Indicate what players, plug-ins, and other extensions are required for accessing multimedia files. Give readers the option of viewing your content without these additional elements.
- ☐ Avoid pages so full of text, graphics, and navigation aids that they make reading difficult and increase loading time.
- ☐ For best visibility, use text and background colors that contrast well. Use textured or patterned backgrounds only if they do not obscure text.
- ☐ Preview your Web site on multiple machines and browsers as well as on both high-speed networks and slower-speed modems.
- ☐ Provide your email address so you can receive feedback from users.

30e Linking Your Content

Hyperlinks are obviously a very important part of Web design. When you provide a link, you are directing people to a particular Web site. For this reason, you should make sure that the site you link to is up and running and that the information appearing there is both accurate and reliable.

It is important to select a visible color for your text-based links to indicate that they are in fact links and not just highlighted text. You will need three colors to indicate the status of a link: one for the link before it is clicked; one for the active link (or the change in color as the link itself is being clicked); and one for the visited link (the color after the link has been successfully accessed).

Finally, make certain that you have the exact URL for the sites to which you are linking. The Web relies on exact URLs to deliver information; if even one letter or directory slash is incorrect, the page will not load.

Close-up: Web Sites and Copyright

As a rule, assume that any material on a Web site is copyrighted unless the author makes an explicit statement to the contrary. This means you must receive written permission if you are going to reproduce this material on your Web site. The only exception to this rule is the **fair use doctrine,** which allows the use of copyrighted material for the purpose of commentary, parody, or research and education. The amount of a particular work you use is also a consideration. You can quote a sentence of an article from the *New York Times* on your Web site for the purpose of commenting on it, but you must get permission from the *New York Times* to reproduce the article in its entirety. The purpose of your use—that is, whether or not you are using it commercially—is important as well: commercial use of any portion of an article always requires permission. As of now, however, you do not have to get permission to provide a link from your own Web site to the article on the *New York Times*'s Web site.

NOTE: The material you quote in a research paper for one of your classes falls under the fair use doctrine and does not require permission.

30f Editing and Previewing Your Web Site

Before you post your Web site, you should proofread and edit it just as you would any other document. (Even if you run a spell check and a grammar check, you must still proofread carefully.)

Checklist: Style Conventions of Writing for the Web

Because of the highly visual nature of the Web, it is important to write and organize information in a way that will catch (and keep) your readers' attention. Follow these guidelines to make your Web site more appealing and navigable to users:

- ☐ Avoid long, wordy sentences. Using active verbs will help keep your sentences short and concise.
- ☐ Avoid long paragraphs. Chunk content into small sections that are easy to read and access online.
- ☐ Speak directly to your audience, using the first person (*I*) and the second person (*you*) to establish a connection with readers.
- ☐ Avoid technical terminology that only a certain segment of your audience will understand.
- ☐ Choose your external links wisely. Do not provide so many that your audience is drawn away from your site.
- ☐ Use headings and bulleted lists to organize information visually and textually.
- ☐ Provide a title in the browser window for each page within your site to help users keep track of where they are.
- ☐ Proofread carefully offline before loading your content online.

30g Publishing Your Web Site

(1) Posting Your Site

Once you have created, edited, and previewed your Web site, you have two options for **posting** or uploading it to a server:

- **Campus Server** Your school may have student accounts you can use for publishing your site on the campus server. Before you can access the server, you will need to apply for an account and a password.
- **Internet Service Provider** An Internet service provider (ISP) such as America Online may offer Web storage space as part of your member benefits. (Alternatively, you can search for free Web servers, but these probably include advertisements that could detract from the purpose and credibility of your site.)

After you have located a server, it is important to determine how much storage space you have and to ensure that your files do not exceed your space limit. Sometimes even one movie clip or audio file can exceed the total amount of space that you have been allocated, so be sure to check space limitations before you try to publish your site.

The most common way to upload your site onto a server is through a file transfer protocol (FTP) program. If you are using a Macintosh, the most widely used software is *Fetch*, which allows you to drag and drop files into specific folders on the Web. On the PC, the most popular program is *WS_FTP*.

Another option for publishing your site is the Publish feature found within many Web authoring packages. Selecting the Publish option in *Netscape Composer*, for example, will upload your site to the Web by calling up a window in which you can indicate the server address and your log-in ID and password.

(2) Publicizing Your Site

Once your site is published on the Web, you should publicize it. Even though many search engines automatically search for new Web sites, you should give formal notification that you have launched a new site. Most search engines have links to pages where you can register new sites. Alternatively, you can access Web sites that automatically send your information to a number of sites. (If you do this, you do not have to repeat the same information each time you register. You can find these sites by doing a keyword search of the phrase *site registration*.)

(3) Maintaining Your Site

A Web site, like many of the documents you will produce in school and on the job, is a work in progress. Links can easily become inactive, and information can quickly become outdated. You should regularly maintain your site, filling in changes in dates, semesters, and years on important documents (such as your online résumé) and updating any inactive or dead links. Finally, always include the date that you update the site to show your users that the site is both active and current.

Exercise 4

Visit your university's Web site or Information Technology Center, and obtain a Web server account. What are your file size limitations, and what content guidelines are provided? What online training or tutorials are available to help you develop and upload your site?

Exercise 5

Select two people to test your Web site from two different locations, one on campus and one off. Ask them to comment on the amount of time it takes the various pages of your Web site to load (particularly if you include any images or movie files), as well as to evaluate the general visual appeal of your site. Based on their recommendations, what changes would you make?

Exercise 6

Ask a classmate to log on to your Web site and perform one task that you consider relatively easy but important to users of your site (for instance, downloading a résumé if the site is personal or locating a shipping policy if the site is commercial). Provide your classmate with only the URL of your site's home page, and ask him or her how long it takes to complete the task. Was the task more difficult than you had originally estimated? If so, what changes could you make to your site to improve ease of use?

Review Checklist: Designing a Web Site

- ☐ Identify the audience and purpose of your Web site.
- ☐ Decide what content and design features you will use.
- ☐ Consider how you want your site to be organized.
- ☐ Draw a basic plan of your site.
- ☐ Lay out text and graphics so they present your ideas clearly and logically.
- ☐ Supply clear and informative links.
- ☐ Make sure all your links are active.
- ☐ Proofread your text.
- ☐ Make sure your site looks the way you want it to.
- ☐ Make sure you have acknowledged all material that you have borrowed from a source.
- ☐ Post your site to an Internet server.
- ☐ Notify search engines that your site is up and running.

Chapter 31

Making Oral Presentations

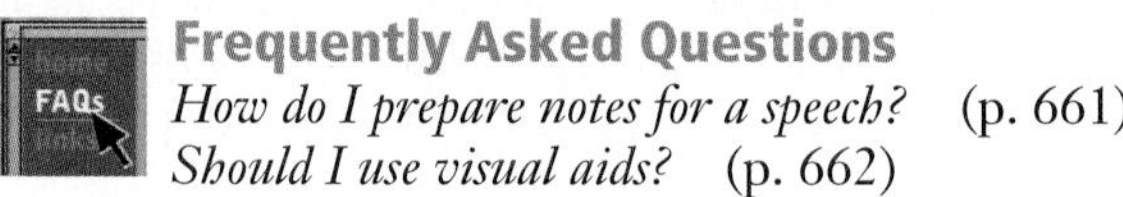

Frequently Asked Questions

How do I prepare notes for a speech? (p. 661)

Should I use visual aids? (p. 662)

At school and on the job, you may be called on to make an **oral presentation**—for example, a speech or a panel discussion. In a college course, you may be asked to explain your ideas, to defend your position, or to present the results of your research. At work, you may be asked to discuss a process, to propose a project, or to solve a problem. Although many people are uncomfortable about giving oral presentations, the guidelines that follow can make the process easier and less stressful.

31a Getting Started

Just as with writing an essay, the preparation phase of an oral presentation is as important as the speech itself. The time you spend on this phase will make your task easier later on.

Identify Your Topic The first thing you should do is to identify the topic of your speech. Sometimes you are given a topic; at other times, you have the option of choosing your own. Once you have a topic, you should decide how much information, as well as what kind of information, you will need to present.

Consider Your Audience The easiest way to determine what kind of information you will need is to consider the nature of your audience. Is your audience made up of experts or of people who know very little about your topic? How much background information will you have to provide? Can you use technical terms, or should you avoid them? Do you think your audience will be interested in your topic, or will you have to create interest? What opinions or ideas about your topic will the members of your audience bring with them?

Close-up: Audience

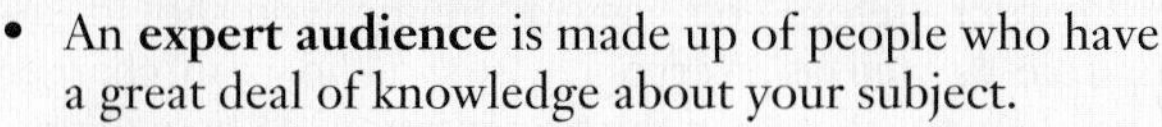

- An **expert audience** is made up of people who have a great deal of knowledge about your subject.
- A **collegial audience** is made up of people who share your frame of reference.
- A **general audience** is made up of people who have no specific knowledge of your subject.
- A **mixed audience** is made up of people who have varying degrees of knowledge about your subject.

ESL Tip

When making oral presentations, some ESL students choose topics related to their cultural backgrounds or home countries. This is a good idea because they are often able to provide insightful information on these topics that is new to their instructor and classmates. If you choose such a topic, try to determine beforehand how much background your audience has on it by speaking with your instructor and classmates.

Consider Your Purpose Your speech should have a specific purpose that you can sum up concisely. To help you zero in on your purpose, ask yourself what you are trying to accomplish with your presentation. Are you trying to inform? to instruct? to stimulate an exchange of ideas? to get support for a project? to solicit feedback? to persuade? It is a good idea to write out this purpose statement and to keep it in front of you on a note card to keep you focused as you plan your speech.

> Purpose statement: to suggest ways to make registration easier for students

Consider Your Constraints How much time do you have for your presentation? (Obviously, a ten-minute presentation requires more information and preparation than a three-minute presentation.) Do you already know enough about your topic, or will you have to do research? Where will you go to find information?

Close-up: Group Presentations

Sometimes you may be required to give a group presentation. Whether you are participating in a panel discussion or delivering one part of a long speech, you should be aware that group presentations involve a lot of preparation and coordination. Before you begin planning, you should understand your role as well as everyone else's: Who is in charge? Who is responsible for each part of the presentation? Who will prepare and display the visuals? In addition, everyone in the group should understand that he or she must stick to a schedule for both research and rehearsal.

31b Planning Your Speech

At the planning phase, you focus on your ideas about your topic and develop a thesis; then, you decide what specific points you will discuss and divide your speech into a few manageable sections.

Develop a Thesis Statement Before you actually plan your speech, you need to develop a thesis statement that clearly and concisely presents your main idea—the key idea you want to communicate to your audience. For example, the student whose purpose statement appears on page 659 came up with this thesis statement for her speech:

```
The university needs to implement a three-step plan
to make registration easier for students.
```

If you know a lot about your topic, you can develop a thesis on your own. If you do not know a lot, you will have to gather information and review it before you can decide on a thesis. As you plan your speech, remember to refer to your thesis to make sure you stay on track.

Decide on Your Points Once you have developed a thesis, you can decide what points you will discuss. Unlike readers, who can reread a passage until they understand it, listeners must understand information the first time they hear it. For this reason, speeches usually make points that are clear and easy to follow. Frequently, your thesis statement states or strongly implies these points.

Gather Support You cannot expect your listeners to simply accept what you say. You must supply details, facts, and examples that will convince them that what you are saying is both accurate and reasonable. You can gather this supporting material in the library, on the

Web, or from your own experience. No matter how much support you supply, however, you should expect your listeners to ask questions, and you should be prepared to answer them.

Outline the Individual Parts of Your Speech Every speech has a beginning, a middle, and an end. Your **introduction** should introduce your subject, engage your audience's interest, and state your thesis—but it should *not* present an in-depth discussion or summary of your topic. The **body,** or middle section, of your speech should present the points that support your thesis. It should also include the facts, examples, and other information that will clarify your points and help convince listeners your thesis is reasonable. As you present your points, use strong topic sentences to lead listeners from one point to another: `The first step . . .`, `The second step . . .`, and so on. Your **conclusion** should bring your speech to a definite end and reinforce your thesis. Because an audience remembers best what it hears last, this section is extremely important. In your conclusion, restate your thesis and reinforce how your speech supports it.

31c Preparing Your Notes

Most people use notes of some form when they give a speech. Each system of notes has advantages and disadvantages. FAQs links

Full Text Some people like to write out the full text of their speech and refer to it during their presentation. If the type is large enough, and if you triple-space, such notes can be useful. One disadvantage of using the full text of your speech is that it is easy to lose your place and become disoriented; another is that you may find yourself simply reading your speech. In either case, you stop making eye contact with your audience—and may also lose their attention.

3″ × 5″ Cards Some people write important parts of their speech—for example, a list of key points or definitions—on 3″ × 5″ note cards. Cards are portable, so they can be rearranged easily. They are also small, so they can be placed inconspicuously on a podium or a table. With some practice, you can learn to use note cards effectively. You have to be careful, however, not to become so dependent on the cards that you lose eye contact with your audience or begin playing with the cards as you give your speech.

Outlines Some people like to refer to an outline when they give a speech. As they speak, they can glance down at the outline to get their bearings or to remind themselves of a point they may have forgotten. Because an outline does not contain the full text of a speech, the temptation to read is eliminated. However, if for some reason you draw a blank, an outline gives you very little to fall back on.

Visual Aids Finally, some people like to use visual aids—such as overhead projectors, slides, or computer presentation software like *Microsoft PowerPoint* to keep them on track.

31d Preparing Visual Aids

(1) Using Visuals

As you plan your speech, decide whether you want to use some type of visual aid. **Visual aids,** such as overhead transparencies, posters, or *PowerPoint* slides, can reinforce important information and make your speech easier to understand. They can also break the monotony of a speech and help focus an audience's attention.

For a simple speech, a visual aid may be no more than a definition or a few key terms, names, or dates written on the board. For a more complicated presentation, you might need charts, graphs, diagrams, or photographs—or even objects.

The major consideration for including a visual aid is whether it actually adds something to your speech. If a poster will help your listeners understand some key concepts, then by all means use one. However, if it will do little to highlight the information in your speech, do not use it. Finally, if you are using equipment such as a slide projector or a laptop, make sure you know how to operate it—and have a contingency plan just in case the equipment does not work the way it should. For example, it is a good idea to back up a *PowerPoint* presentation with overhead transparencies just in case the computer at school or at work will not open your files.

If possible, visit the room in which you will be giving your speech ahead of time, and see whether it has the equipment you need (and whether the equipment works). Some college classrooms are equipped with overhead projectors or computer interfaces; at other schools, you have to make arrangements for equipment in advance.

Finally, make sure that whatever visual aid you use is large enough for everyone in your audience to see. Printing or typing should be neat and free of errors, and graphics should be clearly labeled and easy to see.

(2) Using Presentation Software

Microsoft PowerPoint, the most commonly used presentation software package, enables you to organize an oral presentation and prepare attractive, professional slides (see Figure 31.1). This program contains many options for backgrounds, color schemes, and special effects, including the ability to enhance your slides with sound and video.

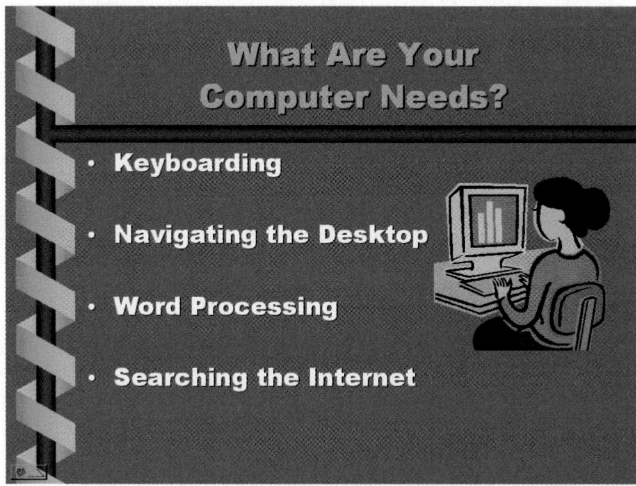

Figure 31.1 Sample *PowerPoint* slide.

http://kirsznermandell.wadsworth.com

Computer Tip: Using *PowerPoint*

If possible, use the computer that you used to prepare your *PowerPoint* slides when you deliver your speech. That way, you will be sure that you will be able to open your files and that all the multimedia effects you included with your slides will work.

- **Organization Aids** If you want to focus on organizing your ideas, you can select the Outline View, which allows you to type text as a list that you can later convert into a slide template. If you want to focus on what your presentation will look like, you can select the Design View, which enables you to type your text directly onto a slide template. You can then select features such as background, text color, and type size.
- **A Notes Feature** *PowerPoint* includes a feature that enables you to create notes, which you can then use during your presentation.
- **An Automatic Slide-Show Feature** Another tool enables you to determine how much time it takes you to talk about each slide.

Using these times as settings, you can automatically change slides during your speech.

- **Multimedia Tools** *PowerPoint's* more advanced features enable you to create multimedia presentations that combine images, video, audio, and animation. You can also use the Insert menu to insert various items—for example, clip art, word art, and image files you have created with a digital camera or scanner—into your slide templates (see Figure 31.2). You can even import charts and tables from *Microsoft Word* and *Excel* and download images from Internet sites directly into your slide templates.

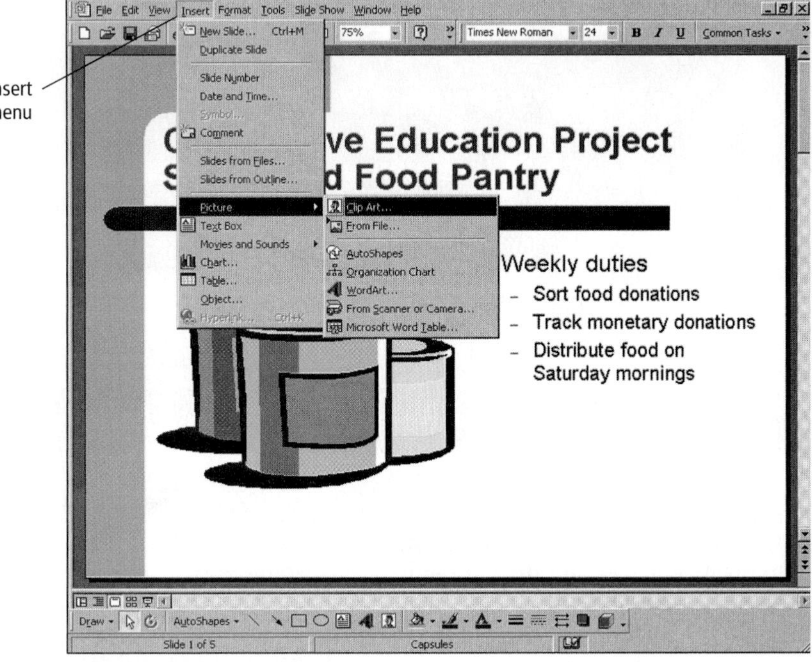

Figure 31.2 ***Microsoft PowerPoint*** **Insert menu.**

- **Audio Narration** Using a microphone that you hook up to your computer (or that may come preinstalled), you can record audio narration directly to *PowerPoint*. You can then set certain audio clips to play alongside specific slides.
- **Animated Transitions** *PowerPoint* can also create animated transitions between slides. These transitions include dissolves, checkerboards, and fades to black. Because of their potential to distract listeners from your content, you should use these effects in moderation.

Using Visual Aids in Your Presentations

Visual Aid	Advantages	Disadvantages
Computer presentations	Clear Easy to read Professional Graphics, video, sound, and animated effects Portable (disk or CD-ROM)	Special equipment needed Expertise needed Special software needed Software might not be compatible with all computer systems
Overhead projectors	Transparencies are inexpensive Transparencies are easily prepared with computer or copier Transparencies are portable Transparencies can be written on during presentation Projector is easy to operate	Transparencies can stick together Transparencies can be placed upside down Some projectors are noisy Transparencies must be placed on projector by hand Speaker must avoid power cord to projector during presentation
Slide projector	Colorful Professional Projector is easy to use Order of slides can be reversed during presentation Portable (slide carousel)	Slides are expensive to produce Special equipment needed for lettering and graphics Dark room needed for presentation Slides can jam in projector
Posters or flip charts	Low-tech and personal Good for small-group presentations Portable	May not be large enough to be seen in some rooms Artistic ability needed May be expensive if prepared professionally Must be secured to an easel
Chalkboards or whiteboards	Available in most rooms Easy to use Easy to erase or change information during presentation	Difficult to draw complicated graphics Handwriting must be legible Must catch errors as you write Cannot face audience when writing or drawing Very informal

Checklist: Designing Visual Aids

- ☐ Do not put more than three or four major points on a single visual.
- ☐ Use single words or short phrases, not sentences or paragraphs.
- ☐ Use bulleted or numbered lists.
- ☐ Use drawings and photographs only when they are large enough and clear enough to be seen.
- ☐ Limit the number of visuals. For a three- to five-minute presentation, five or six visuals are usually enough.
- ☐ Use color to enhance your presentation. Use contrasting colors for backgrounds so lettering or graphics stand out.
- ☐ Use type that is large enough for your audience to see (44- to 50-point type for major headings and 30- to 34-point type for text).
- ☐ Use the same color type and the same typeface and type size for comparable material.
- ☐ Do not use elaborate graphics or special effects just because your computer software enables you to do so (this is especially relevant for users of *PowerPoint*).

Exercise

Create visuals for an oral presentation based on the content of a paper that you have just written for one of your classes. Begin by deciding which points need to be illustrated for your audience. Then, consulting the chart on page 665, decide what kinds of visuals would be most effective.

31e Rehearsing Your Speech

There is a direct relationship between how thoroughly you rehearse and how effective your speech is. For this reason, practice your speech often—at least five times—and make sure you practice delivering your speech with your visuals. (You want to discover problems with your visuals now and not during your presentation.) Do not try to memorize your entire speech, but be sure you know it well enough so you can move from point to point without constantly looking at your notes.

If possible, rehearse your speech in the actual room you will be using, and try standing at the back of the room to make sure your visuals can be seen clearly. You should also practice in front of friends to get some constructive criticism about both the content and the delivery of your speech. Another strategy is to use a tape recorder to help you rehearse. When you play back the tape, you can hear whether you are pronouncing your words clearly and whether you are saying "uh" or "you know" throughout your presentation. Finally, time yourself. Make certain your three-minute speech actually takes three minutes to deliver.

31f Delivering Your Speech

The most important part of your speech is your delivery. Keep in mind that a certain amount of nervousness is normal, so try not to focus on it too much. Channel the nervous energy into your speech, and let it work for you. While you are waiting to begin, take some deep breaths. Once you get to the front of the room, do not start right away. Make sure everything you will need is there and all your equipment is positioned properly.

Before you speak, make sure both feet are flat on the floor and you are facing the audience. Do not begin speaking while you are looking at your notes. When you begin speaking, pace yourself. Speak slowly and clearly, and look at the entire audience, one person at a time. Make sure you speak *to* your audience, not *at* them. Even though your speech is planned, your delivery should be natural and conversational. Speak loudly enough for everyone in the room to hear you, and remember to vary your pitch and your volume so that you do not speak in a monotone. Try using pauses to emphasize important points and to give listeners time to consider what you have said. Repeat key words and phrases to keep your audience focused (and to keep yourself on track). Finally, sound enthusiastic about your subject. If you appear to be bored or distracted, your audience will be too.

As you speak, give listeners cues about where you are in the speech—for example, when you are about to present the main idea, when you will present support for the main idea, and when you are about to finish. Because a speech is more difficult to follow than a piece of writing, you will need to include more transitions than you would in your writing.

Transitions for Speeches

- I believe that . . . ,
- I can give three examples to support my point that . . . ,
- First . . . ,
- Second . . . ,
- Here is the third and most important example . . . ,
- Now that you have heard my three examples . . . ,
- I want to end with the following story . . . ,
- I hope you agree that . . . ,

Do not get flustered if someone asks you to speak louder or if some people in your audience look bored. You can certainly change your pace or volume to get more attention, but remember that a listener may be distracted by factors completely unrelated to your speech.

Your movements should be purposeful and natural. Do not pace or lean against something. Move around only when the need arises—for example, to change a visual, to point to a chart, or to distribute something. Never turn your back to your audience; if you have to write on the board, make sure you are angled toward the audience. Try to use hand movements to emphasize points, but do not play with pens or note cards as you speak, and do not put your hands in your pockets. Also, resist the temptation to deliver your speech from behind a podium or a table; come around to the front, and address the audience directly.

Remember to dress appropriately for the occasion. How you look will be the first thing that listeners notice. (Although shorts and a T-shirt may be appropriate for an afternoon in the park, they are not suitable for a presentation.) Dressing appropriately demonstrates your respect for your audience and shows that you are someone who deserves to be taken seriously.

Finally, do not sit down too quickly. Leave time for questions. Your audience may want to challenge something you have said or ask you to clarify some of your points. If someone asks a question that you have already answered in your speech, repeat the information as briefly as possible. Do not be upset if someone begins to argue with you; an appropriate response might be "That's an interesting angle. I'll be glad to talk to you about it after my presentation is over." If you cannot answer a question, say that you will find the answer and email it.

ESL Tip

Some ESL students are nervous about delivering a speech, especially if they have strong accents. However, even students who have difficulties with English can deliver effective speeches by following the tips in this section on body language, eye contact, and pacing.

Checklist: Delivering Your Speech

- ☐ Take your time before you begin.
- ☐ Make sure your visuals are positioned properly.
- ☐ Make sure your equipment is operating properly.
- ☐ Position yourself effectively.
- ☐ Stand straight.
- ☐ Speak slowly and clearly.
- ☐ Maintain eye contact with the audience.
- ☐ Use natural gestures.
- ☐ Face the audience at all times.
- ☐ Do not let the audience see your visuals before you introduce them or after you finish talking about them.
- ☐ Do not talk to your visuals. Look at and talk to your audience. Even if you have to point to a visual on the screen, make sure you are looking at your audience when you speak.
- ☐ Do not just show or read visuals to your audience. Tell your audience more than they can see or read for themselves.
- ☐ Do not block your visuals.
- ☐ Try to relax.
- ☐ Do not get flustered if something unexpected happens.
- ☐ If you forget something, don't let your audience know. Work the information in later.
- ☐ Do not sit down immediately after your speech. Leave time for questions.
- ☐ Distribute any handouts before or after the speech, not during it.

STUDENT WRITER AT WORK

Applying for a Job

Jonathan C. Wilde, a student at Louisiana State University, is applying for a communications internship at WRZ-TV and Radio. Using the student profile and job description provided below, write a letter of application and a résumé for Jonathan. Begin by reviewing Chapter 28 and selecting the best format for Jonathan's résumé. Next, determine what information from Jonathan's profile you should include in the application letter and résumé and what information (if any) you should omit. Finally, write the letter of application and résumé, consulting the checklists on pages 612 and 616–17 as you revise and edit.

STUDENT PROFILE

Personal Information

Name: Jonathan C. Wilde
Address: Box 45, Highland Hall, Louisiana State University, Baton Rouge, LA 70803-7202
Home Phone: 225-555-4321
Cell Phone: 225-555-0123
School Email: jwilde457@lsu.edu
Personal Email: spideysense@rsn.com

Education

Jonathan is a twenty-year-old junior in the Manship School of Mass Communication at Louisiana State University. He is majoring in advertising with a minor in English literature. He expects to graduate with a Bachelor of Arts in Mass Communication in 2005. He has an overall Grade Point Average (GPA) of 3.45, has been named to the Dean's List for the past two semesters, and is a member of the Golden Key National Honor Society.

He has completed four of the seven core courses required for his major, including Introduction to Mass Media, Media Writing, Visual Communication, and Foundations of Advertising and Public Relations. He is currently enrolled in Foundations of Media Research as well as two modern literature classes and a computer graphics design class.

Employment

In the spring semester of his sophomore year, Jonathan became Promotions Assistant for KLSU, Louisiana State University's student radio station. He collaborates with the Promotions Director to create designs for

T-shirts, bumper stickers, and posters bearing the KLSU logo. He designs and writes copy for KLSU advertisements that appear in the university's student newspaper. He also creates flyers for station-sponsored events, including an annual Battle of the Bands featuring LSU musicians.

In addition to his work at KLSU, Jonathan regularly contributes feature articles to *Legacy*, LSU's quarterly student magazine. He also works five hours a week as a collections assistant at LSU's Middleton Library, a job he has held since his freshman year.

Other Experience and Interests

Jonathan is an avid writer and artist. In high school, he was editor-in-chief of the student literary magazine as well as art director for the yearbook. He knows how to use *Adobe Photoshop*, *Adobe Illustrator*, and *QuarkXPress*, and is currently using *Macromedia Dreamweaver* to experiment with Web design.

JOB DESCRIPTION

WRZ-TV and Radio, Communications Internship (Posted 3/15/04 on university's career services Web site)

The Public Relations and Promotions Department of the WRZ Media Group seeks qualified student candidates for a one-year communications internship.

Responsibilities include assisting the Manager of Communications in the creation of advertisements, annual reports, brochures, flyers, posters, press releases, and other station-related communications; writing and designing a monthly newsletter for WRZ Media Group employees; performing administrative and clerical duties; and providing some customer support.

Candidates should demonstrate strong writing and editorial skills as well as knowledge of the principles of design. Preferred candidates should have experience using computer graphics software (including *Adobe Photoshop* and *Adobe Illustrator*) and desktop publishing applications (such as *QuarkXPress*).

Résumés and cover letters should be submitted to <www.humanresources@wrz.com> with the subject line "communications intern." Résumés may also be mailed to Human Resources, Attention: Richard Davidow, WRZ Media Group, 555 Hilltop Dr., Baton Rouge, LA 70803.

Grammar Checker

Wordiness:

It is important to learn the true facts b
proceed.

PART 6

Sentence Style

Chapter 32

Building Simple Sentences

Frequently Asked Questions

What is a phrase? (p. 677)
What is a clause? (p. 678)
How can I use words and phrases to expand simple sentences? (p. 679)

A **sentence** is an independent grammatical unit that includes a subject and a predicate and expresses a complete thought.

The quick brown fox jumped over the lazy dog.

It has come from outer space.

See 32b1

A **simple subject** is a noun or noun substitute (*fox, it*) that tells who or what the sentence is about. A **simple predicate** is a verb or verb phrase (*jumped, has come*) that tells or asks something about the subject. The **complete subject** of a sentence includes the simple subject plus all its modifiers (*the quick brown fox*). The **complete predicate** includes the verb or verb phrase as well as all the words associated with it—such as modifiers, objects, and complements (*jumped over the lazy dog, has come from outer space*).

ESL Tip

In some languages, such as Spanish, the subject of a sentence can sometimes be omitted (because the form of the sentence's verb clearly indicates who or what the subject of the sentence is). In English, however, every sentence must have a subject.

32a Constructing Simple Sentences

A **simple sentence** consists of at least one subject and one predicate. Simple sentences conform to one of five basic patterns.

(1) Subject + Intransitive Verb (s + v)

The most basic simple sentence consists of just a subject and a verb or **verb phrase** (the main verb plus all its auxiliary verbs).

See 45c1

s v
The price of gold rose.

s v
Stock prices may fall.

Here the verbs *rose* and *may fall* are **intransitive**—that is, they do not need an object to complete their meaning.

(2) Subject + Transitive Verb + Direct Object (s + v + do)

Another kind of simple sentence consists of the subject, a verb, and a direct object.

s v do
Van Gogh created *The Starry Night.*

s v do
Caroline saved Jake.

Here the verbs *created* and *saved* are **transitive**—each requires an object to complete its meaning in the sentence. In each sentence, the **direct object** indicates where the verb's action is directed and who or what is affected by it.

ESL Tip

To determine whether a verb is intransitive or transitive, consult a dictionary. Remember, though, that some verbs, such as *write*, can be intransitive or transitive.

She wrote all night. (intransitive)
She wrote a paper about her experiences studying in Spain. (transitive)

(3) Subject + Transitive Verb + Direct Object + Object Complement (s + v + do + oc)

Some simple sentences include an **object complement,** a word or phrase that renames or describes the direct object.

s v do oc
The class elected Bridget treasurer. (Object complement *treasurer* renames direct object *Bridget.*)

s v do oc
I found the exam easy. (Object complement *easy* describes direct object *exam*.)

(4) Subject + Linking Verb + Subject Complement (s + v + sc)

Another kind of simple sentence consists of a subject, a linking verb (a verb that connects a subject to its complement), and the **subject complement** (the word or phrase that describes or renames the subject).

s v sc
The injection was painless.

s v sc
Tony Blair became prime minister.

Note that the linking verb is like an equal sign, equating the subject with its complement (*Tony Blair* = *prime minister*).

(5) Subject + Transitive Verb + Indirect Object + Direct Object (s + v + io + do)

Some simple sentences include an **indirect object,** which indicates to whom or for whom the verb's action was done.

s v io do
Cyrano wrote Roxanne a poem. (Cyrano wrote a poem for Roxanne.)

s v io do
The officer handed Frank a ticket. (The officer handed a ticket to Frank.)

Exercise 1

In each of the following sentences, underline the subject once and the predicate twice. Then, label direct objects, indirect objects, subject complements, and object complements.

sc
Example: Isaac Asimov was a science fiction writer.

1. Isaac Asimov first saw science fiction stories in his parents' Brooklyn store.
2. He practiced writing by telling his schoolmates stories.
3. Asimov published his first story in *Astounding Science Fiction*.
4. The magazine's editor, John W. Campbell, encouraged Asimov to continue writing.

5. The young writer researched scientific principles to make his stories more accurate.
6. Asimov's "Foundation" series of novels is a "future history."
7. The World Science Fiction Convention gave the series a Hugo Award.
8. Sometimes Asimov used "Paul French" as a pseudonym.
9. *Biochemistry and Human Metabolism* was Asimov's first nonfiction book.
10. Asimov coined the term *robotics*.

32b Identifying Phrases and Clauses

Individual words may be combined into *phrases* and *clauses*.

(1) Identifying Phrases

A **phrase** is a group of related words that lacks a subject or predicate or both and functions as a single part of speech. It cannot stand alone as a sentence.

- A **verb phrase** consists of a main verb and all its auxiliary verbs.

  Time is flying.

- A **noun phrase** includes a noun or pronoun plus all related modifiers.

  I'll climb the highest mountain.

- A **prepositional phrase** consists of a preposition, its object, and any modifiers of that object.

  They discussed the ethical implications of the animal studies.
  He was last seen heading into the orange sunset.

- A **verbal phrase** consists of a **verbal** (participle, gerund, or infinitive) and its related objects, modifiers, or complements. A verbal phrase may be a **participial phrase,** a **gerund phrase,** or an **infinitive phrase.**

  Encouraged by the voter turnout, the candidate predicted a victory. (participial phrase)
  Taking it easy always makes sense. (gerund phrase)
  The jury recessed to evaluate the evidence. (infinitive phrase)

- An **absolute phrase** usually consists of a noun and a participle, accompanied by modifiers. It modifies an entire independent clause rather than a particular word or phrase.

  Their toes tapping, they watched the auditions.

(2) Identifying Clauses

A **clause** is a group of related words that includes a subject and a predicate. An **independent** (main) **clause** can stand alone as a sentence, but a **dependent** (subordinate) **clause** cannot. It must always be combined with an independent clause to form a complex sentence.

See 33b

[Lucretia Mott was an abolitionist.] [She was also a pioneer for women's rights.] (two independent clauses)

[Lucretia Mott was an abolitionist] [who was also a pioneer for women's rights.] (independent clause, dependent clause)

[Although Lucretia Mott is widely known for her support of women's rights,] [she was also a prominent abolitionist.] (dependent clause, independent clause)

Dependent clauses may be *adjective*, *adverb*, or *noun* clauses.

- **Adjective clauses,** sometimes called **relative clauses,** modify nouns or pronouns and always follow the nouns or pronouns they modify. They are introduced by relative pronouns—*that, what, whatever, which, who, whose, whom, whoever,* or *whomever*—or by the adverbs *where* or *when*.

  The television series *M*A*S*H*, which depicted life in an army hospital in Korea during the Korean War, ran for eleven years. (Adjective clause modifies the noun *M*A*S*H*.)

  William Styron's novel *Sophie's Choice* is set in Brooklyn, where the narrator lives in a house painted pink. (Adjective clause modifies the noun *Brooklyn*.)

NOTE: Some adjective clauses, called **elliptical clauses,** are grammatically incomplete but nevertheless can be easily understood from the context of the sentence. Typically, a part of the subject or predicate (or the entire subject or predicate) is missing.

Although [they were] full, they could not resist dessert.

- **Adverb clauses** modify single words (verbs, adjectives, or adverbs), entire phrases, or independent clauses. They are always introduced by subordinating conjunctions. Adverb clauses provide information to answer the questions *how*? *where*? *when*? *why*? and *to what extent*?

Exhausted after the match was over, Kim decided to take a long nap. (Adverb clause modifies *exhausted*, telling *when* Kim was exhausted.)

Mark will go wherever there's a party. (Adverb clause modifies *will go*, telling *where* Mark will go.)

Because 75 percent of its exports are fish products, Iceland's economy is heavily dependent on the fishing industry. (Adverb clause modifies independent clause, telling *why* the fishing industry is so important.)

- **Noun clauses** function as subjects, objects, or complements. A noun clause may be introduced by a relative pronoun or by *whether*, *when*, *where*, *why*, or *how*.

What you see is what you get. (Noun clauses serve as subject and subject complement.)

They finally decided which candidate was most qualified. (Noun clause serves as direct object of verb *decided*.)

Exercise 2

Which of the following groups of words are independent clauses? Which are dependent clauses? Which are phrases? Label each word group *IC*, *DC*, or *P*.

Example: Coming through the rye. (P)

1. Beauty is truth.
2. When knights were bold.
3. In a galaxy far away.
4. He saw stars.
5. I hear a symphony.
6. Whenever you're near.
7. The clock struck ten.
8. The red planet.
9. Slowly I turned.
10. For the longest time.

32c Expanding Simple Sentences

A **simple sentence** is a single independent clause. A simple sentence can consist of just a subject and a verb.

Jessica fell.

Or, a simple sentence can be expanded with modifying words and phrases.

Jessica and her younger sister Victoria almost immediately fell hopelessly in love with the very mysterious Henry Goodyear.

See Ch. 33

NOTE: Joined with other clauses, simple sentences can be expanded into compound and complex sentences.

(1) Expanding Simple Sentences with Adjectives and Adverbs

See 49a

Adjectives and adverbs can expand a simple sentence by modifying nouns, verbs, or other adjectives or adverbs. Read this sentence again:

Jessica and her younger sister Victoria almost immediately fell hopelessly in love with the very mysterious Henry Goodyear.

Here, two adjectives describe nouns.

Adjective	**Noun**
younger	sister
mysterious	Henry Goodyear

Four adverbs describe the action of verbs or modify adjectives or other adverbs.

Adverb	
almost	immediately (adverb)
immediately	fell (verb)
hopelessly	fell (verb)
very	mysterious (adjective)

Exercise 3

Label all the adjectives and adverbs in the following simple sentences.

Example: Marge listened secretly [adv] to the quiet [adj] conversation at the next [adj] table.

1. John swallowed the last of his cold coffee and gently set the thermos down. (Sherman Alexie, *Indian Killer*)
2. Each year I watched the field across from the Store turn caterpillar green, then gradually frosty white. (Maya Angelou, *I Know Why the Caged Bird Sings*)

3. He gingerly held the box and studied the old, familiar pictures. (Alan Lightman, *Good Benito*)
4. Stealthy and alert, he hunkers down like a predator and sneaks right up behind the seal, climbs decisively onto its back, and grips its cheeks in both hands. (Diane Ackerman, *The Rarest of the Rare*)
5. In late mammal times, the body evidently added a third brain. (Robert Bly, *The Sibling Society*)

Exercise 4

Using the following sentences as models, write five original simple sentences. Use adverbs and adjectives where the model sentences use them, and then underline and label these modifiers.

Example: Manek gazed shyly (adv) at the beautiful (adj) girl.

The cat ran wildly (adv) around the empty (adj) house.

1. Walkways from the Washington Monument to the Lincoln Memorial quickly filled.
2. People, shrugging off their winter coats, seemed to step more lightly around the mall.
3. Some sat on benches in carefully pressed white shirts, holding half-eaten sandwiches in pale hands.
4. Others, dressed in shiny spandex or torn T-shirts, spun wildly by on bikes or Rollerblades, sweatily celebrating the first days of spring.
5. Finally, the cherry blossoms were in flower.

(2) Expanding Simple Sentences with Nouns and Verbals

Nouns and verbals that serve as modifiers can help you build richer simple sentences.

Nouns Nouns can act as adjectives modifying other nouns.

He needed two cake pans for the layer cake.

Verbals Verbals (participles, infinitives, and gerunds) may also act as modifiers.

All the living former presidents attended the funeral. (Present participle acts as adjective.)

The Grand Canyon is the attraction to visit. (Infinitive acts as adjective.)

The puzzle was impossible to solve. (Infinitive acts as adverb.)

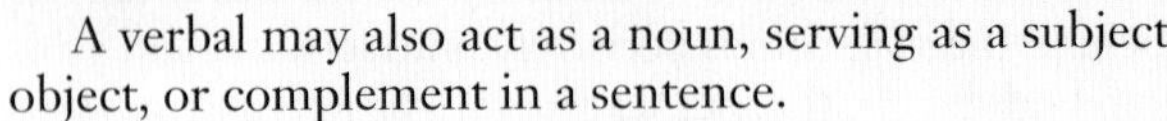

Close-up: Verbals Used as Nouns

A verbal may also act as a noun, serving as a subject, object, or complement in a sentence.

The <u>making</u> of a motion picture can be a complex and lengthy process. (Gerund acts as noun.)

<u>To err</u> is human. (Infinitive acts as noun.)

It took me the entire lab period to identify my <u>unknown</u>. (Past participle acts as noun.)

Exercise 5

For additional practice in building simple sentences with individual words, combine each of the following groups of sentences into one simple sentence that contains several modifiers. You may have to add, delete, or reorder words.

Example: The ~~night was~~ cold, ~~The night was~~ wet, ~~The~~ night scared them, ~~They were~~ terribly ~~scared.~~

1. The ship landed. The ship was from space. The ship was tremendous. It landed silently.
2. It landed in a field. The field was grassy. The field was deserted.
3. A dog appeared. The dog was tiny. The dog was abandoned. The dog was a stray.
4. The dog was brave. The dog was curious. He approached the spacecraft. The spacecraft was burning. He approached it carefully.
5. A creature emerged from the spaceship. The creature was smiling. He was purple. He emerged slowly.
6. The dog and the alien stared at each other. The dog was little. The alien was purple. They stared meaningfully.
7. The dog and the alien walked. They walked silently. They walked carefully. They walked toward each other.
8. The dog barked. He barked tentatively. He barked questioningly. The dog was uneasy.
9. The alien extended his hand. The alien was grinning. He extended it slowly. The hand was hairy.
10. In his hand was a bag. The bag was made of canvas. The bag was green. The bag was for laundry.

(3) Expanding Simple Sentences with Prepositional Phrases

A <u>preposition</u> indicates the relationship between a noun or noun substitute and other words in a sentence. A **prepositional phrase**

consists of the preposition, its object (the noun or noun substitute), and any modifiers of that object. Prepositional phrases can function in a sentence as adjectives or as adverbs.

prep obj
Carry Nation was a crusader for temperance. (Prepositional phrase functions as adjective modifying the noun *crusader*.)

prep mod obj
The Madeira River flows into the mighty Amazon. (Prepositional phrase functions as adverb modifying the verb *flows*.)

Exercise 6

Read the following sentences. Underline each prepositional phrase, and then connect it with an arrow to the word it modifies. Label each prepositional phrase to indicate whether it functions as an adjective or an adverb.

adj adv
Example: The porch of her grandmother's house wraps around all three sides.

1. Carol sat on the front porch and rocked in her grandmother's chair.
2. Age had surprised her in the middle of her life, crept up behind her in the mirror, and attacked her at the joints of her knees and hips.
3. Now she sat on the porch and felt that it too creaked in its joints.
4. Inside the house, her grandmother slept in a narrow bed under a worn chenille spread, the mattress sagging and spilling over the edges of the frame.
5. The slow rocking of the chair soothed the worries from Carol's mind.

Exercise 7

For additional practice in using prepositional phrases, combine each of these sentence pairs to create one simple sentence that includes a prepositional phrase. You may add, delete, or reorder words. Some sentences may have more than one possible correct version.

by toxic
Example: America's drinking water is being contaminated~~. Toxic~~ substances~~ are contaminating it~~.

1. Toxic waste disposal presents a serious problem. Americans have this problem.
2. Hazardous chemicals pose a threat. People are threatened.
3. Some towns, like Times Beach, Missouri, were completely abandoned. Their residents abandoned them.

4. Dioxin is one chemical. It has serious toxic effects.
5. Dioxin is highly toxic. The toxicity affects animals and humans.
6. Toxic chemical wastes like dioxin may be found. Over fifty thousand dumps have them.
7. Industrial parks contain toxic wastes. Open pits, ponds, and lagoons are where the toxic substances are.
8. Toxic wastes pose dangers. The land, water, and air are endangered.
9. In addition, toxic substances are a threat. They threaten our public health and our economy.
10. Immediate toxic waste cleanup would be a tremendous benefit. Americans are the ones who would benefit.

(4) Expanding Simple Sentences with Verbal Phrases

See 32b1

A verbal phrase consists of a **verbal** (participle, gerund, or infinitive) and its related objects, modifiers, or complements.

Some verbal phrases act as modifiers. **Participial phrases** always function as adjectives; **infinitive phrases** may function as adjectives or as adverbs.

Fascinated by Scheherazade's story, they waited anxiously for the next installment. (Participial phrase modifies pronoun *they*.)

It wasn't the ideal time to do homework. (Infinitive phrase modifies noun *time*.)

Henry M. Stanley went to Africa to find Dr. Livingstone. (Infinitive phrase modifies verb *went*.)

Close-up: Using Modifiers

When you use verbal phrases as modifiers, be especially careful not to create misplaced modifiers or dangling modifiers.

See Ch. 39

Other verbal phrases act as nouns. For example, **gerund phrases,** like gerunds themselves, are always used as nouns. **Infinitive phrases** may also be used as nouns.

Making a living is not always easy. (Gerund phrase serves as sentence's subject.)

Wendy appreciated Tom's being honest. (Gerund phrase serves as object of verb *appreciated*.)

The entire town was shocked by their breaking up. (Gerund phrase is object of preposition *by*.)

<u>To know him</u> is <u>to love him</u>. (Infinitive phrase *To know him* serves as sentence's subject; infinitive phrase *to love him* is subject complement.)

Exercise 8

For practice in using verbal phrases, combine each of these sentence pairs to create one simple sentence that contains a participial phrase, a gerund phrase, or an infinitive phrase. Underline the verbal phrase in your sentence. You may have to add, delete, or reorder words, and you may find more than one way to combine each pair.

Example: The American labor movement has helped millions of workers, ~~It has won~~ winning <u>them higher wages and better working conditions</u>.

1. In 1912, the textile workers of Lawrence, Massachusetts, went on strike. They were demonstrating for "Bread and Roses, too."
2. The workers wanted higher wages and better working conditions. They felt trapped in their miserable jobs.
3. Mill workers toiled six days a week. They earned about $1.50 for this.
4. Most of the workers were women and children. They worked up to sixteen hours a day.
5. The mills were dangerous. They were filled with hazards.
6. Many mill workers joined unions. They did this to fight exploitation by their employers.
7. They wanted to improve their lives. This was their goal.
8. Finally, twenty-five thousand workers walked off their jobs. They knew they were risking everything.
9. The police and the state militia were called in. Attacking the strikers was their mission.
10. After sixty-three days, the American Woolen Company surrendered. This ended the strike with a victory for the workers.

(Adapted from William Cahn, *Lawrence 1912: The Bread and Roses Strike*)

(5) Expanding Simple Sentences with Appositives

An **appositive** is a noun or a noun phrase that functions as an adjective, identifying or renaming an adjacent noun or pronoun.

Farrington hated his boss, <u>a real tyrant</u>. (Appositive *a real tyrant* identifies noun *boss*.)

<u>A barrier island off the coast of New Jersey</u>, Long Beach Island is a popular vacation spot. (Appositive *A barrier island off the coast of New Jersey* identifies noun *Long Beach Island*.)

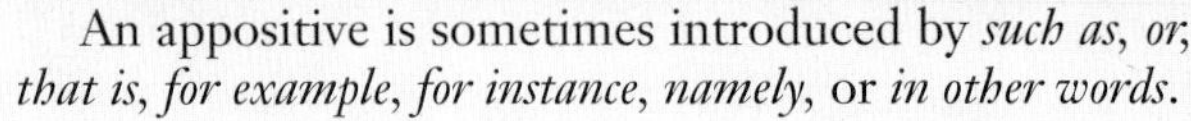

Close-up: Appositives

An appositive is sometimes introduced by *such as*, *or*, *that is*, *for example*, *for instance*, *namely*, or *in other words*.

A regional airline, such as Southwest, may account for more than half the departures at some second-tier airports.

Rabies, or hydrophobia, was nearly always fatal until Pasteur's work.

NOTE: For information on punctuating sentences that include appositives, **see 51d1.**

Exercise 9

For practice in using appositives when you write, build five new simple sentences by combining each of the following pairs, turning one sentence in each pair into an appositive. (Note that each pair can be combined in a variety of different ways and that the appositive can precede or follow the noun it modifies.) You may need to delete or reorder words in some cases.

Example: ~~René Descartes was a~~ A noted French philosopher, René Descartes is best known for his famous declaration, "I think, therefore I am."

1. *I Know Why the Caged Bird Sings* is the first book in Maya Angelou's autobiography. It deals primarily with her life as a young girl in Stamps, Arkansas.
2. Catgut is a tough cord generally made from the intestines of sheep. Catgut is used for tennis rackets, for violin strings, and for surgical stitching.
3. Hermes was the messenger of the Greek gods. He is usually portrayed as an athletic youth wearing a cap and winged sandals.
4. Emiliano Zapata was a hero of the Mexican Revolution. He is credited with effecting land reform in his home state of Morelos.
5. Pulsars are celestial objects that emit regular pulses of radiation. Pulsars were discovered in 1967.

(6) Expanding Simple Sentences with Compound Constructions

See 40a

A **compound construction** consists of two or more grammatically parallel items that are equivalent in importance. Within simple sentences, compound words or phrases—subjects, predicates, complements, or modifiers—may be joined in one of three ways.

- With commas:

  He took one long, loving look at his '57 Chevy.

- With coordinating conjunctions: See 33a1

  They reeled, whirled, flounced, capered, gamboled, and spun. (Kurt Vonnegut Jr., "Harrison Bergeron")

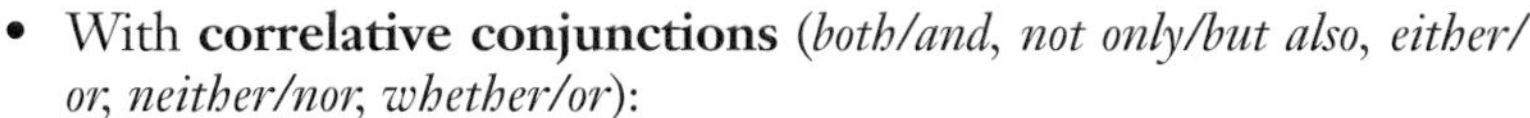

- With **correlative conjunctions** (*both/and, not only/but also, either/or, neither/nor, whether/or*):

  Both milk and carrots contain Vitamin A.

  Neither the twentieth-century poet Sylvia Plath nor the nineteenth-century poet Emily Dickinson achieved recognition during her lifetime.

Exercise 10

A. Expand each of the following sentences by using compound subjects and/or predicates.

Example: Bill ^and Juan^ played guitar ^and sang.^

B. Then, expand your simple sentence with modifying words and phrases, using compound constructions whenever possible.

Example: ^*Despite butterflies in their stomachs and a restless audience,*^ Bill and Juan played guitar and sang.

1. Cortés explored the New World.
2. Virginia Woolf wrote novels.
3. Edison invented the phonograph.
4. PBS airs educational television programming.
5. Thomas Jefferson signed the Declaration of Independence.

Exercise 11

To practice building sentences with compound subjects, predicates, and modifiers, combine each of the following groups of sentences into one.

Example: Marion ^and^ ~~studied.~~ Frank studied ~~. They studied~~ quietly ^and^ ~~. They studied~~ diligently.

1. Robert Ludlum writes best-selling spy thrillers. Tom Clancy writes best-selling spy thrillers. John le Carré writes best-selling spy thrillers.

2. Smoking can cause heart disease. A high-fat diet can cause heart disease. Stress can cause heart disease.
3. Walter Mosley and Sue Grafton write detective novels. They both write about "hard-boiled" detectives.
4. Successful rock bands give concerts. They record albums. They make videos. They license merchandise bearing their names and likenesses.
5. Sports superstars like Tiger Woods and Michael Jordan earn additional income by making personal appearances. They earn money by endorsing products.

Chapter 33

Building Compound and Complex Sentences

Frequently Asked Questions

How do I create a compound sentence? (p. 689)
How do I create a complex sentence? (p. 692)

Writing that includes varied sentences is more interesting than writing that does not. One way to vary your sentences is to use compound and complex sentences along with simple sentences.

33a Building Compound Sentences

A **compound sentence** is created when two or more independent clauses are joined with *coordinating conjunctions*, *transitional words or phrases*, *correlative conjunctions*, *semicolons*, or *colons*.

(1) Using Coordinating Conjunctions

You can join two **independent clauses** with a **coordinating conjunction**—*and*, *or*, *nor*, *but*, *for*, *so*, or *yet*—preceded by a comma.

> The cowboy is a workingman, yet he has little in common with the urban blue-collar worker. (John R. Erickson, *The Modern Cowboy*)
>
> In the fall the war was always there, but we did not go to it any more. (Ernest Hemingway, "In Another Country")
>
> She carried a thin, small cane made from an umbrella, and with this she kept tapping the frozen earth in front of her. (Eudora Welty, "A Worn Path")

ESL Tip

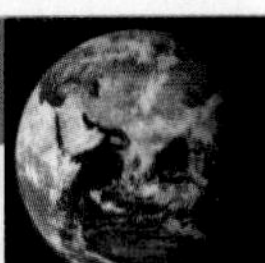

Some languages, such as Arabic, typically use coordination more than English does. If you think you are overusing coordination, try experimenting with subordination, which is explained in 34b2.

(2) Using Transitional Words and Phrases

You can join two independent clauses with a **transitional word or phrase,** preceded by a semicolon (and followed by a comma).

> Aerobic exercise can help lower blood pressure; however, those with high blood pressure should still limit salt intake.
>
> The saxophone does not belong to the brass family; in fact, it is a member of the woodwind family.

See 7b2

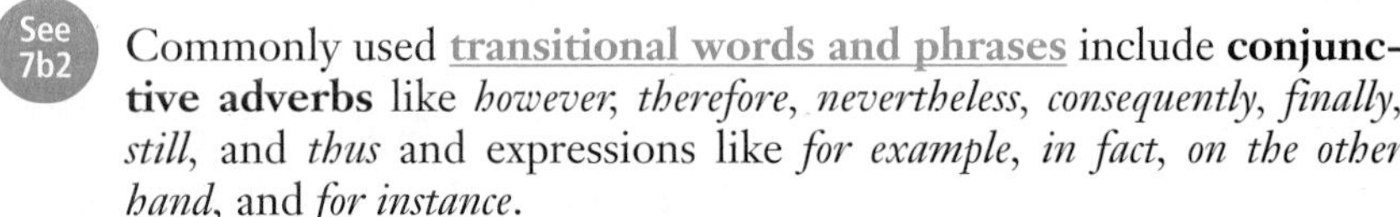

Commonly used transitional words and phrases include **conjunctive adverbs** like *however, therefore, nevertheless, consequently, finally, still,* and *thus* and expressions like *for example, in fact, on the other hand,* and *for instance.*

(3) Using Correlative Conjunctions

See 45g

You can use correlative conjunctions to join two independent clauses into a compound sentence.

> Either he left his coat in his locker, or he left it on the bus.

(4) Using Semicolons

See 52a

A semicolon can join two closely related independent clauses into a compound sentence.

> Alaska is the largest state; Rhode Island is the smallest.
>
> Theodore Roosevelt was president after the Spanish-American War; Andrew Johnson was president after the Civil War.

(5) Using Colons

See 55a

A colon can join two independent clauses.

> He got his orders: he was to leave for France on Sunday.
>
> They thought they knew the outcome: Truman would lose to Dewey.

Close-up: Using Compound Sentences

Joining independent clauses into compound sentences helps to show readers the relationships between the clauses. Compound sentences can indicate the following relationships:

- Addition (*and, in addition, not only . . . but also*)
- Contrast (*but, however*)
- Causal relationships (*so, therefore, consequently*)
- Alternatives (*or, either . . . or*)

Exercise 1

After reading the following paragraph, edit it to create as many compound sentences as you think your readers need to understand the relationships between ideas. When you have finished, bracket the independent clauses and underline the coordinating conjunctions, transitional words and phrases, correlative conjunctions, or punctuation marks that link clauses.

Paolo Soleri came to the United States from Italy. He came as an apprentice to Frank Lloyd Wright. Frank Lloyd Wright's designs celebrate the suburban lifestyle, with stand-alone homes meant for single families. Soleri's Utopian designs celebrate the city. Soleri believes that suburban lifestyles separate people from true nature. He also believes that our lifestyle separates us from the energy of the city. His first theoretical design was called Mesa City. It proposed to house two million people. Soleri is currently building one of his dream cities, Arcosanti, in the desert outside of Scottsdale, Arizona. This project is funded privately by Soleri. He teaches design and building classes to students who help build the city. The students' tuition helps pay for construction. He also makes wind bells and chimes. He sells these all over the world. The profits further finance Arcosanti. The design for Arcosanti evokes images of colonies erected on space stations. It also resembles the hillside towns in Soleri's home country, Italy. The problems with our current city structures grow each year. People are looking for ways to revitalize the city. Some are looking at Soleri's Arcosanti as a model for sustainable urban development and renewal.

Exercise 2

Add appropriate coordinating conjunctions, conjunctive adverbs, or correlative conjunctions as indicated to combine each pair of sentences into one well-constructed compound sentence that retains the meaning of the original pair. Be sure to use correct punctuation.

Example: The American population is aging~~.~~ , so people ~~People~~ seem to be increasingly concerned about what they eat. (coordinating conjunction)

1. The average American consumes 128 pounds of sugar each year. Most of us eat much more sugar than any other food additive, including salt. (conjunctive adverb)

2. Many of us are determined to reduce our sugar intake. We have consciously eliminated sweets from our diets. (conjunctive adverb)
3. Unfortunately, sugar is not found only in sweets. It is also found in many processed foods. (correlative conjunction)
4. Processed foods like puddings and cake contain sugar. Foods like ketchup and spaghetti sauce do too. (coordinating conjunction)
5. We are trying to cut down on sugar. We find limiting sugar intake extremely difficult. (coordinating conjunction)
6. Processors may use sugar in foods for taste. They may also use it to help prevent foods from spoiling and to improve the texture and appearance of food. (correlative conjunction)
7. Sugar comes in many different forms. It is easy to overlook on a package label. (coordinating conjunction)
8. Sugar may be called sucrose or fructose. It may also be called corn syrup, corn sugar, brown sugar, honey, or molasses. (coordinating conjunction)
9. No sugar is more nourishing than the others. It really does not matter which is consumed. (conjunctive adverb)
10. Sugars contain empty calories. Whenever possible, they should be avoided. (conjunctive adverb)

(Adapted from *Jane Brody's Nutrition Book*)

33b Building Complex Sentences

A **complex sentence** consists of one **independent clause** and at least one **dependent clause.**

A dependent clause cannot stand alone; it must be combined with an independent clause to form a sentence. A **subordinating conjunction** or **relative pronoun** links the independent and dependent clauses and indicates the relationship between them.

dependent clause / independent clause
[After the town was evacuated,] [the hurricane began.]

independent clause / dependent clause
[Officials watched the storm,] [which threatened to destroy the town.]

NOTE: Sometimes a dependent clause may be embedded within an independent clause.

dependent clause
Town officials, [who were very concerned], watched the storm.

Frequently Used Subordinating Conjunctions

after	in order that	unless
although	now that	until
as	once	when
as if	rather than	whenever
as though	since	where
because	so that	whereas
before	that	wherever
even though	though	while
if		

Relative Pronouns

that	whatever	who (whose, whom)
what	which	whoever (whomever)

Close-up: Using Complex Sentences

When you join clauses to create complex sentences, you help readers to see the relationships between your ideas. Complex sentences can indicate the following relationships:

- Time relationships (*before, after, until, when, since*)
- Contrast (*however, although*)
- Causal relationships (*therefore, because, so that*)
- Conditional relationships (*if, unless*)
- Location (*where, wherever*)
- Identity (*who, which, that*)

Exercise 3

Bracket the independent and dependent clauses in the following complex sentences. Then, using the five sentences as models, create two new complex sentences in imitation of each. For each pair of new sentences, use the same subordinating conjunction or relative pronoun that appears in the original sentence.

Example: [Although life is sweet,] [it is sometimes hard.]
Although chemistry is difficult, it is often rewarding.
Although a computer may become obsolete, it can often be upgraded.

1. I said what I meant.
2. Savion Glover is the dancer who best exemplifies the phrase "poetry in motion."
3. Because she was considered a heretic, Joan of Arc was burned at the stake.
4. The oracle at Delphi predicted that Oedipus would murder his father and marry his mother.
5. The ghost vanished before Hamlet could question him further.

Exercise 4

Use a subordinating conjunction or relative pronoun to combine each of the following pairs of sentences into one well-constructed complex sentence. Be sure to choose a connecting word that indicates the relationship between the two sentences. You may have to change or reorder words.

Because some *, their*

Example: ~~Some~~ colleges are tightening admissions requirements. ~~Their~~ pool of students is growing smaller.

1. Many high school graduates are currently out of work. They need new skills for new careers.
2. Talented high school students are usually encouraged to go to college. Some high school graduates are now starting to see that a college education may not guarantee them a job.
3. A college education can cost a student more than $100,000. Vocational education is becoming increasingly important.
4. Vocational students complete their work in less than four years. They can enter the job market more quickly.
5. Nurses' aides, paralegals, travel agents, and computer technicians do not need college degrees. They have little trouble finding work.
6. Some four-year colleges are experiencing growth. Public community colleges and private trade schools are growing much more rapidly.
7. The best vocational schools are responsive to the needs of local businesses. They train students for jobs that actually exist.
8. For instance, a school in Detroit might offer advanced automotive design. A school in New York City might focus on fashion design.
9. Other schools offer courses in horticulture, respiratory therapy, and computer programming. They are able to place their graduates easily.

10. Laid-off workers, returning housewives, recent high school graduates, and even college graduates are reexamining vocational education. They all hope to find rewarding careers.

Close-up: Compound-Complex Sentences

Another way to vary your sentences is to create an occasional compound-complex sentence. A **compound-complex sentence** consists of two or more independent clauses and at least one dependent clause.

dependent clause: [When small foreign imports began dominating the US automobile industry,] independent clause: [consumers were very responsive,] but independent clause: [American auto workers were dismayed.]

Chapter 34

Writing Varied Sentences

Frequently Asked Questions

How do I combine choppy sentences to make my writing "flow"? (p. 698)

How do I revise a string of compound sentences? (p. 699)

How do I revise sentences when they all begin the same way? (p. 702)

Using varied sentences can help make your writing livelier and more interesting and can also ensure that you emphasize the most important ideas in your sentences.

34a Varying Sentence Length

To add interest to your writing, try to mix sentences of different lengths.

(1) Mixing Long and Short Sentences

A paragraph consisting entirely of short sentences (or entirely of long ones) can be dull.

> Drag racing began in California in the 1940s. It was an alternative to street racing. Street racing was illegal and dangerous. It flourished in the 1950s and 1960s. Eventually, it became almost a rite of passage. Then, during the 1970s, almost one-third of America's racetracks closed. Today, however, drag racing is making a comeback.

Combining some of the paragraph's short sentences into longer ones creates a more interesting passage.

> Drag racing began in California in the 1940s as an alternative to street racing, which was illegal and dangerous. It flourished in the 1950s and 1960s, eventually becoming almost a rite of passage. Then, during the 1970s, almost one-third of America's racetracks closed. Today, however, drag racing is making a comeback.

(2) Following a Long Sentence with a Short One

Another way to add interest is to follow one or more long sentences with a short one. (This strategy also places emphasis on the short sentence.)

> Over the years, vitamin boosters say, a misconception has grown that as long as there are no signs or symptoms of, say, scurvy, then we have all of the vitamin C we need. Although we know how much of a particular vitamin or mineral will prevent clinical disease, we have practically no information on how much is necessary for peak health. In short, we know how sick is sick, but we don't know how well is well. (*Philadelphia Magazine*)

Exercise 1

Combine each of the following sentence groups into one long sentence. Then, compose a relatively short sentence to follow each long one. Finally, combine all the sentences into a paragraph, adding a topic sentence and any transitions necessary for coherence. Proofread your paragraph to be sure the sentences are varied in length.

1. Chocolate is composed of more than three hundred compounds. Phenylethylamine is one such compound. Its presence in the brain may be linked to the emotion of falling in love.
2. Americans now consume a good deal of chocolate. On average, they eat more than nine pounds of chocolate per person per year. The typical Belgian, however, consumes almost fifteen pounds per year.
3. In recent years, Americans have begun a serious love affair with chocolate. Elegant chocolate boutiques sell exquisite bonbons by the piece. At least one hotel offers a "chocolate binge" vacation. The bimonthly *Chocolate News* for connoisseurs is flourishing.

(Adapted from *Newsweek*)

34b Combining Choppy Simple Sentences

Strings of short simple sentences can be tedious—and sometimes hard to follow, as this paragraph illustrates.

> John Peter Zenger was a newspaper editor. He waged and won an important battle for freedom of the press in America. He criticized the policies of the British governor. He was charged with criminal libel as a result. Zenger's lawyers were disbarred. Andrew Hamilton defended him. Hamilton convinced the jury that

Zenger's criticisms were true. Therefore, the statements were not libelous.

You can revise choppy sentences like these by using *coordination*, *subordination*, or *embedding* to combine them with adjacent sentences.

(1) Using Coordination

Coordination pairs similar elements—words, phrases, or clauses—giving equal weight to each. The following revision links two of the original paragraph's choppy simple sentences with *and* to create a compound sentence.

See 33a

John Peter Zenger was a newspaper editor. He waged and won an important battle for freedom of the press in America. He criticized the policies of the British governor, and as a result, he was charged with criminal libel. Zenger's lawyers were disbarred. Andrew Hamilton defended him. Hamilton convinced the jury that Zenger's criticisms were true. Therefore, the statements were not libelous.

ESL Tip

In order to avoid sentence structure errors, some ESL students rely on simple sentences and coordination in their writing. However, this can make your writing very boring. To add variety, try using subordination and embedding (explained in 34b2 and 34b3) in your sentences.

(2) Using Subordination

Subordination places the more important idea in the independent clause and the less important idea in the dependent clause. The following revision of the preceding paragraph uses subordination to change two simple sentences into dependent clauses, creating two complex sentences.

See 33b

John Peter Zenger was a newspaper editor who waged and won an important battle for freedom of the press in America. He criticized the policies of the British governor, and as a result, he was charged with criminal libel. When Zenger's lawyers were disbarred, Andrew Hamilton defended him. Hamilton convinced the jury that Zenger's criticisms were true. Therefore, the statements were not libelous.

(3) Using Embedding

Embedding is the working of additional words and phrases into a sentence. In the following revision, the sentence *Hamilton convinced the jury . . .* has been reworded to create a phrase (*convincing the jury*) that is embedded into another sentence, where it now modifies the independent clause *Andrew Hamilton defended him*.

> John Peter Zenger was a newspaper editor who waged and won an important battle for freedom of the press in America. He criticized the policies of the British governor, and as a result, he was charged with criminal libel. When Zenger's lawyers were disbarred, Andrew Hamilton defended him, convincing the jury that Zenger's criticisms were true. Therefore, the statements were not libelous.

This final revision of the original string of choppy sentences is a readable paragraph composed of varied and logically linked sentences. The final short simple sentence has been retained for emphasis.

Exercise 2

Using coordination, subordination, and embedding, revise this string of choppy simple sentences into a more varied and interesting paragraph.

> The first modern miniature golf course was built in New York in 1925. It was an indoor course with 18 holes. Entrepreneurs Drake Delanoy and John Ledbetter built 150 more indoor and outdoor courses. Garnet Carter made miniature golf a worldwide fad. Carter built an elaborate miniature golf course. He later joined with Delanoy and Ledbetter. Together they built more miniature golf courses. They abbreviated playing distances. They highlighted the game's hazards at the expense of skill. This made the game much more popular. By 1930, there were 25,000 miniature golf courses in the United States. Courses grew more elaborate. Hazards grew more bizarre. The craze spread to London and Hong Kong. The expansion of miniature golf grew out of control. Then, interest in the game declined. By 1931, most miniature golf courses were out of business. The game was revived in the early 1950s. Today, there are between eight and ten thousand miniature golf courses. The architecture of miniature golf remains an enduring form of American folk art. (Adapted from *Games*)

34c Breaking Up Strings of Compound Sentences

When you write, try to avoid creating an unbroken series of compound sentences. A string of compound sentences can be extremely

monotonous; moreover, if you connect clauses only with coordinating conjunctions, you may find it difficult to indicate exactly how ideas are related and which is most important.

All Compound Sentences: A volcano that is erupting is considered *active*, but one that may erupt is designated *dormant*, and one that has not erupted for a long time is called *extinct*. Most active volcanoes are located in "The Ring of Fire," a belt that circles the Pacific Ocean, and they can be extremely destructive. Italy's Vesuvius erupted in AD 79, and it destroyed the town of Pompeii. In 1883, Krakatoa, located between the Indonesian islands of Java and Sumatra, erupted, and it caused a tidal wave, and more than 36,000 people were killed. Martinique's Mont Pelée erupted in 1902, and its hot gas and ash killed 30,000 people, and this completely wiped out the town of St. Pierre.

Varied Sentences: A volcano that is erupting is considered *active*. (**simple sentence**) One that may erupt is designated *dormant*, and one that has not erupted for a long time is called *extinct*. (**compound sentence**) Most active volcanoes are located in "The Ring of Fire," a belt that circles the Pacific Ocean. (**simple sentence with modifier**) Active volcanoes can be extremely destructive. (**simple sentence**) Erupting in AD 79, Italy's Vesuvius destroyed the town of Pompeii. (**simple sentence with modifier**) When Krakatoa, located between the Indonesian islands of Java and Sumatra, erupted in 1883, it caused a tidal wave that killed 36,000 people. (**complex sentence with modifier**) The eruption of Martinique's Mont Pelée in 1902 produced hot gas and ash that killed 30,000 people, completely wiping out the town of St. Pierre. (**complex sentence with modifier**)

Exercise 3

Revise the compound sentences in this passage so the sentence structure is varied. Be sure that the writer's emphasis and the relationships between ideas are clear.

Dr. Alice I. Baumgartner and her colleagues at the Institute for Equality in Education at the University of Colorado surveyed two thousand Colorado schoolchildren, and they found some startling results. They asked, "If you woke up tomorrow and discovered that you were a (boy) (girl), how would your life be different?" and the answers were sad and shocking. The researchers assumed they would find that boys and girls would see advantages in being either male or female, but instead they found that both boys and girls had a fundamental contempt for females. Many elementary schoolboys titled their answers "The Disaster" or "Doomsday," and they described the terrible lives they would lead as girls, but the girls seemed to feel they would be better off as boys, and they expressed feelings that they would be able to do more and have easier lives. (Adapted from *Redbook*)

34d Varying Sentence Types

Another way to achieve sentence variety is to mix **declarative sentences** (statements) with occasional **imperative sentences** (commands or requests), **exclamations,** and **rhetorical questions** (questions that readers are not expected to answer) as the following paragraph does.

> Local television newscasts seem to be delivering less and less news. Although we stay awake for the late news hoping to be updated on local, national, and world events, only about 30 percent of most newscasts is devoted to news. Up to 25 percent of the typical program—even more during "sweeps weeks"—can be devoted to feature stories, with another 25 percent reserved for advertising. The remaining time is spent on weather, sports, and casual conversation between anchors. Given this focus on "soft" material, what options do those of us wishing to find out what happened in the world have? **(rhetorical question)** Critics of local television have a few suggestions. First, write to your local station's management voicing your concern and threatening to boycott the news if changes are not made; then, try to get others who feel the way you do to sign a petition. **(imperatives)** If changes are not made, try turning off your television and reading the newspaper! **(exclamation)**

Close-up: Varying Sentence Types

Other options for varying sentence types include mixing simple, compound, and complex sentences **(see Chs. 32–33** and **34b–c)**; mixing cumulative and periodic sentences **(see 35b)**; and using balanced sentences **(see 35c).**

Exercise 4

The following paragraph is composed entirely of declarative sentences. To make it more varied, add three sentences—one exclamation, one rhetorical question, and one imperative—anywhere in the paragraph. Be sure the new sentences are consistent with the paragraph's purpose and tone.

When the Fourth of July comes around, the nation explodes with patriotism. Everywhere we look we see parades and picnics, firecrackers and fireworks. An outsider might wonder what all the fuss is about. We could explain that this is America's birthday party, and all the candles are being lit at once. There is no reason for us to hold back our enthusiasm—or to limit the noise that celebrates it. The Fourth of July is watermelon and corn on the cob, American flags and sparklers, brass bands and more. Everyone looks forward to this celebration, and everyone has a good time.

34e Varying Sentence Openings

Rather than begin every sentence with the subject (*I* or *It*, for example) add interest and variety by beginning with a modifying word, phrase, or clause.

(1) Beginning with an Adjective, an Adverb, or a Dependent Clause

Proud and relieved, they watched their daughter receive her diploma. (adjectives)

Hungrily, he devoured his lunch. (adverb)

After Woodrow Wilson was incapacitated by a stroke, his wife unofficially performed many presidential duties. (dependent clause)

(2) Beginning with a Prepositional Phrase, a Participial Phrase, or an Absolute Phrase

For better or worse, credit cards are now readily available to college students. (prepositional phrase)

Located on the west coast of Great Britain, Wales is part of the United Kingdom. (participial phrase)

His interests widening, Picasso designed ballet sets and illustrated books. (absolute phrase)

(3) Beginning with a Coordinating Conjunction or a Transitional Word or Phrase

The Big Bang may be the beginning of the universe, or it may be a discontinuity in which information about the earlier history of the universe was destroyed. But it is certainly the earliest event about which we have any record. (coordinating conjunction) (Carl Sagan, *The Dragons of Eden*)

Pantomime was first performed in ancient Rome. However, it remains a popular dramatic form today. (transitional word)

http://kirsznermandell.wadsworth.com

Computer Tip: Coordinating Conjunctions and Fragments

If you begin a sentence with a coordinating conjunction, use your grammar checker (see Figure 34.1) to make sure that it is a complete sentence and not a **fragment**.

See Ch.37

Spelling and Grammar: English (U.S.)
Fragment:
And then the speaker.
Ignore
Ignore Rule
Next Sentence
Suggestions:
Fragment (consider revising)
Change
Check grammar
Options...
Undo
Cancel

Figure 34.1 Sample grammar checker suggestion.

Exercise 5

Each of these sentences begins with the subject. Revise each so that it has a different opening; then, identify your opening strategy.

Example: ^In *The Names,* N. Scott Momaday, the prominent Native American writer, tells the story of his first fourteen years. ~~in *The Names.*~~ (prepositional phrase)

1. Momaday was taken as a very young child to Devil's Tower, the geological formation in Wyoming that is called Tsoai (Bear Tree) in Kiowa, and there he was given the name Tsoai-talee (Bear Tree Boy).
2. The Kiowa myth of the origin of Tsoai is about a boy who playfully chases his seven sisters up a tree, which rises into the air as the boy is transformed into a bear.
3. The boy-bear becomes increasingly ferocious and claws the bark of the tree, which becomes a great rock with a flat top and deeply scored sides.
4. The sisters climb higher and higher to escape their brother's wrath, and eventually they become the seven stars of the Big Dipper.
5. This story, from which Momaday received one of his names, appears in his works *The Way to Rainy Mountain*, *House Made of Dawn*, and *The Ancient Child*.

34f Varying Standard Word Order

You can vary standard word order (subject-verb-object or subject-verb-complement) either by intentionally inverting this usual order or by inserting words between the subject and the verb.

(1) Inverting Word Order

Sometimes you can place the complement or direct object *before* the verb instead of in its conventional position after the verb, or you can place the verb *before* the subject instead of after it. These strategies draw attention to the word or word group that appears in an unexpected place.

(object) (subject) ↓ (verb) (object) (subject) ↓ (verb)
The north wall he painted red; the other walls he painted white.

(complement) (verb) (subject)
Crucial to the agreement is a clear understanding of the issues.

NOTE: Be careful to use inverted word order in moderation; when it is used in a series of sentences, inverted word order becomes distracting and hard to follow.

(2) Separating Subject from Verb

You can also place words or phrases between subject and verb—but be sure that the word group does not obscure the connection between subject and verb or create an agreement error.

Many states require that infants and young children ride in government-approved child safety seats because they hope this regulation will reduce needless fatalities. (subject and verb together)

Many states, hoping to reduce needless fatalities, require that infants and young children ride in government-approved child safety seats. (subject and verb separated)

Exercise 6

The following five sentences use conventional word order. To vary this standard word order, revise each sentence in one of two ways: either invert the sentence, or insert words between the subject and the verb. After you have completed your revisions, link all the sentences together to create a paragraph.

Example: Dada, ~~was~~ an artistic and literary rebellion, ~~that~~ defied the conventional values of the early twentieth century. (words inserted between subject and verb)

1. The Dada movement first appeared in 1915 and effectively ended in 1925 with the rise of Surrealism.
2. The name *Dada*, French for "hobby horse," was selected at random from a dictionary.
3. The Dadaists ultimately rejected all traditional cultural values, and their goal became to destroy art as an aesthetic cult and replace it with "antiart" and "nonart."
4. The Dadaists rejected traditional art, and they substituted the nonsense poem, the ready-made object, and the collage.
5. The most notorious example of Dada art is the sculpture *Fountain* (1917), which was a urinal Marcel Duchamp found and signed *R. Mutt* and then entered into a gallery exhibit.

Chapter 35

Writing Emphatic Sentences

Frequently Asked Questions

Why shouldn't I begin a sentence with there is *or* there are? (p. 707)

Is repeating words and phrases ever a good idea? (p. 713)

When is it acceptable to use passive voice? (p. 714)

In speaking, we emphasize certain ideas and deemphasize others with intonation and gesture; in writing, we convey **emphasis**—the relative importance of ideas—through the selection and arrangement of words.

35a Conveying Emphasis through Word Order

Readers tend to focus on the beginning and end of a sentence, expecting to find key information there.

(1) Beginning with Important Ideas

Placing key ideas at the beginning of a sentence stresses their importance. The unedited version of the following sentence places emphasis on the study, not on those who conducted it or on those who participated in it. Editing focuses attention on the researcher, not on the study.

> ~~In a landmark study of alcoholism~~, Dr. George Vaillant of Harvard ^*, in a landmark study of alcoholism,* followed two hundred Harvard graduates and four hundred inner-city, working-class men from the Boston area.

Situations that demand a straightforward presentation—laboratory reports, memos, technical papers, business correspondence, and the like—call for sentences that present vital information first and qualifiers later.

Treating cancer with interferon has been the subject of a good deal of research. (emphasizes the treatment, not the research)

Dividends will be paid if the stockholders agree. (emphasizes the dividends, not the stockholders)

Close-up: Writing Emphatic Sentences

Placing an empty phrase like *there is* or *there are* at the beginning of a sentence generally weakens the sentence.

MIT places
~~There is~~ heavy emphasis ~~placed~~ on the development of computational skills ~~at MIT~~.

(2) Ending with Important Ideas

Placing key elements at the end of a sentence is another way to convey their importance.

Using a Colon or a Dash A colon or a dash can add emphasis by isolating an important word or phrase at the end of a sentence.

Beth had always dreamed of owning one special car: a 1953 Corvette.

The elderly need a good deal of special attention—and they deserve that attention.

Close-up: Placing Transitional Expressions

When placed at the end of a sentence, conjunctive adverbs or other transitional expressions lose their power to indicate the relationship between ideas. Place transitional words and phrases earlier in the sentence, where they can perform this function and also add emphasis.

however,
Smokers do have rights; they should not try to impose their habit on others~~, however~~.

Using Climactic Word Order **Climactic word order,** the arrangement of a series of items from the least to the most important, places emphasis on the most important idea at the end.

Binge drinking can lead to unwanted pregnancies, car accidents, and even death. (*Death* is the most serious consequence.)

Exercise 1

Underline the most important idea in each sentence of the following paragraph. Then, identify the strategy that the writer uses to emphasize those ideas. Are the key ideas placed at the beginning or the end of a sentence? Does the writer use climactic order?

Listening to diatribes by angry callers or ranting about today's news, the talk radio host spreads ideas over the air waves. Every day at the same time, the political talk show host discusses national events and policies, the failures of the opposing view, and the foibles of the individuals who espouse those opposing views. Listening for hours a day, some callers become recognizable contributors to many different talk radio programs. Other listeners are less devoted, tuning in only when they are in the car and never calling to voice their opinions. Political radio hosts usually structure their programs around a specific agenda, espousing the party line and ridiculing the opponent's position. With a style of presentation aimed both at entertainment and information, the host's ideas become caricatures of party positions. Sometimes, in order to keep the information lively and interesting, a host may either state the issues too simply or deliberately mislead the audience. A host can excuse these errors by insisting that the show is harmless: it's for entertainment, not information. Many are concerned about how the political process is affected by this misinformation.

(3) Experimenting with Word Order

ESL 61e

In English sentences, the most common word order is subject-verb-object (or subject-verb-complement). By departing from this expected word order, you can call attention to the word, phrase, or clause that you have relocated.

More modest and less inventive than Turner's paintings are John Constable's landscapes.

See 34f1

Here the writer calls attention to the modifying phrase *more modest and less inventive than Turner's paintings* by inverting word order, placing the complement and the verb before the subject.

ESL Tip

If English is your second language, you may be reluctant to experiment with word order. However, to keep your sentences from becoming monotonous, you need to experiment occasionally. When you do, check with a native English speaker or your instructor if you are uncertain about whether or not your sentences are grammatical.

Exercise 2

Revise the following sentences to make them more emphatic. For each, decide which ideas should be highlighted, and place these key ideas at sentence beginnings or endings. Use climactic order or depart from conventional word order where appropriate.

1. Police want to upgrade their firepower because criminals are better armed than ever before.
2. A few years ago, felons used so-called Saturday night specials, small-caliber six-shot revolvers.
3. Now, semiautomatic pistols capable of firing fifteen to twenty rounds, along with paramilitary weapons like the AK-47, have replaced these weapons.
4. Police are adopting such weapons as new fast-firing shotguns and 9mm automatic pistols in order to gain an equal footing with their adversaries.
5. Faster reloading and a hair trigger are among the numerous advantages that automatic pistols, the weapons of choice among law-enforcement officers, have over the traditional .38-caliber police revolver.

35b Conveying Emphasis through Sentence Structure

As you write, you can construct sentences that emphasize more important ideas and deemphasize less important ones.

(1) Using Cumulative Sentences

A **cumulative sentence** begins with an independent clause, followed by additional words, phrases, or clauses that expand or develop it.

> She holds me in strong arms, arms that have chopped cotton, dismembered trees, scattered corn for chickens, cradled infants, shaken the daylights out of half-grown upstart teenagers. (Rebecca Hill, *Blue Rise*)

Because it presents its main idea first, a cumulative sentence tends to be clear and straightforward. (Most English sentences are cumulative.)

(2) Using Periodic Sentences

A **periodic sentence** moves from supporting details, expressed in modifying phrases and dependent clauses, to the key idea, which is placed in the independent clause at the end of the sentence.

Unlike World Wars I and II, which ended decisively with the unconditional surrender of the United States's enemies, the war in Vietnam did not end when American troops withdrew.

NOTE: In some periodic sentences, the modifying phrase or dependent clause comes between subject and predicate: Columbus, after several discouraging and unsuccessful voyages, finally reached America.

Exercise 3

A. Bracket the independent clause(s) in each sentence, and underline each modifying phrase and dependent clause. Label each sentence cumulative or periodic.
B. Relocate the supporting details to make cumulative sentences periodic and periodic sentences cumulative, adding words or rephrasing to make your meaning clear.
C. Be prepared to explain how your revision changes the emphasis of the original sentence.

Example: Feeling isolated, sad, and frightened, [the small child sat alone in the train depot.] (periodic)

Revised: The small child sat alone in the train depot, feeling isolated, sad, and frightened. (cumulative)

1. However different in their educational opportunities, both Jefferson and Lincoln as young men became known to their contemporaries as "hard students." (Douglas L. Wilson, "What Jefferson and Lincoln Read," *Atlantic Monthly*)
2. The road came into being slowly, league by league, river crossing by river crossing. (Stephen Harrigan, "Highway 1," *Texas Monthly*)
3. Without willing it, I had gone from being ignorant of being ignorant to being aware of being aware. (Maya Angelou, *I Know Why the Caged Bird Sings*)

Exercise 4

Combine each of the following sentence groups into one cumulative sentence, subordinating supporting details to more important ideas. Then, combine each group into one periodic sentence. (Each group can be combined in a variety of ways, and you may have to add, delete, change, or reorder words.) How do the two versions of the sentence differ in emphasis?

Example: More women than ever before are running for office. They are encouraged by the success of other female candidates.

Cumulative: More women than ever before are running for office, encouraged by the success of other female candidates.

Periodic: Encouraged by the success of other female candidates, more women than ever before are running for office.

1. Some politicians opposed the prescription drug program. They believed it was too expensive. They felt that a smaller, more limited program was preferable.
2. Smoking poses a real danger. It is associated with various cancers. It is linked to heart disease and stroke. It threatens even nonsmokers.
3. Infertile couples who want children sometimes go through a series of difficult processes. They may try adoption. They may also try artificial insemination or in vitro fertilization. They may even seek out surrogate mothers.
4. The Thames is a river that meanders through southern England. It has been the inspiration for such literary works as *Alice's Adventures in Wonderland* and *The Wind in the Willows*. It was also captured in paintings by Constable, Turner, and Whistler.
5. Black-footed ferrets are rare North American mammals. They prey on prairie dogs. They are primarily nocturnal. They have black feet and black-tipped tails. Their faces have raccoonlike masks.

Exercise 5

Combine each of the following sentence groups into one sentence that subordinates supporting details to the main idea. In each case, create either a periodic or a cumulative sentence, depending on which structure you think will best convey the sentence's emphasis. Add, delete, change, or reorder words when necessary.

, that there are too many students and too few jobs,

Example: The fears of today's college students^ are based on reality. ~~They are afraid there are too many students and too few jobs.~~ (periodic)

1. Today's college students are under a good deal of stress. Job prospects in some fields are not very good. Financial aid is not as easy to come by as it was in the past.
2. Education has grown very expensive. The job market has become tighter. Pressure to get into graduate and professional schools has increased.
3. Family ties seem to be weakening. Students are not always able to count on family support.

4. College students have always had problems. Now, college counseling centers report more—and more serious—problems.
5. The term *student shock* was coined several years ago. This term describes a syndrome that may include depression, anxiety, headaches, and eating and sleeping disorders.
6. Many students are overwhelmed by the vast array of courses and majors offered at their colleges. They tend to be less decisive. They take longer to choose a major and to complete school.
7. Many drop out of school for brief (or extended) periods or switch majors several times. Many take five years or longer to complete their college education.
8. Some colleges are responding to the pressures that students feel. They hold stress-management workshops and suicide-prevention courses. They advertise the services of their counseling centers. They train students as peer counselors. They improve their vocational counseling services.

35c Conveying Emphasis through Parallelism and Balance

See 40a

By reinforcing the similarity between grammatical elements, parallelism can help you convey information clearly and emphatically.

> We seek an individual who is a self-starter, who owns a late-model automobile, and who is willing to work evenings. (classified advertisement)
>
> Do not pass Go; do not collect $200. (instructions)
>
> The Faust legend is central in Benét's *The Devil and Daniel Webster*, in Goethe's *Faust*, and in Marlowe's *Dr. Faustus*. (examination answer)

A **balanced sentence** is neatly divided between two parallel structures—for example, two independent clauses in a compound sentence. The symmetrical structure of a balanced sentence adds emphasis by highlighting correspondences or contrasts between clauses.

> In the 1950s, the electronic miracle was the television; in the 1980s, the electronic miracle was the computer.
>
> Alive, the elephant was worth at least a hundred pounds; dead, he would only be worth the value of his tusks, five pounds, possibly. (George Orwell, "Shooting an Elephant")

35d Conveying Emphasis through Repetition

Unnecessary repetition makes sentences dull and monotonous as well as wordy.

He had a good pitching arm and also could field well and was also a fast runner.

Effective repetition, however, can place emphasis on key words or ideas.

They decided to begin again: to begin hoping, to begin trying to change, to begin working toward a goal.

During those years when I was just learning to speak, my mother and father addressed me only in Spanish; in Spanish I learned to reply. (Richard Rodriguez, *Aria: A Memoir of a Bilingual Childhood*)

Exercise 6

Revise the sentences in this paragraph, using parallelism and balance to highlight corresponding elements and using repetition of key words and phrases to add emphasis. You may combine sentences and add, delete, or reorder words.

Many readers distrust newspapers. They also distrust what they read in magazines. They do not trust what they hear on the radio and what television shows them, either. Of these media, newspapers have been the most responsive to audience criticism. Some newspapers even have ombudsmen. They are supposed to listen to readers' complaints. They are also charged with acting on these grievances. One complaint that many people have is that newspapers are inaccurate. Newspapers' disregard for people's privacy is another of many readers' criticisms. Reporters are seen as arrogant, and readers feel that journalists can be unfair. They feel that reporters tend to glorify criminals, and they believe there is a tendency to place too much emphasis on bizarre or offbeat stories. Finally, readers complain about poor writing and editing. Polls show that despite its efforts to respond to reader criticism, the press continues to face hostility. (Adapted from *Newsweek*)

35e Conveying Emphasis through Active Voice

Active voice verbs are generally more emphatic—and more concise—than passive voice verbs.

Passive: The prediction that oil prices will rise is being made by economists.

Active: Economists now predict that oil prices will rise.

The passive voice tends to focus your readers' attention on the action or on its receiver rather than on who is performing it. The receiver of the action is the subject of a passive sentence, so the actor fades into the background (*by economists*) or is omitted (*the prediction is now being made*).

http://kirsznermandell.wadsworth.com

Computer Tip: Avoiding Passive Voice

Your word processor's grammar checker will highlight passive voice constructions in your writing and offer revision suggestions (see Figure 35.1).

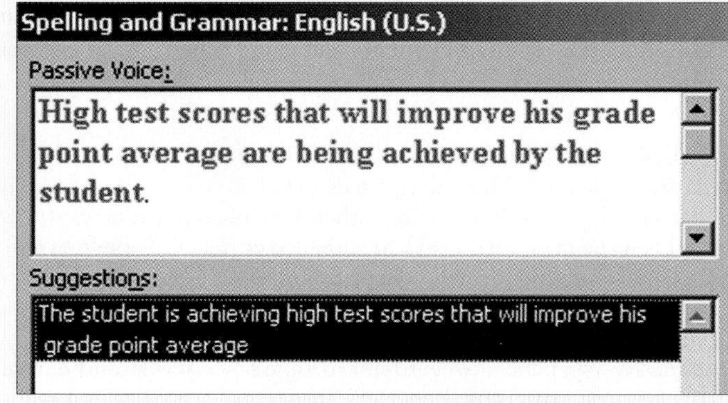
Spelling and Grammar: English (U.S.)
Passive Voice:
High test scores that will improve his grade point average are being achieved by the student.
Suggestions:
The student is achieving high test scores that will improve his grade point average

Figure 35.1 Sample grammar checker suggestion.

FAQs

Sometimes, of course, you *want* to stress the action rather than the actor. If so, it makes sense to use the passive voice.

Passive: The West was explored by Lewis and Clark. (stresses the exploration of the West, not who explored it)

Active: Lewis and Clark explored the West. (stresses the contribution of the explorers)

See Ch. 25

NOTE: Passive voice is also used when the identity of the person performing the action is irrelevant or unknown (*The course was canceled*). For this reason, the passive voice is frequently used in scientific and technical writing: The beaker was filled with a saline solution.

http://kirsznermandell.wadsworth.com

Computer Tip: Using Passive Voice

Sometimes the clearest way to express your ideas is by using passive verbs. For example, the use of passive voice in the sentence below is necessary for clarity. The grammar checker's suggestion is awkward—and incorrect (see Figure 35.2).

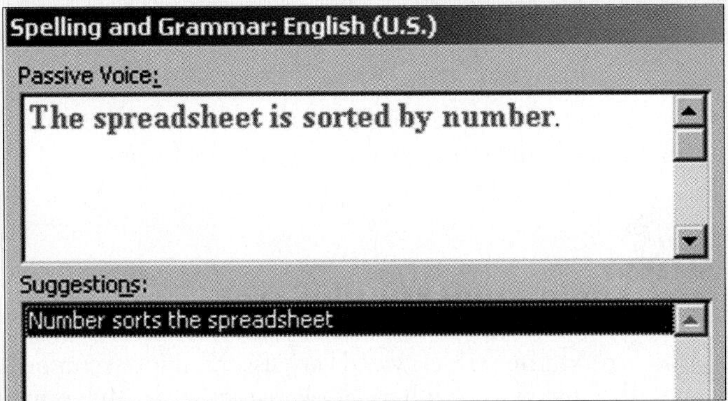
Spelling and Grammar: English (U.S.)
Passive Voice:
The spreadsheet is sorted by number.
Suggestions:
Number sorts the spreadsheet

Figure 35.2 Sample grammar checker suggestion.

Exercise 7

Revise this paragraph to eliminate awkward or excessive use of passive constructions.

Jack Dempsey, the heavyweight champion between 1919 and 1926, had an interesting but uneven career. He was considered one of the greatest boxers of all time. Dempsey began fighting as "Kid Blackie," but his career didn't take off until 1919, when Jack "Doc" Kearns became his manager. Dempsey won the championship when Jess Willard was defeated by him in Toledo, Ohio, in 1919. Dempsey immediately became a popular sports figure; President Franklin D. Roosevelt was one of his biggest fans. Influential friends were made by Jack Dempsey. Boxing lessons were given by him to the actor Rudolph Valentino. He made friends with Douglas Fairbanks Sr., Damon Runyon, and J. Paul Getty. Hollywood serials were made by Dempsey, but the title was lost by him to Gene Tunney, and Dempsey failed to regain it the following year. After his boxing career declined, a restaurant was opened by Dempsey, and many major sporting events were attended by him. This exposure kept him in the public eye until he lost his restaurant. Jack Dempsey died in 1983.

Chapter 36

Writing Concise Sentences

Frequently Asked Questions

How can I tell which words I really need in my sentences and which can be cut? (p. 716)

How do I revise a long, rambling sentence? (p. 721)

A sentence is not concise simply because it is short; a concise sentence contains only the words necessary to make its point.

36a Eliminating Wordiness

A good way to find out which words are essential in a sentence is to underline the key words. Then, look carefully at the remaining words so you can determine which are unnecessary and eliminate wordiness by deleting them.

> It seems to me that it does not make sense to allow any bail to be granted to anyone who has ever been convicted of a violent crime.

The underlining shows you immediately that none of the words in the long introductory phrase are essential. The following revision includes just the words necessary to convey the key ideas:

> Bail should not be granted to anyone who has ever been convicted of a violent crime.

Whenever possible, delete nonessential words—*deadwood*, *utility words*, and *circumlocution*—from your writing.

(1) Eliminating Deadwood

Deadwood is a term used for unnecessary phrases that take up space and add nothing to meaning.

> Many
> ~~There were many~~ factors ~~that~~ influenced his decision to become a priest.

The two plots are ~~both~~ similar in ~~the way~~ that they trace the characters' increasing rage.

Shoppers ~~who are~~ looking for bargains often go to outlets.

They played an exhausting a racquetball game ~~that was exhausting~~.

This ~~In this~~ article ~~it~~ discusses lead poisoning.

The only truly tragic character in *Hamlet* is ~~would have to be~~ Ophelia.

Deadwood also includes unnecessary statements of opinion, such as *I believe*, *I feel*, and *it seems to me*.

~~In my opinion, the~~ The characters seem undeveloped.

~~As far as I'm concerned, this~~ This course looks interesting.

(2) Eliminating Utility Words

Utility words contribute nothing to a sentence. **Utility words** include nouns with imprecise meanings (*factor*, *situation*, *type*, *aspect*, and so on); adjectives so general that they are almost meaningless (*good*, *bad*, *important*); and common adverbs denoting degree (*basically*, *actually*, *quite*, *very*, *definitely*). Often, you can just delete the utility word; if you cannot, replace it with a more precise word.

~~The registration situation~~ Registration was disorganized.

The scholarship ~~basically~~ offered Fran an ~~a good~~ opportunity to study Spanish in Spain.

It was ~~actually~~ a worthwhile book, but I didn't ~~completely~~ finish it.

(3) Avoiding Circumlocution

Taking a roundabout way to say something (using ten words when five will do) is called **circumlocution.** Instead of complicated constructions, use concise, specific words and phrases that come right to the point.

~~It is not unlikely that the~~ The trend will probably continue.

The curriculum was ~~of a~~ unique ~~nature~~.

Joe was in the army while ~~during the same time that~~ I was in college.

Close-up: Revising Wordy Phrases

A wordy phrase can almost always be replaced by a more concise, more direct term.

Wordy	Concise
at the present time	now
at this point in time	now
for the purpose of	for
due to the fact that	because
on account of the fact that	because
until such time as	until
in the event that	if
by means of	by
in the vicinity of	near
have the ability to	be able to

Exercise 1

Revise the following paragraph to eliminate deadwood, utility words, and circumlocution. Whenever possible, delete wordy phrases or replace them with more concise expressions.

For all intents and purposes, the shopping mall is no longer an important factor in the American cultural scene. In the '80s, shopping malls became gathering places where teenagers met, walkers came to get in a few miles, and shoppers who were looking for a wide selection and were not concerned about value went to shop. There are several factors that have worked to undermine the mall's popularity. First, due to the fact that today's shoppers are more likely to be interested in value, many of them have headed to the discount stores. Today's shopper is now more likely to shop in discount stores or bulk-buying warehouse stores than in the small, expensive specialty shops in the large shopping malls. Add to this a resurgence of the values of community, and we can see how malls would have to be less attractive than shopping at local stores. Many malls actually have up to 20 percent empty storefronts, and some have had to close down altogether. Others have met the challenge by expanding their roles from shopping centers into community centers. They have added playgrounds for the children and more amusements and restaurants for the adults. They have also appealed to the growing sense of value shopping by giving gift certificates and discounts to shoppers who spend money in their stores. In the '90s, it seemed as if the huge shopping malls that had become familiar cultural icons were dying out, replaced by catalog and Internet shopping. Now, however, it looks as if some of those icons just might make it and survive by reinventing themselves as more than just places to shop.

36b Eliminating Unnecessary Repetition

Repetition can make your writing more emphatic, but unnecessary repetition and **redundant** word groups (repeated words or phrases that say the same thing, such as *free gift* and *unanticipated surprise*) can obscure your meaning. See 35d

You can correct unnecessary repetition by using any of the following strategies.

(1) Deleting Redundancy

People's clothing ~~attire~~ can reveal a good deal about their personalities.

http://kirsznermandell.wadsworth.com

Computer Tip: Deleting Redundancy

Your word processor's grammar checker will highlight some redundant expressions and offer suggestions for revision (see Figure 36.1).

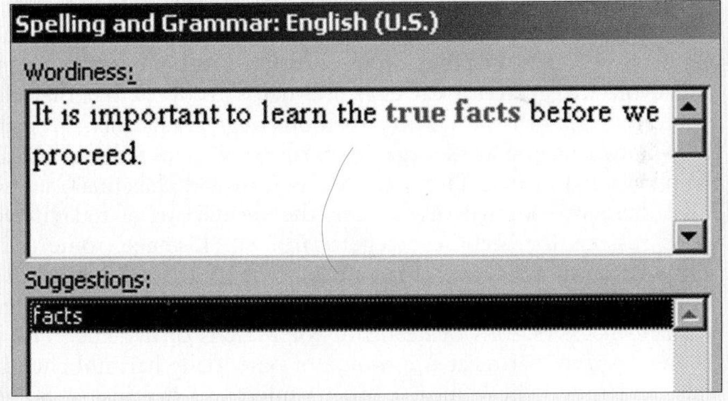
Spelling and Grammar: English (U.S.)
Wordiness:
It is important to learn the true facts before we proceed.
Suggestions:
facts

Figure 36.1 Sample grammar checker suggestion.

(2) Substituting a Pronoun

Fictional detective Miss Marple has solved many crimes. *The Murder at the Vicarage* was one of ~~Miss Marple's~~ her most challenging cases.

(3) Creating an Appositive

Red Barber, ~~was~~ a sportscaster~~.~~, ~~He~~ was known for his colorful expressions.

(4) Creating a Compound

John F. Kennedy was the youngest man ever elected president~~.~~ *and* ~~He was~~ also the first Catholic to hold this office.

(5) Creating a Complex Sentence

Americans value freedom of speech~~.~~*, which* ~~Freedom of speech~~ is guaranteed by the First Amendment.

Exercise 2

Eliminate any unnecessary repetition of words or ideas in this paragraph. Also revise to eliminate deadwood, utility words, or circumlocution.

For a wide variety of different reasons, more and more people today are choosing a vegetarian diet. There are three kinds of vegetarians: strict vegetarians eat no animal foods at all; lactovegetarians eat dairy products, but they do not eat meat, fish, poultry, or eggs; and ovolactovegetarians eat eggs and dairy products, but they do not eat meat, fish, or poultry. Famous vegetarians include such well-known people as George Bernard Shaw, Leonardo da Vinci, Ralph Waldo Emerson, Henry David Thoreau, and Mahatma Gandhi. Like these well-known vegetarians, the vegetarians of today have good reasons for becoming vegetarians. For instance, some religions recommend a vegetarian diet. Some of these religions are Buddhism, Brahmanism, and Hinduism. Other people turn to vegetarianism for reasons of health or for reasons of hygiene. These people believe that meat is a source of potentially harmful chemicals, and they believe meat contains infectious organisms. Some people feel meat may cause digestive problems and may lead to other difficulties as well. Other vegetarians adhere to a vegetarian diet because they feel it is ecologically wasteful to kill animals after we feed plants to them. These vegetarians believe we should eat the plants. Finally, there are facts and evidence to suggest that a vegetarian diet may possibly help people live longer lives. A vegetarian diet may do this by reducing the incidence of heart disease and lessening the incidence of some cancers. (Adapted from *Jane Brody's Nutrition Book*)

36c Tightening Rambling Sentences

The combination of nonessential words, unnecessary repetition, and complicated syntax creates **rambling sentences.** Revising rambling sentences frequently requires extensive editing.

(1) Eliminating Excessive Coordination

When you string a series of clauses together with coordinating conjunctions, you create a rambling, unfocused compound sentence that presents your ideas as if they all have equal weight. To revise such sentences, identify the main idea or ideas, and then subordinate the supporting details.

Wordy: Benjamin Franklin was the son of a candlemaker, but he later apprenticed as a printer, and this experience led to his buying the *Pennsylvania Gazette*, and he managed this periodical with great success.

Concise: Benjamin Franklin, the son of a candlemaker, later apprenticed as a printer, an experience that led to his buying the *Pennsylvania Gazette*, which he managed with great success. (Franklin's apprenticeship as a printer is the sentence's main idea.)

Wordy: Puerto Rico is a large island in the Caribbean, and it is very mountainous, and it has steep slopes, and they fall to gentle plains along the coast.

Concise: A large island in the Caribbean, Puerto Rico is very mountainous, with steep slopes falling to gentle plains along the coast. (Puerto Rico's mountainous terrain is the sentence's main idea.)

(2) Eliminating Adjective Clauses

A series of adjective clauses is also likely to produce a rambling sentence. To revise, substitute more concise modifying words or phrases for the adjective clauses.

Wordy: *Moby-Dick*, which is a novel about a white whale, was written by Herman Melville, who was friendly with Nathaniel Hawthorne, who urged him to revise the first draft.

Concise: *Moby-Dick*, a novel about a white whale, was written by Herman Melville, who revised the first draft at the urging of his friend Nathaniel Hawthorne.

(3) Eliminating Passive Constructions

Excessive use of the passive voice can create rambling sentences. Correct this problem when you revise by changing passive to active voice.

> ~~Water rights are being fought for in court by~~ Indian tribes like the Papago in Arizona and the Pyramid Lake Paiute in Nevada~~.~~ *are fighting in court for water rights.*

(4) Eliminating Wordy Prepositional Phrases

When you revise, substitute adjectives or adverbs for wordy prepositional phrases.

> The trip was *dangerous* ~~one of danger~~ but also *exciting* ~~one of excitement~~.

> He spoke *confidently* ~~in a confident manner~~ and *authoritatively* ~~with a lot of authority~~.

(5) Eliminating Wordy Noun Constructions

Substitute strong verbs for wordy noun phrases.

> We have *decided* ~~made the decision~~ to postpone the meeting until ~~the appearance of~~ all the board members *appear*.

> Sometimes ~~there is an accumulation of~~ water *accumulates* on the roof.

Exercise 3

Revise the rambling sentences in these paragraphs by eliminating excessive coordination; unnecessary use of the passive voice; and overuse of adjective clauses, prepositional phrases, and noun constructions. As you revise, make your sentences more concise by deleting nonessential words and unnecessary repetition.

Some colleges that have been in support of fraternities for a number of years are at this time in the process of conducting a reevaluation of the position of those fraternities on campus. In opposition to the fraternities are a fair number of students, faculty members, and administrators who claim fraternities are inherently sexist, which they say makes it impossible for the groups to exist in a coeducational institution, which is supposed to offer equal opportunities for members of both sexes. More and more members of the college community also see fraternities as elitist as well as sexist and favor their abolition. In addition, many point out that fraternities are associated with dangerous practices, such as hazing and alcohol abuse.

However, some students, faculty, and administrators remain wholeheartedly in support of traditional fraternities, which they believe are responsible for helping students make the acquaintance of people and learn the leadership skills that they believe will be of assistance to them in their future lives as adults. Supporters of fraternities believe that students should retain the right to make their own social decisions and that joining a fraternity is one of those decisions, and they also believe fraternities are responsible for providing valuable services. Some of these are tutoring, raising money for charity, and running campus escort services. Therefore, these individuals are not of the opinion that the abolition of traditional fraternities makes sense.

Student Writer at Work

Improving Sentence Style

The following excerpt is from a draft of an essay for a business law class. It was written in response to an assignment asking students to define a method of conflict resolution and discuss its strengths and weaknesses. Although the draft is clearly written and organized, its sentence style could be improved. Review the chapters in Part 6, and then revise this passage to make its sentences more varied, emphatic, and concise.

The Benefits of Arbitration: When Does It Work Best?

Disputes between businesses, between unrelated individuals, or between family members can require large amounts of time and money in the complex world of litigation. A popular way to resolve these disputes while avoiding costly and expensive litigation is Alternate Dispute Resolution (ADR). ADR is a method of conflict resolution. It is often used in the business world. The parties involved in a dispute choose an impartial, unbiased third party to hear and decide the dispute. This method of conflict resolution is not for everyone, though. Parties involved in a dispute need to get answers to a few questions before deciding to proceed with arbitration. For example, exactly what are the pros and cons of arbitration? When, and under what circumstances, should parties in a dispute opt for arbitration? And finally, when should parties <u>not</u> choose arbitration?

There are many benefits of deciding to enter into arbitration. The benefits of deciding to enter into arbitration can heavily outweigh the benefits of litigation in some cases. Arbitration takes less time than litigation. Because it takes less time, it can save companies money in legal fees and trial fees. Arbitration can also serve as a way for businesses to avoid costly settlements set by juries. Privacy is another benefit of arbitration. The meetings are held privately, and the final decision is not made public.

There are also a few disadvantages associated with arbitration, however. Arbitration, unlike mediation, is binding. This means that the decision made by the arbitrator is final, and this decision must be enforced. This can either be a pro or a con, depending on the decision and depending on the circumstances of the case. If one party feels he or she might be better served by having the dispute heard by a jury, then binding arbitration is not the best route. If the arbitrator's decision is not welcome, all parties are still stuck with it. It is very difficult to appeal an arbitrator's decision. The courts hold these decisions as law and examine them only to see if the decision has actually gone against the law.

Arbitration will usually be the best solution for a business involved in a dispute with another business. It will be quicker and less costly than the litigation process. The matter under dispute and the decision will also be private and stay private. The decision will also be binding, so the end result will be enforced by law. The business will also have the advantage of avoiding the uncertainty of a jury verdict. The settlement amount will probably be lower, and this may be the most important advantage of all.

In disputes between individuals, arbitration does not usually serve the plaintiff well. In such cases—for example, in a divorce—some form of ADR other than arbitration, such as mediation, would be advisable because the recommendation is not binding. For businesses, arbitration is often a wise choice, however.

PART 7

Grammar Checker

Fragment:

Present and past, town and countr

nativeness and foreignness.

Solving Common Sentence Problems

Solving Common Sentence Problems: Using Your Computer's Grammar Checker

The following chart summarizes the ways in which your grammar checker can help you as you write—and the ways in which its usefulness is limited. For more specific explanations and illustrations, consult the Computer Tip boxes in the individual chapters.

Common Sentence Problem	Grammar Checker Advantage	Grammar Checker Limitation
Sentence Fragments (**see Ch. 37**)	Often identifies sentence fragments	Sometimes misses sentence fragments; does not usually offer revision suggestions; often mislabels other sentence problems as fragments
Comma Splices and Fused Sentences (**see Ch. 38**)	Often identifies comma splices and frequently offers revision suggestions	Does not offer revision suggestions for fused sentences; often highlights fused sentences simply as long sentences that need revision (not as errors)
Faulty Modification (**see Ch. 39**)	Identifies some modification problems, including certain awkward split infinitives	Does not offer revision suggestions
Faulty Parallelism (**see Ch. 40**)	Identifies some nonparallel constructions	Mislabels some parallelism problems as wordiness
Awkward or Confusing Sentences (**see Ch. 41**)	Sometimes identifies shifts in voice, person, and number; frequently offers revision suggestions	Misses many unwarranted shifts, mixed constructions, and incomplete or illogical comparisons

Chapter 37

Revising Sentence Fragments

Frequently Asked Questions

A **sentence fragment** is an incomplete sentence—a phrase or clause that is punctuated as if it were a complete sentence. A sentence may be incomplete for any of the following reasons.

- **It lacks a subject.**

  Many astrophysicists now believe that galaxies are distributed in clusters. And even form supercluster complexes.

ESL Tip

In some languages, including Romance languages such as Spanish and Italian, sentences do not always require a subject. (This is because in some sentences in these languages, the verb's form clearly indicates who or what the subject is.) In English, however, a sentence must always have both a subject and a verb.

- **It lacks a verb.**

  Every generation has its defining moments. Usually the events with the most news coverage.

- **It lacks both a subject and a verb.**

  Researchers are engaged in a variety of studies. Suggesting a link between alcoholism and heredity. (*Suggesting* is a **verbal**, which cannot serve as a sentence's main verb.)

- **It is a dependent clause.**

  Bishop Desmond Tutu was awarded the 1984 Nobel Peace Prize. Because he fought to end apartheid.

The pH meter and the spectrophotometer are two scientific instruments. That changed the chemistry laboratory dramatically.

NOTE: A sentence cannot consist of a single clause that begins with a subordinating conjunction (such as *because*) or a relative pronoun (such as *that*); moreover, unless it is a question, a sentence cannot consist of a single clause beginning with *when*, *where*, *who*, *which*, *what*, *why*, or *how*.

Fragments present problems for readers because they convey incomplete thoughts. A fragment is especially confusing when it comes between two independent clauses and readers cannot tell which of the two clauses completes the fragment's thought. For instance, it is impossible to tell to which independent clause the underlined fragment in each of the following sequences belongs.

> The course requirements were changed last year. Because a new professor was hired at the very end of the spring semester. I was unable to find out about this change until after preregistration.
>
> In *The Ox-Bow Incident*, the crowd is convinced that the men are guilty. Even though the men insist they are innocent and Davies pleads for their lives. They are hanged.

FAQs

Close-up: Revising Sentence Fragments

If you identify a fragment in your writing, use one of the following two strategies to revise it:

1. Attach the fragment to an adjacent independent clause.

   According to German legend, Lohengrin is the son of Parzival~~. And~~ *and* a knight of the Holy Grail.

   Pioneers traveled west~~. Because~~ *because* they hoped to find a better life.

2. Turn the fragment into a sentence.

   Lancaster County, Pennsylvania, is home to many Pennsylvania Dutch. ~~Descended~~ *They are descended* from German immigrants. (missing subject and verb added)

   Property taxes rose sharply. ~~Although city~~ *City* services declined. (subordinating conjunction *although* deleted)

http://kirsznermandell.wadsworth.com

Computer Tip: Identifying Fragments

Your grammar checker will be able to help you identify many (although not all) sentence fragments. As you type, they will be underlined in green, and you will be prompted to revise them (see Figure 37.1). However, not every word group identified as a fragment will actually be a fragment. You, not your grammar checker, will have to make the final decision about whether or not a sentence is grammatically complete—and decide how to correct it.

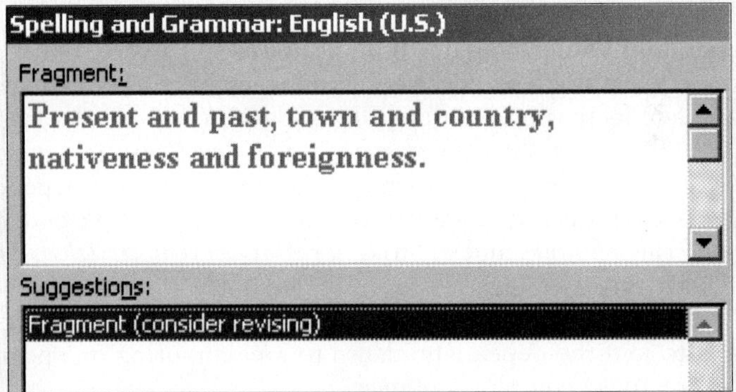

Figure 37.1 Sample grammar checker suggestion.

Exercise 1

Identify each of the following word groups as either a sentence fragment or a complete sentence. Be prepared to explain why each fragment is not a complete sentence. When you have finished, type each sentence into your word-processing program, and run the grammar checker to check your responses.

1. Consisting of shortness of breath, a high fever, and a racing pulse.
2. Held in contempt of court by the presiding judge.
3. Walking to the end of the road and back is good exercise.
4. On her own at last, after many years of struggle for independence.
5. Because he felt torn between two cultures.
6. With boundaries extending from the ocean to the bay.

7. Although language study can be challenging.
8. In addition, a new point guard will be a valuable addition to the team.
9. Defeated by his own greed but not in the least regretful.
10. Moreover, the continued presence of troops in Iraq.

Sections 38a–c identify the grammatical structures most likely to appear as fragments and illustrate the most effective ways of revising each kind.

37a Revising Dependent Clause Fragments

A **dependent clause** contains both a subject and a verb, but it cannot stand alone as a sentence. Because it needs an independent clause to complete its meaning, a dependent clause (also called a *subordinate clause*) must always be attached to at least one independent clause to form a complete sentence. You can recognize a dependent clause because it is always introduced by a subordinating conjunction (*although*, *because*, and so on) or a relative pronoun (*that*, *which*, *who*, and so on).

See 33b

In most cases, the best way to correct a dependent clause fragment is to join the dependent clause to a neighboring independent clause, creating a complex sentence.

because
The United States declared war. ~~Because~~ the Japanese bombed Pearl Harbor. (Dependent clause has been attached to an independent clause, creating a complex sentence.)

, which
The battery is dead. ~~Which~~ means the car won't start. (Dependent clause has been attached to an independent clause, creating a complex sentence.)

Another way to correct a dependent clause fragment is simply to delete the subordinating conjunction or relative pronoun, turning the fragment into a complete independent clause.

The
The United States declared war. ~~Because the~~ Japanese bombed Pearl Harbor. (Subordinating conjunction *because* has been deleted; the result is a new independent clause.)

This
The battery is dead. ~~Which~~ means the car won't start. (Relative pronoun *which* has been replaced by *this;* the result is a new independent clause.)

NOTE: Deleting the subordinating conjunction or relative pronoun, as in the last two examples on page 732, is usually the least desirable way to revise a dependent clause fragment because it is likely to create two choppy sentences.

Exercise 2

Identify the sentence fragments in the following paragraph. Then, correct each fragment either by attaching the fragment to an independent clause or by deleting the subordinating conjunction or relative pronoun to create a sentence that can stand alone. (In some cases, you will have to replace a relative pronoun with another word that can serve as the subject.)

The drive-in movie came into being just after World War II. When both movies and cars were central to the lives of many Americans. Drive-ins were especially popular with teenagers and young families during the 1950s. When cars and gas were relatively inexpensive. Theaters charged by the carload. Which meant that a group of teenagers or a family with several children could spend an evening at the movies for a few dollars. In 1958, when the fad peaked, there were over four thousand drive-ins in the United States. While today there are fewer than three thousand. Many of these are in the Sunbelt, with most in California. Although many Sunbelt drive-ins continue to thrive because of the year-round warm weather. Many northern drive-ins are in financial trouble. Because land is so expensive. Some drive-in owners break even only by operating flea markets or swap meets in daylight hours. While others, unable to attract customers, are selling their theaters to land developers. Soon, drive-ins may be a part of our nostalgic past. Which will be a great loss for many who enjoy them.

37b Revising Phrase Fragments

A **phrase** provides information—description, examples, and so on—about other words or word groups in a sentence. However, because it lacks a subject, a verb, or both, a phrase cannot stand alone. When a phrase is incorrectly punctuated as a sentence, a fragment is created.

Close-up: Fragments Introduced by Transitions

Many phrase fragments are word groups that are introduced by transitional words and phrases, such as *also*, *finally*, *in addition*, and *now*, but are missing subjects and verbs. To correct such a fragment, you need to add the missing subject and verb.

See 7b2

(continued)

Fragments introduced by transitions (continued)

It was also
~~Also~~ a step in the right direction.

he found
Finally, a new home for the family.

we need
In addition, three new keyboards for the computer lab.

I will explain
Now, the first step.

ESL 61d

(1) Prepositional Phrases

A prepositional phrase consists of a preposition, its object, and any modifiers of the object.

To correct a prepositional phrase fragment, attach it to the independent clause that contains the word or word group modified by the prepositional phrase.

> *for*
> President Lyndon Johnson did not seek reelection. ~~For~~ a number of reasons. (Prepositional phrase has been attached to an independent clause, creating a complete sentence.)

> *in*
> He ran sixty yards for a touchdown. ~~In~~ the final minutes of the game. (Prepositional phrase has been attached to an independent clause, creating a complete sentence.)

Exercise 3

Read the following passage, and identify the sentence fragments. Then, correct each one by attaching it to the independent clause that contains the word or word group it modifies.

Most college athletes are caught in a conflict. Between their athletic and academic careers. Sometimes college athletes' responsibilities on the playing field make it hard for them to be good students. Often, athletes must make a choice. Between sports and a degree. Some athletes would not be able to afford college. Without athletic scholarships. Ironically, however, their commitments (training, exercise, practice, and travel to out-of-town games, for example) deprive athletes. Of valuable classroom time. The role of college athletes is constantly being questioned. Critics suggest that athletes exist only to participate in and promote college athletics. Because of the importance of this role to academic institutions, scandals occasionally develop. With coaches and even faculty members arranging to inflate athletes' grades to help them remain eligible. For participation in sports. Some universities even lower admissions standards. To help remedy this and other inequities. The controversial Proposition 48, passed at the NCAA convention in 1982, established minimum College Board scores and grade standards for college students. But many people feel that the NCAA remains overly concerned. With profits rather than with education. As a result, college athletic competition is increasingly coming to resemble pro sports. From the coaches' pressure on the players to win to the network television exposure to the wagers on the games' outcomes.

(2) Verbal Phrases

A verbal phrase consists of a **verbal**—a present participle (*walking*), past participle (*walked*), infinitive (*to walk*), or gerund (*walking*)—plus related objects and modifiers (*walking along the lonely beach*). Because a verbal cannot serve as a sentence's main verb, a verbal phrase is not a complete sentence and should not be punctuated as one.

To correct a verbal phrase fragment, you can attach the verbal phrase to a related independent clause.

> In 1948, India became an independent country~~.~~ ~~Divided~~ [divided] into the nations of India and Pakistan. (Verbal phrase has been attached to a related independent clause, creating a complete sentence.)

> A familiar trademark can increase a product's sales~~.~~ ~~Reminding~~ [, reminding] shoppers that the product has a long-standing reputation. (Verbal phrase has been attached to a related independent clause, creating a complete sentence.)

You can also change the verbal to a verb and add a subject.

> In 1948, India became an independent country. ~~Divided~~ [It was divided] into the nations of India and Pakistan. (Verb *was divided* has replaced verbal *divided*, and subject *it* has been added; the result is a complete sentence.)

> A familiar trademark can increase a product's sales. ~~Reminding~~ [It reminds] shoppers that the product has a long-standing reputation. (Verb *reminds* has replaced verbal *reminding*, and subject *it* has been added; the result is a complete sentence.)

Exercise 4

Identify the sentence fragments in the following paragraph and correct each one. Either attach the fragment to a related independent clause, or add a subject and a verb to create a complete sentence.

Many food products have well-known trademarks. Identified by familiar faces on product labels. Some of these symbols have remained the same, while others have changed considerably. Products like Sun-Maid Raisins, Betty Crocker potato mixes, Quaker Oats, and Uncle Ben's Rice use faces. To create a sense of quality and tradition and to encourage shopper recognition of the products. Many of the portraits have been updated several times. To reflect changes in society. Betty Crocker's portrait, for instance, has changed many times since its creation in 1936. Symbolizing women's changing roles. The original Chef Boy-ar-dee has also changed. Turning from the young Italian chef Hector Boiardi into a white-haired senior citizen. Miss Sunbeam, trademark of Sunbeam Bread, has had her hairdo modified several times since her first appearance in 1942; the Blue Bonnet girl, also created in 1942, now has a more modern look, and Aunt Jemima has also been changed. Slimmed down a bit in 1965. Similarly, the Campbell's Soup kids are less chubby now than in the 1920s when they first appeared. Still, manufacturers are very careful about selecting a trademark or modifying an existing one. Typically spending a good deal of time and money on research before a change is made.

(3) Appositives

An **appositive**—a noun or noun phrase that identifies or renames an adjacent noun or pronoun—cannot stand alone as a sentence.

To correct an appositive fragment, attach the appositive to the independent clause that contains the word or word group the appositive renames.

> Brian was the star forward of the Blue Devils, ~~The~~ the team with the best record. (Appositive has been attached to an independent clause, creating a complete sentence.)

> Piero della Francesca was a leader of the Umbrian school of painting, ~~A~~ a school that remained close to the traditions of Gothic art. (Appositive has been attached to an independent clause, creating a complete sentence.)

Close-up: Lists

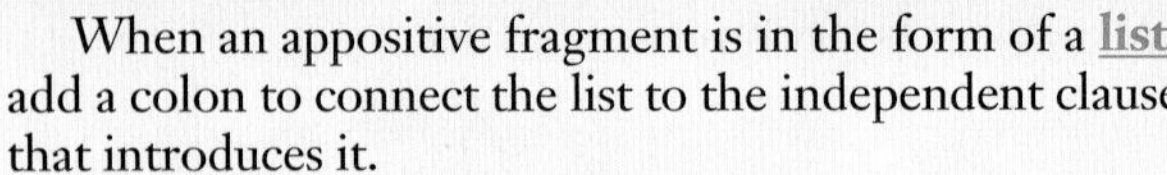

When an appositive fragment is in the form of a list, add a colon to connect the list to the independent clause that introduces it.

> Tourists often outnumber residents in four European cities: Venice, Florence, Canterbury, and Bath.

Close-up: Fragments That Introduce Examples

Sometimes an appositive consists of a word or phrase like *that is*, *for example*, *for instance*, *namely*, or *such as*, followed by an example. To correct this kind of appositive fragment, attach the appositive to the preceding independent clause.

> Fairy tales are full of damsels in distress. ~~Such~~ [, such] as Cinderella and Rapunzel.

NOTE: Sometimes you can correct an appositive fragment by embedding the appositive within an independent clause.

> Some popular novelists [(for example, Charles Dickens and Mark Twain)] are highly respected in later generations. ~~For example, Charles Dickens and Mark Twain.~~

Exercise 5

Identify the fragments in this paragraph, and correct them by attaching each one to the independent clause containing the word or word group the appositive modifies.

Until the early 1900s, communities in West Virginia, Tennessee, and Kentucky were isolated by the mountains that surrounded them. The great chain of the Appalachian Mountains. Set apart from the emerging culture of a growing America and American language, these communities retained a language rich with the dialect of Elizabethan English and sprinkled with hints of a Scotch-Irish influence. In the 1910s and '20s, the communities in these mountains began to long for a better future for their children. The key to that future, as they saw it, was education. In some communities, that education took the form of Settlement Schools. Schools led by the new rash of idealistic young graduates of eastern women's colleges. These teachers taught the basic academic subjects. Such as reading, writing, and mathematics. They also schooled their students in the culture of the mountains. For example, the crafts, music, and folklore of the Appalachians. In addition, they taught them skills that would help them survive when the coal market began to decline. The Settlement Schools attracted artisans from around the world. Quilters, weavers, basketmakers, and carpenters. The schools also opened the mountains to the world, causing the Elizabethan dialect to fade.

37c Revising Compounds

The last part of a **compound predicate, compound object,** or **compound complement** cannot stand alone as a sentence.

To correct this type of fragment, connect the detached part of the compound to the sentence to which it belongs.

> People with dyslexia have trouble reading~~.~~ *and* ~~And~~ may also find it difficult to write. (Detached part of the compound predicate has been connected to the sentence to which it belongs.)

> They took only a compass and a canteen~~.~~ *and* ~~And~~ some trail mix. (Detached part of the compound object has been connected to the sentence to which it belongs.)

> When their supplies ran out they were surprised~~.~~ *and* ~~And~~ hungry. (Detached part of the compound complement has been connected to the sentence to which it belongs.)

Exercise 6

Identify the sentence fragments in this passage, and correct them by attaching each detached compound to the rest of the sentence.

As more and more Americans discover the pleasures of the wilderness, our national parks are feeling the stress. Wanting to get away for a weekend or a week, hikers and backpackers stream from the cities into nearby state and national parks. They bring with them a hunger for wilderness. But very little knowledge about how to behave ethically in the wild. They also do not know how to keep themselves safe. Some of them think of the national parks as inexpensive amusement parks. Without proper camping supplies and lacking enough food and water for their trip, they are putting at risk their lives and the lives of those who will be called on to save them. One family went for a hike up a desert canyon with an eight-month-old infant. And their seventy-eight-year-old grandmother. Although the terrain was difficult, they were not wearing the proper shoes. Or good socks. They did not even carry a first aid kit. Or a map or compass. They were on an unmarked trail in a little-used section of Bureau of Land Management lands. And following vague directions from a friend. Soon, they were lost. They had not brought water or food. Or even rain gear or warm clothes. Luckily for them, they had brought a cell phone. By the time they called for help, however, it was getting dark and a storm was building. A rescue plane eventually located the family. And brought them to safety. Still, a little planning before they hiked in an inhospitable area, and a little awareness and preparedness for the terrain they were traveling in, would have saved this family much worry. And the taxpayers a lot of money.

37d Using Fragments Intentionally

In professional and academic writing, sentence fragments are generally not acceptable except in certain special situations.

Checklist: Using Fragments Intentionally

- ☐ In lists
- ☐ In captions that accompany visuals
- ☐ In topic outlines
- ☐ In quoted dialogue
- ☐ In *PowerPoint* presentations
- ☐ In titles and subtitles of papers and reports
- ☐ In personal email and other informal communication

Fragments are, however, often used in speech and informal writing as well as in journalism, creative writing, and advertising. Magazine advertisements, such as the one for Orange Glo polishing cloths (shown in Figure 37.2), often rely heavily on fragments to isolate (and thereby emphasize) key concepts about the product. Sometimes these fragments are formatted as bulleted lists of the product's selling features; sometimes, as in the ad in Figure 37.2, the fragments are used in a central message or tag line.

Leaves other wipes in the dust is a fragment because it is missing its subject (*Orange Glo*). What makes this fragment effective in this context is how it emphasizes what the product does. The paragraph that describes the product is free of fragments, but the two final phrases (*Orange Glo* and *Your Wood Care Resource*) are both fragments: *Orange Glo* is a subject that lacks a verb, and *Your Wood Care Resource* lacks both a subject and a verb. In both cases, fragments deliver the message succinctly and forcefully.

Figure 37.2 Magazine ad for Orange Glo polishing cloths.

Exercise 7

Select several advertisements from magazines, newspapers, or the Internet. Identify word groups that you think are fragments. Then, type each into your word processor, and run a grammar check. Keep in mind that some statements in ads may look like fragments but may in fact be imperative sentences (commands) that have an implied subject (*you*) and will therefore be recognized as grammatically correct sentences.

See 47c

Revise each fragment you identify so that it is a complete sentence. Then, decide which version—the fragment or your corrected sentence—is more effective for each advertisement's purpose and audience.

Chapter 38

Revising Comma Splices and Fused Sentences

Frequently Asked Questions

What are comma splices and fused sentences, and how are they different from run-ons? (p. 741)

How do I revise a comma splice or fused sentence? (p. 741)

A **run-on sentence** is created when two independent clauses are joined without the necessary punctuation or connective word. A run-on sentence is not just a long sentence—in fact, run-ons can be quite short—but a grammatically incorrect construction. *Comma splices* and *fused sentences* are two kinds of run-on sentences. See 32b2

A **comma splice** is an error that occurs when two independent clauses are joined with just a comma. A **fused sentence** is an error that occurs when two independent clauses are joined with no punctuation.

Comma Splice: Charles Dickens created the character of Mr. Micawber, he also created Uriah Heep.

Fused Sentence: Charles Dickens created the character of Mr. Micawber he also created Uriah Heep.

Close-up: Revising Comma Splices and Fused Sentences

To revise a comma splice or fused sentence, use one of the following four strategies:

1. Add a period between the clauses, creating two separate sentences.
2. Add a semicolon between the clauses, creating a compound sentence.
3. Add an appropriate coordinating conjunction, creating a compound sentence.
4. Subordinate one clause to the other, creating a complex sentence.

http://kirsznermandell.wadsworth.com

Computer Tip: Revising Comma Splices

Your word processor's grammar checker will highlight comma splices and prompt you to revise them (see Figure 38.1). It may also offer suggestions for revision.

Spelling and Grammar: English (U.S.)

Comma Use:

I went to the mall, she went to the beach.

Suggestions:

Comma Use (consider revising)

Figure 38.1 Sample grammar checker suggestion.

Your grammar checker may also highlight fused sentences, but it may identify them as long sentences that need revision. Moreover, it will not offer suggestions for revising fused sentences.

38a Revising with Periods

You can revise a comma splice or fused sentence by adding a period between the independent clauses, creating two separate sentences. This is a good strategy to use when the clauses are long or when they are not closely related.

> In 1894, Frenchman Alfred Dreyfus was falsely convicted of treason~~,~~ ~~his~~ . His struggle for justice pitted the army against civil libertarians.

Close-up: Comma Splices and Fused Sentences

Using a comma to punctuate an interrupted quotation that consists of two complete sentences creates a comma splice. Instead, use a period.

> "This is a good course," Eric said, ~~"in~~ . "In fact, I wish I'd taken it sooner."

38b Revising with Semicolons

You can revise a comma splice or fused sentence by adding a semicolon between two closely related clauses that convey parallel or contrasting information. The result will be a single compound sentence.

See 52a

> In pre–World War II western Europe, only a small elite had access to a university education; this situation changed dramatically after the war.

> Chippendale chairs have straight legs; however, Queen Anne chairs have curved legs.

NOTE: When you use a transitional word or phrase (such as *however*, *therefore*, or *for example*) to connect two independent clauses, the transitional element must be preceded by a semicolon and followed by a comma; if you link the two clauses with just a comma, you create a comma splice. If you omit punctuation entirely, you create a fused sentence.

See 7b2

38c Revising with Coordinating Conjunctions

You can use a coordinating conjunction (*and*, *or*, *but*, *nor*, *for*, *so*, *yet*) to join two closely related clauses of equal importance into one compound sentence. The coordinating conjunction you choose indicates the relationship between the clauses: addition (*and*), contrast (*but*, *yet*), causality (*for*, *so*), or a choice of alternatives (*or*, *nor*). Be sure to add a comma before the coordinating conjunction.

See 33a1

> Elias Howe invented the sewing machine, *and* Julia Ward Howe was a poet and social reformer.

38d Revising with Subordinating Conjunctions or Relative Pronouns

See 33b

When the ideas in two independent clauses are not of equal importance, you can use a subordinating conjunction or relative pronoun to join the clauses into one complex sentence, placing the less important idea in the dependent clause. The subordinating conjunction or relative pronoun you choose establishes the specific relationship between the clauses.

> Stravinsky's ballet *The Rite of Spring* shocked Parisians in 1913~~,~~ *because* its rhythms seemed erotic.

> Lady Mary Wortley Montagu *, who* had suffered from smallpox herself, ~~she~~ helped spread the practice of inoculation.

Close-up: Acceptable Comma Splices

In a few special cases, comma splices are acceptable. For instance, a comma is conventionally used in dialogue between a statement and a tag question, even though each is a separate independent clause.

> This is Ron's house, isn't it?
>
> I'm not late, am I?

In addition, commas may be used to connect two short, balanced independent clauses or two or more short parallel independent clauses, especially when one clause contradicts the other.

> Commencement isn't the end, it's the beginning.

Exercise 1

Identify the comma splices and fused sentences in the following paragraph. Correct each in two of the four possible ways listed in the Close-up box on page 741. If a sentence is correct, leave it alone.

Example: The fans rose in their seats, the game was almost over.

Revised: The fans rose in their seats; the game was almost over.

The fans rose in their seats, for the game was almost over.

Entrepreneurship is the study of small businesses, college students are embracing it enthusiastically. Many schools offer one or more courses in entrepreneurship these courses teach the theory and practice of starting a small business. Students are signing up for courses, moreover, they are starting their own businesses. One student started with a car-waxing business, now he sells condominiums. Other students are setting up catering services they supply everything from waiters to bartenders. One student has a thriving cake-decorating business, in fact, she employs fifteen students to deliver the cakes. All over the country, student businesses are selling everything from tennis balls to bagels, the student owners are making impressive profits. Formal courses at the graduate as well as undergraduate level are attracting more business students than ever, several schools (such as Baylor University, the University of Southern California, and Babson College) even offer degree programs in entrepreneurship. Many business school students are no longer planning to be corporate executives instead, they plan to become entrepreneurs.

Exercise 2

Combine each of the following sentence pairs into one compound sentence without creating comma splices or fused sentences. In each case, connect the clauses either with a semicolon or with a comma and a coordinating conjunction. You may have to add, delete, reorder, or change words or punctuation.

Example: People think of spring when they see crocuses blooming and robins hopping along on their lawns, but I have less traditional methods for telling when spring is imminent.

1. Tiny fragments of broken eggshells are one sign of spring. Dog hair clumping in the corners of my rooms is another.
2. I know it's time to break out the light-blocking shades in mid-March. I move my bed across the room, away from the window.
3. The sound of geese retreating is another clue that spring is approaching. The woodpeckers begin searching for termites again in the sides of my wood-shingled house.
4. The baby mice start to rustle around in the old newspapers in the garage. I have to hide the sugar bowl from the ants.
5. I think T. S. Eliot was right. April is the cruelest month.

Exercise 3

Combine each of the following sentence pairs into one sentence without creating comma splices or fused sentences. In each case, subordinate one clause to the other to create a complex sentence. You may have to add, delete, reorder, or change words or punctuation.

Example: Because I grew up at the New Jersey shore, people ~~People~~ think I'm lucky.

1. Other beach rats know better than to envy me. Inlanders romanticize life by the ocean.
2. The sound of the waves is comforting. The sand gets into everything.
3. In the summer, tourists clog the roads. In the winter, many of the locals are out of work.
4. Beach towns have a difficult time attracting any stable industry. Taxes are often prohibitive.
5. After a while, going to the beach in the summer loses its charm. The beach in winter, empty of other people, is a beautiful sight.

Exercise 4

Combine each of the following sentence pairs into one sentence without creating comma splices or fused sentences. In each case, either connect the clauses into a compound sentence with a semicolon or with a comma and a coordinating conjunction, or subordinate one clause to the other to create a complex sentence. You may have to add, delete, reorder, or change words or punctuation.

1. Several recent studies indicate that many American high school students have little knowledge of history. This is affecting our future as a democratic nation and as individuals.
2. Surveys show that nearly one-third of American seventeen-year-olds cannot identify the countries the United States fought against in World War II. One-third think Columbus reached the New World after 1750.
3. Several reasons have been given for this decline in historical literacy. The main reason is the way history is taught.
4. This problem is bad news. The good news is that there is increasing agreement among educators about what is wrong with current methods of teaching history.
5. History can be exciting and engaging. Too often, it is presented in a boring manner.
6. Students are typically expected to memorize dates, facts, and names. History as adventure—as a "good story"—is frequently neglected.
7. One way to avoid this problem is to use good textbooks. Textbooks should be accurate, lively, and focused.
8. Another way to create student interest in historical events is to use primary sources instead of so-called comprehensive textbooks. Autobiographies, journals, and diaries can give students insight into larger issues.

9. Students can also be challenged to think about history by taking sides in a debate. They can learn more about connections among historical events by writing essays than by taking multiple-choice tests.
10. Finally, history teachers should be less concerned about specific historical details. They should be more concerned about conveying the wonder of history.

Chapter 39

Revising Faulty Modification

Frequently Asked Questions

What are misplaced modifiers, and how do I revise them? (p. 749)

Is a split infinitive ever acceptable? (p. 754)

What are dangling modifiers, and how do I revise them? (p. 755)

A **modifier** is a word, phrase, or clause that describes, limits, or qualifies another word or word group in a sentence. A modifier should be placed close to its **headword,** the word or word group it modifies.

Wendy watched the storm, fierce and threatening.

Faulty modification is the awkward or confusing placement of modifiers or the modification of nonexistent words.

http://kirsznermandell.wadsworth.com

Computer Tip: Revising Faulty Modification

Your grammar checker will identify some modification problems, including certain awkward split infinitives (see Figure 39.1). However, the grammar checker will not offer revision suggestions.

Spelling and Grammar: English (U.S.)

Split Infinitive:

We want **to in a few days climb** Mount Washington.

Suggestions:

Split Infinitive (consider revising)

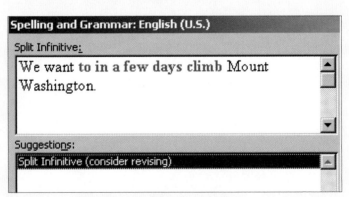

Figure 39.1 Sample grammar checker suggestion.

39a Revising Misplaced Modifiers

A **misplaced modifier** is a word or word group whose placement suggests that it modifies one word or phrase when it is intended to modify another.

Confusing: Flying faster than a speeding bullet, the citizens of Metropolis saw Superman. (Were the citizens of Metropolis flying?)

Revised: The citizens of Metropolis saw Superman flying faster than a speeding bullet.

Confusing: With an IQ of just 52, the lawyer argued that his client should not get the death penalty. (Does the lawyer have an IQ of 52?)

Revised: The lawyer argued that his client, with an IQ of just 52, should not get the death penalty.

When you revise, check to make sure you have placed each modifying word, phrase, and clause in a position that clearly identifies its headword and that does not awkwardly interrupt a sentence.

(1) Placing Modifying Words Precisely

Limiting modifiers—such as *almost*, *only*, *even*, *hardly*, *merely*, *nearly*, *exactly*, *scarcely*, *just*, and *simply*—should always immediately precede the words they modify. Different placements change the meaning of the sentence.

Nick *just* set up camp at the edge of the burned-out town. (He set up camp just now.)

Just Nick set up camp at the edge of the burned-out town. (He set up camp alone.)

Nick set up camp *just* at the edge of the burned-out town. (His camp was precisely at the edge.)

When a limiting modifier is placed so that it is not clear whether it modifies a word before it or one after it, it is called a **squinting modifier.** To avoid ambiguity, place the modifier so it clearly modifies its headword.

Squinting: The life that everyone thought would fulfill her totally bored her. (Was she supposed to be totally fulfilled, or is she totally bored?)

Revised: The life that everyone thought would totally fulfill her bored her. (Everyone expected her to be totally fulfilled.)

Revised: The life that everyone thought would fulfill her bored her totally. (She was totally bored.)

Exercise 1

In the following sentence pairs, the modifier in each sentence points to a different headword. Underline the modifier and draw an arrow to the word it modifies. Then, explain the meaning of each sentence.

Example: She just came in wearing a hat. (She just now entered.)

She came in wearing just a hat. (She wore only a hat.)

1. He wore his almost new jeans.
   He almost wore his new jeans.
2. He had only three dollars in his pocket.
   Only he had three dollars in his pocket.
3. I don't even like freshwater fish.
   I don't like even freshwater fish.
4. I go only to the beach on Saturdays.
   I go to the beach only on Saturdays.
5. He simply hated driving.
   He hated simply driving.

(2) Relocating Misplaced Phrases

Placing a modifying phrase incorrectly can change the meaning of a sentence or create an unclear or confusing sentence. To avoid ambiguity, be sure to place verbal and prepositional phrases right beside the word or word groups they modify.

See 32b1

Verbal Phrases A verbal phrase that acts as a modifier should be placed directly *before* or directly *after* the noun or pronoun it modifies.

Shooting from the foul line, he scored two points.

The two communities, connected by a suspension bridge, are only minutes apart by car.

The incorrect placement of a verbal phrase can make a sentence convey an entirely different meaning or make no sense at all.

Confusing: Jane watched the boats roller-skating along the shore. (Were the boats roller-skating?)

Revised: Roller-skating along the shore, Jane watched the boats.

Prepositional Phrases A prepositional phrase used as an **adjective** nearly always directly *follows* the word it modifies.

See 32b1

This is a Dresden figurine from Germany.

Created by a famous artist, *Venus de Milo* is a statue with no arms.

Incorrect placement of such modifiers can create confusion or even unintended humor.

Venus de Milo is a statue created by a famous artist with no arms. (Did the artist have no arms?)

A prepositional phrase used as an **adverb** also usually *follows* its headword.

Cassandra looked into the future.

Incorrect placement of such phrases can be illogical as well as confusing.

Confusing: She saw the house she built in her mind. (Did she build the house in her mind?)

Revised: In her mind, she saw the house she built.

NOTE: As long as the meaning of the sentence is clear, and as long as the headword is clearly identified, you can place an adverbial modifier in other positions as well.

He had been waiting anxiously at the bus stop for a long time.

Exercise 2

Underline the modifying verbal phrases or prepositional phrases in each sentence and draw arrows to their headwords.

Example: Calvin is the Democrat running for town council.

1. The bridge across the river swayed in the wind.
2. The spectators on the shore were involved in the action.
3. Mesmerized by the spectacle, they watched the drama unfold.
4. The spectators were afraid of a disaster.
5. Within the hour, the state police arrived to save the day.
6. They closed off the area with roadblocks.
7. Drivers approaching the bridge were asked to stop.
8. Meanwhile, on the bridge, the scene was chaos.
9. Motorists in their cars were paralyzed with fear.
10. Struggling against the weather, the police managed to rescue everyone.

Exercise 3

Use the word or phrase that follows each sentence as a modifier in that sentence. Then, underline the modifier, and draw an arrow to indicate its headword.

Example: He approached the lion. (timidly)

Timidly, he approached the lion.

1. The lion paced up and down in his cage, ignoring the crowd. (watching Jack)
2. Jack stared back at the lion. (nervous yet curious)
3. The crowd around them grew. (anxious to see what would happen)
4. Suddenly, Jack heard a growl from deep in the lion's throat. (terrifying)
5. Jack ran from the zoo, leaving the lion behind. (scared to death)

(3) Revising Misplaced Dependent Clauses

A dependent clause that serves as a modifier must be clearly related to its headword. An **adjective clause** usually appears immediately *after* the word it modifies.

> During the Civil War, Lincoln was the president who governed the United States.

An **adverb clause** can appear in any of several positions, as long as its relationship to the word or word group it modifies is clear.

> When Lincoln was president, the Civil War raged.

> The Civil War raged when Lincoln was president.

When you revise a misplaced dependent clause, focus on making the relationship between modifier and headword clear.

Misplaced Adjective Clause: This diet program will limit the consumption of possible carcinogens, which will benefit everyone. (Will carcinogens benefit everyone?)

Revised: This diet program, which will benefit everyone, will limit the consumption of possible carcinogens.

Misplaced Adverb Clause: The parents checked to see that the children were sleeping after they had a glass of wine. (Did the children drink the wine?)

Revised: After they had a glass of wine, the parents checked to see that the children were sleeping.

Exercise 4

Relocate the misplaced verbal phrases, prepositional phrases, or dependent clauses so that they clearly point to the words or word groups they modify.

Example: *Silent Running* is a film ^with Bruce Dern^ about a scientist left alone in space ~~with Bruce Dern.~~

1. She realized that she had married the wrong man after the wedding.
2. *The Prince and the Pauper* is a novel about an exchange of identities by Mark Twain.
3. The energy was used up in the ten-kilometer race that he was saving for the marathon.
4. He loaded the bottles and cans into his new car, which he planned to leave at the recycling center.
5. The manager explained the sales figures to the board members using a graph.

(4) Revising Intrusive Modifiers

Sometimes a long modifier awkwardly interrupts a sentence, making it difficult to understand. Be on the lookout for these **intrusive modifiers** in your writing, and revise them when you find them.

Interrupted Verb Phrases A brief modifier can usually be placed between an auxiliary verb and a main verb.

She had always planned to reenlist.

He will probably be ready to leave on Friday.

Generally, however, you will need to revise when a long modifier interrupts a verb phrase.

Awkward: She had, without giving it a second thought or considering the consequences, planned to reenlist.

Revised: Without giving it a second thought or considering the consequences, she had planned to reenlist.

Awkward: He will, if he ever gets his act together, be ready to leave on Friday.

Revised: If he ever gets his act together, he will be ready to leave on Friday.

Split Infinitives An infinitive is made up of *to* plus the base form of the verb (*to beat*). A **split infinitive**—an infinitive whose parts are separated by a modifier—used to be considered a grammatical error, but now many split infinitives are acceptable. For example, a split infinitive is perfectly acceptable when the intervening modifier is short and when the alternative is awkward or ambiguous.

She expected to not quite beat her previous record.

However, when a modifier awkwardly interrupts an infinitive, it is not acceptable and should be revised.

Awkward: She hoped to in a matter of months, if not days, beat her previous record.

Revised: She hoped to beat her previous record in a matter of months, if not days.

Interrupted Subjects and Verbs or Verbs and Objects or Complements An **adjective phrase or clause**—even a lengthy one—between a subject and a verb or between a verb and its object or complement does not usually cause confusion.

Acceptable: Major films that were financially successful in the1930s include *Gone with the Wind* and *The Wizard of Oz*. (Adjective clause between subject and verb does not obscure sentence's meaning.)

However, an **adverb phrase or clause** in this position may not be clear or sound natural.

Confusing: The election, because officials discovered that some people voted twice, was contested. (Adverb clause intrudes between subject and verb.)

Revised: Because officials discovered that some people voted twice, the election was contested. (Subject and verb are no longer separated.)

Confusing: A. A. Milne wrote, when his son Christopher Robin was a child, *Winnie the Pooh*. (Adverb clause intrudes between verb and object.)

Revised: When his son Christopher Robin was a child, A. A. Milne wrote *Winnie the Pooh*. (Verb and object are no longer separated.)

Exercise 5

Revise these sentences so that the modifying phrases or clauses do not interrupt the parts of a verb phrase or an infinitive or separate a subject from a verb or a verb from its object or complement.

Despite the playwright's best efforts, a
Example: ~~A~~ play can sometimes be~~, despite the playwright's best efforts,~~ mystifying to the audience.

1. The people in the audience, when they saw the play was about to begin and realized the orchestra had finished tuning up and had begun the overture, finally quieted down.
2. They settled into their seats, expecting to very much enjoy the first act.
3. However, most people were, even after watching and listening for twenty minutes and paying close attention to the drama, completely baffled.
4. In fact, the play, because it had nameless characters, no scenery, and a rambling plot that did not seem to be heading anywhere, puzzled even the drama critics.
5. Finally, one of the three major characters explained, speaking directly to the audience, what the play was really about.

39b Revising Dangling Modifiers

A **dangling modifier** is a word or phrase that cannot logically modify any word or word group in the sentence. In fact, its true headword does not appear anywhere in the sentence. In the following sentence, *using this drug* is a dangling modifier.

Using this drug, many undesirable side effects are experienced. (Who is using this drug?)

There are two ways to correct this dangling modifier. The first way is to create a new subject by supplying a word or word group that *using this drug* can logically modify.

Revised: Using this drug, patients experience many undesirable side effects. (Patients are using this drug.)

The second way to correct the dangling modifier is to reword it to create a dependent clause.

Revised: Many undesirable side effects are experienced when this drug is used.

These two options for correcting dangling modifiers are illustrated below.

(1) Creating a New Subject

One way to correct a dangling modifier is by supplying a subject that the modifier can logically describe.

Dangling: Using a pair of forceps, the skin of the rat's abdomen was lifted, and a small cut was made into the body with scissors. (Modifier cannot logically modify *skin*.)

Revised: Using a pair of forceps, the technician lifted the skin of the rat's abdomen and made a small cut into the body with scissors. (Subject of main clause has been changed from *the skin* to *the technician*, a logical headword.)

Dangling: With fifty more pages to read, *War and Peace* was absorbing. (Modifier cannot logically modify *War and Peace*.)

Revised: With fifty more pages to read, Meg found *War and Peace* absorbing. (Subject of main clause has been changed from *War and Peace* to *Meg*, a logical headword.)

Close-up: Dangling Modifiers and the Passive Voice

See 47d1

Most sentences that include dangling modifiers do not include a headword because they are in the passive voice. Changing the passive voice to active voice corrects the dangling modifier by changing the subject of the sentence's main clause to a word that the dangling modifier can logically modify.

(2) Creating a Dependent Clause

Another way to correct a dangling modifier is by rewording the modifier to turn it into a dependent clause.

> **Dangling Phrase:** To implement the new grading system, students were polled. (Modifier cannot logically modify *students*.)
>
> **Revised:** Before the new grading system was implemented, students were polled. (Modifying phrase is now a dependent clause.)
>
> **Dangling:** On the newsstands only an hour, its sales surprised everyone. (Modifier cannot logically modify *sales*.)
>
> **Revised:** Because the magazine had been on the newsstands only an hour, its sales surprised everyone. (Modifying phrase is now a dependent clause.)

Close-up: Revising Dangling Elliptical Clauses

Elliptical clauses are incomplete constructions. Typically, the writer has intentionally omitted part of the subject or predicate (or the entire subject or predicate) from a dependent clause in order to create a more concise sentence. When such a clause cannot logically modify the subject of the sentence's main clause, it dangles. To revise a dangling elliptical clause, add a subject that the elliptical clause can logically modify.

> **Dangling:** While still in the Buchner funnel, you should press the crystals with a clear stopper to eliminate any residual solvent. (Elliptical clause cannot logically modify *you*.)
>
> **Revised:** While still in the Buchner funnel, the crystals should be pressed with a clear stopper to eliminate any residual solvent. (Subject of main clause has been changed from *you* to *crystals*, a word the elliptical clause can logically modify.)

Exercise 6

Eliminate the dangling modifier from each of the following sentences. Either supply a word or word group the dangling modifier can logically modify, or change the dangling modifier into a dependent clause.

Example: Skiing down the mountain, my hat flew off.
(dangling modifier)

Revised: Skiing down the mountain, <u>I</u> lost my hat.
(new subject added)

<u>As I skied down the mountain</u>, my hat flew off.
(dependent clause)

1. Writing for eight hours every day, her lengthy books are published every year or so.
2. As an out-of-state student without a car, it was difficult to get to off-campus cultural events.
3. To build a campfire, kindling is necessary.
4. With every step upward, the trees became sparser.
5. Being an amateur tennis player, my backhand is weaker than my forehand.
6. When exiting the train, the station will be on your right.
7. Driving through the Mojave, the bleak landscape was oppressive.
8. By requiring auto manufacturers to further improve emission-control devices, the air quality will get better.
9. Using a piece of filter paper, the ball of sodium is dried as much as possible and placed in a test tube.
10. Having missed work for seven days straight, my job was in jeopardy.

Chapter 40

Using Parallelism

Frequently Asked Questions

What is parallelism? (p. 759)
What is faulty parallelism, and how do I correct it? (p. 762)

See 40b

Parallelism—the use of matching words, phrases, clauses, or sentence structures to express equivalent ideas—adds unity, balance, and force to your writing. Effective parallelism can help you write clearer sentences, but faulty parallelism can create awkward sentences that obscure your meaning and confuse readers.

40a Using Parallelism Effectively

Effective parallelism makes sentences easy to follow and emphasizes relationships among equivalent ideas. Parallelism highlights the correspondence between *items in a series*, *paired items*, and elements in *lists and outlines*.

(1) With Items in a Series

Coordinate elements—words, phrases, or clauses—in a series should be presented in parallel form. (For information on punctuating elements in a series, **see 51b** and **52c.**)

> Eat, drink, and be merry.
>
> I came; I saw; I conquered.
>
> Baby food consumption, toy production, and school construction are likely to decline as the US population grows older.
>
> Three factors influenced his decision to seek new employment: his desire to relocate, his need for greater responsibility, and his dissatisfaction with his current job.

(2) With Paired Items

Paired points or ideas (words, phrases, or clauses) should be presented in parallel form. Parallelism emphasizes their equivalence and connects the two ideas.

The thank-you note was short but sweet.

Roosevelt represented the United States, and Churchill represented Great Britain.

The research focused on muscle tissue and nerve cells.

Ask not what your country can do for you; ask what you can do for your country. (John F. Kennedy, inaugural address)

Paired items linked by **correlative conjunctions** (such as *not only/but also*, *both/and*, *either/or*, *neither/nor*, and *whether/or*) should be parallel.

The design team paid close attention not only to color but also to texture.

Either repeat physics or take calculus.

Parallelism also highlights the contrast between paired elements linked by *than* or *as*.

Richard Wright and James Baldwin chose to live in Paris rather than to remain in the United States.

Success is as much a matter of hard work as a matter of luck.

(3) In Lists and Outlines

Elements in a list should be presented in parallel form.

The Irish potato famine had four major causes:

1. The establishment of the landlord-tenant system
2. The failure of the potato crop
3. The reluctance of England to offer adequate financial assistance
4. The passage of the Corn Laws

Elements in a formal outline also should be parallel.

Exercise 1

Identify the parallel elements in these sentences by bracketing parallel phrases and clauses.

Example: Manek spent six years in America [going to school] and [working for a computer company].

1. After he completed his engineering degree, Manek returned to India to visit his large extended family and to find a wife.

2. Unfamiliar with marriage practices in India and accustomed to American notions of marriage for love, Manek's American friends frowned on his plans.
3. Not only Manek but also his parents wanted an arranged marriage.
4. He didn't believe that either you married for love or you had a loveless marriage.
5. His parents' marriage, an arranged one, continues happily; his aunt's marriage, also arranged, has lasted thirty years.

Exercise 2

Combine each of the following sentence pairs or sentence groups into one sentence that uses parallel structure. Be sure all paired items and items in a series (words, phrases, or clauses) are expressed in parallel terms.

1. Originally, there were five performing Marx Brothers. One was nicknamed Groucho. The others were called Chico, Harpo, Gummo, and Zeppo.
2. Groucho was very well known. So were Chico and Harpo. Gummo soon dropped out of the act. And later Zeppo did too.
3. They began in vaudeville. That was before World War I. Their first show was called *I'll Say She Is*. It opened in New York in 1924.
4. The Marx Brothers' first movie was *The Cocoanuts*. The next was *Animal Crackers*. And this was followed by *Monkey Business*, *Horse Feathers*, and *Duck Soup*. Then came *A Night at the Opera*.
5. In each of these movies, the Marx Brothers make people laugh. They also exhibit a unique, zany comic style.
6. In their movies, each brother has a set of familiar trademarks. Groucho has a mustache and a long coat. He wiggles his eyebrows and smokes a cigar. There is a funny hat that Chico always wears. And he affects a phony Italian accent. Harpo never speaks.
7. Groucho is always cast as a sly operator. He always tries to cheat people out of their money. He always tries to charm women.
8. In *The Cocoanuts,* Groucho plays Mr. Hammer, proprietor of the run-down Coconut Manor, a Florida hotel. In *Horse Feathers,* his character is named Professor Quincy Adams Wagstaff. Wagstaff is president of Huxley College. Huxley also has financial problems.
9. In *Duck Soup,* Groucho plays Rufus T. Firefly, president of the country of Fredonia. Fredonia was formerly ruled by the late husband of a Mrs. Teasdale. Fredonia is now at war with the country of Sylvania.

10. Margaret Dumont is often Groucho's leading lady. She plays Mrs. Teasdale in *Duck Soup*. In *A Night at the Opera*, she plays Mrs. Claypool. Her character in *The Cocoanuts* is named Mrs. Potter.

40b Revising Faulty Parallelism

Faulty parallelism occurs when equivalent ideas in a sentence are not presented in parallel form.

> **Faulty Parallelism:** Many people in developing countries suffer because the countries lack sufficient housing to accommodate them, sufficient food to feed them, and their health-care facilities are inadequate.

Because the three reasons in the preceding sentence are presented in a series, readers expect them to be expressed in parallel form. The first two elements satisfy this expectation: *sufficient housing to accommodate them* . . . ; *sufficient food to feed them*. . . . The third item in the series, however, breaks this pattern: *their health-care facilities are inadequate*.

Correcting the faulty parallelism creates a clearer, more emphatic sentence, with all three ideas presented in parallel form.

> Many people in developing countries suffer because the countries lack sufficient housing to accommodate them, sufficient food to feed them and sufficient health-care facilities to serve them.

http://kirsznermandell.wadsworth.com

Computer Tip: Revising Faulty Parallelism

Grammar checkers are not very useful for identifying faulty parallelism. Although your grammar checker may highlight some nonparallel constructions, it may label some parallelism problems as wordiness.

(1) Using Parallel Elements

Revise faulty parallelism by matching nouns with nouns, verbs with verbs, and phrases and clauses with similarly constructed phrases and clauses.

Faulty Parallelism	**Revised**
Popular exercises for men and women include spinning, weight lifters, and jogging.	Popular exercises for men and women include spinning, weight lifting, and jogging.
Some of the side effects are skin irritation and eye irritation, and mucous membrane irritation may also develop.	Some of the side effects that may develop are skin, eye, and mucous membrane irritation.
I look forward to hearing from you and to have an opportunity to tell you more about myself.	I look forward to hearing from you and to having an opportunity to tell you more about myself.

(2) Repeating Key Words

Although the use of similar grammatical structures may sometimes be enough to convey parallelism, sentences are often clearer and more emphatic if certain key words (articles, prepositions, and the *to* in infinitives, for example) are repeated in each element of a pair or series.

Faulty Parallelism	**Revised**
Computerization has helped industry by not allowing labor costs to skyrocket, increasing the speed of production, and improving efficiency. (Does *not* apply to all three phrases, or only the first?)	Computerization has helped industry by not allowing labor costs to skyrocket, by increasing the speed of production, and by improving efficiency. (Preposition *by* is repeated to clarify the boundaries of the three parallel phrases.)

(3) Repeating Relative Pronouns

Like correlative conjunctions, the relative pronoun constructions *who . . . and who*, *whom . . . and whom*, and *which . . . and which* are always paired and always introduce parallel clauses. When you revise, check to be sure a relative pronoun introduces each clause.

Faulty: *The Thing*, directed by Howard Hawks, and which was released in 1951, featured James Arness as the monster.

Revised: *The Thing*, which was directed by Howard Hawks and which was released in 1951, featured James Arness as the monster.

Exercise 3

Identify and correct faulty parallelism in these sentences. Then, underline the parallel elements—words, phrases, and clauses—in your corrected sentences. If a sentence is already correct, mark it with a *C*, and underline the parallel elements.

Example: Alfred Hitchcock's films include *North by Northwest*, *Vertigo*, *Psycho*, ~~and he also directed~~ *Notorious*, and *Saboteur*.

1. The world is divided between those with galoshes on and those who discover continents.
2. World leaders, members of Congress, and the American Catholic bishops all pressed the president to limit the arms race.
3. A national task force on education recommended improving public education by making the school day longer, higher teachers' salaries, and integrating more technology into the curriculum.
4. The fast food industry has expanded to include many kinds of restaurants: those that serve pizza, fried chicken chains, some offering Mexican-style menus, and hamburger franchises.
5. The consumption of Scotch in the United States is declining because of high prices, tastes are changing, and increased health awareness has led many whiskey drinkers to switch to wine or beer.

Chapter 41

Revising Awkward or Confusing Sentences

Frequently Asked Questions

What's the difference between direct and indirect discourse? (p. 767)

What's wrong with using the phrase the reason is . . . because*?* (p. 771)

The most common causes of awkward or confusing sentences are *unwarranted shifts*, *mixed constructions*, *faulty predication*, and *illogical comparisons*.

ESL Tip

Some of the faulty example sentences in this chapter are similar to sentences that native English speakers sometimes use in conversation. Keep in mind, however, that although such constructions may be acceptable in informal speech, you should not use them in your writing.

41a Revising Unwarranted Shifts

(1) Shifts in Tense

Verb tense in a sentence (or in a related group of sentences) should not shift without good reason—to indicate changes of time, for example.

See 47b

ESL 61b2

> *The Wizard of Oz* is a classic film that was made in 1939. (acceptable shift from present to past)

Unwarranted shifts in tense, like those in the following sentences, can be confusing.

> I registered for the advanced philosophy seminar because I wanted a challenge. However, after the first week I ~~start~~ started having trouble understanding the reading. (unwarranted shift from past to present)

> Jack Kerouac's novel *On the Road* follows a group of friends who ~~drove~~ drive across the United States. (unwarranted shift from present to past)

NOTE: The present tense is generally used in writing about literature.

(2) Shifts in Voice

Unwarranted shifts from active to passive voice (or from passive to active) can be confusing. In the following sentence, for instance, the shift from active (*wrote*) to passive (*was written*) makes it unclear who wrote *The Great Gatsby.*

> F. Scott Fitzgerald wrote *This Side of Paradise*~~,~~ and later wrote *The Great Gatsby*. ~~was written.~~

Close-up: Shifts in Voice

Sometimes a shift from active to passive voice within a sentence may be necessary to give the sentence proper emphasis.

> Even though consumers protested, the sales tax was increased.

Here the shift from active (*protested*) to passive (*was increased*) keeps the focus on consumer groups and the issue they protested. To say *the legislature increased the sales tax* would change the emphasis of the sentence.

(3) Shifts in Mood

Mood indicates whether a writer is making a statement or asking a question (**indicative mood**), issuing a command or making a request (**imperative mood**), or expressing a wish or hypothetical condition (**subjunctive mood**). Unnecessary shifts in mood also create awkward sentences. The following sentence shifts unnecessarily from the imperative to the indicative mood.

> Next, heat the mixture in a test tube, and ^be ~~you should make~~ sure it does not boil.

(4) Shifts in Person and Number

Person indicates who is speaking (first person—*I*, *we*), who is spoken to (second person—*you*), and who is spoken about (third person—*he*, *she*, *it*, and *they*). Most unwarranted shifts in a sentence occur between second and third person.

> When ^you ~~someone~~ look~~s~~ for a car loan, you should compare the interest rates of several banks. (shift from third to second person)

Number indicates one (singular—*novel*, *it*) or more than one (plural—*novels*, *they*, *them*). Singular pronouns should refer to singular antecedents and plural pronouns to plural antecedents.

> If a person does not study regularly, ^he or she ~~they~~ will have a difficult time passing a course.

(5) Shifts from Direct to Indirect Discourse

Direct discourse reports the exact words of a speaker or writer. It is always enclosed in quotation marks and is often accompanied by an identifying tag (*he says*, *she said*). **Indirect discourse** summarizes the words of a speaker or writer. No quotation marks are used, and the reported words are often introduced with the word *that* or, in the case of questions, with *who*, *what*, *why*, *whether*, *how*, or *if*.

> **Direct Discourse:** My instructor said, "I want your paper by this Friday."
>
> **Indirect Discourse:** My instructor said that he wanted my paper by this Friday.

Shifts between indirect and direct discourse are often confusing.

> During the trial, John Brown repeatedly defended his actions and said that ^he was ~~I am~~ not guilty. (shift from indirect to direct discourse)

"Are you ?"
My mother asked, ~~was I~~ ever going to get a job~~.~~
(neither indirect nor direct discourse)

For information on word order in direct and indirect quotations, see 61e4.

Exercise 1

Read the following sentences, and eliminate any shifts in tense, voice, mood, person, or number. Some sentences are correct, and some can be revised in more than one way.

you
Example: When ~~one~~ examine~~s~~ the history of the women's movement, you see that it had many different beginnings.

1. Some historians see World War II and women's work in the factories as the beginning of the push toward equal rights for women.
2. Women went to work in the fabric mills of Lowell, Massachusetts, in the late 1800s, and her efforts at reforming the workplace are seen by many as the beginning of the equal rights movement.
3. Farm girls from New Hampshire, Vermont, and western Massachusetts came to Lowell to make money, and they wanted to experience life in the city.
4. The factories promised the girls decent wages, and parents were promised that their daughters would live in a safe, wholesome environment.
5. Dormitories were built by the factory owners; they are supposed to ensure a safe environment for the girls.
6. First, visit the loom rooms at the Boot Mills Factory, and then you should tour a replica of a dormitory.
7. When one visits the working loom room at the factory, you are overcome with a sense of the risks and dangers the girls faced in the mills.
8. For a mill girl, moving to the city meant freedom and an escape from the drudgery of farm life; it also meant they had to face many new social situations for which they were not always prepared.
9. Harriet Robinson wrote *Loom and Spindle*, the story of her life as a mill girl, and then a book of poems was published.
10. When you look at the lives of the loom girls, one can see that their work laid part of the foundation for women's later demands for equal rights.

Exercise 2

Change the direct discourse in the following sentences to indirect discourse.

Example: Anna Quindlen explained why she kept her maiden name when she married: "It was a political decision, a simple statement that I was somebody and not an adjunct of anybody, especially a husband."

Anna Quindlen explained that she made a decision to keep her maiden name when she married because it was a simple political statement that she was somebody and not an adjunct to anybody, especially not to a husband.

1. Sally Thane Christensen, advocating the use of an endangered species of tree, the yew, as a treatment for cancer, asked, "Is a tree worth a life?"
2. Stephen Nathanson, considering the morality of the death penalty, asked, "What if the death penalty did save lives?"
3. Martin Luther King Jr. said, "I have a dream that one day this nation will rise up and live out the true meaning of its creed."
4. Benjamin Franklin once stated, "The older I grow, the more apt I am to doubt my own judgment of others."
5. Thoreau said, "The finest qualities of our nature, like the bloom on fruits, can be preserved only by the most delicate handling."

41b Revising Mixed Constructions

A **mixed construction** is created when a dependent clause, prepositional phrase, or independent clause is incorrectly used as the subject of a sentence.

Because she studies every day*,* ~~explains why~~ she gets good grades. (dependent clause incorrectly used as subject)

By calling for information*, you can* ~~is the way to~~ learn more about the benefits of ROTC. (prepositional phrase incorrectly used as subject)

Being ~~He was~~ late made him miss the first act of the play. (independent clause incorrectly used as subject)

Exercise 3

Revise the following mixed constructions so their parts fit together both grammatically and logically.

Example: ~~By investing~~ Investing in commodities made her rich.

1. In implementing the "motor voter" bill has made it easier for people to register to vote.
2. She sank the basket was the reason they won the game.
3. Just because situations change, does not change the characters' hopes and dreams.
4. By dropping the course would be his only chance to avoid a low GPA.
5. Even though she works for a tobacco company does not mean that she is against laws prohibiting smoking in restaurants.

41c Revising Faulty Predication

Faulty predication occurs when a sentence's predicate does not logically complete its subject.

(1) Incorrect Use of *Be*

See 45c1

Faulty predication is especially common in sentences that contain a linking verb—a form of the verb *be*, for example—and a subject complement.

> Mounting costs and decreasing revenues ~~were~~ caused the downfall of the hospital.

This sentence incorrectly states that mounting costs and decreasing revenues *were* the downfall of the hospital when, in fact, they were the *reasons* for its downfall.

(2) *Is When* or *Is Where*

Another kind of faulty predication occurs when a sentence that presents a definition incorrectly includes a construction like *is where* or *is when*.

> Taxidermy is ~~where you construct~~ the construction of a lifelike representation of an animal from its preserved skin. (In a definition, *is* must be preceded and followed by nouns or noun phrases.)

(3) *The Reason . . . Is Because*

A similar type of problem occurs when the phrase *the reason is* precedes *because*. In this situation, *because* (which means "for the reason that") is redundant and should be deleted.

> The reason we drive is ^that ~~because~~ we are afraid to fly.

http://kirsznermandell.wadsworth.com

Computer Tip: Revising Faulty Predication

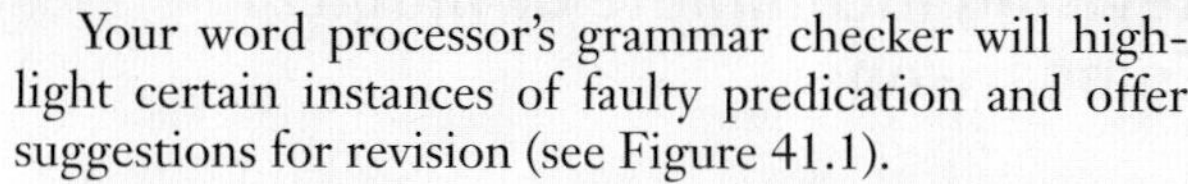

Your word processor's grammar checker will highlight certain instances of faulty predication and offer suggestions for revision (see Figure 41.1).

Spelling and Grammar: English (U.S.)

Colloquialism:

The reason is **because** I could not find my keys.

Suggestions:

that

Figure 41.1 Sample grammar checker suggestion.

Your grammar checker will also highlight some other causes of awkward or confusing sentences, including shifts in voice, person, and number, and will frequently offer revision suggestions. However, the grammar checker will miss many unwarranted shifts, mixed constructions, and incomplete or illogical constructions.

Exercise 4

Revise the following sentences to eliminate faulty predication. Keep in mind that each sentence may be revised in more than one way.

Example: ^Traffic ~~The reason traffic~~ jams occur at 9 a.m. and 5 p.m. ~~is~~ because too many people work traditional rather than staggered hours.

1. Inflation is when the purchasing power of currency declines.
2. Hypertension is where the blood pressure is elevated.
3. Television and the Internet were the decline in students' reading scores.
4. Some people say the reason for the increasing violence in American cities is because guns are too easily available.
5. The reason for all the congestion in American cities is because too many people live too close together.

41d Revising Incomplete or Illogical Comparisons

A comparison tells how two things are alike or unlike. When you make a comparison, be sure it is *complete* (that readers can tell which two items are being compared) and *logical* (that it equates two comparable items).

My chemistry course is harder~~.~~ ^than Nina's^ (What two things are being compared?)

A pig's intelligence is greater than a ~~dog~~ ^dog's^. (illogically compares "a pig's intelligence" to "a dog")

Exercise 5

Revise the following sentences to correct any incomplete or illogical comparisons.

Example: Technology-based industries are concerned about inflation as much as service industries~~.~~ ^are.^

1. Opportunities in technical writing are more promising than business writing.
2. Technical writing is more challenging.
3. In some ways, technical writing requires more attention to detail and is, therefore, more difficult.
4. Business writers are concerned about clarity as much as technical writers.
5. Technology-based industries may one day create more writing opportunities than any other industry.

STUDENT WRITER AT WORK

Solving Common Sentence Problems

In the following draft, written for a composition class, a student writer responds to the question, *How do you define success?* After reading the draft carefully, use the information in Part 7 to help you revise sentence problems such as sentence fragments, comma splices and fused sentences, faulty modification, faulty parallelism, shifts in tense and number, mixed constructions, and faulty predication.

Success Is a Relative Term

A common definition of success is having that which you do not need. This being one definition of success with which I personally do not agree. We as Americans are the wealthiest and the most wasteful people in the world. We are building enormous houses with far too many bedrooms, buying more cars than we can drive, and we accumulate too many luxury items. On the surface, we are a successful nation. But whether we are really successful or not depends on how success is defined.

Many people would agree that what the word <u>success</u> means to most Americans is money, it no longer means achievement of a personal or professional goal. This drive, this need for money, is self-destructive. Because if our society's people simply turn their goals and ambitions into the earning of money, then we will soon see a nation of driven, selfish people. Because people are spending far too much money on things they do not need is a serious problem in our society. Until we solve this problem, we cannot be seen as successful.

There are many other views that can be taken on this complex topic of the meaning of success. Some would argue that doing what we want to with what we have is our right as Americans. Who is to decide when we have crossed over the line of greed? After all, America prospered as a result of our own ingenuity and hard work. If a person has the money and the desire to build himself or herself a three-million-dollar mansion with a swimming pool, then so be it. Many Americans believe that if someone earned that money through their own hard work, then you can do what you want with it.

In fact, this idea of being free to do what one wishes—even if that means spending obscene sums of money on frivolous items—is the basis for our entire country. Through the hardships our ancestors endured, we as a nation turned our land into the most powerful country in the world. Emerging from our struggles, a stronger nation was created. This prosperity, many argue, is success, this is our reward for having survived.

Many others, however, define success not as doing well, but doing good; to them, success is when you are helping other people. In this sense, success may mean making a contribution in our families, in our communities, or we could contribute something where we work. For example, being successful could mean being able to find the time to volunteer in a homeless shelter or tutor children. Not everyone in the United States sees success as purely the ability to make (and spend) money. Doctors, teachers, science, engineering, and, many other fields may attract people who want to achieve success by giving, not taking.

Success should be measured by our contribution to the entire world. Not only to our society, or even to a single individual. It should be every person's responsibility to see that the ideals of liberty, freedom of speech, no oppression, and everyone gets a free education and the right to a job are protected. When a person or a corporation made millions or billions of dollars, they should ask themselves if their prosperity will truly make this world a better place to live. This is how success should be measured. We as a nation should be disgusted with ourselves for being the most wasteful country while representing a small fraction of the world population, this is greed, not success.

manner.
ex·cep′tion·ăl,
ception; out o
uncommon:

PART 8

Using Words Effectively

Chapter 42

Choosing Words

Frequently Asked Questions

How formal should I be in my college writing? (p. 780)
How do I know whether I'm using exactly the right word? (p. 782)
What is a cliché? (p. 788)
What is sexist language, and how can I avoid it? (p. 790)

42a Choosing an Appropriate Level of Diction

Diction, which comes from the Latin word for *say*, refers to the choice and use of words. Different audiences and situations call for different levels of diction.

(1) Formal Diction

Formal diction is grammatically correct and uses words familiar to an educated audience. A writer who uses formal diction often maintains emotional distance from the audience by using the impersonal *one* rather than the more personal *I* and *you.* In addition, the tone of the writing—as determined by word choice, sentence structure, and choice of subject—is dignified and objective.

> We learn to perceive in the sense that we learn to respond to things in particular ways because of the contingencies of which they are a part. We may perceive the sun, for example, simply because it is an extremely powerful stimulus, but it has been a permanent part of the environment of the species throughout its evolution, and more specific behavior with respect to it could have been selected by contingencies of survival (as it has been in many other species). (B. F. Skinner, *Beyond Freedom and Dignity*)

ESL Tip

Some of the expressions you learn from other students or from television are not appropriate for use in formal writing. When you hear new expressions, pay attention to the contexts in which they are used, and try to determine how formal or informal they are.

(2) Informal Diction

Informal diction is the language that people use in conversation and in personal letters and informal emails. You should use informal diction in your college writing only to reproduce speech or dialect or to give a paper a conversational tone.

Colloquial Diction **Colloquial diction** is the language of everyday speech. Contractions—*isn't, I'm*—are typical colloquialisms, as are **clipped forms**—*phone* for *telephone*, *TV* for *television*, *dorm* for *dormitory*. Other colloquialisms include placeholders like *kind of* and utility words like *nice* for *acceptable*, *funny* for *odd*, and *great* for almost anything. Colloquial English also includes expressions like *get across* for *communicate*, *come up with* for *find*, and *check out* for *investigate*.

Slang **Slang,** language that calls attention to itself, is used to establish or reinforce identity within a group—urban teenagers, rock musicians, or computer users, for example. One characteristic of slang vocabulary is that it is usually relatively short-lived, coming into existence and fading out much more quickly than other words do. For example, words like *uptight* and *groovy* emerged in the 1960s. During the 1970s, technology, music, politics, and feminism influenced slang, giving us words like *hacker, disco, stonewalling*, and *macho*. The 1980s contributed expressions like *sound bite*, *yuppie*, and *chocoholic;* slang in the 1990s included expressions such as *wonk*, *downsize*, *spam*, and *flame*. Because slang terms can emerge and disappear so quickly, no dictionary—even a dictionary of slang—can list all or even most of the slang terms currently in use. Some slang words, however, eventually lose their slang status and become accepted as part of the language.

Regionalisms **Regionalisms** are words, expressions, and idiomatic forms that are used in particular geographical areas but may not be understood by a general audience. In eastern Tennessee, for example, a paper bag is a *poke*, and empty soda bottles are *dope bottles*. In Lancaster, Pennsylvania, which has a large Amish population, it is not unusual to hear an elderly person saying *darest* for *dare not* or *daresome* for *adventurous*. And New Yorkers stand *on line* for a movie, whereas people in most other parts of the country stand *in line*.

Nonstandard Diction **Nonstandard diction** refers to words and expressions not generally considered a part of standard English—words like *ain't, nohow, anywheres, nowheres, hisself,* and *theirselves*.

No absolute rules distinguish standard from nonstandard usage. In fact, some linguists reject the idea of nonstandard usage altogether, arguing that this designation relegates both the language and those who use it to second-class status.

NOTE: Keep in mind that colloquial expressions, slang, regionalisms, and nonstandard usages are almost always inappropriate in your college writing.

http://kirsznermandell.wadsworth.com

Computer Tip: Setting the Writing Style Level

Your word processor's grammar checker offers different writing style levels but defaults to the "standard" level. To increase your grammar checker's ability to detect awkward or incorrect constructions in your college writing, you can change the writing style level to Formal or Technical (see Figure 42.1) To change settings, select Options or Preferences from the Tools menu, click the Spelling & Grammar tab, click Settings, and then select Formal or Technical from the Writing Style drop-down menu.

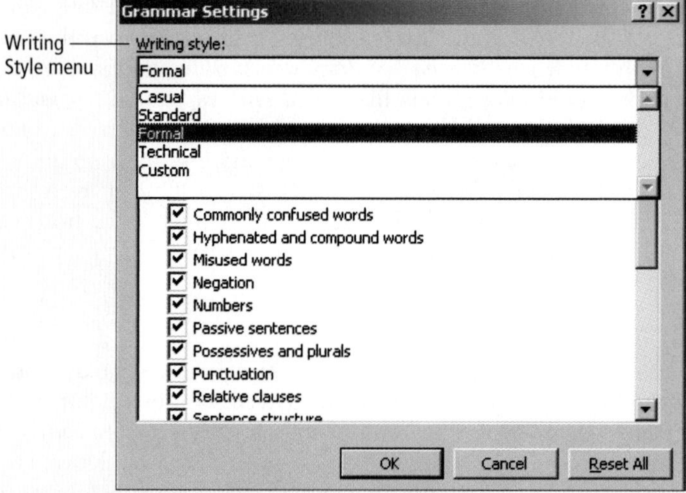

Figure 42.1 ***Microsoft Word*** **Grammar Settings tool.**

(3) College Writing

The level of diction appropriate for college writing depends on your assignment and your audience. A personal-experience essay calls for a somewhat informal style, but a research paper, an exam, or a report requires a more formal vocabulary and a more objective tone. In general, most college writing falls somewhere between formal and informal English, using a conversational tone but maintaining grammatical correctness and using a specialized vocabulary when the situation requires it. (This is the level of diction that is used in this book.)

http://kirsznermandell.wadsworth.com

Computer Tip: Diction and Electronic Communication

In email and instant messages, writers commonly use **emoticons**—typed characters, such as :-) or ;-), that indicate emotions or feelings—and **acronyms,** such as BTW (by the way) or LOL (laughing out loud). Although these typographical devices are common in informal electronic communication, they are inappropriate in formal electronic or print situations, such as academic essays or emails to professors or supervisors.

Exercise 1

The diction of this paragraph, from Toni Cade Bambara's short story "The Hammer Man," is informal. In order to represent the speech of a young girl, the writer intentionally uses slang expressions and nonstandard diction. Underline the words that identify the diction of this paragraph as informal. Then, rewrite the paragraph, using standard diction.

> Manny was supposed to be crazy. That was his story. To say you were bad put some people off. But to say you were crazy, well, you were officially not to be messed with. So that was his story. On the other hand, after I called him what I called him and said a few choice things about his mother, his face did go through some piercing changes. And I did kind of wonder if maybe he sure was nuts. I didn't wait to find out. I got in the wind. And then he waited for me on my stoop all day and all night, not hardly speaking to the people going in and out. And he was there all day Saturday, with his sister bringing him peanut-butter sandwiches and cream sodas. He must've gone to the bathroom right there cause every time I looked out the kitchen window, there he was. And Sunday, too. I got to thinking the boy was mad.

Exercise 2

After reading the following paragraph, underline the words and phrases that identify it as formal diction. Then, rewrite the paragraph, using the level of diction that you would use in your college writing. Consult a dictionary if necessary.

> In looking at many small points of difference between species, which, as far as our ignorance permits us to judge, seem quite unimportant, we must not forget that climate, food, etc., have no doubt produced some direct effect. It is also necessary to bear in mind that owing to the law of correlation, when one part varies and the variations are accumulated through natural selection, other modifications, often of the most unexpected nature, will ensue. (Charles Darwin, *The Origin of Species*)

42b Choosing the Right Word

Choosing the right word to use in a particular context is very important. If you use the wrong word—or even *almost* the right one—you run the risk of misrepresenting your ideas.

(1) Denotation and Connotation

A word's **denotation** is its basic dictionary meaning, what it stands for without any emotional associations. A word's **connotations** are the emotional, social, and political associations it has in addition to its denotative meaning.

Word	Denotation	Connotation
politician	someone who holds a political office	opportunist; wheeler-dealer

Selecting a word with the appropriate connotation can be challenging. For example, the word *skinny* has negative connotations, whereas *thin* is neutral, and *slender* is positive. And words and expressions like *mentally ill*, *insane*, *neurotic*, *crazy*, *psychopathic*, and *emotionally disturbed*, although similar in meaning, have different emotional, social, and political connotations that affect the way people respond. If you use terms without considering their connotations, you run the risk of undercutting your credibility, to say nothing of confusing and possibly angering your readers.

ESL Tip

Learning the connotations of words is a difficult part of learning a second language. Dictionary entries sometimes give a word's connotations as well as its denotations. You can also increase your understanding of a word's connotations by paying attention to the context in which the word appears.

Exercise 3

The following words have negative connotations. For each, list one word with a similar meaning whose connotation is neutral and another whose connotation is favorable.

Example: *Negative* skinny
Neutral thin
Favorable slender

1. deceive
2. antiquated
3. pushy
4. pathetic
5. cheap
6. blunder
7. weird
8. politician
9. shack
10. stench

(2) Euphemisms

A **euphemism** is a polite term used in place of a blunt or harsh term that describes a subject that many people consider offensive or unpleasant. College writing is no place for euphemisms. Say what you mean—*pregnant*, not *expecting; died*, not *passed away;* and *strike*, not *work stoppage*.

(3) Specific and General Words

Specific words refer to particular persons, items, or events; **general** words denote entire classes or groups. *Queen Elizabeth II*, for example, is more specific than *monarch; jeans* is more specific than *clothing;* and *SUV* is more specific than *vehicle*. You can use general words to describe entire classes of items, but you must use specific words to clarify such generalizations.

(4) Abstract and Concrete Words

Abstract words—*beauty*, *truth*, *justice*, and so on—refer to ideas, qualities, or conditions that cannot be perceived by the senses.

Concrete words name things that readers can see, hear, taste, smell, or touch. As with general and specific words, whether a word is abstract or concrete is relative. The more concrete your words and phrases, the more vivid the image you evoke in the reader.

Close-up: Using Specific Words

See 36a2

Take particular care to avoid general words such as *nice*, *great*, and *terrific* that say nothing and could be used in almost any sentence. These utility words convey only enthusiasm, not precise meanings. Replace them with more specific words.

a complex and suspensefully plotted mystery.
The book was ^ ~~good.~~

Exercise 4

Revise the following paragraph from a job application letter by substituting specific, concrete language for general or abstract words and phrases.

> I have had several part-time jobs lately. Some of them would qualify me for the position you advertised. In my most recent job, I sold products in a store. My supervisor said I was a good worker who had a number of valuable qualities. I am used to dealing with different types of people in different settings. I feel that my qualifications would make me a good candidate for your job opening.

42c Using Figures of Speech

Writers often use **figures of speech** (such as *similes* and *metaphors*) to go beyond the literal meanings of words. By doing so, they add interest and variety to their writing. Although you should not overuse figures of speech, do not be afraid to use them when you think they will help you communicate your ideas to your readers.

Close-up: Commonly Used Figures of Speech

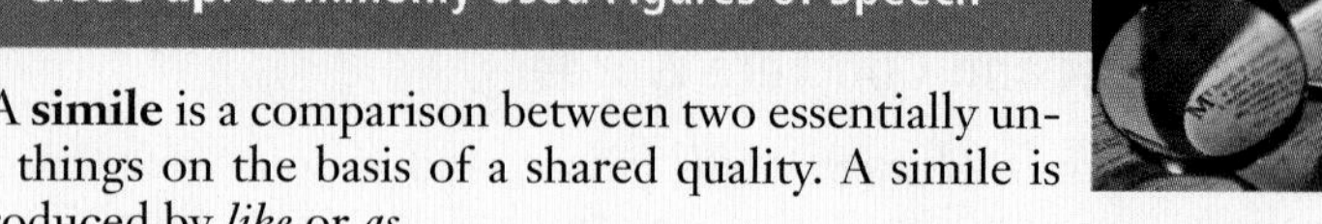

A **simile** is a comparison between two essentially unlike things on the basis of a shared quality. A simile is introduced by *like* or *as*.

Like travelers with exotic destinations on their minds, the graduates were remarkably forgetful. (Maya Angelou, *I Know Why the Caged Bird Sings*)

A **metaphor** also compares two essentially dissimilar things, but instead of saying that one thing is *like* another, it *equates* them.

Perhaps it is easy for those who have never felt the stings and darts of segregation to say, "Wait." (Martin Luther King Jr., "Letter from Birmingham Jail")

An **analogy** explains an unfamiliar item or concept by comparing it to a more familiar one.

According to Robert Frost, writing free verse is like playing tennis without a net.

Personification gives an idea or inanimate object human attributes, feelings, or powers.

Truth strikes us from behind, and in the dark, as well as from before in broad daylight. (Henry David Thoreau, *Journals*)

A **hyperbole** (or overstatement) is an intentional exaggeration for emphasis. For example, Jonathan Swift uses hyperbole in his essay "A Modest Proposal" when he suggests that eating Irish babies would help the English solve their food shortage.

Understatement intentionally downplays the seriousness of a situation or sentiment by saying less than is really meant.

According to Mao Tse-tung, a revolution is not a tea party.

Exercise 5

Read the following paragraph from Mark Twain's *Life on the Mississippi*, and identify as many figures of speech as you can.

Now when I had mastered the language of this water, and had come to know every trifling feature that bordered the great river as familiarly as I knew the letters of the alphabet, I had made a valuable acquisition. But I had lost something, too. I had lost something which could never be restored to me while I lived. All the grace, the beauty, the poetry, had gone out of the majestic river! I still keep in mind a certain wonderful sunset which I witnessed when steamboating was new to me. A broad expanse of the river was turned to blood; in the middle distance the red hue brightened into gold, through which a solitary log came floating black and conspicuous; in one place a long, slanting mark lay sparkling upon the water; in another the surface was broken by boiling, tumbling rings, that were as many-tinted as an opal; where the ruddy flush was faintest, was a smooth spot that was covered with graceful circles and radiating lines, ever so delicately traced; the shore on our left was densely wooded, and the somber shadow that fell from this forest was broken in one place by a long, ruffled trail that shone like silver; and high above the forest wall a clean-stemmed dead tree waved a single leafy bough that glowed like a flame in the unobstructed splendor that was flowing from the sun. There were graceful curves, reflected images, woody heights, soft distances; and over the whole scene, far and near, the dissolving lights drifted steadily, enriching it every passing moment with new marvels of coloring.

Exercise 6

Rewrite the following sentences, adding a figure of speech to each sentence to make the ideas more vivid and exciting. Identify each figure of speech you use. Be careful to avoid ineffective figures of speech.

Example: The room was cool and still. like the inside of a cathedral. (simile)

1. The last of the marathon runners limped toward the finish line.
2. The breeze gently stirred the wind chimes.
3. Jeremy has shoulder-length hair and a high forehead and wears small, red glasses.
4. The computer classroom was quiet.
5. The demolition crew worked slowly but efficiently.
6. Interstate highways often make for tedious driving.
7. Diego found calculus easy.
8. Music is essentially mathematical.
9. Katrina claims her dog is far more intelligent than her brother is.
10. Emotions are curious things.

42d Avoiding Inappropriate Language

(1) Jargon

Jargon, the specialized or technical vocabulary of a trade, a profession, or an academic discipline, is useful for communicating in the field for which it was developed. Outside that field, however, it is often imprecise and confusing. For example, medical doctors may say that a procedure is *contraindicated* or that they are going to carry out a *differential diagnosis*. Business executives may want departments to *interface* effectively, and sociologists may identify the need for *perspectivistic thinking* to achieve organizational goals. If they are addressing other professionals in their respective fields, these terms can facilitate communication. If, however, they are addressing a general audience, these terms have the opposite effect and should be avoided.

ESL Tip

As you read textbooks and journal articles, you will become familiar with the specialized vocabulary of your major. Some ESL writers become so comfortable with the technical vocabulary of their academic disciplines that they do not realize that these terms are probably unfamiliar to many native English speakers. When writing for readers outside your field, try to use words that they will understand. If you are not sure whether a certain term is jargon, ask your instructor (or a native English speaker) for his or her opinion.

(2) Neologisms

Neologisms are newly coined words that are not part of standard English. New situations call for new words, and frequently such words become a part of the language—*email*, *carjack*, and *outsource*, for example. Others, however, are never fully accepted. For example, questionable neologisms are created when the suffix *-wise* is added to existing words—creating nonstandard words like *weatherwise*, *sportswise*, *timewise*, and *productwise*.

If you are not sure whether to use a word, look it up in a current college dictionary. If the word is not there, you probably should not use it.

See Ch. 43

(3) Pretentious Diction

Good writing is clear and direct, not pompous or flowery. Revise to eliminate **pretentious diction,** inappropriately elevated and wordy language.

As I fell ~~into slumber~~ asleep, I ~~cogitated~~ thought about my day ~~ambling through the splendor of~~ hiking the Appalachian Mountains.

Close-up: Pretentious Diction

Frequently, pretentious diction is formal diction used in a relatively informal situation. In such a context, it is always out of place. For every pretentious word, there is usually a clear and direct alternative.

Pretentious	**Clear**
ascertain	discover
commence	start

(continued)

Pretentious diction (continued)

Pretentious	**Clear**
implement	carry out
minuscule	small
reside	live
terminate	end
utilize	use

(4) Clichés

Figures of speech, such as metaphors and similes, stimulate thought by calling up vivid images in a reader's mind. When overused, however, figures of speech lose their power and become clichés—pat, meaningless phrases.

off the beaten path	happy as a clam
sit on the fence	a shot in the arm
free as a bird	smooth sailing
spread like wildfire	fit like a glove
Herculean efforts	fighting like cats and dogs

Writers sometimes resort to clichés when they run out of ideas. If readers sense that you are filling your writing with empty, tired phrases, they will lose interest and disregard your ideas. To keep their attention, you should take the time to think of original expressions that will give your writing the impact and appeal your ideas deserve.

ESL Tip

Many ESL students have learned a long list of English idioms in an ESL class. Some of these idioms, however, have become clichés. Although becoming familiar with these idioms can help you understand them when you encounter them, university instructors discourage students from using clichés in their writing, preferring language that is more original and more precise.

(5) Mixed Metaphors

A **mixed metaphor** is created when a writer combines two or more incompatible images. The result can be illogical, humorous, or both. For this reason, you should revise mixed metaphors to make your imagery consistent.

Mixed: Management extended an olive branch in an attempt to break some of the ice between the company and the striking workers.

Revised: Management extended an olive branch with the hope that the striking workers would take it.

Exercise 7

Rewrite the following passage, eliminating jargon, neologisms, pretentious diction, and clichés. Feel free to add words and phrases and to reorganize sentences to make their meaning clear. If you are not certain about the meaning or status of a word, consult a dictionary.

At a given point in time, there coexisted a hare and a tortoise. The aforementioned rabbit was overheard by the tortoise to be blowing his horn about the degree of speed he could attain. The latter quadruped thereupon put forth a challenge to the former by advancing the suggestion that they interact in a running competition. The hare acquiesced, laughing to himself. The animals concurred in the decision to acquire the services of a certain fox to act in the capacity of judicial referee. This particular fox was in agreement, and, consequently, implementation of the plan was facilitated. In a relatively small amount of time, the hare had considerably outdistanced the tortoise and, after ascertaining that he himself was in a more optimized position distancewise than the tortoise, he arrived at the unilateral decision to avail himself of a respite. He made the implicit assumption in so doing that he would anticipate no difficulty in overtaking the tortoise when his suspension of activity ceased. An unfortunate development racewise occurred when the hare's somnolent state endured for a longer-than-anticipated time frame, facilitating the tortoise's victory in the contest and affirming the concept of unhurriedness and firmness triumphing in competitive situations. Thus, the hare was unable to snatch victory out of the jaws of defeat.

Exercise 8

Go through a newspaper or magazine, and list the examples of jargon, neologisms, pretentious diction, clichés, or mixed metaphors that you find. Then, substitute more appropriate words for the ones you identified. Be prepared to discuss your interpretation of each word and of the word you chose to put in its place.

42e Avoiding Offensive Language

Because the language we use not only expresses our ideas but also shapes our thinking, you all should avoid using words that insult or degrade others.

(1) Stereotypes

Racial and Ethnic When referring to any racial, ethnic, or religious group, use words with neutral connotations or words that the group uses in *formal* speech or writing to refer to itself.

Deciding which term to use is not always easy because the preferred names for specific groups change over time. For example, *African American* is now preferred by many Americans of African ancestry over *black*, which itself replaced *Negro* in the 1960s. People from East Asia—once called *Orientals*—now generally refer to themselves as *Asian* or *Asian American*, or by their country of origin (*Korean*, for example). Many of America's native peoples prefer *Native American*, although some call themselves *Indian*, and others identify themselves as members of a particular tribe—for example, *Kiowa* or *Navajo*. The preferences of people of Spanish descent vary according to their national origin. *Hispanic*—a term coined by the US Bureau of the Census—is often used to refer to anyone of Spanish descent, as are *Latino* and *Latina*. But many individuals prefer other designations—for example, *Chicano* and *Chicana* for people from Mexico. A large number of Americans of Spanish descent, however, prefer to use names that emphasize their dual heritages—*Cuban American*, *Mexican American*, *Dominican American*, and so on.

Age Avoid potentially offensive labels relating to age. Many older people like to call themselves *senior citizens* or *seniors*, and these terms are commonly used by the media and the government.

Class Do not demean certain jobs because they are low paying or praise others because they have impressive titles. Similarly, do not use words—*hick*, *cracker*, *redneck*, or *white trash*, for example—that denigrate people based on their social class.

Sexual Orientation Use neutral terms (such as *gay* and *lesbian*). Do not mention a person's sexual orientation unless it is relevant to your discussion.

(2) Sexist Language

Sexist language entails much more than the use of derogatory words, such as *hunk*, *chick*, and *bimbo*. Assuming that some professions are exclusive to one gender—for instance, that *nurse* denotes only women and that *doctor* denotes only men—is also sexist. So is the use of outdated job titles, such as *postman* for *letter carrier*, *fireman* for *firefighter*, and *stewardess* for *flight attendant*.

Sexist language also occurs when a writer fails to apply the same terminology to both men and women. For example, refer to two scientists with PhDs not as Dr. Sagan and Mrs. Yallow, but as Dr. Sagan and Dr. Yallow. Refer to two writers as James and Wharton, or Henry James and Edith Wharton, not James and Mrs. Wharton.

In your writing, always use *women*—not *girls*, *gals*, or *ladies*—when referring to adult females. Use *Ms.* as the form of address when a woman's marital status is unknown or irrelevant. (If the woman you are addressing refers to herself as *Mrs.* or *Miss*, however, use the form of address she prefers.) Finally, avoid using the generic *he* or *him* when your subject could be either male or female. Use the third-person plural (*they*) or the phrase *he or she* (not *he/she*).

> **Sexist:** Before boarding, each passenger should make certain that he has his ticket.
>
> **Revised:** Before boarding, passengers should make certain that they have their tickets.
>
> **Revised:** Before boarding, each passenger should make certain that he or she has a ticket.

NOTE: Remember not to overuse *his or her* or *he or she* constructions, which can make your writing repetitious and wordy.

Close-up: Eliminating Sexist Language

For every sexist usage, there is usually a nonsexist alternative.

Sexist Usage	**Possible Revisions**
Mankind	People, human beings
Man's accomplishments	Human accomplishments
Man-made	Synthetic
Female engineer/lawyer/accountant, and so on; male model	Engineer/lawyer/accountant, and so on; model
Policeman/woman	Police officer
Salesman/woman/girl	Salesperson, representative
Businessman/woman	Businessperson, executive
Everyone should complete his application by Tuesday.	Everyone should complete his or her application by Tuesday. All students should complete their applications by Tuesday.

NOTE: When trying to avoid sexist use of *he* and *him* in your writing, be careful not to use the plural pronoun *they* or *their* to refer to a singular antecedent.

> Drivers
> ~~Any driver~~ caught speeding should have their driving privileges suspended.

Exercise 9

Suggest at least one alternative form for each of the following words or phrases. In each case, comment on the advantages and disadvantages of the alternative you recommend. If you feel that a particular term is not sexist, explain why.

forefathers
man-eating shark
manpower
workman's compensation
men at work
waitress
first baseman
congressman
manhunt
longshoreman
committeeman
(to) man the battle stations
Girl Friday
point man
draftsman
man overboard
fisherman
foreman
manned space program
gentleman's agreement
no man's land
spinster
old maid
old wives' tale

Exercise 10

Each of the following pairs of terms includes a feminine form that was at one time in wide use; most are still used to some extent. Which do you think are likely to remain in our language for some time, and which do you think will disappear? Explain your reasoning.

heir/heiress
benefactor/benefactress
murderer/murderess
actor/actress
hero/heroine
host/hostess
aviator/aviatrix
executor/executrix
author/authoress
poet/poetess
tailor/seamstress
comedian/comedienne
villain/villainess
prince/princess
widow/widower

Chapter 43

Using a Dictionary

Frequently Asked Questions

What kind of dictionary should I use? (p. 793)
Should I use a thesaurus? (p. 795)
Is an electronic dictionary better than a print dictionary? (p. 798)

43a Understanding a Dictionary Entry

Every writer should own a dictionary. The most widely used type of dictionary is a one-volume **desk dictionary** or **college dictionary.**

To fit a lot of information into a small space, dictionaries use a system of symbols, abbreviations, and typefaces. Each dictionary uses a slightly different system, so consult the preface of your dictionary to determine how its system operates.

As Figure 43.1 on page 794 illustrates, a typical dictionary entry includes a number of different elements, each of which is explained in the pages that follow.

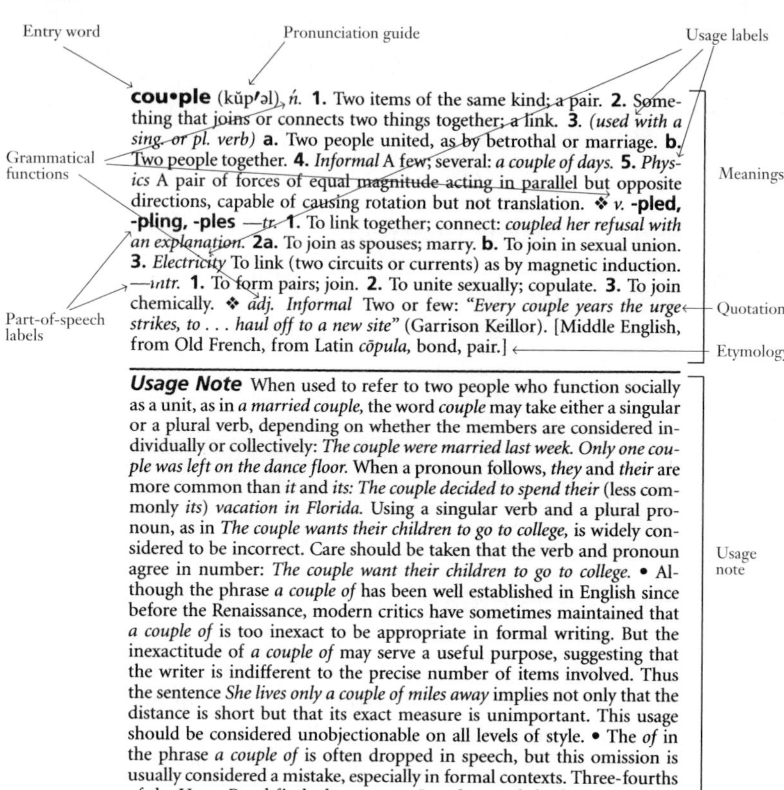

Entry word
Pronunciation guide
Usage labels
Grammatical functions
Meanings
Part-of-speech labels
Quotation
Etymology
Usage note
cou•ple (kŭp′əl) n. 1. Two items of the same kind; a pair. 2. Something that joins or connects two things together; a link. 3. (used with a sing. or pl. verb) a. Two people united, as by betrothal or marriage. b. Two people together. 4. Informal A few; several: a couple of days. 5. Physics A pair of forces of equal magnitude acting in parallel but opposite directions, capable of causing rotation but not translation. ❖ v. -pled, -pling, -ples —tr. 1. To link together; connect: coupled her refusal with an explanation. 2a. To join as spouses; marry. b. To join in sexual union. 3. Electricity To link (two circuits or currents) as by magnetic induction. —intr. 1. To form pairs; join. 2. To unite sexually; copulate. 3. To join chemically. ❖ adj. Informal Two or few: "Every couple years the urge strikes, to . . . haul off to a new site" (Garrison Keillor). [Middle English, from Old French, from Latin cōpula, bond, pair.]
Usage Note When used to refer to two people who function socially as a unit, as in a married couple, the word couple may take either a singular or a plural verb, depending on whether the members are considered individually or collectively: The couple were married last week. Only one couple was left on the dance floor. When a pronoun follows, they and their are more common than it and its: The couple decided to spend their (less commonly its) vacation in Florida. Using a singular verb and a plural pronoun, as in The couple wants their children to go to college, is widely considered to be incorrect. Care should be taken that the verb and pronoun agree in number: The couple want their children to go to college. • Although the phrase a couple of has been well established in English since before the Renaissance, modern critics have sometimes maintained that a couple of is too inexact to be appropriate in formal writing. But the inexactitude of a couple of may serve a useful purpose, suggesting that the writer is indifferent to the precise number of items involved. Thus the sentence She lives only a couple of miles away implies not only that the distance is short but that its exact measure is unimportant. This usage should be considered unobjectionable on all levels of style. • The of in the phrase a couple of is often dropped in speech, but this omission is usually considered a mistake, especially in formal contexts. Three-fourths of the Usage Panel finds the sentence I read a couple books over vacation to be unacceptable; however, another 20% of the Panel finds the sentence to be acceptable in informal speech and writing.

Figure 43.1 Entry from *The American Heritage Dictionary of the English Language*, Fourth Edition.

(1) Entry Word, Pronunciation Guide, and Part-of-Speech Label

The **entry word,** which appears in boldface at the beginning of the entry, gives the spelling of a word and indicates how the word is divided into syllables.

> **col • or** *n.* Also chiefly British **col • our**

The **pronunciation guide** appears in parentheses or between slashes after the main entry. Dictionaries use symbols to represent sounds, and an explanation of these symbols usually appears at the bottom of each page or across the bottom of facing pages throughout the alphabetical listing.

Abbreviations called **part-of-speech labels** indicate parts of speech and grammatical forms.

If a verb is regular, the entry provides only the base form of the verb. If a verb is irregular, the part-of-speech label indicates the irregular principal parts of the verb. See 47a

with • draw . . . *v.* -drew, -drawn, -drawing

In addition, the label indicates whether a verb is transitive (*tr.*), intransitive (*intr.*), or both.

Part-of-speech labels also indicate the plural form of irregular nouns. (When the plural form is regular, it is not shown.)

child . . . *n. pl.* chil · dren

Finally, part-of-speech labels indicate the comparative and superlative forms of both regular and irregular adjectives and adverbs. See 49d

red . . . *adj.* red · der; red · dest

(2) Meanings

Some dictionaries give the most common meaning first and then list less common ones. Others begin with the oldest meaning and move to the most current ones. Check the preface of your dictionary to find out how its entries are arranged.

(3) Etymology

The **etymology** of a word—its history, its evolution over the years—appears in brackets either before or after the list of meanings. For example, *The American Heritage Dictionary of the English Language* shows that *couple* came into Middle English (ME) from Old French (OFr.) and into Old French from Latin (Lat.).

(4) Synonyms and Antonyms

A dictionary entry often lists synonyms (and occasionally antonyms) in addition to definitions. **Synonyms** are words that have similar meanings, such as *well* and *healthy*. **Antonyms** are words that have opposite meanings, such as *courage* and *cowardice*.

Close-up: Using a Thesaurus

When you consult a print or online **thesaurus,** a list of synonyms and antonyms, remember that no two words have exactly the same meanings. Use synonyms carefully, checking your dictionary to make sure the connotation of the synonym is very close to that of the original word.

http://kirsznermandell.wadsworth.com

Computer Tip: Using an Electronic Thesaurus

A good way to find synonyms is to use the Thesaurus tool in your word-processing program. With your cursor, highlight the word you want to find a synonym for, then select Language from the Tools menu, click Thesaurus, and then select a synonym from the list provided (see Figure 43.2). Before replacing the word, check the meaning of the synonym by clicking Look Up.

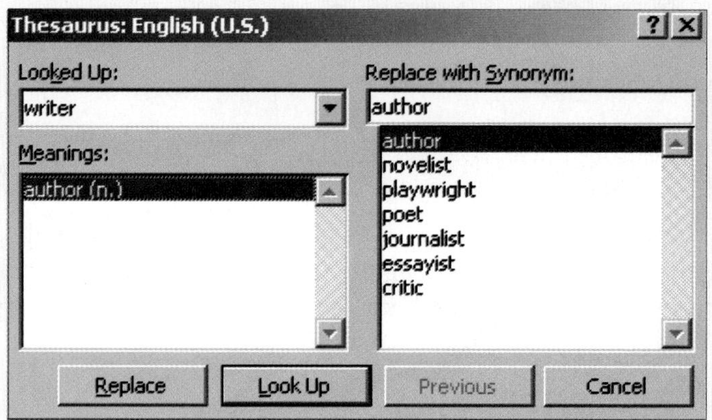

Figure 43.2 *Microsoft Word* **Thesaurus tool.**

(5) Idioms

Dictionary entries often show how certain words are used in set expressions called **idioms.** The meaning of such phrases cannot always be determined from the words alone. For example, what would someone learning English make of the expressions "catch a cold" and "take a walk"?

Dictionaries also indicate the idiomatic use of prepositions.

(6) Usage Labels

Dictionaries use **usage labels** to indicate in what contexts words are acceptable. (Where such labels involve value judgments, dictionaries differ.) Among these labels are *nonstandard* (in wide use but not considered standard usage); *informal/colloquial* (part of the language of conversation and acceptable in informal writing); *slang* (appropriate only in extremely informal situations); *dialect/regional* (limited to a certain geographical region); *obsolete* (no longer in use); *archaic/rare* (once common but now seldom used); and *poetic* (common only in poetry).

Exercise 1

Use your college dictionary to help you answer the following questions about grammatical forms.

1. What are the principal parts of the following verbs: *drink*, *deify*, *carol*, *draw*, and *ring?*
2. Which of the following nouns can be used as verbs: *canter*, *minister*, *council*, *command*, *magistrate*, *mother*, and *lord?*
3. What are the plural forms of these nouns: *silo*, *sheep*, *seed*, *scissors*, *genetics*, and *alchemy?*
4. What are the comparative and superlative forms of the following adverbs and adjectives: *fast*, *airy*, *good*, *mere*, *homey*, and *unlucky?*
5. Are the verbs *bias*, *halt*, *dissatisfy*, *die*, and *turn* transitive, intransitive, or both? Copy from the dictionary the phrase or sentence that illustrates the use of each verb.

Exercise 2

Use your college dictionary to help you determine the restrictions on the use of the following words.

1. irregardless
2. apse
3. flunk
4. lorry
5. kirk
6. gofer
7. whilst
8. sine
9. bannock
10. blowhard

43b Surveying Abridged Dictionaries

An **abridged dictionary** is condensed from a more complete collection of words and meanings. Even so, a good hardback abridged dictionary will contain about 1,500 pages and about 150,000 entries. A paperback dictionary—which contains fewer entries, treated in less detail—is adequate for checking spelling, but for reference, you should consult a hardback abridged dictionary, such as *The American Heritage College Dictionary*, *The Concise Oxford Dictionary*, *The Random House College Dictionary*, *Merriam-Webster's Collegiate Dictionary*, or *Webster's New World College Dictionary*.

NOTE: The name *Webster*, referring to the great lexicographer Noah Webster, is in the public domain. Because it cannot be copyrighted, it appears in the titles of many dictionaries of varying quality.

http://kirsznermandell.wadsworth.com

Computer Tip: Electronic Dictionaries

Electronic dictionaries include the same amount of information that one-volume desk dictionaries have. Electronic dictionaries come in two forms—CD-ROM and online. Typically, you have to download a CD-ROM dictionary into your hard drive before you can use it with your word-processing program. To use an online dictionary, you have to log on to a Web site such as http://www.merriam-webster.com.

ESL Tip

A number of special dictionaries are designed to help ESL writers. Two useful dictionaries are *Heinle's Newbury House Dictionary of American English*, 4th edition (available online at http://nhd.heinle.com) and *Heinle's Basic Newbury House Dictionary of American English*, 2nd edition.

43c Surveying Unabridged Dictionaries

When you are looking for a detailed history of a word or when you want to look up a rare usage, you will need to consult an **unabridged dictionary,** which presents a comprehensive survey of all words in a language.

Close-up: The Oxford English Dictionary (*OED*)

Consisting of twenty volumes plus four supplements, *The Oxford English Dictionary* (also available on CD-ROM and online) is considered one of the foremost English dictionaries in the world. It contains over 500,000 definitions, chronologically arranged, and more than two million supporting quotations. As Figure 43.3 illustrates, the quotations begin with the earliest recorded use of a word and progress to its current meaning.

courage ('kʌridʒ), *sb.* Forms: 4-7 corage, curage, (4-6 corrage, 5 curag, coreage, 6 currage, courra(d)ge, 7 corege), 5- courage. [ME. *corage*, a. OF. *corage, curage*, later *courage* = Pr. and Cat. *coratge*, Sp. *corage*, It. *coraggio*, a Common Romanic word, answering to a L. type **corāticum*, f. cor heart. Cf. the parallel *æta¯ ticum* from *æta¯ t-em* (AGE); and see -AGE.]

†**1.** The heart as the seat of feeling, thought, etc.; spirit, mind, disposition, nature. Obs.

c **1300** K. Alis. 3559 Archelaus, of proud corage. c **1386** CHAUCER *Prol.* 11 Smale fowles maken melodie . . So priketh hem nature in here corages. c **1430** *Pilgr. Lyf Manhode* 1. xxxiii. (1869) 20 What thinkest in thi corage? c **1430** *Stans Puer* 5 To all norture thi corage to enclyne. c **1500** *Knt. Curtesy* 407 in Ritson *Met. Rom.* III. 213 in his courage he was full sad. **1593** SHAKS. 3 *Hen. VI*, ii. ii. 57 This soft courage makes your Followers faint. **1638** DRUMM. OF HAWTH. *Irene* Wks. (1711) 163 Men's courages were growing hot, their hatred kindled. **1659** B. HARRIS *Parival's Iron Age* 41 The Spaniards . . attacked it with all the force and maistry the greatest courages were able to invent.

†**b.** *transf.* Of a plant. *Obs.* (Cf. 'To bring a thing into *good heart*.')

c **1420** *Palladius on Husb.* xi. 90 In this courage Hem forto graffe is goode.

†c. Applied to a person: of. *spirit. Obs.*

1561 T. Hoby tr. *Castiglione's Courtyer* (1577) V j b, The prowes of those diuine courages [viz. Marquesse of Mantua, etc.]. **1647** W. BROWNE *Polex.* ii 197 These two great courages being met, and followed by a small companie of the most resolute pirates.

Figure 43.3 Excerpt for *courage* from *The Oxford English Dictionary.*

Chapter 44

Improving Spelling

Frequently Asked Questions

Why do I still need to proofread if I use a spell checker? (p. 802)
Are there any spelling rules I can memorize? (p. 802)
What can I do to become a better speller? (p. 807)

Most people can spell even difficult words "almost correctly"; usually only a letter or two are wrong. For this reason, memorizing a few rules and their exceptions and learning the correct spelling of the most commonly misspelled words can make a big difference.

44a Understanding Spelling and Pronunciation

Because pronunciation often provides few clues to English spelling, you need to memorize the spellings of many words and use a dictionary or spell checker regularly.

(1) Vowels in Unstressed Positions

Many unstressed vowels sound exactly alike. For instance, it is hard to tell from pronunciation alone that the *i* in *terrible* is not an *a*. In addition, the unstressed vowels *a*, *e*, and *i* are impossible to distinguish in the suffixes *-able* and *-ible*, *-ance* and *-ence*, and *-ant* and *-ent*.

comfortable   brilliance   servant
compatible   excellence   independent

(2) Silent Letters

Some English words contain silent letters, such as the *b* in *climb* and the *t* in *mortgage*.

aisle   depot   pneumonia
climb   knight   silhouette
condemn   mortgage   sovereign

(3) Words That Are Often Pronounced Carelessly

Most of us pronounce words rather carelessly in everyday speech. Consequently, when spelling, we may leave out, add, or transpose letters.

candidate	library	recognize
environment	lightning	specific
February	nuclear	supposed to
government	perform	surprise
hundred	quantity	used to

(4) American and British Spellings

Some words are spelled one way in the United States and another way in Great Britain and the Commonwealth nations.

American	**British**
color	colour
defense	defence
judgment	judgement
theater	theatre
toward	towards
traveled	travelled

(5) Homophones

Homophones are words—such as *accept* and *except*—that are pronounced alike but spelled differently.

accept	to receive
except	other than
affect	to have an influence on (*verb*)
effect	result (*noun*); to cause (*verb*)
its	possessive of *it*
it's	contraction of *it is*
principal	most important (*adjective*); head of a school (*noun*)
principle	a basic truth; rule of conduct.

For a full list of these and other homophones, along with their meanings and sentences illustrating their use, **see the Glossary of Usage.**

NOTE: For a list of commonly confused words that present particular challenges for ESL writers, **see 61g.**

Close-up: One Word or Two?

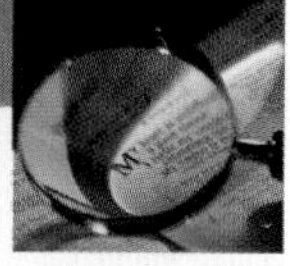

Some words may be written as one word or two, depending on meaning.

any way vs. *anyway*
The early pioneers made the trip west any way they could.
It began to rain, but the game continued anyway.

every day vs. *everyday*
Every day brings new opportunities.
John thought of his birthday as an everyday event.

Other words are frequently misspelled because people are not sure whether they are one word or two.

One Word	Two Words
already	a lot
cannot	all right
classroom	even though
overweight	no one

Consult a dictionary if you have any doubts about whether a word is written as one word or two.

http://kirsznermandell.wadsworth.com

Computer Tip: Running a Spell Check

If you use a spell checker, remember that it will not identify a word that is spelled correctly but used incorrectly—*then* for *than* or *its* for *it's*, for example—or a typo that creates another word, such as *form* for *from*. For this reason, you need to proofread your papers even after you run a spell check.

44b Learning Spelling Rules

Knowing a few reliable rules and their most common exceptions can help you overcome problems caused by the inconsistency between pronunciation and spelling.

(1) The *ie/ei* Combinations

The old rule still stands: use *i* before *e* except after *c* (or when pronounced *ay*, as in *neighbor*).

i* before *e	***ei* after *c***	***ei* pronounced *ay***
belief	ceiling	weigh
chief	deceit	freight
niece	receive	eight

Exceptions: *either, neither, foreign, leisure, weird,* and *seize.* In addition, if the *ie* combination is not pronounced as a unit, the rule does not apply: *atheist, science.*

Exercise 1

Fill in the blanks with the proper *ie* or *ei* combination. After completing the exercise, use your dictionary or spell checker to check your answers.

Example: conc__*ei*__ve

1. rec_____pt
2. var_____ty
3. caff_____ne
4. ach_____ve
5. kal_____doscope
6. misch_____f
7. effic_____nt
8. v_____n
9. spec_____s
10. suffic_____nt

(2) Doubling Final Consonants

The only words that double their consonants before a suffix that begins with a vowel (*-ed, -ing*) are those that pass the following three tests:

1. They have one syllable or are stressed on the last syllable.
2. They contain only one vowel in the last syllable.
3. They end in a single consonant.

The word *tap* satisfies all three conditions: it has only one syllable, it contains only one vowel (*a*), and it ends in a single consonant (*p*). Therefore, the final consonant doubles before a suffix beginning with a vowel (*tapped, tapping*). The word *relent* meets two of the three conditions: it is stressed on the last syllable, and it has one vowel in the last syllable, but it does not end in a single consonant. Therefore, its final consonant is not doubled (*relented, relenting*).

(3) Prefixes

The addition of a prefix never affects the spelling of the root (*mis* + *spell* = *misspell*). Some prefixes can cause spelling problems, however, because they are pronounced alike although they are not spelled alike: *ante-/anti-*, *en-/in-*, *per-/pre-*, and *de-/di-*.

antebellum	antiaircraft
encircle	integrate
perceive	prescribe
deduct	direct

(4) Silent *e* before a Suffix

When a suffix that begins with a consonant is added to a word ending in silent *e*, the *e* is generally kept: *hope/hopeful; lame/lamely; bore/boredom*. **Exceptions:** *argument*, *truly*, *ninth*, *judgment*, and *acknowledgment*.

When a suffix that starts with a vowel is added to a word that ends in a silent *e*, the *e* is generally dropped: *hope/hoping; trace/traced; grieve/grievance; love/lovable*. **Exceptions:** *changeable*, *noticeable*, and *courageous*.

Exercise 2

Combine the following words with the suffixes in parentheses. Keep or drop the silent *e* as you see fit; be prepared to explain your choices.

Example: fate (al)
fatal

1. surprise (ing)
2. sure (ly)
3. force (ible)
4. manage (able)
5. due (ly)
6. outrage (ous)
7. service (able)
8. awe (ful)
9. shame (ing)
10. shame (less)

(5) *y* before a Suffix

When a word ends in a consonant plus *y*, the *y* generally changes to an *i* when a suffix is added (*beauty* + *ful* = *beautiful*). The *y* is kept, however, when the suffix *-ing* is added (*tally* + *ing* = *tallying*) and in some one-syllable words (*dry* + *ness* = *dryness*).

When a word ends in a vowel plus *y*, the *y* is retained (*joy* + *ful* = *joyful*; *employ* + *er* = *employer*). **Exception:** *day* + *ly* = *daily*.

Exercise 3

Add the endings in parentheses to the following words. Change or keep the final *y* as you see fit; be prepared to explain your choices.

Example: party (ing)
partying

1. journey (ing)
2. study (ed)
3. carry (ing)
4. shy (ly)
5. study (ing)
6. sturdy (ness)
7. merry (ment)
8. likely (hood)
9. plenty (ful)
10. supply (er)

(6) *seed* Endings

Endings with the sound *seed* are nearly always spelled *cede*, as in *precede*, *intercede*, *concede*, and so on. **Exceptions:** *supersede*, *exceed*, *proceed*, and *succeed*.

(7) *-able, -ible*

If the root of a word is itself an independent word, the suffix *-able* is most often used. If the root of a word is not an independent word, the suffix *-ible* is most often used.

*comfort*able	*compat*ible
*agree*able	*incred*ible
*dry*able	*plaus*ible

(8) Plurals

Most nouns form plurals by adding *s: savage/savages*, *tortilla/tortillas*, *boat/boats*. There are, however, a number of exceptions.

***Words Ending in* -f *or* -fe** Some words ending in *-f* or *-fe* form plurals by changing the *f* to *v* and adding *es* or *s: life/lives*, *self/selves*. Others add just *s: belief/beliefs*, *safe/safes*. Words ending in *-ff* take *s* to form plurals: *tariff/tariffs*.

***Words Ending in* -y** Most words that end in a consonant followed by *y* form plurals by changing the *y* to *i* and adding *es: baby/babies*. **Exceptions:** proper nouns, such as the *Kennedys* (never the *Kennedies*).

Words that end in a vowel followed by a *y* form plurals by adding *s: day/days, monkey/monkeys.*

Words Ending in -o Words that end in a vowel followed by *o* form the plural by adding *s: radio/radios, stereo/stereos, zoo/zoos.* Most words that end in a consonant followed by *o* add *es* to form the plural: *tomato/tomatoes, hero/heroes.* **Exceptions:** *silo/silos, piano/pianos, memo/memos,* and *soprano/sopranos.*

Words Ending in -s, -ss, -sh, -ch, -x, and -z These words form plurals by adding *es: Jones/Joneses, mass/masses, rash/rashes, lunch/lunches, box/boxes, buzz/buzzes.* **Exceptions:** Some one-syllable words that end in *-s* or *-z* double their final consonants when forming plurals: *quiz/quizzes.*

Compound Nouns **Compound nouns**—nouns formed from two or more words—usually form the plural with the last word in the compound construction: *welfare state/welfare states; snowball/snowballs.* However, where the first word of the compound noun is more important than the others, form the plural with the first word: *sister-in-law/sisters-in-law, attorney general/attorneys general, hole in one/holes in one.*

Foreign Plurals Some words, especially those borrowed from Latin or Greek, keep their foreign plurals. Look up a foreign word's plural form in a dictionary if you do not know it.

Singular	Plural
basis	bases
criterion	criteria
datum	data
larva	larvae
medium	media
memorandum	memoranda
stimulus	stimuli

http://kirsznermandell.wadsworth.com

Computer Tip: Spelling an Unfamiliar Word

Most spell checkers suggest corrections for misspelled words in your documents. Often, the word you meant to use is included in the list of possible words the spell checker generates; sometimes, however, you must determine the correct spelling yourself.

44c Developing Spelling Skills

In addition to studying the rules outlined in 44b, you can take some additional steps to help yourself become a better speller.

(1) Making Your Own Spelling List

Keep a list of your own problem words. When you read through a first draft, circle any words whose spellings you are unsure of. Then, look them up in your dictionary or spell checker as you revise, and add them all (even those you have spelled correctly) to your list. When your instructor returns a paper, add to your list any words you have misspelled. In addition, record problem words that you encounter when reading, including those from class notes and textbooks.

(2) Uncovering Patterns of Misspelling

Do you consistently have a problem with plurals or with *-ible/-able* endings? If so, review the spelling rules that apply to these particular problems. By using this strategy, you can eliminate the need to memorize single words.

(3) Fixing Each Word in Your Mind

Think of associations that will make the correct spellings stick in your mind. For example, you can remember the correct spelling of *definite* (often misspelled *definate*) by remembering that it contains the word *finite*, which suggests the concept of limit, as does *definite*. You can recall the *a* in *brilliance* (often misspelled *brillience*) by remembering that brilliant people often get A's in their classes.

The best way to fix words in your mind is to write them down. When you review your spelling list, don't just *read* the words on it; *write* them.

(4) Learning to Distinguish Commonly Confused Words

Learn to distinguish commonly confused homophones (words that sound exactly alike but have different spellings and meanings, such as *night* and *knight*) and near-homophones (words that sound similar, such as *accept* and *except*). For a list of homophones, **see the Glossary of Usage.**

http://kirsznermandell.wadsworth.com

Computer Tip: Customizing Your Spell Checker

You can customize your spell checker so that it corrects your most common misspellings or typos. Select AutoCorrect from the Tools menu, type the misspelling into the Replace field, and type the correct spelling into the With field (see Figure 44.1). Then, click OK. The spell checker will now automatically check for and correct that misspelling each time it occurs in your documents.

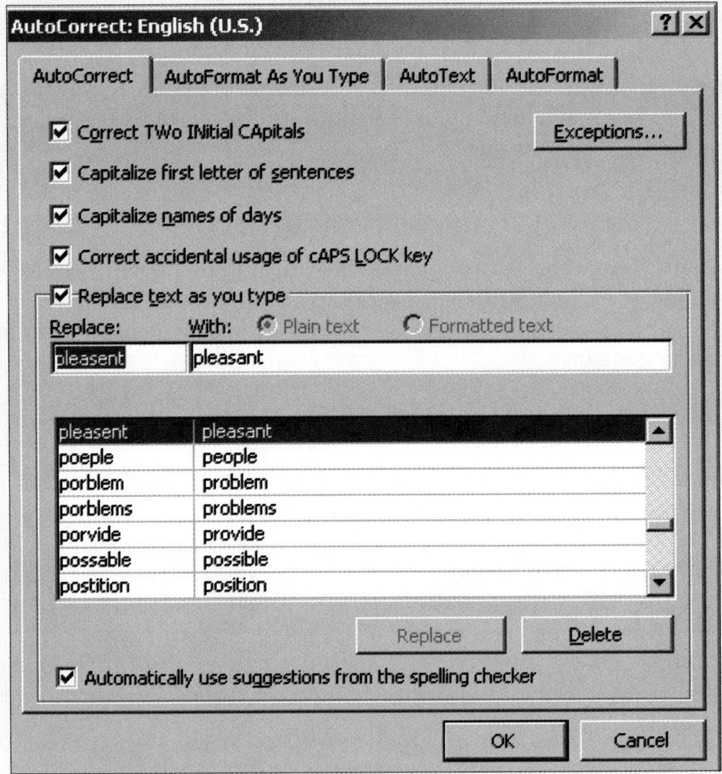

Figure 44.1 ***Microsoft Word*** **AutoCorrect tool.**

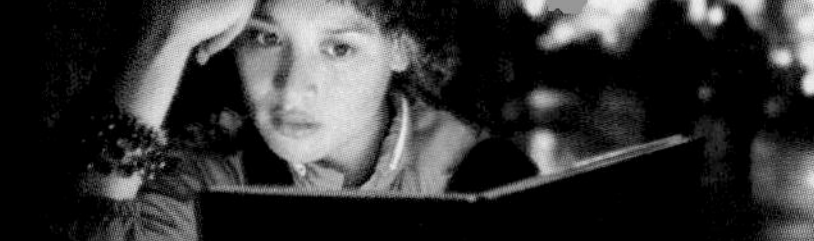

Student Writer at Work

Using Words Effectively

The following draft was written for an education course in response to an assignment asking students to write a position paper on an educational issue. The draft needs a good deal of revision to make its diction more appropriate for a college writing assignment and to correct several spelling errors. As you edit the draft, apply what you have learned in Part 8.

College Is Not for Everyone—Or Is It?

Our educational system in America has a lot of problems. Some guy who doesn't go to college, for whatever reason, will probably find it tuff to prosper either socially or economically. On the one hand, in some other countrys that are industrialized nations, high school graduates all get the same education, whether or not they are college bound. On the other hand, American high schools put all their eggs in one basket and give most resources to college-bound students. Other kids end up leaving high school with nothing accept a sixth- or seventh-grade reading level. This effects our economy alot because some citizens can never earn enough to live on to feed there family well; let's face it, living on minimum wage is like trying to get blood from a stone. We need to make it possible for kids from all kinds of backgrounds to go to college.

My own view on this subject is that it's all about resources and who has them and who doesn't. If taxes could be higher, than perhaps poor schools could give more to there kids; than maybe they could be able to catch up with the schools in the rich areas. Take, for example, my own

high school; it was defiantly not in what you would call a rich area, but it wasn't poor either. Still, we didn't have lots of computers or music classes and extra things like that. It wasn't like they were trying to hold us back, but this lack of resources did make a diffrence in how many of us went on to college. I had a couple of buddies who didn't make it to college, so now they will probably be up the creek when it comes down to getting some kind of job that will pay more than minimum wage. Also, they'll be working everyday just to bring home five fifty an hour.
Now I know for sure that I'll get a way better job then they will after I graduate. My college profs are teaching me skills and knowledge that will put me on the road to success.

I beleive colleges and high school teachers should find ways to let more kids into college and help them graduate. This is especially important for the high schools in the poor part of town where they don't have to much in the way of opportunity for bettering themselves. We need to find a way of educating the undereducated kids. First, we should look at the elementry schools to and see what we can do to help. You can lead a horse to water but you can't make a child drink from the tree of knowledge unless they are ready to hear it. Colleges need to sponser kids from a very young age so they can get them ready for the work they will be asked to do in college. Everyday there are lives being waisted because students think they can't afford to pay for college or they think they aren't smart enough to pass the class. This is defiantly not true! Succeeding in college is just a matter of putting your nose to the grindstone and then realizing that it is time to sink or swim.

So what I am saying here is that college is good for everybody, but the schools need to work harder at preparing kids and letting them know that there is help for the finances and for the dorms and other stuff like that. If these kids can go to college, they can get in gear and graduate.

Grammar Checker

Subject-Verb Agreement:

All of these little details makes the co
hard to understand.

PART 9

Understanding Grammar

Chapter 45

Parts of Speech

Frequently Asked Questions

The eight basic **parts of speech**—the building blocks for all English sentences—are *nouns, pronouns, verbs, adjectives, adverbs, prepositions, conjunctions,* and *interjections.* How a word is classified depends on its function in a sentence.

45a Nouns

Nouns name people, animals, places, things, ideas, actions, or qualities.

A **common noun** names any one of a class of people, places, or things: *artist, judge, building, event, city.*

A **proper noun,** always capitalized, designates a particular person, place, or thing: *Mary Cassatt, World Trade Center, Crimean War.*

A **count noun** names something that can be counted: five *dogs,* two dozen *grapes.*

A **noncount noun** names a quantity that is not countable: *time, dust, work, gold.* Noncount nouns generally have only a singular form.

A **collective noun** designates a group thought of as a unit: *committee, class, navy, band, family.* Collective nouns are generally singular unless the members of the group are referred to as individuals.

An **abstract noun** designates an intangible idea or quality: *love, hate, justice, anger, fear, prejudice.*

45b Pronouns

Pronouns are words used in place of nouns. The word for which a pronoun stands is called its **antecedent.**

If you use a quotation in your paper, you must document it. (Pronoun *it* refers to antecedent *quotation.*)

A **personal pronoun** stands for a person or thing. Personal pronouns include *I, me, we, us, my, mine, our, ours, you, your, yours, he, she, it, its, him, his, her, hers, they, them, their,* and *theirs.*

They made her an offer she couldn't refuse.

An indefinite pronoun does not refer to any particular person or thing, so it does not require an antecedent. Indefinite pronouns include *another, any, each, few, many, some, nothing, one, anyone, everyone, everybody, everything, someone, something, either,* and *neither.*

Many are called, but few are chosen.

A **reflexive pronoun** ends with *-self* and refers to a recipient of the action that is the same as the actor. The reflexive pronouns are *myself, yourself, himself, herself, itself, oneself, themselves, ourselves,* and *yourselves.*

They found themselves in downtown Pittsburgh.

An **intensive pronoun** emphasizes a noun or pronoun that directly precedes it. (Intensive pronouns have the same form as reflexive pronouns.)

Darrow himself was sure his client was innocent.

A **relative pronoun** introduces an adjective clause or a noun clause in a sentence. Relative pronouns include *which, who, whom, that, what, whose, whatever, whoever, whomever,* and *whichever.*

Gandhi was the charismatic man who helped lead India to independence. (introduces adjective clause)

Whatever happens will be a surprise. (introduces noun clause)

An **interrogative pronoun** introduces a question. Interrogative pronouns include *who, which, what, whom, whose, whoever, whatever,* and *whichever.*

Who was that masked man?

A **demonstrative pronoun** points to a particular thing or group of things. *This*, *that*, *these*, and *those* are demonstrative pronouns.

This is one of Shakespeare's early plays.

A **reciprocal pronoun** denotes a mutual relationship. The reciprocal pronouns are *each other* and *one another*. *Each other* indicates a relationship between two individuals; *one another* denotes a relationship among more than two.

Romeo and Juliet declared their love for each other.

Concertgoers jostled one another in the ticket line.

NOTE: Although different types of pronouns may have exactly the same form, they are distinguished from one another by their function in a sentence.

45c Verbs

(1) Recognizing Verbs

A verb may express either action or a state of being.

He ran for the train. (physical action)

He worried about being late. (emotional action)

Elizabeth II became queen after the death of her father, George VI. (state of being)

Verbs can be classified into two groups: *main verbs* and *auxiliary verbs*.

Main Verbs **Main verbs** carry most of the meaning in a sentence. Some main verbs are **action verbs.**

Emily Dickinson wrote poetry.

Other main verbs function as linking verbs. A **linking verb** does not show any physical or emotional action. Its function is to link the sentence's subject to a **subject complement,** a word or phrase that renames or describes the subject.

Carbon disulfide smells bad.

Frequently Used Linking Verbs

appear	believe	look	seem	taste
be	feel	prove	smell	turn
become	grow	remain	sound	

Auxiliary Verbs **Auxiliary verbs** (also called **helping verbs**), such as *be* and *have*, combine with main verbs to form **verb phrases.** Auxiliary verbs indicate tense, voice, or mood.

[auxiliary] [main verb] [auxiliary] [main verb]

The train has started. We are leaving soon.

[verb phrase] [verb phrase]

Certain auxiliary verbs, known as **modal auxiliaries,** indicate necessity, possibility, willingness, obligation, or ability.

In the future, farmers might cultivate seaweed as a food crop.

Coal mining would be safer if dust were controlled in the mines.

Modal Auxiliaries

can	might	ought [to]	will
could	must	shall	would
may	need [to]	should	

(2) Recognizing Verbals

Verbals, such as *known* or *swimming* or *to go*, are verb forms that act as adjectives, adverbs, or nouns. A verbal can never serve as a sentence's main verb unless it is used with one or more auxiliary verbs (*has known*, *should be swimming*). Verbals include *participles*, *infinitives*, and *gerunds*.

Participles Virtually every verb has a **present participle,** which ends in *-ing* (*loving*, *learning*, *going*, *writing*), and a **past participle,** which usually ends in *-d* or *-ed* (*agreed*, *learned*). Some verbs have irregular past participles (*gone*, *begun*, *written*). Participles may function in a sentence as adjectives or as nouns.

See 47a2

Twenty brands of running shoes were displayed at the exhibition. (Present participle *running* serves as adjective modifying noun *shoes*.)

The crowded bus went past those waiting at the corner. (Past participle *crowded* serves as adjective modifying noun *bus*.)

The wounded were given emergency first aid. (Past participle *wounded* serves as a noun, the sentence's subject.)

Infinitives An **infinitive**—the *to* form of the verb—may function as an adjective, an adverb, or a noun.

Ann Arbor was clearly the place to be. (Infinitive serves as adjective modifying noun *place*.)

They say that breaking up is hard to do. (Infinitive serves as adverb modifying adjective *hard*.)

Carla went outside to think. (Infinitive serves as adverb modifying verb *went*.)

To win was everything. (Infinitive serves as noun, the sentence's subject.)

Gerunds **Gerunds** (which, like present participles, end in *-ing*) always function as nouns.

Seeing is believing. (Gerund *seeing* serves as sentence's subject; gerund *believing* serves as subject complement.)

He worried about interrupting. (Gerund *interrupting* is object of preposition *about*.)

Andrew loves skiing. (Gerund *skiing* is direct object of verb *loves*.)

NOTE: When the *-ing* form of a verb is used as a noun, it is a *gerund;* when it is used as an adjective, it is a *present participle.*

45d Adjectives

Adjectives describe, limit, qualify, or in some other way modify nouns or pronouns.

(1) Descriptive Adjectives

Descriptive adjectives name a quality of the noun or pronoun they modify.

After the game, they were exhausted.

They ordered a chocolate soda and a butterscotch sundae.

Some descriptive adjectives are formed from common nouns or from verbs (*friend/friendly*, *agree/agreeable*). Others, called **proper adjectives,** are formed from proper nouns.

A Shakespearean sonnet consists of an octave and a sestet.

Two or more words may be joined (hyphenated before a noun, without a hyphen after a noun) to form a compound adjective: *His parents are very well-read people; most people are not so well read.*

(2) Determiners

When articles, pronouns, numbers, and the like function as adjectives, limiting or qualifying nouns or pronouns, they are referred to as determiners.

Articles (*a*, *an*, *the*)

The boy found a four-leaf clover.

Possessive nouns

Lesley's mother lives in New Jersey.

Possessive pronouns (the personal pronouns *my*, *your*, *his*, *her*, *its*, *our*, *their*)

Their lives depended on my skill.

Demonstrative pronouns (*this*, *these*, *that*, *those*)

This song reminds me of that song we heard yesterday.

Interrogative pronouns (*what*, *which*, *whose*)

Whose book is this?

Indefinite pronouns (*another*, *each*, *both*, *many*, *any*, *some*, and so on)

Both candidates agreed to return another day.

Relative pronouns (*what*, *whatever*, *which*, *whichever*, *whose*, *whoever*)

I forgot whatever reasons I had for leaving.

Numbers (*one*, *two*, *first*, *second*, and so on)

The first time I played baseball, I got only one hit.

45e Adverbs

Adverbs describe the action of verbs or modify adjectives, other adverbs, or complete phrases, clauses, or sentences. They answer the questions "How?" "Why?" "Where?" "When?" "Under what conditions?" and "To what extent?"

He walked rather hesitantly toward the front of the room. (walked *how*?)

Let's meet tomorrow for coffee. (meet *when*?)

Adverbs that modify other adverbs or adjectives limit or qualify the words they modify.

He pitched an almost perfect game.

Interrogative adverbs—*how*, *when*, *why*, and *where*—introduce questions.

Why did the compound darken?

Conjunctive adverbs act as transitional words, joining and relating independent clauses. Conjunctive adverbs may appear in various positions in a sentence.

Jason forgot to register for chemistry. However, he managed to sign up during the drop/add period.

Jason forgot to register for chemistry; however, he managed to sign up during the drop/add period.

Jason forgot to register for chemistry. He managed, however, to sign up during the drop/add period.

Jason forgot to register for chemistry. He managed to sign up during the drop/add period, however.

Frequently Used Conjunctive Adverbs

accordingly	furthermore	meanwhile	similarly
also	hence	moreover	still
anyway	however	nevertheless	then
besides	incidentally	next	thereafter
certainly	indeed	nonetheless	therefore
consequently	instead	now	thus
finally	likewise	otherwise	undoubtedly

45f Prepositions

A preposition introduces a noun or pronoun (or a phrase or clause functioning in the sentence as a noun), linking it to other words in the sentence. The word or word group the preposition introduces is called its **object.**

> They received a postcard from (prep) Bobby (obj) telling about (prep) his trip (obj) to (prep) Canada (obj).

Frequently Used Prepositions

about	beneath	inside	since
above	beside	into	through
across	between	like	throughout
after	beyond	near	to
against	by	of	toward
along	concerning	off	under
among	despite	on	underneath
around	down	onto	until
as	during	out	up
at	except	outside	upon
before	for	over	with
behind	from	past	within
below	in	regarding	without

45g Conjunctions

Conjunctions connect words, phrases, clauses, or sentences.

Coordinating conjunctions (*and*, *or*, *but*, *nor*, *for*, *so*, *yet*) connect words, phrases, or clauses of equal weight.

> The choice was simple: chicken or fish. (*Or* links two nouns.)

> The United States is a government "of the people, by the people, and for the people." (*And* links three prepositional phrases.)

> Thoreau wrote *Walden* in 1854, and he died in 1862. (*And* links two independent clauses.)

Correlative conjunctions, always used in pairs, also link grammatically equivalent items.

Both Hancock and Jefferson signed the Declaration of Independence. (Correlative conjunctions link two nouns.)

Either I will renew my lease, or I will move. (Correlative conjunctions link two independent clauses.)

Correlative Conjunctions

both . . . and	neither . . . nor
either . . . or	not only . . . but also
just as . . . so	whether . . . or

Subordinating conjunctions include *since*, *because*, *although*, *if*, *after*, *when*, *while*, *before*, *unless*, and so on. A subordinating conjunction introduces a dependent (subordinate) clause, connecting it to the sentence's independent (main) clause to form a complex sentence.

See 33b

Although drug use is a serious concern for parents, many parents are afraid to discuss it with their children.

It is best to diagram your garden before you start to plant it.

NOTE: A subordinating conjunction indicates the relationship between clauses.

45h Interjections

Interjections are exclamations used to express emotion: *Oh! Ouch! Wow! Alas! Hey!* These words are grammatically independent; that is, they do not have a grammatical function in a sentence.

An interjection may be set off in a sentence by commas.

The message, alas, arrived too late.

For greater emphasis, an interjection can be punctuated as an independent unit, set off with an exclamation point.

Alas! The message arrived too late.

NOTE: Other kinds of words may also be used in isolation. These include *yes*, *no*, *hello*, *good-bye*, *please*, and *thank you*. All such words, including interjections, are collectively referred to as **isolates.**

Chapter 46

Using Nouns and Pronouns

Frequently Asked Questions

Is I *always more appropriate than* me? (p. 824)

How do I know whether to use who *or* whom? (p. 825)

What is an antecedent? (p. 827)

How do I know whether to use who, which, *or* that? (p. 828)

46a Understanding Case

Case is the form a noun or pronoun takes to indicate its function in a sentence. Nouns change form only in the possessive case: the *cat's* eyes, *Molly's* book. Pronouns, however, have three cases: *subjective*, *objective*, and *possessive*.

Pronoun Case Forms

Subjective						
I	he, she	it	we	you	they	who whoever
Objective						
me	him, her	it	us	you	them	whom whomever
Possessive						
my mine	his, her hers	its	our ours	your yours	their theirs	whose

(1) Subjective Case

A pronoun takes the **subjective case** in the following situations.

Subject of a Verb: I bought a new mountain bike.

Subject Complement: It was he who volunteered to drive.

(2) Objective Case

A pronoun takes the **objective case** in the following situations.

Direct Object: Our supervisor asked Adam and me to work on the project.

Indirect Object: The plumber's bill gave him quite a shock.

Object of a Preposition: Between us, we own ten shares of stock.

Close-up: Pronoun Case in Compound Constructions

I is not necessarily more appropriate than *me*. In compound constructions like the following, *me* is correct.

Just between you and me [not *I*], I think we're going to have a quiz. (*Me* is the object of the preposition *between*.)

(3) Possessive Case

See 45c2

A pronoun takes the **possessive case** when it indicates ownership (*our* car, *your* book). The possessive case is also used before a gerund.

Napoleon gave his approval to their ruling Naples. (*His* indicates ownership; *ruling* is a gerund.)

Exercise 1

Underline the correct form of the pronoun within the parentheses. Be prepared to explain why you chose each form.

Example: Toni Morrison, Alice Walker, and (she, her) are perhaps the most widely recognized African-American women writing today.

1. Both Walt Whitman and (he, him) wrote a great deal of poetry about nature.
2. Our instructor gave Matthew and (me, I) an excellent idea for our project.
3. The sales clerk objected to (me, my) returning the sweater.
4. I understand (you, your) being unavailable to work tonight.
5. The waiter asked Michael and (me, I) to move to another table.

46b Determining Pronoun Case in Special Situations

(1) Comparisons with *Than* or *As*

When a comparison ends with a pronoun, the pronoun's function in the sentence dictates your choice of pronoun case. If the pronoun functions as a subject, use the subjective case; if it functions as an object, use the objective case. You can determine the function of the pronoun by completing the comparison.

Darcy likes John more than I. (*I* is the subject: more than I like John)

Darcy likes John more than me. (*Me* is the object: more than she likes me.)

(2) *Who* and *Whom*

The case of the pronouns *who* and *whom* depends on their function *within their own clause*. When a pronoun serves as the subject of its clause, use *who* or *whoever*; when it functions as an object, use *whom* or *whomever*.

The Salvation Army gives food and shelter to whoever is in need. (*Whoever* is the subject of the dependent clause *whoever is in need*.)

I wonder whom jazz musician Miles Davis influenced. (*Whom* is the object of *influenced* in the dependent clause *whom jazz musician Miles Davis influenced*.)

Close-up: Pronoun Case in Questions

To determine whether to use subjective case (*who*) or objective case (*whom*) in a question, use a personal pronoun to answer the question. If the personal pronoun is the subject, use *who*; if the personal pronoun is the object, use *whom*.

Who wrote *The Age of Innocence?* She wrote it. (subject)

Whom do you support for mayor? I support her. (object)

(3) Appositives

An appositive is a noun or noun phrase that identifies or renames an adjacent noun or pronoun. The case of a pronoun in an appositive depends on the function of the word the appositive identifies.

We heard two Motown recording artists, Smokey Robinson and him. (*Artists* is the object of the verb *heard*, so the pronoun in the appositive *Smokey Robinson and him* takes the objective case.)

Two Motown recording artists, Smokey Robinson and he, recorded for Motown Records. (*Artists* is the subject of the sentence, so the pronoun in the appositive *Smokey Robinson and he* takes the subjective case.)

(4) *We* and *Us* before a Noun

When a first-person plural pronoun directly precedes a noun, the case of the pronoun depends on the way the noun functions in the sentence.

We women must stick together. (*Women* is the subject of the sentence, so the pronoun *we* must be in the subjective case.)

Teachers make learning easy for us students. (*Students* is the object of the preposition *for*, so the pronoun *us* must be in the objective case.)

Exercise 2

Using the word in parentheses, combine each pair of sentences into a single sentence. You may change word order and add or delete words.

Example: After he left the band The Police, bass player Sting continued as a solo artist. He once taught middle-school English. (who)

Revised: After he left the band The Police, bass player Sting, who once taught middle-school English, continued as a solo artist.

1. Herb Ritts has photographed world leaders, leading artistic figures in dance and drama, and a vanishing African tribe. He got his start by taking photographs of Hollywood stars. (who)
2. Tim Green has written several novels about a fictional football team. He played for the Atlanta Hawks and has a degree in law. (who)
3. Some say Carl Sagan did more to further science education in America than any other person. He wrote many books on science and narrated many popular television shows. (who)
4. Jodie Foster has won two Academy Awards for her acting. She was a child star. (who)
5. Sylvia Plath met the poet Ted Hughes at Cambridge University in England. She later married him. (whom)

46c Revising Pronoun Reference Errors

ESL 61f1

An **antecedent** is the word or word group to which a pronoun refers. The connection between a pronoun and its antecedent should always be clear. If the pronoun reference is not clear, you will need to revise the sentence.

(1) Ambiguous Antecedent

Sometimes it is not clear to which antecedent a pronoun—for example, *this*, *that*, *which*, or *it*—refers. In such cases, eliminate the ambiguity by substituting a noun for the pronoun.

> The accountant took out his calculator and completed the tax return. Then, he put ~~it~~ *the calculator* into his briefcase. (The pronoun *it* can refer either to *calculator* or to *tax return*.)

Sometimes a pronoun—for example, *this*—does not seem to refer to any specific antecedent. In such cases, supply a noun to clarify the reference.

> Some one-celled organisms contain chlorophyll yet are considered animals. This *paradox* illustrates the difficulty of classifying single-celled organisms. (Exactly what does *this* refer to?)

(2) Remote Antecedent

The farther a pronoun is from its antecedent, the more difficult it is for readers to make a connection between them. If a pronoun's antecedent is far away from it, replace the pronoun with a noun.

> During the mid-1800s, many Czechs began to immigrate to America. By 1860, about 23,000 Czechs had left their country; by 1900, 13,000 Czech immigrants were coming to ~~its~~ *America's* shores each year.

(3) Nonexistent Antecedent

Sometimes a pronoun refers to an antecedent that does not appear in the sentence. In such cases, replace the pronoun with a noun.

Our township has decided to build a computer lab in the elementary school because ~~they~~ teachers feel that fourth graders should begin using computers. (*They* refers to an antecedent that the writer has neglected to mention.)

Close-up: Pronoun Reference

Expressions such as "*It* says in the paper" and "*They* said on the news," which refer to unidentified antecedents, are not acceptable in college writing. Substitute the appropriate noun for the unclear pronoun: "The *article* in the paper says . . ." and "In his commentary, *Ted Koppel* observes. . . ."

(4) *Who, Which,* and *That*

In general, *who* refers to people or to animals that have names. *Which* and *that* refer to things or to unnamed animals. When referring to an antecedent, be sure to choose the appropriate pronoun (*who, which*, or *that*).

David Henry Hwang, who wrote the Tony Award-winning play *M. Butterfly*, also wrote *Family Devotions* and *FOB*.

The spotted owl, which lives in old growth forests, is in danger of extinction.

Houses that are built today are usually more energy efficient than those built twenty years ago.

Never use *that* to refer to a person.

The man ~~that~~ who holds the world record for eating hot dogs is my neighbor.

NOTE: Make certain that you use *which* in nonrestrictive clauses, which are always set off with commas. In most cases, use *that* in restrictive clauses. *Who* may be used in both restrictive and nonrestrictive clauses.

Exercise 3

Analyze the pronoun reference errors in each of the following sentences. After doing so, revise each sentence by substituting an appropriate noun or noun phrase for the underlined pronoun.

Example: Jefferson asked Lewis to head the expedition, and Lewis selected ~~him~~ Clark as his associate. (*Him* refers to a nonexistent antecedent.)

1. The purpose of the expedition was to search out a land route to the Pacific and to gather information about the West. The Louisiana Purchase increased the need for it.
2. The expedition was going to be difficult. They trained the men in Illinois, the starting point.
3. Clark and most of the men who descended the Yellowstone River camped on the bank. It was beautiful and wild.
4. Both Jefferson and Lewis had faith that he would be successful in this transcontinental journey.
5. The expedition was efficient, and only one man was lost. This was extraordinary.

Chapter 47

Using Verbs

47a Understanding Verb Forms

Every verb has four **principal parts:** a **base form** (the form of the verb used with *I*, *we*, *you*, and *they* in the present tense), a **present participle** (the *-ing* form of the verb), a **past tense form,** and a **past participle.**

NOTE: The verb *be* is so irregular that it is the one exception to this definition; its base form is *be*.

(1) Regular Verbs

A **regular verb** forms both its past tense and its past participle by adding *d* or *ed* to the base form of the verb.

Principal Parts of Regular Verbs

Base Form	Past Tense Form	Past Participle
smile	smiled	smiled
talk	talked	talked
jump	jumped	jumped

(2) Irregular Verbs

Irregular verbs do not follow the pattern discussed above. The chart that follows lists the principal parts of the most frequently used irregular verbs. (When in doubt about the form of a verb, look up the base form in a dictionary. If the dictionary lists only the base form, then the verb is regular.)

See Ch. 43

http://kirsznermandell.wadsworth.com

Computer Tip: Using Correct Verb Forms

Your word processor's grammar checker will highlight incorrect verb forms in your writing and offer revision suggestions (see Figure 47.1).

Spelling and Grammar: English (U.S.)

Verb Form:

Because she was not feeling well, my father had already **drove** her home by the time the party began.

Suggestions:

driven

Figure 47.1 Sample grammar checker suggestion.

Close-up: *Lie/Lay* and *Sit/Set*

Lie means "to recline" and does not take an object ("He likes to *lie* on the floor"); *lay* means "to place" or "to put" and does take an object ("He wants to *lay* a rug on the floor").

Base Form	Past Tense Form	Past Participle
lie	lay	lain
lay	laid	laid

Sit means "to assume a seated position" and does not take an object ("She wants to *sit* on the table"); *set* means "to place" or "to put" and usually takes an object ("She wants to *set* a vase on the table").

Base Form	Past Tense Form	Past Participle
sit	sat	sat
set	set	set

Exercise 1

Complete the sentences in the following paragraph with an appropriate form of the verbs in parentheses.

Example: An air of mystery surrounds many of those who have ___*sung*___ (sing) and played the blues.

The legendary bluesman Robert Johnson supposedly ________ (sell) his soul to the devil in order to become a guitar virtuoso. Myth has it that the young Johnson could barely chord his instrument and annoyed other musicians by trying to sit in at clubs, where he ________ (sneak) onto the bandstand to play every chance he got. He disappeared for a short time, the story goes, and when he returned he was a phenomenal guitarist, having ________ (swear) a Faustian oath to Satan. Johnson's song "Crossroads Blues"—rearranged and recorded by the sixties band Cream as simply "Crossroads"—supposedly recounts this exchange, telling how Johnson ________ (deal) with the devil. Some of his other songs, such as "Hellhound on My Trail," are allegedly about the torment he suffered as he ________ (fight) for his soul.

Exercise 2

Complete the following sentences with appropriate forms of the verbs in parentheses.

Example: Mary Cassatt ___*laid*___ down her paintbrush. (lie, lay)

1. Impressionist artists of the nineteenth century preferred everyday subjects and used to ________ fruit on a table to paint. (sit, set)
2. They were known for their technique of ________ dabs of paint quickly on canvas, giving an "impression" of a scene, not extensive detail. (lying, laying)
3. Claude Monet's *Women in the Garden* featured one woman in the foreground who ________ on the grass in a garden. (sat, set)
4. In Pierre Auguste Renoir's *Nymphs*, two nude figures talk while ________ on flowers in a garden. (lying, laying)
5. Paul Cézanne liked to ________ in front of his subject as he painted and often completed paintings out of doors rather than in a studio. (sit, set)

47b Understanding Tense

Tense is the form a verb takes to indicate when an action occurred or when a condition existed.

English Verb Tenses

Simple Tenses
Present (I *finish*, she or he *finishes*)
Past (I *finished*)
Future (I *will finish*)

Perfect Tenses
Present perfect (I *have finished*, she or he *has finished*)
Past perfect (I *had finished*)
Future perfect (I *will have finished*)

Progressive Tenses
Present progressive (I *am finishing*, she or he *is finishing*)
Past progressive (I *was finishing*)
Future progressive (I *will be finishing*)
Present perfect progressive (I *have been finishing*)
Past perfect progressive (I *had been finishing*)
Future perfect progressive (I *will have been finishing*)

(1) Using the Simple Tenses

The **simple tenses** include *present*, *past*, and *future*.

The **present tense** usually indicates an action that is taking place at the time it is expressed in speech or writing. It can also indicate an action that occurs regularly.

I see your point. (an action taking place when it is expressed)

We wear wool in the winter. (an action that occurs regularly)

Close-up: Special Uses of the Present Tense

The present tense has four special uses.

To Indicate Future Time: The grades arrive next Thursday.

To State a Generally Held Belief: Studying pays off.

To State a Scientific Truth: An object at rest tends to stay at rest.

To Discuss a Literary Work: *Family Installments* tells the story of a Puerto Rican family.

The **past tense** indicates that an action has already taken place.

John Glenn orbited the earth three times on February 20, 1962. (an action completed in the past)

As a young man, Mark Twain <u>traveled</u> through the Southwest. (an action that occurred once or many times in the past but did not extend into the present)

The **future tense** indicates that an action will or is likely to take place.

Halley's Comet <u>will reappear</u> in 2061. (a future action that will definitely occur)

The land boom in Nevada <u>will</u> probably <u>continue</u>. (a future action that is likely to occur)

(2) Using the Perfect Tenses

The perfect tenses designate actions that were or will be completed before other actions or conditions. The perfect tenses are formed with the appropriate tense form of the auxiliary verb *have* plus the past participle.

The **present perfect** tense can indicate two types of continuing action beginning in the past.

Dr. Kim <u>has finished</u> studying the effects of BHA on rats. (an action that began in the past and is finished at the present time)

My mother <u>has invested</u> her money wisely. (an action that began in the past and extends into the present)

The **past perfect** tense indicates an action occurring before a certain time in the past.

By 1946, engineers <u>had built</u> the first electronic digital computer.

The **future perfect** tense indicates that an action will be finished by a certain future time.

By Tuesday, the transit authority <u>will have run</u> out of money.

Close-up: *Could Have, Should Have,* and *Would Have*

Do not use the preposition *of* after *would, should, could,* and *might*. Use the auxiliary verb *have* after these words.

I should ~~of~~ *have* left for class earlier.

(3) Using the Progressive Tenses

The progressive tenses express continuing action. They are formed with the appropriate tense of the verb *be* plus the present participle.

The **present progressive** tense indicates that something is happening at the time it is expressed in speech or writing.

> The volcano is erupting, and lava is flowing toward the town.

The **past progressive** tense indicates two kinds of past action.

> Roderick Usher's actions were becoming increasingly bizarre. (a continuing action in the past)

> The French revolutionary Marat was stabbed to death while he was bathing. (an action occurring at the same time in the past as another action)

The **future progressive** tense indicates a continuing action in the future.

> The treasury secretary will be carefully monitoring the money supply.

The **present perfect progressive** tense indicates action continuing from the past into the present and possibly into the future.

> Rescuers have been working around the clock.

The **past perfect progressive** tense indicates that a past action went on until another one occurred.

> Before President Kennedy was assassinated, he had been working on civil rights legislation.

The **future perfect progressive** tense indicates that an action will continue until a certain future time.

> By eleven o'clock we will have been driving for seven hours.

(4) Using Verb Tenses in a Sentence

You use different tenses in a sentence to indicate that actions are taking place at different times. By choosing tenses that accurately express these times, you enable readers to follow the sequence of actions:

- *When a* ***verb*** *appears in a dependent clause, its tense depends on the tense of the main verb in the independent clause.* When the main verb in the independent clause is in the past tense, the verb in the dependent clause is usually in the past or past perfect tense. When the main verb in the independent clause is in the past perfect tense, the verb in the dependent clause is usually in the past tense. (When the main verb in the independent clause is in any tense except the past or past perfect, the verb in the dependent clause may be in any tense needed for meaning.)

Main Verb	**Verb in Dependent Clause**
George Hepplewhite was (past) an English cabinetmaker	who designed (past) distinctive chair backs.
The battle had ended (past perfect)	by the time reinforcements arrived. (past)

- *When an **infinitive** appears in a verbal phrase, the tense it expresses depends on the tense of the sentence's main verb.* The *present infinitive* (the *to* form of the verb) indicates an action happening at the same time as or later than the main verb. The *perfect infinitive* (*to have* plus the past participle) indicates action happening earlier than the main verb.

Main Verb	**Infinitive**
I went	to see the Rangers play last week. (The going and seeing occurred at the same time.)
I want	to see the Rangers play tomorrow. (Wanting occurs in the present, and seeing will occur in the future.)
I would like	to have seen the Rangers play. (Liking occurs in the present, and seeing would have occurred in the past.)

- *When a **participle** appears in a verbal phrase, its tense depends on the tense of the sentence's main verb.* The *present participle* indicates action happening at the same time as the action of the main verb. The *past participle* or the *present perfect participle* indicates action occurring before the action of the main verb.

Participle	**Main Verb**
Addressing the 1896 Democratic Convention,	William Jennings Bryan delivered his Cross of Gold speech. (The addressing and the delivery occurred at the same time.)
Having written her term paper,	Camille studied for her history final. (The writing occurred before the studying.)

Exercise 3

A verb is missing from each of the following sentences. Fill in the form of the verb indicated in parentheses.

Example: The Outer Banks ___*stretch*___ (stretch: present) along the North Carolina coast for more than 175 miles.

1. Many portions of the Outer Banks of North Carolina ________ (give: present) the visitor a sense of history and timelessness.
2. Many students of history __________ (read: present perfect) about the Outer Banks and its mysteries.
3. It was on Roanoke Island in the 1580s that English colonists __________ (establish: past) the first settlement in the New World.
4. That colony vanished soon after it was settled, __________ (become: present participle) known as the famous "lost colony."
5. By 1718, the pirate Blackbeard __________ (made: past perfect) the Outer Banks a hiding place for his treasures.
6. It was at Ocracoke, in fact, that Blackbeard __________ (meet: past) his death.
7. Even today, fortune hunters __________ (search: present progressive) the Outer Banks for Blackbeard's hidden treasures.
8. The Outer Banks are also famous for Kitty Hawk and Kill Devil Hills; even as technology has advanced into the space age, the number of tourists flocking to the site of the Wright brothers' epic flight __________. (grow: present perfect progressive)
9. Long before that famous flight occurred, however, the Outer Banks __________ (claim: past perfect) countless ships along its ever-shifting shores, resulting in its nickname—the "Graveyard of the Atlantic."
10. If the Outer Banks continue to be protected from the ravages of overdevelopment and commercialization, visitors __________ (enjoy: future progressive) the mysteries of this tiny finger of land for years to come.

47c Understanding Mood

Mood is the form a verb takes to indicate whether a writer is making a statement or asking a question (*indicative mood*), giving a command (*imperative mood*), or expressing a wish or a contrary-to-fact statement (*subjunctive mood*).

The **indicative** mood expresses an opinion, states a fact, or asks a question: Jackie Robinson had a great impact on professional baseball. The indicative is the mood used in most English sentences.

The **imperative** mood is used in commands and direct requests. Usually, the imperative includes only the base form of the verb without a subject: Use a dictionary.

The **subjunctive** mood was common in the past, but it now is used less and less often, and usually only in formal contexts.

(1) Forming the Subjunctive Mood

The **present subjunctive** uses the base form of the verb, regardless of the subject. The **past subjunctive** has the same form as the past tense of the verb. (The auxiliary verb *be*, however, takes the form *were* regardless of the number or person of the subject.)

> Dr. Gorman suggested that I study the Cambrian Period. (present subjunctive)
>
> I wish I were going to Europe. (past subjunctive)

(2) Using the Subjunctive Mood

The present subjunctive may be used in *that* clauses after words such as *ask*, *suggest*, *require*, *recommend*, and *demand*.

> The report recommended that juveniles be given mandatory counseling.
>
> Captain Ahab insisted that his crew hunt the white whale.

The past subjunctive may be used in **conditional statements** (statements beginning with *if* that are contrary to fact, including statements that express a wish).

> If John were here, he could see Marsha. (John is not here.)
>
> The father acted as if he were having the baby. (The father couldn't be having the baby.)
>
> I wish I were more organized. (expresses a wish)

NOTE: In many situations, the subjunctive mood can sound stiff or formal. However, alternative expressions can often eliminate the need for subjunctive constructions.

> The group asked ~~that~~ the mayor ^to ban smoking in public places.

Exercise 4

Complete the sentences in the following paragraph by inserting the appropriate form (indicative, imperative, or subjunctive) of the verb in parentheses. Be prepared to explain your choices.

Harry Houdini was a famous escape artist. He ____________ (perform) escapes from every type of bond imaginable: handcuffs, locks, straitjackets, ropes, sacks, and sealed chests underwater. In Germany, workers ____________ (challenge) Houdini to escape from a packing box. If he ____________ (be) to escape, they would admit that he ____________ (be) the best escape artist in the world. Houdini accepted. Before getting into the box, he asked that the observers ____________ (give) it a thorough examination. He then asked that a worker ____________ (nail) him into the box. "____________ (place) a screen around the box," he ordered after he had been sealed inside. In a few minutes, Houdini ____________ (step) from behind the screen. When the workers demanded that they ____________ (see) the box, Houdini pulled down the screen. To their surprise, they saw the box with the lid still nailed tightly in place.

47d Understanding Voice

Voice is the form a verb takes to indicate whether its subject acts or is acted upon. When the subject of a verb does something—that is, acts—the verb is in the **active voice.** When the subject of a verb receives the action—that is, is acted upon—the verb is in the **passive voice.**

Active Voice: Hart Crane wrote *The Bridge.*

Passive Voice: *The Bridge* was written by Hart Crane.

Close-up: Voice

FAQs links

Because the active voice emphasizes the person or thing performing an action, it is usually briefer, clearer, and more emphatic than the passive voice. Some situations, however, require use of the passive voice. For example, you should use passive constructions when the actor is unknown or unimportant or when the recipient of an action should logically receive the emphasis.

DDT was found in soil samples. (Passive voice emphasizes the discovery of DDT; who found it is not important.)

Grits are eaten throughout the South. (Passive voice emphasizes the fact that grits are eaten, not those who eat them.)

Still, whenever possible, you should use active constructions in your college writing.

(1) Changing Verbs from Passive to Active Voice

You can change a verb from passive to active voice by making the subject of the passive verb the object of the active verb. The person or thing performing the action then becomes the subject of the new sentence.

Passive: The novel *Frankenstein* was written by Mary Shelley.

Active: Mary Shelley wrote the novel *Frankenstein.*

If a passive verb has no object, you must supply one that will become the subject of the active verb.

Passive: Baby elephants are taught to avoid humans. (By whom are baby elephants taught?)

Active: Adult elephants teach baby elephants to avoid humans.

Exercise 5

Determine which sentences in the following paragraph should be in the active voice, and rewrite those sentences.

Rockets were invented by the Chinese about AD 1000. Gunpowder was packed into bamboo tubes and ignited by means of a fuse. These rockets were fired by soldiers at enemy armies and usually caused panic. In thirteenth-century England, an improved form of gunpowder was introduced by Roger Bacon. As a result, rockets were used in battles and were a common—although unreliable—weapon. In the early eighteenth century, a twenty-pound rocket that traveled almost two miles was constructed by William Congreve, an English artillery expert. By the late nineteenth century, thought was given to supersonic speeds by the physicist Ernst Mach, and the sonic boom was predicted by him. The first liquid-fuel rocket was launched by the American Robert Goddard in 1926. A pamphlet written by him anticipated almost all future rocket developments. As a result of his pioneering work, he is called the father of modern rocketry.

(2) Changing Verbs from Active to Passive Voice

You can change a verb from active to passive voice by making the object of the active verb the subject of the passive verb. The subject of the active verb then becomes the object of the passive verb.

Active: Sir James Murray compiled *The Oxford English Dictionary.*

Passive: *The Oxford English Dictionary* was compiled by Sir James Murray.

Remember that an active verb must have an object or else it cannot be put into the passive voice. If an active verb has no object, supply one. This verb will become the subject of the passive sentence.

Active: Jacques Cousteau invented.
Cousteau invented ______?______.

Passive: ______?______ was invented by Jacques Cousteau.
The scuba was invented by Jacques Cousteau.

Exercise 6

Determine which sentences in the following paragraph should be in the passive voice, and rewrite those sentences.

The Regent Diamond is one of the world's most famous and coveted jewels. A slave discovered the 410-carat diamond in 1701 in an Indian mine. Over the years, people stole and sold the diamond several times. In 1717, the regent of France bought the diamond for an enormous sum, but during the French Revolution, it disappeared again. Someone later found it in a ditch in Paris. Eventually, Napoleon had the diamond set into his ceremonial sword. At last, when the French monarch fell, the government placed the Regent Diamond in the Louvre, where it remains today.

Chapter 48

Revising Agreement Errors

Frequently Asked Questions

What do I do if a phrase like along with *comes between the subject and the verb?* (p. 845)

If a subject has two parts, is the verb singular or plural? (p. 845)

Do subjects like anyone *take singular or plural verbs?* (p. 846)

Can I use they *and* their *to refer to words like* everyone? (p. 852)

Agreement is the correspondence between words in number, gender, and person. Subjects and verbs agree in **number** (singular or plural) and **person** (first, second, or third); pronouns and their antecedents agree in number, person, and **gender** (masculine, feminine, or neuter).

48a Making Subjects and Verbs Agree

Singular subjects take singular verbs, and plural subjects take plural verbs.

Singular: Hydrogen peroxide is an unstable compound.

Plural: Characters are not well developed in O. Henry's short stories.

Present tense verbs, except *be* and *have*, add *s* or *es* when the subject is third-person singular. Third-person singular subjects include nouns; the personal pronouns *he*, *she*, *it*, and *one;* and many indefinite pronouns.

The president has the power to veto congressional legislation.

She frequently cites statistics to support her assertions.

In every group, somebody emerges as a natural leader.

Present tense verbs do not add *s* or *es* when the subject is a plural noun, a first-person or second-person pronoun (*I*, *we*, *you*), or third-person plural pronoun (*they*).

Experts recommend that dieters avoid salty processed meat.

In our Bill of Rights, we guarantee all defendants the right to a speedy trial.

At this stratum, you see rocks dating back fifteen million years.

They say that some wealthy people default on their student loans.

In the following special situations, subject-verb agreement can be troublesome for writers.

(1) When Words Come between Subject and Verb

If a modifying phrase comes between subject and verb, the verb should agree with the subject, not with a word in the modifying phrase.

The sound of the drumbeats builds in intensity in *The Emperor Jones.*

The games won by the intramural team are usually few and far between.

NOTE: When phrases introduced by *along with*, *as well as*, *in addition to*, *including*, and *together with* come between subject and verb, these phrases do not change the subject's number: Heavy rain, together with high winds, causes hazardous driving conditions.

(2) When Compound Subjects Are Joined by *And*

Compound subjects joined by *and* usually take plural verbs.

Air bags and antilock brakes are standard on all new models.

There are, however, two exceptions to this rule. First, compound subjects joined by *and* that stand for a single idea or person are treated as a unit and used with singular verbs.

Rhythm and blues is a forerunner of rock and roll.

Second, when *each* or *every* precedes a compound subject joined by *and*, the subject takes a singular verb.

Every desk and file cabinet was searched before the letter was found.

(3) When Compound Subjects Are Joined by *Or*

Compound subjects joined by *or* or by *either . . . or* or *neither . . . nor* may take singular or plural verbs.

If both subjects are singular, use a singular verb; if both subjects are plural, use a plural verb.

Either radiation or chemotherapy is combined with surgery for the most effective results. (Both *radiation* and *chemotherapy* are singular, so the verb is singular.)

Either radiation treatments or chemotherapy sessions are combined with surgery for the most effective results. (Both *treatments* and *sessions* are plural, so the verb is plural.)

If one subject is singular and the other is plural, the verb agrees with the subject that is nearer to it.

Either radiation treatments or chemotherapy is combined with surgery for the most effective results. (Singular verb agrees with *chemotherapy*.)

Either chemotherapy or radiation treatments are combined with surgery for the most effective results. (Plural verb agrees with *treatments*.)

(4) When Indefinite Pronouns Serve as Subjects

Some indefinite pronouns—*both*, *many*, *few*, *several*, *others*—are always plural and take plural verbs. Most others—*another*, *anyone*, *everyone*, *one*, *each*, *either*, *neither*, *anything*, *everything*, *something*, *nothing*, *nobody*, and *somebody*—are singular and take singular verbs.

Anyone is welcome to apply for this grant.

Each of the chapters includes a review exercise.

A few indefinite pronouns—*some*, *all*, *any*, *more*, *most*, and *none*—can be singular or plural, depending on the noun they refer to.

Of course, some of this trouble is to be expected. (*Some* refers to *trouble*.)

Some of the spectators are getting restless. (*Some* refers to *spectators*.)

http://kirsznermandell.wadsworth.com

Computer Tip: Subject-Verb Agreement

Your word processor's grammar checker will highlight and offer revision suggestions for many subject-verb agreement errors, including errors in sentences that have indefinite pronoun subjects (see Figure 48.1).

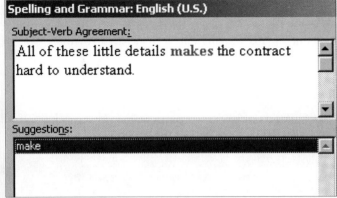

Spelling and Grammar: English (U.S.)

Subject-Verb Agreement:

All of these little details **makes** the contract hard to understand.

Suggestions:

make

Figure 48.1 Sample grammar checker suggestion.

(5) When Collective Nouns Serve as Subjects

A **collective noun** names a group of persons or things—for instance, *navy*, *union*, *association*, *band*. When it refers to a group as a unit (as it usually does), a collective noun takes a singular verb; when it refers to the individuals or items that make up the group, it takes a plural verb.

> To many people, the royal family symbolizes Great Britain. (The family, as a unit, is the symbol.)

> The family all eat at different times. (Each member eats separately.)

NOTE: If a plural verb sounds awkward with a collective noun, reword the sentence: Family members all eat at different times.

ESL Tip

In British English, which you may have learned if you took ESL classes outside the United States, collective nouns tend to take plural verbs more often than they do in American English: Management are considering giving workers a bonus.

Phrases that name fixed amounts—*three-quarters*, *twenty dollars*, *the majority*—are treated like collective nouns. When the amount denotes a unit, it takes a singular verb; when it denotes part of the whole, it takes a plural verb.

Three-quarters of his usual salary is not enough to live on. (*Three-quarters* denotes a unit.)

Three-quarters of workshop participants improve dramatically. (*Three-quarters* denotes part of the group.)

Close-up: Subject-Verb Agreement with Collective Nouns

The number is always singular, and *a number* is always plural.

The number of voters has declined.

A number of students have missed the opportunity to preregister.

(6) When Singular Subjects Have Plural Forms

A singular subject takes a singular verb, even if the form of the subject is plural.

Politics makes strange bedfellows.

Statistics deals with the collection, classification, analysis, and interpretation of data.

When such a word has a plural meaning, however, use a plural verb.

Her politics are too radical for her parents. (*Politics* refers not to the science of political government but, rather, to political principles or opinions.)

The statistics prove him wrong. (*Statistics* denotes not a body of knowledge but the numerical facts or data themselves.)

NOTE: The title of an individual work takes a singular verb even if the title's form is plural: *The Grapes of Wrath* describes the journey of migrant workers and their families from the Dust Bowl to California.

NOTE: Some words retain their Latin plural forms, which do not look like English plural forms. Be particularly careful to use the correct verbs with such words: *criterion is, criteria are; medium is, media are; bacterium is, bacteria are*.

(7) When Subject-Verb Order Is Inverted

Even when word order is inverted so that the verb comes before the subject (as it does in questions and in sentences beginning with *there is* or *there are*), the subject and verb must agree.

Is either answer correct?

There is a monument to Emiliano Zapata in Mexico City.

There are currently thirteen federal circuit courts of appeals.

(8) With Linking Verbs

A linking verb should agree with its subject, not with the subject complement.

The problem was termites.

Here, the verb *was* correctly agrees with the subject *problem*, not with the subject complement *termites*. If *termites* were the subject, the verb would be plural.

Termites were the problem.

(9) With Relative Pronouns

When you use a relative pronoun (*who, which, that*, and so on) to introduce a dependent clause, the verb in that clause should agree in number with the pronoun's **antecedent** (the word to which the pronoun refers).

The farmer is among the ones who suffer during a grain embargo. (Verb *suffer* agrees with plural antecedent *ones*.)

The farmer is the only one who suffers during the grain embargo. (Verb *suffers* agrees with singular antecedent *one*.)

Exercise 1

Each of these ten correct sentences illustrates one of the conventions just explained. Read each sentence carefully, and explain why each verb form is used.

Example: Obedience in our schools is at an all-time low. (The verb is singular because *obedience*, not *schools*, is the subject.)

1. Jack Kerouac, along with Allen Ginsberg and William S. Burroughs, was a major figure in the "beat" movement.
2. Every American boy and girl needs to learn basic computational skills.
3. Aesthetics is not an exact science.
4. The audience was restless.
5. The Beatles' *Sergeant Pepper* album is one of those albums that remain popular long after they are issued.
6. All is quiet.
7. The subject was roses.
8. When he was young, Benjamin Franklin's primary concern was books.
9. Eighty dollars is too much to spend on one concert ticket.
10. "There are more things in heaven and earth, Horatio, than are dreamt of in your philosophy."

Exercise 2

Some of the following sentences are correct, but others contain common errors in subject-verb agreement. If a sentence is correct, mark it with a *C;* if it has an error, correct it.

1. *I Love Lucy* is one of those television shows that almost all Americans have seen at least once.
2. The committee presented its findings to the president.
3. Neither Western novels nor science fiction appeal to me.
4. Stage presence and musical ability makes a rock performer successful today.
5. *It's a Wonderful Life*, like many old Christmas movies, seems to be shown on television every year.
6. Hearts are my grandmother's favorite card game.
7. The best part of B. B. King's songs are the guitar solos.
8. Time and tide waits for no man.
9. Sports are my main pastime.
10. *Vincent and Theo* is Robert Altman's movie about the French Impressionist painter Vincent van Gogh and his brother.

48b Making Pronouns and Antecedents Agree

See 45b

ESL 61f

A pronoun must agree with its **antecedent**—the word or word group to which the pronoun refers. Singular pronouns—such as *he*, *him*, *she*, *her*, *it*, *me*, *myself*, and *oneself*—should refer to singular antecedents. Plural pronouns—such as *we*, *us*, *they*, *them*, and *their*—should refer to plural antecedents.

In the following special situations, pronoun-antecedent agreement can cause problems for writers.

(1) With Compound Antecedents

In most cases, use a plural pronoun to refer to a **compound antecedent** (two or more antecedents connected by *and*).

> Mormonism and Christian Science were influenced in their beginnings by Shaker doctrines.

However, if a compound antecedent denotes a single unit—one person, thing, or idea—use a singular pronoun to refer to the compound antecedent.

> In 1904, the husband and father brought his family from Germany to the United States.

Use a singular pronoun when a compound antecedent is preceded by *each* or *every*.

> Every programming language and software package has its limitations.

Use a singular pronoun to refer to two or more singular antecedents linked by *or* or *nor*.

> Neither Thoreau nor Whitman lived to see his work read widely.

When one part of a compound antecedent is singular and one part is plural, the pronoun agrees in person and number with the closer antecedent.

> Neither the child nor her parents wore their seatbelts.

(2) With Collective Noun Antecedents

If the meaning of the collective noun antecedent is singular (as it will be in most cases), use a singular pronoun. If the meaning is plural, use a plural pronoun.

> The nurses' <u>union</u> announced <u>its</u> plan to strike. (All the members acted as one.)

> The <u>team</u> ran onto the court and took <u>their</u> positions. (Each member acted individually.)

(3) With Indefinite Pronoun Antecedents

Most indefinite pronouns—*each*, *either*, *neither*, *one*, *anyone*, and the like—are singular and require singular pronouns.

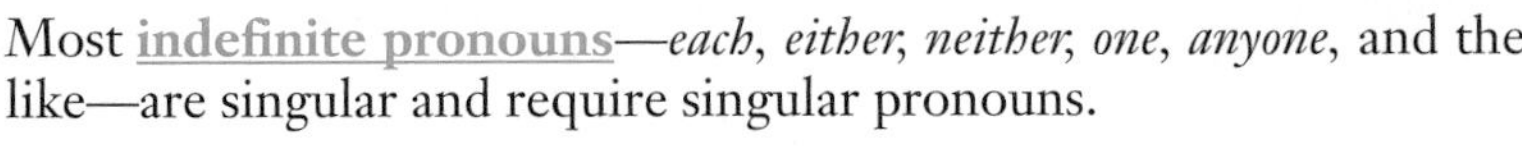

> <u>Neither</u> of the men had <u>his</u> proposal ready by the deadline.

> <u>Each</u> of these neighborhoods has <u>its</u> own traditions and values.

Close-up: Pronoun-Antecedent Agreement

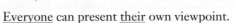

In speech and in informal writing, many people use the plural pronouns *they* or *their* with singular indefinite pronouns that refer to people, such as *someone*, *everyone*, and *nobody*.

> <u>Everyone</u> can present <u>their</u> own viewpoint.

In college writing, however, you should try to avoid using a plural pronoun to refer to a singular subject. Instead, you can use both the masculine and the feminine pronoun.

> <u>Everyone</u> can present <u>his or her</u> own viewpoint.

Or, you can make the sentence's subject plural.

> <u>All participants</u> can present <u>their</u> own viewpoints.

The use of *his* alone to refer to a singular indefinite pronoun (Everyone can present *his* own viewpoint) is considered sexist language.

http://kirsznermandell.wadsworth.com

Computer Tip: Pronoun-Antecedent Agreement

Your word processor's grammar checker will highlight and offer revision suggestions for many pronoun-antecedent agreement errors (see Figure 48.2).

Figure 48.2 Sample grammar checker suggestion.

Exercise 3

In the following sentences, find and correct any errors in subject-verb or pronoun-antecedent agreement.

1. The core of a computer is a collection of electronic circuits that are called the central processing unit.
2. Computers, because of advanced technology that allows the central processing unit to be placed on a chip, a thin square of semiconducting material about one-quarter of an inch on each side, has been greatly reduced in size.
3. Computers can "talk" to each other over phone lines through a modem, an acronym for *modulator-demodulator*.
4. Pressing keys on keyboards resembling typewriter keyboards generate electronic signals that are input for the computer.
5. Computers have built-in memory storage, and equipment such as disks or tapes provide external memory.
6. RAM (random-access memory), the erasable and reusable computer memory, hold the computer program, the computations executed by the program, and the results.
7. After computer programs are "read" from a disk or tape, the computer uses the instructions as needed to execute the program.

8. ROM (read-only memory), the permanent memory that is "read" by the computer but cannot be changed, are used to store programs that are needed frequently.
9. A number of video games with impressive graphics, sound, and color is available for home computers.
10. Although some computer users write their own programs, most buy ready-made software programs such as the ones that allows a computer to be used as a word processor.

Exercise 4

The following ten sentences illustrate correct subject-verb and pronoun-antecedent agreement. Following the instructions in parentheses after each sentence, revise each so its verbs and pronouns agree with the newly created subject.

Example: One child in ten suffers from a learning disability. (Change *One child in ten* to *Ten percent of all children*.)

Revised: Ten percent of all children suffer from a learning disability.

1. The governess is seemingly pursued by evil as she tries to protect Miles and Flora from those she feels seek to possess the children's souls. (Change *The governess* to *The governess and the cook*.)
2. Insulin-dependent diabetics are now able to take advantage of new technology that can help alleviate their symptoms. (Change *diabetics* to *the diabetic*.)
3. All homeowners in coastal regions worry about the possible effects of a hurricane on their property. (Change *All homeowners* to *Every homeowner*.)
4. Federally funded job-training programs offer unskilled workers an opportunity to acquire skills they can use to secure employment. (Change *workers* to *the worker*.)
5. Foreign imports pose a major challenge to the American textile market. (Change *Foreign imports* to *The foreign import*.)
6. *Brideshead Revisited* tells how one family and its devotion to its Catholic faith influence Charles Ryder. (Delete *and its devotion to its Catholic faith*.)
7. *Writer's Digest* and *The Writer* are designed to aid writers as they seek markets for their work. (Change *writers* to *the writer*.)
8. Most American families have access to television; in fact, more have televisions than have indoor plumbing. (Change *Most American families* to *Almost every American family*.)
9. In Montana, it seems as though every town's elevation is higher than its population. (Change *every town's elevation* to *all the towns' elevations*.)
10. A woman without a man is like a fish without a bicycle. (Change *A woman/a man* to *Women/men*.)

Chapter 49

Using Adjectives and Adverbs

49a Understanding Adjectives and Adverbs

Adjectives modify nouns and pronouns. **Adverbs** modify verbs, adjectives, or other adverbs—or entire phrases, clauses, or sentences. Both adjectives and adverbs describe, limit, or qualify other words, phrases, or clauses.

The *function* of a word in a sentence, not its *form*, determines whether it is an adjective or an adverb. Although many adverbs (such as *immediately* and *hopelessly*) end in *-ly*, others (such as *almost* and *very*) do not. Moreover, some words that end in *-ly* (such as *lively*) are adjectives. Only by locating the modified word and determining what part of speech it is can you determine whether a modifier is an adjective or an adverb.

ESL Tip

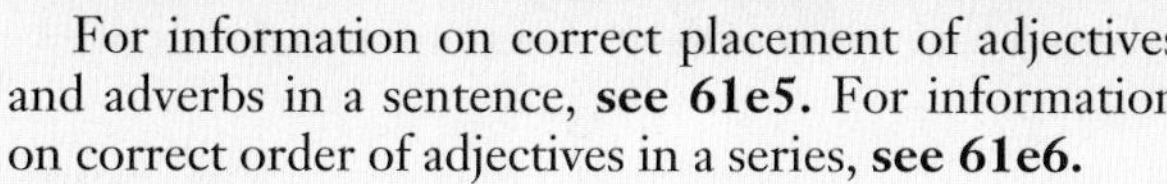

For information on correct placement of adjectives and adverbs in a sentence, **see 61e5.** For information on correct order of adjectives in a series, **see 61e6.**

49b Using Adjectives

Be sure to use an **adjective**—not an adverb—as a subject complement. A **subject complement** is a word that follows a linking verb and modifies the sentence's subject, not its verb. A linking verb does

See 45c1

not show physical or emotional action. *Seem, appear, believe, become, grow, turn, remain, prove, look, sound, smell, taste, feel,* and the forms of the verb *be* are or can be used as linking verbs.

Michelle seemed brave. (*Seemed* shows no action, so it is a linking verb. Because *brave* is a subject complement that modifies the subject *Michelle*, it takes the adjective form.)

Michelle smiled bravely. (*Smiled* shows action, so it is not a linking verb. *Bravely* modifies *smiled*, so it takes the adverb form.)

NOTE: Sometimes the same verb can function as either a linking verb or an action verb: He remained stubborn. (He was still stubborn.) He remained stubbornly. (He remained, in a stubborn manner.)

Also, be sure to use an adjective—not an adverb—as an **object complement,** a word that follows a sentence's direct object and modifies that object and not the verb. Objects are nouns or pronouns, so their modifiers must be adjectives.

Most people called him timid. (People consider him to be timid; here *timid* is an object complement that modifies *him*, the sentence's direct object, so the adjective form is correct.)

Most people called him timidly. (People were timid when they called him; here *timidly* modifies the verb *called*—not the object—so the adverb form is correct.)

49c Using Adverbs

Be sure to use an **adverb**—not an adjective—to modify verbs, adjectives, or other adverbs—or entire phrases, clauses, or sentences.

Most students did ~~great~~ *very well* on the midterm.

My parents dress a lot more ~~conservative~~ *conservatively* than my friends do.

Close-up: Using Adjectives and Adverbs

In informal speech, adjective forms such as *good, bad, sure, real, slow, quick,* and *loud* are often used to modify verbs, adjectives, and adverbs. Avoid these informal modifiers in college writing.

The program ran ~~real good~~ *really well* the first time we tried it, but the new system performed ~~bad~~ *badly*.

Exercise 1

Revise each of the incorrect sentences in the following paragraph so that only adjectives modify nouns and pronouns and only adverbs modify verbs, adjectives, or other adverbs.

A popular self-help trend in the United States today is subliminal tapes. These tapes, with titles like *How to Attract Love*, *Freedom from Acne*, and *I Am a Genius*, are intended to address every problem known to modern society—and to solve these problems quick and easy. The tapes are said to work because their "hidden messages" bypass conscious defense mechanisms. The listener hears only music or relaxing sounds, like waves rolling slow and steady. At decibel levels perceived only subconsciously, positive words and phrases are embedded, usually by someone who speaks deep and rhythmic. The top-selling cassettes are those that help listeners lose weight or quit smoking. The popularity of such tapes is not hard to understand. They promise easy solutions to complex problems. But the main benefit of these tapes appears to be for the sellers, who are accumulating profits real fast.

Exercise 2

Being careful to use adjectives—not adverbs—as subject complements and object complements, write five sentences in imitation of each of the following sentences. Consult the list of linking verbs in 45c1, and use a different linking verb in each of your sentences.

1. Julie looked worried.
2. Dan considers his collection valuable.

49d Using Comparative and Superlative Forms

Most adjectives and adverbs have **comparative** and **superlative** forms that can be used with nouns to indicate degree.

Comparative and Superlative Forms

Form	Function	Example
Positive	Describes a quality; does not indicate a comparison	big, lovely
Comparative	Indicates a comparison between *two* qualities (greater or lesser)	bigger, lovelier
Superlative	Indicates a comparison among *more than two* qualities (greatest or least)	biggest, loveliest

NOTE: Some adverbs, particularly those indicating time, place, and degree (*almost*, *very*, *here*, and *immediately*), do not have comparative or superlative forms.

(1) Comparative Forms

To form the comparative, all one-syllable adjectives and many two-syllable adjectives (particularly those that end in *-y*, *-ly*, *-le*, *-er*, and *-ow*) add *-er*: slower, funnier. (Note that a final *y* becomes *i* before *-er* is added.)

Other two-syllable adjectives and all long adjectives form the comparative with *more:* more famous, more incredible.

Adverbs ending in *-ly* also form the comparative with *more*: more slowly. Other adverbs use the *-er* ending to form the comparative: sooner.

All adjectives and adverbs indicate a lesser degree with *less:* less lovely, less slowly.

(2) Superlative Forms

Adjectives that form the comparative with *-er* add *-est* to form the superlative: nicest, funniest. Adjectives that indicate the comparative with *more* use *most* to indicate the superlative: most famous, most challenging.

The majority of adverbs use *most* to indicate the superlative: most quickly. Others use the *-est* ending: soonest.

All adjectives and adverbs use *least* to indicate the least degree: least interesting, least willingly.

Close-up: Using Comparatives and Superlatives

- Never use both *more* and *-er* to form the comparative or both *most* and *-est* to form the superlative.

  Nothing could have been ~~more~~ easier.

  Jack is the ~~most~~ meanest person in town.

- Never use the superlative when comparing only two things.

  Stacy is the ^taller ~~tallest~~ of the two sisters.

- Never use the comparative when comparing more than two things.

  We chose the ^earliest ~~earlier~~ of the four appointments.

(3) Irregular Comparatives and Superlatives

Some adjectives and adverbs have irregular comparative and superlative forms. Instead of adding a word or an ending to the positive form, they use different words to indicate the comparative and the superlative.

Irregular Comparatives and Superlatives

	Positive	**Comparative**	**Superlative**
Adjectives:	good	better	best
	bad	worse	worst
	a little	less	least
	many, some, much	more	most
Adverbs:	well	better	best
	badly	worse	worst

Close-up: Illogical Comparative and Superlative Forms

Many adjectives and adverbs can logically exist only in the positive degree. For example, words like *perfect*, *unique*, *excellent*, *impossible*, and *dead* can never be used in the comparative or superlative degree.

(continued)

Illogical comparative and superlative forms (continued)

I read ~~the most~~ *an* excellent story.

The vase in the museum's collection is ~~very~~ unique.

These words can, however, be modified by words that suggest approaching the absolute state—*nearly* or *almost*, for example.

He revised until his draft was almost perfect.

Exercise 3

Supply the correct comparative and superlative forms for each of the following adjectives or adverbs. Then, use each form in a sentence.

Example: strange stranger strangest

The story had a *strange* ending.
The explanation sounded *stranger* each time I heard it.
This is the *strangest* gadget I have ever seen.

1. difficult
2. eccentric
3. confusing
4. bad
5. mysterious
6. softly
7. embarrassing
8. well
9. often
10. tiny

49e Avoiding Double Negatives

Be careful not to create a **double negative** by using a negative modifier (such as *never*, *no*, or *not*) with another negative word (such as *nearly*, *hardly*, *none*, or *nothing*).

Old dogs cannot learn ~~no~~ new tricks.

Remember that many contractions include the negative word *not*.

The instructor doesn't give ~~no~~ partial credit.

http://kirsznermandell.wadsworth.com

Computer Tip: Revising Double Negatives

Your word processor's grammar checker will highlight double negatives and offer suggestions for revision (see Figure 49.1).

Spelling and Grammar: English (U.S.)

Negation Use:

Never walk alone in **no** dark alleys.

Suggestions:

any

Figure 49.1 Sample grammar checker suggestion.

STUDENT WRITER AT WORK

Understanding Grammar

The following draft of a student essay, which was written for a business marketing course, contains a variety of grammatical errors. After reading the draft carefully, proofread to correct the writer's errors in subject-verb and pronoun-antecedent agreement as well as any errors in verb tense, pronoun reference, and use of adjectives and adverbs.

The Science of Good Marketing

The County Museum of Science and Industry (CMSI) is like many family-oriented nonprofit science museums across the country: visitors would pay to see different exhibits, demonstrations, and shows, and the museum channeled money that does not go to their staffing expenses back into the museum. As a nonprofit, the museum must engage in activities that promote some religious, charitable, educational, literary, or scientific purpose. The main difference between nonprofit and for-profit, or capital-oriented, businesses are that nonprofit organizations cannot never offer stock in exchange for capital investments, while capital-oriented companies can. One of the advantages of being a nonprofit organization is that the museum is eligible for certain federal and state tax exemptions if they have profits to report after expenses.

With a lot of competition from capital-oriented companies, nonprofit organizations (especially museums) that generate revenue from repeat visitors and tourism is turning to corporate sponsorship to more better fund and maintain the attractions that keep people coming. Major corporate donors are constantly sought out, and when not enough funds are raised by this, the museum turns to advertising. For example, when a local radio station sponsors one of the movies playing in the museum's theater, this brings people who listen to that station in to see the movie frequently.

Usually, however, corporate sponsorship is all that is needed. The museum has an official soft drink; it also has an official airline. The two companies concerned are "official" because they have paid to have their names flashed on the screen during the museum's preshow. This approach works real well because consumers enjoy seeing a product of a company that they already know and like associated with the museum they are visiting.

At CMSI, most exhibits are underwritten by a local or national corporation. For example, a multi-billion-dollar international pharmaceutical corporation sponsored a recent exhibit on microbes and diseases. The current featured exhibit, called "Moneyville," is sponsored by a multi-billion-dollar banking company, and it educates visitors on the benefits of investing and banking. Other recent exhibits have also been sponsored by various businesses. For example, ticket sellers have handed out promotional material for a company that makes photo printer paper, and theater presenters have mentioned a travel company that had supplied a movie to the museum. Finally, a child that leaves the museum often carries a sample of sponsor advertising, in the form of keychains or small toys, in their hand.

All of these marketing strategies work to keep the museum's income up and help it to remain competitive with other local and national attractions. There are definitely worst ways to make a profit, but if the museum wants to do more than simply staying solvent, they will need to increase their marketing strategies to include more exhibits as well as more advertising.

Grammar Checker

Comma Use:

Although the library is usually open y
round; it will be closed this fall due t

PART 10

Understanding Punctuation and Mechanics

OVERVIEW OF SENTENCE PUNCTUATION: COMMAS, SEMICOLONS, COLONS, DASHES, PARENTHESES

(Further explanations and examples are located in the sections listed in parentheses after each example.)

Separating Independent Clauses

With a Comma and a Coordinating Conjunction
The House approved the bill, but the Senate rejected it. (**51a**)

With a Semicolon
Paul Revere's *The Boston Massacre* is traditional American protest art; Edward Hicks's paintings are socially conscious art with a religious strain. (**52a**)

With a Semicolon and a Transitional Word or Phrase
Thomas Jefferson brought two hundred vanilla beans and a recipe for vanilla ice cream back from France; thus, he gave America its all-time favorite ice-cream flavor. (**52b**)

With a Colon
A *U.S. News & World Report* survey revealed a surprising fact: Americans spend more time at malls than anywhere else except at home and at work. (**55a2**)

Separating Items in a Series

With Commas
Chipmunk, *raccoon*, and *Mugwump* are Native American words. (**51b**)

With Semicolons
Laramie, Wyoming; Wyoming, Delaware; and Delaware, Ohio, were three of the places they visited. (**52c**)

Setting Off Examples, Explanations, or Summaries

With a Colon

She had a dream: to play professional basketball. (**55a2**)

With a Dash

"Study hard," "Respect your elders," "Don't talk with your mouth full"—Sharon had often heard her parents say these things. (**55b2**)

Setting Off Nonessential Material

With a Single Comma

His fear increasing, he waited to enter the haunted house. (**51d4**)

With a Pair of Commas

Mark McGwire, not Sammy Sosa, was the first to break Roger Maris's home-run record. (**51d3**)

With Dashes

Neither of the boys—both nine-year-olds—had any history of violence. (**55b1**)

With Parentheses

In some European countries (notably Sweden and France), high-quality day care is offered at little or no cost to parents. (**55c1**)

Solving Common Punctuation Problems: Using Your Computer's Grammar Checker

The following chart presents an overview of the advantages and disadvantages of using a grammar checker to identify and correct punctuation errors in your writing. For more specific explanations and illustrations, consult the Computer Tip boxes in the individual chapters.

Punctuation Mark	Common Punctuation Problem	Grammar Checker Advantage	Grammar Checker Limitation
Periods (**50a**)	Failure to capitalize after a period	Automatically capitalizes the first word of a sentence	Does not always detect missing, misplaced, or misused periods
Question Marks (**50b**)	Missing question mark at the end of a direct question	Highlights possible questions; sometimes offers revision suggestions	Does not identify some common misuses of question marks
Commas (**Ch. 51**)	Misuse of a comma alone to join two independent clauses	Often identifies misused commas and offers revision suggestions	Does not detect some common misuses of commas; does not always correctly distinguish between restrictive and nonrestrictive modifiers
Semicolons (**Ch. 52**)	Misuse of a semicolon between a dependent and an independent clause	Highlights semicolon and suggests using a comma	Does not identify some common misuses of semicolons; mislabels some semicolon errors as other types of errors
Apostrophes (**Ch. 53**)	Misuse of an apostrophe with a plural noun that is not possessive	Highlights noun and suggests deleting apostrophe	Does not recognize plurals of letters and plurals of words referred to as words

Punctuation Mark	Common Punctuation Problem	Grammar Checker Advantage	Grammar Checker Limitation
Quotation Marks **(Ch. 54)**	Missing punctuation after an identifying tag that introduces a quoted passage	Offers revision suggestions	Does not detect missing quotation marks or misplaced punctuation with quotation marks
Colons **(55a)**	Comma or semicolon incorrectly used in place of a colon	Sometimes identifies error	Does not usually offer revision suggestions; does not identify misused colons after expressions like *such as* and *for example* or in certain verb and prepositional constructions
Dashes **(55b)**	Misuse of a single hyphen surrounded by one space on each side to represent a dash	Automatically converts hyphen to a dash	Does not detect single hyphens misused as dashes when no space surrounds them; does not identify overused dashes

Chapter 50

Using End Punctuation

Frequently Asked Questions

50a Using Periods

(1) Ending a Sentence

Use a period to signal the end of a statement, a mild command or polite request, or an indirect question.

Something is rotten in Denmark. (statement)

Be sure to have the oil checked before you start out. (mild command)

When the bell rings, please exit in an orderly fashion. (polite request)

They wondered whether the water was safe to drink. (indirect question)

(2) Marking an Abbreviation

Use a period in most abbreviations.

Mr. Spock	1600 Pennsylvania Ave.	9 p.m.
Dr. Who	Aug.	etc.

If an abbreviation ends the sentence, do not add another period.

He promised to be there at 6 a.m./

However, do add a question mark if the sentence is a question.

Did he arrive at 6 p.m.?

If the abbreviation falls *within* a sentence, use normal punctuation after the period.

He promised to be there at 6 p.m., but he forgot.

Close-up: Abbreviations without Periods

Abbreviations composed of all capital letters do not usually require periods unless they are the initials of people's names (E. B. White).

MD RN BC

Familiar abbreviations of the names of corporations or government agencies and abbreviations of scientific and technical terms do not require periods.

IBM EPA DNA CD-ROM

Acronyms—new words formed from the initial letters or first few letters of a series of words—do not include periods.

modem	op-ed	scuba	radar
OSHA	AIDS	NAFTA	CAT scan

Clipped forms (commonly accepted shortened forms of words, such as *flu*, *dorm*, *math*, and *fax*) do not include periods.

Postal abbreviations do not include periods.

NY CA MS FL TX

(3) Marking Divisions in Dramatic, Poetic, and Biblical References

Use periods to separate act, scene, and line numbers in plays; book and line numbers in long poems; and chapter and verse numbers in biblical references. (Do not space between the periods and the elements they separate.)

Dramatic Reference: *Hamlet* 2.2.1–5

Poetic Reference: *Paradise Lost* 7.163–67

Biblical Reference: *Judges* 4.14

NOTE: In MLA parenthetical references, titles of literary and biblical works are often abbreviated: `Ham. 2.2.1-5; Judg. 4.14.`

(4) Marking Divisions in Electronic Addresses

Periods, along with other punctuation marks (such as slashes and colons), are frequently used in electronic addresses (URLs).

http://kirsznermandell.wadsworth.com

NOTE: When you type a URL, do not end it with a period; do not add spaces after periods within the address.

Exercise 1

Correct these sentences by adding missing periods and deleting unnecessary ones. If a sentence is correct, mark it with a *C*.

Example: Their mission changed the war.

1. Julius Caesar was killed in 44 B.C.
2. Dr. McLaughlin worked hard to earn his Ph.D..
3. Carmen was supposed to be at A.F.L.-C.I.O. headquarters by 2 p.m.; however, she didn't get there until 10 p.m.
4. After she studied the fall lineup proposed by N.B.C., she decided to work for C.B.S.
5. Representatives from the U.M.W. began collective bargaining after an unsuccessful meeting with Mr. L Pritchard, the coal company's representative.

50b Using Question Marks

(1) Marking the End of a Direct Question

Use a question mark to signal the end of a direct question.

Who was that masked man? (direct question)

"Is this a silver bullet?" they asked. (declarative sentence opening with a direct question)

(2) Marking Questionable Dates or Numbers

Use a question mark in parentheses to indicate that a date or number is uncertain.

Aristophanes, the Greek playwright, was born in 448 (?) BC and died in 380 (?) BC.

(3) Editing Misused Question Marks

Do not use question marks in the following situations.

After an Indirect Question Use a period, not a question mark, with an **indirect question** (a question that is not quoted directly).

The personnel officer asked whether he knew how to type?.

With Other Punctuation Do not use other punctuation marks along with question marks.

"Can it be true?," he asked.

With Another Question Mark Do not end a sentence with more than one question mark.

You did what?? Are you crazy??

To Convey Sarcasm Do not use question marks to convey sarcasm. Instead, suggest your attitude through word choice.

not-so-very
I refused his generous (?) offer.

In an Exclamation Do not use a question mark after an exclamation that is phrased as a question.

!
Will you please stop that at once?

http://kirsznermandell.wadsworth.com

Computer Tip: Replacing Punctuation Marks

Microsoft Word's Find and Replace tool allows you to search for certain punctuation marks and replace them with others (see Figure 50.1). Select Find from the Edit menu, click the Replace tab, type a punctuation mark into the Find What box, and then type the replacement mark into the Replace With box. Clicking Replace will replace this punctuation mark one time; clicking Replace All will replace it each time it appears in your document.

Figure 50.1 ***Microsoft Word*** **Find and Replace tool.**

Exercise 2

Correct the use of question marks and other punctuation in the following sentences.

Example: She asked whether Freud's theories were accepted during his lifetime?

1. He wondered whether he should take a nine o'clock class?
2. The instructor asked, "Was the Spanish-American War a victory for America."
3. Are they really going to China??!!
4. He took a modest (?) portion of dessert—half a pie.
5. "Is *data* the plural of *datum*?," he inquired.

50c Using Exclamation Points

Use an exclamation point to signal the end of an emotional or emphatic statement, an emphatic interjection, or a forceful command.

Remember the *Maine*!

No! Don't leave!

Finish this job at once!

NOTE: Except for recording dialogue, exclamation points are almost never appropriate in college writing. Even in informal writing, you should use exclamation points sparingly.

Exercise 3

Add appropriate punctuation to this passage.

Dr Craig and his group of divers paused at the shore, staring respectfully at the enormous lake Who could imagine what terrors lay beneath its surface Which of them might not emerge alive from this adventure Would it be Col Cathcart Capt Wilks, the MD from the naval base Her husband, P L Fox Or would they all survive the task ahead Dr Craig decided some encouraging remarks were in order

"Attention divers," he said in a loud, forceful voice "May I please have your attention The project which we are about to undertake—"

"Oh, no" screamed Mr Fox suddenly "Look out It's the Loch Ness Monster"

"Quick" shouted Dr Craig "Move away from the shore" But his warning came too late

Chapter 51

Using Commas

Frequently Asked Questions

Do I need a comma before the word and *when it comes between the last two items in a series?* (p. 876)

How do I know whether to put a comma after a word or phrase that opens a sentence? (p. 878)

How do I use commas with that *and* which*?* (p. 881)

How do I use commas with words and phrases like however *and* in fact*?* (p. 883)

How do I use commas with quotations? (p. 884)

Should I always use a comma before the words and *and* but*?* (p. 889)

51a Setting Off Independent Clauses

Use a comma when you form a compound sentence by linking two independent clauses with a **coordinating conjunction** (*and*, *but*, *or*, *nor*, *for*, *yet*, *so*) or a pair of correlative conjunctions. See 45g

The House approved the bill, but the Senate rejected it.

Either the hard drive is full, or the modem is too slow.

NOTE: You may omit the comma if two clauses connected by a coordinating conjunction are very short.

Seek and ye shall find.

Love it or leave it.

Close-up: Separating Independent Clauses

Use a semicolon—not a comma—to separate two independent clauses linked by a coordinating conjunction when at least one of the clauses already contains a comma or when the clauses are especially complex.

The tourists visited Melbourne, the capital of Australia, for three days; and they toured Wellington, New Zealand, for two.

Exercise 1

Combine each of the following sentence pairs into one compound sentence, adding commas where necessary.

Example: Emergency medicine became an approved medical specialty in 1979, and now ~~. Now,~~ pediatric emergency medicine is becoming increasingly important. (and)

1. The Pope did not hesitate to visit Cuba. He did not hesitate to meet with President Fidel Castro. (nor)
2. Agents place brand-name products in prominent positions in films. The products will be seen and recognized by large audiences. (so)
3. Unisex insurance rates may have some drawbacks for women. These rates may be very beneficial. (or)
4. Cigarette advertising no longer appears on television. It does appear in print media. (but)
5. Dorothy Day founded the Catholic Worker movement in the 1930s. Her followers still dispense free food, medical care, and legal advice to the needy. (and)

51b Setting Off Items in a Series

(1) Coordinate Elements

Use commas between items in a series of three or more **coordinate elements** (words, phrases, or clauses joined by a coordinating conjunction).

Chipmunk, *raccoon*, and *Mugwump* are Native American words.

You may pay by check, with a credit card, or in cash.

Brazilians speak Portuguese, Colombians speak Spanish, and Haitians speak French and Creole.

NOTE: If phrases or clauses in a series already contain commas, use semicolons to separate the items.

Do not use a comma to introduce or to close a series.

Three important criteria are~~,~~ fat content, salt content, and taste.

Quebec, Ontario, and Alberta~~,~~ are Canadian provinces.

NOTE: To avoid ambiguity, always use a comma before the *and* (or other coordinating conjunction) that separates the last two items in a series.

The party was made special by the company, the subdued light from the hundreds of twinkling candles, and the excellent hors d'oeuvres.

(2) Coordinate Adjectives

Use a comma between items in a series of two or more **coordinate adjectives**—adjectives that modify the same word or word group—unless they are joined by a conjunction.

She brushed her long, shining hair.

The baby was tired and cranky and wet. (adjectives joined by conjunctions; no commas required)

Checklist: Punctuating Adjectives in a Series

- ☐ If you can reverse the order of the adjectives or insert *and* between the adjectives without changing the meaning, the adjectives are coordinate, and you should use a comma.

  She brushed her long, shining hair.

  She brushed her shining, long hair.

  She brushed her long [and] shining hair.

- ☐ If you cannot reverse the order of the adjectives or insert *and*, the adjectives are not coordinate, and you should not use a comma.

  Ten red balloons fell from the ceiling.

  Red ten balloons fell from the ceiling.

  Ten [and] red balloons fell from the ceiling.

NOTE: Numbers—such as *ten*—are not coordinate with other adjectives.

ESL Tip

If you have difficulty determining the order of two or more adjectives, **see 61e6** for tips to help you with this problem.

Exercise 2

Correct the use of commas in the following sentences, adding or deleting commas where necessary. If a sentence is punctuated correctly, mark it with a *C*.

Example: Neither dogs, snakes, bees, nor dragons frighten her.

1. Seals, whales, dogs, lions, and horses, all are mammals.
2. Mammals are warm-blooded vertebrates that bear live young, nurse them, and usually have fur.
3. Seals are mammals, but lizards, and snakes, and iguanas are reptiles, and salamanders are amphibians.
4. Amphibians also include frogs, and toads and newts.
5. Eagles geese ostriches turkeys chickens and ducks are classified as birds.

Exercise 3

Add two coordinate adjectives to modify each of the following phrases, inserting commas where required.

Example: *strong, beautiful* classical music

1. distant thunder
2. silver spoon
3. New York Yankees
4. miniature golf
5. Rolling Stones
6. loving couple
7. computer science
8. wheat bread
9. art museum
10. new math

51c Setting Off Introductory Elements

In most cases, an introductory element is followed by a comma. If the sentence's meaning will be clear without it, the comma can be omitted. When in doubt, however, you should include the comma.

(1) Dependent Clauses

An introductory dependent clause is generally set off from the rest of the sentence by a comma.

Although the CIA used to call undercover agents *penetration agents*, they now routinely refer to them as *moles*.

When war came to Baghdad, many victims were children.

If a dependent clause is short and designates time, you may omit the comma—provided the sentence will be clear without it.

> When I exercise I drink plenty of water.

NOTE: Do not use a comma to set off a dependent clause at the *end* of a sentence.

(2) Verbal and Prepositional Phrases

An introductory verbal phrase is usually set off by a comma.

> Thinking that this might be his last chance, Peary struggled toward the North Pole. (participial phrase)
>
> To write well, one must read a lot. (infinitive phrase)

An introductory prepositional phrase is also usually set off by a comma.

> During the Depression, movie attendance rose. (prepositional phrase)

However, if an introductory prepositional phrase is short and no ambiguity is possible, you may omit the comma.

> After the exam I took a four-hour nap.

Close-up: Using Commas with Verbal Phrases

A verbal phrase that serves as a subject is not set off by a comma.

See 32b1

> Laughing out loud, can release tension. (gerund phrase)
>
> To know him, is to love him. (infinitive phrase)

(3) Transitional Words and Phrases

When a transitional word or phrase begins a sentence, it is usually set off from the rest of the sentence with a comma.

> However, any plan that is enacted must be fair.
>
> In other words, we cannot act hastily.

Exercise 4

Add commas in the following paragraph where necessary to set off an introductory element from the rest of a sentence.

While childhood is shrinking adolescence is expanding. Whatever the reason girls are maturing earlier. The average onset of puberty is now two years earlier than it was only forty years ago. What's more both boys and girls are staying in the nest longer. At present, it is not unusual for children to stay in their parents' home until they are twenty or twenty-one, delaying adulthood and extending adolescence. To some who study the culture this increase in adolescence portends dire consequences. With teenage hormones running amuck for longer the problems of teenage pregnancy and sexually transmitted diseases loom large. Young boys' spending long periods of their lives without responsibilities is also a recipe for disaster. However others see this "youthing" of American culture in a more positive light. Without a doubt adolescents are creative, lively, and more willing to take risks. If we channel their energies carefully they could contribute, even in their extended adolescence, to American culture and technology.

51d Setting Off Nonessential Material

Sometimes words, phrases, or clauses *contribute* to the meaning of a sentence but are not *essential* for conveying the sentence's main point or emphasis. Use commas to set off such nonessential material whether it appears at the beginning, in the middle, or at the end of a sentence.

(1) Nonrestrictive Modifiers

Use commas to set off **nonrestrictive modifiers,** which supply information that is not essential to the meaning of the word or word group they modify. (Do *not* use commas to set off **restrictive modifiers,** which supply information that is essential to the meaning of the word or word group they modify.)

Nonrestrictive (commas required): Actors, who have inflated egos, are often insecure. (*All* actors—not just those with inflated egos—are insecure.)

Restrictive (no commas): Actors who have inflated egos are often insecure. (Only those actors with inflated egos—not all actors—are insecure.)

Adjective Clauses

Nonrestrictive: He ran for the bus, which was late as usual.

Restrictive: Speaking in public is something that most people fear.

Prepositional Phrases

Nonrestrictive: The clerk, with a nod, dismissed me.

Restrictive: The man with the gun demanded their money.

Verbal Phrases

Nonrestrictive: The marathoner, running her fastest, beat her previous record.

Restrictive: The candidates running for mayor have agreed to a debate.

Appositives

Nonrestrictive: *Citizen Kane*, Orson Welles's first film, made him famous.

Restrictive: The film *Citizen Kane* made Orson Welles famous.

Checklist: Restrictive and Nonrestrictive Modifiers

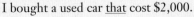

To determine whether a modifier is restrictive or nonrestrictive, ask yourself these questions:

- ☐ Is the modifier essential to the meaning of the noun it modifies (*The man with the gun*, not just any man)? If so, it is restrictive and does not take commas.
- ☐ Is the modifier introduced by *that* (*something that most people fear*)? If so, it is restrictive. *That* cannot introduce a nonrestrictive clause.
- ☐ Can you delete the relative pronoun without causing ambiguity or confusion (*something [that] most people fear*)? If so, the clause is restrictive.
- ☐ Is the appositive more specific than the noun that precedes it (*the film* Citizen Kane)? If so, it is restrictive.

Close-up: Using Commas with *That* and *Which*

That introduces only restrictive clauses, which are not set off by commas.

I bought a used car that cost $2,000.

Which can introduce both restrictive and nonrestrictive clauses.

Restrictive (no comma): I bought a used car which cost $2,000.

(continued)

Using commas with* that *and* which *(continued)

Nonrestrictive (commas needed): The used car I bought, which cost $2,000, broke down after a week.

NOTE: Many writers prefer to use *which* only to introduce nonrestrictive clauses.

http://kirsznermandell.wadsworth.com

Computer Tip: *That* or *Which*

Your word processor's grammar checker may label the use of *which* as an error when it introduces a restrictive clause (see Figure 51.1). It will prompt you to add commas, using *which* to introduce a nonrestrictive clause, or to change *which* to *that.* Review the meaning of your sentence, and revise accordingly.

Spelling and Grammar: English (U.S.)
"That" or "Which":
Only the books which are in the attic must be moved.
Suggestions:
books, which are in the attic,
OR
books that are in the attic

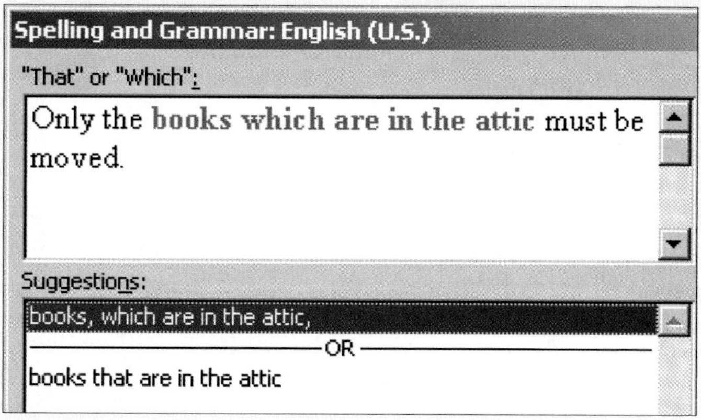

Figure 51.1 Sample grammar checker suggestion.

Exercise 5

Insert commas where necessary to set off nonrestrictive modifiers.

The Statue of Liberty which was dedicated in 1886 has undergone extensive renovation. Its supporting structure whose designer was the French engineer Alexandre Gustave Eiffel is made of iron. The Statue of Liberty created over a period of nine years by sculptor Frédéric-Auguste Bartholdi stands 151 feet tall. The people of France who were grateful for American help in the French Revolution raised the money to pay the sculptor who created the statue. The people of the United States contributing over $100,000 raised the money for the pedestal on which the statue stands.

(2) Transitional Words and Phrases

Transitional words and phrases—which include conjunctive adverbs like *however, therefore, thus,* and *nevertheless* as well as expressions like *for example* and *on the other hand*—qualify, clarify, and make connections. However, they are not essential to meaning. For this reason, they are always set off by commas when they interrupt a clause (as well as when they begin or end a sentence).

The Outward Bound program, for example, is considered safe.

In fact, Outward Bound has an excellent reputation.

Other programs are not so safe, however.

Close-up: Transitional Words and Phrases

When a transitional word or phrase joins two independent clauses, it must be preceded by a semicolon and followed by a comma.

Laughter is the best medicine; of course, penicillin also comes in handy sometimes.

(3) Contradictory Phrases

A phrase that expresses contradiction is usually set off by commas.

This medicine is taken after meals, never on an empty stomach.

Mark McGwire, not Sammy Sosa, was the first to break Roger Maris's home-run record.

(4) Absolute Phrases

An **absolute phrase,** which includes a noun or pronoun and a participle and modifies an entire independent clause, is always set off by a comma from the clause it modifies.

His fear increasing, he waited to enter the haunted house.

Many soldiers were lost in Southeast Asia, their bodies never recovered.

(5) Miscellaneous Nonessential Material

Other nonessential material usually set off by commas includes tag questions, names in direct address, mild interjections, and *yes* and *no.*

This is your first day on the job, isn't it?

I wonder, Mr. Honeywell, whether Mr. Albright deserves a raise.

Well, it's about time.

Yes, we have no bananas.

Exercise 6

Set off the nonessential elements in these sentences with commas. If a sentence is correct, mark it with a *C*.

Example: Piranhas, like sharks, will attack and eat almost anything if the opportunity arises.

1. Kermit the Frog is a Muppet a cross between a marionette and a puppet.
2. The common cold a virus is frequently spread by hand contact not by mouth.
3. The account in the Bible of Noah's Ark and the forty-day flood may be based on an actual deluge.
4. Many US welfare recipients, such as children, the aged, and the severely disabled, are unable to work.
5. The submarine *Nautilus* was the first to cross under the North Pole wasn't it?
6. The 1958 Ford Edsel was advertised with the slogan "Once you've seen it, you'll never forget it."
7. Superman was called Kal-El on the planet Krypton; on earth however he was known as Clark Kent not Kal-El.
8. Its sales topping any of his previous singles "Heartbreak Hotel" was Elvis Presley's first million-seller.
9. Two companies Nash and Hudson joined in 1954 to form American Motors.
10. A firefly is a beetle not a fly and a prairie dog is a rodent not a dog.

51e Using Commas in Other Conventional Contexts

(1) With Direct Quotations

In most cases, use commas to set off a direct quotation from the **identifying tag**—the phrase that identifies the speaker (*he said*, *she answered*, and so on).

Emerson said to Whitman, "I greet you at the beginning of a great career."

"I greet you at the beginning of a great career," Emerson said to Whitman.

"I greet you," Emerson said to Whitman, "at the beginning of a great career."

When the identifying tag comes between two complete sentences, however, the tag is introduced by a comma but followed by a period.

"Winning isn't everything," Vince Lombardi said. "It's the only thing."

If the first sentence of an interrupted quotation ends with a question mark or exclamation point, do not use commas.

"Should we hold the front page over?" she asked. "After all, it's a slow news day."

"Hold the front page over!" he cried. "This is the biggest story of the decade."

(2) With Titles or Degrees Following a Name

Hamlet, prince of Denmark, is Shakespeare's most famous character.

Michael Crichton, MD, wrote *Jurassic Park*.

(3) In Addresses and Dates

When a date or an address falls within a sentence, a comma follows the last element.

On August 30, 1983, the space shuttle *Challenger* was launched.

No comma separates the street number from the street or the state name from the ZIP code.

Her address is 600 West End Avenue, New York, NY 10024.

NOTE: When only the month and year are given, no commas are used: August 1983.

(4) In Salutations and Closings

In informal correspondence, use commas following salutations and closings. Also use commas in both informal and business correspondence following the complimentary close.

Dear John,	Love,
Dear Aunt Sophie,	Sincerely,

See 28a

NOTE: In business letters, always use a colon, not a comma, after the salutation.

(5) In Long Numbers

For a number of four digits or more, place a comma before every third digit, counting from the right.

1,200	120,000
12,000	1,200,000

NOTE: Commas are not used in long page and line numbers, address numbers, telephone numbers, or ZIP codes (or in four-digit year numbers).

ESL Tip

In some countries, writers use commas in decimal numbers where US writers use periods. When writing in English, remember to use periods in decimal numbers.

The total bill was $53,75.

The number $1\frac{3}{4}$ can be represented as the decimal number 1,75.

Exercise 7

Add commas where necessary to set off quotations, names, dates, addresses, and numbers.

1. India became independent on August 15 1947.
2. The UAW has more than 1500000 dues-paying members.
3. Nikita Khrushchev, former Soviet premier, once said "We will bury you!"
4. Mount St. Helens, northeast of Portland Oregon, began erupting on March 27 1980 and eventually killed at least thirty people.
5. Located at 1600 Pennsylvania Avenue Washington DC, the White House is a popular tourist attraction.
6. In 1956, playing before a crowd of 64519 fans in Yankee Stadium in New York New York, Don Larsen pitched the first perfect game in World Series history.
7. Lewis Thomas MD was born in Flushing New York and attended Harvard Medical School in Cambridge Massachusetts.
8. In 1967 2000000 people worldwide died of smallpox, but in 1977 only about twenty people died.

9. "The reports of my death" Mark Twain remarked "have been greatly exaggerated."
10. The French explorer Jean Nicolet landed at Green Bay Wisconsin in 1634, and in 1848 Wisconsin became the thirtieth state; it has 10355 lakes and a population of more than 4700000.

51f Using Commas to Prevent Misreading

In some cases, you need to use a comma to avoid ambiguity. Consider the following sentence.

> Those who can, sprint the final lap.

Without the comma, *can* appears to be an auxiliary verb ("Those who can sprint . . ."), and the sentence seems incomplete. Because the comma tells readers to pause, it eliminates confusion.

Also use a comma to acknowledge the omission of a repeated word, usually a verb, and to separate words repeated consecutively.

> Pam carried the box; Tim, the suitcase.
>
> Everything bad that could have happened, happened.

Exercise 8

Add commas where necessary to prevent misreading.

Example: Whatever will be, will be.

1. According to Bob Frank's computer is obsolete.
2. Da Gama explored Florida; Pizarro Peru.
3. By Monday evening students must begin preregistration for fall classes.
4. Whatever they built they built with care.
5. When batting practice carefully.
6. Brunch includes warm muffins topped with whipped butter and freshly brewed coffee.
7. Students go to school to learn not to play sports.
8. Technology has made what once seemed not possible possible.

Exercise 9

Add commas to the following sentences where needed, and be prepared to explain why each is necessary. If a sentence is correct, mark it with a *C*.

Example: Once again ^ Congress is looking to make changes in immigration law.

1. According to some critics this test which new citizens must take before they are naturalized is simple and shallow.
2. Others claim that making the test more difficult would be unfair because many graduates of American high schools cannot answer the basic civics questions about the design of the American flag the structure of the US government and the events of American political history required by the test.
3. Some fear that too many new citizens from foreign countries will undermine core American values but others argue that those values came from earlier immigrants and that change is not necessarily bad.
4. Fear of immigrants while seemingly unfounded is not new.
5. In the 1940s the American government forced immigrants from Japan and their American-born children into internment camps after the Japanese bombed Pearl Harbor initiating America's involvement in World War II.

51g Editing Misused Commas

Do not use commas in the following situations.

(1) To Join Two Independent Clauses

A comma alone cannot join two independent clauses; it must be followed by a coordinating conjunction. Using just a comma to connect two independent clauses creates a comma splice.

The season was unusually cool, ^but the orange crop was not seriously harmed.

(2) To Set Off Restrictive Modifiers

Commas are not used to set off restrictive modifiers.

Women, who seek to be equal to men, lack ambition.

The film, *Malcolm X*, was directed by Spike Lee.

(3) Between Inseparable Grammatical Constructions

Do not place a comma between grammatical elements that cannot be logically separated: a subject and its predicate, a verb and its complement or direct object, a preposition and its object, or an adjective and the word or phrase it modifies.

A woman with dark red hair, opened the door. (comma incorrectly placed between subject and predicate)

Louis Braille developed, an alphabet of raised dots for the blind. (comma incorrectly placed between verb and object)

They relaxed somewhat during, the last part of the obstacle course. (comma incorrectly placed between preposition and object)

Wind-dispersed weeds include the well-known and plentiful, dandelions, milkweed, and thistle. (comma incorrectly placed between adjective and words it modifies)

(4) Between a Verb and an Indirect Quotation or Indirect Question

Do not use commas between verbs and indirect quotations or between verbs and indirect questions.

General Douglas MacArthur vowed, that he would return. (comma incorrectly placed between verb and indirect quotation)

The landlord asked, if we would sign a two-year lease. (comma incorrectly placed between verb and indirect question)

(5) Between Phrases Linked by Correlative Conjunctions

Commas are not used to separate two phrases linked by **correlative conjunctions**.

Forty years ago, most college students had access to neither photocopiers, nor pocket calculators.

Both typewriters, and tape recorders were generally available, however.

(6) In Compounds That Are Not Composed of Independent Clauses

Do not use commas before coordinating conjunctions like *and* or *but* when they join two elements of a compound subject, predicate, object, complement, or auxiliary verb.

Plagues, and pestilence were common during the Middle Ages. (compound subject)

Many women thirty-five and older are returning to college, and tend to be good students. (compound predicate)

Mattel has marketed a doctor's lab coat, and an astronaut suit for its Barbie doll. (compound object)

People buy bottled water because it is pure, and fashionable. (compound complement)

She can, and will be ready to run in the primary. (compound auxiliary verb)

(7) Before a Dependent Clause at the End of a Sentence

Commas are generally not used before a dependent clause that falls at the end of a sentence.

Jane Addams founded Hull House, because she wanted to help Chicago's poor.

Exercise 10

Unnecessary commas have been intentionally added to some of the sentences that follow. Delete any unnecessary commas. If a sentence is correct, mark it with a *C*.

Example: Spring fever, is a common ailment.

1. A book is like a garden, carried in the pocket. (Arab proverb)
2. Like the iodine content of kelp, air freight, is something most Americans have never pondered. (*Time*)
3. Charles Rolls, and Frederick Royce manufactured the first Rolls-Royce Silver Ghost, in 1907.
4. The hills ahead of him were rounded domes of grey granite, smooth as a bald man's pate, and completely free of vegetation. (Wilbur Smith, *Flight of the Falcon*)
5. Food here is scarce, and cafeteria food is vile, but the great advantage to Russian raw materials, when one can get hold of them, is that they are always fresh and untampered with. (Andrea Lee, *Russian Journal*)

Chapter 52

Using Semicolons

Frequently Asked Questions

When do I use a semicolon? (p. 891)
Do I introduce a list with a semicolon or a colon? (p. 897)

The **semicolon** is used only between items of equal grammatical rank: two independent clauses, two phrases, and so on.

52a Separating Independent Clauses

Use a semicolon between closely related independent clauses that convey parallel or contrasting information but are not joined by a coordinating conjunction.

> Paul Revere's *The Boston Massacre* is traditional American protest art; Edward Hicks's paintings are socially conscious art with a religious strain.

NOTE: Using only a comma or no punctuation at all between independent clauses creates a comma splice or fused sentence.

See Ch.38

Exercise 1

Add semicolons where necessary to separate independent clauses. Then, reread the paragraph to make certain no comma splices or fused sentences remain.

Example: *Birth of a Nation* was one of the earliest epic movies; it was based on the book *The Klansman*.

During the 1950s movie attendance declined because of the increasing popularity of television. As a result, numerous gimmicks were introduced to draw audiences into theaters. One of the first of these was Cinerama, in this technique three pictures were shot side by side and projected onto a curved screen. Next came 3-D, complete with special glasses, *Bwana Devil* and *The Creature from the Black Lagoon* were two early 3-D ventures. *The Robe* was the first picture filmed in Cinemascope in this technique a shrunken image was projected on a screen twice as wide as it was tall. Smell-O-Vision (or Aroma-rama) was a short-lived gimmick that enabled audiences to smell what they were viewing problems developed when it became impossible to get one odor out of the theater in time for the next smell to be introduced. William Castle's *Thirteen Ghosts* introduced special glasses for cowardly viewers who wanted to be able to control what they saw, the red part of the glasses was the "ghost viewer" and the green part was the "ghost remover." Perhaps the ultimate in movie gimmicks accompanied the film *The Tingler* when this film was shown seats in the theater were wired to generate mild electric shocks. Unfortunately, the shocks set off a chain reaction that led to hysteria in the theater. During the 1960s, such gimmicks all but disappeared, viewers were able once again to simply sit back and enjoy a movie. In 1997, *Mr. Payback*, a short interactive film that contained elements of a videogame, brought back the gimmick, it allowed viewers to vote on how they wanted the plot to unfold.

Exercise 2

Combine each of the following sentence groups into one sentence that contains only two independent clauses. Use a semicolon to join the two clauses. You will need to add, delete, relocate, or change some words; keep experimenting until you find the arrangement that best conveys the sentence's meaning.

Example: The Congo River Rapids is a ride at the Dark Continent in Tampa, Florida~~.~~ *; riders* ~~Riders~~ raft down the river~~.~~ *, gliding* ~~They glide~~ alongside jungle plants and animals.

1. Theme parks offer exciting rides. They are thrill packed. They flirt with danger.
2. Free Fall is located in Atlanta's Six Flags over Georgia. In this ride, riders travel up a 128-foot-tall tower. They plunge down at fifty-five miles per hour.
3. In the Sky Whirl, riders go 115 feet up in the air and circle about seventy-five times. This ride is located in Great America. Great America parks are in Gurnee, Illinois, and Santa Clara, California.
4. The Kamikaze Slide can be found at the Wet'n Wild parks in Arlington, Texas, and Orlando, Florida. This ride is a slide three hundred feet long. It extends sixty feet into the air.
5. Viper is an exciting ride. It is found at Six Flags Great Adventure in Jackson, New Jersey. Its outside loop has a 360-degree spiral.
6. Astroworld in Houston, Texas, boasts Greezed Lightnin'. This ride is an eighty-foot-high loop. The ride goes from zero to sixty miles per hour in four seconds and moves forward and backward.

7. The Beast is at Kings Island near Cincinnati, Ohio. The Beast is a wooden roller coaster. It has a 7,400-foot track and goes seventy miles per hour.
8. Busch Gardens in Williamsburg, Virginia, features Escape from Pompeii. This is a water ride. It allows riders to explore ruins and see Mount Vesuvius.
9. Wild Arctic is at Sea World in Orlando, Florida. This ride includes a simulated helicopter flight. The flight goes to Base Station Wild Arctic. The ride also goes to a wrecked ship.
10. At Busch Gardens Tampa Bay in Tampa, Florida, Egypt is a thrill-packed attraction. It features an inverted roller coaster with cars hanging from the top. A replica of King Tut's tomb is also featured.

52b Separating Independent Clauses Introduced by Transitional Words and Phrases

Use a semicolon before a transitional word or phrase that joins two independent clauses. (The transitional element is followed by a comma.)

Thomas Jefferson brought two hundred vanilla beans and a recipe for vanilla ice cream back from France; thus, he gave America its all-time favorite ice-cream flavor.

Exercise 3

Combine each of the following sentence groups into one sentence that contains only two independent clauses. Use a semicolon and the transitional word or phrase in parentheses to join the two clauses, adding commas within clauses where necessary. You will need to add, delete, relocate, or change some words. There is no one correct version; keep experimenting until you find the arrangement you feel is most effective.

Example: The Aleutian Islands, ~~are~~ located off the west coast of Alaska, ~~They~~ are an extremely remote chain of islands; in fact, they ~~They~~ are sometimes called America's Siberia. (in fact)

1. The Aleutians lie between the North Pacific Ocean and the Bering Sea. The weather there is harsh. Dense fog, 100-mph winds, and even tidal waves and earthquakes are not uncommon. (for example)

2. These islands constitute North America's largest network of active volcanoes. The Aleutians boast some beautiful scenery. The islands are relatively unexplored. (still)
3. The Aleutians are home to a wide variety of birds. Numerous animals, such as fur seals and whales, are found there. These islands may house the largest concentration of marine animals in the world. (in fact)
4. During World War II, thousands of American soldiers were stationed on Attu Island. They were stationed on Adak Island. The Japanese eventually occupied both islands. (however)
5. The islands' original population of native Aleuts was drastically reduced in the eighteenth century by Russian fur traders. Today the total population is only about 8,500. US military employees comprise more than half of this. (consequently)

(Adapted from *National Geographic*)

52c Separating Items in a Series

Use semicolons between items in a series when one or more of these items include commas.

Three papers are posted on the bulletin board outside the building: a description of the exams**;** a list of appeal procedures for students who fail**;** and an employment ad from an automobile factory, addressed specifically to candidates whose appeals are turned down. (Andrea Lee, *Russian Journal*)

Laramie, Wyoming**;** Wyoming, Delaware**;** and Delaware, Ohio, were three of the places they visited.

Exercise 4

Replace commas with semicolons where necessary to separate internally punctuated items in a series. (For information on use of semicolons with quotation marks, **see 54e2.**)

Example: Luxury automobiles have some strong selling points: they are status symbols; some, such as the Corvette, appreciate in value; and they are usually comfortable and well appointed.

1. The history of modern art seems at times to be a collection of "isms": Impressionism, a term that applies to painters who

attempted to depict contemporary life by reproducing an "impression" of what the eye sees, Abstract Expressionism, which applies to artists who stress emotion and the unconscious in their nonrepresentational works, and, more recently, Minimalism, which applies to painters and sculptors whose work reasserts the physical reality of the object.

2. Although the term *Internet* is widely used to refer only to the World Wide Web and email, the Internet consists of a variety of discrete elements, including newsgroups, which allow users to post and receive messages on an unbelievably broad range of topics, interactive communication forums, such as blogs, discussion forums, and chat rooms, and FTP, which allows users to download material from remote computers.
3. Three of rock and roll's best-known guitar heroes played with the "British Invasion" group The Yardbirds: Eric Clapton, the group's first lead guitarist, went on to play with John Mayall's Bluesbreakers, Cream, and Blind Faith, and is now a popular solo act, Jeff Beck, the group's second guitarist, though not as visible as Clapton, made rock history with the Jeff Beck Group and inventive solo albums, and Jimmy Page, the group's third and final guitarist, transformed the remnants of the original group into the premier heavy metal band, Led Zeppelin.
4. Some of the most commonly confused words in English are *aggravate*, which means "to worsen," and *irritate*, which means "to annoy," *continual*, which means "recurring at intervals," and *continuous*, which means "an action occurring without interruption," *imply*, which means "to hint, suggest," and *infer*, which means "to conclude from," and *compliment*, which means "to praise," and *complement*, which means "to complete or add to."
5. Tennessee Williams wrote *The Glass Menagerie*, which is about Laura Wingfield, a disabled young woman, and her family, *A Streetcar Named Desire*, which starred Marlon Brando, and *Cat on a Hot Tin Roof*, which won a Pulitzer Prize.

Exercise 5

Combine each of the following sentence groups into one sentence that includes a series of items separated by semicolons. You will need to add, delete, relocate, or change words. Try several versions of each sentence until you find the most effective arrangement.

Example: Collecting baseball cards is a worthwhile hobby, ~~It~~ because it helps children learn how to bargain and trade, ~~It also~~ ; it encourages them to compare data about ballplayers, ; and, most ~~Most~~ important, it introduces them to positive role models.

1. A good dictionary offers definitions of words, including some obsolete and nonstandard words. It provides information about synonyms, usage, and word origins. It also offers information on pronunciation and syllabication.
2. The flags of the Scandinavian countries all depict a cross on a solid background. Denmark's flag is red with a white cross. Norway's flag is also red, but its cross is blue, outlined in white. Sweden's flag is blue with a yellow cross.
3. Over one hundred international collectors' clubs are thriving today. One of these associations is the Cola Clan, whose members buy, sell, and trade Coca-Cola memorabilia. Another is the Citrus Label Society. There is also a Cookie Cutter Collectors' Club.
4. Listening to the radio special, we heard "Shuffle Off to Buffalo" and "Moon over Miami," both of which are about eastern cities. We heard "By the Time I Get to Phoenix" and "I Left My Heart in San Francisco," which mention western cities. Finally, we heard "The Star-Spangled Banner," which seemed to be an appropriate finale.
5. There are three principal types of contact lenses. Hard contact lenses, also called "conventional lenses," are easy to clean and handle and quite sturdy. Soft lenses, which are easily contaminated and must be cleaned and disinfected daily, are less durable. Gas-permeable lenses, sometimes advertised as "semihard" or "semisoft" lenses, look and feel like hard lenses but are more easily contaminated and less durable.

52d Editing Misused Semicolons

Do not use semicolons in the following situations.

(1) Between a Dependent and an Independent Clause

Use a comma, not a semicolon, between a dependent and an independent clause.

Because new drugs can now suppress the body's immune reaction~~;~~, fewer organ transplants are rejected by the body.

http://kirsznermandell.wadsworth.com

Computer Tip: Editing Misused Semicolons

Your word processor's grammar checker will highlight certain misused semicolons and frequently offer suggestions for revision (See Figure 52.1).

Spelling and Grammar: English (U.S.)

Comma Use:

Although the library is usually open year-**round;** it will be closed this fall due to renovations.

Suggestions:

round,

Figure 52.1 Sample grammar checker suggestion.

(2) Between a Phrase and a Clause

Use a comma, not a semicolon, between a phrase and a clause.

Increasing rapidly~~;~~, computer crime poses a challenge for government, financial, and military agencies.

(3) To Introduce a List

FAQs

Use a colon, not a semicolon, to introduce a list.

See 55a1

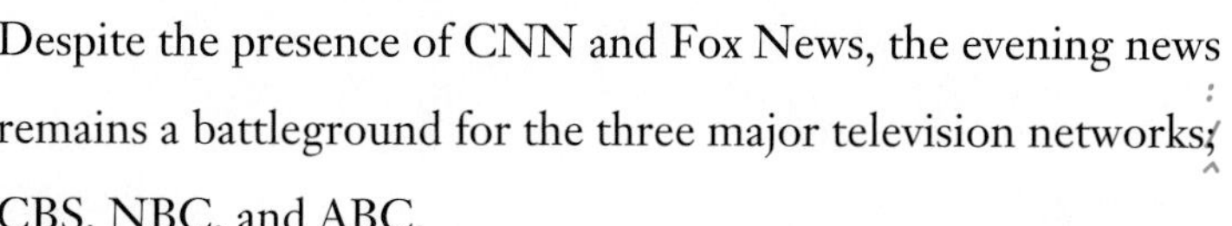

Despite the presence of CNN and Fox News, the evening news remains a battleground for the three major television networks~~;~~: CBS, NBC, and ABC.

NOTE: Always use a complete sentence before a colon that introduces a list.

(4) To Introduce a Quotation

Do not use a semicolon to introduce quoted speech or writing.

Marie Antoinette may not have said~~;~~, “Let them eat cake.”

Exercise 6

Read the following paragraph carefully. Then, add semicolons where necessary, and delete incorrectly used ones, substituting other punctuation where necessary.

> Barnstormers were aviators; who toured the country after World War I, giving people short airplane rides and exhibitions of stunt flying, in fact, the name *barnstormer* was derived from the use of barns as airplane hangars. Americans' interest in airplanes had all but disappeared after the war. The barnstormers helped popularize flying; especially in rural areas. Some were pilots who had flown in the war; others were just young men with a thirst for adventure. They gave people rides in airplanes; sometimes charging a dollar a minute. For most passengers, this was their first ride in an airplane, in fact, sometimes it was their first sight of one. After Lindbergh's 1927 flight across the Atlantic; Americans suddenly needed no encouragement to embrace aviation. The barnstormers had outlived their usefulness; and an era ended. (Adapted from William Goldman, *Adventures in the Screen Trade*)

Chapter 53

Using Apostrophes

Frequently Asked Questions

How do I form the possessive of a singular word that already ends in -s? (p. 899)
How do I form the possessive of plural words that end in -s? (p. 900)
What's the difference between its *and* it's? (p. 903)

Use an apostrophe to form the possessive case, to indicate omissions in contractions, and to form certain plurals.

53a Forming the Possessive Case

The possessive case indicates ownership. In English, the possessive case of nouns and indefinite pronouns is indicated either with a phrase that includes the word *of* (the hands *of* the clock) or with an apostrophe and, in most cases, an *s* (the clock'*s* hands).

(1) Singular Nouns and Indefinite Pronouns

To form the possessive case of singular nouns and indefinite pronouns, add *'s*.

> "The Monk's Tale" is one of Chaucer's *Canterbury Tales*.
>
> When we would arrive was anyone's guess.

(2) Singular Nouns Ending in *-s*

To form the possessive case of singular nouns that end in *-s*, add *'s* in most cases.

> Reading Henry James's *The Ambassadors* was not Maris's idea of fun.
>
> The class's time was changed to 8 a.m.

NOTE: With some singular nouns that end in *-s*, pronouncing the possessive ending as a separate syllable can sound awkward. In such cases, it is acceptable to use just an apostrophe: Crispus Attucks' death, Aristophanes' *Lysistrata*.

An apostrophe is not used to form the possessive case of a title that already contains an *'s* ending; use a phrase instead.

Awkward: *A Midsummer Night's Dream*'s staging

Revised: the staging of *A Midsummer Night's Dream*

(3) Plural Nouns Ending in *-s*

To form the possessive case of regular plural nouns (those that end in *-s* or *-es*), add only an apostrophe.

The Readers' Guide to Periodical Literature is available online.

Laid-off employees received two weeks' severance pay and three months' medical benefits.

The Lopezes' three children are triplets.

(4) Irregular Plural Nouns

To form the possessive case of nouns that have irregular plurals, add *'s*.

Long after they were gone, the geese's honking could still be heard.

The Children's Hour is a play by Lillian Hellman; *The Women's Room* is a novel by Marilyn French.

The two oxen's yokes were securely attached to the cart.

(5) Compound Nouns or Groups of Words

To form the possessive case of compound nouns or of word groups, add *'s* to the last word.

The editor-in-chief's position is open.

He accepted the secretary of state's resignation under protest.

This is someone else's responsibility.

(6) Two or More Items

To indicate individual ownership of two or more items, add *'s* to each item.

Ernest Hemingway's and Gertrude Stein's writing styles have some similarities. (Hemingway and Stein have two separate writing styles.)

To indicate joint ownership, add *'s* only to the last item.

Gilbert and Sullivan's operettas include *The Pirates of Penzance* and *The Mikado*. (Gilbert and Sullivan collaborated on both operettas.)

Exercise 1

Change the modifying phrases that follow the nouns to possessive forms that precede the nouns.

Example: the pen belonging to my aunt

my aunt's pen

1. the songs recorded by Ray Charles
2. the red glare of the rockets
3. the idea Warren had
4. the housekeeper Rick and Leslie hired
5. the first choice of everyone
6. the dinner given by Harris
7. furniture designed by William Morris
8. the climate of the Virgin Islands
9. the sport the Russells play
10. the role created by the French actress

Exercise 2

Change each word or phrase in parentheses to its possessive form. In some cases, you may have to use a phrase to indicate the possessive.

Example: The (children) toys were scattered all over their (parents) bedroom.

The children's toys were scattered all over their parents' bedroom.

1. Jane (Addams) settlement house was called Hull House.
2. (*A Room of One's Own*) popularity increased with the rise of feminism.
3. The (chief petty officer) responsibilities are varied.
4. Vietnamese (restaurants) numbers have grown dramatically in ten (years) time.
5. (Charles Dickens) and (Mark Twain) works have sold millions of copies.

53b Indicating Omissions in Contractions

(1) Omitted Letters

Apostrophes replace omitted letters in contractions that combine a pronoun and a verb (*he* + *will* = *he'll*) or the elements of a verb phrase (*do* + *not* = *don't*).

Frequently Used Contractions

it's (it is, it has)
he's (he is, he has)
she's (she is, she has)
who's (who is, who has)
isn't (is not)
wouldn't (would not)
couldn't (could not)
don't (do not)
won't (will not)

let's (let us)
we've (we have)
they're (they are)
we'll (we will)
I'm (I am)
we're (we are)
you'd (you would)
we'd (we would)
they'd (they had)

NOTE: Contractions are generally not used in college writing.

http://kirsznermandell.wadsworth.com

Computer Tip: Revising Contractions

If you set your word processor's writing style to Formal or Technical, the grammar checker will highlight contractions and offer suggestions for revision (see Figure 53.1).

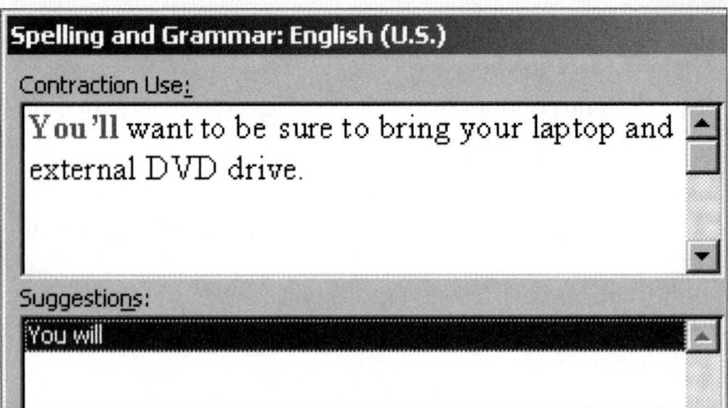
Spelling and Grammar: English (U.S.)
Contraction Use:
You'll want to be sure to bring your laptop and external DVD drive.
Suggestions:
You will

Figure 53.1 Sample grammar checker suggestion.

Close-up: Using Apostrophes

Be careful not to confuse contractions (which always include apostrophes) with the possessive forms of personal pronouns (which never include apostrophes).

Contractions	**Possessive Forms**
Who's on first?	Whose book is this?
They're playing our song.	Their team is winning.
It's raining.	Its paws were muddy.
You're a real pal.	Your résumé is very impressive.

(2) Omitted Numbers

In informal writing, an apostrophe may be used to represent the century in a year.

Crash of '29   class of '06   '57 Chevy

In college writing, however, write out the year in full: *the Crash of 1929, the class of 2006, a 1957 Chevrolet.*

Exercise 3

In the following sentences, correct any errors in the use of apostrophes. (Remember, apostrophes are used in contractions but not in possessive pronouns.) If a sentence is correct, mark it with a *C*.

Example: ~~Who's~~ *Whose* troops were sent to Korea?

1. Its never easy to choose a major; whatever you decide, your bound to have second thoughts.
2. Olive Oyl asked, "Whose that knocking at my door?"
3. Their watching too much television; in fact, they're eyes are glazed.
4. Whose coming along on the backpacking trip?
5. The horse had been badly treated; it's spirit was broken.
6. Your correct in assuming its a challenging course.
7. Sometimes even you're best friends won't tell you your boring.
8. They're training had not prepared them for the hardships they faced.
9. It's too early to make a positive diagnosis.
10. Robert Frost wrote the poem that begins, "Who's woods these are I think I know."

53c Forming Plurals

In a few special situations, add *'s* to form plurals.

Forming Plurals with Apostrophes

Plurals of Letters

The Italian language has no *j*'s or *k*'s.

Plurals of Words Referred to as Words

The supervisor would accept no *if*'s, *and*'s, or *but*'s.

See 57c

NOTE: Elements spoken of as themselves (letters, numerals, or words) are set in italic type; the plural ending, however, is not.

NOTE: Apostrophes are not used in plurals of abbreviations (including acronyms) or numbers.

DVDs WACs 1960s

Exercise 4

In the following sentences, form correct plurals for the letters and words in parentheses. Underline to indicate italics where necessary.

Example: The word *bubbles* contains three (b).
The word *bubbles* contains three *b*'s.

1. She closed her letter with a row of (x) and (o) to indicate kisses and hugs.
2. The three (R) are reading, writing, and 'rithmetic.
3. The report included far too many (maybe) and too few (definitely).
4. The word bookkeeper contains two (o), two (k), and three (e).
5. His letter included many (please) and (thank you).

53d Editing Misused Apostrophes

Do not use apostrophes with plural nouns that are not possessive.

The Thompson's are not at home.

Down vest's are very warm.

The Philadelphia Seventy Sixer's are exciting to watch.

Do not use apostrophes to form the possessive case of personal pronouns.

This ticket must be your's or her's.

The next turn is their's.

Her doll had lost it's right eye.

The next great moment in history is our's.

NOTE: Be especially careful not to confuse the possessive forms of personal pronouns with contractions.

See 53b1

Exercise 5

In the following sentences, correct all errors in the use of apostrophes to form noun plurals or the possessive case of personal pronouns.

Example: Dr. Sampson's lecture's were more interesting than her's.

1. The Schaefer's seats are right next to our's.
2. Most of the college's in the area offer computer courses open to outsider's as well as to their own students.
3. The network completely revamped it's daytime programming.
4. Is the responsibility for the hot dog concession Cynthia's or your's?
5. Romantic poets are his favorite's.
6. Debbie returned the books to the library, forgetting they were her's.
7. Cultural revolution's do not occur very often, but when they do they bring sweeping change's.
8. Roll-top desk's are eagerly sought by antique dealer's.
9. A flexible schedule is one of their priorities, but it isn't one of our's.
10. Is your's the red house or the brown one?

Chapter 54

Using Quotation Marks

Frequently Asked Questions

How do I punctuate quotations that are introduced by phrases like he said*?* (p. 907)

Do I use quotation marks with a long quotation? (p. 909)

Are lines of poetry always set off with quotation marks? (p. 910)

Which titles require quotation marks? (p. 911)

Do I put commas and periods inside or outside quotation marks? (p. 912)

What do I do about a quotation inside another quotation? (p. 913)

Use quotation marks to set off brief passages of quoted speech or writing, to set off certain titles, and to set off words used in special ways. Do not use quotation marks when quoting long passages of prose or poetry.

54a Setting Off Quoted Speech or Writing

When you quote a word, phrase, or brief passage of someone else's speech or writing, enclose the quoted material in a pair of quotation marks.

> Gloria Steinem said, "We are becoming the men we once hoped to marry."
>
> In an essay about advertising in women's magazines, Gloria Steinem wrote, "When *Ms.* began, we didn't even consider *not* taking ads."

Close-up: Using Quotation Marks with Dialogue

When you record **dialogue** (conversation between two or more people), enclose the quoted words in quotation marks. Begin a new paragraph each time a new speaker is introduced.

When you are quoting several paragraphs of dialogue by one speaker, begin each new paragraph with quotation marks. However, use closing quotation marks only at the end of the *entire quoted passage*, not at the end of each paragraph.

Special rules govern the punctuation of a quotation when it is used with an **identifying tag,** a phrase (such as *he said*) that identifies the speaker or writer. Punctuation guidelines for various situations involving identifying tags are outlined below.

(1) Identifying Tag in the Middle of a Quoted Passage

Use a pair of commas to set off an identifying tag that interrupts a quoted passage.

"In the future," pop artist Andy Warhol once said, "everyone will be world famous for fifteen minutes."

If the identifying tag follows a completed sentence but the quoted passage continues, use a period after the tag, and begin the new sentence with a capital letter and quotation marks.

"Be careful," Erin warned. "Reptiles can be tricky."

(2) Identifying Tag at the Beginning of a Quoted Passage

Use a comma after an identifying tag that introduces quoted speech or writing.

The Raven repeated, "Nevermore."

Use a colon instead of a comma before a quotation if the identifying tag is a complete sentence.

She gave her final answer: "No."

http://kirsznermandell.wadsworth.com

Computer Tip: Checking Punctuation with Quotation Marks

Your word processor's grammar checker will often highlight missing punctuation in sentences containing quotation marks and offer suggestions for revision (see Figure 54.1).

(continued)

Checking punctuation with quotation marks (continued)

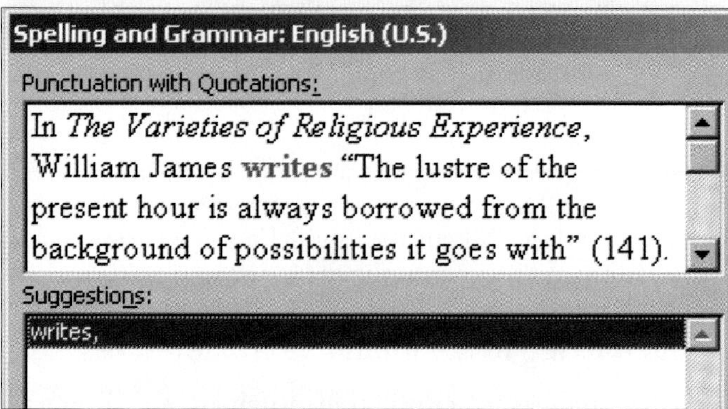
Spelling and Grammar: English (U.S.)
Punctuation with Quotations:
In The Varieties of Religious Experience, William James writes "The lustre of the present hour is always borrowed from the background of possibilities it goes with" (141).
Suggestions:
writes,

Figure 54.1 Sample grammar checker suggestion.

(3) Identifying Tag at the End of a Quoted Passage

Use a comma to set off a quotation from an identifying tag that follows it.

> "Be careful out there," the sergeant warned.

If the quotation ends with a question mark or an exclamation point, use that punctuation mark instead of the comma. In this situation, the tag begins with a lowercase letter even though it follows end punctuation.

> "Is Ankara the capital of Turkey?" she asked.
>
> "Oh boy!" he cried.

NOTE: Commas and periods are always placed *inside* quotation marks. For information on placement of other punctuation marks with quotation marks, **see 54e.**

Exercise 1

Add quotation marks to these sentences where necessary to set off quotations from identifying tags.

Example: Wordsworth's phrase "splendour in the grass" was used as the title of a movie about young lovers.

1. Few people can explain what Descartes's words I think, therefore I am actually mean.

2. Gertrude Stein said, You are all a lost generation.
3. Freedom of speech does not guarantee anyone the right to yell fire in a crowded theater, she explained.
4. There's no place like home, Dorothy insisted.
5. If everyone will sit down the teacher announced the exam will begin.

54b Setting Off Long Prose Passages and Poetry

(1) Long Prose Passages

When you quote a short prose passage, set it off in quotation marks, and run it into the text.

> Galsworthy describes Aunt Juley as "prostrated by the blow" (329).

However, do not enclose a **long prose passage** (a passage of more than four lines) in quotation marks. Instead, set it off by indenting the entire passage one inch (or ten spaces) from the left-hand margin. Double-space above and below the quoted passage, and double-space between lines within it. Introduce the passage with a colon.

> The following portrait of Aunt Juley illustrates several of the devices Galsworthy uses throughout The Forsyte Saga, such as a journalistic detachment that is almost cruel in its scrutiny, a subtle sense of the grotesque, and an ironic stance:
>
>> Aunt Juley stayed in her room, prostrated by the blow. Her face, discoloured by tears, was divided into compartments by the little ridges of pouting flesh which had swollen with emotion. . . . At fixed intervals she went to her drawer, and took from beneath the lavender bags a fresh pocket-handkerchief. Her warm heart could not bear the thought that Ann was lying there so cold. (329)
>
> Many similar portraits of characters appear throughout the novel.

NOTE: With long prose passages, parenthetical documentation is placed one space *after* the end punctuation. (With short prose passages, parenthetical documentation goes *before* the end punctuation.)

Close-up: Quoting Long Prose Passages

When you quote a long prose passage that is a single paragraph, do not indent the first line. When quoting two or more paragraphs, however, indent the first line of each paragraph (including the first) *three* additional spaces. If the first sentence of the quoted passage does not begin a paragraph in the source, do not indent—but do indent the first line of each subsequent paragraph. If the passage you are quoting includes material set in quotation marks, keep the quotation marks.

(2) Poetry

Treat one line of poetry like a short prose passage: enclose it in quotation marks and run it into the text.

```
One of John Donne's best-known poems begins with
the line, "Go and catch a falling star."
```

If you quote two or three lines of poetry, separate the lines with slashes (/), and run the quotation into the text. (Leave one space before and one space after the slash.)

```
Alexander Pope writes, "True Ease in Writing comes
from Art, not Chance, / As those move easiest who
have learned to dance."
```

If you quote more than three lines of poetry, set them off like a long prose passage. (For special emphasis, you may set off fewer lines in this manner.) Do not use quotation marks, and be sure to reproduce punctuation, spelling, capitalization, and indentation *exactly* as they appear in the poem.

```
     Wilfred Owen, a poet who was killed in action in World
War I, expressed the horrors of war with vivid imagery:
          Bent double, like old beggars under sacks,
          Knock-kneed, coughing like hags, we cursed
             through sludge,
          Till on the haunting flares we turned our backs
          And towards our distant rest began to trudge.
             (lines 1-4)
```

54c Setting Off Titles

Titles of short works and titles of parts of long works are enclosed in quotation marks. Other titles are italicized.

Titles Requiring Quotation Marks

Articles in Magazines, Newspapers, and Professional Journals
"Why Johnny Can't Write"

Essays, Short Stories, Short Poems, and Songs
"Fenimore Cooper's Literary Offenses" "Flying Home"
"The Road Not Taken" "The Star-Spangled Banner"

Chapters or Sections of Books
"Miss Sharp Begins to Make Friends"

Episodes of Radio or Television Series
"Lucy Goes to the Hospital"

See 57a for a list of titles that require italics.

NOTE: MLA style recommends underlining to indicate italics.

Exercise 2

Add quotation marks to the following sentences where necessary to set off titles. If italics are incorrectly used, substitute quotation marks. Place commas and periods inside quotation marks.

Example: Canadian author Margaret Atwood has written stories, such as ~~Rape Fantasies,~~ "Rape Fantasies," and poems, such as "You Fit Into Me."

1. One of the essays from her new book *Good Bones and Simple Murder* was originally published in *Harper's* magazine.
2. Her collection of poems, *Morning in the Burned House*, contains the moving poem *In the Secular Night*.
3. You may have seen the movie *The Handmaid's Tale*, starring Robert Duvall, based on her best-selling novel.
4. *Surfacing* was the first book of hers I read, but my favorite work of hers is the short story Hair Ball.
5. I wasn't surprised to find her poems The Animals in the Country and This Is a Photograph of Me in our English textbook last year.

54d Setting Off Words Used in Special Ways

Enclose a word used in a special or unusual way in quotation marks. (If you use the phrase *so-called* before an unusual usage, do not also use quotation marks.)

> It was clear that adults approved of children who were "readers," but it was not at all clear why this was so. (Annie Dillard)

Also enclose a **coinage**—an invented word—in quotation marks.

> After the twins were born, the minivan became a "babymobile."

54e Using Quotation Marks with Other Punctuation

At the end of a quotation, punctuation is sometimes placed inside quotation marks and sometimes placed outside them.

(1) With Final Commas or Periods

At the end of a quotation, place a comma or period *inside* the quotation marks.

> Many, like the poet Robert Frost, think about "the road not taken," but not many have taken "the one less traveled by."

(2) With Final Semicolons or Colons

At the end of a quotation, place a semicolon or colon *outside* the quotation marks.

> Students who do not pass the test receive "certificates of completion"; those who pass are awarded diplomas.
>
> Taxpayers were pleased with the first of the candidate's promised "sweeping new reforms": a balanced budget.

(3) With Question Marks, Exclamation Points, and Dashes

If a question mark, exclamation point, or dash is part of the quotation, place the punctuation mark *inside* the quotation marks.

> "Who's there?" she demanded.
>
> "Stop!" he cried.
>
> "Should we leave now, or—" Vicki paused, unable to continue.

If a question mark, exclamation point, or dash is *not* part of the quotation, place the punctuation mark *outside* the quotation marks.

> Did you finish reading "The Black Cat"?
>
> Whatever you do, don't yell "Uncle"!
>
> The first story—Updike's "*A & P*"—provoked discussion.

If both the quotation and the sentence are questions or exclamations, place the punctuation mark *outside* the quotation marks.

> Who asked, "Is Paris burning"?

Close-up: Quotations within Quotations

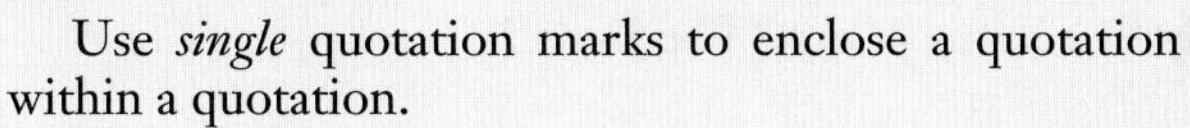

Use *single* quotation marks to enclose a quotation within a quotation.

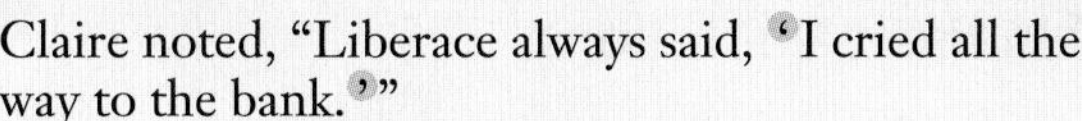

> Claire noted, "Liberace always said, 'I cried all the way to the bank.'"

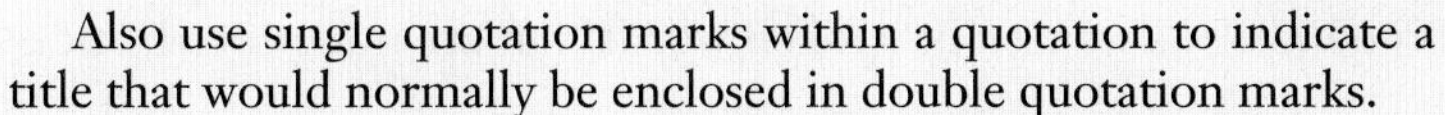

Also use single quotation marks within a quotation to indicate a title that would normally be enclosed in double quotation marks.

> I think what she said was, "Play it, Sam. Play 'As Time Goes By.'"

Use double quotation marks around quotations or titles within a long prose passage.

See 54b1

54f Editing Misused Quotation Marks

Quotation marks should not be used in the following situations.

(1) To Convey Emphasis

Do not use quotation marks to convey emphasis.

> William Randolph Hearst's ~~"~~fabulous~~"~~ home is a castle called San Simeon.

(2) To Set Off Slang or Technical Terms

Do not use quotation marks to set off slang or technical terms. (Note that slang is almost always inappropriate in college writing.)

> Dawn is ~~"into"~~ *very involved in* running.
>
> ~~"~~Biofeedback~~"~~ is sometimes used to treat migraine headaches.

(3) To Enclose Titles of Long Works

See 57a

Titles of long works are italicized (or underlined to indicate italics), not set in quotation marks.

> The classic novel "War and Peace" is even longer than the epic poem "Paradise Lost."

NOTE: Do not use quotation marks (or italics) to set off titles of your own papers.

(4) To Set Off Terms Being Defined

Terms being defined are italicized (or underlined to indicate italics).

> The word "tintinnabulation," meaning the ringing sound of bells, was used by Poe in his poem "The Bells."

(5) To Set Off Indirect Quotations

Quotation marks should not be used to set off **indirect quotations** (someone else's written or spoken words that are not quoted exactly).

> Freud wondered "what a woman wanted."

Exercise 3

In the following paragraph, correct the use of single and double quotation marks to set off direct quotations, titles, and words used in special ways. Supply quotation marks where they are required, and delete those that are not required, substituting italics where necessary.

In her essay 'The Obligation to Endure' from the book "Silent Spring," Rachel Carson writes: As Albert Schweitzer has said, 'Man can hardly even recognize the devils of his own creation.' Carson goes on to point out that many chemicals have been used to kill insects and other organisms which, she writes, are "described in the modern vernacular as pests." Carson believes such "advanced" chemicals, by contaminating our environment, do more harm than good. In addition to "Silent Spring," Carson is also the author of the book "The Sea Around Us." This work, divided into three sections (Mother Sea, The Restless Sea, and Man and the Sea About Him), was published in 1951.

Exercise 4

Correct the use of quotation marks in the following sentences. If a sentence is correct, mark it with a *C*.

Example: The "Watergate" incident brought many new expressions into the English language.

1. Kilroy was here and Women and children first are two expressions *Bartlett's Familiar Quotations* attributes to "Anon."
2. Neil Armstrong said he was making a small step for man but a giant leap for mankind.
3. "The answer, my friend", Bob Dylan sang, "is blowin' in the wind".
4. The novel was a real "thriller," complete with spies and counterspies, mysterious women, and exotic international chases.
5. The sign said, Road liable to subsidence; it meant that we should look out for potholes.
6. One of William Blake's best-known lines—To see a world in a grain of sand—opens his poem Auguries of Innocence.
7. In James Thurber's short story The Catbird Seat, Mrs. Barrows annoys Mr. Martin by asking him silly questions like Are you tearing up the pea patch? Are you scraping around the bottom of the pickle barrel? and Are you lifting the oxcart out of the ditch?
8. I'll make him an offer he can't refuse, promised "the godfather" in Mario Puzo's novel.
9. What did Timothy Leary mean by "Turn on, tune in, drop out?"
10. George, the protagonist of Bernard Malamud's short story, A Summer's Reading, is something of an "underachiever."

Chapter 55

Using Other Punctuation Marks

Frequently Asked Questions

55a Using Colons

The **colon** is a strong punctuation mark that points readers ahead.

(1) Introducing Lists or Series

Colons set off lists or series, including those introduced by phrases like *the following* or *as follows*.

> Waiting tables requires three skills: memory, speed, and balance.

NOTE: When a colon introduces a list or series, explanatory material, or a quotation, it must be preceded by a complete sentence.

(2) Introducing Explanatory Material

Use a colon to introduce material that explains, exemplifies, or summarizes. Frequently, this material is presented as an **appositive,** a word group that identifies or renames an adjacent noun or pronoun.

> Diego Rivera painted a controversial mural: the one commissioned for Rockefeller Center in the 1930s.
>
> She had one dream: to play professional basketball.

Sometimes a colon separates two independent clauses, the second illustrating or explaining the first.

> A *U.S. News & World Report* survey revealed a surprising fact: Americans spend more time at malls than anywhere else except at home and at work.

Close-up: Using Colons

When a complete sentence follows a colon, it may begin with either a capital or a lowercase letter. However, if the sentence is a quotation, the first word is always capitalized (unless it was not capitalized in the source).

(3) Introducing Quotations

When you quote a long prose passage, always introduce it with a colon. Also use a colon before a short quotation when it is introduced by a complete sentence.

See 54b1

FAQs

> With dignity, Bartleby repeated the familiar words: "I prefer not to."

Other Conventional Uses of Colons

To Separate Titles from Subtitles
Family Installments: Memories of Growing Up Hispanic

To Separate Minutes from Hours
6:15 a.m.

After Salutations in business letters
Dear Dr. Evans:

See 28a

To Separate Place of Publication from Name of Publisher in a Works-Cited List
Boston: Wadsworth, 2005

See 18a2

(4) Editing Misused Colons

Do not use colons in the following situations.

***After Expressions Like* Such As *and* For Example** Do not use colons after the expressions *such as*, *namely*, *for example*, and *that is*. Remember that when a colon introduces a list or series, a complete sentence must precede the colon.

> The Eye Institute treats patients with a wide variety of conditions, such as: myopia, glaucoma, and cataracts.

In Verb and Prepositional Constructions Do not place colons between verbs and their objects or complements or between prepositions and their objects.

James A. Michener wrote: *Hawaii*, *Centennial*, *Space*, and *Poland*.

Hitler's armies marched through: the Netherlands, Belgium, and France.

Exercise 1

Add colons where appropriate in the following sentences, and delete any misused colons.

Example: There was one thing he really hated: getting up at 7:00 every morning.

1. Books about the late John F. Kennedy include the following *A Hero for Our Time; Johnny, We Hardly Knew Ye; One Brief Shining Moment;* and *JFK: Reckless Youth*.
2. Only one task remained to tell his boss he was quitting.
3. The story closed with a familiar phrase "And they all lived happily ever after."
4. The sergeant requested: reinforcements, medical supplies, and more ammunition.
5. She kept only four souvenirs a photograph, a matchbook, a theater program, and a daisy pressed between the pages of *William Shakespeare The Complete Works*.

55b Using Dashes

(1) Setting Off Nonessential Material

Like commas, **dashes** can set off nonessential material, but unlike commas, dashes call attention to the material they set off. Indicate a dash with two unspaced hyphens (which most word-processing programs will automatically convert to a dash).

For emphasis, you may use dashes to set off explanations, qualifications, examples, definitions, and appositives.

Neither of the boys—both nine-year-olds—had any history of violence.

Too many parents learn the dangers of swimming pools the hard way—after their toddler has drowned.

(2) Introducing a Summary

Use a dash to introduce a statement that summarizes a list or series before it.

"Study hard," "Respect your elders," "Don't talk with your mouth full"—Sharon had often heard her parents say these things.

(3) Indicating an Interruption

In dialogue, a dash can mark a hesitation or an unfinished thought.

"I think—no, I know—this is the worst day of my life," Julie sighed.

(4) Editing Overused Dashes

Because too many dashes can make a passage seem disorganized and out of control, you should be careful not to overuse them.

Registration was a nightmare~~—most~~ [. Most] of the courses I wanted to take—geology and conversational Spanish, for instance—met at inconvenient times~~—~~or were closed by the time I tried to sign up for them~~—it~~ [. It] was really depressing~~—~~[,] even for registration.

Exercise 2

Add dashes where needed in the following sentences. If a sentence is correct, mark it with a *C*.

Example: World War I [—] called "the war to end all wars" [—] was, unfortunately, no such thing.

1. Tulips, daffodils, hyacinths, lilies all these flowers grow from bulbs.
2. St. Kitts and Nevis two tiny island nations are now independent after 360 years of British rule.
3. "But it's not" She paused and thought about her next words.
4. He considered several different majors history, English, political science, and business before deciding on journalism.
5. The two words added to the Pledge of Allegiance in the 1950s "under God" remain part of the Pledge today.

55c Using Parentheses

(1) Setting Off Nonessential Material

Use parentheses to enclose material that expands, clarifies, illustrates, or supplements.

In some European countries (notably Sweden and France), high-quality day care is offered at little or no cost to parents.

When a complete sentence set off by parentheses falls within another sentence, it should not begin with a capital letter or end with a period.

The area is so cold (temperatures average in the low twenties) that it is virtually uninhabitable.

If the parenthetical sentence does *not* fall within another sentence, however, it must begin with a capital letter and end with appropriate punctuation.

The area is very cold. (Temperatures average in the low twenties.)

Close-up: Using Parentheses with Other Punctuation

When parentheses fall within a sentence, punctuation never precedes the opening parenthesis. Punctuation may follow the closing parenthesis, however.

George Orwell's *1984*, (1949), which focuses on the dangers of a totalitarian society, is required reading.

(2) Using Parentheses in Other Situations

Parentheses are used around letters and numbers that identify points on a list, dates, cross-references, and documentation.

All reports must include the following components: (1) an opening summary, (2) a background statement, and (3) a list of conclusions.

Russia defeated Sweden in the Great Northern War (1700–1721).

Other scholars also make this point (see p. 54).

One critic has called the novel "puerile" (Arvin 72).

Exercise 3

Add parentheses where appropriate in the following sentences. If a sentence is correct, mark it with a *C*.

Example: The greatest battle of the War of 1812 (the Battle of New Orleans) was fought after the war was declared over.

1. During the Great War 1914–1918, Britain censored letters written from the front lines.
2. Those who lived in towns on the southern coast like Dover could often hear the mortar shells across the channel in France.
3. Wilfred Owen wrote his most famous poem "Dulce et Decorum Est" in the trenches in France.
4. The British uniforms with bright red tabs right at the neck were responsible for many British deaths.
5. It was difficult for the War Poets as they are now called to return to writing about subjects other than the horrors of war.

55d Using Brackets

(1) Setting Off Comments within Quotations

Brackets within quotations tell readers that the enclosed words are yours and not those of your source. You can bracket an explanation, a clarification, a correction, or an opinion.

"Even at Princeton he [F. Scott Fitzgerald] felt like an outsider."

If a quotation contains an error, indicate that the error is not yours by following the error with the Latin word *sic* ("thus") in brackets.

"The octopuss [sic] is a cephalopod mollusk with eight arms."

NOTE: Use brackets to indicate changes that you make in order to fit a quotation smoothly into your sentence.

See 15d1

(2) Replacing Parentheses within Parentheses

When one set of parentheses falls within another, use brackets in place of the inner set.

In her study of American education between 1945 and 1960 (*The Trouble Crusade* [New York: Basic, 1963]), Diane Ravitch addresses issues like progressive education, race, educational reforms, and campus unrest.

55e Using Slashes

(1) Separating One Option from Another

When separating one opinion from another with a slash, do not leave a space before or after the slash.

> The either/or fallacy is a common error in logic.
>
> Writer/director Spike Lee will speak at the film festival.

(2) Separating Lines of Poetry Run Into the Text

When separating lines of poetry run into the text, leave one space before and one space after the slash.

> The poet James Schevill writes, "I study my defects / And learn how to perfect them."

55f Using Ellipses

Use ellipses in the following situations.

(1) Indicating an Omission in Quoted Prose

Use an **ellipsis**—three *spaced* periods—to indicate you have omitted words from a prose quotation. An ellipsis in the middle of a quoted passage can indicate the omission of a word, a sentence or two, or even a whole paragraph or more. When deleting material from a quotation, be very careful not to change the meaning of the original passage.

> **Original:** "When I was a young man, being anxious to distinguish myself, I was perpetually starting new propositions." (Samuel Johnson)
>
> **With Omission:** "When I was a young man, . . . I was perpetually starting new propositions."

Note that when you delete words immediately after an internal punctuation mark (such as the comma in the above example), you retain the punctuation before the ellipsis.

When you delete material *at the end of a sentence*, place the sentence's period or other end punctuation before the ellipsis.

According to humorist Dave Barry, "from outer space Europe appears to be shaped like a large ketchup stain. . . ."

NOTE: Never begin a quoted passage with an ellipsis.

Deletion from Middle of One Sentence to End of Another
According to Donald Hall, "Everywhere one meets the idea that reading is an activity desirable in itself. . . . People surround the idea of reading with piety and do not take into account the purpose of reading."

Deletion from Middle of One Sentence to Middle of Another
"When I was a young man, . . . I found that generally what was new was false." (Samuel Johnson)

NOTE: If a quoted passage already contains ellipses, MLA recommends that you enclose your own ellipses in brackets to distinguish them from those that appear in the original quotation.

Close-up: Using Ellipses

If a quotation ending with an ellipsis is followed by parenthetical documentation, the final punctuation *follows* the documentaton.

As Jarman argues, "Compromise was impossible . . ." (161).

(2) Indicating an Omission in Quoted Poetry

Use an ellipsis when you omit a word or phrase from a line of poetry. When you omit one or more lines of poetry, use a line of spaced periods. (The length may be equal either to the line above it or to the missing line—but it should not be longer than the longest line of the poem.)

Original:

Stitch! Stitch! Stitch!
In poverty, hunger, and dirt,
And still with a voice of dolorous pitch,
Would that its tone could reach the Rich,
She sang this "Song of the Shirt"!
(Thomas Hood)

With Omission:

Stitch! Stitch! Stitch!
In poverty, hunger, and dirt,
. . . .
She sang this "Song of the Shirt"!

Exercise 4

Read the following paragraph, and follow the instructions after it, taking care in each case not to delete essential information.

> The most important thing about research is to know when to stop. How does one recognize the moment? When I was eighteen or thereabouts, my mother told me that when out with a young man I should always leave a half-hour before I wanted to. Although I was not sure how this might be accomplished, I recognized the advice as sound, and exactly the same rule applies to research. One must stop *before* one has finished; otherwise, one will never stop and never finish. (Barbara Tuchman, *Practicing History*)

1. Delete a phrase from the middle of one sentence, marking the omission with ellipses.
2. Delete words from the middle of one sentence to the middle of another, marking the omission with ellipses.
3. Delete words at the end of any sentence, marking the omission with ellipses.
4. Delete one complete sentence from the middle of the passage, marking the omission with ellipses.

Exercise 5

Add appropriate punctuation—colons, dashes, parentheses, brackets, or slashes—to the following sentences. If a sentence is correct, mark it with a *C*.

Example: There was one thing she was sure of^:^ if she did well at the interview, the job would be hers.

1. Mark Twain Samuel L. Clemens made the following statement "I can live for two months on a good compliment."
2. Liza Minnelli, the actress singer who starred in several films, is the daughter of Judy Garland.
3. Saudi Arabia, Oman, Yemen, Qatar, and the United Arab Emirates all these are located on the Arabian Peninsula.
4. John Adams 1735–1826 was the second president of the United States; John Quincy Adams 1767–1848 was the sixth.
5. The sign said "No tresspassing sic."
6. *Checkmate* a term derived from the Persian phrase meaning "the king is dead" announces victory in chess.
7. The following people were present at the meeting the president of the board of trustees, three trustees, and twenty reporters.
8. Before the introduction of the potato in Europe, the parsnip was a major source of carbohydrates in fact, it was a dietary staple.
9. In the well-researched book *Crime Movies* (New York Norton, 1980), Carlos Clarens studies the gangster genre in film.
10. I remember reading though I can't remember where that Upton Sinclair sold plots to Jack London.

Chapter 56

Capitalization

Frequently Asked Questions

http://kirsznermandell.wadsworth.com

Computer Tip: Revising Capitalization Errors

In *Microsoft Word,* the AutoCorrect tool will automatically capitalize certain words—such as the first word of a sentence or the days of the week. In addition, you can designate certain words to be automatically capitalized for you as you type. To do this, select AutoCorrect from the Tools menu, and type in the words. Be sure to proofread your documents after using the AutoCorrect tool, though, since it can actually introduce capitalization errors into your writing.

56a Capitalizing the First Word of a Sentence

Capitalize the first word of a sentence, including a sentence of quoted speech or writing.

As Shakespeare wrote, "Who steals my purse steals trash."

Do not capitalize a sentence set off within another sentence by dashes or parentheses.

Finding the store closed—it was a holiday—they went home.

The candidates are Frank Lester and Jane Lester (they are not related).

Capitalization is optional when a complete sentence is introduced by a colon.

See 55a

Close-up: Using Capital Letters in Poetry

Remember that the first word of a line of poetry is generally capitalized. If the poet uses a lowercase letter to begin a line, however, you should follow that style when you quote the line.

56b Capitalizing Proper Nouns

Proper nouns—the names of specific persons, places, or things—are capitalized, and so are adjectives formed from proper nouns.

ESL Tip

If you are not sure whether a noun should be capitalized, look it up in a dictionary. Do not capitalize a word simply because you want to emphasize its importance.

(1) Specific People's Names

Eleanor Roosevelt Medgar Evers

Capitalize a title when it precedes a person's name (Senator Olympia Snowe) or is used instead of the name (Dad). Do not capitalize titles that *follow* names (Olympia Snowe, the senator from Maine) or those that refer to the general position, not the particular person who holds it (a stay-at-home dad).

You may, however, capitalize titles that indicate very high-ranking positions even when they are used alone or when they follow a name: the Pope; George W. Bush, President of the United States. Never capitalize a title denoting a family relationship when it follows an article or a possessive pronoun (an uncle, his mom).

Capitalize titles that represent academic degrees or abbreviations of those degrees even when they follow a name: Dr. Benjamin Spock; Benjamin Spock, MD.

(2) Names of Particular Structures, Special Events, Monuments, and So On

the Brooklyn Bridge	the Taj Mahal
the Eiffel Tower	Mount Rushmore
the World Series	the *Titanic*

NOTE: Capitalize a common noun, such as *bridge*, *river*, *county*, or *lake*, when it is part of a proper noun (Lake Erie, Kings County).

(3) Places and Geographical Regions

Saturn	the Straits of Magellan
Budapest	the Fiji Islands
Walden Pond	the Western Hemisphere

Capitalize *north*, *south*, *east*, and *west* when they denote particular geographical regions, but not when they designate directions.

There are more tornadoes in Kansas than in the East. (*East* refers to a specific region.)

Turn west at Broad Street and continue north to Market. (*West* and *north* refer to directions, not specific regions.)

(4) Days of the Week, Months, and Holidays

Saturday	Cinco de Mayo
January	Rosh Hashanah

(5) Historical Periods, Events, Documents, and Names of Legal Cases

the Industrial Revolution	the Treaty of Versailles
the Reformation	the Voting Rights Act
the Battle of Gettysburg	*Brown* v. *Board of Education*

NOTE: Names of court cases are italicized (or underlined to indicate italics) in the text of your papers but not in works-cited entries.

(6) Philosophic, Literary, and Artistic Movements

Naturalism	Dadaism
Neoclassicism	Expressionism

(7) Races, Ethnic Groups, Nationalities, and Languages

African American	Korean
Latino/Latina	Dutch

NOTE: When the words *black* and *white* denote races, they have traditionally not been capitalized. Current usage is divided on whether to capitalize *black*.

(8) Religions and Their Followers; Sacred Books and Figures

Islam	the Koran	Buddha
the Talmud	the Scriptures	God

NOTE: It is not necessary to capitalize pronouns referring to God (although some people do so as a sign of respect).

(9) Political, Social, Athletic, Civic, and Other Groups and Their Members

the Democratic Party

the International Brotherhood of Electrical Workers

the New York Yankees

the American Civil Liberties Union

the National Council of Teachers of English

the Rolling Stones

See 59b

NOTE: When the name of a group or institution is abbreviated, the abbreviation uses capital letters in place of the capitalized words.

IBEW ACLU NCTE

(10) Businesses, Government Agencies, and Other Institutions

Bank of America	Lincoln High School
the Environmental Protection Agency	the University of Maryland

(11) Brand Names and Words Formed from Them

Velcro Coke Post-it Rollerblades Astroturf

NOTE: Brand names that over long use have become synonymous with the product—for example, *nylon* and *aspirin*—are no longer capitalized. (Consult a dictionary to determine whether to capitalize a familiar brand name.)

Close-up: Using Brand Names

In general, use generic references, not brand names, in college writing—*photocopy*, not *Xerox*, for example. These generic names are not capitalized.

(12) Specific Academic Courses

Sociology 201	English 101

NOTE: Do not capitalize a general subject area (sociology, zoology) unless it is the name of a language (English, Spanish).

(13) Adjectives Formed from Proper Nouns

Freudian slip	Elizabethan era
Platonic ideal	Shakespearean sonnet
Aristotelian logic	Marxist ideology

When words derived from proper nouns have lost their original associations, do not capitalize them: china bowl, french fries.

http://kirsznermandell.wadsworth.com

Computer Tip: Checking Proper Nouns

Your word processor's spell checker may not recognize many of the proper nouns you use in your documents, particularly those that require irregular capitalization, such as *Leonardo da Vinci* (see Figure 56.1), and therefore will identify these nouns as spelling errors. To solve this problem, click Ignore to instruct the spell checker to ignore the word one time, and Ignore All to instruct the spell checker to ignore all uses of the word in your document.

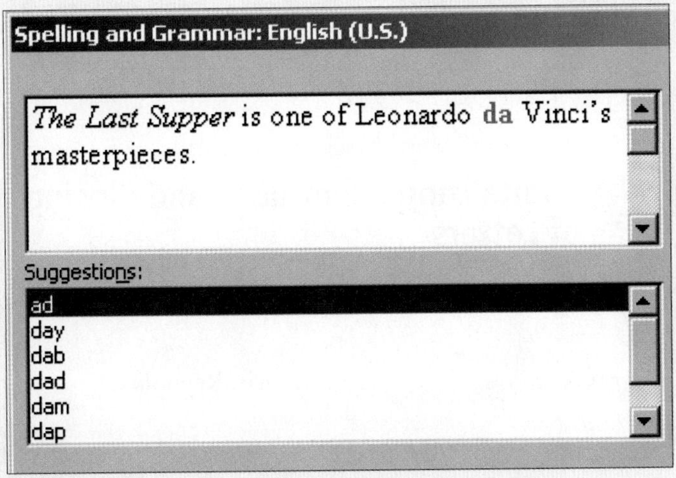

Spelling and Grammar: English (U.S.)

The Last Supper is one of Leonardo da Vinci's masterpieces.

Suggestions:

ad
day
dab
dad
dam
dap

Figure 56.1 Sample spell checker suggestion.

56c Capitalizing Important Words in Titles

In general, capitalize all words in titles with the exception of articles (*a*, *an*, and *the*), prepositions, coordinating conjunctions, and the *to* in infinitives (unless they are the first or last word in the title or subtitle).

"Dover Beach"

The Declaration of Independence

Across the River and into the Trees

On the Waterfront

Madame Curie: A Biography

What Friends Are For

56d Capitalizing the Pronoun *I*, the Interjection *O*, and Other Single Letters in Special Constructions

Always capitalize the pronoun *I* even if it is part of a contraction (*I'm*, *I'll*, *I've*).

> Sam and I finally went to the Grand Canyon, and I'm glad we did.

Always capitalize the interjection *O*.

> Give us peace in our time, O Lord.

However, capitalize the interjection *oh* only when it begins a sentence.

NOTE: Many other single letters are capitalized in certain usages: U-boat, D day, Model T, vitamin B, an A in history, C major. Consult your dictionary to determine whether or not to use a capital letter.

56e Capitalizing Salutations and Closings of Letters

Always capitalize the first word of the salutation of a personal or business letter.

Dear Fred,

Dear Mr. Reynolds:

Always capitalize the first word of the complimentary close.

Sincerely,

Very truly yours,

56f Editing Misused Capitals

Do not capitalize words for emphasis or as an attention-getting strategy. If you are uncertain about whether or not a word should be capitalized, consult a dictionary.

(1) Seasons

Do not capitalize the names of the seasons—summer, fall, winter, spring—unless they are personified, as in *Old Man Winter.*

(2) Centuries and Loosely Defined Historical Periods

Do not capitalize the names of centuries or general historical periods.

seventeenth-century poetry   the automobile age

Do, however, capitalize names of specific historical, anthropological, and geological periods.

Iron Age   Paleozoic Era

(3) Diseases and Other Medical Terms

Do not capitalize names of diseases or medical tests or conditions unless a proper noun is part of the name or unless the name of the disease is an acronym.

smallpox	Apgar test	AIDS
Lyme disease	mumps	SIDS

Exercise

Capitalize words where necessary in these sentences.

Example: John F. Kennedy won the pulitzer prize for his book *profiles in courage.* [handwritten corrections: P P P C]

1. Two of the brontë sisters wrote *jane eyre* and *wuthering heights,* nineteenth-century novels that are required reading in many english classes that focus on victorian literature.
2. It was a beautiful day in the spring—it was april 15, to be exact—but all Ted could think about was the check he had to write to the internal revenue service and the bills he had to pay by friday.
3. Traveling north, they hiked through british columbia, planning a leisurely return on the cruise ship *canadian princess.*

4. Alice liked her mom's apple pie better than aunt nellie's rhubarb pie, but she liked grandpa's punch best of all.
5. A new elective, political science 30, covers the vietnam war from the gulf of tonkin to the fall of saigon, including the roles of ho chi minh, the viet cong, and the buddhist monks; the positions of presidents johnson and nixon; and the influence of groups like the student mobilization committee and vietnam veterans against the war.
6. When the central high school drama club put on a production of shaw's *pygmalion*, the director xeroxed extra copies of the parts for eliza doolittle and professor henry higgins so he could give them to the understudies.
7. Shaking all over, Bill admitted, "driving on the los angeles freeway is a frightening experience for a kid from brooklyn, even in a bmw."
8. The new united federation of teachers contract guarantees teachers many paid holidays, including columbus day, veterans day, and washington's birthday; a week each at christmas and easter; and two full months (july and august) in the summer.
9. The sociology syllabus included the books *beyond the best interests of the child*, *regulating the poor: the functions of public welfare*, and *a welfare mother*; in anthropology, we were to begin by studying the stone age; and in geology, we were to focus on the Mesozoic era.
10. Winners of the nobel peace prize include lech walesa, former leader of the polish trade union solidarity; the reverend dr. martin luther king jr., founder of the southern christian leadership conference; and archbishop desmond tutu of south africa.

Chapter 57

Italics

Frequently Asked Questions

What kinds of titles are italicized? (p. 933)
Should I underline to indicate italics in my papers? (p. 934)
Can I use italics to emphasize certain words or phrases? (p. 935)

57a Setting Off Titles and Names

Use italics for the titles and names listed in the following box. Most other titles are set off with quotation marks.

Titles and Names Set in Italics

Books: *David Copperfield*, *The Bluest Eye*

Newspapers: the *Washington Post*, the *Philadelphia Inquirer*
(According to MLA style, introductory articles are not italicized in titles of newspapers.)

Magazines and Journals: *Rolling Stone*, *Scientific American*

Online Magazines and Journals: *salon.com*, *theonion.com*

Web Sites or Home Pages: *urbanlegends.com*, *movie-mistakes.com*

Pamphlets: *Common Sense*

Films: *The Matrix*, *Citizen Kane*

Television Programs: *60 Minutes*, *The Bachelor*, *Fear Factor*

Radio Programs: *All Things Considered*, *A Prairie Home Companion*

Long Poems: *John Brown's Body*, *The Faerie Queen*

Plays: *Macbeth*, *A Raisin in the Sun*

Long Musical Works: *Rigoletto*, *Eroica*

Software Programs: *Microsoft Word*, *PowerPoint*

(continued)

Titles and names set in italics (continued)

Search Engines and Web Browsers: *Google, Netscape Communicator*

Databases: *Academic Search Premier, Expanded Academic ASAP Plus*

Paintings and Sculpture: *Guernica, Pietà*

Ships: *Lusitania,* U.S.S. *Saratoga* (S.S. and U.S.S. are not italicized.)

Trains: *City of New Orleans, The Orient Express*

Aircraft: *The Hindenburg, Enola Gay* (Only particular aircraft, not makes or types such as Piper Cub or Boeing 757, are italicized.)

Spacecraft: *Challenger, Enterprise*

NOTE: Names of sacred books, such as the Bible and the Koran, and well-known documents, such as the Constitution and the Declaration of Independence, are neither italicized nor placed within quotation marks.

Close-up: Using Italics

MLA guidelines recommend that you underline to indicate italics. However, you may italicize if your instructor prefers. (Note that style guides in other may disciplines require italics.)

57b Setting Off Foreign Words and Phrases

Italics are often used to set off foreign words and phrases that have not become part of the English language.

"*C'est la vie,*" Madeline said when she saw the long line for the concert.

Spirochaeta plicatilis is a corkscrewlike bacterium.

If you are not sure whether a foreign word has been assimilated into English, consult a dictionary.

57c Setting Off Elements Spoken of as Themselves and Terms Being Defined

Use italics to set off letters, numerals, and words that refer to the letters, numerals, and words themselves.

Is that a *p* or a *g?*

I forget the exact address, but I know it has a *3* in it.

Does *through* rhyme with *cough?*

Also use italics to set off words and phrases that you go on to define.

A *closet drama* is a play meant to be read, not performed.

NOTE: When you quote a dictionary definition, put the word you are defining in italics and the definition itself in quotation marks.

To *infer* means "to draw a conclusion"; to *imply* means "to suggest."

57d Using Italics for Emphasis

Italics can occasionally be used for emphasis.

Initially, poetry might be defined as a kind of language that says *more* and says it *more intensely* than does ordinary language. (Lawrence Perrine, *Sound and Sense*)

However, overuse of italics is distracting. Instead of italicizing, try to indicate emphasis with word choice and sentence structure.

Exercise

Underline to indicate italics where necessary, and delete any italics that are incorrectly used. If a sentence is correct, mark it with a *C*.

Example: <u>However</u> is a conjunctive adverb, not a coordinating conjunction.

1. I said Carol, not Darryl.
2. A *deus ex machina*, an improbable device used to resolve the plot of a fictional work, is used in Charles Dickens's novel Oliver Twist.
3. He dotted every i and crossed every t.

4. The Metropolitan Opera's production of Carmen was a tour de force for the principal performers.
5. *Laissez-faire* is a doctrine holding that government should not interfere with trade.
6. Antidote and anecdote are often confused because their pronunciations are similar.
7. Hawthorne's novels include Fanshawe, The House of the Seven Gables, The Blithedale Romance, and The Scarlet Letter.
8. Words like mailman, policeman, and fireman have been replaced by nonsexist terms like letter carrier, police officer, and firefighter.
9. A classic black tuxedo was considered de rigueur at the charity ball, but Jason preferred to wear his *dashiki*.
10. Thomas Mann's novel Buddenbrooks is a bildungsroman.

Chapter 58

Hyphens

Frequently Asked Questions

Where do I put the hyphen if I divide a compound word at the end of a line? (p. 937)

Should I use a hyphen to divide an electronic address at the end of a line? (p. 937)

Hyphens have two conventional uses: to break a word at the end of a line and to link words in certain compounds.

58a Breaking a Word at the End of a Line

A computer never breaks a word at the end of a line; if the full word will not fit, it is brought down to the next line. Sometimes, however, you will want to break a word with a hyphen—for example, to fill in space at the end of a line. When you break a word at the end of a line, divide it only between syllables, consulting a dictionary if necessary. Never divide a word at the end of a page, and never hyphenate a one-syllable word. In addition, never leave a single letter at the end of a line or carry only one or two letters to the next line.

If you divide a compound word at the end of a line, put the hyphen between the elements of the compound (*snow-mobile*, not *snowmo-bile*).

See 58b

http://kirsznermandell.wadsworth.com

Computer Tip: Dividing Electronic Addresses (URLs)

Never insert a hyphen to divide an electronic address (URL) at the end of a line. (Readers might think the hyphen is part of the address.) MLA style recommends that you break the URL after a slash. If this is not possible, break it in a logical place—after a period, for example—or avoid the problem altogether by moving the entire URL to the next line.

58b Dividing Compound Words

A **compound word** consists of two or more words. Some familiar compound words are always hyphenated: *no-hitter*, *helter-skelter*. Other compounds are always written as one word: *fireplace*, *peacetime*. Finally, some compounds are always written as two separate words: *labor relations*, *bunk bed*. Your dictionary can tell you whether a particular compound requires a hyphen.

http://kirsznermandell.wadsworth.com

Computer Tip: Hyphenating Compound Words

Your word processor's grammar checker will highlight certain compound words with incorrect or missing hyphenation and offer suggestions for revision (see Figure 58.1).

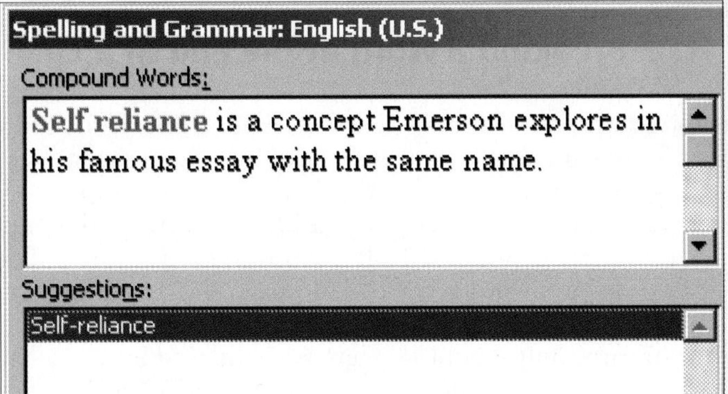
Spelling and Grammar: English (U.S.)
Compound Words:
Self reliance is a concept Emerson explores in his famous essay with the same name.
Suggestions:
Self-reliance

Figure 58.1 Sample grammar checker suggestion.

(1) Hyphenating with Compound Adjectives

A **compound adjective** is a series of two or more words that function together as an adjective. When a compound adjective *precedes* the noun it modifies, use hyphens to join its elements.

> The research team tried to use nineteenth-century technology to design a space-age project.

When a compound adjective *follows* the noun it modifies, do not use hyphens to join its elements.

The three government-operated programs were run smoothly, but the one that was not government operated was short of funds.

NOTE: A compound adjective formed with an adverb ending in *-ly* is not hyphenated, even when it precedes the noun.

Many upwardly mobile families are on tight budgets.

Use **suspended hyphens—**hyphens followed by a space or by appropriate punctuation and a space—in a series of compounds that have the same principal elements.

Graduates of two- and four-year colleges were eligible for the grants.

The exam called for sentence-, paragraph-, and essay-length answers.

(2) Hyphenating with Certain Prefixes and Suffixes

Use a hyphen between a prefix and a proper noun or proper adjective.

mid-July   pre-Columbian

Use a hyphen to connect the prefixes *all-*, *ex-*, *half-*, *quarter-*, *quasi-*, and *self-* and the suffixes *-elect* to a noun.

ex-senator   self-centered   president-elect

NOTE: The words *selfhood*, *selfish*, and *selfless* do not include hyphens. In these cases, *self* is the root, not a prefix.

(3) Hyphenating in Compound Numerals and Fractions

Hyphenate compounds that represent numbers below one hundred (even if they are part of a larger number).

the twenty-first century   three hundred sixty-five days

Also hyphenate the written form of a fraction when it modifies a noun.

a two-thirds share of the business

(4) Hyphenating for Clarity

Hyphenate to prevent readers from misreading one word for another.

Before we can reform criminals, we must re-form our ideas about prisons.

Hyphenate to avoid hard-to-read combinations, such as two *i*'s (*semi-illiterate*).

In most cases, hyphenate between a capital initial and a word when the two combine to form a compound: *A-frame*, *T-shirt*.

(5) Hyphenating in Coined Compounds

A **coined compound,** one that uses a new combination of words as a unit, requires hyphens.

He looked up with a who-do-you-think-you-are expression.

Exercise 1

Form compound adjectives from the following word groups, inserting hyphens where necessary.

Example: a contract ~~for three years~~ [three-year inserted before contract]

1. a relative who has long been lost
2. someone who is addicted to video games
3. a salesperson who goes from door to door
4. a display calculated to catch the eye
5. friends who are dearly beloved
6. a household that is centered on a child
7. a line of reasoning that is hard to follow
8. the border between New York and New Jersey
9. a candidate who is thirty-two years old
10. a computer that is friendly to its users

Exercise 2

Add hyphens to the compounds in these sentences wherever they are required. Consult a dictionary if necessary.

Example: Alaska was the forty-ninth state to join the United States.

1. One of the restaurant's blue plate specials is chicken fried steak.
2. Virginia and Texas are both right to work states.
3. He stood on tiptoe to see the near perfect statue, which was well hidden by the security fence.
4. The five and ten cent store had a self service makeup counter and stocked many up to the minute gadgets.
5. The so called Saturday night special is opposed by pro gun control groups.
6. He ordered two all beef patties with special sauce, lettuce, cheese, pickles, and onions on a sesame seed bun.

7. The material was extremely thought provoking, but it hardly presented any earth shattering conclusions.
8. The Dodgers Phillies game was rained out, so the long suffering fans left for home.
9. Bone marrow transplants carry the risk of what is known as a graft versus host reaction.
10. The state funded child care program was considered a highly desirable alternative to family day care.

Chapter 59

Abbreviations

Frequently Asked Questions

Can I abbreviate technical terms? (p. 943)

Can I use abbreviations like e.g. *and* etc. *in college writing?* (p. 945)

Generally speaking, **abbreviations** are not appropriate in college writing except in tables, charts, and works-cited lists. Some abbreviations are only acceptable in scientific, technical, or business writing, or only in a particular discipline. If you have any questions about the appropriateness of a particular abbreviation, check a style manual in your field.

http://kirsznermandell.wadsworth.com

Computer Tip: Shorthand and Text Messaging

Like emoticons and acronyms, which are popular in email and instant messages, shorthand abbreviations and symbols—such as GR8 (great) and 2NITE (tonight)—are common in text messages between mobile phones and in other forms of electronic communication. Although they are acceptable in informal electronic communication, such abbreviations are not appropriate in college writing or in business communications.

59a Abbreviating Titles

Titles before and after proper names are usually abbreviated.

Mr. Homer Simpson	Rep. Chaka Fattah
Henry Kissinger, PhD	Prof. Elie Weisel

Do not, however, use an abbreviated title without a name.

The ~~Dr.~~ *doctor* diagnosed hepatitis.

59b Abbreviating Organization Names and Technical Terms

You may refer to well-known businesses and to government, social, and civic organizations by capitalized initials. These abbreviations fall into two categories: those in which the initials are pronounced as separate units (MTV) and **acronyms,** in which the initials are pronounced as a word (NATO).

To save space, you may use accepted abbreviations for complex technical terms that are not well known, but be sure to spell out the full term the first time you mention it, followed by the abbreviation in parentheses.

> Citrus farmers have been using ethylene dibromide (EDB), a chemical pesticide, for more than twenty years. Now, however, EDB has contaminated water supplies.

NOTE: Spell out a term if you think the abbreviation will confuse readers.

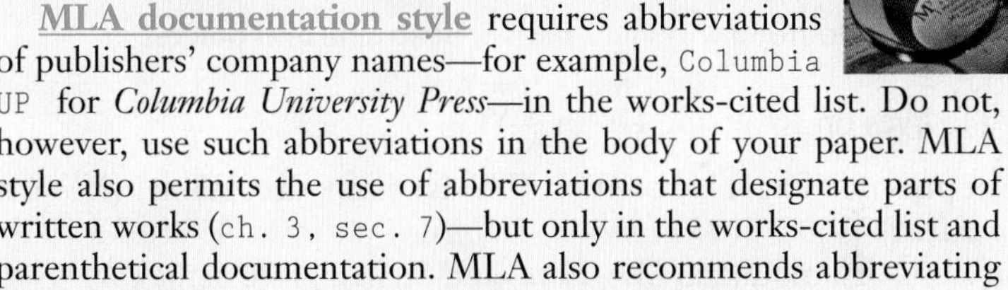

Close-up: Abbreviations in MLA Documentation

MLA documentation style requires abbreviations of publishers' company names—for example, `Columbia UP` for *Columbia University Press*—in the works-cited list. Do not, however, use such abbreviations in the body of your paper. MLA style also permits the use of abbreviations that designate parts of written works (`ch. 3, sec. 7`)—but only in the works-cited list and parenthetical documentation. MLA also recommends abbreviating literary works and books of the Bible: `Oth.` (*Othello*), `Exod.` (Exodus). These words should not be abbreviated in the text of your paper.

59c Abbreviating Dates, Times of Day, and Temperatures

Dates, times of day, and temperatures are often abbreviated.

50 BC (*BC* follows the date.)	AD 432 (*AD* precedes the date.)
6 a.m.	3:03 p.m.
20°C (Centigrade or Celsius)	180°F (Fahrenheit)

Always capitalize *BC* and *AD*. (The more neutral alternatives *BCE*, for "before the common era," and *CE*, for "common era," are also capitalized.) Use lowercase letters for a.m. and p.m., but use these abbreviations only when they are accompanied by numbers.

> We will see you in the ~~a.m.~~ morning.

NOTE: Avoid the abbreviation *no.* (written either *no.* or *No.*), except in technical writing, and then use it only before a specific number.

59d Editing Misused Abbreviations

In college writing, abbreviations are not used in the following cases.

(1) Names of Days, Months, or Holidays

Do not abbreviate days of the week, months, or holidays.

> On ~~Sat., Dec.~~ Saturday, December 23, I started my ~~Xmas~~ Christmas shopping.

(2) Names of Streets and Places

In general, do not abbreviate names of streets and places.

> He lives on Riverside ~~Dr.~~ Drive in ~~NYC.~~ New York City.

Exceptions: The abbreviation *US* is often acceptable (*US Coast Guard*), as is *DC* in *Washington, DC*. Also permissible are *Mt.* before the name of a mountain (*Mt. Etna*) and *St.* in a place name (*St. Albans*).

(3) Names of Academic Subjects

Do not abbreviate names of academic subjects.

> ~~Psych.~~ Psychology and English ~~lit.~~ literature are required courses.

(4) Names of Businesses

Write company names exactly as the firms themselves write them, including the distinction between the ampersand (&) and the word *and: AT&T, Charles Schwab & Co., Inc.* Abbre-viations for *company, corporation*, and the like are used only along with a company name.

> The ~~corp.~~ corporation merged with a ~~co.~~ company in Ohio.

(5) Latin Expressions

Abbreviations of the common Latin phrases *i.e.* ("that is"), *e.g.* ("for example"), and *etc.* ("and so forth") are not appropriate in college writing.

for example,
Other musicians (~~e.g.,~~ Bruce Springsteen) have also been influenced by Bob Dylan.

and other poems.
Poe wrote "The Raven," "Annabel Lee," ~~etc.~~

(6) Units of Measurement

In technical writing, some units of measurement are abbreviated when they are preceded by a numeral.

The hurricane had winds of 35 mph.

One new Honda gets over 50 mpg.

NOTE: MLA style requires that you write out units of measurement and spell out words such as *inches*, *feet*, *years*, *miles*, *pints*, *quarts*, and *gallons*.

(7) Symbols

The symbols =, +, and # are acceptable in technical and scientific writing but not in nontechnical college writing. The symbols % and $ are acceptable only when used with numerals (15%, $15,000), not with spelled-out numbers.

See 60b4, 60b7

Exercise

Correct any incorrectly used abbreviations in the following sentences, assuming that all are intended for a college audience. If a sentence is correct, mark it with a *C*.

Example: *Romeo* ~~&~~ and *Juliet* is a play by Shakespeare.

1. The committee meeting, attended by representatives from Action for Children's Television (ACT) and NOW, Sen. Putnam, & the pres. of ABC, convened at 8 A.M. on Mon. Feb. 24 at the YWCA on Germantown Ave.
2. An econ. prof. was suspended after he encouraged his students to speculate on securities issued by a corp. under investigation by the SEC.
3. Benjamin Spock, the MD who wrote *Baby and Child Care*, was a respected dr. known throughout the USA.

4. The FDA banned the use of Red Dye no. 2 in food in 1976, but other food additives are still in use.
5. The Rev. Dr. Martin Luther King Jr., leader of the SCLC, led the famous Selma, Ala., march.
6. Wm. Golding, a novelist from the U.K., won the Nobel Prize in lit.
7. The adult education center, financed by a major computer corp., offers courses in basic subjects like introductory bio. and tech. writing as well as teaching HTML and XML.
8. All the bros. in the fraternity agreed to write to Pres. Dexter appealing their disciplinary probation under Ch. 4, Sec. 3, of the IFC constitution.
9. A 4 qt. (i.e., 1 gal.) container is needed to hold the salt solution.
10. According to Prof. Morrison, all those taking the exam should bring two sharpened no. 2 pencils to the St. Joseph's University auditorium on Sat.

Chapter 60

Numbers

Frequently Asked Question

When do I spell out a number, and when do I use a numeral? (p. 947)

Convention determines when to use a **numeral** (22) and when to spell out a number (twenty-two). Numerals are commonly used in scientific and technical writing and in journalism, but they are used less often in the humanities.

NOTE: The guidelines in this chapter are based on the *MLA Handbook for Writers of Research Papers*, 6th ed. (2003). APA style, however, requires that all numbers below ten be spelled out if they do not represent specific measurements and that numbers ten and above be expressed in numerals.

60a Spelled-Out Numbers versus Numerals

Unless a number falls into one of the categories listed in 60b, spell it out if you can do so *in one or two words.*

The Hawaiian alphabet has only twelve letters.

Class size stabilized at twenty-eight students.

The subsidies are expected to total about two million dollars.

Numbers *more than two words* long are expressed in figures.

The dietitian prepared 125 sample menus.

The developer of the community purchased 300,000 doorknobs and 153,000 faucets.

Never begin a sentence with a numeral. If necessary, reword the sentence.

Faulty: 250 students are currently enrolled in World History 106.

Revised: Current enrollment in World History 106 is 250 students.

NOTE: When one number immediately precedes another in a sentence, spell out the first, and use a numeral for the second: *five 3-quart containers.*

http://kirsznermandell.wadsworth.com

Computer Tip: Spelled-Out Numbers versus Numerals

Your word processor's grammar checker will often highlight numerals in your writing and suggest that you spell them out (see Figure 60.1). Before clicking Change, be sure that the number does not fall into one of the categories listed in 60b.

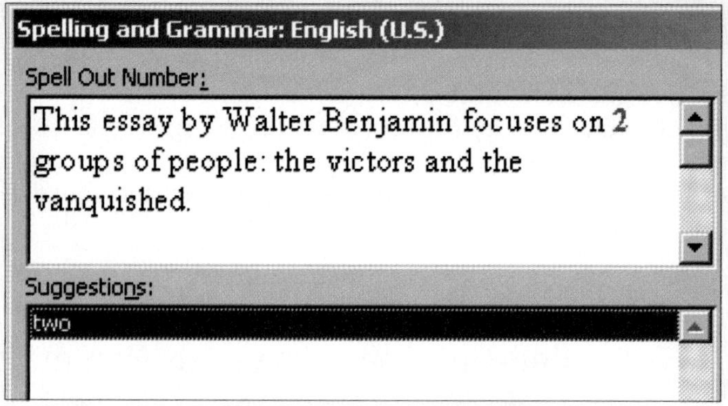
Spelling and Grammar: English (U.S.)
Spell Out Number:
This essay by Walter Benjamin focuses on 2 groups of people: the victors and the vanquished.
Suggestions:
two

Figure 60.1 Sample grammar checker suggestion.

60b Conventional Uses of Numerals

(1) Addresses

111 Fifth Avenue, New York, NY 10003

(2) Dates

January 15, 1929   1914–1919

(3) Exact Times

9:16   10 a.m. (or 10:00 a.m.)

Exceptions: Spell out times of day when they are used with *o'clock:* *eleven o'clock*, not *11 o'clock*. Also spell out times expressed in quarter and half hours: *half-past eight, a quarter to ten.*

(4) Exact Sums of Money

$25.11 $6,752.00

NOTE: Always use a numeral (not a spelled-out number) with a $ symbol. You may spell out a round sum of money if you use sums infrequently in your paper, provided you can do so in two or three words.

five dollars two thousand dollars

(5) Divisions of Written Works

Use arabic (not roman) numerals for chapter and volume numbers; acts, scenes, and lines of plays; chapters and verses of the Bible; and line numbers of long poems.

(6) Measurements before an Abbreviation or Symbol

12″ 55 mph
32° 15 cc

(7) Percentages and Decimals

80% 3.14

NOTE: You may spell out a percentage (*eighty percent*) if you use percentages infrequently in your paper, provided the percentage can be expressed in two or three words. Always use a numeral (not a spelled-out number) with a % symbol.

(8) Ratios, Scores, and Statistics

In a paper that follows APA or CSE style, use numerals for numbers presented as a comparison.

See Ch. 19, Ch. 21

Children preferred Fun Flakes over Graino by a ratio of 20 to 1.
The Orioles defeated the Phillies 6 to 0.
The median age of the voters was 42; the mean age was 40.

(9) Identification Numbers

Route 66 Track 8 Channel 12

NOTE: When writing out large numbers, insert a comma every three digits from the right, beginning after the third digit.

3,000 25,000 6,751,098

Do not, however, use commas in four-digit page and line numbers, addresses, or year numbers.

page 1202 3741 Laurel Ave. 1968

Exercise

Following MLA guidelines, revise the use of numbers in these sentences, making sure usage is correct and consistent. If a sentence uses numbers correctly, mark it with a *C*.

Example: The Empire State Building is ^102^ ~~one hundred and two~~ stories high.

1. *1984*, a novel by George Orwell, is set in a totalitarian society.
2. The English placement examination included a 30-minute personal-experience essay, a 45-minute expository essay, and a 150-item objective test of grammar and usage.
3. In a control group of two hundred forty-seven patients, almost three out of four suffered serious adverse reactions to the new drug.
4. Before the Thirteenth Amendment to the Constitution, slaves were counted as $^{3}/_{5}$ of a person.
5. The intensive membership drive netted 2,608 new members and additional dues of over 5 thousand dollars.
6. They had only 2 choices: either they could take the yacht at Pier Fourteen, or they could return home to the penthouse at Twenty-seven Harbor View Drive.
7. The atomic number of lithium is three.
8. Approximately 3 hundred thousand schoolchildren in District 6 were given hearing and vision examinations between May third and June 26.
9. The United States was drawn into the war by the Japanese attack on Pearl Harbor on December seventh, 1941.
10. An upper-middle-class family can spend over 250,000 dollars to raise each child up to age 18.

STUDENT WRITER AT WORK

Understanding Punctuation

The essay that follows was written for a composition course in response to an assignment asking students to write a personal narrative about a life-changing experience. Commas, semicolons, apostrophes, quotation marks, dashes, and parentheses have been intentionally deleted; only the end punctuation has been retained. Review Chapters 51–55; then, read the essay carefully, and add all appropriate punctuation marks.

The Day I Learned to Hunt

The dry pine needles crunched like eggshells under our thick boots.

Wont the noise scare them away Dad?

He smiled knowingly and said No deer rely mostly on smell and sight.

I thought That must be why were wearing fluorescent orange jumpsuits but I didn't feel like arguing the point.

It was a perfect day for my first hunting experience. The biting winds were caught by the thick bushy arms of the tall pines and I could feel a numbing redness in my face. Now I realized why Dad always grew that ugly gray beard that made him look ten years older. A few sunbeams managed to carve their way through the layers of branches and leaves creating pools of white light on the dark earth.

How far have we come? I asked.

Oh only a couple of miles. We should be meeting Joe up ahead.

Joe was one of Dads hunting buddies. He always managed to go off on his own for a few hours and come back with at least a four-pointer. Dad was envious of Joe and liked to tell people what he called the real story.

You know Joe paid a fortune for that buck at the checking station hed tell his friends. Dad was sure that this would be his lucky year.

We trudged up a densely wooded hill for what seemed like hours. The sharp-needled branches whipped my bare face as I followed close behind my father occasionally I wiped my cheeks to discover a new cut in my frozen flesh.

All this for a deer I thought.

The still pine air was suddenly shattered by four rapid gunshots echoing across the vast green valley below us.

Joes got another one. Come on! Dad yelled. It seemed as if I were following a young kid as I watched my father take leaping strides down the path we had just ascended. I had never seen him so enthusiastic before. I plodded breathlessly along trying to keep up with my father.

Suddenly out of the corner of my eye I caught sight of an object that didnt fit in with the monotony of trunks and branches and leaves and needles. I froze and observed the largest most majestic buck I had ever seen. It too stood motionless apparently grazing on some leaves or berries. Its coloring was beautiful with alternating patches of tan brown and snow-white fur. The massive antlers towered proudly above its head as it looked up and took notice of me. What struck me most were the tearful brown eyes almost feminine in their gaze.

Once again the silence was smashed this time by my fathers thundering call and I watched as the huge deer scampered gracefully off through the trees. I turned and scurried down the path after my father. I decided not to mention a word of my encounter to him. I hoped the deer was far away by now.

Finally I reached the clearing from where the shots had rung out. There stood Dad and Joe smiling over a fallen six-point buck. The purple-red blood dripped from the wounds to form a puddle in the dirt. The bucks sad brown eyes gleamed in the sun but no longer smiled and blinked.

Where have you been? asked Dad. Before I could answer he continued Do you believe this guy? Every year he bags the biggest deer in the whole state!

While they laughed and talked I sat on a tree stump to rest my aching legs. Maybe now we can go home I thought.

But before long I heard Dad say Come on Bob I know theres one out there for us.

We headed right back up that same path and sure enough that same big beautiful buck was grazing in that same spot on the same berry bush. The only difference was that this time Dad saw him.

This is our lucky day he whispered.

I froze as Dad lifted the barrel of his rifle and took careful aim at the silently grazing deer. I closed my eyes as he squeezed the trigger but instead of the deadly gun blast I heard only a harmless click. His rifle had jammed.

Use your rifle quick he whispered.

As I took aim through my scope the deer looked up at me. Its soulful brown eyes were magnified in my sight like two glassy bulls-eyes. My finger froze on the trigger.

Shoot him! Shoot him!

But instead I aimed for the clouds and fired. The deer vanished along with my fathers dreams. Dad never understood why this was the proudest moment of my life.

PART 11

Bilingual and ESL Writers

Chapter 61

Grammar and Style for ESL Writers

Frequently Asked Questions

See 3a

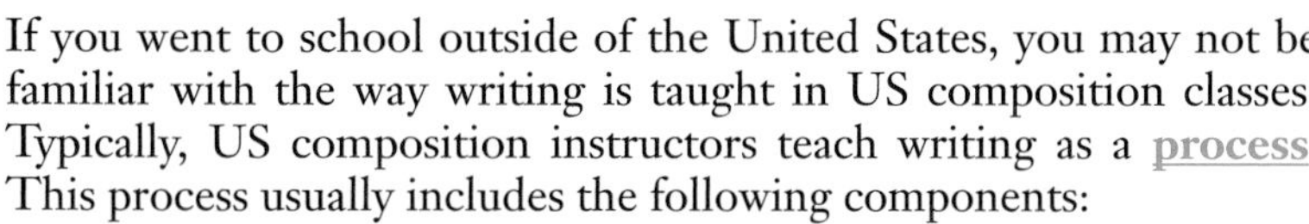

If you went to school outside of the United States, you may not be familiar with the way writing is taught in US composition classes. Typically, US composition instructors teach writing as a process. This process usually includes the following components:

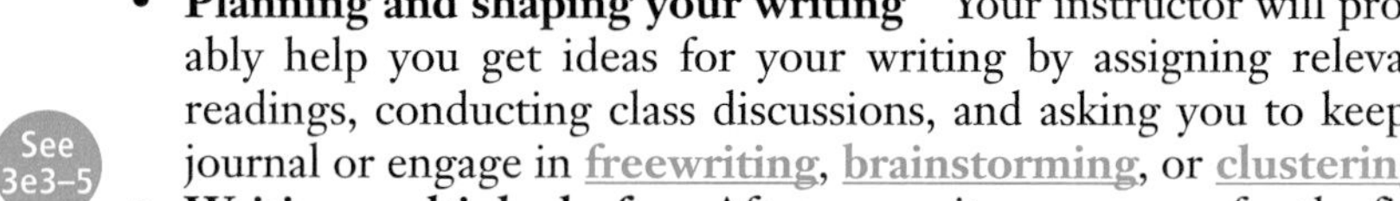

See 3e3–5

- **Planning and shaping your writing** Your instructor will probably help you get ideas for your writing by assigning relevant readings, conducting class discussions, and asking you to keep a journal or engage in freewriting, brainstorming, or clustering.
- **Writing multiple drafts** After you write your paper for the first time, you will probably get feedback from your teacher or your classmates so that you can **revise** (improve) your paper before receiving a grade on it. Instructors expect students to use the suggestions they receive to make significant improvements to their papers. (For more information on the drafting process, **see Chapter 5.**)
- **Looking at sample papers** Your instructor may provide the class with sample papers of the type that he or she has assigned. Such samples can help you understand how to complete the assigned paper. Sometimes the samples are strong papers that can serve as good examples of what to do. However, most samples will have both strengths and weaknesses, so be sure you understand your instructor's opinion of the samples he or she provides.

See 5d2

- **Engaging in** peer review (sometimes called peer editing) Your instructor may ask the class to work in small groups or individually to exchange ideas about an assigned paper. You will be expected to provide other students with feedback on the strengths and weaknesses of their papers. Afterward, you should think carefully about your classmates' comments and make changes to improve your paper.

- **Attending conferences** Your instructor may schedule one or more appointments with you to discuss your writing and may ask you to bring a draft of the paper you are working on. Your instructor may also be available to help you with your paper without an appointment during his or her office hours. In addition, many educational institutions have **writing centers**, where tutors help students get started on their papers or improve their drafts. When you meet with your instructor or writing center tutor, bring a list of specific questions about your paper, and be sure to make careful notes about what you discuss. You can refer to these notes when you revise your paper.

Close-up: Using Your Native Language

FAQs links

Depending on your language background and skills, you may find it helpful to use your native language in some stages of your writing. When you are making notes about the content of your paper, you may be able to generate more ideas and record them more quickly if you do some of the work in your native language. Additionally, when you are drafting your paper and cannot think of a particular word in English, it may be better simply to write the word in your native language (and come back to it later) so you do not lose your train of thought. However, if you use another language a great deal as you draft your writing and then try to translate your work into English, the English may sound awkward or be hard to understand. The best strategy when you draft your papers is to write in English as much as you can, using the vocabulary and structures that you already know.

Close-up: Characteristics of US Classrooms

Here are some other aspects of US classrooms that may be unfamiliar to you:

- **Punctuality** Students are expected to be in their seats and ready to begin class at the scheduled time. If you are late repeatedly, your grade may be lowered.

(continued)

Characteristics of US classrooms (continued)

- **Student–Instructor Relationships** The relationship between students and instructors may be more casual or friendly than you are used to. However, instructors still expect students to abide by the rules they set.
- **Class Discussion** Instructors typically expect students to volunteer ideas in class and may even enjoy it when students disagree with instructors' opinions (as long as the students can make good arguments for their positions). Rather than being a sign of disrespect, this is usually considered to be evidence of interest and involvement in the topic under discussion.

For ESL writers (as for many native English writers), grammar can be a persistent problem. Grammatical knowledge in a second language usually develops slowly, with time and practice, and much about English is idiomatic (not subject to easy-to-learn rules). The rest of this chapter is designed to provide you with the tools you will need to address some of the most common grammatical errors made by ESL writers.

61a Editing Your Work

Editing your paper involves focusing on grammar, spelling, punctuation, and mechanics. The approach you take to editing for grammar errors should depend on your strengths and weaknesses in English.

Checklist: Editing Strategies

- ☐ **If you learned English mostly by speaking it, if you have strong oral skills, and if you usually make correct judgments about English by instinct,** the best approach for you may be reading your paper aloud and listening for mistakes, correcting them by deciding what sounds right. You may even find that as you read aloud, you automatically correct your written mistakes as you speak. (Be sure to transfer those corrections to your paper.) In addition to proofreading your paper from beginning to end, you might find it helpful to start from the end of the paper, reading and proofreading sentence by sentence. This strategy can keep you from being distracted by your ideas, allowing you to focus on grammar alone.

- ☐ **If you learned English mostly by reading, studying grammar rules, and/or translating between your native language and English,** you may not feel that you have good instincts about what sounds right in English. If this is the case, you should take a different approach to editing your papers. First, identify the errors you make most frequently by looking at earlier papers your instructor has marked or by asking your instructor for help. Once you have identified your most common errors, read through your paper, checking each sentence for these errors. Try to apply the grammar and mechanics rules you already know, or check the relevant grammar explanations in this chapter for help.

After you check your paper for grammar errors, you should check again to make sure that you have used proper punctuation, capitalization, and spelling. If you have difficulty with spelling, you can use a spell checker to help you, but remember that spell checkers cannot catch every error. After you have made grammar and mechanics corrections on your own, you can seek outside help in identifying errors you might have missed. You should also keep a notebook with a list of your most frequent grammatical errors and review these errors frequently.

Exercise 1

An ESL student in a composition course wrote the following paragraph as part of a draft of a paper about his experiences learning to write in English. After his instructor corrected the errors in the paragraph, the student made a chart and recorded them.

A. Read the paragraph, referring when necessary to the correction symbols on the inside back cover of this book. Then, examine the student's chart (see Figure 61.1).

In elementary school, my teachers used to teach us how to write ~~the~~ (b)Basic English. [For example, how to write the l(e)itters from A to Z and also some basic (frag) vocabular(y)~~ies~~.] I was young at that time and learning how to write in a second language ~~is~~ (was) very difficult(,). even writing in ~~the~~ (b)Basic English. My teachers helped me to improve my writing by using cards(and), posters(and), giving me quizzes and a lot of assignment^s^. In the ~~bingeing~~ beginning of my study of English writing, I was always receiving low grades. But after a while I made my grades move~~d~~ up by not ^being^ afraid of English and by doing what my teachers asked me to do. For example, when the teacher gave me a new word in English to memorize~~;~~, I wrote it many times on paper to make it stick ~~on~~ in my mind.

Word/phrase problems

error	*error type*	*correct form*
the Basic English	*article, capitalization*	*basic English*
litters	*spelling*	*letters*
vocabularies	*singular/plural*	*vocabulary*
is	*verb form*	*was*
a lot of assignment	*singular/plural*	*a lot of assignments*
bingeing	*spelling*	*beginning*
I made my grades moved up	*verb form*	*I made my grades move up*
by not afraid	*missing verb*	*by not being afraid*
repeating strategy	*article*	*a repeating strategy*
stick on my mind	*preposition*	*stick in my mind*

Sentence problems

problem: sentence fragment, sentence 2

solution: Reword and join the fragment to the sentence before it: In elementary school, my teachers used to teach us how to write basic English, including how to write the letters from A to Z and also some basic vocabulary.

problem: confusing list, sentence 4

solution: Add "and" twice:

. . . by using cards and posters and by giving me quizzes and a lot of assignments.

List of punctuation problems

missing comma, sentence 3

semicolon should be a comma, sentence 9

Figure 61.1 Student writer's chart.

B. Now, examine a piece of your own writing that has been corrected by your instructor. Make a chart similar to the one in Figure 61.1. To record your errors, either choose error types from the following list, or make up labels of your own that make sense to you.

Possible Error Types

verb form	preposition	spelling
singular/plural	wrong word	capitalization
article (*a*, *an*, *the*)		

Checklist: Getting Outside Help with Editing

- ☐ **Ask a tutor or a friend for help.** After you have done your best to edit your own paper, you may want to ask for help from a Writing Center tutor, from your instructor, or from a friend whose English skills you trust. Begin by asking your helper to tell you about any errors that keep him or her from understanding the meaning of your paper, and work together to revise your writing so that your ideas are clear. Next, ask your helper to underline or circle the errors in your paper that are distracting, and then try to correct them (with your helper's assistance, when necessary). You will learn more this way than you will if your helper corrects your errors for you.
- ☐ **Use a grammar checker.** Your computer's grammar checker may give you some help with editing, but you may not find it very helpful since such grammar checkers are usually not designed to catch the types of errors typically made by ESL students.
- ☐ **Use a dictionary.** The dictionary can also be a good source of grammar help, especially if you use a dictionary designed for nonnative English speakers.

Exercise 2

This exercise is designed to familiarize you with an online dictionary for ESL learners so that you can use such a dictionary to help you edit your writing. To complete this exercise, you will need to log on to the online version of *Heinle's Newbury House Dictionary of American English*, 4th edition (http://nhd.heinle.com).

A. Examine the online dictionary entry for the word *tuition* (see Figure 61.2).

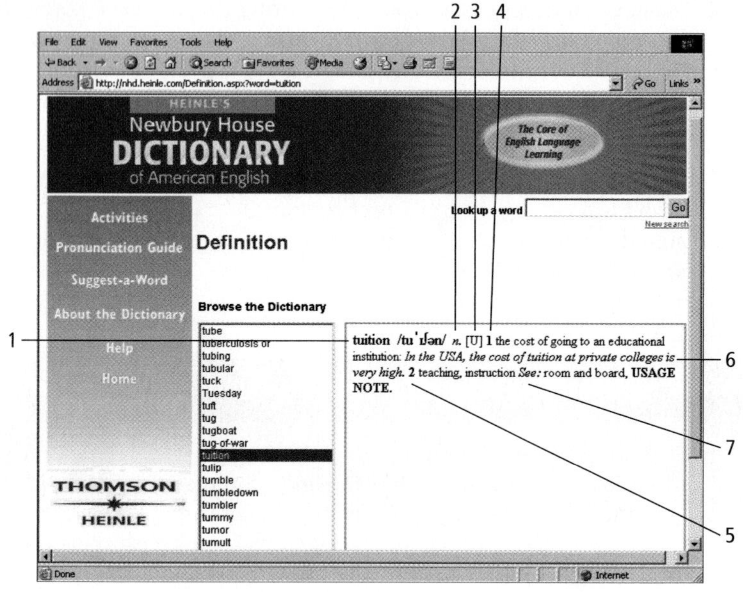

Figure 61.2 Online dictionary entry for *tuition*.

This entry gives you several pieces of information:

1. spelling
2. indication (with the abbreviation *n.*) that the word is a noun
3. indication (with the abbreviation [U]) that this noun is uncountable (noncount).

See 61c1

4., 5. definitions of the word
6. example sentence
7. usage note about the related phrase *room and board*

Now, look up the online dictionary entry for *room and board*, and write an explanation of the difference between *tuition* and *room and board.*

B. Examine the online dictionary entry for the word *ride* (see Figure 61.3).

This entry gives you the following information:

1. indication (with the abbreviation *v.*) that the word can be used as a verb
2. that the simple past form of *ride* is *rode:* I rode my bike yesterday.
3. that the past participle of *ride* is *ridden:* She has ridden the same bike for ten years.
4. that the present participle of *ride* is *riding:* He's out riding his horse.

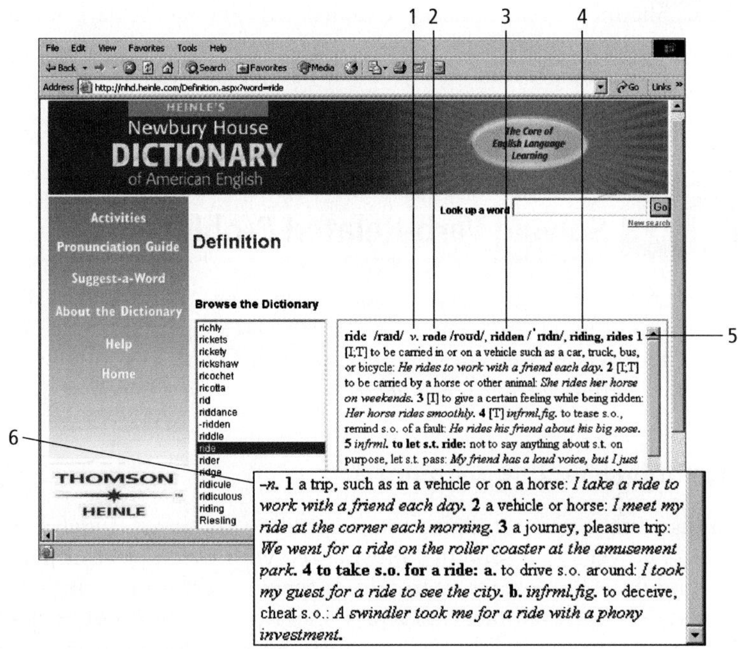

Figure 61.3 Online dictionary entry for *ride*.

5. that the third person conjugation of *ride* is *rides:* He <u>rides</u> to school with the neighbors.
6. indication (with the abbreviation *n.*) that *ride* can also be used as a noun

Now, go to http://nhd.heinle.com to read the complete entry for *ride*, and answer the following questions:

1. What does the sentence, "The teacher rode them about their poor attendance." mean?
2. If someone calls "Shotgun!" on the way to the car, what does it mean?
3. If I say my investment advisor "took me for a ride," what do I probably mean?

C. Using the online version of *Heinle's Newbury House Dictionary of American English*, 4th edition (http://nhd.heinle.com), look up the answers to the following questions:

1. What does the word *paternalistic* mean? (You will need to look up its root word, *paternalism*, to find out.)
2. Which preposition—*at*, *with*, or *in*—is usually used with the verb *participate*?

3. Should the season *spring* be capitalized? Should the days of the week be capitalized?
4. Have you ever had *cabin fever*? What does it mean?

61b Solving Verb-Related Problems

Although verbs in all languages perform similar functions, they differ in form and usage from language to language—perhaps more than any other part of speech or grammatical unit. The most common ESL errors related to verbs involve *subject-verb agreement* and *verb tense.*

(1) Subject-Verb Agreement

English verbs change their form according to *person*, *number*, and *tense*. The verb in a sentence must agree with the subject in person and number. **Person** refers to *who* or *what* is performing the action of the verb (for example, *I*, *you*, or someone else). **Number** refers to *how many* people or things are performing the action (one or more than one).

In English, the rules for subject-verb agreement are fairly straightforward. With regular verbs in the present tense, for third-person singular subjects (for example, *he*, *she*, *it*, *the dog*, *Mary*), add *s* or *es* to the base form of the verb. If you are not sure whether to add *s* or *es*, consult a dictionary. For all other subjects (for example, *I*, *you*, *we*, *they*, *the dogs*), use the base form of the verb.

I *write*	we *write*
you (singular) *write*	you (plural) *write*
he, she, it *writes*	they *write*

Two very common **irregular verbs** are *be* and *have*, which take the following forms in the present tense.

I *am*	we *are*
you (singular) *are*	you (plural) *are*
he, she, it *is*	they *are*
I *have*	we *have*
you (singular) *have*	you (plural) *have*
he, she, it *has*	they *have*

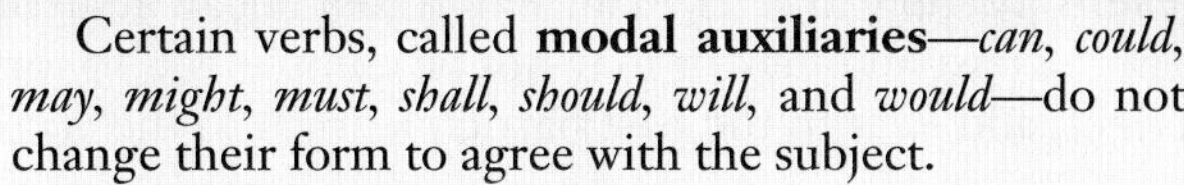

Close-up: Modal Auxiliaries

Certain verbs, called **modal auxiliaries**—*can*, *could*, *may*, *might*, *must*, *shall*, *should*, *will*, and *would*—do not change their form to agree with the subject.

I *can* buy the props, and then Myria and Emma *can* paint them tomorrow.

Mr. Lam and Ms. Boyer *might* be able to attend, but Mr. Esposito *might* not be able to make it.

Roisin *would* enjoy law school, but his brothers probably *would* not.

(2) Forming Past, Present, and Future Verbs

In English, the form of a verb changes according to *when* the action of the verb takes place—in the **past, present,** or **future.** For example, adding *ed* to many English verbs creates a past tense and places the action of the verb in the past. One problem that many nonnative English speakers have with English verb tenses results from the large number of irregular verbs in English: for example, the first-person singular simple past form of the verb *to sing* is not "I singed," but "I sang," and the first-person singular simple past form of the verb *to fight* is not "I fighted," but "I fought." See 47b

The following examples demonstrate how to create various verb forms related to the past, present, and future tenses. The verb that is used to illustrate the various forms is *eat*, which is an irregular verb. The simple past form of *eat* is *ate*, and the past participle is *eaten*.

Use the **simple present form** for something that happens regularly or that is true over time.

I eat lunch at noon every day.

Use the **simple past** to refer to an action completed in the past. To form the simple past, add *d* or *ed* to regular verbs. **Irregular verbs,** like *eat*, have special past tense forms, which you can find in a dictionary.

I ate lunch at noon yesterday.

Use the **simple future** to refer to an action that will occur in the future. To form the simple future, add *will* before the simple present verb form.

I will eat lunch at noon tomorrow.

Use the **present perfect** to refer to an action that began at an unspecified time in the past and may or may not be completed. To form the present perfect, add *have* to the past participle form of the verb.

I have eaten lunch.

Use the **past perfect** to refer to an action that occurred at a particular time in the past, often before another action. To form the past perfect, add *had* to the past participle form of the verb.

I had already eaten lunch when my mother arrived.

Use the **future perfect** to refer to an action in the future that will occur before another action in the future. To form the future perfect, add *will have* before the past participle form of the verb.

I will have eaten lunch when the meeting starts.

Use the **present progressive** to refer to an action that is occurring at the time it is expressed in speech or writing. To form the present progressive, add a form of the present verb *be* before the verb, and add *ing* to the simple present form of the verb.

I am eating lunch right now.

Use the **past progressive** to indicate a continuous activity in the past or an action occurring in the past at the same time as another past action. To form the past progressive, add a form of the simple past verb *be* before the verb, and add *ing* to the simple present form of the verb.

I was eating lunch when someone knocked on the door.

Use the **future progressive** to indicate a continuing action in the future. To form the future progressive, add a future form of the verb *be* before the verb, and add *ing* to the simple present form of the verb.

I will be eating lunch when Maria delivers the package tomorrow. (Note that the simple present verb form is used in the second part of the sentence to refer to an action that will occur in the future.)

Use the **present perfect progressive** to indicate an action continuing from the past into the present and possibly into the future.

To form the present perfect progressive, add *have been* before the verb, and add *ing* to the simple present form of the verb.

I have been eating lunch at noon every day for three years.

Use the **past perfect progressive** to indicate that a past action continued until another action occurred. To form the past perfect progressive, add *had been* before the verb, and add *ing* to the simple present form of the verb.

I had been eating lunch at noon every day until my work schedule changed.

Use the **future perfect progressive** to indicate that an action will continue until a certain future time. To form the future perfect progressive, add *will have been* before the verb, and add *ing* to the simple present form of the verb.

On December 8, I will have been eating lunch at noon every day for four years.

Close-up: Choosing the Simplest Verb Forms

Some nonnative English speakers use verb forms that are more complicated than they need to be. They may do this because their native language uses more complicated verb forms than English does or because they "over-correct" their verbs into complicated forms. Specifically, nonnative speakers tend to use progressive and perfect verb forms instead of simple verb forms. To communicate your ideas clearly to an English-speaking audience, choose the simplest possible verb form.

(3) Using Auxiliary Verbs to Form Past, Present, and Future Verbs

The **auxiliary verbs** (also known as helping verbs) *be*, *have*, and *do* are used to create some present, past, and future forms of verbs in English: "Julio *is taking* a vacation"; "I *have been* tired lately"; "He *does* not *need* a license." The auxiliary verbs *be*, *have*, and *do* change form to reflect the time frame of the action or situation and to agree with the subject; however, the main verb remains in simple present or simple past form.

I *am* ready to go to the meeting.

They *were* ready to go to the meeting.

Mr. Chuen *has lived* in that house for eight years.

They *have lived* near downtown for only one year.

Ms. Trepagnier *does* not *like* the opera.

My brothers *do* not *want* to see a Broadway musical.

NOTE: Remember, only auxiliary verbs, not the verbs they "help," change form to indicate person, number, and tense.

Present: We have to eat.

Past: We had to eat. (not "We had to ate.")

Exercise 3

A student wrote the following two paragraphs as part of a paper for his ESL composition I class. He was asked to write about several interviews he conducted with people in his future profession, hotel management. The paragraphs contain errors in subject-verb agreement and verb tense, which the student's instructor underlined. Correct the underlined verbs by changing their form: begin by considering when the action took place, and then choose the simplest appropriate verb form to express that time. (Be sure to pay attention to the meaning and context of the sentences to determine which verb form is appropriate.)

In the past, when someone (1) ask me why I was interested in the hotel business, I always (2) have a hard time answering that question. I do not know exactly when and why I (3) decide to be a hotel manager. The only reason I can think of is my father. In his current job, he (4) travel a lot, and I have had a few chances to follow him and see other cities. Every time I went with him on a business trip, we (5) spended the night in a hotel, and I was surprised at how much hotels (6) does to satisfy their customers. All the employees are always friendly and polite. This gave me a positive image of hotels that made me (7) decided that the hotel business would be right for me.

For this paper, I (8) spended almost two weeks interviewing department heads at a local Hilton Hotel. Mr. Andrew Plain, the person who (9) spend the most time with me, (10) share an experience related to when he first got into the business. One of his first jobs was to plan a wedding, and he (11) feel a lot of responsibility because he (12) believe that a wedding is a one-time life experience for most people. So he wanted to take care of everything and make sure that everything was on track. To prepare for the wedding, he (13) need to work almost every Sunday, and one night he even (14) have to sleep in his office to attend the early wedding ceremony the next morning. From my experience with this interview, I realized that the people who are interested in the hotel business (15) needs great dedication to their career.

Getting Help from the Dictionary

You may have trouble with items 5, 8, and 9 of Exercise 3 if you do not know the correct past tense forms of the verb *spend*, which is irregular. For help, look up the word *spend* in the dictionary. The first word after the word *spend* is the simple past form of *spend*.

(4) Negative Verbs

The meaning of a verb may be made **negative** in English in a variety of ways, chiefly by adding the words *not* or *does not* to the verb (is, *is not;* can ski, *cannot* ski; drives a car, *does not* drive a car).

Nonnative English speakers (and some native speakers) sometimes use double negatives. A double negative is an error that occurs when the meaning of a verb is made negative not just once but twice in a single sentence. In some languages, a double structure is actually required in order to negate a verb; for example, the French phrase *je ne sais pas* ("I don't know") uses the double structure *ne/pas* around the verb *sais*. However, a double negative is incorrect in written English.

See 49e

Henry doesn't have ~~no~~ *any* friends at all. (*or* Henry ~~doesn't have~~ *has* no friends at all.)

I looked for articles in the library, but there weren't ~~none~~ *any*.
(*or* I looked for articles in the library, but there were~~n't~~ none.)

(5) Phrasal Verbs

Many verbs in English are composed of two or more words—for example, *check up on, run for, turn into,* and *wait on.* These verbs are called **phrasal verbs.** It is important to become familiar with phrasal verbs and their definitions so you will recognize these verbs as phrasal verbs instead of as verbs that are followed by prepositions. Knowing the definitions of the individual words that make up these verbs is not always enough to enable you to define the phrasal verbs accurately. Even after consulting a dictionary, you will need to pay close attention to the use of these verbs in speech and writing.

Sometimes the words that make up a phrasal verb can be separated from each other by a direct object. In these **separable phrasal verbs,** the object can come either before or after the preposition. For example, "Ellen *turned down* the job offer" and "Ellen *turned* the job offer *down*" are both correct. However, when the object is a pronoun, the pronoun must come before the preposition. Therefore, "Ellen turned *it* down " is correct; "Ellen turned down *it*" is incorrect.

Close-up: Separable Phrasal Verbs

Verb	Definition
call off	cancel
carry on	continue
cheer up	make happy
clean out	clean the inside of
cut down	reduce
figure out	solve
fill in	substitute
find out	discover
give back	return something
give up	stop doing something or stop trying
leave out	omit
pass on	transmit
put away	place something in its proper place
put back	place something in its original place
put off	postpone
start over	start again
talk over	discuss
throw away/out	discard
touch up	repair

However, some phrasal verbs—such as *look into*, *make up for*, and *break into*—consist of words that can never be separated. With these **inseparable phrasal verbs,** you do not have a choice about where to place the object; the object must always follow the preposition. For example, "Anna *cared for* her niece" is correct, but "Anna *cared* her niece *for*" is incorrect.

Close-up: Inseparable Phrasal Verbs

Verb	Definition
come down with	develop an illness
come up with	produce
do away with	abolish
fall behind in	lag
get along with	be congenial with
get away with	avoid punishment
keep up with	maintain the same achievement or speed
look up to	admire
make up for	compensate
put up with	tolerate
run into	meet by chance
see to	arrange
show up	arrive
stand by	wait *or* remain loyal to
stand up for	support
watch out for	beware of *or* protect

(6) Voice

Verbs may be in either active or passive voice. When the subject of a sentence performs the action of the verb, the verb is in **active voice.** When the action of the verb is performed on the subject, the verb is in **passive voice.**

See 47d

Karla and Miguel purchased the plane tickets. (active voice)

The plane tickets were purchased by Karla and Miguel. (passive voice)

Because your writing will usually be clearer and more concise if you use the active voice, you should use the passive voice only when you have a good reason to do so. For example, in scientific writing, it is often common for writers to use the passive voice in order to convey the idea of scientific objectivity (lack of bias).

(7) Using Infinitives and Gerunds as Nouns

In English, two verb forms may be used as nouns: **infinitives,** which always begin with *to* (as in *to work, to sleep, to eat*), and **gerunds,** which always end in *-ing*, (as in *working, sleeping, eating*).

To bite into this steak requires better teeth than mine. (infinitive used as a noun)

Cooking is one of my favorite hobbies. (gerund used as a noun)

Sometimes the gerund and the infinitive form of the same verb can be used interchangeably. For example, "He continued *to sleep*" and "He continued *sleeping*" convey the same meaning. However, this is not always the case. Saying, "Marco and Lisa stopped *to eat* at Julio's Café" is not the same as saying, "Marco and Lisa stopped *eating* at Julio's Café." In this example, the meaning of the sentence changes depending on whether a gerund or infinitive is used.

(8) Using Participles as Adjectives

In English, verb forms called **present participles** and **past participles** are frequently used as adjectives. Present participles usually end in *-ing*, as in *working*, *sleeping*, and *eating*, and past participles usually end in *-ed*, *-t*, or *-en*, as in *worked*, *slept*, and *eaten*.

According to the Bible, God spoke to Moses from a *burning* bush. (present participle used as an adjective)

Some people think raw fish is healthier than *cooked* fish. (past participle used as an adjective)

A **participial phrase** is a group of words consisting of the participle plus the noun phrase that functions as the object or complement of the action being expressed by the participle. To avoid confusion, the participial phrase must be placed as close as possible to the noun it modifies.

Having visited San Francisco last week, Jim and Lynn showed us pictures from their vacation. (The participial phrase is used as an adjective that modifies *Jim and Lynn*.)

See 51d

NOTE: When a participial phrase falls at the beginning of a sentence, a comma is used to set it off. When a participial phrase is used in the middle of a sentence, commas should be used only if the phrase is *not* essential to the meaning of the sentence. No commas should be used if the participial phrase is essential to the meaning of the sentence.

(9) Transitive and Intransitive Verbs

Many nonnative English speakers find it difficult to decide whether or not a verb needs an object and in what order direct and indirect objects should appear in a sentence. Learning the difference between transitive verbs and intransitive verbs can help you with such problems.

A **transitive verb** is a verb that has a direct object: "My father asked a question" (subject + verb + direct object). In this example, *asked* is a transitive verb; it needs an object to complete its meaning.

An **intransitive verb** is a verb that does not take an object: "The doctor smiled" (subject + verb). In this example, *smiled* is an intransitive verb; it does not need an object to complete its meaning.

A transitive verb may be followed by a direct object or by both an indirect object and a direct object. (An indirect object answers the question "To whom?" or "For whom?") The indirect object may come before or after the direct object. If the indirect object follows the direct object, the preposition *to* or *for* must precede the indirect object.

s v do
Keith wrote a letter. (subject + verb + direct object)

s v io do
Keith wrote his friend a letter. (subject + verb + indirect object + direct object)

s v do io
Keith wrote a letter *to* his friend. (subject + verb + direct object + *to/for* + indirect object)

Some verbs in English look similar and have similar meanings, except that one is transitive and the other is intransitive. For example, *lie* is intransitive, *lay* is transitive; *sit* is intransitive, *set* is transitive; *rise* is intransitive, *raise* is transitive. Knowing whether a verb is transitive or intransitive will help you with troublesome verb pairs like these and help you place the words in the correct order.

NOTE: It is also important to know whether a verb is transitive or intransitive because only transitive verbs can be used in the passive voice. To determine whether a verb is transitive or intransitive—that is, to determine whether or not it needs an object—consult the example phrases in a dictionary. See 47d

(10) Verbs Formed from Nouns

In English, nouns can sometimes be used as verbs, with no change in form (other than the addition of an *s* for agreement with third-person singular subjects or the addition of past tense endings). For example, the nouns *chair*, *book*, *frame*, and *father* can all be used as verbs.

She *chairs* a committee on neighborhood safety.

We *booked* a flight to New York for next week.

I will *frame* my daughter's diploma after she graduates.

He *fathered* several children out of wedlock.

61c Solving Noun-Related Problems

Nouns name things: people, objects, places, feelings, and ideas. In English, most nouns have different forms for **singular** and **plural** number (such as singular *star* and plural *stars*), but there are exceptions to this rule. In English, two or more nouns may be used to form a single **compound noun:** "She ate a *cheese sandwich*."

The most common ESL errors related to nouns involve the singular-plural distinction and the use of articles with nouns.

(1) The Singular-Plural Distinction

In English, nouns may have **number;** that is, they may change in form according to whether they name one thing or more than one thing. If a noun names one thing, it is a singular noun; if a noun names more than one thing, it is a plural noun.

To change most singular nouns to plural, add *s* or *es* to the singular form. For example, *pencil* changes to *pencils*, and *bench* changes to *benches*.

However, many nouns in English are irregular. To change an irregular noun from singular to plural, you need to change the spelling of the word instead of just adding a suffix to the word. For example, *mouse* changes to *mice*, *tooth* changes to *teeth*, and *child* changes to *children*.

Close-up: Noncount Nouns

Some English nouns do not have a plural form. These are called **noncount nouns** because what they name cannot be counted. (**Count nouns** name items that can be counted, such as *woman* or *desk*.) The following commonly used nouns are noncount nouns. These words have no plural forms. Therefore, you should never add *s* or *es* to them.

advice
clothing
education
enthusiasm
equipment
evidence
furniture
homework
information
knowledge
luggage
merchandise
revenge

NOTE: Some noncount nouns—such as *luggage* or *furniture*—seem like items that can be counted. To avoid confusion, consult the example phrases in a dictionary in order to determine whether a noun takes a regular plural form or an irregular plural form and to determine whether it is a count or a noncount noun.

Exercise 4

An ESL student wrote the following paragraph as part of a composition paper about her experiences learning English. Read the paragraph, and decide which of the underlined words need to be made plural and which should remain unchanged. If a word should be made plural, make the necessary correction. If a word is correct as is, mark it with a *C*.

Visiting Ireland for three (1) month expanded my (2) knowledge of English. I took a part-time English (3) course, which was the key to improving my writing. The (4) course helped me understand the essential (5) rule of English, and I learned a lot of new (6) vocabulary and expressions. In the first three (7) lecture, the teacher, Mr. Nelson, explained the fundamentals of writing in English. My (8) enthusiasm for the English language increased because I realized the importance of this (9) language for my (10) future. Mr. Nelson recommended that I read more English (11) book. I took his advice, and my English got better.

Getting Help from the Dictionary

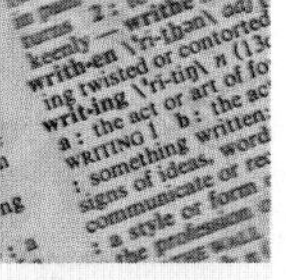

Some of the nouns in Exercise 4 are noncount nouns, which cannot be made plural. If you are not sure whether a noun is countable or not, look it up in a dictionary.

(2) Using Articles with Nouns

English has two types of **articles,** indefinite and definite. Use an **indefinite article** (*a* or *an*) with a noun when readers are not familiar with the noun you are naming—for example, when you are introducing a noun for the first time. To say, "Jatin entered *a* building," signals to the audience that you are introducing the idea of the building into your speech or writing for the first time. The building is unspecific, or indefinite, until it has been identified.

The indefinite article *a* is used when the word following it (which may be a noun or an adjective) begins with a consonant or with a consonant sound: *a tree, a onetime offer*. The indefinite article *an* is used if the word following it begins with a vowel (*a, e, i, o,* or *u*) or with a vowel sound: *an apple, an honor*.

Use the **definite article** (*the*) when the noun you are naming has already been introduced, when the noun is already familiar to readers, or when the noun to which you refer is specific. To say, "Jatin entered *the* building," signals to readers that you are referring to the same building you mentioned earlier. The building has now become specific and may be referred to by the definite article.

Close-up: Using Articles with Nouns

There are three main exceptions to the rules governing the use of articles with nouns:

1. A **plural noun** does not require an **indefinite article:** "I love horses," not "I love *a* horses." (A plural noun does, however, require a definite article when you have already introduced the noun to your readers or when you are referring to a specific plural noun: "I love *the* horses in the national park near my house.")
2. A **noncount noun** may or may not require an article.

   "Love conquers all," not "*A* love conquers all" or "*The* love conquers all."

   "*A* good education is important," not "Good education is important."

   "*The* homework is difficult" or "Homework is difficult," not "*A* homework is difficult."

   To help determine whether or not a noncount noun requires an article, look up that noun in a dictionary and consult the sample sentences provided.
3. A **proper noun,** which names a particular person, place, or thing, sometimes takes an article and sometimes does not. When you use an article with a proper noun, do not capitalize the article unless the article is the first word of the sentence.

   "*The* Mississippi River is one of the longest rivers in the world," not "Mississippi River is one of the longest rivers in the world."

   "Teresa was born in *the* United States," not "Teresa was born in United States."

   "China is the most populous nation on earth," not "*The* China is the most populous nation on earth."

To find out whether or not a proper noun requires an article, look up that noun in a dictionary, and consult the sample sentences provided.

Exercise 5

The following introductory paragraph of a paper about renewable energy power sources was written for an ESL composition course. Read the paragraph, and decide whether or not each of the underlined noun phrases requires an article. If a noun phrase is correct as is, mark it with a *C*. If a noun phrase needs an article, indicate whether that article should be *a*, *an*, or *the*.

(1) Use of electrical power has increased dramatically over (2) last thirty years and continues to rise. (3) Most ordinary sources of (4) electricity require (5) oil, (6) gas, or (7) uranium, which are not (8) renewable resources. Living without (9) electrical power is not feasible as long as everything in our lives depends on (10) electricity, but (11) entire world will be in (12) big crisis if (13) ignorance regarding renewable energy continues. (14) Renewable energy, including (15) solar energy, (16) wind energy, (17) hydro energy, and (18) biomass energy, need (19) more attention from (20) scientists.

Getting Help from the Dictionary

If you are uncertain whether or not to use an article with a certain noun, look up that noun in a dictionary, and use the sample sentences provided as a guide. When dealing with a noun phrase, be sure to look up the main noun. For example, in item (1), look up *use*, and in item (2), look up *year*.

Close-up: Learning to Use Articles with Nouns

The rules for using articles are complicated. In fact, even linguists sometimes have trouble explaining why a certain noun in a certain context does or does not require an article. The rules for article usage outlined in this section may be helpful, but they will not work all the time. For people who speak first languages that do not have an article system (or that have an article system that works very differently from that of English), articles are one of the hardest aspects of the English language to acquire.

(3) Using Other Determiners with Nouns

Determiners are words that function as adjectives to limit or qualify the meaning of nouns. In addition to articles, nouns may be identified by other determiners that function in ways similar to articles, such as demonstrative pronouns, possessive nouns and pronouns, numbers (both cardinal and ordinal), and other words indicating amount or number order.

Close-up: Using Other Determiners with Nouns

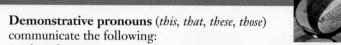

- **Demonstrative pronouns** (*this, that, these, those*) communicate the following:
  1. the relative nearness or farness of the noun from the speaker's position. Use *this* and *these* for things that are near, *that* and *those* for things that are far: *this* book on my desk, *that* book on your desk; *these* shoes on my feet, *those* shoes in the closet.
  2. the number of things indicated. Use *this* and *that* for singular nouns, *these* and *those* for plural nouns: *this* (or *that*) flower in the vase; *these* (or *those*) flowers in the garden.
- **Possessive nouns and pronouns** (*Ashraf's, his, their*) show who or what the noun belongs to: *Maria's* courage, *everybody's* fears, the *country's* natural resources, *my* personality, *our* groceries.
- **Cardinal numbers** (*three, fifty, a thousand*) indicate the quantity of the noun: *seven* continents, *twelve* apples, *a hundred* lakes.
- **Ordinal numbers** (*first, tenth, thirtieth*) indicate in what order the noun appears among other items: *third* planet from the sun, *first* date, *tenth* anniversary.
- Words other than numbers may indicate **amount** (*many, few*) or **order** (*next, last*) and function in the same ways as cardinal and ordinal numbers: *few* opportunities, *last* chance.

61d Using Prepositions

In English, prepositions (such as *to, from, at, with, among,* and *between*) link noun phrases to other parts of a sentence. Prepositions convey several different kinds of information:

- Relations to **time** (*at* nine o'clock, *in* five minutes, *for* a month)
- Relations to **place** (*in* the classroom, *at* the library, *beside* the chair) and **direction** (*to* the market, *onto* the stage, *toward* the freeway)
- Relations of **association** (go *with* someone, the tip *of* the iceberg)
- Relations of **purpose** (working *for* money, dieting *to* lose weight)

In some languages, prepositions may be used quite differently, may exist in forms quite different from English, or may not exist at all. Therefore, speakers of those languages may have difficulty with English prepositions. Speakers of languages with prepositions very similar to those in English—especially Romance languages such as Spanish, French, and Italian—have a different problem: they may be tempted to translate their own languages' prepositional phrases directly into English. Instead of doing this, it is better to try to remember which prepositions are used in common prepositional phrases.

(1) Commonly Used Prepositional Phrases

In English, the use of prepositions is often idiomatic rather than governed by grammatical rules. In many cases, therefore, learners of English as a second language need to memorize which prepositions are used in which phrases.

In English, some prepositions that relate to time have specific uses with certain nouns, such as days, months, and seasons:

- *On* is used with days and specific dates: *on* Monday, *on* September 13, 1977.
- *In* is used with months, seasons, and years: *in* November, *in* the spring, *in* 1999.
- *In* is also used when referring to some parts of the day, as in the following cases: *in* the morning, *in* the afternoon, *in* the evening.
- *At* is used to refer to other parts of the day: *at* noon, *at* night, *at* seven o'clock.

Close-up: Difficult Prepositional Phrases

The following phrases (accompanied by their correct prepositions) sometimes cause difficulties for ESL writers:

according *to* | *at* least | relevant *to*
apologize *to* | *at* most | similar *to*
appeal *to* | refer *to* | subscribe *to*
different *from*

(2) Commonly Confused Prepositions

The prepositions *to*, *in*, *on*, *into*, and *onto* are very similar to one another and are therefore easily confused.

Close-up: Basic Definitions of Common Prepositions

- *To* is the basic preposition of direction. It indicates movement toward a physical place: "She went *to* the restaurant"; "He went *to* the meeting." *To* is also used to form the infinitive of a verb: "He wanted *to deposit* his paycheck before noon"; "Irene offered *to drive* Maria to the baseball game."
- *In* indicates that something is within the boundaries of a particular space or period of time: "My son is *in* the garden"; "I like to ski *in* the winter"; "The map is *in* the car."
- *On* indicates position above or the state of being supported by something: "The toys are *on* the porch"; "The baby sat *on* my lap"; "The book is *on* top of the magazine."
- *Into* indicates movement to the inside or interior of something: "She walked *into* the room"; "I threw the stone *into* the lake"; "He put the photos *into* the box." Although *into* and *in* are sometimes interchangeable, note that usage depends on whether the subject is stationary or moving. *Into* usually indicates movement, as in "I jumped *into* the water." *In* usually indicates a stationary position relative to the object of the preposition, as in "Mary is swimming *in* the water."
- *Onto* indicates movement to a position on top of something: "The cat jumped *onto* the chair"; "Crumbs are falling *onto* the floor." Both *on* and *onto* can be used to indicate a position on top of something (and therefore they can sometimes be used interchangeably), but *onto* specifies that the subject is moving to a place from a different place or from an outside position.

(3) Pronouns in Prepositional Phrases

Both native and nonnative English speakers sometimes have difficulty choosing which pronoun should follow a preposition. The pronoun that is the object of a preposition should be in the objective case.

> Would you like to go to a movie with me? (not "Would you like to go to a movie with *I*?")
>
> Would you like to eat lunch with Felix and me ? (not "Would you like to eat lunch with Felix and *I*?")
>
> Just between you and me, I think you won the contest. (not "Just between *you* and *I*, I think you won the contest.")

Exercise 6

An ESL student in a composition class wrote the following paragraphs as part of a paper about her experiences learning to write in English. In several cases, she chose the wrong prepositions. The student's instructor has underlined the misused prepositions. Your task is to replace each underlined preposition with a correct preposition. (In some cases, there may be more than one possible correct answer.) If you have trouble, see the "Getting Help from the Dictionary" box, which follows the exercise.

My first experience writing (1) <u>of</u> English took place (2) <u>at</u> my early youth. I don't remember what the experience was like, but I do know that I have improved my writing skills since then. The improvement stems from various reasons. One major impact (3) <u>to</u> my writing was the fact that I attended an American school (4) <u>of</u> my country. This helped a lot because the first language (5) <u>to</u> the school was English. Being surrounded (6) <u>in</u> English helped me improve both my verbal skills and my writing skills. Another major factor that helped me develop my English writing skills, especially my grammar and vocabulary, was reading novels.

(7) <u>At</u> the future, I plan to improve my writing skills in English by participating (8) <u>to</u> several activities. I plan to read more novels so I can further develop the grammar and vocabulary skills that will help me earn my degree. I also plan to communicate verbally with native speakers and to listen (9) <u>at</u> public speeches (such as the president's state of the union address), which usually contain rich vocabulary. But my main plan is to keep writing more papers and discussing my writing (10) <u>to</u> my instructor. The more I write, the more confident I will become and the more my writing will improve. And there is always room for improvement.

Getting Help from the Dictionary

In some cases, you can determine which preposition to use by consulting a dictionary. For example, you can find the answers to items 3, 6, 7, 8, 9, and 10 in Exercise 7 by consulting a dictionary. Look up a noun or verb that is part of the phrase in question, and within the dictionary entry for each of these words, you will find example phrases containing the correct preposition. *Hint:* For item (3), look up the word *impact*, and for item (6), look up *surround*.

61e Understanding Word Order

Word order is extremely important in English sentences. For example, word order may indicate which word is the subject of the sentence and which is the object, or it may indicate whether the sentence is a question or a statement.

(1) Standard Word Order

Like Chinese, English is an "SVO" language, one in which the most typical sentence pattern is "subject-verb-object." (Arabic, by contrast, is an example of a "VSO" language.) If you deviate from the SVO pattern, you may not communicate your ideas clearly. There are times, however, when writers in English do deviate from the SVO pattern. For information on some of these instances, **see 61e2–6.**

(2) Word Order in Questions

Word order in questions can be particularly troublesome for speakers of languages other than English because there are so many different ways to arrange words when questions are formed in English.

Close-up: Word Order in Questions

- To create a **yes/no question** from a statement using the verb *be*, simply move the helping verb so it precedes the subject.

    Rasheem is researching the depletion of the ozone layer.

    Is Rasheem researching the depletion of the ozone layer?

- To create a **yes/no question** from a statement using a verb other than *be*, use a form of the auxiliary verb *do* before the subject, and do not invert the subject and verb.

    Does Rasheem want to research the depletion of the ozone layer?

    Do Rasheem's friends want to help him with his research?

    Did Rasheem's professors approve his research proposal?

- You can also form a question by adding a **tag question** (such as *won't he?* or *didn't I?*) to the end of a statement. If the verb of the main statement is *positive*, then the verb of the tag question is *negative*; if the verb of the main statement is *negative*, then the verb of the tag question is *positive*.

Rasheem is researching the depletion of the ozone layer, isn't he?

Rasheem doesn't intend to write his dissertation about the depletion of the ozone layer, does he?

- To create a **question asking for information,** use **interrogative** words (*who, what, where, when, why, how*), and invert the order of the subject and verb (note that *who* functions as the subject of the question in which it appears). Do not move the helping verb to precede the subject.

  Who is researching the depletion of the ozone layer?

  What is Rasheem researching?

  Where is Rasheem researching the depletion of the ozone layer?

(3) Word Order in Imperative Sentences

Imperative sentences state commands. It is common for the subject of an imperative sentence to be left out because the word *you* is understood to be the subject: "Go to school"; "Eat your dinner." Therefore, the word order pattern in an imperative sentence is often "verb-object," or "VO."

(4) Word Order with Direct and Indirect Quotations

Direct quotations use the exact words that the original writer or speaker used; consequently, the order of the words in a direct quotation cannot be changed. However, you can vary the placement of the **identifying tag,** the phrase that identifies the writer or speaker you are quoting. The identifying tag can be placed **before, in the middle of,** or **after** the quotation. (Note that direct quotations are always placed within quotation marks.)

He said, "Before I return the shoes to the department store, I must find the receipt." (identifying tag before the quotation)

"Before I return the shoes to the department store," he said, "I must find the receipt." (identifying tag in the middle of the quotation)

"Before I return the shoes to the department store, I must find the receipt," he said. (identifying tag after the quotation)

With **indirect quotations,** which summarize what the speaker or writer said, quotation marks are not used. Because you are simply reporting to your audience what the speaker or writer said, not quoting directly, you may change the words the speaker or writer used so long as you retain the original meaning of the source. With indirect quotations, it is often necessary to change the order of the words as well as the pronouns and the verb tenses used in the source.

> **Direct quotation:** "Before I return the shoes to the department store, I must find the receipt."
>
> **Indirect quotation:** He said that he needed to find the receipt for the shoes before he could return them to the department store.

(5) Position of Adjectives and Adverbs

Adjectives and adverbs are modifiers that describe or provide additional information about other words in a sentence. Adjectives provide information about nouns, and adverbs provide information about verbs, adjectives, and other adverbs.

See 45d, Ch. 49

Adjectives generally describe nouns. A book might be *large* or *small*, *red* or *blue*, *expensive* or *cheap*. Unlike adjectives in other languages, English adjectives change their form only to indicate degree (*fast*, *faster*, *fastest*). In English, adjectives do not have to agree in number or gender with the nouns they describe (as they must in French and German, for example).

Adverbs in English are easily identified; nearly all end in *-ly* (*calmly*, *loudly*, *rapidly*), except for a small number of "intensifiers," such as *very*, *rather*, and *quite*. Adverbs generally describe verbs. A person may walk *slowly* or *quickly*, *shyly* or *confidently*, *elegantly* or *clumsily*. Adverbs may also modify adjectives (*very* blue eyes, *truly* religious man) or other adverbs (answer *rather* stupidly, investigate *extremely* thoroughly).

In Arabic and in Romance languages such as French, Spanish, and Italian, adjectives generally **follow** the nouns they describe. In English, however, adjectives usually appear **before** the nouns they describe. In English, one would say, "*Red and black cars* are involved in more accidents than *blue, green, or white cars*."

Adverbs may appear before or after the verbs they describe, but they should be placed as close to the verb as possible: not "I *told* John that I couldn't meet him for lunch *politely*," but "I *politely told* John that I couldn't meet him for lunch" or "I *told* John *politely* that I couldn't meet him for lunch." When an adverb describes an adjective or another adverb, it usually comes *before* that adjective or adverb: "The essay has *basically sound* logic"; "You must express yourself *absolutely clearly*." Never place an adverb between the verb and the direct object.

Incorrect: Rolf drank *quickly* the water.

Correct: Rolf drank the water *quickly* (or, Rolf *quickly* drank the water).

Incorrect: Suong took *quietly* the test.

Correct: Suong *quietly* took the test (or, Suong took the test *quietly*.)

NOTE: To avoid confusion about whether to use an adjective or an adverb, remember that adjectives modify nouns, and adverbs modify verbs, adjectives, and other adverbs. An adjective always follows a form of the verb *be* if the adjective modifies the subject of the sentence. For example, "I was *careful*" (not "I was *carefully*").

(6) Order of Adjectives

A single noun may be described by more than one adjective—sometimes even by a list of adjectives in a row. Given a list of three or four adjectives, native English speakers would arrange them in a sentence in the same order. If shoes are to be described as *green* and *big*, numbering *two*, and of the type worn for playing *tennis*, native speakers would say, "two big green tennis shoes." Generally, the adjectives most important in completing the meaning of the noun are placed closest to the noun.

Close-up: Order of Articles, Adjectives, and Other Words

- Articles (*a*, *an*, *the*), demonstrative pronouns (*this*, *that*, *these*, *those*), or possessive nouns or pronouns (*his*, *our*, *Maria's*, *everybody's*)
- Amounts (*one*, *five*, *many*, *few*) and order (*first*, *next*, *last*)
- Personal opinions (*nice*, *ugly*, *crowded*, *pitiful*)
- Sizes and shapes (*small*, *tall*, *straight*, *crooked*)
- Ages (*young*, *old*, *modern*, *ancient*)
- Colors (*red*, *blue*, *dark*, *light*)
- Nouns that compound to form a noun phrase (*soccer* ball, *cardboard* box, *history* class)

Exercise 7

Write five original sentences in which two or three adjectives describe a noun. Be sure that the adjectives are in the right order.

61f Using Pronouns

See 45b, Ch. 46

Any English noun may be replaced by a pronoun. For example, *doctor* may be replaced by *he* or *she*, *books* by *them*, and *computer* by *it*. The English language uses more pronouns than most other languages. In Japanese, for example, it is common to repeat the noun again and again without using a pronoun replacement, but such repetition would sound odd to a native English speaker. (Note that a pronoun, like the noun it replaces, must agree with the verb in number.)

See 48a

(1) Pronoun Reference

See 46c

Pronoun reference is very important in English sentences, where the noun the pronoun replaces (the **antecedent**) must be easily identified. In general, then, you should place the pronoun as close as possible to the noun it replaces so the noun to which the pronoun refers is clear. If this is impossible, it is best to use the noun itself instead of replacing it with a pronoun.

Unclear: When Tara met Emily, she was nervous. (Does *she* refer to Tara or Emily?)

Clear: When Tara met Emily, Tara was nervous.

Unclear: Stefano and Victor love his DVD collection. (Whose DVD collection—Stefano's, Victor's, or someone else's?)

Clear: Stefano and Victor love Emilio's DVD collection.

(2) Pronoun Placement

Never use a pronoun immediately after the noun it replaces. For example, do not say, "Most of my classmates they are smart"; instead, say, "Most of my classmates are smart." The only exception to this rule occurs with an **intensive pronoun,** which ends in *-self* and emphasizes the preceding noun or pronoun: "Marta *herself* was eager to hear the results."

(3) Indefinite Pronouns

Unlike **personal pronouns** (*I, you, he, she, it, we, they, me, him, her, us*, and *them*), **indefinite pronouns** do not refer to a particular person, place, or thing. Therefore, an indefinite pronoun does not require an antecedent. **Indefinite pronoun subjects** (*anybody, nobody,* *each*, *either*, *someone*, *something*, *all*, *some*), like personal pronouns, must agree in number with the sentence's verb.

Nobody ~~have~~ has failed the exam. (*Nobody* is a singular subject and requires a singular verb.)

(4) Appositives

Appositives are nouns or noun phrases that identify or rename an adjacent noun or pronoun. An appositive usually follows the noun it explains or modifies but can sometimes precede it.

My parents, Mary and John, live in Louisiana. (*Mary and John* identifies *parents*.)

The event organizers, William and I, attended the banquet. (*William and I* identifies *the event organizers*.)

Alpha Centauri, one of the brightest stars in the sky, is the closest star to the sun. (*One of the brightest stars in the sky* identifies *Alpha Centauri*.)

NOTE: The case of a pronoun in an appositive depends on the case of the word it describes.

If an appositive is *not* necessary to the meaning of the sentence, use commas to set off the appositive from the rest of the sentence. If an appositive *is* necessary to the meaning of the sentence, do not use commas.

His aunt Trang is in the hospital. (*Trang* is necessary to the meaning of the sentence because it identifies which aunt is in the hospital.)

Akta's car, a 1994 Jeep Cherokee, broke down last night, and she had to walk home. (*a 1994 Jeep Cherokee* is not necessary to the meaning of the sentence.)

(5) Pronouns and Gender

A pronoun must agree in **gender** with the noun to which it refers.

My *sister* sold *her* old car.

Your *uncle* is walking *his* dog.

NOTE: In English, most nonhuman nouns are referred to as *it* because they do not have grammatical gender. However, exceptions are sometimes made for pets, ships, and countries. Pets are often referred to as *he* or *she*, depending on their sex, and ships and countries are sometimes referred to as *she*.

Exercise 8

There are no pronouns in the following passage. The repetition of the nouns again and again would seem strange to a native English speaker. Rewrite the passage, replacing as many of the nouns as possible with appropriate pronouns. Be sure that the connection between the pronouns and the nouns they replace is clear.

> The young couple seated across from Daniel at dinner the night before were newlyweds from Tokyo. The young couple and Daniel ate together with other guests of the inn at long, low tables in a large dining room with straw mat flooring. The man introduced himself immediately in English, shook Daniel's hand firmly, and, after learning that Daniel was not a tourist but a resident working in Osaka, gave Daniel a business card. The man had just finished college and was working at the man's first real job, clerking in a bank. Even in a sweatsuit, the man looked ready for the office: chin closely shaven, bristly hair neatly clipped, nails clean and buffed. After a while the man and Daniel exhausted the man's store of English and drifted into Japanese.
>
> The man's wife, shy up until then, took over as the man fell silent. The woman and Daniel talked about the new popularity of hot springs spas in the countryside around the inn, the difficulty of finding good schools for the children the woman hoped to have soon, the differences between food in Tokyo and Osaka. The woman's husband ate busily. From time to time the woman refilled the man's beer glass or served the man radish pickles from a china bowl in the middle of the table, and then returned to the conversation.

61g Distinguishing Commonly Confused Words

A number of word pairs in English have similar meanings. These word pairs can be confusing to nonnative English speakers because the ways in which the expressions are used in sentences are different although their meanings may be similar.

No and *Not*

No is an adjective; *not* is an adverb. Therefore, use *no* with nouns, and use *not* with verbs, adjectives, and other adverbs.

She has no desire to go to the football game.

Sergio's sisters are not friendly.

Too **and** ***Very***

Too is an intensifier. It is used to add emphasis in a sentence and to indicate excess.

It is too cold outside to go swimming.

Very is also an intensifier. It means greatly or intensely, but not to excess.

It was very cold outside, but not cold enough to keep us from playing in the backyard.

Even, Even If, **and** ***Even Though***

When used as an adverb, *even* is used to intensify or indicate surprise.

Greta felt even worse than she looked.

Even my little brother knows how to figure that out!

Even if is used in a sentence where there is a condition that may or may not occur.

Even if it rains tomorrow, I'm going to the park.

Even though is similar in meaning to *although.*

Even though Christopher is a very fast runner, he did not make the national track team.

A Few/A Little **and** ***Few/Little***

A few and *a little* mean not much, but some or enough. *A few* is used with count nouns. *A little* is used with noncount nouns.

We have a few screws remaining from the project.

There is a little bit of paint left in the can.

Few and *little* mean a small number—there are some, but perhaps not as much as one would like.

Few singers are as talented as Kelly.

I have little hope that this situation will change.

Much **and** ***Many***

Both *much* and *many* mean "a great quantity" or "to a great degree." Use *much* to modify noncount nouns: "much experience"; "much money." Use *many* to modify count nouns: "many people"; "many incidents."

Most of, Most, and *The Most*

Most and *most of* have similar meanings. *Most of* means "nearly all of something." Use *most of* when the noun that follows is a specific plural noun. When you use *most of,* be sure to use the definite article *the* before the noun.

> Most of the children had cookies for dessert.

Most is used for more general observations and means nearly all.

> Most houses in the United States have electricity.

The most is used for comparing more than two of something.

> Thomas has the most jellybeans.
>
> Pedro is the most experienced of the engineers.

Some and *Any*

Some denotes an unspecified amount or quantity that may be part of a larger amount. It can modify both count and noncount nouns: "some water"; "some melons." *Any* indicates an unspecified amount, which may be none, some, or all. It can modify both count and noncount nouns: "any person"; "any luggage."

61h Understanding Spelling, Punctuation, and Capitalization

In English, spelling, punctuation, and capitalization are important because all three help readers to understand your meaning.

(1) Spelling

See Ch. 44

Misspelled words can confuse and distract readers. Spelling in English is not perfectly phonetic and sometimes may seem illogical. In many languages that use a phonetic alphabet or syllabary, such as Japanese, Korean, or Persian script, words are spelled as they are pronounced. In contrast, spelling in English may be related more to the history of the word and its origins in other languages than to the way a word is pronounced. Therefore, learning to spell correctly is often a matter of memorization, not sounding out the word phonetically. For example, "ough" is pronounced differently in the words *tough*, *though*, and *thought*. In addition to memorizing the spelling of words, you can use your computer's spell checker to help you, but remember that spell checkers do not identify all misspelled words.

(2) Punctuation

Punctuation provides readers with hints to the meaning a writer is trying to convey. Since punctuation rules vary from language to language, it is important to learn how punctuation is used in American English.

(3) Capitalization

Different languages have different rules for capitalization; in fact, in the writing systems of some languages, capitalization does not exist at all. English has very specific rules for the use of capital letters, and when a writer violates them, it can distract or confuse a reader.

Exercise 9

An ESL student in a composition course wrote the following paragraph as part of a paper about his experiences learning to write in English. Rewrite the paragraph, correcting errors in spelling, punctuation, and capitalization.

My first experience started when I was studying english as a second language in Collage, I had to write essays as part of the course. The teacher assigned us to write about something such as Winter, football games or living in the dessert. It is not so hard to write about these things, but I did not have the necesary tools for arranging the information in my mind. Therefore when I submitted my assignment, I got a low grade. However the teacher did not write enough comments on my paper when he corrected it. I remember one day when he asked the class to write about new technology. I spent a long time writing in order to turn in a high-quality essay. In the end I got a c and he wrote at the end of my paper "you need to work harder". That made me so disapointed; I knew I had a very long way to go to improve my writing.

STUDENT WRITER AT WORK

Editing for ESL Writers

The following personal experience essay, written by a composition student about his process of learning to write English as a second language, contains some grammatical and mechanical errors. His instructor has underlined the errors in the first paragraph, but not those in the remaining paragraphs. Make necessary corrections to the entire paper, referring back to Chapter 61 when necessary. Revise further to strengthen coherence, unity, and style.

My Way

To begin this paper, I have to search through my memories back to August 1999, the time when I arrived <u>to</u> the United <u>states</u> and began to attend <u>High School</u>. Unlike other international <u>student</u>, I did not have any English skills when I came here. I was really scared about the fact <u>tha</u> I had to go to high school without any English skills. But I survived the last four years, and I would like to write about how I came to improve my English writing skills and the three ways that helped me <u>over the next few paragraphs</u>.

Getting professional help from an expert is one of the ways to learn your second language. Couple of months after I started my sophomore year of high school, I began to work with a teacher who had ESL (English as a Second Language) teaching experience. She told me that the best way to learn a second language is to live with a native speaker of the language you want to learn. Because of her experience with international students, she knew what I needed, and how to encourage me. I worked with her every days after school and learned correct pronunciation, grammar, and paper writing. I also had to listen a lot. She told me once that learning a second language is like being a baby learning a first language.

This idea of "Being a baby" showed me how could I learn English in an entertaining way. I began to watch more TV shows and movies, and I listen to music almost all day. I probably watched every single episode of The Simpsons. I watched the episodes over and over again. When I began to understand what the characters saying, I wrote down the words that I could not understand and looked it up in the dictionary after the show. I tried to memorize every single sentence in the episodes and said those sentences aloud, imitating the characters' accent. After a few months of training by "being a baby," many people recognized the improvement in my vocabulary and pronunciation. I gained more confidence in this way, and I was really happy about the fact that I begin to enjoy what I had to do.

I lived with an American family for about two year. They helped me a lot in improving my English writing skills because they gave me lots of opportunities to speak and listen to English. Listening to language is a good way to learn how to write, but one must be careful. Some people speak proper English as it is taught in schools, and some talk using colloquial terms. I am not saying that using colloquial terms are bad, but that one should know where and when it is appropriate to use them. When a person learn a language by listening to a speaker who might use colloquial terms, the listener might mistakes these as proper English and use them in writing. To learn to note when and where to use colloquial terms, I spend as much time as possible talking to my host family. Most people would disagree with me if I told them that I had to learn more slang terms in order to learn how to write better. But you have to know what is wrong to do what is right.

There are a hundred of ways to improve second language writing skill, but there is no best way because every individual learns differently and have their own way and pace. Living with native speakers, getting help from an expert, and watching TV shows helped me, but I do not think these ways apply to everyone. I believe that you have to find which way works best for you. I used to think that learning second language writing is hard and scary, but it is a pleasant experience if you follow your own plan with confidence.

Glossary of Usage

This glossary of usage lists words and phrases that writers often find troublesome and explains how they are used.

ESL Tip

For a list of commonly confused words that present particular challenges for ESL writers, **see 61g.**

a, an Use *a* before words that begin with consonants and words with initial vowels that sound like consonants: *a* person, *a* historical document, *a* one-horse carriage, *a* uniform. Use *an* before words that begin with vowels and words that begin with a silent *h: an* artist, *an* honest person.

accept, except *Accept* is a verb that means "to receive"; *except* as a preposition or conjunction means "other than" and as a verb means "to leave out": The auditors will *accept* all your claims *except* the last two. Some businesses are *excepted* from the regulation.

advice, advise *Advice* is a noun meaning "opinion or information offered"; *advise* is a verb that means "to offer advice to": The broker *advised* her client to take his attorney's *advice.*

affect, effect *Affect* is a verb meaning "to influence"; *effect* can be a verb or a noun—as a verb it means "to bring about," and as a noun it means "result": We know how the drug *affects* patients immediately, but little is known of its long-term *effects.* The arbitrator tried to *effect* a settlement between the parties.

all ready, already *All ready* means "completely prepared"; *already* means "by or before this or that time": I was *all ready* to help, but it was *already* too late.

all right, alright Although the use of *alright* is increasing, current usage calls for *all right.*

allusion, illusion An *allusion* is a reference or hint; an *illusion* is something that is not what it seems: The poem makes an *allusion* to the Pandora myth. The shadow created an optical *illusion.*

a lot *A lot* is always two words.

among, between *Among* refers to groups of more than two things; *between* refers to just two things: The three parties agreed *among* themselves to settle the case. There will be a brief intermission *between* the two acts. (Note that *amongst* is British, not American, usage.)

amount, number *Amount* refers to a quantity that cannot be counted; *number* refers to things that can be counted: Even a small *amount* of caffeine can be harmful. Seeing their commander fall, a large *number* of troops ran to his aid.

an, a See **a, an.**

and/or In business or technical writing, use *and/or* when either or both of the items it connects can apply. In college writing, however, avoid the use of *and/or.*

as . . . as . . . In such constructions, *as* signals a comparison; therefore, you must always use the second *as:* John Steinbeck's *East of Eden* is *as* long *as* his *The Grapes of Wrath*.

as, like *As* can be used as a conjunction (to introduce a complete clause) or as a preposition; *like* should be used as a preposition only: In *The Scarlet Letter,* Hawthorne uses imagery as (not *like*) he does in his other works. After classes, Fred works *as* a manager of a fast food restaurant. Writers *like* Carl Sandburg appear once in a generation.

at, to Many people use the prepositions *at* and *to* after *where* in conversation: *Where* are you working *at*? *Where* are you going *to*? This usage is redundant and should not appear in college writing.

awhile, a while *Awhile* is an adverb; *a while*, which consists of an article and a noun, is used as the object of a preposition: Before we continue, we will rest *awhile*. (modifies the verb *rest*); Before we continue, we will rest for *a while* (object of the preposition *for*)

bad, badly *Bad* is an adjective, and *badly* is an adverb: The school board decided that *Huckleberry Finn* was a *bad* book. American automobile makers did not do *badly* this year. After verbs that refer to any of the senses or after any other linking verb, use the adjective form: He looked *bad*. He felt *bad*. It seemed *bad*.

being as, being that These awkward phrases add unnecessary words, thereby weakening your writing. Use *because* instead.

beside, besides *Beside* is a preposition meaning "next to"; *besides* can be either a preposition meaning "except" or "other than" or an adverb meaning "as well": *Beside* the tower was a wall that ran the length of the city. *Besides* its industrial uses, laser technology has many other applications. Edison invented not only the lightbulb but the phonograph *besides*.

between, among See **among, between.**

bring, take *Bring* means "to transport from a farther place to a nearer place"; *take* means "to carry or convey from a nearer place to a farther place": *Bring* me a souvenir from your trip. *Take* this message to the general, and wait for a reply.

can, may *Can* denotes ability; *may* indicates permission: If you *can* play, you *may* use my piano.

capital, capitol *Capital* refers to a city that is an official seat of government; *capitol* refers to a building in which a legislature meets: Washington, DC, is the *capital* of the United States. When we were there, we visited the *Capitol* building.

center around This imprecise phrase is acceptable in speech and informal writing but not in college writing. Use *center on* instead.

cite, site *Cite* is a verb meaning "to quote as an authority or example"; *site* is a noun meaning "a place or setting"; it is also a shortened form of *Web site:* Jeff *cited* five sources in his research paper. The builder cleared the *site* for the new bank. Marisa uploaded her *site* to the Web.

climactic, climatic *Climactic* means "of or related to a climax"; *climatic* means "of or related to climate": The *climactic* moment of the movie occurred unexpectedly. If scientists are correct, the *climatic* conditions of Earth are changing.

coarse, course *Coarse* is an adjective meaning "inferior" or "having a rough, uneven texture"; *course* is a noun meaning "a route or path," "an area on which a sport is played," or "a unit of study": *Coarse* sandpaper is used to smooth the surface. The *course* of true love never runs smoothly. Last semester I had to drop a *course.*

complement, compliment *Complement* means "to complete or add to"; *compliment* means "to give praise": A double-blind study would *complement* their preliminary research. My instructor *complimented* me on my improvement.

conscious, conscience *Conscious* is an adjective meaning "having one's mental faculties awake"; *conscience* is a noun that means the moral sense of right and wrong: The patient will remain *conscious* during the procedure. His *conscience* would not allow him to lie.

continual, continuous *Continual* means "recurring at intervals"; *continuous* refers to an action that occurs without interruption: A pulsar is a star that emits a *continual* stream of electromagnetic radiation. (It emits radiation at regular intervals.) A small battery allows the watch to run *continuously* for five years. (It runs without stopping.)

could of, should of, would of The contractions *could've, should've,* and *would've* are often misspelled as the nonstandard constructions *could of, should of,* and *would of.* Use *could have, should have,* and *would have* in college writing.

council, counsel A *council* is "a body of people who serve in a legislative or advisory capacity"; *counsel* means "to offer advice or guidance": The city *council* argued about the proposed ban on smoking. The judge *counseled* the couple to settle their differences.

couple, couple of *Couple* means "a pair," but *couple of* is often used colloquially to mean "several" or "a few." In your college writing, specify "four points" or "two examples" rather than using "a couple of."

criterion, criteria *Criteria,* from the Greek, is the plural of *criterion,* meaning "standard for judgment": Of all the *criteria* for hiring graduating seniors, class rank is the most important *criterion.*

data *Data* is the plural of the Latin *datum,* meaning "fact." In everyday speech and writing, *data* is often used as the singular as well as the plural form. In college writing, use *data* only for the plural: The *data* discussed in this section *are* summarized in Appendix A.

different from, different than *Different than* is widely used in American speech. In college writing, use *different from.*

discreet, discrete *Discreet* means "careful or prudent"; *discrete* means "separate or individually distinct": Because Madame Bovary was not *discreet,* her reputation suffered. Atoms can be broken into hundreds of *discrete* particles.

disinterested, uninterested *Disinterested* means "objective" or "capable of making an impartial judgment"; *uninterested* means "indifferent or unconcerned": The American judicial system depends on *disinterested* jurors. Finding no treasure, Hernando de Soto was *uninterested* in going farther.

don't, doesn't *Don't* is the contraction of *do not; doesn't* is the contraction of *does not.* Do not confuse the two: My dog *doesn't* (not *don't*) like to walk in the rain. (Note that contractions are generally not acceptable in college writing.)

effect, affect See **affect, effect.**

e.g. *E.g.* is an abbreviation for the Latin *exempli gratia,* meaning "for example" or "for instance." In college writing, do not use *e.g.* Instead, use "for example" or "for instance."

emigrate from, immigrate to To *emigrate* is "to leave one's country and settle in another"; to *immigrate* is "to come to another country and reside there." The noun forms of these words are *emigrant* and *immigrant:* My great-grandfather *emigrated from* Warsaw along with many other *emigrants* from Poland. Many people *immigrate* to the United States for economic reasons, but such *immigrants* still face great challenges.

eminent, imminent *Eminent* is an adjective meaning "standing above others" or "prominent"; *imminent* means "about to occur": Oliver Wendell Holmes Jr. was an *eminent* jurist. In ancient times, a comet signaled *imminent* disaster.

enthused *Enthused,* a colloquial form of *enthusiastic,* should not be used in college writing.

etc. *Etc.*, the abbreviation of *et cetera*, means "and the rest." Do not use it in your college writing. Instead, use "and so on"—or, better yet, specify exactly what *etc.* stands for.

everyday, every day *Everyday* is an adjective that means "ordinary" or "commonplace"; *every day* means "occurring daily": In the Gettysburg Address, Lincoln used *everyday* language. She exercises almost *every day.*

everyone, every one *Everyone* is an indefinite pronoun meaning "every person"; *every one* means "every individual or thing in a particular group": *Everyone* seems happier in the spring. *Every one* of the packages had been opened.

except, accept See **accept, except.**

explicit, implicit *Explicit* means "expressed or stated directly"; *implicit* means "implied" or "expressed or stated indirectly": The director *explicitly* warned the actors to be on time for rehearsals. Her *implicit* message was that lateness would not be tolerated.

farther, further *Farther* designates distance; *further* designates degree: I have traveled *farther* from home than any of my relatives. Critics charge that welfare subsidies encourage *further* dependence.

fewer, less Use *fewer* with nouns that can be counted: *fewer* books, *fewer* people, *fewer* dollars. Use *less* with quantities that cannot be counted: *less* pain, *less* power, *less* enthusiasm.

firstly (secondly, thirdly, . . .) Archaic forms meaning "in the first . . . second . . . third place." Use *first, second, third* instead.

further, farther See **farther, further.**

good, well *Good* is an adjective, never an adverb: She is a *good* swimmer. *Well* can function as an adverb or as an adjective. As an adverb, it means "in a good manner": She swam *well* (not *good*) in the meet. *Well* is used as an adjective with verbs that denote a state of being or feeling. Here *well* can mean "in good health": I feel *well.*

got to *Got to* is not acceptable in college writing. To indicate obligation, use *have to, has to,* or *must.*

hanged, hung Both *hanged* and *hung* are past participles of *hang*. *Hanged* is used to refer to executions; *hung* is used to mean "suspended": Billy Budd was *hanged* for killing the master-at-arms. The stockings were *hung* by the chimney with care.

he, she Traditionally *he* has been used in the generic sense to refer to both males and females. To acknowledge the equality of the sexes, however, avoid the generic *he*. Use plural pronouns whenever possible. **See 42e2.**

hopefully The adverb *hopefully*, meaning "in a hopeful manner," should modify a verb, an adjective, or another adverb. Do not use *hopefully* as a sentence modifier meaning "it is hoped." Rather than "*Hopefully*, scientists will soon discover a cure for AIDS," write "*I hope* scientists will soon discover a cure for AIDS."

i.e. *I.e.* is an abbreviation for the Latin *id est*, meaning "that is." In college writing, do not use *i.e.* Instead, use its English equivalent.

if, whether When asking indirect questions or expressing doubt, use *whether:* He asked *whether* (not *if*) the flight would be delayed. The flight attendant was not sure *whether* (not *if*) it would be delayed.

illusion, allusion See **allusion, illusion.**

immigrate to, emigrate from See **emigrate from, immigrate to.**

implicit, explicit See **explicit, implicit.**

imply, infer *Imply* means "to hint" or "to suggest"; *infer* means "to conclude from": Mark Antony *implied* that the conspirators had murdered Caesar. The crowd *inferred* his meaning and called for justice.

infer, imply See **imply, infer.**

inside of, outside of *Of* is unnecessary when *inside* and *outside* are used as prepositions. *Inside of* is colloquial in references to time: He waited *inside* (not *inside of*) the coffee shop. He could run a mile in *under* (not *inside of*) eight minutes.

irregardless, regardless *Irregardless* is a nonstandard version of *regardless.* Use *regardless* or *irrespective* instead.

is when, is where These constructions are faulty when they appear in definitions: A playoff is (not *is when*) an additional game played to establish the winner of a tie.

its, it's *Its* is a possessive pronoun; *it's* is a contraction of *it is: It's* no secret that the bank is out to protect *its* assets.

kind of, sort of *Kind of* and *sort of* to mean "rather" or "somewhat" are colloquial and should not appear in college writing: It is well known that Napoleon was *rather* (not *kind of*) short.

lay, lie See **lie, lay.**

leave, let *Leave* means "to go away from" or "to *let* remain"; *let* means "to allow" or "to permit": *Let* (not *leave*) me give you a hand.

less, fewer See **fewer, less.**

let, leave See **leave, let.**

lie, lay *Lie* is an intransitive verb (one that does not take an object) meaning "to recline." Its principal forms are *lie, lay, lain, lying:* Each afternoon she would *lie* in the sun and listen to the surf. *As I Lay Dying* is a novel by William Faulkner. By 1871, Troy had *lain* undisturbed for two thousand years. The painting shows a nude *lying* on a couch.

Lay is a transitive verb (one that takes an object) meaning "to put" or "to place." Its principal forms are *lay, laid, laid, laying:* The Federalist Papers *lay* the foundation for American conservatism. In October 1781, the British *laid* down their arms and surrendered. He had *laid* his money on the counter before leaving. We watched the stonemasons *laying* a wall.

like, as See **as, like.**

loose, lose *Loose* is an adjective meaning "not rigidly fastened or securely attached"; *lose* is a verb meaning "to misplace": The marble facing of the building became *loose* and fell to the sidewalk. After only two drinks, most people *lose* their ability to judge distance.

lots, lots of, a lot of These words are colloquial substitutes for *many*, *much*, or *a great deal of*. Avoid their use in college writing: The students had many (not *lots of* or *a lot of*) options for essay topics.

man Like the generic pronoun *he*, *man* has been used in English to denote members of both sexes. This usage is being replaced by *human beings*, *people*, or similar terms that do not specify gender. **See 42e2.**

may, can See **can, may.**

may be, maybe *May be* is a verb phrase: *maybe* is an adverb meaning "perhaps": She *may be* the smartest student in the class. *Maybe* her experience has given her an advantage.

media, medium *Medium*, meaning "a means of conveying or broadcasting something," is singular; *media* is the plural form and requires a plural verb: The *media* have distorted the issue.

might have, might of *Might of* is a nonstandard spelling of the contraction of *might have* (*might've*). Use *might have* in college writing.

number, amount See **amount, number.**

OK, O.K., okay All three spellings are acceptable, but this term should be avoided in college writing. Replace it with a more specific word or words: The lecture was *adequate* (not *okay*), if uninspiring.

outside of, inside of See **inside of, outside of.**

passed, past *Passed* is the past tense of the verb *pass; past* means "belonging to a former time" or "no longer current": The car must have been going eighty miles per hour when it *passed* us. In the envelope was a bill marked *past* due.

percent, percentage *Percent* indicates a part of a hundred when a specific number is referred to: "*10 percent* of his salary." *Percentage* is used when no specific number is referred to: "a *percentage* of next year's receipts." In technical and business writing, it is permissible to use the % sign after percentages you are comparing. Write out the word *percent* in college writing.

phenomenon, phenomena A *phenomenon* is a single observable fact or event. It can also refer to a rare or significant occurrence. *Phenomena* is the plural form and requires a plural verb: Many supposedly paranormal *phenomena* are easily explained.

plus As a preposition, *plus* means "in addition to." Avoid using *plus* as a substitute for *and:* Include the principal, *plus* the interest, in your calculations. Your quote was too high; moreover (not *plus*), it was inaccurate.

precede, proceed *Precede* means "to go or come before"; *proceed* means "to go forward in an orderly way": Robert Frost's *North of Boston* was *preceded* by an earlier volume. In 1532, Francisco Pizarro landed at Tumbes and *proceeded* south.

principal, principle As a noun, *principal* means "a sum of money (minus interest) invested or lent" or "a person in the leading position"; as an adjective, it means "most important"; a *principle* is a noun meaning a rule of conduct or a basic truth: He wanted to reduce the *principal* of the loan. The *principal* of the high school is a talented administrator. Women are the *principal* wage earners in many American households. The Constitution embodies certain fundamental *principles*.

quote, quotation *Quote* is a verb. *Quotation* is a noun. In college writing, do not use *quote* as a shortened form of *quotation:* Scholars attribute these *quotations* (not *quotes*) to Shakespeare.

raise, rise *Raise* is a transitive verb, and *rise* is an intransitive verb—that is, *raise* takes an object, and *rise* does not: My grandparents *raised* a large family. The sun will *rise* at 6:12 this morning.

real, really *Real* means "genuine" or "authentic"; *really* means "actually." In your college writing, do not use *real* as an adjective meaning "very."

reason is that, reason is because *Reason* should be used with *that* and not with *because*, which is redundant: The *reason* he left is *that* (not *because*) you insulted him.

regardless, irregardless See **irregardless, regardless.**

respectably, respectfully, respectively *Respectably* means "worthy of respect"; *respectfully* means "giving honor or deference"; *respectively* means "in the order given": He skated quite *respectably* at his first Olympics. The seminar taught us to treat others *respectfully*. The first- and second-place winners were Tai and Kim, *respectively*.

rise, raise See **raise, rise.**

set, sit *Set* means "to put down" or "to lay." Its principal forms are *set* and *setting*: After rocking the baby to sleep, he *set* her down carefully in her crib. After *setting* her down, he took a nap.

Sit means "to assume a sitting position." Its principal forms are *sit*, *sat*, and *sitting:* Many children *sit* in front of the television five to six hours a day. The dog *sat* by the fire. We were *sitting* in the airport when the flight was canceled.

shall, will *Will* has all but replaced *shall* to express all future action.

should of See **could of, should of, would of.**

since Do not use *since* for *because* if there is any chance of confusion. In the sentence "*Since* President Nixon traveled to China, trade between China and the United States has increased," *since* could mean either "from the time that" or "because." To be clear, use *because*.

sit, set See **set, sit.**

so Avoid using *so* as a vague intensifier meaning "very" or "extremely." Follow *so* with *that* and a clause that describes the result: She was *so* pleased with their work *that* she took them out to lunch.

sometime, sometimes, some time *Sometime* means "at some time in the future"; *sometimes* means "now and then"; *some time* means "a period of time": The president will address Congress *sometime* next week. All automobiles, no matter how reliable, *sometimes* need repairs. It has been *some time* since I read that book.

sort of, kind of See **kind of, sort of.**

stationary, stationery *Stationary* means "staying in one place"; *stationery* means "materials for writing" or "letter paper": The communications satellite appears to be *stationary* in the sky. The secretaries supply departmental offices with *stationery*.

supposed to, used to *Supposed to* and *used to* are often misspelled. Both verbs require the final *d* to indicate past tense.

take, bring See **bring, take.**

than, then *Than* is a conjunction used to indicate a comparison; *then* is an adverb indicating time: The new shopping center is bigger *than* the old one. He did his research; *then*, he wrote a report.

that, which, who Use *that* or *which* when referring to a thing, use *who* when referring to a person: It was a speech *that* inspired many. The movie, *which* was a huge success, failed to impress her. Anyone *who* (not *that*) takes the course will benefit.

their, there, they're *Their* is a possessive pronoun; *there* indicates place and is also used in the expressions *there is* and *there are; they're* is a contraction of *they are:* Watson and Crick did *their* DNA work at Cambridge University. I love Los Angeles, but I wouldn't want to live *there*. *There* is nothing we can do to resurrect an extinct species. When *they're* well treated, rabbits make excellent pets.

themselves; theirselves, theirself *Theirselves* and *theirself* are nonstandard variants of *themselves*.

then, than See **than, then.**

till, until, 'til *Till* and *until* have the same meaning, and both are acceptable. *Until* is preferred in college writing. *'Til*, a contraction of *until*, should be avoided.

to, at See **at, to.**

to, too, two *To* is a preposition that indicates direction; *too* is an adverb that means "also" or "more than is needed"; *two* expresses the number 2: Last year we flew from New York *to* California. "Tippecanoe and Tyler, *too*" was William Henry Harrison's campaign slogan. The plot was *too* complicated for the average reader. Just north of *Two* Rivers, Wisconsin, is a petrified forest.

try to, try and *Try and* is the colloquial equivalent of the more formal *try to*: He decided to *try to* (not *try and*) do better. In college writing, use *try to*.

-type Deleting this empty suffix eliminates clutter and clarifies meaning. Found in the wreckage was an *incendiary* (not *incendiary-type*) device.

uninterested, disinterested See **disinterested, uninterested.**

unique Because *unique* means "the only one," not "remarkable" or "unusual," never use constructions like "the most unique" or "very unique."

until See **till, until, 'til.**

used to See **supposed to, used to.**

utilize In most cases, replace *utilize* with *use* (*utilize* often sounds pretentious).

wait for, wait on To *wait for* means "to defer action until something occurs." To *wait on* means "to act as a waiter": I am *waiting for* (not *on*) dinner.

weather, whether *Weather* is a noun meaning "the state of the atmosphere"; *whether* is a conjunction used to introduce an alternative: The *weather* will improve this weekend. It is doubtful *whether* we will be able to ski tomorrow.

well, good See **good, well.**

were, we're *Were* is a verb; *we're* is the contraction of *we are:* The Trojans *were* asleep when the Greeks attacked. We must act now if *we're* going to succeed.

whether, if See **if, whether.**

which, who, that See **that, which, who.**

who, whom When a pronoun serves as the subject of its clause, use *who* or *whoever;* when it functions in a clause as an object, use *whom* or *whomever:* Sarah, *who* is studying ancient civilizations, would like to visit Greece. Sarah, *whom* I met in France, wants me to travel to Greece with her. To determine which to use at the beginning of a question, use a personal pronoun to answer the question: *Who* tried to call me? *He* called. (subject); *Whom* do you want for the job? I want *her*. (object)

who's, whose *Who's* means "who is" or "who has"; *whose* indicates possession: *Who's* going to take calculus? *Who's* already left for the concert? The writer *whose* book was in the window was autographing copies.

will, shall See **shall, will.**

would of See **could of, should of, would of.**

your, you're *Your* indicates possession; *you're* is the contraction of *you are*: You can improve *your* stamina by jogging two miles a day. *You're* certain to be the winner.

Glossary of Grammatical and Rhetorical Terms

absolute phrase See **phrase.**

abstract noun See **noun.**

acronym A word formed from the first letters or initial sounds of a group of words: *NATO* = North Atlantic Treaty Organization.

active voice See **voice.**

adjective A word that describes, limits, qualifies, or in any other way modifies a noun or pronoun. A **descriptive adjective** names a quality of the noun or pronoun it modifies: *junior* year. A **proper adjective** is formed from a proper noun: *Hegelian philosophy*. **45d, 49b**

adjective clause See **clause.**

adverb A word that describes the action of verbs or modifies adjectives, other adverbs, or complete phrases, clauses, or sentences. Adverbs answer the questions "How?" "Why?" "Where?" "When?" and "To what extent?" Adverbs are formed from adjectives, many by adding *ly* to the adjective form (*dark/darkly, solemn/solemnly*), and may also be derived from prepositions (*Joe carried on*.). Other adverbs that indicate time, place, condition, cause, or degree are not derived from other parts of speech: *then, never, very,* and *often,* for example. The words *how, why, where,* and *when* are classified as **interrogative adverbs** when they ask questions (*How did we get into this mess*?). See also **conjunctive adverb. 45e, 49c**

adverb clause See **clause.**

adverbial conjunction See **conjunctive adverb.**

agreement The correspondence between words in number, person, and gender. Subjects and verbs must agree in number (singular or plural) and person (first, second, or third): *Soccer is a popular European sport; I play* soccer too. **48a** Pronouns and their antecedents must agree in number, person, and gender (masculine, feminine, neuter): *Lucy loaned Charlie her car.* **48b**

allusion A reference to a well-known historical, literary, or biblical person or event that readers are expected to recognize.

analogy A kind of comparison in which the writer explains an unfamiliar idea or object by comparing it to a more familiar one: *Sensory pathways of the central nervous system are bundles of nerves rather like telephone cables that feed information about the outside world into the brain for processing.*

antecedent The word or word group to which a pronoun refers: *Brian finally bought the stereo he had always wanted.* (*Brian* is the antecedent of the pronoun *he*.)

appositive A noun or noun phrase that identifies or renames the noun or pronoun it follows: *Columbus, the capital of Ohio, is in the central part of the state.* Appositives may be used without special introductory phrases, as in the preceding example, or they may be introduced by *such as, or, that is, for example,* or *in other words: Japanese cars, such as Hondas, now have a large share of the US automobile market.* **32c5** In a **restrictive appositive,** the appositive precedes the noun or pronoun it modifies: *Singing cowboy Gene Autry was once the owner of the California Angels.* **51d1**

article The word *a, an,* or *the*. Articles signal that a noun follows and are classified as **determiners. 61c2–3**

auxiliary verb See **verb.**

balanced sentence A sentence neatly divided between two parallel structures. Balanced sentences are typically **compound sentences** made up of two parallel clauses (*The telephone rang, and I answered*), but the parallel clauses of a **complex sentence** can also be balanced. **35c**

base form See **principle parts.**

cardinal number A number that expresses quantity—*seven, thirty, one hundred*. (Contrast **ordinal number.**)

case The form a noun or pronoun takes to indicate how it functions in a sentence. English has three cases. A pronoun takes the **subjective** (or **nominative**) **case** when it acts as the subject of a sentence or a clause: *I am an American.* **46a1** A pronoun takes the **objective case** when it acts as the object of a verb or of a preposition: *Fran gave me her dog.* **46a2** Both nouns and pronouns take the **possessive case** when they indicate ownership: *My house is brick, Brandon's T-shirt is red.* This is the only case in which nouns change form. **46a3**

clause A group of related words that includes a subject and a predicate. An **independent (main) clause** may stand alone as a sentence (*Yellowstone is a national park in the West*), but a **dependent (subordinate) clause** must always be accompanied by an independent clause (*Yellowstone is a national park in the West that is known for its geysers*). Dependent clauses are classified according to their function in a sentence. An **adjective clause** (sometimes called a **relative clause**) modifies nouns or pronouns: *The ficus, which grew to be twelve feet tall, finally died* (the clause modifies *ficus*). An **adverb clause** modifies single words (verbs, adjectives, or adverbs) or an entire phrase or clause: *The film was exposed when Bill opened the camera* (the clause modifies *exposed*). A **noun clause** acts as a noun (as subject, direct object, indirect object, or complement) in a sentence: *Whoever arrives first wins the prize* (the clause is the subject of the sentence). An **elliptical clause** is grammatically incomplete—that is, part or all of the subject or predicate is missing. If the missing part can be inferred from the context of the sentence, such a construction is acceptable: *When (they are) pressed, the committee members will act.* **32b2**

climactic word order The writing strategy of moving from the least important to the most important point in a sentence and ending with the key idea. **35a2**

collective noun See **noun.**

comma splice An error created when two independent clauses are incorrectly joined by a comma. Correct comma splices by separating the independent clauses with a period, a semicolon, or a comma and a coordinating conjunction, or by using subordination. **Ch. 38**

Comma Splice: The Mississippi River flows south, the Nile River flows north.

Revised: The Mississippi River flows south. The Nile River flows north.

Revised: The Mississippi River flows south; the Nile River flows north.

Revised: The Mississippi River flows south, and the Nile River flows north.

Revised: Although the Mississippi River flows south, the Nile River flows north.

common noun See **noun.**

comparative degree See **degree.**

complement A word or word group that describes or renames a subject, an object, or a verb. A **subject complement** is a word or phrase that follows a linking verb and renames the subject. It can be an adjective (called a **predicate adjective**) or a noun (called a **predicate nominative**): *Clark Gable was a movie star.* An **object complement** is a word or phrase that describes or renames a direct object. Object complements can be either adjectives or nouns: *We call the treehouse our hideout.*

complete predicate See **predicate.**

complete subject See **subject.**

complex sentence See **sentence.**

compound Two or more words that function as a unit, such as **compound nouns:** *attorney-at-law, boardwalk;* **compound adjectives:** *hard-hitting editorial;* **compound prepositions:** *by way of, in addition to;* **compound subjects:** *April and May are spring months.;* and **compound predicates:** *Many try and fail to climb Mount Everest.*

compound adjective See **compound.**

compound noun See **compound.**

compound predicate See **compound.**

compound preposition See **compound.**

compound sentence See **sentence.**

compound subject See **compound.**

compound-complex sentence See **sentence.**

conjunction A word or words used to connect single words, phrases, clauses, and sentences. **Coordinating conjunctions** (*and, or, but, nor, for, so, yet*) connect words, phrases, or clauses of equal weight: *crime and* punishment (coordinating conjunction *and* connects two words). **Correlative conjunctions** (*both . . . and, either . . . or, neither . . . nor,* and so on), always used in pairs, also link items of equal weight: *Neither Texas nor Florida crosses the Tropic of Cancer.* **Subordinating conjunctions** (*since, because, although, if, after,* and so on) introduce adverb clauses: *You will have to pay for the tickets now because I will not be here later.* **45g**

conjunctive adverb An adverb that joins and relates independent clauses in a sentence (*also, anyway, besides, hence, however, nevertheless, still,* and so on): *Howard tried out for the Yankees; however, he didn't make the team.* **45e**

connotation The emotional associations that surround a word. (Contrast **denotation.**) **42b1**

contraction The combination of two words with an apostrophe replacing the missing letters: *We + will = we'll; was + not = wasn't.*

coordinate adjective One of a series of adjectives that modify the same word or word group: *The park was quiet, shady, and cool.* **51b2**

coordinating conjunction See **conjunction.**

coordination The pairing of similar elements (words, phrases, or clauses) to give equal weight to each. Coordination is used in simple sentences to link similar elements into compound subjects, predicates, complements, or modifiers. It can also link two independent clauses to form a compound sentence: *The sky was cloudy, and it looked like rain.* (Contrast **subordination.**)

correlative conjunction See **conjunction.**

count noun See **noun.**

cumulative sentence A sentence that begins with a main clause followed by additional words, phrases, or clauses that expand or develop it: *On the hill stood a schoolhouse, paint peeling, windows boarded, playground overgrown with weeds.* **35b1**

dangling modifier A modifier for which no logical headword appears in the sentence. To correct dangling modifiers, either create a new subject that can logically serve as the headword of the dangling modifier, or change the dangling modifier into a dependent clause. **39b**

After pumping they continued the trip.
~~Pumping~~ up the tire, ~~the trip continued.~~

deductive argument An argument that begins with a general statement or proposition and establishes a chain of reasoning that leads to a conclusion. **9f**

degree Most adjectives and adverbs change form to indicate degree. The **positive degree** describes a quality without indicating a comparison (*Frank is tall*). The **comparative degree** indicates a comparison between two persons or things (*Frank is taller than John*). The **superlative degree** indicates a comparison between one person or thing and two or more others (*Frank is the tallest boy in his scout troop*). **49d**

demonstrative pronoun See **pronoun;** see also **determiner.**

denotation The dictionary meaning of a word. (Contrast **connotation.**) **42b1**

dependent clause See **clause.**

descriptive adjective See **adjective.**

determiner Determiners are words that function as adjectives to limit or qualify nouns. Determiners include **articles** (*a, an, the*): *the book, a peanut;* **possessive nouns** (*Janet's*): *Janet's dog;* **possessive pronouns** (*my, your, his*, and so on): *their apartment, my house;* **demonstrative pronouns** (*this, these, that, those*): *that table, these chairs;* **interrogative pronouns** (*what, which, whose*, and so on): *Which car is yours?*; **indefinite pronouns** (*another, each, both, many*, and so on): *any minute, some day;* **relative pronouns** (*what, whatever, which, whichever, whose, whosoever*): *Bed rest was what the doctor ordered;* and **ordinal** and **cardinal numbers** (*one, two, first, second*, and so on): *Claire saw two robins.* **45d2; 49a; 61c2–3**

direct object See **object.**

direct quotation See **quotation.**

documentation The formal acknowledgment of the sources used in a piece of writing. **Pt. 3**

documentation style A format for providing information about the sources used in a piece of writing. Documentation formats vary from discipline to discipline. **Pt. 3**

double negative A nonstandard combination of two negative words:

Double Negative: She didn't have no time.

Revised: She had no time *or* She didn't have any time. **49e; 61b4**

ellipsis Three spaced periods used to indicate the omission of a word or words from a quotation: "*The time has come . . . and we must part.*" **55f**

elliptical clause See **clause.**

embedding A strategy for varying sentence structure that involves changing some sentences into modifying phrases and working them into other sentences. **34b3**

enthymeme A syllogism in which one of the premises—usually the major premise—is implied rather than stated. **9f3**

expletive A construction in which *there* or *it* is used with a form of the verb *be*: *There is no one here by that name.*

faulty parallelism See **parallelism.**

figurative language Language that departs from the literal meaning or order of words to create striking effects or new meanings. Types of figurative language (called **figures of speech**) include **simile, metaphor,** and **personification. 42c**

figure of speech See **figurative language.**

finite verb A verb that can serve as the main verb of a sentence. Unlike **participles, gerunds,** and **infinitives** (see also **verbal**), finite verbs do not require an auxiliary in order to function as the main verb: *The rooster crowed.*

fragment See **sentence fragment.**

function word An article, a preposition, a conjunction, or an auxiliary verb that indicates the function of and the grammatical relationships among the nouns, verbs, and modifiers in a sentence.

fused sentence A type of **run-on sentence** that occurs when two independent clauses are joined without punctuation. Correct fused sentences by separating the independent clauses with a period, a semicolon, or a comma and a coordinating conjunction, or by using subordination. **Ch. 38**

Fused Sentence: Protein is needed for good nutrition lipids and carbohydrates are too.

Revised: Protein is needed for good nutrition. Lipids and carbohydrates are too.

Revised: Protein is needed for good nutrition; lipids and carbohydrates are too.

Revised: Protein is needed for good nutrition, but lipids and carbohydrates are too.

Revised: Although protein is needed for good nutrition, lipids and carbohydrates are too.

gender The classification of nouns and pronouns as masculine (*father, boy, he*), feminine (*mother, girl, she*), or neuter (*radio, kitten, them*).

gerund A special verb form ending in *-ing* that is always used as a noun: *Fishing is relaxing* (gerund *fishing* serves as subject; gerund *relaxing* serves as subject complement). **Note:** When the *-ing* form of a verb is used as a modifier, it is considered a **present participle.** See also **verbal.**

gerund phrase See **phrase.**

headword The word or phrase in a sentence that is described, defined, or limited by a modifier.

helping verb See **verb.**

idiom An expression that is characteristic of a particular language and whose meaning cannot be predicted from the meaning of its individual words: *lend a hand.*

imperative mood See **mood.**

indefinite pronoun See **pronoun;** see also **determiner.**

independent clause See **clause.**

indicative mood See **mood.**

indirect object See **object.**

indirect question A question that tells what has been asked but, because it does not report the speaker's exact words, does not take quotation marks or end with a question mark: *He asked whether he could use the family car.*

indirect quotation See **quotation.**

inductive argument An argument that begins with observations or experiences and moves toward a conclusion. **9e**

infinitive The base form of the verb preceded by *to.* An infinitive can serve as an adjective (*He is the man to watch*), an adverb (*Chris hoped to break the record*), or a noun (*To err is human*). See also **verbal.**

infinitive phrase See **phrase.**

intensifier A word that adds emphasis but not additional meaning to words it modifies. *Much, really, too, very,* and *so* are typical intensifiers.

intensive pronoun See **pronoun.**

interjection A grammatically independent word, expressing emotion, that is used as an exclamation. An interjection can be set off by a comma, or, for greater emphasis, it can be punctuated as an independent unit, set off by an exclamation point: *Ouch! That hurt.* **45h**

interrogative adverb See **adverb.**

interrogative pronoun See **pronoun;** see also **determiner.**

intransitive verb See **verb.**

irregular verb A verb that does not form both its past tense and past participle by adding *d* or *ed* to the base form of the verb. **47a2**

isolate Any word, including an **interjection,** that can be used in isolation: *Yes. No. Hello. Good-bye. Please. Thanks.*

linking verb A verb that connects a subject to its complement: *The crowd became quiet.* Words that can be used as linking verbs include *seem, appear, believe, become, grow, turn, remain, prove, look, sound, smell, taste, feel,* and forms of the verb *be.*

main clause See **clause.**

main verb See **verb.**

metaphor A **figure of speech** in which the writer makes an implied comparison between two unlike items, equating them in an unexpected way: *The subway coursed through the arteries of the city.* (Contrast **simile.**) **42c**

misplaced modifier A modifier that has no clear relationship with its headword, usually because it is placed too far from it. **39a**

Dan learned much about his new baby son by
~~By~~ changing his diapers~~,~~. ~~Dan learned much about his new baby son.~~

mixed construction A sentence made up of two or more parts that do not fit together grammatically. **41b**

Mixed: The Great Chicago Fire caused terrible destruction was what prompted changes in the fire code. (independent clause used as a subject)

Revised: The terrible destruction of the Great Chicago Fire prompted changes in the fire code.

Revised: Because of the terrible destruction of the Great Chicago Fire, the fire code was changed.

mixed metaphor The combination of two or more incompatible images in a single figure of speech: *During the race, John kept a stiff upper lip as he ran like the wind.* **42d5**

modal auxiliary See **verb.**

modifier A word, phrase, or clause that acts as an adjective or an adverb, describing, limiting, or qualifying another word or word group in the sentence.

mood The verb form that indicates the writer's basic attitude. There are three moods in English. The **indicative mood** is used for statements and questions: *Nebraska became a state in 1867.* The **imperative mood** specifies commands or requests and is often used without a subject: (*You*) *Pay the rent.* The **subjunctive mood** expresses wishes or hypothetical conditions: *I wish the sun were shining.* **47c**

nominal A word, phrase, or clause that functions as a noun.

nominative case See **case.**

noncount noun See **noun.**

nonfinite verb See **verbal.**

nonrestrictive modifier A modifying phrase or clause that does not limit or particularize the words it modifies, but rather supplies additional information about them. Nonrestrictive modifiers are set off by commas: *Oregano, also known as marjoram or suganda, is a member of the mint family.* (Contrast **restrictive modifier.**) **51d1**

noun A word that names people, places, things, ideas, actions, or qualities. A **common noun** names any of a class of people, places, or things: *lawyer, town, bicycle.* A **proper noun,** always capitalized, refers to a particular person, place, or thing: *Mother Teresa, Chicago, Schwinn.* A **count noun** names something that can be counted: a *a dozen eggs, two cats in the yard.* A **noncount noun** names a quantity that is not countable: *sand, time, work.* An **abstract noun** refers to an intangible idea or quality: *bravery, equality, hunger.* A **collective noun** designates a group of people, places, or things thought of as a unit: *Congress, police, family.* **45a**

noun clause See **clause.**

noun phrase See **phrase.**

number The form taken by a noun, pronoun, or verb to indicate one (singular): *car, he, this, boast,* or many (**plural**): *cars, they, those, boasts.* **41a4**

object A noun, pronoun, or other noun substitute that receives the action of a **transitive verb, verbal,** or **preposition.** A **direct object** indicates where the verb's action is directed and who or what is affected by it: *John caught a butterfly.* An **indirect object** tells to or for whom the verb's action was done: *John gave Nancy the butterfly.* An **object of a preposition** is a word or word group introduced by a preposition: *John gave Nancy the butterfly for an hour.*

object complement See **complement.**

object of a preposition See **object.**

objective case See **case.**

ordinal number A number that indicates position in a series: *seventh, thirtieth, one-hundredth.* (Contrast **cardinal number.**)

parallelism The use of similar grammatical elements in sentences or parts of sentences: *We serve beer, wine, and soft drinks.* Words, phrases, clauses, or complete sentences may be parallel, and parallel items may be paired or presented in a series. When elements that have the same function in a sentence are not presented in the same terms, the sentence is flawed by **faulty parallelism. 35c; Ch. 40**

participial phrase See **phrase.**

participle A verb form that generally functions in a sentence as an adjective. Virtually every verb has a **present participle,** which ends in *-ing* (*breaking, leaking, taking*), and a **past participle,** which usually ends in *-d* or *-ed* (*agreed, walked, taken*). (See also **verbal.**) *The heaving seas swamped the dinghy* (present participle *heaving* modifies noun *seas*); *Aged people deserve respect* (past participle *aged* modifies noun *people*).

parts of speech The eight basic building blocks for all English sentences: *nouns, pronouns, verbs, adjectives, adverbs, prepositions, conjunctions,* and *interjections.*

passive voice See **voice.**

past participle See **participle.**

periodic sentence A sentence that moves from a number of specific examples to a conclusion, gradually building in intensity until a climax is reached in the main clause: *Sickly and pale and looking ready to crumble, the marathoner headed into the last mile of the race.* **35b2**

person The form a pronoun or verb takes to indicate the speaker (**first person**): *I am/we are;* those spoken to (**second person**): *you are;* and those spoken about (**third person**): *he/she/it is; they are.* **41a4**

personal pronoun See **pronoun.**

personification A form of **figurative language** in which the writer describes an idea or inanimate object in human terms: *The big feather bed beckoned to my tired body.* **42c**

phrase A grammatically ordered group of related words that lacks a subject or a predicate or both and functions as a single part of speech. A **verb phrase** consists of an auxiliary (helping) verb and a main verb: *The wind was blowing hard.* A **noun phrase** includes a noun or pronoun plus all related modifiers: *She broke the track record.* A **prepositional phrase** consists of a preposition, its object, and any modifiers of that object: *The ball sailed over the fence.* A **verbal phrase** consists of a verbal and its related objects, modifiers, or complements. A verbal phrase may be a **participial phrase** (*Undaunted by the sheer cliff, the climber scaled the rock*), a **gerund phrase** (*Swinging from trees is a monkey's favorite way to travel*), or an **infinitive phrase** (*Wednesday is Bill's night to cook spaghetti*). An **absolute phrase** includes a noun or pronoun and a participle, accompanied by modifiers: *His heart racing, he dialed her number.* It modifies an entire independent clause. **32b1**

plural See **number.**

positive degree See **comparison.**

possessive case See **case.**

possessive noun See **determiner.**

possessive pronoun See **determiner.**

predicate A verb or verb phrase that tells or asks something about the subject of a sentence is called a **simple predicate:** *Well-tended lawns grow green and thick.* (*Grow* is the simple predicate.) A **complete predicate** includes all the words associated with the predicate: *Well-tended lawns grow green and thick.* (*Grow green and thick* is the complete predicate.)

predicate adjective See **complement.**

predicate nominative See **complement.**

prefix A letter or group of letters put before a root or a word that adds to, changes, or modifies it.

preposition A part of speech that introduces a noun or pronoun (or a phrase or clause functioning in the sentence as a noun), linking it to other words in the sentence: *Jeremy crawled under the bed.* **45f**

prepositional phrase See **phrase.**

present participle See **participle.**

principal parts The forms of a verb from which all other forms can be derived. The principal parts are the **base form** (*give*), the **present participle** (*giving*), the **past tense** (*gave*), and the **past participle** (*given*).

pronoun A word that may be used in place of a noun in a sentence. The noun for which a pronoun stands is called its **antecedent.** There are eight types of pronouns. Some have the same form but are distinguished by their function in the sentence. A **personal pronoun** stands for a person or thing: *I, me, we, us, my,* and so on (*They broke his window*). A **reflexive pronoun** ends in *-self* or *-selves* and refers to the subject of the sentence or clause: *myself, yourself, himself,* and so on (*They painted the house themselves*). An **intensive pronoun** ends in *-self* or *-selves* and emphasizes a preceding noun or pronoun (*Custer himself died in the battle*). A **relative pronoun** introduces an adjective or noun clause in a sentence: *which, who, whom,* and so on (*Sitting Bull was the Sioux chief who defeated Custer*). An **interrogative pronoun** introduces a question: *who, which, what, whom,* and so on (*Who won the lottery?*). A **demonstrative pronoun** points to a particular thing or group of things: *this, that, these, those* (*Who was that masked man?*). A **reciprocal pronoun** denotes a mutual relationship: *each other, one another* (*We still have each other*). An **indefinite pronoun** refers to persons or things in general, not to specific individuals. Most indefinite pronouns are singular—*anyone, everyone, one, each*—but some are always plural—*both, many, several* (*Many are called, but few are chosen*). **45b**

proper adjective See **adjective.**

proper noun See **noun.**

quotation The use of the written or spoken words of others. A **direct quotation** is a passage borrowed word for word from another source. Quotation marks (" ") establish the boundaries of a direct quotation: "*Those tortillas taste like cardboard,*" *complained Beth.* **54a** An **indirect quotation** reports someone else's written or spoken words without quoting that person directly. Quotation marks are not used: *Beth complained that the tortillas tasted like cardboard.*

reciprocal pronoun See **pronoun.**

reflexive pronoun See **pronoun.**

regular verb A verb that forms both its past tense and past participle by the addition of *d* or *ed* to the base form of the verb. **47a1**

relative clause See **clause.**

relative pronoun See **pronoun.**

restrictive appositive See **appositive.**

restrictive modifier A modifying phrase or clause that limits the meaning of the word or word group it modifies. Restrictive modifiers are not set off by commas: *The Ferrari that ran over the fireplug was red.* (Contrast **nonrestrictive modifier.**) **51d1**

root A word from which other words are formed. An understanding of a root word increases a reader's ability to understand unfamiliar words that incorporate the root.

run-on sentence An incorrect construction that results when the proper connective or punctuation does not appear between independent clauses.

A run-on occurs either as a **comma splice** or as a **fused sentence.** **Ch. 38**

sentence An independent grammatical unit that contains a *subject* and a *predicate* and expresses a complete thought: *Carolyn sold her car*. A **simple sentence** consists of one subject and one predicate: *The season ended*. **32a;** a **compound sentence** is formed when two or more simple sentences are connected with coordinating conjunctions, conjunctive adverbs, semicolons, or colons: *The rain stopped, and the sun began to shine.* **33a;** a **complex sentence** consists of one simple sentence, which functions as an independent clause in the complex sentence, and at least one dependent clause, which is introduced by a subordinating conjunction or a relative pronoun: *When he had sold three boxes* [dependent clause], *he was halfway to his goal.* [independent clause] **33b;** and a **compound-complex sentence** consists of two or more independent clauses and at least one dependent clause: *After he prepared a shopping list* [dependent clause], *he went to the store* [independent clause], *but it was closed.* [independent clause]. **33b**

sentence fragment An incomplete sentence, phrase, or clause that is punctuated as if it were a complete sentence. **Ch. 37**

shift A change of *tense, voice, mood, person, number,* or *type of discourse* within or between sentences. Some shifts are necessary, but problems occur with unnecessary or illogical shifts. **41a**

simile A **figure of speech** in which the writer makes a comparison, introduced by *like* or *as,* between two unlike items on the basis of a shared quality: *Like sands through the hourglass, so are the days of our lives. The wind was as savage as his neighbor's Doberman.* (Contrast **metaphor.**) **42c**

simple predicate See **predicate.**

simple sentence See **sentence.**

simple subject See **subject.**

singular See **number.**

split infinitive An infinitive whose parts are separated by a modifier. **39a4**

She expected ~~to~~ ultimately to swim the channel.

squinting modifier A modifier that seems to modify either a word before it or one after it and that conveys a different meaning in each case. **39a1**

Squinting: The task completed simply delighted him.

Revised: He was delighted to have the task completed simply.

Revised: He was simply delighted to have the task completed.

subject A noun or noun substitute that tells who or what a sentence is about is called a **simple subject:** *Healthy thoroughbred horses run like* *the wind*. (*Horses* is the simple subject.) The **complete subject** of a sentence includes all the words associated with the subject: *Healthy thoroughbred horses run like the wind*. (*Healthy thoroughbred horses* is the complete subject.) **32a**

subject complement See **complement.**

subjective case See **case.**

subjunctive mood See **mood.**

subordinate clause See **clause.**

subordinating conjunction See **conjunction.**

subordination Making one or more clauses of a sentence grammatically dependent upon another element in a sentence: *Preston was only eighteen when he joined the firm*. (Contrast **coordination.**) **33b**

suffix A syllable added at the end of a word or root that changes its part of speech.

superlative degree See **degree.**

suspended hyphen A hyphen followed by a space or by the appropriate punctuation and a space: *The wagon was pulled by a two-, four-, or six-horse team.*

syllogism A three-part set of statements or propositions, devised by Aristotle, that contains a major premise, a minor premise, and a conclusion. **9f2**

tag question A question, consisting of an auxiliary verb plus a pronoun, that is added to a statement and set off by a comma: *You know it's going to rain, don't you?*

tense The form of a verb that indicates when an action occurred or when a condition existed. **47b**

transitive verb See **verb.**

verb A word or phrase that expresses action (*He painted the fence*) or a state of being (*Henry believes in equality*). A **main verb** carries most of the meaning in the sentence or clause in which it appears: *Winston Churchill smoked long, thick cigars*. A main verb is a **linking verb** when it is followed by a **subject complement:** *Dogs are good pets.* An **auxiliary verb** (sometimes called a **helping verb**) combines with the main verb to form a **verb phrase:** *Graduation day has arrived*. The auxiliaries *be* and *have* are used to indicate the tense and voice of the main verb. The auxiliary *do* is used for asking questions and forming negative statements. Other auxiliary verbs, known as **modal auxiliaries** (*must, will, can, could, may, might, ought* [*to*], *should,* and *would*), indicate necessity, possibility, willingness, obligation, and ability: *It might rain next Tuesday.* A **transitive verb** requires an **object** to complete its meaning in the sentence: *Pete drank all the wine* (*wine* is the direct object). An **intransitive verb** has no direct object: *The candle flame glowed.* **45c1; Ch. 47**

verb phrase See **phrase.**

verbal (**nonfinite verb**) Verb forms—**participles, infinitives,** and **gerunds**—that are used as nouns, adjectives, or adverbs. Verbals do not behave like verbs. Only when used with an auxiliary can such verb forms serve as the main verb of a sentence. *The wall painted* is not a sentence; *The wall was painted* is. **45c2**

verbal phrase See **phrase.**

voice The form that determines whether the subject of a verb is acting or is acted upon. When the subject of a verb performs the action, the verb is in the **active voice:** *Tiger Woods sank a thirty-foot putt.* When the subject of a verb receives the action—that is, is acted upon—the verb is in the **passive voice:** *A thirty-foot putt was sunk by Tiger Woods.* **35e; 41a2; 47d, 61b6**

CREDITS

The pages that follow constitute an extension of the copyright page. We have made every effort to trace the ownership of all copyrighted material and to secure permission from copyright holders. In the event of any question arising as to the use of any material, we will be pleased to make the necessary corrections in future printings. Thanks are due to the following authors, publishers, and agents for permission to use the material indicated.

Text and Illustrations

p. 3: Figure 1.1. Reprinted by permission of National Center for Family Literacy.

p. 5: From "The War at Home" by Ethan Brown from *New York* magazine, April 28, 2003.

p. 7: Review by Charles H. Peterson of *The King of Torts* by John Grisham. Reprinted by permission of the author.

p. 9: "What Makes a Credit Score Rise or Fall?" by Jennifer Bayot from the *New York Times*, June 29, 2003. Copyright © 2003 The New York Times Co. Reprinted by permission.

p. 10: Figure 1.3. Screen shot copyright 2003 by Consumers Union of U.S., Inc. Yonkers, NY 10703-1057, a nonprofit organization. Reprinted with permission from the July 2003 issue of *Consumer Reports®* for educational purposes only. No commercial use or reproduction permitted. To learn more about Consumers Union, log onto www.ConsumerReports.org.

pp. 21–22: "Undecided—and Proud of It" by Michael Finkel from the *New York Times*, November 24, 1989. Copyright © 1989 by Michael Finkel. Reprinted by permission of The New York Times.

pp. 23–25: "The Case Against Joe Nocera: How People Like Me Helped Ruin the Public Schools" by Joseph Nocera from the *Washington Monthly*. Reprinted by permission.

pp. 25–26: "Whose Legacy Is It, Anyway?" by Jake Lamar from the *New York Times*, October 9, 1991. Copyright © 1991 by Jake Lamar. Reprinted by permission of The New York Times.

p. 28: Figure 2.1. "The Whole World is Watching . . . Member of Marine honor guard passes the Vietnam memorial on which names of casualties of the war are inscribed" from *Philadelphia Inquirer*, November 14, 1982. Reprinted by permission of Philadelphia Newspapers.

p. 29: Figure 2.2. Courtesy of The Phoenix Companies, Inc.

p. 31: Figure 2.3. Reprinted by permission of New Balance.

pp. 37–38: From *Born on the Fourth of July* by Ron Kovic. Copyright © 1976. Reprinted by permission of The McGraw-Hill Companies.

p. 156: Screen shot from Women's Basketball Hall of Fame Web site, www.wbhof.com.

pp. 165–167: "Questioning the Motives of Home-Schooling Parents" by Froma Harrop as appeared in *The Seattle Times*, June 28, 2001. Reprinted by permission of The Providence Journal Company.

p. 171: Figure 9.5. Salary chart from Christchurch Polytechnic Institute of Technology, New Zealand, Web site. Reprinted by permission.

p. 171: Figure 9.6. Salary chart from Christchurch Polytechnic Institute of Technology, New Zealand, Web site. Reprinted by permission.

pp. 180–181: "English Comes First" by Richard D. Lamm from the *New York Times*, July 1, 1986. Copyright © 1986 by Richard D. Lamm. Reprinted by permission of The New York Times.

pp. 189–190: Excerpt from article, "The World of Hunting," by William R. Quimby. From *Safari Magazine*, July/August 1992. Copyright © 1992 by William R. Quimby. Reprinted courtesy of Safari Club International.

p. 200: Figure 10.1. Reprinted by permission of Dick Adair.

p. 201: Figure 10.2. © Reprinted with special permission of King Feature Syndicate.

p. 214: Figure 10.3. Reprinted by permission of Reason, www.reason.com.

p. 246: Figure 12.1. Screen shot from Southeastern Louisiana University Library Catalog Web site.

p. 247: Figure 12.2. Screen shot from Southeastern Louisiana University Library Catalog Web site.

p. 252: "The Supply Side of the Digital Divide: Is There Equal Availability in the Broadband Internet Access Market?" by James E. Prieger from *Economy Inquiry*, April 2003, Vol. 41, No. 2, p. 346. Reprinted by permission of Oxford University Press.

p. 253: Figure 12.5. Screen shot reproduced with the permission of LexisNexis.

p. 256: Figure 12.6. Screen shot used by permission of The General Libraries, The University of Texas at Austin.

p. 274: Figure 13.2. Screen shot from http://home.netscape.com. An AOL company.

p. 276: Figure 13.3. Screen shot reproduced with permission of Yahoo! Inc. © 2004 by Yahoo! Inc. *Yahoo!* and the *Yahoo!* logo are trademarks of Yahoo! Inc.

p. 277: Figure 13.4. Screen shot reprinted by permission of Google.

p. 280: Figure 13.5. Screen shot copyright © 1998–2003 InfoSpace, Inc. All rights reserved. Reprinted with permission of InfoSpace, Inc.

p. 289: Figure 14.1. Screen shot used with permission. Copyright © 2004 Mothers Against Drunk Driving. All rights reserved. www.madd.org.

p. 292: Figure 14.2. Screen shot copyright © 2003, The Washington Post, reprinted with permission.

p. 293: Figure 14.3. Screen shot courtesy of the American Cancer Society. Copyright 2003 American Cancer Society, Inc. All rights reserved.

p. 293: Figure 14.4. Screen shot courtesy of CancerSource. www .cancersource.com.

pp. 297–298: Excerpt from "Freedom of Hate Speech?" by Phil Sudo from *Scholastic Update*, 124.14 (1992), pp. 17–20. Copyright © 1992 by Scholastic Inc. Reprinted by permission of Scholastic Inc.

pp. 302–303: Courtesy Landon Y. Jones, *Great Expectations: America and the Baby-Boom Generation*, © 1980.

p. 309: Figure 16.1. "The Red Wheelbarrow" by William Carlos Williams from *Collected Poems: 1909–1939, Volume 1*, copyright 1938 by New Directions Publishing Corp. Reprinted by permission of New Directions Publishing Corp.

p. 319: Screen shot reprinted by permission of Google.

p. 320: Screen shot from InfoTrac® by Gale Group. Reprinted by permission of The Gale Group.

p. 321: Screen shot used by permission of The General Libraries, The University of Texas at Austin.

p. 328: Screen shot reprinted by permission of Google.

p. 369: "a song in the front yard" by Gwendolyn Brooks from *Blacks*. Reprinted by consent of Brooks Permissions.

p. 381: Figure 18.1. Screen shot from "Will Genetic Engineering Kill Us?" by Mark Baard from *Wired News*, April 16, 2003.

p. 491: "A Dream Deferred" by Langston Hughes. Used by permission of Random House.

p. 507: From SeeItandStopIt.org.

pp. 519–521: "Sleepy Time Gal" from *The Crush* by Gary Gildner. Copyright © 1983 by Gary Gildner. Reprinted by permission of the author.

pp. 531–532: "The True-Blue American" by Delmore Schwartz, from *Selected Poems: Summer Knowledge*, Copyright © 1959 by Delmore Schwartz. Reprinted by permission of New Directions Publishing Corp.

p. 575: Lines from "A Pink Wool Knitted Dress" by Ted Hughes from *Birthday Letters*. Used by permission of Farrar, Straus and Giroux, LLC.

p. 575: "Wreath for a Bridal" from *The Collected Poems of Sylvia Plath*, edited by Ted Hughes. Copyright © 1960, 1965, 1971, 1981 by the Estate of Sylvia Plath. Editorial Material copyright © 1981 by Ted Hughes. Reprinted by permission of HarperCollins Publishers Inc.

p. 636: Figure 29.3. 90.9 WBUR-FM, Boston's NPR® News Station. Reprinted by permission.

p. 639: Figure 29.7. Screen shot from www.lyricoperaofwaco.org.

p. 650: Figure 30.5. Screen shot reprinted with permission from National Family, Career and Community Leaders of America.

p. 651: Figure 30.6. Screen shot reprinted by permission of School of Music, Northern Illinois University, DeKalb, IL.

p. 652: Figure 30.8. Screen shot from www.csus.edu/org/labsa/members.htm.

p. 740: Figure 37.2. Reprinted by permission of BRW Legrand.

p. 794: *Couple*, definition, copyright © 2000 by Houghton Mifflin Company. Adapted and reproduced by permission from *The American Heritage Dictionary of the English Language*, Fourth Edition.

p. 799: *Courage*, definition, copyright © 1989 by Oxford University Press. Reprinted by permission from *Oxford English Dictionary*, 2nd edition. Edited by John Simpson and Edmund Weiner.

p. 962: Figure 61.2. Screen shot of definition of *tuition* from *Heinle's Newbury House Dictionary of American English.*

p. 963: Figure 61.3. Screen shot of definition of *ride* from *Heinle's Newbury House Dictionary of American English.*

Photos

Part Openers

p. 1: © Photodisc Green/Getty Images **p. 219:** © Photodisc Red/Getty Images **p. 359:** © John Coletti **p. 495:** © Photodisc Blue/Getty Images **p. 777:** © Royalty-Free/Corbis **p. 955:** Courtesy NASA Goddard Space Flight Center. Image by Reto Stockli. Enhancement by Robert Simmon

Icons

Computer tips, p. xii: © Keith Brofsky/Photodisc/Getty Images

Checklists, p. xii: © John Coletti

Close-up boxes, p. xii: © Photodisc/Getty Images

Print sources, p. xii: © Simon Battensby/Stone/Getty Images

ESL tips, p. xiii: © NASA Goddard Space Flight Center. Image by Reto Stockli. Enhancement by Robert Simmon

Student Writer at Work exercises, p. xiii: © Taxi/Getty Images

Photos

Chapter 2, p. 28: Figure 2.1. Photo by Bryan Grigsby

Chapter 3, p. 38: Figure 3.1. © Rolf Bruderer/Corbis

Chapter 6, p. 104: © 2003 Heinle Division of Thomson Learning

Chapter 7, p. 124: Figure 7.1. © Philip Gould/Corbis **p. 125:** Figure 7.2

© Buddy Mays/Corbis **p. 125:** Figure 7.3. © Taxi/Getty Images **p. 126:** Figure 7.4. © Bettmann/Corbis **p. 127:** Figure 7.5. © Richard T. Nowitz/Corbis **p. 128:** Figure 7.6. © Bettmann/Corbis **p. 128:** Figure 7.7. © Corbis **p. 128:** Figure 7.7. © Corbis **p. 129:** Figure 7.8. © Images.com/Corbis **p. 129:** Figure 7.9. © Anthony Bannister/Gallo Images/Corbis **p. 130:** Figure 7.10. © Jim Zuckerman/Corbis **p. 131:** Figure 7.11. © Peabody Museum of Archaeology and Ethnology/Harvard University **p. 131:** Figure 7.12. © Alan Schein Photography/Corbis **p. 134tr:** Figure 7.13. © Leonard de Selva/Corbis **p. 134tl:** Figure 7.14. © Steve Prezant/Corbis **p. 134bl:** Figure 7.15. © Gideon Mendel/Corbis **p. 134br:** Figure 7.16. © Bettmann/Corbis

Chapter 9, p. 168: Figure 9.1. © Joe Rosenthal/Corbis **p. 169:** Figure 9.2. © Bettmann/Corbis **p. 169:** Figure 9.3. © Stephanie Maze/Corbis **p. 170:** Figure 9.4. © Stephanie Maze/Corbis

Chapter 17, p. 345: © The Daily Texan/The University of Texas at Austin

Chapter 18, p. 402: © Smithsonian American Art Museum, Washington, DC/Art Resource, NY **p. 404:** © High Museum of Art, Atlanta, Georgia. T. Marshall Hahn Collection, 1997.114

Chapter 19, p. 430: © 2003 Heinle Division of Thomson Learning

Chapter 29, p. 640: Figure 29.8. © Deb Martin

INDEX

Page numbers in blue refer to definitions.

A

D

N

T

V

X

Y

Z

The Research Process

Activity	Date Due	Date Completed
Move from a General Assignment to a Narrow Topic, **11a**	____________	____________
Map Out a Search Strategy, **11b**	____________	____________
Do Exploratory Research and Formulate a Research Question, **11c**	____________	____________
Assemble a Working Bibliography, **11d**	____________	____________
Develop a Tentative Thesis, **11e**	____________	____________
Do Focused Research, **11f**	____________	____________
Take Notes, **11g**	____________	____________
Fine-Tune Your Thesis, **11h**	____________	____________
Outline Your Paper, **11i**	____________	____________
Draft Your Paper, **11j**	____________	____________
Revise Your Paper, **11k**	____________	____________
Prepare Your Final Draft, **11l**	____________	____________

Checklist: Avoiding Plagiarism

- ☐ **Take careful notes.** Be sure you have recorded information from your sources carefully and accurately.
- ☐ **In your notes, clearly identify borrowed material.** In handwritten notes, put all words borrowed from your sources inside circled quotation marks, and enclose your own comments within brackets. If you are taking notes on a computer, boldface all quotation marks.
- ☐ **In your paper, differentiate your ideas from those of your sources** by clearly introducing borrowed material with an identifying tag and by following it with documentation.
- ☐ **Enclose all direct quotations** used in your paper within quotation marks.
- ☐ **Review all paraphrases and summaries** in your paper to make certain they are in your own words and that any distinctive words and phrases from a source are quoted.
- ☐ **Document all quoted material and all paraphrases and summaries** of your sources.
- ☐ **Document all information** that is open to dispute or that is not common knowledge.
- ☐ **Document all opinions, conclusions, figures, tables, statistics, graphs, and charts** taken from a source.
- ☐ **Never submit the work of another person as your own.** Do not buy a paper from an online paper mill or use a paper given to you by a friend. In addition, do not include in your paper passages that have been written by a friend, relative, or writing tutor.